# Advances In
# Real-Time Systems

# Advances In
# Real-Time Systems

**Sang H. Son,** *Editor*

*University of Virginia*

Prentice Hall, Englewood Cliffs, NJ 07632

Library of Congress Cataloging-in-Publication Data

Advances in real-time systems / Sang H. Son, editor.
     p.   cm.
   Includes bibliographical references and index.
   ISBN 0-13-083348-7
   1. Real-time data processing.   I. Son, Sang H.
QA76.54.A39  1995
005.2--dc20                                                    94-26844
                                                                  CIP

Acquisitions Editor: Bill Zobrist
Production Editor: Joe Scordato
Copy Editor: Barbara Zeiders
Cover Designer: Bruce Kenselaar
Buyer: Lori Bulwin
Editorial Assistant: Phyllis Morgan


Cover art: DALI, Salvador. The Persistence of Memory. (Peristance de la memoire). 1931. Oil on canvas, 9-1/2 x 13". The Museum of Modern Art, New York. Given annonymously. Photograph copyright 1994 The Museum of Modern Art, New York.

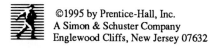 ©1995 by Prentice-Hall, Inc.
A Simon & Schuster Company
Englewood Cliffs, New Jersey 07632

The author and publisher of this book have used their best efforts in preparing this book. These efforts include the development, research, and testing of the theories and programs to determine their effectiveness. The author and publisher make no warranty of any kind, expressed or implied, with regard to these programs or the documentation contained in this book. The author and publisher shall not be liable in any event for incidental or consequential damages in connection with, or arising out of, the furnishing, performance, or use of these programs.

Printed in the United States of America

10  9  8  7  6  5  4  3  2  1

ISBN 0-13-083348-7

Prentice-Hall International (UK) Limited, London
Prentice-Hall of Australia Pty. Limited, Sydney
Prentice-Hall Canada Inc., Toronto
Prentice-Hall Hispanoamericana, S.A., Mexico
Prentice-Hall of India Private Limited, New Delhi
Prentice-Hall of Japan, Inc., Tokyo
Simon & Schuster Asia Pte. Ltd., Singapore
Editora Prentice-Hall do Brasil, Ltda., Rio de Janeiro

# About the Editor

**Sang Hyuk Son** is an associate professor of computer science at the University of Virginia. His research interests include real-time computing, database systems, distributed systems, and fault-tolerant computing. He has written or co-authored over 80 papers and several book chapters in these areas. He received the B.S. degree in electronics engineering from Seoul National University in 1976, and the M.S. degree in electrical engineering from the Korea Advanced Institute of Science and Technology in 1978. He earned the M.S. and Ph.D. degrees in computer science from the University of Maryland, College Park, in 1984 and 1986, respectively.

Dr. Son has served as a guest editor for the *ACM SIGMOD Record*, Special Issue on Real-Time Database Systems, and as the Program Chair of the 10th IEEE Workshop on Real-Time Operating Systems and Software (RTOSS), held in May 1993. He has also served as an ACM National Lecturer for 1991-1993. He was the General Chair of the 11th RTOSS Workshop held in May 1994. He is a member of the Association for Computing Machinery and the IEEE Computer Society.

# Contributors

**Ashok Agrawala**
Department of Computer Science
University of Maryland
College Park, MD 20742

**Alan Burns**
Real-Time Systems Research Group
Department of Computer Science
University of York, UK

**Duncan Clarke**
Department of Computer and
Information Science
University of Pennsylvania
Philadelphia, PA 19104

**Paul S. Dodd**
Real-Time Computing Laboratory
Computer Science and Engineering Division
Department of Electrical Engineering and
Computer Science
The University of Michigan
Ann Arbor, MI 48109

**Domenico Ferrari**
The Tenet Group
Computer Science Division
EECS Department
University of California at Berkeley and
International Computer Science Institute
Berkeley, CA 94720

**Hector Garcia-Molina**
Stanford University
Stanford, CA 94305

**Richard Gerber**
University of Maryland
College Park, MD 20742

**Ahmed Gheith**
AWD Future Systems Technology
International Business Machines
Austin, TX 78758

**Rhan Ha**
Department of Computer Science
University of Illinois
Urbana, IL 61801

**Seongsoo Hong**
University of Maryland
College Park, MD 20742

**Atri Indiresan**
Real-Time Computing Laboratory
Computer Science and Engineering Division
Department of Electrical Engineering and
Computer Science
The University of Michigan
Ann Arbor, MI 48109

**Farnam Jahanian**
Computer Science and Engineering Division
Department of Electrical Engineering and
Computer Science
University of Michigan
Ann Arbor, MI 48109

**Sanjay Kamat**
Department of Computer Science
Texas A&M University
College Station, TX 77843

**Dilip D. Kandlur**
Real-Time Computing Laboratory
Computer Science and Engineering Division
Department of Electrical Engineering and
Computer Science
The University of Michigan
Ann Arbor, MI 48109

**Ben Kao**
Princeton University
Princeton, NJ 08544

**K. H. (Kane) Kim**
Department of Electrical and
Computer Engineering
University of California
Irvine, CA 92717

**Young-Kuk Kim**
Computer Science Department
University of Virginia
Charlottesville, VA 22903

**Daniel L. Kiskis**
Real-Time Computing Laboratory
Computer Science and Engineering Division
Department of Electrical Engineering and
Computer Science
The University of Michigan
Ann Arbor, MI 48109

**Insup Lee**
Department of Computer and
Information Science
University of Pennsylvania
Philadelphia, PA 19104

**John P. Lehoczky**
Department of Statistics
Carnegie Mellon University
Pittsburgh, PA 15213

**Kwei-Jay Lin**
Department of Electrical and
Computer Engineering
University of California, Irvine
Irvine, CA 92717

**Jane W. S. Liu**
Department of Computer Science
University of Illinois
Urbana, IL 61801

**Nancy Lynch**
Department of Electrical Engineering and
Computer Science
Massachusetts Institute of Technology
Cambridge, MA 02139

**Bhaskar Purimetla**
Department of Computer Science
University of Massachusetts
Amherst, MA 01003

**Ragunathan Rajkumar**
Software Engineering Institute
Carnegie Mellon University
Pittsburgh, PA 15213

**Krithi Ramamritham**
Department of Computer Science
University of Massachusetts
Amherst, MA 01003

**Harold A. Rosenberg**
Real-Time Computing Laboratory
Computer Science and Engineering Division
Department of Electrical Engineering and
Computer Science
The University of Michigan
Ann Arbor, MI 48109

**Manas Saksena**
Department of Computer Science
University of Maryland
College Park, MD 20742

**Shirish S. Sathaye**
Network Architecture and
Performance Group
Digital Equipment Corporation
Littleton, MA 01460

**Karsten Schwan**
College of Computing
Georgia Institute of Technology
Atlanta, GA 30332

**Lui Sha**
Software Engineering Institute
Carnegie Mellon University
Pittsburgh, PA 15213

**Alan Shaw**
Department of Computer Science and
Engineering, FR-35
University of Washington
Seattle, WA 98195

**Kang G. Shin**
Real-Time Computing Laboratory
Computer Science and Engineering Division
Department of Electrical Engineering and
Computer Science
The University of Michigan
Ann Arbor, MI 48109

**James da Silva**
Department of Computer Science
University of Maryland
College Park, MD 20742

**Rajendran M. Sivasankaran**
Department of Computer Science
University of Massachusetts
Amherst, MA 01003

**Sang H. Son**
Computer Science Department
University of Virginia
Charlottesville, VA 22903

**John A. Stankovic**
Department of Computer Science
University of Massachusetts
Amherst, MA 01003

**Sandra R. Thuel**
AT&T Bell Laboratories
Holmdel, NJ 07733

**Hong-Liang Xie**
Department of Computer and
Information Science
University of Pennsylvania
Philadelphia, PA 19104

**Wei Zhao**
Department of Computer Science
Texas A&M University
College Station, TX 77843

# Contents

**4   Design and Implementation of Maruti-II                      73**
    *Manas Saksena, James da Silva, and Ashok Agrawala*

**II   Real-Time Communication                                  103**

**5   A New Admission Control Method for Real-Time
    Communication in an Internetwork                          105**
    *Domenico Ferrari*

**6   Real-Time Performance of Two Token Ring Protocols         117**
    *Sanjay Kamat and Wei Zhao*

**7   A Systematic Approach to Designing Distributed Real-Time
    Systems                                                   149**
    *Lui Sha and Shirish S. Sathaye*

## III   Scheduling and Resource Management                    **173**

# IV   Formal Methods                                          273

## 12 The Algebra of Communicating Shared Resources and Its Toolkit                                                         275

*Insup Lee, Duncan Clarke, and Hong-Liang Xie*

## 13 Simulation Techniques for Proving Properties of Real-Time Systems                                                          299

*Nancy Lynch*

# V   Programming Language and Tools                          333

## 14 Issues on Real-Time Systems Programming: Language, Compiler, and Object Orientation                               335

*Kwei-Jay Lin*

## 15 Compiler Support for Real-Time Programs                   353

*Richard Gerber and Seongsoo Hong*

**20  Real-Time Databases: Issues and Applications                487**

*Bhaskar Purimetla et al.*

**21  Predictability and Consistency in Real-Time Database Systems  509**

*Young-Kuk Kim and Sang H. Son*

**Index                                                           533**

# Preface

A real-time system is one whose basic specification and design correctness arguments must include its ability to meet its timing constraints. This implies that its correctness depends not only on the logical correctness, but also on the timeliness of its actions. To function correctly, it must produce a correct result within a specified time, called deadline. In these systems, an action performed too late (or even too early) may be useless or even harmful, even if it is functionally correct. If timing requirements coming from certain essential safety-critical applications would be violated, the results could be catastrophic. They may cause serious damage to the system or to its environment, including injury or even death of people involved. These are called *hard real-time* systems. By contrast, there are applications that also have deadlines but are noncritical. For example, one can define a transmission system to have failed if voice packets are not delivered within a certain deadline during a teleconference session. However, in those applications, such failures will not be catastrophic. They are called *soft real-time* systems.

The realm of real-time computing applications is expanding rapidly. The importance of real-time computing in a large number of applications, such as aerospace and defense systems, industrial automation, instrumentation, traffic control, and telecommunication, has resulted in an increased research effort in this area.

Although it is commonly believed that meeting the timing requirements is a matter of increasing system throughput sufficiently, research in real-time systems has discredited this notion. In fact, the computational structures appropriate for systems requiring bounded response time are fundamentally different from those requiring high throughput. The progress in hardware technology in recent years has made high-performance computing and communication feasible. However, it became clear that high-speed execution alone may not solve all the problems real-time computing needs to address. The challenges and tradeoffs faced by the designers of real-time systems are quite different from those who design general-purpose computing systems. To achieve the fundamental requirements of timeliness and predictability, not only do conventional methods for scheduling and resource management have to be redesigned, but new concepts that have not been considered in conventional systems need to be added. New paradigms are necessary to specify and validate real-time systems.

Some of the important issues that need to be considered for a successful real-time system are as follows:

- Formal methods for specifying and verifying requirements.

- Scheduling and resource management to ensure that timing requirements are met.

- Programming languages and tools to support a powerful yet predictable software development process.

- Operating systems for predictable operations in a complex and unpredictable environment with distributed and multiprocessor systems.

- Real-time communication to support real-time traffic in satisfying timing constraints of individual messages.

- Fault tolerance to ensure adequate reliability and timeliness in spite of failures.

- Real-time databases to support time-constrained access to data and access to data that has temporal validity.

The purpose of this book is twofold: to present new developments in the real-time computing systems field and to summarize the current state of the art. This book contains a selection of contributed chapters that cover most areas of importance for the design and development of real-time systems. Each chapter is written by contributing authors who are leading researchers in the area. They attempt to include key issues and approaches to address essential requirements in designing a large, next-generation real-time system. They provide in-depth discussion of design alternatives and technical details in real-time systems. The chapters are grouped into several technical areas, based on their relevance.

The book is aimed at professionals in the field of real-time systems. It will be useful to researchers and engineers who have to deal with several aspects of real-time systems. It is particularly suitable for graduate or advanced undergraduate courses, as it presents many novel ideas and advanced technologies.

Throughout the relatively brief history of real-time computing, research efforts have concentrated on a number of topic areas spanning the broadening spectrum of real-time systems and their applications. It is now beginning to emerge as a robust, credible, and important research discipline in computer science and engineering. It is my hope that this book will convey many important ideas and results developed by the real-time systems research community to a wide audience, and contribute to the discovery of even deeper understanding of principles of real-time systems.

# Acknowledgments

This book would not have been possible without the cooperation of the contributing authors. I would like to acknowledge their understanding and help in shaping the contents of this book. Special thanks go to Young-Kuk Kim for painstakingly formatting all the manuscripts into a beautiful volume. Thanks also go to Bill Zobrist, my editor at Prentice Hall, and to Prof. Vijay Kumar, of the University of Missouri, for encouragement and guidance in completing this project. I would also like to acknowledge the support for my research in real-time systems from the Office of Naval Research, IBM Federal Systems Company, and Virginia Center for Innovative Technology. Finally, my special thanks go to my wife, Inhye, and my children, Daniel and Yena, for their love, understanding, and encouragement, and for the joy they bring to my life.

*Sang H. Son*

# Part I

# Real-Time Operating Systems

# Chapter 1

# A Software Overview of HARTS: A Distributed Real-Time System[1]

Kang G. Shin, Dilip D. Kandlur,
Daniel L. Kiskis, Paul S. Dodd,
Harold A. Rosenberg, and Atri Indiresan

This chapter presents an overview of the software environment of HARTS, a distributed real-time system being developed in the Real-Time Computing Laboratory, the University of Michigan. The environment is comprised of an operating system called HARTOS and three evaluation tools. In addition to the usual non-real-time services like remote procedure calls and naming, HARTOS provides services necessary to support time-constrained and fault-tolerant communication. These include the real-time channel service, deadline-based scheduling, clock synchronization, and group communication.

The three evaluation tools collectively create a facility for various experiments on HARTS and HARTOS. The first tool is a synthetic workload generator (SWG) which provides a means for measuring the performance of architectural and OS designs and real-time and fault-tolerant mechanisms while varying system workloads in a controlled environment. The second tool is a real-time monitor (HMON) that is used to debug and measure the performance of distributed real-time applications. The third tool is a software fault injector that will be used in conjunction with the SWG and HMON to validate the fault-tolerance mechanisms of HARTS.

---

[1]This chapter is based on "A Distributed Real-Time Operating System," by the same authors that appeared in *IEEE Software*, vol. 9, no. 5, pp. 58–68, September 1992, ©1992 IEEE.

## 1.1   Introduction

It has become a common practice to use digital computers for such embedded real-time applications as computer-integrated manufacturing, industrial process control, defense systems, and electric power distribution and monitoring. These applications usually impose stringent timing *and* reliability requirements on the computer system to be used, because a system failure could lead to catastrophe. Distributed systems with point-to-point interconnection networks are natural candidate architectures for these applications due mainly to their potential for meeting the stringent timeliness and reliability requirements of such applications. The key to success in using a distributed system for these applications is the timely execution of computational tasks which usually reside on different nodes and communicate with one another to accomplish a common goal. Providing deadline guarantees for real-time tasks is very difficult since it involves interaction among various elements, such as high- and low-level hardware architectures, operating systems, and performance/dependability evaluation tools. To study these interactions, we have been designing, implementing, and evaluating a 19-node hexagonal mesh, called HARTS (Hexagonal Architecture for Real-Time Systems), in the Real-Time Computing Laboratory (RTCL), the University of Michigan.

The architectural aspects of HARTS have been treated in a companion paper [25]. The main intent of this chapter is to cover the software environment of HARTS, which is comprised of operating systems and evaluation tools. Two versions of the HARTS operating system, called HARTOS, have been developed. The first version of HARTOS primarily extends the functionality of the uniprocessor pSOS[2] [26] real-time operating system kernel to work in a multiprocessor and distributed environment. pSOS services are enhanced to provide interprocessor communication (both unreliable datagram and RPC) and a distributed name service. The second version of HARTOS extends the services of the first version to provide real-time fault-tolerant communication. The extensions and modifications include the real-time channel service and a deadline-based message scheduling policy to replace round-robin/priority message scheduling. This version also provides other important services, such as reliable broadcasting, clock synchronization, and group communication.

In addition to the operating systems, we are developing a number of software tools for evaluating the performance and dependability of HARTS, HARTOS, and other systems. To date we have developed three evaluation tools. The first is the synthetic workload generator (SWG). The SWG compiles a high-level description of a workload to produce a synthetic workload (SW) which will execute on HARTS during evaluation experiments. The second tool is a monitor called HMON. HMON is a real-time monitor that is used to debug and measure the performance of distributed real-time applications. It provides transparent, continuous monitoring using dedicated hardware and integrated operating system-level software. The third tool is a software fault injector. The fault injector provides a

---

[2]pSOS is a trademark of Software Components Group, Inc.

mechanism for inserting errors into an otherwise error-free system. The type and location of the errors can be controlled by the user. The fault injector will be used to validate the dependability mechanisms that are, and will be, implemented on HARTS.

Together, these tools create a facility in which a wide range of experiments may be performed. The SW may be used to exercise those parts of the system which are being studied. The monitor may be used to collect the performance/dependability data, and the fault injector may be used to simulate faulty behavior whose effects may then be studied.

The chapter begins in Section 1.2 with a brief introduction of the HARTS environment. The two versions of HARTOS are described in Section 1.3. HARTOS support for non-real-time, real-time, and fault-tolerant services is detailed there. Section 1.4 is devoted to the three tools for evaluating HARTS and HARTOS: the synthetic workload generator, the real-time monitor, and the software fault injector. The chapter concludes in Section 1.5 with remarks on the current status and future directions of the overall project.

## 1.2   HARTS Environment

HARTS is an experimental distributed real-time system, comprised of multiprocessor nodes connected by a point-to-point interconnection network. Each HARTS node consists of several Application Processors (APs), which are used for running application tasks, and a Network Processor (NP). The NP contains the interface to the network, buffer memory, and a RISC processor, which handles most of the processing related to communication.

The HARTS interconnection has a *continuously wrapped hexagonal mesh* topology [5, 27], which is a regular, homogeneous graph where each node has six neighbors. The graph can be visualized as a simple hexagonal (H-) mesh with wrap links added to the nodes on the periphery. Figure 1.1 illustrates the wrapping scheme for the peripheral nodes, where the dimension of an H-mesh is the number of nodes on a peripheral edge. An analysis of important topological properties of HARTS, and its comparison with other topologies, can be found in [5]. The version of HARTS under construction is a hexagonal mesh of dimension 3 and contains 19 nodes.

In the current configuration, HARTS consists of VMEbus-based nodes (see Figure 1.2). Each node has 1-3 APs, a System Controller card, a Network Processor card, and an Ethernet processor card. The processor cards have a Motorola 68020 32-bit processor and 4 Mbytes of dual-ported RAM which can be accessed from the VMEbus. The Ethernet Processor card (ENP) uses a 10-MHz 68000 processor and an AMD Ethernet Controller device (LANCE). The Ethernet serves as a link to the workstations used for software development. A custom NP board is currently under development. An important component of this NP is the programmable routing controller (PRC) chip [8], which supports high-speed switching mechanisms such as virtual cut-through. This chip is used in the NP card as the front-end interface to the hexagonal mesh. While the custom NP is under development, the ENP is being used to execute the HARTOS communication software. Once the NP is completed,

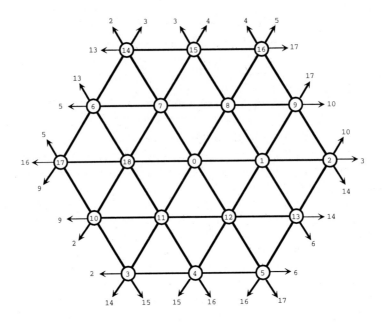

**Figure 1.1** A Wrapped Hexagonal Mesh of Dimension 3

the HARTOS software will be ported to it.

## 1.3 HARTOS: The Operating System of HARTS

HARTOS is designed to exploit the NP on each HARTS node. Currently, HARTOS consists of pSOS executing on the APs, the HARTOS protocol code executing on the ENP, and an interface between the APs and the ENP. The design will be the same when the custom NP is completed. Therefore, in the following discussion, the term NP will refer to the ENP, as the description will still hold once the custom NP is implemented.

The first version of HARTOS primarily extends the functionality of the uniprocessor pSOS kernel [26] to work in a multiprocessor and distributed environment. pSOS services are enhanced to provide interprocessor communication (both unreliable datagram and RPC) and a distributed name service. This version is built on top of the K1 kernel [6]. The K1 kernel provides the basic facilities necessary for protocol support. These include the interface with the Ethernet and mechanisms for setting timeouts and handling interrupts.

The second version extends the services of the first version to provide real-time communication services. The extensions and modifications include the real-time

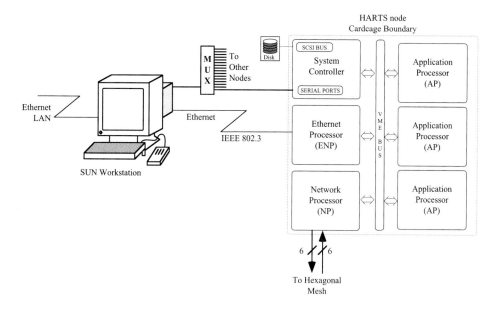

**Figure 1.2** The HARTS Software Development Environment

channel service and changing round-robin/priority message scheduling to deadline-based scheduling. The K1 kernel used in the first version provides only primitive support for the NP. In the second version, we use a derivative of the $x$-Kernel [11] as the executive for the NP since it is much better suited to building complex communication protocols. Besides communication services, it also allows various applications to be implemented as protocol modules that can be integrated in the protocol stack. HARTOS version 2 also includes fault-tolerant services such as reliable broadcasting and group communication.

### 1.3.1   pSOS Node Kernel

pSOS serves as the executive on each AP and provides facilities for process and memory management, event handling, and inter-process communication. A *process* is the unit for sequential execution, resource ownership, and scheduling. Processes are named and use a name to locate a process with which they wish to communicate. The kernel employs a preemptive priority-based scheduler with a provision for cyclic service for processes of equal priority. Processes can dynamically change their priority and also protect themselves from interruption while in critical sections by setting their mode to non-preemptive.

The primary mechanism used for inter-process communication is the *message exchange*. A message exchange is an object at which messages or processes can be queued. The exchange thus allows many-to-many process communication. The *signal* facility is an alternative low-cost mechanism for inter-process communication by which *events* can be posted to a process.

## 1.3.2   HARTOS, Version 1

HARTOS extends the pSOS process control, inter-process communication, time queries, and name lookup functions to work between processors on the same node and across the network. Calls may be blocking or nonblocking, and the user may specify a timeout and maximum number of retries to be used for each remote call. Nonblocking calls are not queued. This policy is consistent with the requirements of many real-time applications, like control applications in which sensor data is gathered periodically and only current data is of value to the application. A function is available to allow the sending process to block until completion of an outstanding operation.

pSOS provides exchanges for passing short messages between processes on the same processor. Shared memory may be used to pass larger blocks of data. The extension of pSOS message passing primitives in HARTOS handles small messages. However, an alternate mechanism is needed for large data transfers across the network. For large messages HARTOS includes operations which transfer up to 16 Kbytes of data between processes. Data transfers may be prioritized to order operations from different processes. Assignment of priorities for other operations is not required since the resource and time requirements of those operations are small, and no timeliness guarantees are supported in this version of HARTOS.

Destinations for HARTOS system calls are specified using an internal address which consists of an AP ID and an exchange or process ID. These addresses are obtained by processes from the HARTOS naming service. The NPs maintain a distributed name table which is used to map logical names to internal addresses. Each NP maintains a table of map entries for entities that were declared on that node by the associated APs. Names are entered explicitly into the table by the application. A process may locate a named server by submitting a find request to the NP. On a find operation, the local name table is first searched for a match. If there is no local match, a request for a name mapping is broadcast to other NPs on behalf of the process that made the request. Only NPs which detect a match reply to the request and the first reply received is taken. The request is handled entirely by the NPs and is not visible to the APs.

## 1.3.3   HARTOS, Version 2

In the second version of HARTOS, we have expanded the services provided by the communication subsystem. As in the first version, it provides blocking and nonblocking interprocess communication and a name service. In addition, it provides a real-time channel service to provide communication with guaranteed delays and maintains a global time base in the system using the clock synchronization algorithm described in [23]. The global time base is essential for the real-time channel service.

As the communication services became more complex, we needed a more sophisticated environment for implementing and experimenting with different communication protocols. We have employed a derivative of the $x$-Kernel [11] as the executive for the NP, since it is well suited for supporting communication protocols.

The $x$-Kernel provides several facilities for implementing protocols like a uniform protocol interface and libraries to manipulate messages efficiently and maintain mappings. It also comes with utilities to configure and test different protocol stacks.

Communication services are provided in the form of protocols running on the $x$-Kernel. Figure 1.3 gives an overview of the communication subsystem and shows the dependencies between various protocols. At the lowest level is the link-level protocol, which uses a multi-class Earliest Due Date (EDD) scheduling algorithm [13] to support a mix of normal (best-effort) and real-time (guaranteed maximum latency) traffic. In addition, the normal link-level protocol supports a reliable broadcast mechanism. The real-time channel (RTC) link-level is shown to be logically distinct from the normal link level mainly because of the differences in buffer management and in-transit message handling. The clock synchronization protocol maintains a system-wide synchronized time base, which can be accessed by application tasks and by other protocol modules. The FRAG protocol fragments large messages into link-level-size packets and transports them. On reception, it collects the fragments and coalesces them into a single message. The User Datagram Protocol (UDP) supports the unreliable datagram service.

The higher-level protocols include real-time channel control, HARTOS protocol (which provides the HARTOS version 1 equivalent system call interface), a name service whose functions are described in the preceding section, user datagram service, and a request-reply service. In the remainder of this section, we sketch the services provided by these protocols.

**Reliable Broadcast.**    Although broadcasting is a very simple operation for broadcast networks like the Ethernet and the Token Ring, where a message transmitted can be "seen" by every other node in the network, it is more involved for point-to-point interconnection networks. For this type of network, a simple non-redundant broadcast algorithm, which delivers a single copy of a message to every node, essentially constructs a spanning tree for the network graph rooted at the source node. It is desirable to minimize the number of store-and-forward communication steps, i.e., the height of the spanning tree. The number of required store-and-forward communication steps can be further reduced in this type of network based on the virtual cut-through switching scheme [16]. We provide support for such broadcasting in the HARTS programmable routing controller (PRC) [8].

The functionality of reliable broadcasting is essential for implementing algorithms for clock synchronization, distributed fault diagnosis, and distributed agreement in the presence of faults [19, 20]. In such applications, it is necessary to ensure that a non-faulty node can correctly deliver its private value to all other non-faulty nodes in the system. This is difficult because faulty nodes can discard, corrupt, and possibly alter the information passing through them. On-line distributed diagnosis schemes are available for identifying faults. However, these schemes do not always give 100% fault coverage. Therefore, it is highly desirable that these broadcast algorithms should work even when the identity of all the faulty processors is not known. This can be accomplished by delivering multiple copies of the message through disjoint paths to every node in the system. The receiving nodes can then identify the original message from the multiple copies using a scheme which is ap-

APPLICATION LEVEL

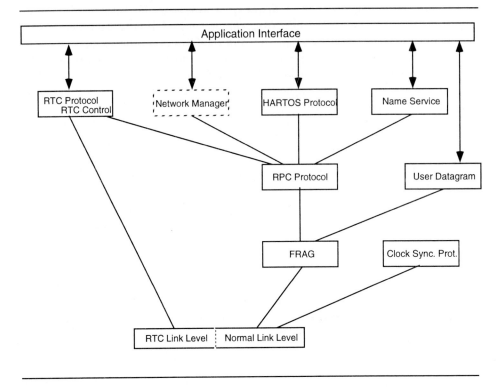

PHYSICAL LEVEL

**Figure 1.3**  Simplified View of the Communication Subsystem

propriate for the fault model, such as majority voting. This enables us to develop broadcasting algorithms for meshes which are resilient to node/link faults.

We have already developed a *k-reliable* broadcast algorithm to deliver $k$ copies of the message to each node through disjoint paths [14]. Assuming that encryption is used to guard against message corruption, a $k$-reliable broadcast will be resilient to the loss of $k - 1$ message copies.

**Clock Synchronization.**  Clock synchronization is supported by the Clock Synchronization Protocol (CP). The CP module interacts with its peers on other nodes to provide a global time base for the system. It relies on a hardware time-stamping mechanism to disseminate the clock value of a local node to other nodes [23] and uses the interactive convergence algorithm [19] on the clock values that it receives from other nodes. The PRC affixes a transmit time-stamp to a clock packet just before its transmission and it appends a receive time-stamp to any clock packet that it receives. This hardware time-stamping ensures that delays in the processing and propagation of clock messages can be factored out such that they do not affect the tightness of the synchronization. The protocol also employs a hardware-maintained local clock, which has a resolution of 1 microsecond.

The clock maintained by this protocol can be read directly by processes running on the NP. It is used to set deadlines for messages and processes, and to determine the order of services. The protocol also provides control operations that processes on the APs can use to access the time.

**Remote Procedure Call.** This protocol implements a request-reply operation with *at most once* semantics, using the technique in [3]. The protocol handles only the RPC transport mechanism. Clients of this protocol are expected to marshal the call arguments into a request packet, and subsequently extract the return results from the reply packet.

We implement the HARTOS version 1 calls [12] using a client protocol module sitting on top of RPC. Some of these calls are now redundant because their functions have been subsumed in other protocols. For example, the name service calls are handled by the Name Service Protocol. Similarly, the data transfer operations can be implemented trivially using UDP and the fragmentation protocol, FRAG.

**Real-Time Channel.** Communication in real-time systems has to be predictable, because unpredictable delays in the delivery of messages can adversely affect the execution of real-time tasks dependent on these messages. Predictable communication is difficult to achieve since network delays can be non-deterministic for numerous types of networks. The Real-Time Channel Protocol (RTCP) provides *a priori* guarantees for timely delivery of messages. The clients of this protocol are processes running on the APs. It handles the transmission and reception of both large and small messages; large messages are fragmented into packets for transmission. However, RTCP does not expect any acknowledgment and does not attempt to retransmit packets. A real-time channel is a unidirectional connection between two end-points. To support bidirectional communication, RTCP can be extended to allow the user to create a pair of real-time channels simultaneously in two opposing directions. The parameters for these two channels would be specified separately, as they are expected to be different. RTCP is responsible for transferring data to and from the local memory of the APs and the overhead incurred for this (and other functions) has to be accounted for in the computation of the end-to-end delivery time.

To establish a channel, it is necessary to specify the source and destination of the channel, the worst-case traffic patterns, and the maximum allowable delay in end-to-end message transit. The channel establishment procedure has to establish a route through the network from source to destination, ensuring that adequate communication bandwidth, buffer space, and processing bandwidth are available at all intermediate nodes in the path. Details of the channel establishment procedure may be found in [13, 15]. Channel establishment is a complex operation because it involves reservation of resources at multiple nodes in the network. It is therefore preferable to place the channel establishment function into a separate service. By making this function centralized, it is possible to make better use of network resources since we can select routes appropriately to balance network load.

This approach also makes it easier to handle network reconfiguration in the event of network failures. This service, called the Network Manager (NM), is provided by a special node (or a set of nodes) in the system. It is represented by a dashed-line block in Figure 1.3 to indicate that it is not present on all nodes in the system. Fault-tolerance of NM is achieved by assigning redundant copies of NM on multiple nodes and maintaining consistency among these copies with atomic broadcasts [13].

The control functions of RTCP are handled by the real-time channel control module, which uses an RPC mechanism to contact the NM. When a channel is successfully established, the NM returns the selected route for the channel and the worst-case delay for each link on the route. This information is recorded in data structures which are used to set deadlines for messages belonging to real-time channels.

RTCP usually treats each send request as a separate message. It enforces a rate-based flow control mechanism and adjusts the time constraints of the message accordingly. Long messages are split into fragments and these fragments are all assigned a common deadline. On the receive side, RTCP collects the fragments of a message and delivers the message to the client. If some fragments of a message do not arrive within the deadline for the message, the partial message will be delivered to the client with an appropriate warning.

## 1.4   Evaluation Tools

In addition to our work in operating systems, we are developing three software tools for performance and fault-tolerance evaluation. These tools provide us with an environment in which we can test and evaluate the hardware and software being developed for HARTS. The tools have been developed to be mutually independent. They may be used separately or in cooperation, depending on the requirements of the evaluation.

The first tool is the synthetic workload generator (SWG). The SWG compiles a high-level description of a workload to produce a synthetic workload (SW) which will execute on HARTS. The behavior and structure of the SW is controlled by the user. In this way the system may be evaluated under various workload conditions. To aid in debugging and to measure the performance of distributed real-time applications, we have developed a real-time monitor, HMON. HMON provides transparent, continuous monitoring using dedicated hardware and integrated operating system-level software. Finally, we are developing a software fault injector. The fault injector is a mechanism which inserts errors into an otherwise error-free system. The type and location of the errors can be controlled by the user. It provides a means for validating dependability mechanisms that are implemented on HARTS.

Together these tools create a facility in which a wide range of experiments may be performed. The SW may be used to exercise those parts of the system which are being studied. The monitor may be used to collect the performance data, and the fault injector may be used to simulate faulty behavior whose effects may then be studied. These tools are discussed in the following subsections.

## 1.4.1   Synthetic Workload Generation

Since HARTS is an experimental testbed, it is anticipated that a wide range of system features will be implemented and evaluated on it. We will need to evaluate these features under a range of workload conditions. Therefore, we have developed the SWG to create workloads for these evaluations. The SWG [18] compiles a high-level description of the workload into an executable synthetic workload (SW) [17]. An SW is a set of programs which execute on the target computer while performance measurements are being made. The SW produces the load on the system's resources and thus directly affects the performance indices being measured. The programs that compose the SW are not taken from an application, but are instead written such that their structure and behavior models that of the programs in an application. The tasks of the SW are parameterized such that the workload characteristics may easily be changed to suit the needs of the experimenter and the application. The SWG can produce SWs which accurately represent real workloads, or it may produce SWs which represent specific (possibly anomalous) workload conditions.

To specify the SWs, we have developed a language called the Synthetic Work-load Specification Language (SWSL). SWSL describes the workload in a form which may be used as the input to an SWG. SWSL is based on a number of Structured Analysis (SA) notations, e.g., [4, 30, 10], and rapid prototyping notations [21]. It enhances these notations to provide greater flexibility and to include structures to facilitate the specification of SWs. SWSL provides the means to specify parameters for the workload components. For example, the tasks in our workload model have parameters which specify their execution and resource usage characteristics. Of particular importance are the parameters which specify real-time characteristics of the tasks. Examples of these parameters include invocation periods, deadlines, and other real-time scheduling requirements. No previous workload model used to specify SWs had such parameters.

SWSL specifies the functions which are executed by the tasks. A function is defined as a sequence of operations which exercise different system resources. In practice, these operations will be taken from a library of synthetic operations. This library contains parameterized operations, each of which utilizes a specific resource. Synthetic operations may be interspersed with user-supplied C code to produce customized functions. SWSL also allows the specification of control constructs within the function. Using these constructs, the synthetic tasks can simulate the data-dependent branching and looping behavior of actual application tasks. Through the combination of synthetic operations, control constructs, and user-supplied C code, SWSL provides the mechanisms to specify a wide range of task behaviors.

This approach to specifying real-time workloads was taken for two reasons. First, a high-level specification of the application software, such as the SA (Structured Analysis) model, will generally be a good approximation of the structure of the workload. Thus, by using a similar model, we can produce an SW which will closely approximate the structure and behavior of the workload being modeled. The experimental evaluations performed using this SW should then provide useful and meaningful results. Second, as real-time software becomes more complex, the use of structured methods to design the software will become widespread. The design process will be supported by computer-aided software engineering (CASE) tools [9]. Our approach allows the SWG to become an integral part of a CASE tool. SWSL is similar to currently used design notations. Hence, high-level designs created by CASE tools can be used by the SWG to create SWs. The SWs thus produced will be akin to a rapid prototype. The difference is that while the rapid prototype is aimed at demonstrating the functionality of the software from the user's viewpoint, the SW is aimed at demonstrating the resource utilization behavior of the software from the system's viewpoint. As components of the application software are completed, they may be integrated into the SW specification. Therefore, the SWG may be used at all stages of system development, and the effects of design decisions at each stage may be evaluated experimentally.

The SW is intended for use in evaluating embedded distributed real-time systems. As such, it is assumed that the SW will be compiled on a workstation and the executable code downloaded to the system. In support of this scenario, we have built facilities into SWSL which make this process more efficient. SWSL defines an experiment as consisting of a number of statistically independent runs. During each run, the SW executes and performance data may be collected. A specification of a workload may contain parameter values for a number of runs. For each run, the user may define different values for the workload parameters, or a single value may be defined for a parameter for a set of consecutive runs. This single specification is compiled and downloaded at the beginning of the experiment. The SW pauses between each run to allow the user to upload performance data or to reset or adjust data collection instruments. To provide flexibility, the experiments are parameterized. The user can specify values such as the duration of each run and the random number generators used to produce stochastic behavior in the SW.

To define SWs for a distributed system, SWSL specifies on which processor each workload component is located. Components are statically allocated and can easily be moved from one processor to another between executions of the SW. This feature allows the user to change the distribution of load within the system between experiments. SWSL also provides replicated objects. Multiple identical objects may be defined on multiple processors. Such objects may be used to represent objects which have been replicated for fault-tolerance purposes, or they may be representative members of a particular class of objects within the workload being modeled.

The SWG compiles the SWSL workload description and generates the specified SW. The design of the SWG is shown in Figure 1.4. In addition to compiling the task graph and parameters, it performs connectivity and correctness checking on the task graph. It determines if the workload components are connected legally and reports any errors. One output of the SWG is a set of data structures describing the task graph and workload and experiment parameters. The second output is the C code for the application tasks. These files are compiled and linked with the SW driver object code and the library of synthetic operations to produce an executable SW, ready to be downloaded to the various processors of HARTS. No intermediate user intervention is required.

The SW is composed of a driver and the synthetic application tasks. The

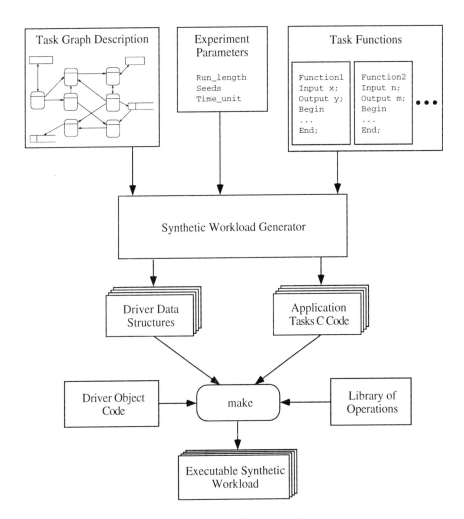

**Figure 1.4** Synthetic Workload Generation

driver performs the control functions related to the experiment. Based on the data structures produced by the SWG, it creates, initializes, and activates all the objects in the SW task graph. It also communicates with the drivers on other processors to allow synchronous SW control on the distributed system. The synthetic application tasks are responsible for creating the resource demands on the system. They execute during the experiment with little interference from the driver.

## 1.4.2   Monitoring Tools

A distributed real-time system is a complex environment from the perspectives of software design, development, testing, and operation. Monitoring distributed real-time systems is a difficult challenge that must be met if software designers, system architects, and performance evaluators are to measure, debug, test, and develop systems efficiently.

   *Monitoring* can be defined as the measurement, collection, and processing of information about the execution of tasks in a computer system. System characteristics may complicate this task. A real-time system requires the monitor itself to operate under strict reliability and performance constraints. The reliability constraints require that the monitored system and the monitor continue to operate in the presence of static or dynamic failures. The performance constraints require that the interference caused to the system by the monitor's presence must be predictable, minimal, and bounded.

   Distribution also imposes constraints on the monitor. Distributed systems lack both global state information and a sense of global simultaneity. There is no total ordering defined over events that occur on different nodes. Monitored data must be collected from several sites and integrated to obtain a coherent view of the system. Further, when tasks run in parallel, their behavior can be nondeterministic. The monitor must support deterministic reproducibility for effective debugging.

   To address these issues, we have developed HMON, a monitor for distributed real-time systems [7]. Our goal is to provide a real-time monitor integrated with its environment to support services like debugging distributed real-time applications, aiding real-time task scheduling, and measuring performance. We perform the monitoring transparently so that the programmer is not forced to add special code to applications. The monitor provides continuous monitoring capabilities throughout a real-time system's life cycle, from design and testing to production. Our monitor is flexible enough to observe both high-level events that are operating system- and application- specific as well as low-level events like shared variable references.

   HMON is a distributed software monitor that runs on a dedicated processor. The monitor uses software integrated into the HARTOS interface for flexible, transparent monitoring. We dedicate some system hardware to the monitor to minimize interference with the measured system. Predictability is maintained by keeping interference deterministic. Intrusive debugging is done only during replay, not on-line. Replay is done deterministically to make debugging feasible. Our approach is unique in that we perform transparent monitoring and deterministic replay on a distributed real-time system without adding any special hardware, such as a bus probe or a hardware instruction counter.

Monitoring and debugging are topics of active research. Software monitors are popular because they allow users to view the monitored system at various levels of complexity or abstraction. However, typically, such monitors are invasive and not applicable to real-time systems because of their unpredictable interference. Ad hoc solutions such as turning off the real-time clock or altering timeout values during monitoring operations will not work when the system interacts with the real world or uses asynchronous interrupts.

Passive hardware monitors can provide detailed, low-level information about a system, such as communication activities, memory accesses, and I/O patterns. They also cause little interference to the monitored system. However, hardware monitors do not support the interactive modification of task execution that is necessary to support debugging.

A number of monitoring and debugging systems have been developed specifically for real-time systems [22, 24, 28, 29]. However, interactive debugging of real-time programs without deterministic replay is not sufficient because debugging commands destroy the timing-dependent nature of real-time systems. Similarly, breakpoints must only be inserted during replay, not normal execution, to maintain the consistent timing behavior of the system. Fortunately, techniques developed for debugging distributed systems may safely be applied to real-time systems during replay since interference during replay does not alter program execution.

The HMON runs on a dedicated AP, called the *monitor processor* (MP), on each node of HARTS. Additional code to collect data runs on the NP and the APs of each node (see Figure 1.5). Each processor's local memory is accessible to other processors. The MP logs the data on an external user workstation. Though the data collection code interferes with the system being monitored, in our system, this interference is low, predictable, and accounted for in CPU and network scheduling. Since the interference is the same during normal execution as during development and debugging, the debugging code is a predictable part of the application.

The monitoring system can be divided into three phases: data extraction on the APs and NP, data compression on the monitoring processor, and data logging on an external workstation. Data on monitored events is acquired through code inserted into the monitored system. We acquire much of our data by monitoring system calls and context switches transparently by modifying the existing HARTOS system call interface. HMON also monitors interrupts and shared variable references to allow deterministic replay of tasks for debugging. All extracted data is sent to the MP. Each MP orders and compresses the log data and sends it from its node to an external user-level process running on a workstation outside HARTS. This process receives and archives data coming in from all MPs so that the events can be replayed for debugging. The MPs use the Ethernet controller on each node to send their data to the user workstation. The HARTS interconnection network remains unaffected by the transmission of data over the Ethernet.

## 1.4.3    Fault Injection

Real-time systems employed in life- and mission-critical tasks employ a variety of fault-tolerance and fault-recovery mechanisms to ensure high dependability. These

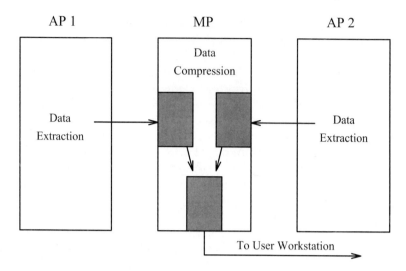

**Figure 1.5** Monitor Data Collection

mechanisms must be rigorously tested to verify that the system meets its dependability goals. This can be very difficult, given the large mean-time-between-failure (MTBF) of highly dependable systems. In order to verify the properties of such a system experimentally, there must be some way to accelerate the occurrence of faults or errors. A fault injector is a tool which allows the user to introduce faults or errors into the system.

Most previously published fault injection experiments (e.g., [1, 2]) fall into one of two categories, hardware fault injection or software fault injection. In hardware fault injection, faults are typically inserted into the system at the pin level. In software fault injection, errors are typically inserted by altering the contents of memory or registers. Errors can also be introduced by corrupting messages or altering object code.

In order to facilitate the evaluation of dependability mechanisms on HARTS, we have developed the Software Fault Injector (SFI). SFI supports a variety of faults and errors, each of which can be injected as transient, intermittent, or hard faults. In addition, SFI allows different faults to be injected at each node in the system. The injection time and duration can also be specified. This can greatly simplify the testing of dependable distributed applications, which often must be able to tolerate erroneous behavior by multiple nodes in the system over an extended period of time. In addition, SFI is easy to integrate with any workload developed for HARTS.

SFI provides a suite of tools that simplify and automate the design and execution of dependability experiments. SFI consists of two main components. These are the SFI Experiment Generator (SEG) and the SFI Control Modules (SCM). The SEG takes a user-supplied experiment description file and creates the executable files and script files used to run the fault injection experiments. The SCM consists of the routines that provide the actual fault injection capability. The SEG compiles the appropriate portions of the SCM with the workload for each node.

In order to create and run an experiment using SFI, the user only needs to create an experiment description file that provides SFI with the names of the HARTS nodes to be used, and the location of the workload and the type of faults to be injected on each node. The workload can be any application that runs on HARTS. It can be a real application, or a synthetic workload generated with the SWG. Once the experiment description file is created, the user runs SEG to create all of the executable and script files necessary to run the fault injection experiment. During the experiment, performance data may be collected using HMON.

The fault types used by SFI are memory faults, communication faults, and processor faults. The memory faults are injected as single bit or burst errors. Communication faults cause lost, altered, or delayed messages. Processor faults represent faults in functional units of the CPU.

Each fault type has a number of possible variations that can be specified by the user. The injection of memory and communication faults can be transient, intermittent, or permanent. If the fault is to occur intermittently, the user can specify a probability distribution that describes the interarrival times between faults. For memory faults, permanent faults are emulated by specifying small interarrival times for an intermittent fault. Note that this is not the same as a true permanent fault, as the faulted location can be overwritten between injections. Combinations of these faults can be used on each node, allowing the user to implement a variety of failure semantics.

## 1.5    Future Directions

Version 1 of HARTOS is completed and has been running stably for over two years. A detailed description, including performance measurements, may be found in [12]. This version was used to provide interprocessor communication for the development of the SWG and HMON. No further development of this version is planned.

Version 2 of HARTOS is under development. It currently provides all the functionality of version 1. The clock synchronization protocol has not yet been implemented since it depends on the PRC, which is under development. In addition, many of the functions of the real-time channel service have been implemented and their performance measured. The real-time channel described in this chapter deals with one-to-one communication. While it provides guarantees of real-time performance, it does so under the assumption of the absence of faults. At present, we are considering alternatives to relax this restriction and provide a fault-tolerant real-time service.

One option is to reroute a real-time channel in case of component failure, but this could take more than the guaranteed delay. In addition, failure of an application node would cause total loss of service. A more promising alternative is to extend the real-time channel concept to one-to-many communication. This could be used to provide a group channel for replicated applications to communicate in real time. The issues that need to be addressed in this extension are multicast route selection, message consistency, and message ordering.

The various evaluation tools are at different stages of completion. The SWG is operational and has been used for the performance measurements obtained for HARTOS version 1. As HARTS and HARTOS develop, the SWG will be used extensively to evaluate them. A range of experiments have been planned. First, simple SWs will be created to measure basic performance values and to test functionality. Later, the SWG will be used to generate SWs which are representative of actual workloads. We will then use these SWs to measure the performance of HARTS under the load offered by each example application. Performance indices to be studied include the performance of the network communication facilities of HARTOS, the effects of asynchronous tasks on task schedulability, message scheduling, and the performance of fault-tolerance mechanisms.

The debugging features of the monitor are incomplete and will be expanded. An improved debugger user interface will be developed. The monitor processor will also be further developed to enhance deterministic replays and support CPU scheduling. Finally, a utility to analyze monitored data on a user workstation will be explored.

The fault injector is partially complete. The experiment generator has been implemented, as has the injection of most of the fault types. Current work is on implementing the rest of the fault types and on improving the data collection and analysis tools. The fault injector is intended as a support tool for dependability experiments on HARTS. As a result, it will be continuously expanded as new applications require different capabilities.

## Acknowledgments

The work reported here is supported in part by the Office of Naval Research under Contract N00014-92-J-1080 and Grant N00014-91-J-1115, and the National Science Foundation under Grant MIP-9012549. Any opinions, findings, and conclusions or recommendations expressed in this chapter are those of the authors and do not necessarily reflect the views of the funding agencies.

## References

[1] J. Arlat, Y. Crouzet, and J.-C. Laprie, "Fault injection for dependability validation of fault-tolerant computing systems," in *Proc. Int. Symp. on Fault-Tolerant Computing*, pp. 348–355, June 1989.

[2] J. Barton, E. Czeck, Z. Segall, and D. Siewiorek, "Fault injection experiments using fiat," *IEEE Trans. Computers*, vol. 39, no. 4, pp. 575–581, April 1990.

[3] A. D. Birrell and B. J. Nelson, "Implementing remote procedure calls," *ACM Trans. Computer Systems*, vol. 2, no. 1, pp. 39–59, February 1984.

[4] W. Bruyn, R. Jensen, D. Keskar, and P. Ward, "ESML: An extended systems modeling language based on the data flow diagram," *ACM Software Engineering Notes*, vol. 13, no. 1, pp. 58–67, 1988.

[5] M.-S. Chen, K. G. Shin, and D. D. Kandlur, "Addressing, routing and broadcasting in hexagonal mesh multiprocessors," *IEEE Trans. Computers*, vol. 39, no. 1, pp. 10–18, January 1990.

[6] *ENP K1 Kernel Software User's Guide*, Communication Machinery Corp., May 1986.

[7] P. S. Dodd and C. V. Ravishankar, "Monitoring and debugging distributed real-time programs," *Software-Practice and Experience*, 1992.

[8] J. W. Dolter, P. Ramanathan, and K. G. Shin, "A microprogrammable VLSI routing controller for HARTS," in *Int. Conf. on Computer Design: VLSI in Computers*, pp. 160–163, October 1989.

[9] H. Falk, "CASE tools emerge to handle real-time systems," *Computer Design*, vol. 27, no. 1, pp. 53–74, January 1988.

[10] D. J. Hatley and I. A. Pribhai, *Strategies for Real-Time System Specification*, Dorset House Publishing, New York, 1987.

[11] N. C. Hutchinson and L. L. Peterson, "The $x$-Kernel: An architecture for implementing network protocols," *IEEE Trans. Software Engineering*, vol. 17, no. 1, pp. 1–13, January 1991.

[12] D. D. Kandlur, D. L. Kiskis, and K. G. Shin, "HARTOS: A distributed real-time operating system," *ACM SIGOPS Operating Systems Review*, vol. 23, no. 3, pp. 72–89, July 1989.

[13] D. D. Kandlur and K. G. Shin, "Design of a communication subsystem for HARTS," Technical Report CSE-TR-109-91, CSE Division, Department of EECS, The University of Michigan, Ann Arbor, MI, October 1991.

[14] D. D. Kandlur and K. G. Shin, "Reliable broadcast algorithms for HARTS," *ACM Trans. Computer Systems*, vol. 9, no. 4, pp. 374–398, November 1991.

[15] D. D. Kandlur, K. G. Shin, and D. Ferrari, "Real-time communication in multi-hop networks," in *Proc. 11th Int. Conf. on Distributed Computer Systems*, pp. 300–307, IEEE, May 1991.

[16] P. Kermani and L. Kleinrock, "Virtual cut-through: A new computer communication switching technique," *Computer Networks*, vol. 3, no. 4, pp. 267–286, September 1979.

[17] D. L. Kiskis and K. G. Shin, "A synthetic workload for real-time systems," in *Proc. 7th IEEE Workshop on Real-Time Operating Systems and Software*, pp. 77–81, May 1990.

[18] D. L. Kiskis and K. G. Shin, "Generating synthetic workloads for real-time systems," in *Proc. IEEE Workshop on Real-Time Operating Systems and Software*, pp. 109–113, May 1991.

[19] L. Lamport and P. M. Melliar-Smith, "Synchronizing clocks in the presence of faults," *Journal of the ACM*, vol. 32, no. 1, pp. 52–78, January 1985.

[20] L. Lamport, R. Shostak, and M. Pease, "The byzantine generals problem," *ACM Trans. Programming Languages and Systems*, vol. 4, no. 3, pp. 382–401, July 1982.

[21] Luqi, V. Berzins, and R. T. Yeh, "A prototyping language for real-time software," *IEEE Trans. Software Engineering*, vol. 14, no. 10, pp. 1409–1423, October 1988.

[22] D. Lyttle and R. Ford, "A symbolic debugger for real-time embedded Ada software," *Software-Practice and Experience*, vol. 20, no. 5, pp. 499–514, May 1990.

[23] P. Ramanathan, D. D. Kandlur, and K. G. Shin, "Hardware assisted software clock synchronization for homogeneous distributed systems," *IEEE Trans. Computers*, vol. 39, no. 4, pp. 514–524, April 1990.

[24] J. D. Schoeffler, "A real-time programming event monitor," *IEEE Trans. Education*, vol. 31, no. 4, pp. 245–250, November 1988.

[25] K. G. Shin, "HARTS: A distributed real-time architecture," *IEEE Computer*, vol. 24, no. 5, pp. 25–35, May 1991.

[26] *pSOS User's Guide*, Software Components Group.

[27] K. S. Stevens, "The communication framework for a distributed ensemble architecture," AI Technical Report 47, Schlumberger Research Laboratory, February 1986.

[28] H. Tokuda, M. Kotera, and C. W. Mercer, "A real-time monitor for a distributed real-time operating system," *Proc. ACM SIGPLAN/SIGOPS Workshop on Parallel and Distributed Debugging*, published in *ACM SIGPLAN Notices*, vol. 24, no. 1, pp. 68–77, January 1989.

[29] J. J. P. Tsai, K.-Y. Fang, H.-Y. Chen, and Y.-D. Bi, "A noninterference monitoring and replay mechanism for real-time software testing and debugging," *IEEE Trans. Software Engineering*, vol. 16, no. 8, pp. 897–916, August 1990.

[30] P. T. Ward, "The transformation schema: An extension of the data flow diagram to represent control and timing," *IEEE Trans. Software Engineering*, vol. 12, no. 2, pp. 198–210, February 1986.

# Chapter 2

# A Reflective Architecture for Real-Time Operating Systems

## John A. Stankovic and Krithi Ramamritham

This chapter describes how the notion of a reflective architecture can serve as a central principle for building complex and flexible real-time systems, contributing to making them more dependable. A reflective system is one that reasons about and reflects upon its own current state and that of the environment to determine the right course of action. By identifying reflective information, exposing it to application code, and retaining it at run time, a system is capable of providing predictable performance with respect to timing constraints, of reacting in a flexible manner to changing dynamics within the system as well as in the environment, to be more robust to violations of initial assumptions and to faults, to better evolve over time, and also for better monitoring, debugging, and understanding of the system. Advantages of this approach are given and details of a specific implementation of a reflective architecture in a real-time operating system are provided. Several open questions are also presented.

## 2.1 Introduction

In the field of complex real-time systems, it is a common understanding that we want integrated system-wide solutions so that design, implementation, testing, monitoring, dependability, and validation (both functional and timing) are all addressed. However, building real-time systems for critical applications and showing that they meet functional, fault tolerance, and timing requirements are complex tasks. At the heart of this complexity there exist several opposing factors. These include:

- the desire for predictability versus the need for flexibility to handle non-deterministic environments, failures, and system evolution,

- the need for abstraction to handle complexity versus the need to include implementation details in order to assess timing properties,

- the need for efficient performance and low cost versus understandability, and

- the need for autonomy (to deal better with faults and scaling) versus the need for cooperation (to achieve application semantics).

This chapter argues that one good approach for addressing such opposing requirements is a reflective system architecture that **exposes** the **correct** meta-level information. Exactly what this information should be and how it should be supported will be the subject of research for many years. However, in this chapter we provide details of our current view of this information and its implementation structures within a real-time operating system. Once a system has this information, it can be dynamically altered as system conditions change (increasing the coverage of the system dynamically), or as the system evolves over time, or is ported to another platform. In particular, the system is built with the idea that it cannot know the environment completely, but must nevertheless be dependable. The hypothesis is that with a reflective architecture the necessary flexibility for complex real-time systems can be attained. Further, we argue that this powerful type of flexibility contributes to many other things that are required, including understandability, analyzability (and therefore predictability), high performance, monitoring, debugging, and dependability. While reflection contributes to addressing all these issues, in the interest of space we focus primarily on showing how reflection supports the first two points listed above. We note that much of what is discussed in this chapter has been implemented in the Spring kernel [22], and is now being used on a robotic automated assembly testbed in non-deterministic environments.

In Section 2.2 we briefly discuss the notion of reflection and present the state of the art. In Section 2.3 we outline a methodology for real-time systems where reflection is a central principle. In Section 2.4 we identify ingredients of such a reflective architecture and provide details of its implementation in a real-time operating system. In Section 2.5 we summarize our contributions, the status of the implementation, and identify required future work.

## 2.2   State of the Art — Reflection

Reflection, as a concept, is not new and almost all systems have some reflective information in them. However, identifying reflection as a *key architectural principle* and exploiting it in real-time systems is very new. In simple terms, reflection can be defined as the computational process of reasoning about and acting upon the system itself. Normally, a computation solves an application problem such as sorting a file or filtering important signals out of radar returns. If, in addition, there is a system computation dealing with the dynamic setting of the parameters and policies of the sorting process or the filtering process itself, then we have a meta-level structure and possibilities for reflection. Consequently, when using a reflective architecture, we can consider a system to have a computational part and a reflective part. The reflective part is a self-representation of the system, exposing the system state and semantics of the application. For example, for the filtering process this might include choosing the most appropriate filter, setting parameters for the process, checking ranges of input data, executing it on most suitable processor, and so on. To best support flexibility over the long lifetimes of complex, real-time systems, we believe that it is absolutely essential to have general architecture structures capable of holding *current* state and semantics of both the application and system software, primitives for changing that information, and general (modifiable) on-line methods for using that information. In other words, such reflective information can be monitored, used in decision making during system operation, and easily changed, thereby supporting many flexibility features. Much research is still required to identify exactly what reflective information is important, how to represent it, and to determine the performance implications of using reflection, including its impact on the computational part of the system.

Reflection has appeared in AI systems, e.g., within the context of rule-based and logic-based languages [12, 21]. More recently it is being used in object-oriented languages and object-oriented databases in order to increase their flexibility [6, 13]. Combining object-oriented programming with reflection seems to be very important since object-oriented programming supports abstraction and good design and adding reflection supplies flexibility. Reflection also has been touted as valuable to distributed systems for supporting transparency and flexibility [24], but details and open research problems have not been worked out. Reflection has also been used to some extent in our past work on real-time systems [23]. This chapter discusses a greatly expanded view of the impact of reflection on real-time systems.

One problem in discussing reflection is that reflection is a term used somewhat differently in three different areas: AI, object-oriented programming, and object-oriented databases. The differences emerge from two issues: one, it is a matter of degree as to what is considered reflective and what is considered computational; not always easy to identify, and two, some definitions require reflection to be able to generate code at run time similar to how LISP has a duality between code and data. In this chapter we explicitly identify what information and processing we consider reflective for complex, dependable, real-time, distributed computing systems.

## 2.3    Methodology

While most of this chapter deals with reflection, here we briefly present an overview of a design methodology for real-time systems. We do this, in part, to emphasize that reflection by itself is **not** sufficient to address the problems raised in the Introduction, and, in part, to place what it does provide in perspective. Reflection can be used independently of the overall design paradigm, e.g., it can be used with an object-oriented design and implementation or with a more classical procedure-oriented design and implementation. Because of the obvious advantages of an object-oriented design at the functional level, we briefly discuss a vision of how a real-time system could be developed under this approach. This would contribute to dependability. However, significant performance questions still exist for object-oriented real-time systems. In particular, open questions remain in the areas of interaction of concurrency and inheritance, overheads for support of objects, and predictability of these run-time structures which has not been established nor even seriously considered. Because of these reasons, in the actual prototype reflective system that we have developed [14, 15, 22], we currently employ a procedure based design and programming paradigm which is extended to integrate with reflection.

*A vision for the design of complex real-time systems might begin with the use of a concurrent object-oriented approach subject to the integrating theme that the system is reflective.* Concurrent programming support is required to handle the highly asynchronous, event-driven nature of many real-time systems. The object-oriented aspects provide modularity, abstraction, information hiding, library modules with different properties, and so on. The hierarchies created within object classes can contain the application-level reflective information and proceed from more abstract levels down to specific implementations where the implementations may have varying run-time costs and different fault semantics as a function of the actual compilers, operating systems, and hardware used. Information on the system configuration and implementation is supplied by a separate language such as our System Description Language (SDL) [14]. In this way the (programming-level) objects can encapsulate the high-level timing and fault tolerance requirements as well as the application-level reflective information; and the SDL will capture implementation details and system-level reflective information. Various tools then combine information from these languages for analysis of predictability and for creating a reflective run-time system.

Reflection supports flexibility, but flexibility is a doubled-edged sword. Too much flexibility can destroy predictability. Consequently, control must be exercised over the use of flexibility both via constraints at design time and via the use of scheduling paradigms which provide for predictability. We believe that the object-oriented paradigm may provide the structure necessary to constrain builders of critical applications, even when we allow a high degree of flexibility (supported by reflection). And dynamic real-time scheduling can produce a run-time, system-wide schedule for executing the objects to meet timing and fault requirements.

Since the reflective paradigm should be used across all levels of the system, what information is reflective is application dependent. However, most complex real-time systems will require features found in operating systems, so we can apply this architecture to the operating system in a more generic manner than for higher-level application code; we do this in the remainder of this chapter.

## 2.4   A Reflective Architecture

Can a flexible real-time system architecture be significantly different from a general timesharing system architecture? It can, and it must be, to handle the added complexity of time constraints, flexible operation, and dependability. As systems get large we can no longer handcraft solutions, but require architectures that support algorithmic analysis along functional, time, and dependability dimensions. This analysis can and should be done for a dynamic system, as a completely static approach relies too much on *a priori* identification of fault and load hypotheses which are invariably wrong in complex, critical applications.

One problem we have in real-time systems is that the time dimension reaches across all levels of abstraction. Reflection has an advantage here in that at design time, at programming time, and at run time, one can reach across those layers. For example, if the programmer knows that the system retains the task importance, worst-case execution time as a function of a system state, and fault semantics for use at run time, then that user may program policies that make adaptive use of this information, including exact execution-time costs. This allows for more efficient use of resources, all information can be dynamically altered, and new policies can be added more easily, than *a priori* choosing one policy and mapping to a priority where all information on how that priority was achieved is lost!

Building a real-time system based on a reflective architecture means that first we must identify reflective information regarding the system. This information includes:

- importance of a task, group of tasks, and how tasks' importance relates to each other and to system modes,

- time requirements (deadlines, periods, jitter, etc.),

- time profiles, such as the worst-case execution times or formulas depicting the execution time of the module,

- resource needs,

- precedence constraints,

- communication requirements,

- objectives or goals of the system,

- consistency and integrity constraints,

- policies to guide system-wide scheduling,

- fault tolerance requirements and policies to guide adaptive fault tolerance,

- policies to guide tradeoff analyses, and

- performance monitoring information.

Implementation structures in the operating system then retain this information and primitives allow it to be dynamically changed. We have implemented this in the Spring kernel [22] by defining process control blocks where much of the above information is kept, and other data structures that keep more system-wide information, such as properties of groups of processes.

## 2.4.1   Specification of Reflective Information

Given that we choose to use a reflective architecture, we must be able to specify the reflective information. It is obvious that in real-time systems we must be able to specify real-time and fault tolerance requirements. To keep system costs reasonable and address the needs of individual tasks, we would also like to be able to specify adaptive fault tolerance policies. Further, we want to be able to analyze the system to meet predictability requirements and allow flexibility at run time. To do this, what is required is the ability to separate what can be specified at a higher, more abstract level from implementation details. However, in a real-time system the implementation details are critical to the analysis and cannot be overlooked or relegated to *unimportant details*.

As a result, we are developing three related and integrated languages that are then used by various tools for design and analyses. The three complementary languages are as follows. First, we need a high-level programming language that is efficient in producing source code and capable of specifying reflective information such as timing requirements (deadlines, periods, etc.) and the need for *guarantees* with respect to these requirements. In the spirit of research, we have developed two versions of such languages, Spring-C [15] and Real-Time Concurrent C (RTCC) [5]. Spring-C is currently implemented and used with our current overall reflective system implementation. However, it is very simple. In parallel, together with colleagues at ATT Bell Labs, we have developed a more sophisticated real-time language with the necessary features for timing specification and guarantee semantics, but it has not been integrated with the Spring kernel. Second, we require a system description language that provides enough details about the implementation so that careful, detailed, and accurate timing analysis can be performed. We have already designed and implemented this language (mentioned above), called the System Description Language (SDL) [14]. Third, we require a notation for specifying fault tolerance requirements on a task-by-task basis, where it is possible to describe adaptive management of redundancy. In this area, we have a preliminary design of such a language, called Fault Tolerant Entities for Real-Time (FERT) [2].

At the present time we want to keep the timing specification in the high-level language and the fault tolerance specification of redundancy strategies in another language, for separation of concerns and abstraction reasons. An open research question is whether this separation is suitable or whether we should merge the specifications of time and fault tolerance into one language.

In SDL we can specify details regarding the network, each node in the network, memory layout, bus characteristics, device characteristics and locations, kernel features, and other aspects related to performing accurate timing analysis. As we add timing requirements, extensions will be required and descriptions of primitives dealing with support for fault tolerance are also necessary. We would also like to add greater support for describing the environment which is being controlled by the real-time system. This feature is severely lacking in state-of-the-art tools and languages today.

FERT allows a designer to treat each FERT object as a fault-tolerant entity with protection boundaries (fault containment units), initially without worrying about timing and redundancy issues. The designer of the FERT itself then specifies a set of application modules as part of a single *entity*. The application modules represent user code for redundant operations, or voters, or more general adjudication code. Each of these application modules would be written in Spring-C or RTCC with associated timing requirements. In addition to application modules, the FERT designer also supplies one or more adaptive control polices using four basic primitives which *explicitly* interact with scheduling and analysis algorithms, both off-line analysis and on-line algorithms that provide dynamic guarantees. Finally, FERTs carefully control input and output via PORTS. Timing, task value information, and so on, can be input via the PORTS and used by the adaptive control strategies. We consider more details of FERTs in Sections 2.4.3 and 2.4.4.

Therefore, when programming with real-time languages, in our case Spring-C (or eventually with RTCC), the System Description Language (SDL) [14], and FERT [2], we identify and provide reflective information and write code that modifies it. Tools can use this information for analysis and design *knowing* that such information is also available at run time. We now provide more specific examples of the reflective architecture for scheduling, fault tolerance, and their interaction.

## 2.4.2   Real-Time Scheduling

Most real-time kernels provide a fixed-priority scheduling mechanism. This works when tasks' priorities are fixed. However, in general, this mechanism is *inadequate* because many systems require dynamic priorities and mapping a dynamic scheme onto a fixed-priority mechanism can be very inefficient, and significant information can be lost in the process. In other words, the run-time system has no information as to how the fixed priority was calculated, e.g., it might have been some weighted formula that combined importance and deadline and resource needs.

Fixed-priority scheduling is also *incomplete* because it deals only with the CPU resource. Since we are interested in when a task completes, we must consider all the resources that a task requires. An integrated view of resource management should be part of the reflective architecture interface, including the ability to specifically identify the needed resources and to reserve them for the (future) time when they will be needed. So, reservations of sets of resources should be part of the architecture.

Fixed-priority scheduling has *missing functionality* because it substitutes a single priority number for possibly a set of issues, such as the semantic value of completing the task, the timing constraint of the task, and fault properties of the task. Further, a fixed priority ignores the fact that semantic information is often dynamic, i.e., a function of the state of the system.

When using priority-based scheduling, the analysis either assumes a static system and shows that *logically* the system works (but assumption coverages are often unknown and if something unexpected occurs, then the system is uncategorized), or assumes a completely dynamic approach with average-case performance; this is unacceptable for critical applications.

In order to deal with predictability versus flexibility, there is a need for **multi-**

**level, multi-dimensional** scheduling algorithms that explicitly categorize the performance, including when there is system degradation or unexpected events. It is multi-level in the sense that we categorize the tasks into critical (missing the deadline causes loss of life or total system failure), essential (these tasks have hard deadlines and no value is accrued if the deadline is missed, but the tasks are not critical), soft real-time (task values drop after the deadline but not to zero or some negative number), and non-real-time (these tasks have no deadlines).

Each category has its own performance metric. Critical tasks must be shown to meet their deadlines and fault requirements in the worst case based on the most intelligent assessment of environmental conditions that we can make at deployment time, but **in addition** we must be able to dynamically borrow processing power and resources from the other classes of work so as to understand how much additional load and faults can be handled. This additional work could be categorized as *in the worst case*, e.g., where all tasks run to worst-case times, and as *average case* where tasks execute to average execution times and where it is likely that even greater unexpected loads can be handled. Of course, no one wants to run the system in these difficult loads, but if such loads exist, the approach allows for categorization of what happens in excess load and likelihood of being able to continue. This is in contrast to some static solutions where any excess critical load is *guaranteed* to cause failure! It is also true that in many static designs all tasks are equated to critical tasks, thereby increasing the cost of the system or even making it infeasible due to the combinatorial explosion of schedules that have to be accounted for in large, complex, dynamic environments.

We have developed and analyzed an algorithm for classes of tasks and where time can be borrowed from non-critical tasks in a categorized manner [4]. This permits a degree of *safety* because critical tasks are guaranteed, *robustness* because unexpected events (of a certain class, i.e., excess load) are handled in a categorized manner, and *availability* because the system gracefully degrades rather than failing catastrophically. Details of the algorithm and its analysis are beyond the scope of this chapter, but can be found in [4]. It is important to note that while this algorithm has these nice attributes, the algorithm assumes a very simple task model. It is necessary to derive new algorithms with the same attributes, but with more sophisticated task characteristics.

Essential tasks, soft real-time tasks, and non-real-time tasks each have a probabilistic performance metric, but these can be a function of load. For example, in the absence of failures and overloads it may be that 100% of essential tasks also make their deadline, but this degrades as unexpected loads occur. Interesting approaches have been developed, including [19], where dynamic arrivals are accounted for when doing static allocation of critical periodic tasks. Other possibilities include bounding the performance, such as discussed in [7, 10].

The algorithms are multi-dimensional [17] in that they must consider all resources needed by a task, not just the CPU, and they must consider precedence constraints and communication requirements, not just independent tasks. Providing algorithm support for this level of scheduling improves productivity and reduces errors compared to having a very primitive priority mechanism and requiring the designer to map tasks to priorities accounting for worst cases blocking times over resources and interrupts. While the details of this type of algorithm are beyond the scope of this chapter, what is important about it is that it dynamically uses reflective information about the tasks requirements (importance, deadline, precedence constraints, resource requirements, fault semantics, etc.). See [17, 19, 20] for more details.

We also use scheduling in planning mode as opposed to myopic scheduling.[1] When tasks arrive, the planning based scheduling algorithm uses the reflective information about active tasks and creates a full schedule for the active tasks and predicts if one or more deadlines will be missed. If deadlines would be missed, error handling can occur before the deadline is missed, often simplifying error recovery. Further, because reflective information is available, the decision as to how to handle the predicted timing failure can be made more intelligently and as a function of the current state of the system as opposed to some *a priori* chosen policy. The planning based scheduling with its inherent advantages is implemented in the Spring kernel [17, 22] and a scheduling co-processor has been implemented to reduce its run time overhead [3].

### 2.4.3   Fault Tolerance

Many real-time systems require adaptive fault tolerance [8] in order to operate in complex, highly variable environments, to keep costs low (rather than a brute force static approach that replicates everything regardless of environmental conditions), and so that redundancy and control can be tailored to the individual application functions as is required by those individual functions. The reflective architecture is a suitable structure for adaptive fault tolerance. We now briefly discuss some of the details of what constitutes our current view of a reflective architecture for adaptive fault tolerance based on a three-level framework.

At the highest level of this framework is the overall design process, which starts with the specification of the physical inputs and outputs to and from the external world, a first specification of the important functional blocks in the system and the flow of data and interactions among them, a first definition of timing requirements (periods, deadlines, and response times of event-response chains), an identification of which functions are critical indicating that their execution must be guaranteed off-line, and a specification of mode changes. This top-level functional design ignores the issue of software redundancy.

To manage redundancy, we introduce an intermediate level of design decomposition inside the functional blocks and above the application code. Redundancy is added inside the individual functional blocks, using a general scheme called FERT (Fault-Tolerant Entity for Real Time) [2] which adheres to the reflective architecture approach. The FERT level extends previous fault tolerance work [1, 11, 16] in two main ways: by including in the notation features that explicitly address real-time constraints, and by a flexible and adaptable control strategy for managing

---

[1]Myopic scheduling refers to those algorithms which only choose what the next task to execute should be. At run time these algorithms do not have any concept of total load, or whether any or all of the tasks are likely to miss their deadlines.

redundancy.

The third level of the framework is the coding of the application modules themselves. The three levels must be consistent with each other.

While it is the highest level of the framework that creates the intermodule (inter FERT) system structure, we now concentrate on the FERT level itself because this is where many reflective aspects of adaptive fault tolerance reside. The reflective aspects of FERT can be divided into two parts: the reflective information itself and the overall structure. Information regarding timing constraints, importance of tasks (specified as values and penalties), levels and types of redundancy, and adaptive control of redundancy are all part of the reflective information. All this information is visible at design, implementation, and run time, allowing it to be dynamically updated and used by on-line policies. For design time, the generic design notation can specify information such as whether $n$-copies and a voter, or primary backups, or imprecise computations are required for each individual FERT, and to notify the scheduling mechanisms (both off-line and on-line algorithms) of relative importance of tasks, their timing requirements, and their worst-case and average-case use of resources. This specification is part of the reflective architecture which links the design to both off-line analysis and on-line scheduling. Additionally, a FERT has its own structure, which is exposed to all levels. The structure consists of (1) ports through which all inputs and outputs pass, (2) application modules which implement the functionality and voting or adjudication of the FERT, if needed, and (3) a control module which specifies how application modules interact with each other and with the run-time system. The control part is meant to specify adaptive strategies that take into account available resources, deadlines, importance, and observed faults.

The control part uses four generic primitives which we believe should be visible in a reflective architecture supporting dependable computing:

- **possible**: asks whether a collection of tasks can be feasibly scheduled; multiple **possible** requests can be issued in parallel; this allows dynamic analyzability with respect to meeting timing constraints;

- **exec**: identifies a list of tasks that must be executed subject to various constraints; typically used by the control when finally deciding what should execute given the results of the **possible** queries;

- **unused**: identifies resources which were planned to be used but no longer required, e.g., because the initial version of the task completed successfully and the backups are no longer required; improves performance of the system;

- **output**: finally commit the produced results.

Even though we have developed a notation for adaptive fault tolerance under time constraints, many open research questions remain, including:

- how allocation decisions for the redundant copies are made and specified,

- how system-wide considerations will be included rather than the entity-by-entity redundancy and timing design now supported,

- determining what information must be retained, at run time (what should be the interface to the run-time kernel),

- replica determinism definition and support,

- recovery semantics that should exist within the FERT itself, and

- flexibility provided by FERT is very powerful, but if not *controlled,* analysis will be impossible. Therefore, we need to develop controls on the specification of flexible operations that allow high adaptivity and reliability, yet is predictable and analyzable.

In summary, the reflective architecture for supporting adaptive fault tolerance permits the designer to specify time, importance, redundancy, and control information *knowing* that the run-time structure will retain this information, so that the adaptive control policies implementer can use and modify such information. In particular, the interaction with the off-line and on-line schedulers permits more flexibility while preserving timing-related predictability. Since the intent of this section is to focus on reflective architectures for fault tolerance, we are brief and do not discuss many other issues related to fault tolerance. Interested readers should see [2].

## 2.4.4   Integrating Scheduling and Fault Tolerance

Scheduling must explicitly address real-time constraints for guaranteeing deadlines for redundant copies, voters, error handlers, and so on. It must also address different classes of tasks, such as critical tasks, hard deadline but not critical tasks, soft deadline tasks, and non-real-time tasks. Scheduling will also be part of the off-line analysis, e.g., to guarantee minimum levels of guarantee for critical tasks. It is necessary to integrate the off-line scheduling decisions with the dynamic operation of the system in a manner such that the off-line guarantees are not violated at run time, and such that the system maximizes its effectiveness beyond the minimum guaranteed part.

Off-line support is necessary to create *a priori* guarantees that the minimum performance and reliability of the system are achieved. This may be accomplished in a number of ways. Here we discuss briefly one way to accomplish this task using a form of *reservation of flexible time slots.*

The off-line algorithm works with the following assumptions:

- the Spring-C or RTCC, SDL, and FERT languages describe the timing and fault behavior of modules on an individual basis as well as other module requirements, such as precedence constraints and general resource requirements;

- a system-level specification details the minimum level of guaranteed performance and reliability required;

- the workload requirements are specified; and

- some knowledge of the run-time algorithms and environment is utilized.

The environment information includes the hardware resources available and a distributed, real-time, fault-tolerant system kernel that has (i) a global time base, (ii) run-time data structures that contain the flexibility and adaptability requirements of the application, (iii) predictable primitives, (iv) run-time scheduling support, and (v) a basic guarantee paradigm which uses on-line planning.

The off-line guarantee algorithm takes as input all the information listed above and attempts to find a feasible allocation and schedule for the modules that are part of the minimum guaranteed requirements, as well as accounting for other requirements in order to obtain good performance beyond the minimum. In particular, the interaction between the FERT specifications and the off-line algorithm is as follows. FERTs are typed as being critical or non-critical. All critical FERTS are guaranteed by the off-line scheduling algorithm. In many cases the critical FERTS will have a single strategy defined and therefore this is what must be guaranteed. If more than one strategy is defined for a critical FERT, then the minimum strategy is *a priori* guaranteed by the off-line algorithm, and at run time, if it is possible, a more comprehensive and valuable strategy may be dynamically guaranteed each time the FERT executes. Non-critical FERTS are dynamically guaranteed using the options specified in the FERT, but some overall time and resource availability may be guaranteed for all non-critical FERTs.

Since this algorithm executes off-line and for the critical tasks, significant compute time can and should be devoted to this problem. If the heuristic is having difficulty in producing feasible allocations and schedules, the designer can choose to add resources to the system or modify requirements and re-run the algorithm. The output is a flexible timetable with earliest and latest scheduled start times, and finish times for all the critical tasks and their minimum redundant copies and/or voters, and idle intervals.

Various heuristics for static allocation and scheduling exist in the literature [9, 18, 19, 26]. We base the discussion of what is required in a new heuristic on a set of extensions to the heuristic found in [19]. That heuristic is able to schedule complex periodic tasks in distributed systems. It handles periodic time constraints, worst-case execution time, general resource needs, precedence constraints, communicating tasks, and replication requirements. The communicating tasks, when allocated across nodes of the distributed system, are scheduled in conjunction with a time-slotted subnet. The algorithm as it now exists has been evaluated by simulation. Further, extensions to the algorithm have been developed which attempt to balance load and spread out (in time) scheduled tasks to avoid clustered computation time which could cause long latency. In other words, some results have been developed which account for the dynamic operation of the system when performing the static allocation and scheduling off-line.

We need to enhance the current algorithm in the following ways:

- considering aperiodic tasks with minimum guarantees,

- enhancing the fault semantics to include those supported by FERTs,

- accounting for the dynamics in a more sophisticated manner, including creating a window for each statically guaranteed task composed of an earliest start time, latest start time, and deadline,

- addressing tasks of different importance, and

- addressing mode changes.

The on-line algorithm runs in parallel with application processes. It uses the *a priori* generated flexible timetable (that accounts for all resources, not just the CPU) to insert newly invoked work (above the minimum reserved). If newly invoked work can be placed in the table, then the work is dynamically guaranteed, else various actions are taken based on the current policy. The planner also uses the on-line descriptions of the fault behaviors of the active FERTS, compiled from their control components. For example, suppose that a certain FERT is invoked, and the on-line scheduling algorithm (a planner) identifies the preferred strategy as requiring a primary and two backups to be scheduled prior to the deadline, all on different nodes. If the planner can find open intervals for this requirement, in time, then that strategy is dynamically guaranteed. If not, the planner applies the designer-specified action, e.g., the information associated with this FERT might indicate just to abort the FERT, or alternatively, it might indicate that a strategy consisting of a simple error handler with no redundancy should be scheduled. The planner for a given system must be sufficiently powerful to support the level of adaptability of fault semantics specified by the designer, and in general, planners on different nodes must cooperate to find feasible task assignments to time slots, including subnet time slots. A key problem is making the planner fast enough (and bounded) to be usable in many systems. However, the cost of distributed planning may be reduced by using a scheduling chip [3].

## 2.5   Conclusions

Current real-time systems platforms present inadequate, incomplete, and missing functionality in their architectures, including at the interface to scheduling and for fault tolerance. As a result of these poor interfaces, critical real-time systems are difficult to design, maintain, analyze, and understand. The systems tend to be inflexible and productivity is low. We need to raise the level of functionality that the run-time platform provides to better provide portability, productivity, and lower costs. A reflective architecture has potential in these areas.

Further, in order to support dependable real-time systems in complex and unfriendly environments, the current goals, policies, and state of the system must be available for dynamic access and modification. However, the dynamics must be carefully controlled. Establishing designs and solutions that engineer good tradeoffs among the opposing factors listed in the Introduction will be difficult and the subject of research for many years. However, the reflective architecture has many nice properties that provide a structure for engineering those tradeoffs.

More specifically, in this chapter we presented a view of how complex real-time systems for critical applications might be built based on a reflective architecture.

While many systems contain various amounts of information that are used dynamically, in many cases such information and its use is ad hoc and piecemeal. Here we identified specific reflective information as well as describing integrated and more complete architectural designs for both real-time and fault tolerance requirements. We discussed how using reflection as an architectural principle enhances certain aspects of dependability because it (i) addresses time constraints at all levels of the system so that more accurate timing analysis can be done even early in the design, (ii) facilitates the use of scheduling algorithms that are robust even under violations in the initial assumptions, (iii) supports planning-based scheduling that allows detection of timing errors early and application of state- and time-dependent recovery strategies, and (iv) supports adaptive fault tolerance so that there is flexible management of redundancy subject to time constraints.

While final verification that this approach will succeed in practice remains to be demonstrated (i.e., it has not been used on real safety critical applications), we have demonstrated many aspects of it in many ways. For example, a System Description Language (SDL) has been designed and implemented [14] along with extensions to the programming language C, called Spring-C. A more sophisticated real-time language, RTCC, has also been designed. These languages provide specification of and access to reflective information. A compiler [15] has been implemented that accumulate this information and make it part of the run-time structures of the Spring kernel [22]. The kernel contains the planning-based scheduling algorithms [17] that dynamically create predictable execution, and to lower the overhead of on-line planning, a hardware scheduling chip has been designed and implemented [3]. Many aspects of the algorithms and implementation details have been studied and shown to be valuable both via simulation [4, 17] and in an actual distributed testbed system composed of three multiprocessor nodes (15 processors) [22]. The adaptive fault tolerance aspects of the reflective architecture have not been implemented, and are still in the design stage [2].

Finally, systems which support flexibility and adaptability are usually more difficult to understand and control. Without good constraints and guidelines a designer could program haphazardly, making it almost impossible to analyze. Future work includes developing good engineering tradeoffs between what is necessary for adaptability and what is necessary for analyzability. It is also necessary to embed the approach we discussed here in an overall design methodology, such as object-oriented programming.

# Acknowledgments

This work has been supported, in part, by NSF under Grants IRI 9208920 and CDA 8922572, by ONR under Grant N00014-92-J-1048, and by CNR-IEI under the PDCS project.

We would like to thank Doug Niehaus for his various contributions to the project, including major parts of the design and implementation of the system. Many others in the Spring project also deserve thanks. We thank them all. We also thank A. Bondavalli and L. Strigini for their contributions to our joint work on adaptive fault tolerance.

# References

[1] A. Bondavalli, F. Giandomenico, and J. Xu, A Cost Effective and Flexible Scheme for Software Fault Tolerance, Univ. of Newcastle, TR 372, Feb. 1992.

[2] A. Bondavalli, J. Stankovic, and L. Strigini, Adaptable Fault Tolerance for Real-Time Systems, *Proc. Third International Workshop on Responsive Computer Systems*, Sept. 1993.

[3] W. Burleson, J. Ko, D. Niehaus, K. Ramamritham, J. Stankovic, Wallace, and C. Weems, The Spring Scheduling Co-processor: A Scheduling Accelerator, *Proc. ICCD*, Cambridge, MA, Oct. 1993.

[4] G. Buttazzo and J. Stankovic, RED: A Robust Earliest Deadline Scheduling Algorithm, *Proc. Responsive Systems Workshop*, Sept. 1993.

[5] N. Gehani and K. Ramamritham, Real-Time Concurrent C: A Language for Programming Dynamic Real-Time Systems, *Real-Time Systems*, Vol. 3, No. 4, Dec. 1991.

[6] M. Ibrahim, editor, *Proc. OOPLSA '91 Workshop on Reflection and Metalevel Architectures in Object Oriented Programming*, Oct. 1991.

[7] R. Karp, On-line versus Off-line Algorithms: How Much Is It Worth to Know the Future, *Information Processing*, North-Holland, Amsterdam, Vol. 1, 1992.

[8] K. Kim and T. Lawrence, Adaptive Fault Tolerance: Issues and Approaches, *Proc. Second IEEE Workshop on Future Trends in Distributed Computing Systems*, Cairo, Egypt, 1990.

[9] C. Koza, Scheduling of Hard Real-Time Tasks in the Fault Tolerant Distributed Real-Time System MARS, *Proc. Fourth IEEE Workshop on Real-Time Operating Systems*, Boston, pp. 31-36, 1987.

[10] G. Le Lann, Why Should We Keep Using Precambrian Design Approaches at the Dawn of the Third Millennium? *Proc. Workshop on Large, Distributed, Parallel Architecture Real-Time Systems*, March 1993.

[11] C. Liu, A General Framework for Software Fault Tolerance, PDCS Second Year Project Report, ESPRIT Project 3092, 1991.

[12] P. Maes, Concepts and Experiments in Computational Reflection, *OOPSLA '87, Sigplan Notices*, Vol. 22, No. 12, pp. 147-155, 1987.

[13] S. Matsuoka, T. Watanabe, Y. Ichisugi, and A. Yonezawa, Object Oriented Concurrent Reflective Architectures, 1992.

[14] D. Niehaus, J. Stankovic, and K. Ramamritham, The Spring System Description Language, UMASS TR-93-08, 1993.

[15] D. Niehaus, Program Representation and Translation for Predictable Real-Time Systems, *Proc. RTSS*, pp. 43-52, Dec. 1991.

[16] D. Powell et al., The Delta-4 Approach to Dependability on Open Distributed Computing Systems, *Proc. 18th International Symposium on Fault Tolerant Computing*, Tokyo, Japan, 1988.

[17] K. Ramamritham, J. Stankovic, and P. Shiah, Efficient Scheduling Algorithms For Real-Time Multiprocessor Systems, *IEEE Transactions on Parallel and Distributed Computing*, Vol. 1, No. 2, pp. 184-194, Apr. 1990.

[18] K. Ramamritham, Scheduling Complex Periodic Tasks, *Proc. International Conference on Distributed Computing Systems*, 1990.

[19] K. Ramamritham and J. Adan, Providing for Dynamic Arrivals During the Static Allocation and Scheduling of Periodic Tasks, *Proc. Real-Time Operating System and Software*, May 1993.

[20] K. Ramamritham and J. Stankovic, Scheduling Strategies Adopted in Spring: An Overview, chapter in *Foundations of Real-Time Computing: Scheduling and Resource Management*, edited by Andre van Tilborg and Gary Koob, Kluwer Academic Publishers, Dordrecht, The Netherlands, pp. 277-306, 1991.

[21] B. Smith, Reflection and Semantics in a Procedural Language, MIT TR 272, 1982.

[22] J. Stankovic and K. Ramamritham, The Spring Kernel: A New Paradigm for Real-Time Systems, *IEEE Software*, Vol. 8, No. 3, pp. 62-72, May 1991.

[23] J. Stankovic, On the Reflective Nature of the Spring Kernel, invited paper, *Proc. Process Control Systems '91*, Feb. 1991.

[24] R. Stroud, Transparency and Reflection in Distributed Systems, position paper for *Fifth ACM SIGOPS European Workshop*, April 1992.

[25] B. Wyatt, K. Kavi, and S. Hufnagel, Parallelism in Object Oriented Languages: A Survey, *IEEE Software*, Vol. 6, Nov. 1992.

[26] J. Xu and D. Parnas, Scheduling Processes with Release Times, Deadlines, Precedence, and Exclusion Relations in Real-Time Systems, *IEEE Trans. on Software Engineering*, Vol. 16, pp. 360-369, 1990.

# Chapter 3

# CHAOS$^{arc}$ : Real-Time Objects and Atomicity for Multiprocessors[1]

## Ahmed Gheith and Karsten Schwan

CHAOS$^{arc}$ is an object-based multiprocessor operating system kernel that provides primitives with which programmers may easily construct objects of differing types and object invocations of differing semantics, targeting multiprocessor systems and real-time applications. The CHAOS$^{arc}$ kernel can *guarantee* desired performance and functionality levels of selected computations in real-time applications. Such guarantees can be made despite possible uncertainty in execution environments by allowing programs to *adapt* in performance and functionality to varying operating conditions. This chapter reviews the primitives offered by CHAOS$^{arc}$ and it demonstrates how the required elements of the CHAOS$^{arc}$ real-time kernel are constructed with those primitives.

## 3.1 Reliability in Real-Time Systems

In contrast to other parallel or distributed application software, the control software of real-time systems cannot be termed *reliable* unless it exhibits two key attributes [27]: (1) computations must complete within well-defined timing constraints typically captured by execution *deadlines* [20], and (2) programs must exhibit predictable behavior in the presence of uncertain operating environments

[1]This chapter is based on "CHAOS$^{arc}$ : Kernel Support for Multi-weight Objects, Invocations, and Atomicity in Real-Time Multiprocessor Applications," by Ahmed Gheith and Karsten Schwan, which appeared in *ACM Transactions on Computer Systems*, vol. 11, no. 1, pp. 33–72, February 1993, ©1993, Association for Computing Machinery, Inc.

[1]. CHAOS$^{arc}$ [2] is an object-based operating system kernel that addresses (1) and (2) by provision of constructs with which programmers may *guarantee* desired performance and functionality levels of selected computations in real-time applications.

CHAOS$^{arc}$ deals with uncertainty by permitting programs to *adapt* [1] (i.e., change at run time) in performance and functionality to varying operating conditions. Our past research has addressed adaptations that anticipate changes in the operating environment—termed *preventive adaptations*. Such adaptations attempt to guarantee certain levels of performance or functionality in operating software by making assumptions regarding future system behavior based on past behavior [1, 10, 27]. The mechanisms of CHAOS$^{arc}$ are motivated by experiences with a complex real-time application (the ASV autonomous suspension vehicle [23]). A novel element of CHAOS$^{arc}$ is its support for *reactive adaptations* performed in response to external or exceptional events like failures, temporary overloads, and so on.

As with the CHAOS operating system [27], CHAOS$^{arc}$ supports an object model of software tailored to real-time systems. Namely, real-time software—termed *operating software*—consists of a number of autonomous *objects*, each providing a number of *operations* (entry points) that can be invoked by other objects. Operations are executed by multi-grain tasks ranging from procedures executed synchronously in the caller's address space, to single or multiple execution threads, which may be executed asynchronously and in parallel with the invoking task. Multi-grain tasks are complemented by multi-grain invocations, which range from reliable invocations that maintain parameters and return information (or even communication 'streams' [27]) to invocations that implement unreliable 'control signals' or 'pulses' [27]. Furthermore, invocation semantics can be varied by attachment of real-time attributes like delays and deadlines, where deadline semantics may vary from *guaranteed deadlines*, which are hard deadlines [20] that must not be missed, to *soft deadlines* that may be missed occasionally, to *recoverable deadlines* that cause programmed recovery actions when missed, to *weak deadlines* [15, 16], which specify that partial or incomplete results are acceptable when the deadline is missed. Thus, the first contribution of the CHAOS$^{arc}$ kernel is its configurability, namely, its support for the assembly of efficient representations of multi-grain objects and multi-type invocations. Configurability is a property CHAOS$^{arc}$ shares with most high-performance operating systems, including the Synthesis kernel [17] and Amber [3].

The second contribution of CHAOS$^{arc}$ is its specific support for real-time programming, such as the provision of deadlines and the associated real-time scheduling mentioned above. Such support culminates in the notion of real-time, atomic computations—for simplicity, henceforth termed 'atomic computations'—consisting of sets of atomic, real-time invocations. Each set defines a grouping of related invocations that is to be viewed as a single execution unit. Clearly, atomic computations

---

[2]A **C**oncurrent, **H**ierarchical, **A**daptable **O**perating **S**ystem supporting atomic, real-time computations.

in CHAOS$^{arc}$ are related to similar concepts in distributed databases and network operating systems [33], in that CHAOS$^{arc}$ must be capable of performing exception and event handling, synchronization, scheduling [2, 11, 34], and atomic computations [21] in a manner similar to what must be done for any parallel and distributed application. In addition, for each atomic computation in CHAOS$^{arc}$, three different classes of attributes must be maintained: real-time, concurrency control, and recovery attributes. *Real-time attributes* specify temporal restrictions on computation execution. *Concurrency control attributes* are constraints regarding the execution of concurrent atomic computations caused by the sharing of resources, such as serializability [33]. Finally, *recovery attributes* are application-dependent properties required to guarantee that an incomplete (aborted) atomic computation leaves the system in a state semantically equivalent to the state before its execution. The dynamic concurrency control and task scheduling policies [28, 29] offered by CHAOS$^{arc}$ jointly address the potentially unpredictable operating conditions of complex real-time applications. These policies must themselves be *predictable* [24], which implies that arbitrary delays due to locking [12] in concurrency control protocols or due to cascaded aborts in timestamping-based protocols are not acceptable.

The primary motivation for the development of CHAOS$^{arc}$ is our experience with real-time applications that were or are being constructed in conjunction with researchers in academic and industrial environments [18]. In that work, it has become clear that the programming of such applications requires programming and run-time support ranging from notions of parallel tasks and task communication, to objects and object invocations [27], to finally, atomic computations. Atomic computations permit programmers to state and maintain statically determined global properties of their multi-object applications, thus enabling them to cope better with dynamic, unpredictable variations in operating environments.

## 3.2    A Real-Time, Robotics Application

The example presented in this section is derived from the operating software of the ASV robot and other walking machines [23]. Similar software characteristics can be found in many other, real-time applications, such as manipulator control [27] or the control of subsystems consisting of multiple actuators and sensors. Other real-time applications for which CHAOS$^{arc}$ has been used include the control software of a robot arm tracking parts on a moving conveyor [27], and a real-time simulation.

**A Stylized Robotics Application.**    Consider a six-legged walking machine. Each leg is controlled by a separate actuator. The robot moves by making a sequence of steps. One way of taking a step is first to move legs forward individually and then push all legs backward. Given the robot's mechanical design, certain constraints are associated with the sequencing and timing of the operations involved in taking a step. These constraints are conveniently modeled using concurrency, real-time, and recovery attributes of 'step' computations, as explained below.

*Consistency constraints.* To maintain the robot's stability, only certain combinations of legs may be moved simultaneously, which implies the association of concurrency control attributes with computations that move legs. A sample attribute is that only one leg may be moved at a time, with the exception that any of the two middle legs may be moved at the same time as any other leg. When stability is threatened due to violations of this consistency constraint (e.g., due to failure of a leg), recovery actions must be taken (e.g., forced placement of the failed leg on the ground). Recovery does not entail rollback and re-computation. Instead, recovery attributes specify certain computations and ensuing actions that attempt to achieve some future consistent state.

*Timing constraints.* A leg cannot be in transition (off the ground) for more than a specified amount of time, $\tau$, in order to prevent excess strain on the robot body. This real-time attribute may be modeled as a *recoverable* deadline, where recovery consists of actions that result in the leg being placed on the ground. In addition, a minimum speed in a certain operating mode may be established by definition of deadlines for individual leg movements. When such *weak* deadlines are missed, recovery may consist of allowing one leg to initiate its move as long as another leg is already sufficiently close to the ground.

*Recovery and adaptation.* The recovery actions—or reactive adaptations— noted above concern forward recovery, since the effects of actions on the external environment cannot simply be 'undone' by rolling back and restarting. However, there is also a need for backward recovery, in cases where the external environment is not affected or where time that cannot be 'unspent' is not an issue. For example, motion planning can be performed as an atomic computation that starts with a 'safe' initial plan and tries to improve on it. Obviously, such planning is not guaranteed to succeed; it might, for example, violate its timing constraints. If a plan cannot be generated within the allotted time, motion planning fails and recovers by reverting back to the original 'safe' plan.

**Objects, Object Invocations, and Atomic Computations.**  CHAOS$^{arc}$ concurrent objects have one of two *types*: they may be (1) *passive* (executed in the address space and by the execution thread of the invoker) or (2) *active* (executed by other execution threads in their own address spaces). Active objects may consist of single or multiple threads used for the execution of the objects' invocations. For a concrete example, consider the invocations among active objects when moving the robot depicted in Figure 3.1. These sample invocations can be grouped into atomic computations that capture the consistency and timing requirements mentioned above. In this example, object invocations are grouped hierarchically, where the atomic computation on top is defined by a single, atomic invocation of the operation 'Robot$move' of the 'Robot' object. This atomic computation repeatedly performs synchronous, atomic invocations of 'Robot$step' of the 'Robot' object, thereby defining one sub-computation for each step. The parent atomic computation ('Robot$move') commits after all sub-computations have committed. In turn, each 'Robot$step' defines two separable sub-computations, the first consisting of six atomic invocations of the 'move' operations of legs 1 to 6. If all such 'move' operations complete, six concurrent 'push' operations of objects 'leg1' to 'leg6' are

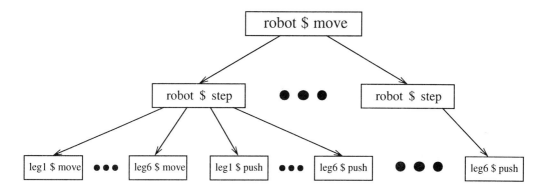

**Figure 3.1** Invocation Hierarchy for Robot Movement

performed.

In this example, all knowledge of constraints regarding the coordinated forward or backward movement of legs is hidden in the 'Leg' objects' operations (we are assuming that the two middle legs may be moved simultaneously), whereas 'Robot$step' possesses the knowledge that all forward 'move' operations must complete prior to the initiation of any backward 'push' operation. Timing information concerning the desired speed of the robot is passed as deadlines from the 'Robot$move' operation to 'Robot$step' and 'Leg$move', respectively.

The following code fragments from 'Robot$move', 'Robot$step', and 'Leg$move' illustrate atomic invocations. In the program text outlined below, italics are used to describe program functionality and comments, whereas actual fragments of program text are written in COLD$^{arc}$, the language used to write CHAOS$^{arc}$ applications. COLD$^{arc}$ is not a complete language; it extends the C language with object-oriented features (classes, objects, states, and operations) as well as object types, attributes, and multiple invocation semantics. The COLD$^{arc}$ compiler translates COLD$^{arc}$ programs to C. Statements not specific to CHAOS$^{arc}$ are written in C. For brevity, some of the internal data structures of objects and details of operations are not shown.

**The 'Leg' Class.**    The 'Leg' class is described as follows:

```
active CLASS Leg <locks = 1> IS
  USE Robot;
  STATE
     legnum :  int;
  END
  LOCK LegLock;

  OPERATION move(dest :  IN position)
     <xlock = LegLock, recovery = unmove>
  BEGIN
     bool ok;
```

```
    /* get control over the robot body */
    if ((legnum==3) or (legnum==4)) /* middle leg */
        INVOKE$sync Robot$shared_control(ok) <atomic>;
    else
        INVOKE$sync Robot$exclusive_control(ok) <atomic>;
    if (not ok) POLICY$abort;
    move the leg
END


OPERATION unmove(dest:position)
    <exectime = UNMOVE_TIME>
BEGIN
    if (leg is up) {
        put leg down
    }
END


OPERATION push()
    <xlock = LegLock, recovery = unpush>
BEGIN
    push leg (legnum) backwards;
END


OPERATION unpush()
BEGIN
    if (this is the first failure) {
        raise that leg
    }
    else
        INVOKE$fast Robot$unstable;
END
```

The 'move' in the 'Leg' class operation attempts to set a lock that gives it either exclusive or shared control of a leg. In the case of a middle leg being moved, the lock may be acquired by invocation of the operation 'shared_control' in the 'robot' object (lock 'RobotLock' resides in the 'robot' object and therefore can be acquired only by invocation of an operation in the 'robot' object). All other legs must be moved one at a time and therefore require acquisition of an exclusive lock ('exclusive_control').

After locking has been performed, 'move' checks whether it should proceed with the move, by checking the value returned by the locking operation, and then it interacts with the actuators to move the leg. An interesting note regarding the 'Leg' object is that the 'move' operation may be *undone* simply by lowering a raised leg. Thus, for *forward recovery*, a 'recovery' operation for 'move'—termed 'unmove'—is listed in the attribute list of 'move' and defined as part of the 'Leg' class.

A closer examination of the 'Leg' class demonstrates the importance of object types and attributes. First, since the class 'Leg' is 'active', all of that class are going to have their own execution threads. Second, the name-value pair '<locks = 1>' declares a *class attribute*, which is associated with all instances of that class. The 'locks' attribute specifies the number of locks associated with each object of that class. These locks are local to the objects; that is, they are not directly accessible from other objects and they are acquired and released automatically by declaring them as operation attributes (see below). '<Locks = 1>' appears as an attribute specification rather than as a declaration internal to the 'Leg' class because it is not manipulated explicitly by application code. Instead, this specification is an input to the implementation known to CHAOS$^{arc}$ of any complex active class (complex classes are explained in more detail in Section 3.3.1).

As with the class attribute 'Locks', the operation declaration for 'move' not only defines 'dest' to be an *input formal* argument of type 'position', but it also has two attributes: 'xlock' and 'recovery'. Again, these attributes are not processed by user-written code; they are inputs to code implementing atomic invocations. Specifically, the 'xlock' attribute states that the specified lock(s) (i.e., 'LegLock') is to be acquired in *exclusive* mode when the operation is invoked and is to be released when the invocation terminates. The other attribute, 'recovery', specifies the name of another operation of the same class that will perform forward recovery for this operation (i.e., the operation 'unmove'). The 'unmove' operation has the attribute 'exectime', which specifies a fixed upper bound on its execution time.

The attributes listed above are creation-time attributes on classes or operations. CHAOS$^{arc}$ also permits the specification of attribute values at other times, as in the invocation request:

```
INVOKE$sync Robot$shared_control (ok) <atomic>;
```

which invokes the operation 'shared_control' of an object of class 'Robot' (in this case, the object is implicitly found rather than explicitly specified) passing 'ok' as an *actual argument*. The invocation *mode* is 'sync' and it has the attribute 'atomic'. The 'sync' invocation mode specifies that the invoker waits until the invocation returns. The 'atomic' attribute specifies that the invocation is to be executed as a *sub-computation*, which implies that it terminates only after its parent has terminated. Furthermore, resources acquired by the invocation will not be released until the enclosing computation terminates. In general, an invocation mode is an attribute of the invocation used to determine the invocation semantics.

The statements 'POLICY$abort' and 'POLICY$commit'[3] are kernel requests. They terminate the invocation successfully and unsuccessfully, respectively. The general form for a kernel request is

```
POLICY$request <named arguments>
```

**The 'Robot' Class.**    For brevity, we elide the code of the class 'Robot', and simply describe its functionality and salient features. The class 'Robot' has the 'Leg' objects as *components*, it contains a number of interesting state variables used for keeping track of the states of the robot's legs, and it offers the operations 'move', 'moveTime', 'step', 'exclusive_control', 'shared_control', 'check_stability', 'unstable',

---

[3]The reason for using the keyword 'POLICY' is related to the implementation of CHAOS$^{arc}$ and will be explained in Section 3.3.2.

and 'initialize'. The class' initialization code creates two execution threads, one executing the operation 'check_stability' and the other executing the operation 'panic'. The 'panic' operation is invoked in *event-driven* mode, which implies that the invocation is activated whenever a certain event (specified as an attribute to the operation) occurs. This event is expressed and implemented within the operation as a *synchronization point*, which is the main synchronization primitive used in CHAOS$^{arc}$ . For this discussion, it is sufficient to know that a synchronization point is an entity that can be in one of two states: *enabled* or *disabled*. The execution of an invocation can be suspended until a given synchronization point is enabled. Furthermore, synchronization points can be *connected* to each other, such that the state of one synchronization point is a boolean function of the state of a number of other synchronization points.

The operations 'panic' and 'check_stability' in class 'Robot' are used for handling exceptional conditions. The 'panic' operation requires access to the internal state of the 'Robot' object, namely its lock, 'RobotLock', in exclusive mode. However, 'panic' is invoked in event-driven mode, which means that 'panic' does not compete for the lock until the event specified in the invocation actually occurs. At that time, since the 'panic' operation's invocation has the 'urgent' attribute, 'panic' *revokes* the lock from conflicting invocations, thereby forcing them to *abort*. As a result, whenever the 'Robot''s operation 'unstable' is called, which in turn enables the synchronization point 'unstable_sp', the 'panic' operation is activated and immediately aborts any invocations holding the lock. In the sample code implemented with CHAOS$^{arc}$ , aborted leg movement operations simply result in the immediate placement of all legs on the ground. In addition, aborts are also caused by detection of unexpected instabilities using the explicitly defined operation 'check_stability'. This operation is invoked at initialization time in *periodic* mode, so that it checks for instabilities at fixed periods. Upon detection, the operation enables the 'unstable_sp' synchronization point, thereby triggering the 'panic' sequence of actions. Note that the 'Robot' class also exports an operation called 'unstable', which may be used by other objects for signaling robot instability.

The operations 'shared_control' and 'exclusive_control' defined in class 'Robot' demonstrate some important properties of locks. Specifically, as with all locks in CHAOS$^{arc}$ , the 'Robot' class's locks are only accessible to the class's local operations. As a result, the 'Leg' objects have to invoke operations 'shared_control' and 'exclusive_control' to acquire the lock 'Robotlock' that is part of the class state, in shared or exclusive mode, respectively. Since locks are released automatically when an operation returns, these operations must be invoked with the 'atomic' attribute, which causes each invocation to hold on to its resources (e.g., locks) until the whole computation terminates.

We are now ready to explain the major operations 'step' and 'move' of class 'Robot'. The 'step' operation implements two distinct phases of movement. First, it invokes 'Leg$move' for each of the legs. Second, if all move operations have completed successfully, 'step' goes into the 'Leg$push' phase. Specifically, 'step' waits for a condition that expresses that (1) all leg movements have been completed successfully or (2) that any one (or more) movements have failed. Upon failure, the 'step' operation immediately *aborts* and forces the rest of its 'Leg$move' sub-computations to abort, as well. Synchronization points are used to implement the two phases of leg movement (i.e., the required waiting condition).

The 'Robot$move' operation defines a timing operation, 'moveTime', and a recovery operation, 'unmove'. The timing operation is invoked automatically upon invocation of its containing operation in order to provide an upper bound on the operation's execution time. This bound is used for making on-line scheduling decisions [28]. The recovery operation, on the other hand, is invoked if the invocation aborts either explicitly (with the 'abort' statement) or implicitly (e.g., when missing its deadline). The recovery operation is invoked in the same context as the aborted invocation (parameters and state) and is expected to undo the (partial) effect of the invocation.

Last, the 'move' operation invokes 'step' using a synchronous, streaming invocation. In CHAOS$^{arc}$ , multiple invocations occurring in a single stream are viewed as a single execution unit (atomic computation) with common attributes. For example, the 'move' operation is treated as a sequence of 'step' operations that either succeed or fail as a single unit. Furthermore, the 'Leg$move' and 'Leg$push' invocations have the 'top_level' attribute, which means that they execute as independent computations and can release their resources once they return.

**Discussion.**    Several properties of real-time, atomic computations differentiate our work from past work in distributed databases and operating systems.

*Nested atomic computations with multiple abort and recovery actions.* Atomic computations may be nested, as exemplified by the 'step' sub-computations of the 'move' computation. As with nested transactions in distributed systems [33], the atomic computation 'move' will not commit until all of its 'step' sub-computations have committed, and it may abort if any of its sub-computations abort. In this example, 'step' attempts to recover if any of its sub-computations ('Leg$move' or 'Leg$push') abort. However, the recovery actions taken by 'step' will differ in case of failure of a 'Leg$move' vs. a 'Leg$push' operation. Thus, in CHAOS$^{arc}$ , multiple recovery actions may be used with atomic invocations (e.g., two different recovery actions are indicated for each 'Robot$step' invocation). Furthermore, the specifics of forward recovery may depend on the state of the aborted sub-computations. In this example, an abort during the 'move' phase may result in forward recovery that attempts to complete the 'move' without one of the legs, whereas an abort during the 'push' phase may require a failed leg to be raised off the ground before forward recovery with the remaining legs is attempted.

*Atomic computations and resource management.* Aborting a parent atomic computation will cause aborts of its sub-computations. This requires that all sub-computations retain their resources until the parent atomic computation has committed, which is not always viable or desirable. As an example, consider the consistency constraints of leg movements to be enforced by 'Leg$move' sub-computations. These constraints need to be applied only during the actual movements of the legs. Thus, once a specific 'Leg$move' operation has been completed, it should be able to release its resource (a specific leg), thereby making it available to other invocations (e.g., to a 'push' operation).

CHAOS$^{arc}$ addresses such resource management issues by permitting sub-computations to be invoked as *top-level* atomic computations. All such atomic computations commit independently of all other atomic computations. Once committed, a sub-computation cannot be aborted (e.g., due to its parent aborting). If necessary, the sub-computation's effects must be 'undone' using forward recovery. In the case of an aborted 'Robot$move' or 'Robot$step' (e.g., an abort issued by the vehicle's operator), only those sub-computations that have not yet committed will be aborted; the effects of previously committed sub-computations cannot be 'undone' simply by reversing the effects of previous actions. For example, if a move is aborted after a few steps, then recovery may entail stopping the vehicle or even taking a few steps backward, but it will not consist of the reverse execution of all steps taken during the move.

*Attribute inheritance.* The example exhibits real-time attributes of atomic computations that are inherited by sub-computations. In CHAOS$^{arc}$ , the transmission of timing constraints from atomic computations to sub-computations may either be determined by the application program or inherited automatically using an algorithm explained in [6, 7].

*Partial invocation execution.* Most of the invocations shown in the sample program are executed asynchronously and potentially in parallel with the invoker. Since atomic invocations exhibit substantial setup cost (see the measurements reported in Section 3.3.4.1), CHAOS$^{arc}$ 's implementation and its applications make use of synchronization points to implement most invocations as three phases: (1) initiation, (2) execution, and (3) completion. During initiation, name resolution, addressing, scheduling of the thread executing the invocation, and all other setups are performed, followed by the execution of initialization code (if any). This phase typically ends by waiting for permission (using a synchronization point) to proceed with the second phase, which is the execution of the actual code body of the invoked operation. This permission is given either as soon as possible (i.e., the invocation is *pre-scheduled* prior to the time at which its results are actually required) or when the invoker requires the results of the invoked object's operation (the invocation has only been *partially executed*). In the latter case, the latency of invocation is determined by the operation's code and not by the operating system's overhead associated with the invocation construct [10]. In the former case, invocation results are available almost immediately after permission has been granted. In the sample program, the 'Robot$step' and 'Leg$push' operations may be rewritten such that all 'Leg$push' operations are partially executed while 'Leg$move' is in progress, so that pushing can be performed as soon as all leg movements have completed. Similar strategies may be used for the implementation of invocation 'completion'. See [6, 7] for a more complete description of the robot application, including the complete code for the 'Robot' object.

## 3.3    The CHAOS$^{arc}$ Kernel Mechanisms

The preceding section demonstrates the importance of real-time, atomic computations and invocations. This section describes CHAOS$^{arc}$ 's object-oriented operating system kernel.

Two major aims of the kernel's design and implementation are *predictability* and high *performance*. Predictability means that kernel mechanisms and policies have "well-behaved timing properties", that is, there should be known upper bounds on the execution times of all kernel functions. Also, the kernel must be *accountable*, which means that it must either honor its critical commitments or report its failure to do so to higher software levels before such knowledge becomes obsolete (provided that the underlying hardware remains in application-specific "safe states"). For example, an unanticipated change in the system noted by the kernel might cause an invocation to miss its hard deadline. This fact should be reported to the invoker within a time bound that enables the application to react accordingly. High performance requires that the guaranteed upper bounds on the execution times of the kernel mechanisms be as tight as possible.

The requirements of predictability and performance result in the following restrictions on the kernel's mechanisms. First, limits are imposed on the complexity of the decision-making policies used within the kernel. Second, mechanisms that provide statistical performance improvements (e.g., a cache) cannot be used, since an accountable kernel must schedule activities based on their worst-case performance. However, we do use predictable variations of such techniques, such as making local copies of globally accessible data. Third, resource sharing between different kernel components (e.g., exclusive accesses to shared variables) must be organized such that the performance of one component depends on the resource but not on other components accessing the resource.

### 3.3.1    Objects, Classes, Attributes

Two concepts permit CHAOS$^{arc}$ to support multiple kinds of objects and invocation semantics: *classes* and *attributes*.

**Classes.**    A *class* is an abstraction for a number of similar objects. It defines the application-level view of the objects in terms of their internal state and external interface (operations). Sample classes are shown in the example for the 'Leg' object (see page 43). Classes are used to define the complex structure of objects, such as the structure of the *active*, multi-threaded 'Leg' object capable of supporting atomic invocations depicted in Figure 3.2.

The complex object's *state* is partitioned into a number of components, each of which can either be *shared* or *copied* (specified as a state attribute). The *shared* component is accessible to all invocations of the same object. It is the task of the object's concurrency control and failure recovery to ascertain that multiple invocations have a consistent view of the resulting shared state. In contrast, at invocation time, a separate copy is made of the *copied* component. This copy is used by the invocation and is copied back (atomically) into the object's state when the invocation terminates if and only if the invocation is successful (commits). Otherwise, the copy is discarded. Copied state components are used in objects that can recover by restoring their state (or parts of it) to its original value (backward recovery), whereas shared state components are intended for use with forward recovery as discussed in Section 3.3.5.

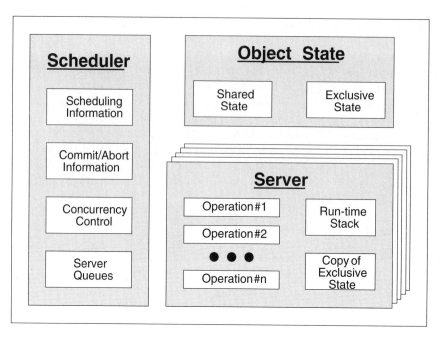

**Figure 3.2** Object Structure

The object *scheduler* receives and schedules all invocations to the object. It employs some scheduling policy to assign invocations to internal, multiple execution threads. This assignment is based on scheduling attributes (e.g., deadline) and is performed in cooperation with processor schedulers (e.g., to attempt to guarantee deadlines [28]). Multi-thread scheduling typically consists of both the assignment of threads to processors and the determination of an exact schedule for the assigned thread on its target processor [2, 28, 34, 36]. However, each such scheduling decision is checked for legality by the object's *concurrency control* algorithm, which must ensure object consistency when invoked by concurrent, atomic invocations. The *commit/abort protocol* of the object ensures that a committed atomic computation has a permanent effect on the object, whereas the abort of an atomic computation leaves either no changes (backward recovery) or results in the attainment of some equivalent state regarding this object (forward recovery).

Server queues describe all available servers (i.e., threads), each of which is generic in that it may execute any of the object's operations (in contrast to CHAOS [27]) and has its own execution environment and copy of the object's exclusive state. Not shown in the figure are queues used for the temporary storage of received invocations.

**Attributes.**    Figure 3.2 does not expose the object attributes used at the time of object creation to control the various options associated with complex objects, atomic invocations, and so on. However, it should be apparent from the figure that components like the 'scheduler' require inputs in addition to the actual parameters specified for operation invocations (e.g., the number of server threads it can employ for invocation execution). In general, CHAOS$^{arc}$ permits the association of *attributes* with classes, objects, state variables, operations, or invocations, and the specific permissible attributes and the interpretation of their values depend on the object type (i.e., *active* or *passive*). As stated earlier, if all attribute values had to be specified at the time of object creation, then attributes could not generate the appropriate inputs for activities like on-line scheduling and dynamic resource allocation. Therefore, many attribute values can be specified at run time (e.g., the number of execution threads for a dynamically created object, the deadline for an invocation,...). Several different types of attributes are used in the example in Section 3.2. A complete list appears in [6, 7].

### 3.3.2   Object Representation

The objective of this section is to explain the implementation of complex objects like the 'Leg' object, thereby providing a basis for interpretation of the performance measurements appearing in Section 3.3.4.2.

**Kernel Structure.**   Three levels of abstraction exist in the CHAOS$^{arc}$ system. The first and lowest level—termed CHAOS$^{base}$—hides most of the details of the target architecture using a user-level multiprocessor threads package compatible with Mach Cthreads. CHAOS$^{arc}$ can execute on any machine on which such a threads package exists, currently including a Sequent Symmetry, a BBN Butterfly, SUN and SGI workstations, and a Kendall Square Research KSR-1 supercomputer. Two extensions of the threads package concern (1) the inclusion of real-time scheduling algorithms for use by CHAOS$^{arc}$ [2, 28, 36] and (2) improvements in the package's lack of predictability (mostly due to memory management in the underlying Mach operating system) and efficiency by its re-implementation on the bare hardware of the BBN Butterfly [35].

The second level of abstraction in the CHAOS$^{arc}$ kernel—termed CHAOS$^{min}$—implements the basic mechanisms needed to manipulate objects. Specifically, it provides the notions of *classes*, *objects*, *invocations*, and *attributes*. The CHAOS$^{min}$ layer does not associate semantics with attributes. Instead, CHAOS$^{min}$ permits the addition of special objects, called *policies*, that interpret all explicitly specified attributes and thereby enforce the properties of the object stated by its attributes and implied by its type (e.g., *active* or *passive*). As a result, CHAOS$^{min}$ maintains a uniform kernel interface when it is *extended* by defining new policy classes and linking them with the kernel. Furthermore, CHAOS$^{min}$ facilitates *customization* in that existing kernel abstractions and functions can be specialized and/or modified easily.

**Primitive Objects.**   Four built-in classes define the *primitive* objects offered by CHAOS$^{min}$ : 'ADT', 'TADT', 'Monitor', and 'Task'. An 'ADT' (abstract data type) defines a passive object (i.e., without execution threads) without synchronization for concurrent calls. The call of such an object is performed in the address space of the caller, and it does not involve migration of the calling thread (for reasons of predictability and performance). Conversely, calling the active 'TADT' (threaded abstract data type) creates a new execution thread that starts executing the called operation, again without automatic synchronization of concurrent calls. A 'MONITOR' is an object without execution threads that only allows a single call to be active at a time. It can implement arbitrary scheduling policies using *condition variables* on which wait and signal operations may be performed. A 'TASK' (like Ada tasks) is an active object with a single execution thread. It defines a number of *entries* that can be called from other objects. All calls are performed in the context of the 'TASK' and are executed one at a time using some well-defined (and variable) policy for entry selection.

**Complex Objects.**  The third level of abstraction is called CHAOS$^{arc}$–it implements complex classes, objects, invocations, and atomic computations. This level uses *primitive* objects and the policy object called 'ca_policy' to implement all CHAOS$^{arc}$ functionality. It is at this level that application programmers declare, instantiate, and invoke objects (see Section 3.2) for use in real-time applications. Furthermore, non-real-time complex objects may be constructed at this third level, if desired, by implementation of policies other than 'ca_policy'.

To motivate the performance results reported in Section 3.3.4.1 and to illustrate the manner in which the 'ca_policy' object and *primitive* objects are used in the composition of objects and of alternative invocation semantics, we next describe the composition of the 'Leg' object (see Figure 3.3).

As with any other CHAOS$^{arc}$ object, the 'ca_policy' object implemented as an ADT intercepts all invocations to the 'Leg' object. Specifically, the 'ca_policy' ADT accepts invocations with attributes specific to CHAOS$^{arc}$ (e.g., *atomic, stream, . . .*), interprets those attributes, performs any necessary resource analysis and scheduling, and then initiates the execution of the body of code implementing the invocation. For resource management, the 'ca_policy' of the 'Leg' object interacts with three other components of the complex object shown in Figure 3.3: (1) an ADT containing the leg's shared state (not shown in the figure), (2) a 'scheduler' (or 'resource manager') of class *task*, (3) a 'pool' object, and (4) multiple 'server' TADTs (as many as desired for internal concurrency of the 'Leg' object).[4] Sample information maintained in the leg's shared state includes the locking requirements of different operations (which are statically specified in the class definition) and information about currently active/pending invocations (which is dynamically manipulated).

To schedule each invocation, the 'ca_policy' ADT invokes its 'scheduler' (or 'resource_manager') component. Since the 'scheduler' is of class *task*, the invoker of the complex object can continue its execution in parallel to the target object's decision making concerning this invocation. The concurrency control and scheduling decisions regarding each 'Leg' object made by the 'scheduler' concern the two resources present in CHAOS$^{arc}$ : *processors* and *locks*. Regarding processors, the

---

[4]In general, a policy object may also interact with non-component objects, such as the policies of other complex objects.

scheduler interacts with the lower-level scheduling policy (at the thread level) to perform schedulability analysis and processor allocation for each incoming invocation. For locks, the scheduler maintains information that is used by the concurrency control policy (see Section 3.3.5) to accept, reject, or abort individual invocations.

The 'ca_policy' creates the threads for code execution and performs the mapping of invocations to threads using its 'Servers' component. 'Server' threads can be either dynamically created at invocation time or statically created at the time of object initialization. In the case of the 'Leg' object, the 'servers' are multiple TADTs, each of which contains code for all of the leg's operations. Therefore, each such TADT may remove any invocation from the object's 'pool'. When performing an invocation, a 'server' TADT updates its internal component object of class ADT representing the copy of the leg state's exclusive component (not shown in Figure 3.3). Note that a 'server' TADT must always be located on a processor to which the leg sensors and actuators are physically accessible. The number and locations of 'server' TADTs are specified as attributes of the complex object.

An invocation is placed into the 'pool' by the 'ca_policy' once it has been scheduled by the 'resource manager'. Pending invocations are removed from the 'pool' by the object's active threads.

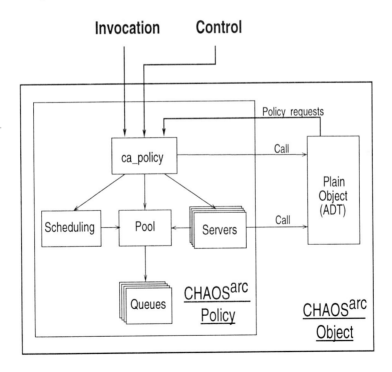

**Figure 3.3** Internal Representation of the Leg Object

### 3.3.3    Synchronization

The structure and representation of complex objects has been explained in the preceding section. Not yet apparent from that explanation are the mechanisms with which objects interact, which are: (1) explicit synchronization by use of *synchronization points*, which are CHAOS$^{arc}$ 's means of expressing events, (2) invocations of individual object operations, and (3) atomic computations spanning multiple objects and operations. Such interaction mechanisms are explained next.

CHAOS$^{min}$ offers two different synchronization mechanisms: locks and synchronization points. Locks are used for the maintenance of state during backward recovery in atomic computations (as with transactions in database systems); their semantics and use are explained in Section 3.3.5. Synchronization points, on the other hand, are used both by CHAOS$^{arc}$ itself in the implementation of invocation primitives and by users for the representation of and reaction to arbitrary events in real-time applications.

Synchronization points are used to express dependencies of activities like object invocations on both *external* and *internal*, simple or composite, events. Simple external events represent directly measurable changes in the external environment (e.g., the robot becoming unstable), while simple internal events correspond to changes to the system state generated either at the application or system level. Composite events are expressed in terms of other simple and composite events using logical operators ($\lor$, $\land$, $\neg$). Recalling the walking machine example, it is apparent that the events and the resulting patterns of synchronization to be stated may be quite complex, involving a large number of concurrent activities. For example, it should be possible to state a composite condition expressing that no 'Leg$push' computations may proceed until all 'moves' have been completed. Furthermore, when considering failures, a more complex condition may be stated, such as:

$$\bigwedge_{i=1}^{6} S_i \lor \bigvee_{i=1}^{6} F_i$$

Here, $S_i$ ($F_i$) represent the success (failure) event of the leg movement operation $i$. The condition states that the control program in 'step' should wait for either all six legs to move successfully or for any leg to report a failure.

A *synchronization point* is a passive entity (again implemented with an ADT) that can be in one of two states: *enabled* or *disabled*. There is a single, global synchronization point name space per application, which implies that synchronization point identifiers can be freely passed among objects. Furthermore, synchronization points can be dynamically created and deleted, but synchronization point identifiers are guaranteed to be unique over time. An invocation can wait until a synchronization point is enabled using the statement:

```
POLICY$sp_wait <name = spname>
```

In order to express complex conditions, a synchronization point, 'sp', can be connected to a set of synchronization points, 'sps', in one of four different modes: 'SP_ANY', 'SP_ALL', 'SP_SOME', or 'SP_NONE', which implement the boolean functions OR, AND, NOR, and NAND, respectively. The semantics of the connection is that whenever one of the synchronization points in 'sps' changes its state, the state of 'sp' is re-evaluated. The new state is a boolean function of the states of the points in 'sps' with an enabled synchronization point set to 'true' and an disabled one set to 'false'. Notice that the state of 'sp' is not guaranteed to always reflect the states of 'sps'. Specifically, the state can change as a side effect to a 'wait' request or by explicitly issuing 'enable' or 'disable' requests.

Clearly, synchronization points permit formulation of complex synchronization patterns. However, for real-time applications, synchronization points must fulfill additional requirements. First, the overhead and latency of synchronization points must be low, and unbounded delays due to the use of synchronization points are not acceptable. Second, multiple semantics of signaling using synchronization points are of importance. Specifically, changing the state of a synchronization point has two effects. First, the conditions for all synchronization points connected to it are evaluated and their states are updated. This process is repeated recursively for all synchronization points for which there is a change of state. Second, the activities waiting on the synchronization points being enabled are signaled in several fashions, depending on the synchronization point's *mode*. One of these modes is *SP_AutoDisable*. In this mode, the synchronization point is disabled after all activities waiting on it have been signaled. AutoDisabling a synchronization point is useful for signaling single events to activities, as with the example of signaling the 'step' computation that all 'move' sub-computations have been completed. When this mode is not specified, the synchronization point will remain enabled until explicitly disabled. In this fashion, different 'permanent' operating modes [25] may be programmed. For instance, a 'rough terrain' operating mode can be specified as staying in effect as long as a certain synchronization point remains enabled.

**Implementation of Synchronization Points.**   A CHAOS$^{arc}$ synchronization point is an ADT with internal data structures consisting of (1) a control block recording the state of the synchronization point (enabled or disabled) and its mode (AutoDisable, MustEnable, JustOne) and (2) two queues: the *connected* queue and the *delayed* queue. The connected queue reflects permanent dependencies between different synchronization points, while the delayed queue represents dependencies among multiple invocations of a single synchronization point.

CHAOS$^{arc}$ implements a pool of synchronization points as a complex object available to the programmer. This complex object's 'ca_policy' ADT uses a number of components of class *monitor* each of which pre-allocates an area of memory as a pool of synchronization points and descriptors. Measurements demonstrate that the costs of creation, waiting, and connection are functions of the number of synchronization points involved in the operation, whereas the cost of enabling a synchronization point is a function of the number of invocations waiting for it as well as the number of activities connected to it, and the cost of disabling is simply a function of the number of activities connected to the synchronization point. Measurements also show that the minimum cost of accessing a synchronization point is roughly comparable to the cost of accessing a mutex lock. This high performance is important due to the extensive use of synchronization points in the implementation of CHAOS$^{arc}$ 's invocation primitives and atomic invocations described next.

### 3.3.4   Atomic Real-Time Invocations

Invocation is the only mechanism for inter-object interaction in CHAOS$^{arc}$ . Invoking an operation of an object involves both data transfers (for parameters) and control transfers (to execute the operation's code). The exact nature of these transfers is defined by the invocation's semantics. CHAOS$^{arc}$ supports a variety of invocation semantics tailored to real-time applications.

**Invocation Primitives.**   As in other object-based systems, an invocation request specifies the object, the operation, and the arguments to be passed to that operation. In addition, and in order to express the different interaction patterns typical of real-time systems [27], CHAOS$^{arc}$ supports a number of invocation *attributes*. Therefore, an invocation request has the form:

    INVOKE$*mode* obj$op  (*params*)  <*attributes*>

where 'obj' and 'op' uniquely identify an operation to which the parameters specified by *params* are passed. CHAOS$^{arc}$ supports six invocation *modes*: 'async', 'sync', 'periodic', 'event', 'stream', and 'fast'. Each invocation mode defines and interprets a number of *attributes*.

   **Asynchronous** (mode = 'async') is the default invocation mode. It is used to represent sporadic (one-time) activities that can execute concurrently with the invoker. Asynchronous invocation attributes fall into different categories. *Timing* attributes specify desired timing properties of the invocations. The 'delay' attribute specifies an amount of time by which the invocation should be delayed (relative to invocation time). The 'deadline' specifies a limit on the execution time of the invocation relative to the time of the invocation. 'dlmode' specifies the deadline mode: 'SL_HARD' specifies a hard deadline that must be met. An invocation request will be rejected if CHAOS$^{arc}$ cannot guarantee its hard deadline either for the lack of resources (e.g., processor cycles) or the inability of its schedulability analysis algorithm to guarantee its deadline (e.g., liberal use of locks). 'DL_SOFT' specifies a soft deadline that can be violated.

   The CHAOS$^{arc}$ scheduling policy tries to maximize the chances of invocations meeting their soft deadlines. 'DL_RECOVERABLE' specifies that if the invocation misses its deadline it should be forced to *abort* and, as a result, execute its recovery action. Invocations with recoverable deadlines are always accepted and, as with soft deadlines, CHAOS$^{arc}$ tries to maximize their chances of meeting their deadlines. Finally, 'DL_PARTIAL' specifies that if an invocation exceeds its deadline, it should be terminated successfully. This is useful in utilizing partial results of computations [15]. For example, to specify an asynchronous invocation with a hard deadline of '100', we state:

    INVOKE$async Robot$move (position)
       <
          deadline = 100,
          dlmode = DL_HARD,
       >

*Feedback* attributes allow the invoker to monitor the progress of the invocation. This information is available through a number of synchronization points representing significant events in the lifetime of the invocation. The invoker specifies the events that should be reported and can use the corresponding synchronization points to check those conditions. Significant events that can be specified are: invocation is ready ('ready_sp'), invocation is running ('running_sp'), invocation is successful ('succ_sp'), invocation failed ('fail_sp'), invocation is done ('done_sp' = 'succ_sp' ∨ 'fail_sp'), and invocation terminated ('term_sp'). For any of the feedback attributes, if a valid synchronization point is specified, it will be used to signal that condition. If the synchronization point specified is 'SP_NULL' (default), the condition is ignored. Finally, if it is 'SP_NONE', a synchronization point is created for that condition, returned in the specified attribute, then deleted when the invocation terminates. Feedback information can be used to synchronize concurrent activities (e.g., wait until all leg movements are done in the robot example).

*Control* attributes specify synchronization points that control the execution of the invocation. 'go_sp' is a synchronization point that has to be enabled in order for the invocation to start execution. It is used in the robot example to force all 'push' operations to execute simultaneously. 'abort_sp' is a synchronization point which, when enabled, forces the invocation to terminate as if it failed.

*Atomicity* attributes specify whether the new invocation should start a new atomic computation and where to place it in the computation hierarchy. 'Atomic' specifies that the invocation is to be executed as a sub-computation of the current one. A sub-computation, if it terminates successfully, cannot commit until its parent computation commits. If the parent aborts, all sub-computations are forced to abort. As a result, sub-computations that obtain locks during their execution do not release them until the whole computation hierarchy terminates, thus observing strict two-phase locking [14]. 'Top_level' specifies that the invocation should be executed as an independent atomic computation. Namely, it becomes the root of a new computation hierarchy and can terminate independently of its parent. Finally, 'must_succeed' specifies that the invocation's parent should be forced to fail if the invocation fails. The default is to report the failure and allow the parent to react to it.

A complete list of invocation attributes appears in [7]. As an example, consider the *feedback* attribute, which specifies events of interest to the invoker expressed in terms of synchronization points that are to be enabled/disabled based on those events. For that attribute, *running_sp* specifies a synchronization point which should be enabled while the invocation is active and disabled when it terminates.

More complex invocation semantics include periodic, stream, and event-driven invocations. A **periodic** invocation causes the named operation to be executed repeatedly every 'period' (an attribute) units of time as long as the 'go_sp' attribute is enabled. Attributes to periodic invocations are similar to those for asynchronous invocations with a few exceptions: 'period' is a timing attribute that specifies the period for the invocation. 'Abort_sp', when enabled, terminates the entire request. There is no direct way of terminating individual activities. All invocation instances within a periodic invocation share the same execution environment and the same parameter block, which can be used to pass information between the invoker and the invokee as well as between different instances of the same invocation. As a result, all instances of a periodic invocation are viewed as a single computation. That is, if the invocation fails, they will recover as one unit.

**Stream** invoke (mode = 'stream') establishes a master-slave channel between two activities in which the master activity (invoker) can successively start different instances of the slave activity (invokee), thereby (1) amortizing the invocation setup cost over a number of invocations and (2) allowing a number of invocations to the same operations to be treated as a single computation that either commits or aborts as a unit. Communication between the two activities is achieved through the parameter block and the feedback information from the invokee. Once the channel is established between the two activities, the invoker can re-invoke the invokee any number of times. A stream invocation is explicitly terminated by the invoker using the 'POLICY$purge' statement.

**Event-driven** invocations (mode = 'event') are used to implement event-handling actions. An event-driven invocation specifies an operation that is to be executed every time a synchronization point ('go_sp') is enabled. All instances of the invocation share the same execution environment and parameter block and are viewed as a single computation. The whole invocation is terminated by enabling the 'stop_sp' synchronization point.

### 3.3.4.1   Invocation Building Blocks

Previous work has shown that it is desirable to allow users to synthesize new primitives from basic building blocks offered by a real-time operating system kernel. CHAOS$^{arc}$ adopts this building block approach, but offers additional functionality compared to other research [3, 27]. Specifically, in CHAOS$^{arc}$ , users can construct arbitrary invocation primitives by use of existing building blocks as well as by creation of their own building blocks.

**Invocation States.**   All invocation semantics offered by CHAOS$^{arc}$ are implemented with the basic building blocks of CHAOS$^{min}$ and using policies like the one created above. As a result, the performance of an invocation is determined both by the performance of basic building blocks as well as by the semantics-dependent states transitioned by the invocation. Below, we identify the resulting generic and semantics-dependent states of each invocation. Invocation performance is reviewed in the next section.

Consider the asynchronous invocation of 'Leg$push' appearing in the example in Section 3.2. This invocation has states that reflect both the implementation of all CHAOS$^{arc}$ invocations as well as the specific semantics of the 'push' operation's invocation stated by its creation- and invocation-time attributes and implemented by the 'ca_policy' policy object. Recall that these semantics even include execution of the leg object's scheduler, concurrency control algorithm, servers, and so on. Of course, the exact sequence of state transitions taken by each invocation is defined by the operation's creation time and invocation-time attributes and modes.

*Issued state.*   The 'Leg$push' operation starts in the *issued* state. At this stage, the invocation is represented by an an ADT called *invocation block*, which specifies the invoked object, operation, arguments, and attributes.

*Invocation queueing.* Next, an invocation request is placed in the appropriate invocation queue. The target object's scheduler is responsible for dequeuing and processing the invocation request. Thus, the delay between the posting and the processing of an invocation is a function not only of the invoker and the object scheduler but also of all other invocations handled by the same scheduler. CHAOS$^{arc}$ provides a separate queueing structure for invocations with hard deadlines; this permits the computation of a guaranteed upper bound on the time which a request will spend in the queue before request queueing. This upper bound is a function of the maximum processing time for each single request (which is fixed for each object scheduler) and the queue size (which is known at request queueing time). If the guaranteed upper bound exceeds the invocation deadline, the request is not queued and the invocation is rejected. Note that queueing the request does not mean that the invocation will be successful; it might still be rejected by the object scheduler. Nevertheless, this scheme guarantees that an invoker is notified of a rejected request prior to the invocation's deadline.

*Queued, accepted, rejected states.* Next, the invocation block is passed to the appropriate object scheduler, which places the invocation in the *queued* state. This state signifies that the request has been submitted to, and is being queued for processing, by the object scheduler. The scheduler processes incoming requests one at a time. Once a request is processed, it can be *rejected* if it is an invocation with a hard deadline that cannot be guaranteed, else it is *accepted*.

*Ready state: resource allocation.* Once accepted, a request is made ready to run by allocation of two kinds of resources: an execution thread and possibly, some locks. Since unpredictable performance may results from shared resources, CHAOS$^{arc}$ restricts the resource usage of invocations with hard deadlines. Specifically, invocations with hard deadlines must have upper bounds on their execution time. These upper bounds are made available (to the scheduler) through the 'time' functions that can be defined for object operations (see Section 3.2 for examples regarding the use of timing function). Given this information, the object scheduler inspects the individual processor schedulers' commitments in order to guarantee that the execution of the invocation will complete before its deadline. For brevity, this chapter does not discuss sample scheduling algorithms capable of solving this two-level scheduling problem (i.e., invocation scheduling followed by thread scheduling) or the three-level scheduling problem (i.e., scheduling atomic computations, their sub-computations, and the threads implementing them). Sample dynamic multiprocessor algorithms capable of both assigning time-constrained individual and groups of threads to processors and for performing processor scheduling for each assigned individual or group of threads are described in [2, 28]. Such algorithms may be used with CHAOS$^{arc}$ by on-line translation of the timing constraints of atomic computations to timing constraints of their sub-computations (i.e., timing constraints of individual invocations) to timing constraints of the threads created for invocation execution using algorithms like the ones developed by Bihari [1] or Gopinath [10]. A sample translation of an invocation's timing constraints to the timing constraints associated with a real-time thread implementing the invocation appears in [26].

Invocations are also not allowed to make locking requests at random; all locking requests are known to the scheduler before the invocation starts execution (using shared or exclusive locks). Using this information, the object scheduler employs a deterministic algorithm based on maintaining the "guaranteed earliest available time" for each lock and thus accepting or rejecting invocations based on that knowledge and on their locking requests (see Section 3.3.5 for a brief description of this algorithm).

*Ready, running states.* When all resources required by an invocation are allocated, the invocation is in the *ready* state. It remains in this state as long as it has the resources (not preempted) and it is not allocated to a server (execution thread). Once the invocation is assigned to a server, it enters the *running* state. Server assignment is performed using a preemptive earliest deadline first algorithm [4]. Once running, each execution thread first makes a local copy of the exclusive component of its object's state, then performs the desired function.

*Failure, success, commit, and abort states.* A running invocation can either succeed, fail, or go back to the ready state (periodic and event-driven invocations). An invocation enters the *success* state if its execution terminates successfully. The *failure* state can be entered voluntary or by force. Voluntary failure is caused by external or internal conditions detected by the application. An invocation signals such detected failures by using the 'abort' statement. Forced failures may be caused by violated deadlines, by the occurrence of unexpected external events, by violation of consistency constraints, or by preemption by more critical activities. The *abort* state is entered by an invocation if its execution fails and/or if its parent computation aborts. Aborting an invocation results in the local copy of the copied components being discarded and initiates the forward recovery procedure for the invoked operation. An atomic invocation enters the *commit* state if and only if its execution was successful and its parent computation commits. Committing an invocation updates the *copied* state components from the local copy, thus making changes made by the invocation permanent.

*Generality of invocation primitives.* As with all invocation primitives supported by the system, CHAOS$^{arc}$ 's complex 'ca_policy' contains code for interpretation of both alternate invocation semantics and of concurrency control and scheduling attributes. In this fashion, object implementors can design both custom object representations as well as invocation semantics matching those representations. This has been shown quite important in most multiprocessor operating systems. As an example of a customized object invocation, consider the invocation of 'leg$push' by the 'robot' object:

```
INVOKE leg$move (i,legDest) INVID: inv[i]
     top-level, atomic,
     feedback :   success+failure;
```

For this invocation, the specific operation of the 'ca_policy' object to be invoked is selected using the default (not explicitly stated) *attribute* 'regular' of the invocation. The resulting stub for the regular invocation of 'leg$move' includes:

```
ipb = get a parameter block for ''ca_policy $ regular'';
ipb->object = leg;
 .  .ipb->arguments = leg_move_pb(i,legDest);
ipb->regular, top-level, atomic = 1;
ipb->feedback = success + failure;
INVOKE ''leg->policy''$regular (ipb);
```

which is an invocation of the operation 'regular' of the 'ca_policy' object associated with the 'leg' object. In this invocation, 'ipb' is the *invocation block* (parameter block from the point of view of the policy object) describing the invocation. Its fields 'object' and 'operation' concern the 'leg' object being invoked, 'arguments' is a pointer to a parameter block containing the values of 'i' and 'legDest' being passed to the 'leg$push' operation. The fields 'regular', 'top-level', and 'atomic' are *attributes* of the invocation; they are passed as arguments to the policy object. Additional parameters, such as deadlines, may also be specified as attributes of the invocation.

In general, the invocation mechanism offered by CHAOS$^{arc}$ may be used to build any number of different invocation primitives and semantics, and to change the behavior of invocations during run time as well as at compile time. This capability remains unique among multiprocessor and real-time operating systems.

### 3.3.4.2    Invocation Performance

Two attributes of the CHAOS$^{arc}$ kernel are demonstrated next. First, CHAOS$^{arc}$'s objects are quite efficient, so that their use in high-performance real-time applications is possible. However, the attainment of high performance requires that programmers use the multiple granularities of objects offered by CHAOS$^{arc}$. Otherwise, significant performance losses may be incurred. Second, the different invocation types directly supported by CHAOS$^{arc}$ offer not only the functionalities required by real-time applications but also exhibit significant differences in performance, so that the proper use of invocation types may result in significant performance gains [27] for parallel real-time applications.

All measurements reported below are attained with the prototype of the CHAOS$^{arc}$ kernel implemented on a 32-node GP1000 BBN Butterfly. The Butterfly is a MIMD, shared-memory parallel processor. Each processor node contains a 25-MHz Motorola MC68020 processor, a 68881 floating point processor, a 68851 Memory Management Unit (MMU), 4M bytes of RAM, and a microcoded co-processor called the Processor Node Controller (PNC) which handles shared memory requests. Processor nodes are connected by a 32 megabits per second per path multistage switch which allows processor nodes to share their local memories with other nodes. For reference, a procedure call without parameters costs approximately 3 microseconds on the BBN Butterfly, and a call to a local ADT costs only 18 microseconds. The Mach operating system and a Cthreads package developed by our group are being used.

*Primitive objects.* Since *primitive* objects are the basis of all CHAOS$^{arc}$ functionality, their invocation performance is measured first, followed by an evaluation of the complex objects visible to typical users of CHAOS$^{arc}$. The measurements

**Table 3.1  Timing for *primitive* Objects (in microseconds)**

|          | Local | | Global | |
|----------|-----------|---------------|-----------|---------------|
|          | One Way | Round Trip | One Way | Round Trip |
| ADT      | 18      | 26         | 45      | 55         |
| MONITOR  | 90      | 150        | 110     | 190        |
| TADT     | 270+    | 150        | 450     | 340        |
| TASK     | 280+    | 280+       | 350     | 320        |

in Table 3.1 list the costs of both local (same processor) and global (remote processor) invocations (numbers with an appended '+' denote minimum measured
costs).[5] They show that CHAOS$^{arc}$ 's small grain, primitive objects may be used
for low-level control in real-time applications (such control tasks execute at rates of
100 MHz or above [25]). Monitor invocations cost more than ADT invocations due
to locking. TADT invocation cost includes the cost of thread creation, and both
TADT invocation and task invocation include thread activation cost. For tasks
and TADTs, one-way costs exceed round-trip costs due to the additional overheads
of thread context switching necessitated by creation and immediate execution of
a thread on the same processor (those costs are not accounted for in the round-
trip measurements). For remote calls, the target processor is assumed idle, so that
queueing and waiting in the target's ready queue do not occur. Note that a call to
a global task object is cheaper than to a global TADT object (assuming the task is
currently idle) due to the fact that thread creation need not be performed (a task
consists of a single thread repeatedly selecting entries for execution). Of the 320
microseconds reported for the remote task call, 70 microseconds is the overhead
for entry selection and queueing. In both calls, the main cost in the invocation of
active objects arises (a) from resource allocation (acquisition of a new thread) in
the case of a TADT and from (b) invocation queueing in the case of a task. This is
the motivation for the non-queued, no-resource invocation primitive (FastInvoke)
offered in CHAOS and CHAOS$^{arc}$ .

   *Complex objects.* As stated above, the objects visible to the users of CHAOS$^{arc}$
are complex objects constructed from the primitive objects listed above. Similarly,
the invocation primitives used by CHAOS$^{arc}$ programmers are implemented using
*primitive* objects. Next, we evaluate the cost of a regular invocation in CHAOS$^{arc}$ .
We then use this evaluation to explain the costs of CHAOS$^{arc}$ 's other invocation
primitives.

   Consider the different stages of an invocation identified in the previous section, again using the example of the 'Leg$push' operation. In the first stage of an
invocation, construction of the invocation block is performed in the address space of

---

[5]All reported measurements are averages of some large number of calls (typically 1000),
and all Mach pages are locked in memory, so that the costs of page swapping does not
perturb our results.

the invoker (115 microseconds), in part by using the code resident in the 'ca_policy' ADT implementing the invocation. Next, the latter ADT also performs the queueing of the invocation at the *monitor* object that implements the object's resource manager (scheduling and concurrency control). The minimum time within which the queued invocation is selected and dequeued by the resource manager is 60 microseconds, resulting in a total of 175 microseconds from the time the invocation is issued to its being processed for *acceptance* (assuming a 'zero' scheduling algorithm in the resource manager). Thus, an invocation can be rejected in a minimum of 175 microseconds. Run-time averages for this time can be improved by elision of schedulability analysis for invocations with extremely tight deadlines. In such cases, rejection can be performed within 30 microseconds. These measurements define the limitations of accountability in the current implementation of CHAOS$^{arc}$ : an invocation cannot be rejected before at least 175 microseconds has been spent on it.

Following the invocation's acceptance, resources are allocated for its execution. Such resource allocation (in this case, lock acquisition) for an atomic invocation consumes 30* #locks microseconds; it is performed by the 'ca_policy' object, as well. Since locks are fairly cheaply acquired, a substantial number of locks may be associated with each invocation without undue performance losses. After resource allocation, the invocation reaches its *ready* state, from which the cost of making it *running* is essentially thread activation cost (110 microseconds). Termination consists of reporting *success* via a synchronization point and resource release (20 microseconds per lock).

Several interesting observations can be made regarding invocation performance. First, it is important that CHAOS$^{arc}$ support the *pre-scheduling* of invocations. Namely, in anticipation of an invocation, it should be possible to take all steps up to the invocation's *ready* state before some source object actually issues the invocation. In this fashion, the latency of a regular invocation can be reduced significantly. Pre-scheduling may be performed during idle times of the processors used by the real-time application. Currently, CHAOS$^{arc}$ allows users to explicitly implement such pre-scheduling using synchronization points. Our future work may include the design of scheduling algorithms automatically able to perform pre-scheduling.

A second observation regarding invocation performance is that alternative invocation primitives may be implemented such that the costs of *queueing, acceptance,* and so on, are not incurred with each invocation, as shown in Table 3.2. For instance, a 'stream' invocation incurs the cost of acceptance and resource allocation only once for a whole set of invocations, so that those costs can be amortized over that set (see the costs of 'reinvoke' in Table 3.2). A similar optimization applies for a periodic invocation, in which resource allocation can be performed once. Additional invocation primitives and their performance are described in [6, 7].

## 3.3.5    Atomic Real-Time Computations

It has been shown that atomic transactions facilitate distributed programming [33], in part by isolating the programmer from the details of concurrency con-

**Table 3.2  Timing for Invocations**

|                    | Sync |  | Async |  | Periodic |  | Stream |  |
|--------------------|-------|--------|-------|--------|-------|--------|-------|--------|
|                    | Local | Global | Local | Global | Local | Global | Local | Global |
| Find policy        | 10    | 30     | 10    | 30     | 10    | 30     | 10    | 30     |
| Build invocation block | 20 | 30   | 40    | 60     | 50    | 70     | 50    | 70     |
| Invoke policy      | 26    | 55     | 26    | 55     | 26    | 55     | 26    | 55     |
| Accept / reject    | 40+   | 60+    | 40+   | 60+    | 40+   | 60+    | 40+   | 60+    |
| Obtain locks       | 30*n  | 30*n   | 30*n  | 30*n   | 30*n  | 30*n   | 30*n  | 30*n   |
| Enqueue            | N.A.  | N.A.   | 50    | 70     | 50    | 70     | 50    | 70     |
| Submit             | 18    | 45     | 110+  | 110    | 110+  | 110    | 110+  | 110    |
| Unlock             | 20*n  | 20*n   | 20*n  | 20*n   | 20*n  | 20*n   | 20*n  | 20*n   |
| Terminate          | 70    | 70     | 70    | 70     | 70    | 70     | 70    | 70     |
| Total              | 184   | 290    | 346   | 445    | 346   | 435    | 356   | 445    |
|                    | +50*n |        |       |        |       |        |       |        |
| Reinvoke           | 18    | 45     | N.A.  | N.A.   | 230   | 250    | 200   | 220    |

trol and failure recovery. *Atomic real-time computations* in CHAOS$^{arc}$–henceforth termed atomic computations—are an adaptation of the concept of atomic transactions [14, 21] to real-time systems. In CHAOS$^{arc}$ , an atomic computation is an abstraction for a hierarchy of atomic invocations of object operations. Namely, an atomic computation represents a group of object invocations with common timing, consistency, and recovery requirements. The computation is guaranteed to terminate in one of the two states *success* or *failure*. A successful computation can *commit* to make its effects observable to other activities, whereas a *failed* computation *aborts*, thereby initiating any required recovery actions that either restore the system to its pre-computation state or to some "equivalent" state. Timing requirements may be stated as deadlines on the execution of the computation and its sub-computations. Consistency requirements address both the internal state of the application and the state of the external environment within which the application operates. Similarly, recovery must also concern itself with the external environment's state (e.g., current position of a robot vehicle), which implies that both backward and forward [32] recovery must be supported.

The performance of atomic computations strictly depends on the performance of atomic invocations, which is reported in the preceding section. In the remainder of this section, we discuss the correct implementation of the timing and consistency requirements of atomic computations. Namely, we describe how (1) the concurrency control algorithms enforcing consistency constraints stated as mutual exclusion constraints on concurrent activities interacts with (2) the scheduling algorithm seeking to meet the deadlines of those concurrent activities. More specifically, this means that CHAOS$^{arc}$ 's scheduling algorithm must take into account the worst-case times resulting from locks being held for reasons of concurrency control. It also implies that we cannot use concurrency-control policies that permit locks to be held for arbitrary durations [12]. Furthermore, optimistic concurrency control policies like time stamping cannot be used since unpredictable execution times may result from cascaded aborts.

**Concurrency Control and Locking.**  CHAOS$^{arc}$ addresses scheduling and concurrency control as follows: (1) all locks are local to objects and can be acquired only via explicit operations defined on those objects and (2) such operations must explicitly declare their locking requirements using operation attributes. As a result of (1) and (2), the object scheduler can compute bounds on execution times due to locking. Specifically, regarding (1), each class declaration includes a specification of the number of locks to be associated with objects of that class (declared using the class attribute 'locks'). When an object of this class is created, the object scheduler allocates and initializes the desired number of locks. Regarding (2), the two locking attributes used with operations are 'slock' for locks required in the shared mode and 'xlock' for locks required in the exclusive mode. When an atomic operation is invoked, the object scheduler satisfies that operation's locking requirements before its execution starts and releases them when the operation terminates. To observe strict two-phase locking, an atomic invocation does not release its locks until the computation that started it terminates.

The algorithm for concurrency control and scheduling informally described above assumes that operations hold locks for the entire duration of their execution. In order to accommodate urgent, unexpected requests common in dynamic real-time systems, CHAOS$^{arc}$ permits a lock to be revoked. This results in the abort of the operation (and therefore, the computation) holding the lock. Such lock preemption is performed by the object scheduler level, so that the decision to preempt a lock is made based on both the scheduling attributes and the criticalness of computations. Lock preemption may cause backward or forward recovery, where forward recovery is performed by a recovery operation (specified as an operation attribute) assigned to each operation. The recovery operation is executed when the computation issuing the invocation aborts, and it is expected to *undo* the effects of an invocation by executing in the same context as the original operation's invocation (i.e., parameters and object state). CHAOS$^{arc}$ also offers a mechanism that permits programmers to use semantic information to improve concurrency in atomic computations [5, 30] (see [7]).

**Termination.**    Two-phase locking requires that CHAOS$^{arc}$ must distinguish two terminal states of execution, as discussed in Section 3.3.4: *done* and *terminated*. An invocation is *done* when it enters the states *success* or *failure*. The success state is entered when an invocation either explicitly uses the 'POLICY\$succ' statement or when it returns, thereby signaling an implied success. An invocation can fail for a number of reasons, including exceeding a recoverable deadline, failure of its parent computation, and explicit failure indicated with the 'POLICY\$fail' statement. A *done* 'top_level' atomic invocation releases all of its locks. A *done* atomic invocation transfers its locks to its parent computation.

A computation *terminates* and releases all locks when it enters states *commit* or *abort*. The termination state is entered when (1) the computation's invocation is done, (2) its parent computation has terminated, and (3) the invocations executing its sub-computations are done. A computation terminates in the *abort* state if its invocation fails or if its parent aborts, else it *commits*. Upon termination, the computation either makes its effects permanent by updating the object state from the 'copied' components (commit) or it discards those components and initiates the recovery operation as discussed above.

## 3.4   Related Research

CHAOS$^{arc}$ 's major contributions are the notions of atomic, real-time invocations and computations and the ability to build custom objects and invocation primitives. While CHAOS$^{arc}$ re-implements some of the functionality offered by CHAOS [27], its implementation and implementation concepts (e.g., classes and their use in the construction of complex objects and new types of invocations) result in its increased predictability compared to CHAOS and its ability to support a much larger variety of invocation types and complex object classes [10, 27]. In addition, CHAOS$^{arc}$ is portable to any machine offering a Mach-compatible threads package.

The CHAOS$^{arc}$ kernel's main contribution is the fashion in which different types of objects and invocations are composed from primitive objects, thereby leading to substantial flexibility in the upper layers of CHAOS$^{arc}$ and offering substantially increased flexibility of operating system primitives compared to other research addressing remote procedure calls in networks or on multiprocessors. The Synthesis kernel addresses adaptability at a lower-level than CHAOS$^{arc}$ [17]. It is concerned with adaptations of code segments used for the implementation of objects, whereas CHAOS$^{arc}$ adapts object and invocation implementations at the level of primitive objects.

The Spring kernel [31], also developed concurrently with CHAOS$^{arc}$ and CHAOS, initially targeted distributed systems consisting of sets of workstations, followed by a second implementation for a uniform memory, small-scale multiprocessor. Its current implementation does not address the highly dynamic real-time applications that are the focus of CHAOS$^{arc}$ (e.g., it does not offer atomic invocations or computations), nor does it have the thread-based portability of CHAOS$^{arc}$ . The notion of 'resource managers' in Spring is implemented in the GEM and CHAOS operating systems [25, 27] as part of their process schedulers; they may be implemented in CHAOS$^{arc}$ using specialized objects at the user level, in the CHAOS$^{arc}$ kernel, or even at the thread level.

Other real-time operating systems [25] are process-based and primarily address the static scheduling of real-time applications. The GEM system [25] also addresses program adaptation, but not to the extent to which it is explored in CHAOS or CHAOS$^{arc}$ . For reasons of performance and predictability, CHAOS$^{arc}$ does not offer support for the run-time inheritance of arbitrary object attributes. Currently, only timing attributes are propagated along computation hierarchies. For static timing analyses, the reader is referred to the object-based work in [10] and to the Arts project [32], and to the graphical programming environment of Sartor [19]—called "CONSORT"—which supports the partially automatic, static synthesis of arbitrary time-constrained program components.

*Guardians* and *actions* in Argus [33] are quite similar to CHAOS$^{arc}$ objects regarding backward recovery, but do not address forward recovery and real-time issues. Also complementary to our work is the research performed as part of the Arts projects at Carnegie-Mellon University [32], where researchers are investigating the detailed effects of architectural attributes (e.g., caches or bus contention) on the predictability of program execution. However, recent extensions of the Arts real-time kernel addressing an object-oriented interface implemented with a real-time version of C++ interfaces appear directly compatible with the concepts advanced by CHAOS and CHAOS$^{arc}$ . A good summary of current research in real-time operating systems appears in [9].

## 3.5     Conclusions and Future Research

CHAOS$^{arc}$ demonstrates the viability of using the notion of atomic computations for programming complex, real-time, embedded applications. Atomic computations appear to be a natural paradigm for grouping multiple activities into related units (computations) with guaranteed properties (e.g., deadlines, mutual exclusion, etc.), but additional experiences with their use for real-time applications would be a valuable addition to this research. The mechanisms implemented by the CHAOS$^{arc}$ kernel provide a predictable, accountable, and efficient basis for programming with real-time atomic computations. These mechanisms are predictable because they have well-defined upper bounds on their execution times that are (can be) determined before their execution. They are accountable because their decisions are guaranteed to be honored as long as the system is in an application-specific "safe state". Finally, they are efficient because of their low execution overhead, concurrency exploitation, and tightness of their guaranteed upper bounds.

The kernel mechanisms of CHAOS$^{arc}$ may be used to compose different classes of objects and different types of object invocations, at small performance penalties. This makes the *synthesis* of object invocations possible. Prototypes of CHAOS$^{arc}$ were first implemented on a BBN Butterfly using both the Chrysalis and MACH operating systems. Currently, CHAOS$^{arc}$ runs on a KSR1 supercomputer, on Sparcstations, and on SGI workstations. Another version of CHAOS$^{arc}$ may run as a native kernel on one of the new IBM multiprocessor supercomputers.

The future research of our group concerns additional experimentation with the CHAOS$^{arc}$ kernel and its COLD$^{arc}$ programming system using programs from the 'intelligent' components of real-time systems. In addition, we are continuing to develop (1) the predictable CHAOS$^{arc}$ kernel and its underlying threads package, (2) the CHAOS$^{arc}$ programming system based on the COLD$^{arc}$ real-time programming langage, and (3) dynamic scheduling algorithms and models.

Regarding (1), a predictable, real-time threads package has been developed [29] and most its components were implemented on the bare hardware of the GP1000 BBN Butterfly multiprocessor, in order to demonstrate that such a package can be the basis of a predictable implementation of the CHAOS$^{arc}$ kernel [35]. We have completed implementation of this package for the KSR1 supercomputer and portable versions running on Sparcstations and SGI machines. In addition, we are currently investigating kernel configuration at both the object and threads levels of the CHAOS$^{arc}$ system [22]. Regarding (2), the programming system of CHAOS$^{arc}$ implements the COLD$^{arc}$ language, which extends the C language in order to express objects, classes, and real-time attributes of both. We are now implementing additional tools for the construction, testing, and tuning of CHAOS$^{arc}$ applications. The resulting programming environment will include (1) a visual display of timing and performance attributes and of monitoring information concerning both [13], and (2) a visual program change facility that may be used with COLD$^{arc}$ to change performance-related aspects of the real-time application and can therefore be used to predict or guarantee such application characteristics (e.g., execution timing).

The scheduling and concurrency control algorithms developed as part of this research are rather conservative algorithms. More sophisticated algorithms may be useful, including a lock guarantee algorithm that utilizes more information about locks by maintaining a *lock profile* that contains information about future as well as current locking requests and uses this information to perform lock acquisition to maximize concurrency without jeopardizing system accountability [37]. In addition, we have developed dynamic scheduling algorithms [28], have investigated the effects of concurrency on scheduling [36], and are considering long-term dynamic scheduling algorithms in the context of real-time simulations, which use recent system information to predict future developments [8].

# Acknowledgments

Prabha Gopinath and Harold Forbes have implemented additional real-time programs used with CHAOS$^{arc}$ . Hongyi Zhou implemented selected components of the real-time threads package for CHAOS$^{arc}$ on the bare hardware of the GP1000 BBN Butterfly, and Bodhi Mukherjee and Kaushik Ghosh have constructed multiple versions of Cthreads for the Sequent Symmetry, Silicon Graphics, and KSR multiprocessors, and for various uniprocessor workstations. Dilma Silva and Greg Eisenhauer constructed the version of CHAOS$^{arc}$ now running on the KSR, SGI, and Sparc machines.

# References

[1] T. Bihari and K. Schwan. Dynamic adaptation of real-time software. *ACM Transactions on Computer Systems*, 9(2):143–174, May 1991.

[2] Ben Blake and Karsten Schwan. Experimental evaluation of a real-time scheduler for a multiprocessor system. *IEEE Transactions on Software Engineering*, 17(1):34–44, Jan. 1991.

[3] Jeffrey S. Chase, Franz G. Amador, E. Lazowska, H. Levy, and R. Littlefield. The amber system: Parallel programming on a network of multiprocessors. In *Twelfth ACM Symposium on Operating System Principles. SIGOPS Notices* 23(5):147–158. ACM SIGOPS, Dec. 1989.

[4] Michael L. Dertouzos and Aloysius K. Mok. Multiprocessor on-line scheduling of hard-real-time tasks. *IEEE Transactions on Software Engineering*, 15(12):1497–1506, Dec. 1989.

[5] H. Garcia-Molina. Using semantic knowledge for transaction processing in a distributed database. *ACM Transactions on Database Systems*, 8(2), June 1983.

[6] Ahmed Gheith. *Support for Multi-weight Objects, Invocations, and Atomicity in Real-Time Systems*. Ph.D. thesis, Georgia Institute of Technology, College of Computing, Aug. 1990.

[7] Ahmed Gheith and Karsten Schwan. Chaos-arc: Kernel support for multi-weight objects, invocations, and atomicity in real-time applications. *ACM Transactions on Computer Systems*, 11(1):33–72, Apr. 1993.

[8] Kaushik Ghosh, Richard M. Fujimoto, and Karsten Schwan. A testbed for optimistic execution of real-time simulations. *Proceedings of the IEEE Workshop on Parallel and Distributed Real-Time Systems*, Apr. 1993.

[9] Kaushik Ghosh, Bodhi Mukherjee, and Karsten Schwan. A survey of real-time operating systems. GIT-CC-93/18, College of Computing, Georgia Institute of Technology, Atlanta, Ga., Feb. 1994.

[10] Prabha Gopinath. *Programming and Execution of Object-Based, Parallel, Hard Real-Time Applications*. Ph.D. thesis, Department of Computer and Information Sciences, The Ohio State University, June 1988.

[11] E. Douglas Jensen, C. Douglass Locke, and Hideyuki Tokuda. A time-driven scheduling model for real-time operating systems. In *IEEE Real-Time Systems Symposium*, pages 112–122, 1985.

[12] Zvi M. Kedem. Locking protocols: From exclusive to shared locks. *Journal of the Association for Computing Machinery*, 30(4):787–804, Oct. 1983.

[13] Carol Kilpatrick and Karsten Schwan. Chaosmon: Application-specific monitoring and display of performance information for parallel and distributed systems. In *ACM Workshop on Parallel and Distributed Debugging*, pages 57–67. *ACM SIGPLAN Notices*, 26(12), May 1991.

[14] Butler W. Lampson. Atomic transactions. In *Distributed Systems: Architecture and Implementation, an Advanced Course*, chapter 14, Butler T. Lampson, editor. Springer-Verlag, New York, 1981.

[15] Kwei-Jay Lin, Swaminthan Natarajan, and Jane W.-S. Liu. Imprecise results: Utilizing partial computations in real-time systems. In *IEEE Real-Time Systems Symposium*, pages 210–217, 1987.

[16] C. Douglas Locke. *Best-Effort Decision Making for Real-Time Scheduling*. Ph.D. thesis, Carnegie Mellon University, 1986.

[17] Henry Massalin and Calton Pu. Threads and input/output in the synthesis kernel. In *Proceedings of the 12th Symposium on Operating Systems Principles*, pages 191–201. ACM SIGOPS, Dec. 1989.

[18] R.B. McGhee, D.E. Orin, D.R. Pugh, and M.R. Patterson. A hierarchically-structured system for computer control of a hexapod walking machine. In *Proceedings of 5th IFTOMM Symposium on Robots and Manipulator Systems*, Udine, Italy. IFTOMM, June 1984.

[19] Aloysius K. Mok. Sartor: A design environment for real-time systems. In *IEEE Real-Time Systems Symposium*, pages 174–181, 1985.

[20] Aloysius K. Mok. *Fundamental Problems of Distributed Systems for the Hard Real-Time Environment.* Ph.D. thesis, Laboratory for Computer Science, Massachussetts Institute of Technology, May 1983.

[21] J. Eliot and B. Moss. *Nested Transactions: An Approach to Reliable Distributed Computing.* Series in Information Systems. MIT Press, Cambridge, Mass. and London, 1985.

[22] Bodhisattwa Mukherjee and Karsten Schwan. Improving performance by use of adaptive objects: Experimentation with a configurable multiprocessor thread package. In *Proceedings of 2nd International Symposium on High Performance Distributed Computing (HPDC-2)*, pages 59–66, July 1993.

[23] David E. Orin. Supervisory control of a multilegged robot. *International Journal of Robotic Research*, 1(1), Spring 1982.

[24] K. Ramamritham and J.A. Stankovic. Dynamic task scheduling in hard real-time distributed systems. *IEEE Software*, 1(3):65–75, July 1984.

[25] Karsten Schwan, Tom Bihari, Bruce W. Weide, and Gregor Taulbee. High-performance operating system primitives for robotics and real-time control systems. *ACM Transactions on Computer Systems*, 5(3):189–231, Aug. 1987.

[26] Karsten Schwan, Ahmed Gheith, and Hongyi Zhou. From chaos-min to chaos-arc: A family of real-time multiprocessor kernels. In *Proceedings of the Real-Time Systems Symposium*, Orlando, Fla., pages 82–92. IEEE, Dec. 1990.

[27] Karsten Schwan, Prabha Gopinath, and Win Bo. Chaos: Kernel support for objects in the real-time domain. *IEEE Transactions on Computers*, 36(8):904–916, July 1987.

[28] Karsten Schwan and Hongyi Zhou. Dynamic scheduling of hard real-time tasks and real-time threads. *IEEE Transactions on Software Engineering*, 18(8):736–748, Aug. 1992.

[29] Karsten Schwan, Hongyi Zhou, and Ahmed Gheith. Multiprocessor real-time threads. *Operating Systems Review*, 25(4):35–46, Oct. 1991. Also appears in the Jan. 1992 issue of *Operating Systems Review*.

[30] L. Sha, J.P. Lehoczky, and E.D. Jensen. Modular concurrency control and failure recovery. *IEEE Transactions on Computers*, 37(2), 1988.

[31] John A. Stankovic. The design of the spring kernel. In *IEEE Real-Time Systems Symposium*, pages 146–157, 1987.

[32] Hideyuki Tokuda and Clifford W. Mercer. Arts: A distributed real-time kernel. *Operating Systems Review*, 23(3):29–53, July 1989.

[33] William Weihl and Barbara Liskov. Implementation of resilient, atomic data types. *ACM Transactions on Programming Languages and Systems*, 7(2):244–269, Apr. 1985.

[34] W. Zhao, K. Ramamarith, and J. Stankovic. Scheduling tasks with resource requirements in hard real-time systems. *IEEE Transactions on Software Engineering*, 13(5):564–577, May 1987.

[35] Hongyi Zhou. *Task Scheduling and Synchronization for Multiprocessor Real-Time Systems*. Ph.D. thesis, College of Computing, Georgia Institute of Technology, May 1992.

[36] Hongyi Zhou, Karsten Schwan, and Ian Akyildiz. Performance effects of information sharing in a distributed multiprocessor real-time scheduler. Technical report, College of Computing, Georgia Tech., GIT-CC-91/40, Sept. 1991. Abbreviated version in *1992 IEEE Real-Time Systems Symposium*, Phoenix, Ariz.

[37] Hongyi Zhou, Karsten Schwan, and Ahmed Gheith. The dynamic synchronization of real-time threads for multiprocessor systems. In *Symposium on Experiences with Distributed and Multiprocessor Systems*, Newport Beach, Calif. pages 93–107. Usenix, ACM, Mar. 1992.

# Chapter 4

# Design and Implementation of Maruti-II

## Manas Saksena, James da Silva, and Ashok Agrawala

The design and development of integrated systems that support dependable operation of mission-critical applications with real-time requirements poses challenging problems for systems designers and developers. The Maruti system is being designed to address integrated solutions for such applications, from the development of the application to the operating system support for their execution. Maruti has been designed as a time-driven system to provide temporal determinacy. In this chapter, we present the design philosophy of the Maruti system, as well as discuss the design and implementation of Maruti-II.

## 4.1 Introduction

Many complex, mission-critical systems depend not only on correct functional behavior, but also on correct temporal behavior [2, 13]. These systems are called *real-time systems*. The most critical systems in this domain are those which must support applications with *hard real-time* constraints, in which missing a deadline may cause a fatal error. Due to their criticality, jobs with hard real-time constraints must always execute satisfying the user-specified timing constraints, despite the presence of faults such as site crashes or link failures.

A real-time operating system, besides having to support most functions of a conventional operating system, carries the extra burden of guaranteeing the execution of its requested jobs satisfying their timing constraints. In order to carry out real-time processing, the requirements of the jobs have to be specified to the system, so that a suitable schedule can be made for the job execution. Thus, conventional application development techniques must be enhanced to incorporate support for specification of timing and resource requirements. Further, tools must be made available to extract these requirements from the application programs, and analyze them for schedulability.

Based on the characteristics of its jobs, a real-time system can be classified as *static*, *dynamic*, or *reactive*. In a static system, all (hard real-time) jobs and their execution characteristics are known ahead of time, and thus can be statically analyzed prior to system operation. Many such systems are built using the cyclic executive or static priority architecture. In contrast, there are many systems in which new processing requests may be made while the system is in operation. In a dynamic system, new requests arrive asynchronously and must be processed immediately. However, since new requests demand immediate attention, such systems must either have "soft" constraints, or be lightly loaded and rely on exception mechanisms for violation of timing constraints. In contrast, reactive systems have certain lead time to decide whether or not to accept a newly arriving processing request. Due to the presence of the lead time, a reactive system can carry out analysis without adversely affecting the schedulability of currently accepted requests. If adequate resources are available, then the job is accepted for execution. On the other hand, if adequate resources are not available, then the job is rejected and does not execute. The ability to reject new jobs distinguishes a reactive system from a completely dynamic system.

The goal of the Maruti project is to create an environment for the development and deployment of applications with hard real-time constraints in a reactive environment. Such applications must typically be able to execute on a platform consisting of distributed and heterogeneous resources, and operate continuously in the presence of faults. The Maruti project started in 1988 and the first version of the system was designed as an object-oriented system with suitable extensions for the objects to support real-time operation. The proof-of-concept version of this design was implemented to run on top of the Unix operating system and supported hard and non-real-time applications running in a distributed, heterogeneous environment. The feasibility of the fault-tolerant concepts was also demonstrated with that implementation. No changes to the Unix kernel were made in that implementation, which was operational in 1990. We realized that Unix is not a very hospitable host for real-time applications, as very little control over the use of resources can be exercised in that system without extensive modifications to the kernel. Therefore, based on the lessons learned from the first design, we proceeded with the design of the current version of Maruti and changed the base to be Mach, which does permit a more direct control of resources.

In this chapter, we summarize the design philosophy of the Maruti system and discuss the design and implementation of Maruti-II. We also present the development tools and operating system support for mission-critical applications. While the system is being designed to provide integrated support for multiple requirements of mission critical applications, we focus our attention on real-time requirements on a single-processor system.

The rest of the chapter is organized as follows. In the remainder of this section, we outline our design goals and principles. In Section 4.2, we present an overview of the Maruti system. Section 4.3 describes the Maruti computational model. In Sections 4.4, 4.5, and 4.6 we present details of the application development, system integration, and run-time system, respectively. Concluding remarks are presented in Section 4.7.

## 4.1.1    Design Goals

The design of a real-time system must take into consideration the primary characteristics of the applications which are to be supported. The design of Maruti has been guided by the following application characteristics and requirements [2, 12, 13].

**Real-Time Requirements.** The most important requirement for real-time systems is the capability to support timely execution of applications. In contrast, with many existing systems, the next generation systems will require support for hard, soft, and non-real-time applications on the same platform.

**Fault Tolerance.** Many of the mission-critical systems are safety critical, and therefore have fault-tolerance requirements. In this context, *fault tolerance* is the ability of a system to support continuous operation in the presence of faults. Although a number of techniques for supporting fault-tolerant systems have been suggested in the literature, they rarely consider the real-time requirements of the system. A real-time operating system must provide support for fault tolerance and exception-handling capabilities for increased reliability, while continuing to satisfy the timing requirements.

**Distributivity.** The inherent characteristics of many systems require that multiple autonomous computers, connected through a local area network, cooperate in a distributed manner. The computers and other resources in the system may be homogeneous or heterogeneous. Due to the autonomous operation of the components which cooperate, system control and coordination become a much more difficult task than if the system were implemented in a centralized manner. The techniques learned in the design and implementation of centralized systems do not always extend to distributed systems in a straightforward manner.

**Scenarios.** Many real-time applications undergo different modes of operation during their life cycle. A *scenario* defines the set of jobs executing in the system at any given time. A hard real-time system must be capable of switching from one scenario to another, maintaining the system in a safe and stable state at all times, without violating the timing constraints.

**Integration of Multiple Requirements.** The major challenge in building operating systems for mission-critical computing is the integration of multiple requirements. Because of the conflicting nature of some of the requirements and the solutions developed to date, integration of all the requirements in a single system is a formidable task. For example, the real-time requirements preclude the use of many of the fault-handling techniques used in the fault-tolerant systems.

## 4.1.2   Design Approach and Principles

Maruti is a time-based system in which the resources are reserved prior to execution. The resource reservation is done on the timeline, thus allowing for reasoning about real-time properties in a natural way. The time-driven architecture provides a predictable execution for real-time systems, a necessary requirement for hard real-time applications. The basic design approach is outlined below.

**Resource Reservation for Hard Real-Time Jobs.** Hard real-time applications in Maruti have advance resource reservation: this results in a priori guarantees about the timely execution of hard real-time jobs. This is achieved through a *calendar* data structure which keeps track of all resource reservations and the assigned time-intervals. The resource requirements are specified as early as possible in the development stage of an application and are manipulated, analyzed, and refined through all phases of application development.

**Predictability through Reduction of Resource Contention.** Hard real-time jobs are scheduled using a time-driven scheduling paradigm in which the resource contention between jobs is eliminated through scheduling. This results in reduced run-time overheads and leads to a high degree of predictability. However, not all jobs can be pre-scheduled. Since resources may be shared between jobs in the "calendar" and other jobs in the system, such as non-real-time activities, there may be resource contention leading to lack of predictability. This is countered by eliminating as much of resource contention as possible and reducing it whenever it is not possible to eliminate it entirely. The lack of predictability is compensated by allowing enough slack in the schedule.

**Integrated Support for Fault Tolerance.** Fault tolerance objectives are achieved by integrating the support for fault tolerance at all levels in the system design. The fault tolerance is supported by (i) early fault detection, (ii) resilient application structures through redundancy, and (iii) capability to switch modes of operation. Fault detection capabilities are integrated with the application during its development, permitting the use of application-specific fault detection and fault-handling. As fault-handling may result in violation of temporal constraints, replication is used to make the application resilient. Failure of a replica may not affect the timely execution of other replicas and thereby the interactions of the system it may be controlling. Under anticipated load and failure conditions, it may become necessary for the system to revoke the guarantees given to the hard real-time applications and change its mode of operation dynamically so that an accepted degraded mode of operation may continue.

**Separation of Mechanisms and Policies.** In the design of Maruti, emphasis has been placed on separating mechanisms from policies. Thus, for instance, the system provides basic dispatching mechanisms for a time-driven system, keeping the design of specific scheduling policies separate. The same approach is followed in other aspects of the system. By separating the mechanisms from the policies, the system can be tailored to different environments, and optimized for them.

**Portability, Extensibility.** Unlike many other real-time systems, the aim of the Maruti project has been to develop a system which can be tailored to use in a wide variety of situations, from small embedded systems to complex mission-critical systems. With the rapid change in hardware technology, it is imperative that the design be such that it is portable to different platforms and makes minimal assumptions about the underlying hardware platform. The portability and extensibility are also enhanced by using modular design with well-defined interfaces. This allows for integration of new techniques into the design with relative ease.

## 4.2    Maruti Overview

### 4.2.1    Application Life Cycle

The life cycle of an application program can be divided into *design*, *development*, and *operational* phases. For real-time applications we need to carry out some additional stages during the phases of the life cycle. In the following we present the steps we explicitly recognize for Maruti applications. Figure 4.1 shows the three phases of the application life cycle.

1. **Design Phase:** This stage is the starting point of the development of an application during which the overall design is carried out. The activities during this stage include requirements specification, conceptual design, and detailed design.

2. **Development Phase:**  This phase is broken down into two stages, compilation and integration.

   - **Compilation**. The source code modules are created at this stage, along with their interface specifications. The resource requirements for the modules are identified at this level itself, and are supplied to the integration environment.

   - **Integration**. In the integration stage, modules created in the compilation stage are interconnected to form a complete program. The remaining resource requirements for the application are identified and recorded with the application. Resilient applications are also created at this stage should the application have resiliency requirements.

   The result of this phase is an executable application program, along with its resource and timing requirements.

3. **Operational Phase:**  The operational phase consists of resource allocation and execution, and is initiated after an invocation request is made. For hard real-time applications, we require that resource allocation be done prior to execution.

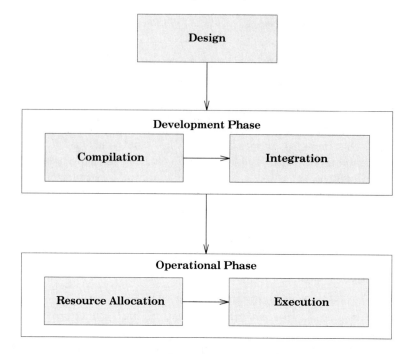

**Figure 4.1**  Application Life Cycle

- **Resource allocation**. The allocation and reservation of resources is carried out at this stage.
- **Execution**. During this stage the operating system performs dispatching, message passing, and reservation enforcement. Previous stages prepare the application for this stage, such that the run-time overheads are minimal.

The resource requirements and timing information are identified and tracked as the application progresses through its life cycle, and are explicitly used during run-time. When such information is not available during the early phases of the life cycle, place holders are provided for the information.

## 4.2.2   Maruti Components

The Maruti system may be seen as comprised of three major component systems, as identified below:

**Application Development.**   To support applications in a real-time system, conventional application development techniques must be augmented with support for specification and extraction of resource requirements and timing constraints. The application development system provides a set of programming tools to support and facilitate the development of real-time applications with diverse requirements. It consists of tools that support both phases of application development, compilation and integration. The Maruti Programming Language (MPL) is used during the compilation stage to develop program modules. A precompiler extracts resource, control, and timing information from the source program modules, which serves as input to application integration. The Maruti Configuration Language (MCL) is used to specify how individual program modules are to be connected together to form an application. Integration tools are used for this purpose.

**System Integration.**   The system integration involves analyzing the resource allocation and scheduling of a collection of applications, in terms of their real-time and fault-tolerance properties. The properties of the system are analyzed with respect to the system configuration and the characteristics of the run-time system, which are specified using the Maruti configuration language.

**Run-Time System.**   The run-time system provides the conventional functionality of an operating system in a manner that supports the timely dispatching of jobs. There are two major components of the run-time system: the Maruti kernel, which enforces the scheduling and allocation decisions, and the run-time dispatcher, which performs resource allocation and scheduling for dynamic arrivals.

## 4.3   Maruti Computation Model

In this section we describe the Maruti computation model, from a run-time perspective, and discuss its properties and key features. The computational model is driven by the time-driven scheduling paradigm using non-blocking resource control policies [14, 15].

### 4.3.1   Elemental Units

The basic building block of the Maruti computation model is an Elemental Unit (EU). An elemental unit is triggered by incoming data and signals, operates on the input data, and produces some output data and signals. The behavior of an EU is *atomic*, with respect to its environment, in the following sense:

- All resources needed by an elemental unit are assumed to be required for the entire length of its execution.

- The interaction of an EU with other entities of the systems is either (logically) before it starts executing or after it finishes execution.

The components of an EU are illustrated in Figure 4.2 and are described below:

1. **Input and Output Ports**. Each EU may have several input and/or output ports. Each port specifies a part of the interface of the EU. The input ports are used to accept incoming input data to the EU, while the output ports are used for feeding the output of the EU to other entities in the system.

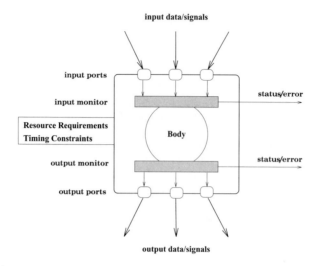

**Figure 4.2** Elemental Unit Structure

2. **Input and Output Monitors.** An input monitor collects the data from the input ports, and provides it to the main body. In doing so, it acts as a filter, and may also be used for error detection and debugging. The input monitors are also used for supporting different triggering conditions for the EU. Similar to input monitors, the output monitors act as filters to the outgoing data. The output monitor may be used for error detection and timing constraint enforcement. The monitors may be connected to other EUs in the system, and may send (asynchronous) messages to them reporting errors or status messages.

3. **Main Body.** The main body accepts the input data from the input monitor, acts on it, and supplies the output to the output monitor. It defines the functionality provided by the EU.

Annotated with an elemental unit are its resource requirements and timing constraints, which are supplied to the resource schedulers. The resource schedulers must ensure that the resources are made available to the EU at the time of execution, and that its timing constraints are satisfied.

## 4.3.2   Composition of EUs

In order to define complex executions, the EUs may be composed together and properties specified on the composition. Elemental units are composed by connecting an output port of an EU with an input port of another EU. A valid connection requires that the input and output port types be compatible, e.g., carry the same message type. Such a connection marks a one-way flow of data or control, depending on the nature of the ports.

A composition of EUs can be viewed as a directed acyclic graph (henceforth,

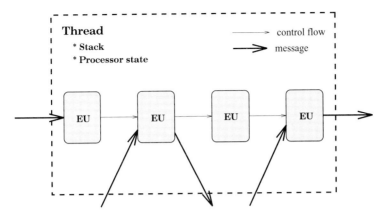

**Figure 4.3** Thread Structure

referred to as an *Elemental Unit Graph* (EUG)), in which the nodes are the EUs, and the edges are the connections between EUs. A partially specified EUG in which all input and output ports are not connected is termed a *partial* EUG. A partial EUG may be viewed as a higher-level EU. In a complete EUG, all input and output ports are connected, and there are no cycles in the graph. The acyclic requirement comes from the required time determinacy of execution and thereby a need to prevent unbounded cycles or recursions. Bounded cycles in an EUG are converted into an acyclic graph by loop unrolling.

The composition of EUs allows for definitions of higher-level abstractions, and the properties associated with them. By carefully choosing the abstractions, the task of developing applications and ensuring that the timing and other operational constraints are satisfied can be greatly simplified. In Maruti, we have chosen the following abstractions:

- A *thread* is a sequential composition of elemental units, as illustrated in Figure 4.3. It has a sequential flow of control which is triggered by data/control messages to the first EU in the thread. The flow of control is terminated with the last EU in the thread. Two adjacent EUs of a thread are connected by a single link carrying the flow of control. The component elemental units may receive messages, or send messages to elemental units outside the thread. All EUs of a thread share the execution stack and processor state.

- A *job* is a collection of threads which cooperate with each other to provide some functionality. The partial EUGs of the component threads are connected together in a well-defined manner to form a complete EUG. All threads within a job operate under a global timing constraint specified for the job. Figure 4.4 shows the structure of a job, in terms of its component threads, elemental units, and the connections between elemental units.

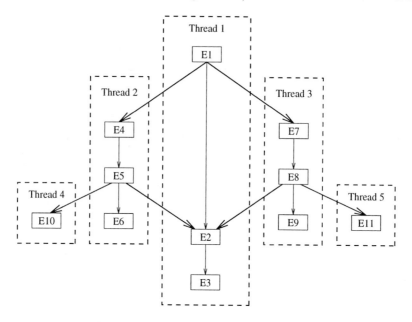

**Figure 4.4** Elemental Unit Graph for a Job

### 4.3.3   Communication Model

Maruti supports message passing and shared memory models for communication.

**Message Passing.**   Maruti supports the notion of one-way message passing between elemental units. The message passing paradigm provides a location and architecture transparent communication paradigm. A *channel* abstraction is used to specify a one-way message communication path between the sender and receiver (Figure 4.5). A one-way message passing channel is set up by declaring the output port on the sender EU, the input port on the receiver EU, and the type of message. The communication is asynchronous with respect to the sender; i.e., the sender does not block. Depending on the nature of the communication channel, the receiver may block:

- *Synchronous communication* is used for tightly coupled communication between elemental units of the same job. For every invocation of the sender, there is an invocation of the receiver which accepts the message sent by the sender. The receiver is blocked (de-scheduled) until message arrival under normal circumstances. If the receiver is unblocked and there is no message, then it is indicative of failure. The messages in a synchronous communication channel are delivered in FIFO order.

- *Asynchronous communication* may be used for message passing communication between elemental units not belonging to the same job. It may also be used between real-time and non-real-time jobs. In such communication, neither the sender nor the receiver is blocked (i.e., there is no synchronization).

**Figure 4.5** Channel

Since the sender and receiver may execute at different rates, it is possible that no finite amount of buffers suffice. Hence, an asynchronous communication channel is inherently lossy. The receiver may specify its input port to be *in-First*, or *inLast*, to indicate which messages to drop when the buffers are full. The first message is dropped in an inLast channel, while the last message is dropped in an inFirst channel.

There may be multiple receivers of a message, thus allowing for multi-cast messages. Similar to a one-to-one channel, a multicast channel may also be synchronous or asynchronous. All receivers of a multi-cast message must be of the same type.

**Shared Memory.**  The other communication paradigm supported in Maruti is the shared memory paradigm. The simplest way to share memory between EUs is to allow them to exist within the same address space. We use the *task* abstraction for this purpose. A task consists of multiple threads operating within it, sharing the address space (Figure 4.6). The task serves as an execution environment for the component threads. A thread may belong to only one task.

In addition to the shared memory within a task, inter-task sharing is also supported through the creation of *shared memory partitions*. A shared memory partition is a shared buffer which can be accessed by any EU permitted to do so. The shared memory partitions provide an efficient way to access data shared between multiple EUs.

The shared memory communication paradigm provides just the shared memory; it is the user's responsibility to ensure safe access to the shared data. This can be done by defining a logical resource, and by ensuring that the resource is acquired every time the shared data is accessed. By providing appropriate restrictions on the logical resource, safe access to data can be obtained.

## 4.3.4  Resource Model

A distributed system consists of a collection of autonomous processing nodes, connected via a local area network. Each processing node has resources classified as (i) processors, (ii) logical resources, and (iii) peripheral devices. The logical resources are used to provide safe access to shared data structures, and are passive in nature. The peripheral devices include sensors and actuators.

Restrictions may be placed on the preemptability of resources to maintain resource consistency. The type of the resource determines the restrictions that are placed on the preemptability of the resource, and serves to identify operational constraints for the purpose of resource allocation and scheduling. We classify the resources into the following types based on the restrictions that are imposed on their usage.

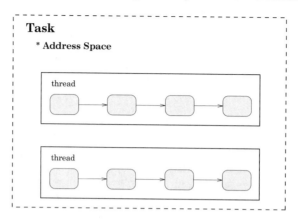

**Figure 4.6** Task Structure

- **Non-preemptable**. The inherent characteristics of a resource may be such that it prevents preemptability, i.e., any usage of the resource must be in a non-preemptive manner. Many devices require non-preemptive scheduling. For resources which require the use of CPU, this implies non-preemptive execution from the time the resource is acquired until the time the resource is released.

- **Exclusive**. Unlike a non-preemptive resource, an exclusive resource can be preempted. However, the resource may not be granted to anyone else in the meanwhile. A critical section is an example of a resource, which must be used in exclusive mode.

- **Serially Reusable**. A serially reusable resource cannot only be preempted but may also be granted to another EU. The state of such resources can be preserved and restored when the resource is granted back. The processors are examples of serially reusable resources.

- **Shared**. A shared resource may be used by multiple entities simultaneously. In a single-processor system, since only one entity is executing at a given time, there is no distinction between a shared resource and a serially reusable resource.

Clearly, a non-preemptable resource is the most restrictive, and a shared resource is the least restrictive in terms of the type of usage allowed. An application requesting the use of a resource must specify when the resource is to be acquired, when it is to be released, and the restrictions on the preemptability of the resource. The resource requirements for applications may be specified at different levels of computational abstractions, as identified below.

- **EU level**. The lowest level a resource requirement can be specified at is the EU level. A resource specified at the EU level implies that the resource is acquired and released within the EU. For scheduling purposes, it is assumed that the resource is required for the entire duration of the execution of the EU.

- **Thread Level.** Resource specification at the thread level is used for resources which are acquired and released by different EUs belonging to the same thread. For instance, a critical section may be acquired in one EU, and released in another one.

- **Job Level.** Job-level resource specifications are used to specify resources which are not acquired and released for each invocation of a periodic or sporadic job. Instead, these resources are acquired at the job initialization and released at job termination. For a periodic job, an implicit resource associated with each thread are the thread data structures (including processor stack and registers).

## 4.3.5    Operational Constraints

The execution of EUs is constrained through various kinds of operational constraints (Table 4.1). Such constraints may arise out of restricted resource usage or through the operational requirements of the application. Examples of such constraints are: precedence, mutual exclusion, ready time, and deadline. They may be classified into the following categories:

- **Synchronization Constraints.** Synchronization constraints arise out of data and control dependencies, or through resource preemptability restrictions. Typical examples of such constraints are precedence and mutual exclusion.

- **Timing Constraints.** Many types of timing constraints may be specified at different levels of specification, i.e., at job level, thread level, or EU level. At the job level, the invocation pattern of the job may be specified, i.e., whether the job is periodic, sporadic, or aperiodic, its ready time and deadline, and so on. For threads, a ready time and deadline may be specified, relative to the job arrival. Likewise, a ready time and deadline may be specified for an individual EU. We also support the notion of relative timing constraints [4, 5, 7] i.e., constraints which constrain the temporal distance between the execution of two EUs.

- **Allocation Constraints.** In our model, tasks are allocated to processing nodes. Allocation constraints are used to restrict the task allocation decisions. Allocation constraints often arise due to fault-tolerance requirements, where the redundant computations must be allocated on different processing nodes. Similarly, when two tasks share memory, they must be allocated on the same processing node. Sometimes a task must be bound to a processing node since it uses a particular resource (e.g., a sensor) bound to the node.

The operational constraints are made available to the resource allocation and scheduling tools, which must ensure that the allocation and scheduling maintains the

**Table 4.1  Operational Constraints**

| Operational Constraint | Interpretation |
|---|---|
| $E_1$ **precedes** $E_2$ | $E_1$ precedes $E_2$; i.e., the execution of $E_1$ must finish before the execution of $E_2$ starts. |
| $(E_1, \ldots, E_k)$ **excludes** $(E'_1, \ldots, E'_m)$ | The execution of all elemental units $E_1$ through $E_k$, taken as a group, must not overlap with execution of all elemental units $E'_1$ through $E'_m$. |
| **readytime** $X$ $R$ | The execution of $X$ must not start before $R$, where $X$ may be a job, a thread, or an EU. The execution of a job refers to execution of any of its threads; the execution of a thread refers to execution of its first elemental unit. |
| **deadline** $X$ $D$ | The execution of $X$ must finish before $D$. |
| **relative deadline** $E_1$ $E_2$ $D$ | $E_2$ must finish within $D$ time of $E_1$ starting. |
| **delay** $E_1$ $E_2$ $\Delta$ | $E_2$ must start no sooner than $\Delta$ time after $E_1$ finishes. |
| **together** $X$ $Y$ | Tasks $X$ and $Y$ must be on the same processing node. |
| **separate** $X$ $Y$ | Tasks $X$ and $Y$ must be on different processing nodes. |
| **on** $X$ $P$ | Task $X$ must be allocated on processor $P$. |

restrictions imposed by the constraints. The model does not place any a priori restriction on the nature of the constraints that may be specified. However, the development of the resource allocator and scheduler will depend on the type of constraints that can be specified.

## 4.4    Applications Development System

In this section, we describe the programming paradigm used and supported in Maruti. Programming in Maruti is a two-stage process: (i) compilation, in which individual program modules are created and their interfaces specified, and (ii) integration, where the program modules are configured together to build a complete Maruti application.

From a functional perspective, an application program is viewed as a set of modules cooperating together to provide the desired functionality. On the other hand, from a temporal perspective, the application consists of a cooperating set of jobs, executing within some timing constraints. Each module consists of local data and source code. A module exports an interface, consisting of entry points and services, which are used during configuration to bind modules and create the jobs of the application. While modules provide the source code and data for an application, the jobs (and their components threads) provide the manner in which the modules are executed. Jobs and threads are the active entities of an application.

### 4.4.1    Compilation

#### 4.4.1.1    Maruti Programming Language

Rather than develop completely new programming languages, we have taken the approach of using existing languages as base programming languages, and augmenting them with Maruti primitives needed to provide real-time support. In the current version, the base programming language used is ANSI C. Clearly, to be suitable for use in a real-time environment, the full generality of C cannot be permitted. Various restrictions are placed on the language to assure that programs can execute in bounded and known time, and to be able to analyze the control flow and resource usage of program. Examples of such restrictions are: unbounded loops and recursion are not allowed, no "goto" statements are allowed, and no dynamic memory allocation is permitted.

The code of an application is divided into modules. In loose terms, a module is a collection of procedures, functions, and local data structures. A module forms an independently compiled unit and may be linked with other modules to form a complete application. At run time, a module maps to a task. All procedures and functions within the module share the address space and hence may communicate using shared variables.

The base programming language (i.e., ANSI C) has been augmented with Maruti primitives to extract out resource and timing information, and to create elemental units out of the program. Primitives are also provided to support the communication paradigm. Table 4.2 presents a sampling of the primitives used in MPL.

Each module exports an interface, which is extracted by the compilation tools during the process of compilation. The interface includes the entries, services, ports, and so on, and is used during the configuration stage to create a complete application program.

**Module Interface**

- An *entry point* defines a start point for a job. A single thread may be created out of each entry point, and assigned to a job during the application configuration.

- A *service* defines a function to be executed on behalf of a client. It is triggered by the reception of one or more messages. At run time each call to the service maps to a different thread. Thus, unlike an entry point, multiple threads may be executing the same service, one thread servicing each invoking client.

- *Ports* are the end-points of channels used for message passing. For each entry and service in the module, the input and output ports, the type of each port, and the type of the message form parts of the module interface.

- Each module may have an *initialization function,* which is invoked to initialize the module when it is loaded in the memory. The initialization function may be called with arguments.

- *Actions* are the externally observable actions of the modules. Actions are used to specify (fine-grained) timing constraints.

- *Logical resources* are used to safely access and maintain data consistency. For each logical resource used within the module, the EUs using the resource and the type of usage is recorded in the interface.

#### 4.4.1.2   Compilation of Modules

A program module can be independently compiled. The compilation process for a program is shown in Figure 4.7. In addition to the generation of the object code, the compilation also results in the creation of partial EUGs for the modules (i.e., for the services and entries in the module), as well as the extraction of resource requirements, such as stack sizes for threads, memory requirements, and logical resource requirements.

**Generation of Partial EUG.**   As mentioned before, invocation of an entry point and service call starts a new thread of execution. A control flow graph is generated for each service and entry. The control flow graph and the MPL primitives are used to delineate EU boundaries. Recall that an EU execution is atomic; i.e., all resources required by the EU are assumed to be used for the entire duration of its execution. Further, all input messages are assumed to be logically received at the start of an EU and all output messages are assumed to be logically sent at the end

Table 4.2  Maruti Programming Language Primitives

| MPL Primitive | Interpretation |
|---|---|
| **send** (port,&msg)<br>**receive** (port,&msg)<br>**opt-receive** (port,&msg) | Send a message on "port".<br>Synchronous receive.<br>Asynchronous receive; "port" may be in-First or inLast |
| **service** foo (&msg,...)<br>  **in** in-port: in-msg-type,<br>  **out** out-port: out-msg-type,<br>  { *body* } | Service foo. The input and output ports for the service are identified along with the type of message on each port. The arguments to the service give the input message buffers. |
| **entry** foo (&msg,...)<br>  **in** in-port: in-msg-type,<br>  **out** out-port: out-msg-type,<br>  { *body* } | Entry foo. Arguments are the same as service arguments. |
| **module** name<br>**maruti_main**<br>  (int argc, char **argv) | Name of the module.<br>The initialization function for the module. |
| **observable action** { *body* } | The "body" forms an observable action. |
| **region** (resource,option) { *body* } | The "resource" is acquired at the start of the "body" and released at the end of it. The access restrictions are specified in the "options". |
| **shared** type variable | A named shared memory buffer of type "type". The buffer may be accessed through the named "variable". |

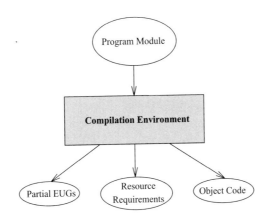

**Figure 4.7**  Compilation Environment

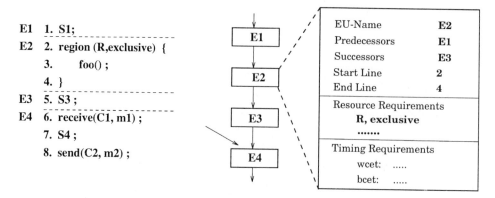

**Figure 4.8** Elemental Unit Boundaries

of an EU. At compilation time, the code for each entry and service is broken up into one or more elemental units. The delineation of EU boundaries must be done in a manner that ensures that no cycles are formed in the resultant EUG. Thus, for instance, a *send* followed by a receive within the same EU may result in a cyclic precedence, and hence must not be allowed. We follow certain rules of thumb to delineate EU boundaries, which may be overridden and explicitly changed by the user. The EU boundaries are created at (i) a receive statement, (ii) the beginning and end of a resource block, (iii) the beginning and end of an observable action, and (iv) a send statement. An example of how such EU boundaries are created is shown in Figure 4.8.

Figure 4.8 also illustrates the information that is maintained for each elemental unit created as a result of the compilation process. For each elemental unit a symbolic name is generated and is used to identify it. The predecessors and successors of the EU as well the source code line numbers associated with the EU are identified and stored. The resource and timing requirements that can be identified during compilation are also stored, and placeholders are created for the remaining information.

## 4.4.2    Integration

### 4.4.2.1    Maruti Configuration Language

The Maruti Configuration Language (MCL) is used to build complete applications from independently created program modules. The language is used to specify communication between program modules, the timing constraints of the application program, and allocation and replication constraints. It is a high-level language which supports modularity, hierarchical description, and modifiability. The program modules merely provide the functional blocks by whose use complex application programs may be developed. In this section, we illustrate the key features of the configuration language using which complete application programs are put together. Table 4.3 gives a sampling of MCL primitives.

Table 4.3  Maruti Configuration Language Primitives

| MCL Primitive | Interpretation |
|---|---|
| **application** name *body* | Create an application whose description is given by the "body". |
| **job** name : **period** value | Specification of a periodic job. |
| **task** name:   module [module-params] | Defines a new instantiation of a task from "module"; "module-params" give the initialization arguments for the "module". |
| **channel name** | Specifies a new channel variable. |
| *in-channels*  module.entry   *out-channels* **in** job | Instantiate a new thread from an entry point in "job". All "in-channels" and "out-channels" must be channel variables. |
| *in-channels*  module.service  *out-channels* | Thread instantiation from a service. |
| **interval** (**start** action1, **end** action2) < time | The temporal interval between the start of "action1" and end of "action2" must be no more than "time". |
| **interval** (**end** action1, **start** action2) > time | The temporal interval between the end of "action1" and start of "action2" must be no less than "time". |
| **together** names | Allocate all the tasks specified in "names" on the same machine. |
| **separate** names | Allocate all the tasks specified in "names" on separate machines. |

**Tasks, Threads, and Channel Binding.** Each module may be instantiated any number of times to generate tasks. The threads of a task are created by instantiating the entries and services of the corresponding module. An entry may be instantiated only once, while a service may be instantiated any number of times. An entry instantiation also indicates the job to which the entry belongs. A service instantiation belongs to the job of its client. The instantiation of a service or entry requires binding the input and output ports to a channel. A channel has a single input port indicating the sender, and one or more output ports indicating the receivers. The configuration language uses *channel variables* for defining the channels. The definition of a channel also includes the type of communication it supports, i.e., synchronous or asynchronous.

**Resources.** All global resources (i.e., resources which are visible outside a module) are specified in the configuration file, along with the access restrictions on the resource. The configuration language allows for binding of resources in a module to the global resources. Any resources used by a module which are not mapped to a global resource are considered local to the module.

**Timing Requirements/Constraints.** The timing requirements and constraints are used to specify the temporal requirements and constraints of the program. As mentioned before, an application consists of a set of cooperating jobs. A job is a set of *entries* (and the services called by the entries) which closely cooperate. Associated with each job are its invocation characteristics, i.e., whether it is periodic or aperiodic. For a periodic job, its period and optionally the readytime and deadline within the period are specified. The constraints of a job apply to all component threads.

In addition to constraints on jobs and threads, finer-level timing constraints may be specified on the observable actions. An observable action may be specified in the code of the program. For any observable action, a ready time and a deadline may be specified. These are relative to the job arrival. An action may not start executing before the ready time, and must finish before the deadline. Each thread is an implicitly observable action, and hence may have a ready time and a deadline.

Apart from the ready time and deadline constraints, programs in Maruti can also specify relative timing constraints [4], those which constrain the interval between two events. For each action, the start and end of the action mark the observable events. A relative constraint is used to constrain the temporal separation between two such events, and may be a relative deadline constraint which specifies the upper bound on time between two events, or a delay constraint which specifies the lower bound on time between the occurrence of the two events (refer to Table 4.1). The interval constraints are closer to the event-based real-time specifications, which constrain the minimum/maximum distance between two events [6] and allow for a rich expression of timing constraints for real-time programs.

**Replication and Fault Tolerance.** At the application level fault tolerance is achieved by creating resilient applications [8]. A resilient application is created by allowing redundant computations. The configuration language eases the task of achieving fault tolerance, by allowing mechanisms to replicate the modules and

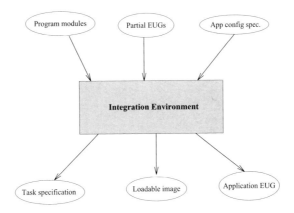

**Figure 4.9** Integration Environment

services, thus achieving the desired amount of resiliency. By specifying allocation constraints, a programmer can ensure that the replicated modules are executed on different partitions.

A replicated application can be represented by a resilient elemental unit graph, a graph in which several units have been replicated to provide the desired resiliency. Modules may be replicated by creating multiple instances of the module. It is the programmer's responsibility to ensure replica determinism. When modules are replicated, support must be provided for replicated communications, especially voting mechanisms. Each replicated service also replicates its input and output ports.

### 4.4.2.2   Program Integration

Given an application specification in the Maruti Configuration Language and the component application modules, the integration tools are responsible for creating a completion application program and extracting out the resource and timing information for scheduling and resource allocation. Figure 4.9 shows the basic activities performed during the integration stage. The input to the integration environment are the program modules the partial EUGS corresponding to the modules and the application configuration specification. The output of the integration environment are (i) a specification for the loader for creating tasks, populating their address spaces, creating the threads and channels, and initializing the task; (ii) loadable executables of the program; and (iii) the complete application EUG along with the resource descriptions for the resource allocation and scheduling subsystem.

## 4.5   System Integration

During the system integration phase, the feasibility of the system resources to support a given set of applications is evaluated. In the simplest case, this results in resource allocation and scheduling for the applications to execute. The Maruti Configuration Language is used to specify a high-level description of the system in terms of its resources, the nature and characteristics of the resources, and so on. In this section, we give a flavor of the system description, as well as the resource allocation and scheduling.

### 4.5.1   System Specification

The Maruti Configuration Language (MCL) is used to specify system resources, the component applications and their scenarios, the allocation and scheduling restrictions and so on. We give a brief description of the entities that may be specified using the configuration language. The system specification is used by the resource allocation and scheduling components for allocation and scheduling of resources.

**Node Description.**   Since Maruti supports a distributed execution environment, the system may consist of multiple nodes (machines) connected through a communications network. For each node, a logical name of the node, the number and type of processors, the size of the main memory, and descriptions of peripheral devices connected to the node are specified.

**Communication Network Specifications.**   The communications network provides the communication paths between nodes. Similar to each node-description, a specification of the communication network, the protocol used, and the parameters of the protocol are provided in the description of the communications network. For instance, in a broadcast bus supporting a *Time-Division Multiplexed Access* (TDMA) protocol, one may specify the TDMA slot size, the machines connected to the broadcast bus, the transmission speed of the bus, and so on.

**Scenarios.**   Most real-time systems undergo several modes of operation. From one mode to another, the set of active jobs may change for a part of the system. A *scenario* describes a mode of operation for a system, and describes a collection of jobs and their real-time constraints. The scenario changes are different from dynamic job arrivals in that the characteristics of the scenarios are statically known, even though the exact time of a change is not known. However, since the description of a system before and after a mode change is well known, it is amenable to schedulability analysis.

   A scenario change is requested from the application, and may be triggered by some internal or external condition. When a scenario change is requested, the change cannot always take place instantaneously. Correct times are pre-determined where the change can take place with no effect on the scheduling, data, and system integrity. In some cases the scenario change must take place very quickly. The *priority scenarios* have been defined for these cases. When such a scenario is requested, the scenario change takes place immediately and replaces the complete application. Of course such an operation may leave the data in an inconsistent state. It is the responsibility of the programmer to provide a recovery for such cases.

## 4.5.2    Resource Allocation and Scheduling

Maruti follows a time-driven scheduling paradigm in which resources are reserved "in time" for hard real-time jobs. For each resource, a "calendar" is maintained which gives the mapping of each elemental unit instance to time. The calendar is used by the kernel for timely dispatching of EUs. Given a complete description of the applications and the system architecture, the task of the resource allocation and scheduling subsystem is to create the calendars for the different resources in the system. In this section, we discuss the basic issues involved and address some of the policy issues.

Given an application and a system architecture, the resource allocation problem is to map the application structures onto the resources in the system. We consider primarily the resource allocation problem of assigning tasks to processing nodes. Given an allocation of tasks to processing nodes, the scheduling problem is to produce calendars for each processing node, as well as analyze the schedulability of communications between different processing nodes.

## 4.5.3    Node Scheduling

At the core of the scheduling subsystem is the scheduling of a single processing node with multiple resources. Many real-time systems may have only a single processing node connected to various input/output devices. Even in a distributed system, single-node scheduling forms a central part of the entire resource scheduling paradigm.

The schedule for a single node is created for the least common multiple of the periods of the jobs executing on that node. This schedule is repeated cyclically. We use primarily non-preemptive scheduling techniques since the scheduling is done at fine-grained units (EUs), such that preemption is not likely to improve schedulability significantly. The non-preemptive scheduling is essentially a sequencing problem, in which an optimal sequence of execution must be determined. To reduce the complexity problem, we have developed search space reduction techniques. The idea behind search space reduction techniques is to perform simple polynomial time analysis on the timing constraints, and eliminate as many schedule sequences as possible. The techniques developed include *decomposition scheduling* [16] and *temporal analysis* [11]; both have been shown to help improve the performance of scheduling techniques.

## 4.5.4    Communications Scheduling

In a distributed system, the communication protocol and its scheduling form a central part of the resource allocation and scheduling system. The communication links may be point-to-point or multiple access links. Point-to-point links may be treated in the same way as processors, and a calendar created for them. However, a calendar-based mechanism is not very suitable for multiple access links in a complex system. The calendar approach for a multiple access communication medium results in very tight coupling of the processing nodes. Instead, real-time commu-

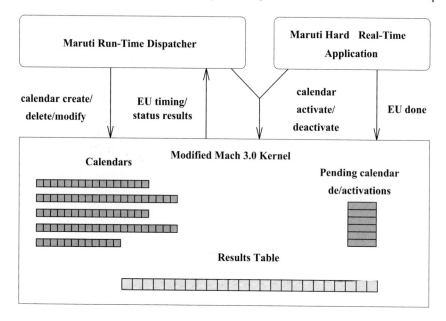

**Figure 4.10** Maruti-II Run-Time Organization

nication protocols based on time-division multiplexing schemes (e.g., [3, 9, 10]) provide better control over the network resources and allow for decoupling of communication medium from the processing nodes. The design of Maruti permits both approaches for communication scheduling.

## 4.5.5   Task Allocation and Global Scheduling

In a distributed real-time system, the problem of task allocation must be solved with a view to provide global schedulability. The global scheduling refers to the scheduling of all processing nodes as well as the communication network. The end-to-end processing requirements must be satisfied through global scheduling. We are exploring the use of heuristic techniques such as simulated annealing to solve the task allocation and global scheduling problem.

## 4.6   Maruti Run-Time System

The run-time organization of Maruti-II is shown in Figure 4.10. The lowest level of the Maruti run-time system is based on the Mach 3.0 Kernel from Carnegie Mellon [1]. Mach is modified to support the execution of elemental units in hard real-time calendars. In this section, we overview the run-time support provided for hard real-time applications in Maruti.

## 4.6.1    The Dispatcher

On top of the modified kernel is the *Maruti Dispatcher*, a Mach server that manages much of the activity of the running system. Among the dispatcher's tasks are:

- *Resource Management.* The dispatcher handles requests to load applications. This involves creating all the tasks and threads of the application, reserving memory, and loading the code and data into the memory. All the resources are reserved before an application is considered successfully loaded and ready to run.

- *Calendar Management.* The dispatcher creates and loads the kernel calendars used by applications, and activates them when the application run-time arrives. The application itself can activate and deactivate calendars for scenario changes.

- *Connection Management.* A Maruti application can consist of many different tasks using channels for communication. The dispatcher sets up the connections between the application tasks using direct shared buffers for local connections, or a shared buffer with a communications agent for remote connections.

- *Exception-Handling.* Rogue application threads can generate exceptions such as missed deadlines, arithmetic exceptions, stack overflows, and stray accesses to unreserved memory. These exceptions are normally handled by the dispatcher for all the Maruti application threads. Various exception-handling behaviors can be configured, from terminating the entire application or just the errant thread, to simply invoking a task-specific handler.

## 4.6.2    Multiple Scenarios

The Maruti design includes the concept of *scenarios*, implemented at run-time as sets of alternative calendars that can be switched quickly to handle an emergency or a change in operating mode. These calendars are pre-scheduled, and able to begin execution without having to invoke a lot of user-level machinery. While handling scenarios is a complicated problem for the higher-level Maruti subsystems, the kernel-level support is easily provided.

The Dispatcher loads the initial scenarios specified by the application and activates one of them to begin normal execution. However, the application itself can activate and deactivate scenarios. For example, an application might need to respond instantaneously to the pressing of an emergency shutdown button. A single system call then causes the immediate suspension of normal activity and the running of the shutdown code sequence.

Calendar activation and deactivation commands can be issued before the desired switch time. The requests are recorded and the switches occur at the precise moment specified. This allows the application to ensure smooth transitions at safe points in the execution.

### 4.6.3   Kernel Organization

The hard real-time portion of the modified Mach kernel consists of three data structures:

- The *calendars* are created and loaded by the Dispatcher. Kernel memory is reserved for each calendar at the time it is created. Several system calls serve to create, delete, modify, activate, and deactivate calendars.

- The *results table* holds timing and status results for the execution of each elemental unit. The `maruti_calendar_results` system will report these results back up to the user level, usually to the dispatcher. The dispatcher can then keep statistics or write a trace file.

- The *pending activation table* holds all outstanding calendar activation and deactivation requests. Since the requests can come before the switch time, the kernel must track the requests and execute them at the correct time in the correct order.

The kernel scheduler gains control of the CPU at every clock tick interrupt. At that time, if a Maruti thread is currently running and its deadline has arrived, its execution is stopped and an exception raised.

If any pending activations are due to be executed, those requests are handled, changing the set of active calendars. Then the next calendar entry is checked to see if it is scheduled to execute at this time. If so, the kernel switches immediately to the specified thread. If no Maruti threads are scheduled to execute, the kernel falls through to the normal Mach clock tick handler to schedule any non-real-time Mach threads.

Maruti threads indicate to the kernel that they have successfully reached the end of their elemental unit with the `maruti_unit_done` system call. This causes the kernel to mark the current calendar entry as done and fill in the time actually used by the thread. The Maruti thread is then suspended until it next appears in the calendars. Non-real-time Mach threads can be run until the next Maruti calendar entry is scheduled.

At all times the kernel knows which calendar entry will be the next one to run, so that the calendars are not continually searched for work. This is recalculated when `maruti_unit_done` is called or whenever the set of active calendars changes.

### 4.6.4   Maruti System Calls

Maruti provides new system calls which are outlined in Table 4.4, primarily for manipulation of calendars. These system calls require the *privileged host port*, a Mach capability that is roughly equivalent to the *root* access in Unix. A task with the privileged host capability can access devices, reboot the machine, assign processors, and access other tasks and threads.

Most system calls in the current system relate to calendar manipulation. The kernel provides support to create, delete, activate, and deactivate calendars. A calendar consists of scheduling entries: each entry identifies the scheduled elemental

### Table 4.4  Maruti System Calls

| System Call | Description |
|---|---|
| maruti_calendar_create | Creates a fresh calendar in the kernel. The calendar remains in dormant state until activated. |
| maruti_calendar_delete | Deletes a given calendar and frees its resources. It is an error to delete an active calendar. |
| maruti_calendar_set_entry | Sets an entry in the calendar. The call is used to add new entries in the calendar. |
| maruti_calendar_activate | Activates the given calendar at a specified switch time.  If switch time is in the past, the calendar is activated immediately. |
| maruti_calendar_deactivate | Deactivates a given calendar at a specified switch time. |
| maruti_calendar_results | Retrieves elemental unit execution results from the results table. The information for each elemental unit includes its execution time and exit status. |
| maruti_unit_done | Called by Maruti threads to indicate an elemental unit boundary to the kernel. The thread sleeps inside this call until it is reactivated by the kernel. When the call returns, a new elemental unit is running. |

unit and its associated scheduled start and finish times. It is implemented as a table wired down in kernel memory. The kernel stores the actual execution times of the elemental units in the results table, which may be queried from the application.

## 4.7  Concluding Remarks

In this chapter, we have focused attention on the support provided in Maruti for executing hard real-time applications on a single machine. We have implemented the current version on DECstations, and on Dell 433/MX PC-compatible machines. Clearly, the current implementation does not have all the capabilities required for mission-critical applications as discussed in this chapter. The design, however, has all the hooks necessary to add these capabilities, many of which have been designed and are at different stages of implementation.

For dependable operation of a mission-critical system the fault handling and recovery must be integrated in the system. The design of Maruti supports early detection of faults through the use of monitors, which may be included with every elemental unit if so desired. The current implementation of MPL does not provide separate facilities to attach monitors to elemental units; however, monitors can be explicitly included in the elemental units by the applications programmer. To continue to meet hard real-time requirements in the face of unexpected hardware and software failures, replication of components is necessary. Maruti, through the integration process, makes replication of pre-existing software components relatively straightforward. *Forkers* can be inserted to distribute channel communications to several replicas, and *Joiners* can vote on the output from the replicas and pass on the result.

The current implementation of the kernel supports the switching of calendars at predetermined times, thereby permitting the changing of applications and scenarios. To make use of this facility for a degraded mode of operation, additional support software is necessary to analyze the implications of such a change. Note that while many of the changes can be analyzed prior to the run-time, some such analysis support may be necessary at the run-time also.

Maruti has been designed to support the execution of applications with hard, soft, and non-real-time requirements. Soft and non-real-time components can be written in MPL, or can be normal Mach/Unix tasks that attach themselves to asynchronous Maruti channels and shared memory blocks. Soft real-time components can be placed into the Maruti calendars to guarantee them a certain percentage of CPU time without imposing deadlines. Components can also be scheduled on an as-available basis, i.e., when there is slack time in the Maruti calendars. The Mach/Unix scheduler takes over, managing both fixed priority and floating priority threads. Maruti components can be inserted into this non-real-time queue with a specified priority. The generality of the low-level mechanisms implemented in Maruti permit the use of other mechanisms to support soft and non-real-time operation of applications also.

In a reactive system, an online scheduler is responsible for adding new jobs to the existing set of jobs. The online scheduler serves the purpose of providing an interface between the user and the kernel, and must verify the schedulability of a new job before inserting it into the kernel's calendar. Reactivity at the kernel level is provided through two mechanisms: (i) the capability to switch from one calendar to another, and (ii) the capability to add new entries into the calendar. The kernel support for such mechanisms is easily provided. The first capability is useful for adding new periodic jobs when the resultant calendar may be of a different length than the currently active calendar. The second facility is more useful for adding aperiodic jobs into the calendar, which are inserted into the calendar for a single execution, and then removed.

In order to meet the temporal requirements of complex mission-critical systems, we believe that temporal determinacy is an important aspect. The design of Maruti has established the feasibility of this approach, which will permit the dependable control of systems of tomorrow.

# Acknowledgments

This work is supported in part by ARPA and Philips Labs under contract DASG60-92-0055 to Department of Computer Science, University of Maryland. The views, opinions, and/or findings contained in this report are those of the author(s) and should not be interpreted as representing the official policies, either expressed or implied, of the Advanced Research Projects Agency, PL, or the U.S. government.

# References

[1] M. Accetta, R. Baron, W. Bolosky, D. Golub, R. Rashid, A. Tevanian, and M. Young. Mach: A New Kernel Foundation for Unix Development. In *Proceedings of Summer Usenix*, July 1986.

[2] A. K. Agrawala and S. T. Levi. *Real-Time System Design*. McGraw-Hill, New York, 1990.

[3] B. Chen, G. Agrawal, and W. Zhao. Optimal Synchronous Capacity Allocation for Hard Real-Time Communications with the Timed Token Protocol. In *Proceedings, IEEE Real-Time Systems Symposium*, pages 198–207, December 1992.

[4] B. Dasarathy. Timing Constraints of Real-Time Systems: Constructs for Expressing Them, Methods of Validating Them. *IEEE Transactions on Software Engineering*, SE-11(1):80–86, January 1985.

[5] R. Gerber, W. Pugh, and M. Saksena. Parametric Dispatching of Hard Real-Time Tasks. Technical Report CS-TR-2985, UMIACS-TR-92-118, Department of Computer Science, University of Maryland, College Park, MD, October 1992.

[6] F. Jahanian and A. K. Mok. Safety Analysis of Timing Properties in Real-Time Systems. *IEEE Transactions on Software Engineering*, SE-12(9):890–904, September 1986.

[7] R. R. Lutz and J. S. K. Wong. Detecting Unsafe Error Recovery Schedules. *IEEE Transactions on Software Engineering*, SE-18(8):749–760, August 1992.

[8] D. Mossé. *A Framework for Development and Deployment of Fault-Tolerant Applications in Real-Time Systems*. Ph.D. thesis, University of Maryland, College Park, August 1993.

[9] S. Mukherjee, D. Saha, M. Saksena, and S. K. Tripathi. A Bandwidth Allocation Scheme for Time Constrained Message Transmission on a Slotted Ring LAN. In *Proceedings, IEEE Real-Time Systems Symposium*, pages 44–53, December 1993.

[10] D. Saha, M. Saksena, S. Mukherjee, and S. K. Tripathi. On Guaranteed Delivery of Time-Critical Messages in DQDB. Technical Report CS-TR-3149, UMIACS-TR-93-96, Department of Computer Science, University of Maryland, College Park, MD, October 1993.

[11] M. Saksena and A. K. Agrawala. Temporal Analysis for Hard Real-Time Scheduling. In *Proceedings, 12th International Phoenix Conference on Computers and Communications*, pages 538–544, March 1993.

[12] J. A. Stankovic. Misconceptions about Real-Time Computing: A Serious Problem for Next-Generation Systems. *IEEE Computer*, 21(10):10–19, Oct. 1988.

[13] J. A. Stankovic. Real-Time Computing Systems: The Next Generation. In J. A. Stankovic and K. Ramamritham, editors, *Tutorial: Hard Real-Time Systems*, page 14:38, IEEE, New York, 1988.

[14] S. K. Tripathi and V. Nirkhe. Synchronization in Hard Real-Time Systems. In S. K. Tewksbury, editor, *Frontiers in Computing Systems Research: Essays on Emerging Technologies, Architectures and Theories*. Plenum Press, New York, 1990.

[15] S. K. Tripathi and V. Nirkhe. Synchronization in Hard Real-Time Systems (position paper). In *Operating Systems of the 90's and Beyond*, July 1991.

[16] X. Yuan, M. Saksena, and A. K. Agrawala. A Decomposition Approach to Real-Time Scheduling. *Journal of Real-Time Systems*, January 1994.

# Part II

# Real-Time Communication

# Chapter 5

# A New Admission Control Method for Real-Time Communication in an Internetwork

## Domenico Ferrari

Admission control is a necessary component of a real-time communication service. The admission control method adopted so far in the Tenet approach to real-time communication was based on a very simple, not very realistic node model. The method described here can be applied to a wide variety of node models with a wide spectrum of accuracies, and is therefore much more general than the previous one. The admission control tests and computations for the case of the Earliest Due Date scheduling discipline are shown as an example of application of the new method. The main advantages and drawbacks of this method are discussed; the predominance of the advantages is expected to be confirmed by experience with testbed implementations.

## 5.1  Introduction

Admission control for connections is now universally recognized as a necessary component of a real-time communication service. Without a limitation of the number of real-time connections[1] admitted to share simultaneously the resources of a packet-switching network, the absence of congestion, hence the quality of the received message streams, could not be guaranteed.

---

[1]The term *real-time connection*, strictly speaking, denotes a connection characterized by an upper bound on packet delays; however, it has for several years been applied to connections offering bounds on some other performance or reliability indices (e.g., throughput, loss rate) as well, or instead. It will be used here with the latter, extended meaning.

Many methods can be resorted to in order to determine whether a new real-time connection can be added to those already existing in the network, and in fact several have been proposed in the literature (see, for example, [7] and [8]). One of the earliest algorithms presented [5] is the first method based on the Tenet approach, a method which was later called Scheme 0 [2]; this scheme, which had been developed for simple homogeneous networks, was subsequently extended to complex heterogeneous internetworks, and became Tenet's Scheme 1 [3]. The principle on which both schemes are based is that of verifying, at the time a request for a new connection is made, whether the resources available along the path of the new connection are sufficient, even in the worst possible case, to

(i)   provide the new connection with the performance guarantees it needs, and

(ii)  allow the guarantees offered to all the existing real-time connections to continue being satisfied.

These conditions are tested in each of the nodes along the path, and the request message is allowed to proceed to the next node only if all tests in a node are satisfied. Since the Tenet schemes have been designed to reach an admission or rejection decision in only one round trip, the final tests take place in the destination[2] of the connection. Both types of tests (node tests and destination tests) depend on the types of bounds the client wants for the new connection, and on the model assumed for the node. In building Scheme 0 and then Scheme 1, we implicitly assumed that a node could be represented by a single queueing server with a finite amount of buffer space in its queues and with a Multi-Class Earliest Due Date (EDD) scheduler [5]. However, when Scheme 1 had to be applied to a real internetworking testbed such as Xunet 2 [6], we found that our node model was inadequate, primarily because nodes did not just consist of one processor, but included other processors on their network interface boards. A more realistic model for a node consisting of a general-purpose computer system is shown in Figure 5.1 as an example.

This problem was temporarily circumvented by introducing in some of the tests a variable representing, rather than the packet service time of the central processor, the packet service time of the bottleneck processor among all those included in the new node model. This solution was obviously unsatisfactory: it lacked generality, and required determining where, in each node, was the bottleneck processor, a designation that could clearly change with the load on the node.

A general, clean solution was obviously needed. Such a solution is described here. Section 5.2 provides the background of our investigation by summarizing the Tenet approach. The new admission control method is presented in Section 5.3, and its characteristics are discussed in Section 5.4. Section 5.5 contains concluding remarks.

---

[2]This discussion assumes that the request message is issued by the source of the new connection. A trivial modification of the schemes allows them to be used also when the message starts from the destination and proceeds backward toward the source.

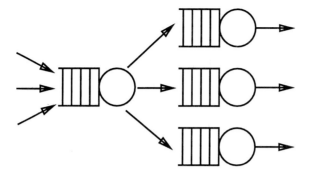

**Figure 5.1** A Node Model Showing the Three Interface Processors Serving the Three Output Links

## 5.2     The Tenet Approach

The Tenet real-time communication Schemes 0 and 1 are based on a simplex unicast network-layer abstraction, the *real-time channel*, characterized by traffic and performance bounds specified by the client. The traffic bounds for channel $i$ are the following:

- $x_{min,i}$ : the minimum inter-packet interval,

- $x_{ave,i}$ : the minimum of the average inter-packet intervals,

- $I_i$ : the averaging interval used in the definition of $x_{ave,i}$,

- $s_{max,i}$ : the maximum packet size.

  The performance bounds for channel $i$ are:

- $D_{max,i}$ : the end-to-end delay bound,

- $Z_{min,i}$ : the minimum probability that packet delay is not greater than $D_{max,i}$,

- $J_{max,i}$ : the end-to-end delay jitter bound,

- $W_{min,i}$ : the minimum probability that a packet is lost due to buffer overflow.

  The Tenet approach is connection-oriented and reservation-based: before a real-time channel can be used by its requestor, it must be established (i.e., resources for the channel must be set aside along its route), so that the desired performance guarantees are supported. Note that these resources are not reserved for the channel's exclusive use; the channel only has higher priority for using them, but in keeping with the principles of packet switching, they can be used by non-real-time traffic whenever no packets from the channel are present.

Channel establishment is a distributed process. A message issued by the source (though it could be issued by the destination instead) visits each node (switch, router, gateway) on the route of the channel. This message causes several admission tests and computations to be performed at each node. If the new channel passes all the tests in a node, the message is forwarded, with some state information about the current node, to the next node on the route. The final tests are performed by the destination; if they are successful, a channel-established message is sent by the destination to the source along the reverse route; when each node is revisited, the message corrects the tentative reservations made in that node by the forward message, and informs the node about the performance bounds assigned to it. Some of these bounds will be used during data transfer operations, others in tests for the admission of future channels, and some in both types of circumstances.

If any of the tests in the nodes or in the destination fails, the channel cannot be established, and a channel-rejected message is immediately sent back to the source. This message removes in each node it visits the tentative reservations made for the new channel.

A new channel's route may be computed by the source (or destination) if this host has the necessary topological information; knowledge by this host of the current real-time load (i.e., a measure of how much of each resource is currently earmarked for use by a real-time channel), and of such additional information as propagation delays and error rates of the links involved, is also quite useful to increase the probability that the chosen route will be able to support the new channel. An alternative is the construction of the route in a hop-by-hop fashion, with individual nodes usually not knowing much beyond the real-time loads of their immediate neighbors.

To complete this general description of the Tenet approach, we only have to mention two special aspects of data transfers: scheduling and distributed rate control. Most scheduling policies can be used for real-time communication under fairly liberal conditions [3]. Since some of the tests to be performed in a node during channel establishment are dependent on the scheduling discipline implemented in that node, we have chosen to restrict this discussion to the case of the Multi-class EDD discipline in its two versions: the so-called Delay-EDD (or D-EDD) [5, 9] and Jitter EDD (or J-EDD) [4, 9].[3] Rate control, either at the periphery of the network or in all of its nodes, is needed to protect well-behaving channels from the misbehavior of faulty or malicious sources, and from the occasional bunching of packets on a channel due to traffic fluctuations. While the latter effect is automatically cured by the J-EDD scheduling discipline, which restores the original traffic pattern in each node implementing this policy, the former effect (and both effects in a D-EDD node) can be eliminated by suitably postponing the offending packets'

---

[3]D-EDD chooses for transmission the packet with the earliest deadline on a deterministic channel if transmitting the one with the earliest deadline on a statistical channel were to violate the former's deadline; otherwise, it chooses the latter, unless the first non-real-time packet can be transmitted without violating the statistical packet's deadline, in which case the non-real-time packet is shipped. J-EDD is based on the same discipline but holds each packet that has arrived too early before giving it to the scheduler.

deadlines in the node's scheduler [5].

# 5.3   The New Admission Control Method

Figure 5.2 illustrates the model that we adopt for a simplex unicast real-time channel. The additional arrows symbolically allude to the fact that each server is shared among many channels. The crucial difference, with respect to the one used in the original Schemes 0 and 1, is that here each node visited by the channel may be represented by more than one single server. Thus, the new model is a much more general one.

For example, the node model in Figure 5.1 will contribute two servers for each node to the channel model in Figure 5.2. Each server is of one of two types:

(i)   *J-type*, if it is scheduled by a discipline that can control jitter (in our example, the J-EDD discipline); and

(ii)  *NJ-type* otherwise.

The admission tests we discuss here assume that the NJ-type servers are scheduled by the D-EDD discipline, but both D-EDD and J-EDD can easily be replaced by other disciplines, as long as the tests are modified appropriately. There is no need for all servers of either type to be homogeneous: servers may be scheduled by a variety of policies even within the same network and the same channel route, but of course we have to use the correct set of tests for each one of them.

Each server is endowed with given amounts of the following resources:

- buffer space,

- computing power,

- *delay resource*,

where, depending on the component modeled by the server, computing power may represent the processor power or the link bandwidth, and where the *delay resource* refers to the feasibility of scheduling all packets by the server's scheduler within the respective local delay bounds.

A server on the modeled channel's route is in general traversed by a number of other, already established real-time channels. Each channel's end-to-end characterization is the 8-tuple of traffic and performance parameters listed in Section 5.2. In each server $n$, an established channel $k$ has the following characterization:

- $d_{n,k}$ : local delay bound (used to compute the EDD deadline),

- $z_{n,k}$ : local minimum probability of delay bound violation,

- $w_{n,k}$ : local minimum probability of buffer overflow,

- $t_{n,k}$ : maximum packet service time.

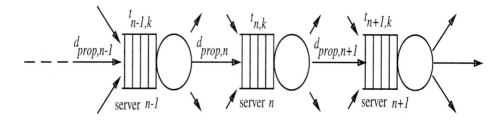

**Figure 5.2**  The Model of a Channel's Path

While the first three parameters of this 4-tuple are computed during the establishment procedure, $t_{n,k}$ is assumed to be known in each server before the server is visited by the establishment message during its forward trip. In a J-type server, a channel whose delay jitter bound $J_{max}$ is specified is characterized also by the canonical delay $D_{n,i}^*$ , which is the delay with respect to the departure time from the source each packet on that channel will be forced to have when it is given to the scheduler in that server.

Another quantity that is known beforehand (and that we assume is transmitted to the destination through the establishment message for each visited server) is the propagation delay $d_{prop,n}$ of the link preceding server $n$ along the new channel's route. Note that this quantity is the only one that characterizes each link in the model in Figure 5.2.

During the forward trip of the establishment message, we can see whether in each server

(a) the addition of a new channel with a deterministic delay bound (i.e., $Z_{min,i} = 1$ ) would cause the worst-case utilization of the server by deterministic channels to rise above 1 (**deterministic test**);

(b) the addition of the new channel would cause the worst-case utilization of the server by all channels to reach a point where the probability of violating the local delay bound of an established channel would be greater than its local bound for that probability (**statistical test**);

(c) the amount of buffer space that is available for the new channel in the server would allow its packets to spend there a maximum amount of time larger than the minimum local delay bound the server can offer the new channel (**buffer space test**).

The minimum local delay bound $dmin_{n,i}$ offered by server $n$ to new channel $i$ is the minimum value of $d_{n,i}$ that makes the packets on channel $i$ schedulable. Computing $dmin_{n,i}$ is the goal of the **delay bound computation** to be performed by the server before the buffer space test. As shown in Table 5.1, which summarizes the admission tests for EDD-scheduled servers, this computation entails sorting the established channels in order of increasing local delay bound, and determining the first position in this list where the new channel can be inserted without causing any of the local delay bounds of the channels below it to violate the condition

$$d_{n,h} \geq \sum_{l=1}^{h} t_{n,l} + T_n + t_{n,c_n+1} \ (h = k, k+1, \ldots, c_n; k = 1, 2, \ldots, c_n), \qquad (5.1)$$

where $T_n$ is the maximum service time server $n$ may give to any packet (including the non-real-time packets), $c_n$ is the number of channels established in server $n$, and $c_n + 1$ is the index locally assigned to the new channel. The value of $dmin_{n,i}$ is the value of the right-hand side of (1) for $h = k_o$, where $k_o$ is the smallest value of $k$ such that inequalities (1) are all satisfied. The proof of this result can be found in [5].

The admission tests and computations to be performed by the destination are collected in Table 5.2. Note that there are several different ways of organizing the tests and computations; the choices made in building Tables 5.1 and 5.2 have been dictated by the desire to simplify understanding and to avoid local computations during the reverse trip; they are by no means optimum in any sense of the term.

## 5.4    Discussion

The admission control method described in the preceding section is much more general than that on which the Tenet Schemes 0 and 1 have been based so far. The assumption made by the latter, that each node could be satisfactorily represented as a single queueing server, is clearly inadequate in most practical cases. The new method replaces it with a single server to be used as a building block for much more complicated and realistic node models. Since the new tests and computations pertain to this building block and not to the node model, the node model can be changed without having to modify the tests or the computations to be performed for admission control. Some of the tests and computations depend on the scheduling discipline implemented by the server; the correct ones will obviously have to be used during the channel establishment procedure in each server, the only condition (fortunately an easy one to satisfy) being that different tests and computations in different servers will interoperate, so that the destination will receive all the information it needs to make correct admission and allocation decisions.

It should be noted that most of the tests and computations devised for Schemes 0 and 1 are valid for each single server, as they were developed for nodes that were represented by single servers. This observation has allowed us to benefit greatly from our previous work; for instance, we did not have to prove inequalities (1), since the proof had already been given in [5]. The only difference, but a non-trivial one, is that tests and computations are now to be applied to each server, not to each node. Since it is to be expected that there will be one processor in each node running tests and computations whenever a channel establishment request is received, that processor will have to run as many sets of tests and computations as there are single servers in the model chosen for that node. One could argue that this will increase the overhead and the time of channel establishment; the counter-argument, however, is that the new method is reliable, while the old one was rather

**Table 5.1  Server Tests for Admission Control**

| Name | Condition | Computation | Test | Record | Forward |
|---|---|---|---|---|---|
| Deterministic test | $Z_{min,i} = 1$ | $U_{det,n} \leftarrow U_{det,n} + \dfrac{t_{n,i}}{x_{min,i}}$ <br> where $U_{det,n}$ is initialized to 0 | $U_{det,n} < 1$ | $U_{det,n}$ | — |
| Statistical test | $U_n \geq 1$ <br> where <br> $U_n = \displaystyle\sum_{k=1}^{c_n+1} \dfrac{t_{n,k}}{x_{min,k}}$ | $p_k = \dfrac{x_{min,k}}{x_{ave,k}}$ <br> for $k = 1, 2, \ldots, c_n + 1$ <br> H: overflow combination of channels <br> $P_{do,n} \leftarrow$ <br> $\displaystyle\sum_H \left[ \prod_{k \in H} p_k \prod_{l \notin H} (1 - p_l) \right]$ <br> $zmax_{n,i} \leftarrow 1 - P_{do,n}$ <br> if $Z_{min,i} < 1$ ; <br> $z_{n,i} = zmax_{n,i} \leftarrow 1$ <br> if $Z_{min,i} = 1$ | $z_{n,k} \leq$ <br> $1 - P_{do,n}$ <br> (for $k = 1, 2,$ <br> $\ldots, c_n$, and <br> $z_{n,k} < 1$ ) | $P_{do,n}$ | $zmax_{n,i}$ |
| Delay bound computation | — | Let <br> $d_{n,1} \leq d_{n,2} \leq \cdots \leq d_{n,c_n}$ <br> for $k = 1, 2, \ldots, c_n$ <br> if $d_{n,h} - \displaystyle\sum_{l=1}^{h} t_{n,l}$ <br> $-T_n - t_{n,c_n+1} \geq 0$ <br> for $h = k, k + 1, \ldots, c_n,$ <br> then $dmin_{n,i}$ <br> $\leftarrow \displaystyle\sum_{l=1}^{k} t_{n,l} + T_n + t_{n,c_n+1}$ | — | $dmin_{n,i}$ | $dmin_{n,i}$ |
| Buffer space test | — | $bmax_{n,i} \leftarrow B$ where <br> $B \leq B_n - \displaystyle\sum_{k=1}^{c_n} b_{n,k}$ <br> $b_{n,i} \leftarrow bmax_{n,i}$ <br> $dmax_{n,i} \leftarrow \dfrac{bmax_{n,i} x_{min,i}}{s_{max,i}}$ <br> $- \displaystyle\sum_{k=m}^{n-1} (dmax_{k,i} - t_{k,i})$ <br> (i) if $J_{max,i}$ is undefined, then $m = 1$; <br> (ii) if $J_{max,i}$ is defined, then $m = $ position of the previous J-type server | $dmax_{n,i} \geq$ <br> $dmin_{n,i}$ | $b_{n,i}$ <br> $dmax_{n,i}$ | $dmax_{n,i}$ |

## Table 5.2  Destination Tests for Admission Control

| Name | Computation | Test | Forward |
|---|---|---|---|
| D-Test | $D_{prop,i} \leftarrow \sum_{n=1}^{N} d_{prop,n}$ ;<br><br>$D_{min,i} \leftarrow \sum_{n=1}^{N} dmin_{n,i}$ | $D_{min,i} \leq$<br><br>$D_{max,i} - D_{prop,i}$ | — |
| W-Test | if $W_{min,i} < 1, w_{n,i} \leftarrow W_{min,i}^{\ 1/N}$ $(n = 1, \ldots, N)$<br>if $W_{min,i} = 1, w_{n,i} \leftarrow 1$ $(n = 1, \ldots, N)$ | — | $w_{n,i}$<br>$(n = 1, \ldots, N)$ |
| Z-Test | if $Z_{min,i} < 1, Z_{max,i} \leftarrow \prod_{n=1}^{N} zmax_{n,i}$ ,<br><br>$z_{n,i} = zmax_{n,i} \left( \dfrac{Z_{min,i}}{\prod_{n=1}^{N} zmax_{n,i}} \right)^{1/N}$ $(n = 1, \ldots, N)$ | $Z_{min,i} \leq Z_{max,i}$ | $z_{n,i}$<br><br>$(n = 1, \ldots, N)$ |
| d-Comp | if $\sum_{n=1}^{N} dmax_{n,i} \leq D_{max,i}$ , then<br><br>$D'_{max,i} \leftarrow \sum_{n=1}^{N} dmax_{n,i}$ ,<br>$d_{n,i} \leftarrow dmax_{n,i}$ $(n = 1, \ldots, N)$<br>if $\sum_{n=1}^{N} dmax_{n,i} > D_{max,i}$ , then<br>$D'_{max,i} \leftarrow D_{max,i}$<br>$d_{n,i} \leftarrow dmin_{n,i} + \frac{1}{N}(D_{max,i} - D_{min,i})$<br>$(n = 1, \ldots, N)$ | — | $d_{n,i}$<br>$(n = 1, \ldots, N)$<br><br>$D'_{max,i}$ |
| J-Test | if $J_{max,i}$ is defined, then $m =$ position<br>of the last J-type server<br>and $J_{N,i} \leftarrow \sum_{k=m}^{N} (d_{k,i} - t_{k,i})$ ;<br><br>$D_{prop,n,i} \leftarrow \sum_{k=1}^{n} d_{prop,k}$ $(n = 1, \ldots, N)$<br><br>$D^*_{n,i} \leftarrow D_{prop,n,i} + \sum_{k=1}^{n-1} d_{k,i}$ $(n = 1, \ldots, N)$ | $J_{N,i} \leq J_{max,i}$ | $D^*_{n,i}$<br><br>$(n = 1, \ldots, N)$ |
| b-Comp | $\Delta_{n,i} \leftarrow \sum_{k=m}^{n} (d_{k,i} - t_{k,i})$<br>if $J_{max,i}$ is undefined, then $m = 1$<br>if $J_{max,i}$ is defined, then $m =$ position<br>of the previous J-type server<br>$b_{n,i} \leftarrow s_{max,i} \left\lceil \dfrac{d_{n,i} + \Delta_{n,i}}{x_{min,i}} w_{n,i} \right\rceil$ $(n = 1, \ldots, N)$ | — | $b_{n,i}$<br>$(n = 1, \ldots, N)$ |

shaky, either because it reduced the entire, possibly quite complicated, node to a single server, or because it relied on the assumption that the node had a severe bottleneck that could be correctly identified and would never change.

Another important consequence of the new approach is found in the implementation of admission control within an internetwork. With the old method, heterogeneous internetworks were treated in a hierarchical way: each subnetwork had its own characterization, and was dealt with, to a large extent, independently of the rest of the internetwork. The channel's destination allocated resources (i.e., assigned local performance bounds) only to highest-level subnetworks and links; within each subnetwork, such assignment was done by the "local destination" (the endpoint of the channel's path within the subnetwork), and so on recursively [1, 3]. All of this can be done without violating the single-round-trip requirement of the Tenet channel establishment procedure. However, while the hierarchical procedure is elegant and efficient, its implementation, debugging, and testing are quite complicated. The new method does not require resorting to such a procedure, as long as each internetwork component along a channel's path can be modeled as a cascade of single servers as in Figure 5.2. If all heterogeneity can be absorbed by the modeling generality of the new method, a condition that is likely to be satisfied in practical cases, we can deal with one-level paths even when the internetwork is complex. This, of course, makes the tasks of the destination heavier (and reduces those of the "intermediate destinations" to zero), as well as calling for much longer establishment messages, but simplifies the channel establishment code very substantially. It should also be easier to design and implement this code so that it is truly portable to a wide variety of internetworking environments.

All of these considerations should obviously (and will) be confirmed by experience with applying the new admission control method in several internetworking testbeds.

## 5.5   Conclusions

A more general and intellectually satisfying approach than the one previously proposed by the Tenet Group to admission control for real-time communication services in packet-switching internetworks has been presented. The new approach is based on a real-time channel model consisting of a cascade of single queueing servers, each of which may be of one of two types (J or NJ) and contains given amounts of three types of resources; the connections between servers are characterized only by their (constant) delay. The admission tests and computations are designed and have to be executed for each server along the path of the channel to be established. The only aspect of a server that influences (some of) the tests and computations is the scheduling discipline implemented by the server. Servers with different scheduling disciplines can coexist along a channel's route, but the appropriate tests and computations will have to be run in each server during the establishment procedure. J-type and NJ-type servers can also coexist, of course. To show an example of tests and computations, we have presented those for the case of the D-EDD and J-EDD disciplines.

The advantages and the drawbacks of the new method have been briefly discussed. The method's generality is its most important characteristic: it is at the root of such advantages as the portability of the tests and computations as well as of the code, and the simpler one-level approach to admission control in internetworks; it is also responsible for such relative disadvantages as the higher establishment overhead and the longer establishment messages.

It seems clear, on the basis of these considerations, that the new method makes a positive and useful contribution to the technology of real-time communication. Only careful testbed implementation and experimentation, however, can confirm the validity of this conclusion.

# Acknowledgments

This work was supported by the National Science Foundation and the Defense Advanced Research Projects Agency (DARPA) under Cooperative Agreement NCR-8919038 with the Corporation for National Research Initiatives, by AT&T Bell Laboratories, Hitachi, Ltd., Hitachi America, Ltd., Pacific Bell, the University of California under a MICRO grant, and the International Computer Science Institute. The views and conclusions contained in this document are those of the author, and should not be interpreted as representing official policies, either expressed or implied, of the U.S. government or any of the sponsoring organizations.

The author is grateful to the members of the Tenet Group for being intelligent and creative sounding boards in several discussions of these topics. He is particularly indebted to Amit Gupta, who provided many suggestions and substantially simplified the formulation of the delay bound computation (inequality (1)), and to Eberhard Mueller-Menrad, who discovered several bugs in an earlier version of Tables 5.1 and 5.2. He is also thankful to Ellen Boyle for her invaluable help with the preparation of the manuscript.

# References

[1] A. Banerjea and B. Mah. "The Real-Time Channel Administration Protocol." *Proc. Second International Workshop on Network and Operating System Support for Digital Audio and Video*, Springer-Verlag, Heidelberg, Germany, pp. 160–170, November 1991.

[2] D. Ferrari, A. Banerjea, and H. Zhang. "Network Support for Multimedia - A Discussion of the Tenet Approach." Technical Report TR-92-072, International Computer Science Institute, Berkeley, Calif., October 1992.

[3] D. Ferrari. "Real-Time Communication in an Internetwork." *Journal of High Speed Networks*, 1(1):79–103, 1992.

[4] D. Ferrari. "Distributed Delay Jitter Control in Packet-Switching Internetworks." *Journal of Internetworking: Research and Experience*, 4(1):1–20, 1993.

[5]  D. Ferrari and D. Verma. "A Scheme for Real-Time Channel Establishment in Wide-Area Networks." *IEEE Journal on Selected Areas of Communication*, 8(4):368–379, April 1990.

[6]  A. G. Fraser, C. R. Kalmanek, A. E. Kaplan, W. T. Marshall, and R. C. Restrick. "Xunet 2: A Nationwide Testbed in High-Speed Networking." *Proc. INFOCOM'92*, Florence, Italy, 1992.

[7]  S. Jamin, S. Shenker, L. Zhang, and D. D. Clark. "An Admission Control Algorithm for Predictive Real-Time Service." *Proc. Third International Workshop on Network and Operating System Support for Digital Audio and Video*, Springer-Verlag, Heidelberg, Germany, pp. 349–356, 1992.

[8]  A. A. Lazar and G. Pacifici. "Control of Resources in Broadband Networks with Quality of Service Guarantees." *IEEE Communications*, 29(10):66–73, October 1991.

[9]  H. Zhang and S. Keshav. "Comparison of Rate-Based Service Disciplines." *Proc. ACM SIGCOMM '91*, Zurich, Switzerland, pp. 113–122, September 1991.

# Chapter 6

# Real-Time Performance of Two Token Ring Protocols

## Sanjay Kamat and Wei Zhao

When designing real-time communication protocols, the primary objective is to guarantee the deadlines of synchronous messages while sustaining a high aggregate throughput. In this chapter, we study two token ring protocols for their suitability in real-time systems. The priority-driven protocol (e.g., IEEE 802.5) allows implementation of a priority-based real-time scheduling discipline like the rate monotonic algorithm. The timed token protocol (e.g., FDDI) provides guaranteed bandwidth and bounded access time for synchronous messages. We study these two protocols by deriving their schedulability conditions, i.e., the conditions which determine whether a given message set can be guaranteed. Using these conditions, we evaluate the average performance of these protocols under different operating conditions. We observe that neither protocol dominates the other for the entire range of the system parameter space. We conclude that the priority-driven protocol performs better for bandwidths in the range of 1-10 Mbit/s, while the timed token protocol has a superior performance at higher bandwidths.

## 6.1 Introduction

Advances in computer and communication technology have led to the widespread use of digital computers in embedded real-time systems such as space vehicle systems, automated manufacturing, industrial process control, and so on. The design and evaluation of such systems is difficult due to the stringent timing requirements of these applications. The challenge is further compounded by the distributed nature of the systems. The success of a *distributed real-time* system depends on the timely execution of computational tasks which usually reside on different nodes and communicate with each other to accomplish a common goal. It is impossible for the individual tasks to meet their timing requirements without the support of an

117

underlying network which ensures timely delivery of inter-task messages.

In this chapter, we study two approaches to the problem of guaranteeing the deadlines of *synchronous messages* on token ring networks. Synchronous messages are the most common time-critical messages in distributed real-time systems. A real-time synchronous message stream is a sequence of messages arriving periodically at a network node, with each message having a deadline for transmission. The most important goal in building a real-time network is to *guarantee* the deadlines of synchronous messages; that is, to ensure that they are always transmitted before their deadlines.

### 6.1.1   Token Ring Protocols

This study concentrates on token ring-networks. Ring-based networks have become popular in recent years because of their simplicity and their potential use of high-speed transmission media. The choice of Media Access Control (MAC) protocol determines how real-time messages can be scheduled for transmission over the ring. A MAC protocol can be considered to be an entity which implements two specific policies: an *access arbitration* policy and a *capacity control* policy [16]. In token ring networks, a station gains access to a transmission medium by capturing a circulating token. The access arbitration policy determines when a station on the ring may capture the token, influencing the order in which stations receive service. The capacity control policy determines the duration for which a station may transmit after capturing the token. Two token-based MAC protocols have emerged as design alternatives:

- *The Priority-Driven Protocol (PDP)*
  This protocol uses a priority-based access arbitration policy. Individual messages can be assigned priorities. A token with a priority field is used to regulate the access to the ring in a manner that allows the node with the highest-priority message to transmit first. Capacity control is achieved by setting a token-holding timer at each station. Messages are divided into fixed-sized frames and the station holding the token can transmit its frames until its token-holding timer expires. This protocol has been employed in the IEEE 802.5 standard [8].

- *The Timed Token Protocol (TTP)*
  This protocol uses a simple access arbitration policy. A token is passed from node to node around the ring, allowing the stations to transmit in a round-robin fashion. Capacity control in this protocol is also implemented using timers. This protocol has been employed in network standards such as the Fiber Distributed Data Interface (FDDI) [1], the High-Speed Data Bus and the High-Speed Ring Bus (HSDB/HSRB) [19, 20, 32], and the Survivable Adaptable Fiber Optic Embedded Network (SAFENET) [6, 17].

## 6.1.2    Objectives of This Study

The objectives of this study are twofold. First, we derive schedulability conditions for the priority-driven protocol and the timed token protocol. Schedulability conditions specify if a set of synchronous messages will meet their deadlines for a given system. These conditions are indispensable for network administration.

The schedulability of a message set depends on the message and network parameters: the individual message lengths and their periods, the relative positions of the nodes where the messages arrive, the arrival phasings, the disturbance caused by asynchronous messages, the size of the message set, the network bandwidth, and so on. We should aim at deriving schedulability conditions that are simple and can be tested efficiently.

The second objective of this study is to carry out a quantitative comparison of the real-time performance of the priority-driven and timed token protocols. Through this study, we want to identify the operational domain in which one protocol has a superior performance compared to the other. This would provide concrete guidelines for choosing a particular protocol at system design time.

At design time, a detailed knowledge of the message set is often unavailable. The designer of a real-time network, however, may have an estimate of the real-time traffic in terms of its utilization. Hence, we will use utilization-based metrics for performance evaluation. In particular, we are interested in the following two utilization-based metrics:

1. *Average Breakdown Utilization (ABU)*
   The average breakdown utilization of a protocol is defined as the expected value of the utilization at which real-time messages begin to miss their deadlines.

2. *Guarantee Probability (GP(U))*
   The guarantee probability of a protocol at utilization $U$ is defined as the probability that a message set with utilization $U$ is guaranteed by the protocol.

The metrics defined above measure the protocol performance over the entire population of message sets. They can be considered as alternatives to the *minimum breakdown utilization*[1] which has been used to quantify the performance of a protocol in [2, 3]. The minimum breakdown utilization of a protocol is defined as the smallest utilization below which real-time messages are always guaranteed. The minimum breakdown utilization indicates the *worst-case* performance of a protocol. Knowledge of this bound simplifies run-time network administration—schedulability tests are not needed as long as the offered load is below this bound. Unfortunately, this metric does not provide any information about the network performance when the utilization exceeds the minimum breakdown utilization. Thus, at the design stage, it is more appropriate to select a protocol based on its average-case performance using measures such as the average breakdown utilization or the guarantee probability.

---

[1] Also referred in the literature as *worst-case achievable utilization* [2–4, 15].

The average breakdown utilization is a *point* measure and hence can be used as a single figure of merit to evaluate protocol performance. It represents how high the utilization can be, on average, without missing any deadlines. The guarantee probability provides additional information about the sensitivity of the performance to system utilization. Being defined as a function of utilization, it provides a detailed picture of the system performance as the load is varied.

Based on these measures, we evaluate and compare the performance of the priority-driven protocol and the timed token protocol. We find that neither protocol is superior to the other under all operating conditions. The priority-driven protocol allows implementation of an optimal scheduling policy such as the rate monotonic scheduling algorithm [15]. This implementation has a better performance at low transmission speeds. However, at high transmission speeds, the overheads due to priority arbitration become predominant, lowering its performance. It is seen that the timed token protocol, which implements a simpler access arbitration policy, has a superior performance for high-speed real-time networks.

### 6.1.3    Previous Relevant Work

Our work complements previous studies on communication protocols for real-time applications. The worst-case performance for asynchronous real-time messages in a token ring environment has been investigated in [14, 33], while the average-case performance is studied in [25]. Implementation of the *rate monotonic algorithm* on an IEEE 802.5 token ring was first proposed by Strosnider, Lehoczky, and Sha [29]. The *timed token protocol* was first proposed by Grow in [7]. Sevcik and Johnson [22] formally demonstrated that this protocol ensures a bounded access time for all stations on the ring. The issue of guaranteeing the deadlines of synchronous real-time messages with this protocol has been addressed recently in [2–4]. The average breakdown utilization measure was introduced by Lehoczky, Sha, and Ding [13] to evaluate the average-case performance of the *rate monotonic algorithm* in a CPU scheduling environment. We extend the methodology adopted in [13] to the token ring environment for obtaining the average breakdown utilization of the two protocols. The notion of guarantee probability has been introduced recently to analyze synchronous bandwidth allocation schemes for the FDDI protocol [11, 12]. A preliminary comparison of the two protocols based on average breakdown utilization alone was presented in [10].

For further references on recent advances in the field of real-time systems, the reader is referred to [27, 28, 30, 31]. Additional information on designing real-time communication systems can be found in [5, 16, 18, 24].

### 6.1.4    Chapter Outline

The rest of this chapter is organized as follows. In Section 6.2, we describe the system model and introduce the notations employed in this chapter. Section 6.3 deals with the priority-driven protocol. The basic protocol is described, followed by a discussion of an implementation of the *rate monotonic scheduling* algorithm. Schedulability conditions for this scheme are then derived. In parallel with Section 6.3, Section 6.4 deals with the timed token protocol. In Section 6.5, we present a geometric representation of message sets which helps us to formalize the notions of average breakdown utilization and guarantee probability. Efficient methods of estimating these measures are described. Numerical results of a comparison between these protocols are presented in Section 6.6. We conclude with a summary in Section 6.7.

## 6.2    System Model

In this section we describe the network and message models and introduce the notations used in this chapter.

### 6.2.1    Network Model

We consider a network of $n$ nodes (stations) connected using a ring topology. A special bit pattern called token circulates around the ring regulating the right to transmit for individual stations. Some notations relevant to our model are as follows:

- $BW$ = Bandwidth of the transmission medium.

- $W_T$ = Token walk time around the ring. $W_T$ consists of the ring and buffer latency and the propagation delay around the ring.

- $\Theta = W_T$ + time to transmit a token. $\Theta$ represents the time spent in completing one round of priority arbitration[2] for the priority-driven protocol.

- $\tau = \Theta$ + time to transmit one asynchronous frame. $\tau$ represents the portion of a token cycle that is unavailable for transmission of synchronous frames in the context of the timed token protocol.[3]

### 6.2.2    Message Model

Messages may be classified as *synchronous* messages or *asynchronous* messages. We assume that there are $n$ streams of synchronous messages, $S_1, S_2, \ldots, S_n$, one on each node in the system. These streams form a synchronous *message set*, $M$, i.e.,

$$M = \{S_1, S_2, \ldots, S_n\}. \tag{6.1}$$

The characteristics of messages are as follows:

---

[2]The priority arbitration process will be described in Section 6.3.1.

[3]The time to transmit a single asynchronous frame is known as *asynchronous overrun* [22]. It reduces the amount of time available for transmission of synchronous messages during a token cycle of the timed token protocol.

1. Synchronous messages are *periodic*, i.e., they have a constant inter-arrival time. We denote by $P_i$ the period length of stream $S_i$ $(i = 1, 2, \ldots, n)$. We assume that all of the $P_i$'s are bounded below by $P_{min}$.

2. The *deadline* of a synchronous message is defined as the time by which the message must be transmitted. We assume that the deadline of a message is the end of the period in which it arrives; that is, if a message in stream $S_i$ arrives at time $t$, then its deadline is at time $t + P_i$.

3. The *payload length* of each message in stream $S_i$ is $C_i$, which is the amount of *time* needed to transmit this message. A message can also be measured by its *size* $C_i^b$—the number of bits in the message. Hence, we have

$$C_i = \frac{C_i^b}{BW}. \tag{6.2}$$

In practice, the time spent in completing the transmission of a message is more than the payload length. The extra time is due to various protocol overheads such as transmission of packet headers, checksum bits, and so on. We will denote by $C_i'$ the augmented message length which takes these overheads into account. The method of computing $C_i'$ for each protocol will be discussed later.

We will use the term *active interval* of a message to denote the interval of time between the arrival of the message and the completion of its transmission.

The *utilization* of a synchronous message stream $S_i$ is defined as the fraction of time spent by the network in the transmission of synchronous messages from this stream and is given by

$$U_i = \frac{C_i}{P_i}. \tag{6.3}$$

The *utilization* of the entire set, $U(M)$, is obtained as

$$U(M) = \sum_{i=1}^{n} U_i = \sum_{i=1}^{n} \frac{C_i}{P_i}. \tag{6.4}$$

We consider asynchronous messages to be ones without real-time constraints.

## 6.3   Schedulability of the Priority-Driven Protocol

In this section we describe the priority-driven protocol. This protocol has been incorporated into the IEEE 802.5 standard [8]. We then discuss an implementation of the *rate monotonic algorithm* [15] with this protocol. We also consider a modified version of the IEEE 802.5 standard which provides a more efficient implementation of priority arbitration. The schedulability conditions are then derived.

## 6.3.1    Protocol Description

The access arbitration policy and the capacity control policy implemented by this protocol are described below.

- *Access arbitration policy*

  The access arbitration policy of this protocol ensures that the message with the highest priority is transmitted first. This is achieved by using priority fields in the token and frame headers. The token has a priority field which indicates the current service priority. A node captures the token only if the node has a pending message with priority greater than or equal to that of the token.

  The header of every frame (token and data) also contains another priority field, called the priority reservation field. Each station examines the priority reservation field in the frame header as the frame passes by. A node replaces the contents of the reservation field by the highest priority of its pending messages whenever the latter is higher than the value currently present in the reservation field. This enables the reservation field to represent the highest priority of messages waiting in the system. When the transmitting station receives the frame back, it uses the contents of the reservation field to update its knowledge of the highest-priority message pending in the network. This knowledge is used to set the priority of a new token when the transmitting station releases the token.

- *Capacity control policy*

  Once a station captures the token, it can transmit its frames one after the other until its token holding timer expires. It then transmits a fresh token with the token priority field set to the highest-known priority of messages pending on the ring.

The reader is referred to [8, 26] for further details on the protocol operation.

## 6.3.2    Parameter Settings

The effectiveness of this protocol in guaranteeing the deadlines of synchronous messages depends on the choice of proper values for three parameters: the *message priorities*, the *message frame length,* and the *token holding timer* value at each station.

- *Assignment of message priorities*

  In order to guarantee their deadlines, the messages must be assigned priorities in a proper manner. This problem is similar to the problem of assigning priorities to periodic tasks in the context of CPU scheduling. It is well known that the *rate monotonic algorithm* [15], which assigns higher priorities to tasks with shorter periods, is the optimal static priority preemptive CPU scheduling algorithm for this problem. Further, this algorithm can be applied to token rings [29]. Thus, the synchronous messages are assigned priorities in the inverse order of their periods.

- *Choice of frame size*

The rate monotonic algorithm requires that a node with a high-priority message be able to preempt the transmission of a lower-priority message. However, arbitrary preemption of transmission is not feasible in a network. Preemption can be approximated by dividing messages into frames. The transmitting station examines the header of the transmitted frame when the frame returns, to check the contents of the priority reservation field. It releases a token of appropriate priority if the reservation field indicates that a higher-priority message is active at some other node. This means that preemption takes place at the boundaries of frame transmission.

A small frame size provides a better approximation of preemption. However, there are fixed overheads associated with the transmission of each frame. Thus, a smaller frame size implies a higher overhead. Hence, the choice of frame size is a trade-off between the enhanced responsiveness provided by the fine granularity of small frames and the low overhead incurred by large frames.

We assume that the synchronous and asynchronous message frames have the same size. We use the notations $F^b_{info}$ and $F^b_{ovhd}$ for the sizes of the payload part and the overhead part of a frame, respectively. $F^b$ denotes the total size of a frame in bits and $F = F^b/BW$ denotes the length of time needed to transmit a frame. We will also use the notations $K_i$ and $L_i$ to denote respectively the total number of frames and the number of full-length frames into which a message of payload size $C^b_i$ is divided. These quantities are obtained as

$$K_i = \left\lceil \frac{C^b_i}{F^b_{info}} \right\rceil \quad \text{and} \quad L_i = \left\lfloor \frac{C^b_i}{F^b_{info}} \right\rfloor . \tag{6.5}$$

Note that when $K_i = L_i$ all frames are of maximum size, while $K_i = L_i + 1$ implies that the last frame is of smaller length.

- *Token-holding timer*

The IEEE 802.5 standard specifies a token-holding timer at each station. Once a station captures the token, it can continue transmitting frames as long as the token-holding timer has not expired. Because we intend to implement rate monotonic scheduling, we need frame-level priority arbitration. This can be achieved by setting the token-holding timer at each station to allow for the transmission of only one frame.

The standard also specifies that a free token is released by the transmitting node after its timer expires. Hence, the overhead of passing a token is incurred for every transmitted frame when the standard protocol is used.

The overhead of token circulation can be reduced to one per message if a slightly modified version of the standard protocol is adopted. In this modified version, the transmitting station is not required to release the token after the transmission of every frame. If the reservation field in the returned frame indicates that the transmitting station still has the highest-priority pending messages, then it continues to transmit instead of releasing the token. We will analyze this modified version along with the one based on the standard. Throughout the rest of this chapter, we will use the term *priority-driven protocol* (PDP) to mean either the IEEE 802.5 standard or the modified version of the standard.

## 6.3.3    Schedulability Conditions

Our objective is to derive precise criteria to test whether a given message set is schedulable by the priority-driven protocol. We assume that the parameters of a PDP are selected as discussed above. In deriving these conditions, we focus on the lengths and periods of synchronous messages while assuming the worst possible impact of message arrival phasings and asynchronous message transmissions.

We will derive the desired schedulability conditions by extending the schedulability conditions for the rate monotonic algorithm in a CPU scheduling environment [13, 23] to the network environment. It was shown in [23] that a set of $n$ periodic tasks can be scheduled by the rate monotonic algorithm for all task phasings if

$$\forall i, \ 1 \leq i \leq n, \ \min_{(k,l) \in R_i} \left[ \sum_{j=1}^{i-1} \frac{C_j}{lP_k} \left\lceil \frac{lP_k}{P_j} \right\rceil + \frac{C_i}{lP_k} + \frac{B_i}{lP_k} \right] \leq 1 \tag{6.6}$$

where $R_i = \{(k,l) | 1 \leq k \leq i, \ l = 1, \ldots, \lfloor P_i/P_k \rfloor \}$, $C_i$ and $P_i$ are the computation time and the period of task $T_i$, respectively, and $B_i$ is the worst-case *blocking* time for the first $i$ highest-priority tasks. *Blocking* means priority inversion; that is, a low-priority task is executed even though a higher-priority task is ready for execution.

This result assumes that there are no overheads associated with priority arbitration or preemption. Although this is a reasonable assumption for a centralized environment, it is not valid for the network environment. To extend the above result to token rings, we need to replace the computation times in (6.6) by the *augmented* message transmission times, which take into account the various overheads associated with message transmission. We also need to derive the maximum *blocking* time for a set of high-priority messages.

Recall that messages are transmitted in units of frames. Hence, to compute the augmented message lengths, it is useful first to obtain the effective time required to complete the transmission of a single frame. The following lemma provides the necessary result.

**Lemma 6.3.1** *If a priority-driven protocol is used, the effective time needed to complete the transmission of one frame of length $F$ is $\max(F, \Theta)$.*

**Proof:** Once the transmission of a frame begins, the transmitting station will not release the token until (1) it transmits the last bit of the frame, and (2) it receives the header of the already transmitted frame. The second condition is necessary because the transmitting station has to examine the requested priority in the reservation field of the header to determine its subsequent action. In case of the standard IEEE 802.5 protocol, a new token with requested priority will be released. In the modified version, a new token will not be released if the transmitting station has a message frame with priority higher than the requested priority. Hence, for both the versions, the effective time needed to complete the transmission of one frame is $\max(F, \Theta)$. □

The augmented transmission time for a message is obtained by taking into account the effective transmission times of all its frames and the token-passing overheads (amortized per message). This is the sum of all the time intervals during which the transmission medium is not available for transmitting any other messages.

The following two lemmas provide the augmented message transmission times for the IEEE 802.5 standard and the modified version.

**Lemma 6.3.2** *For the priority-driven protocol using the IEEE 802.5 standard, $C_i'$, the augmented message length for a message in stream $S_i$ is obtained as follows:*

$$C_i' = \begin{cases} K_i \cdot \Theta + K_i \cdot \frac{\Theta}{2} & \text{if } F \leq \Theta, \\[2mm] L_i \cdot F + (K_i - L_i) \cdot \max\left(C_i - L_i \cdot F_{info} + F_{ovhd}, \Theta\right) \\ +K_i \cdot \frac{\Theta}{2} & \text{otherwise.} \end{cases} \quad (6.7)$$

**Proof:** The computation of $C_i'$ is based on the following equation:

$$C_i' = \sum_{j=1}^{K_i} \text{Effective transmission time for } j\text{th frame}$$

$$+ \text{ Token passing overhead per message} \quad (6.8)$$

where $K_i$ defined by (6.5) denotes the total number of frames into which the original message is divided. If $K_i = L_i$, then all the frames have the full length ($F$), while $K_i = L_i + 1$ implies that the last frame is of less than full length. When $F \leq \Theta$, the effective transmission time for all the frames is $\Theta$ by Lemma 6.3.1. When $F > \Theta$, the effective transmission time for all but the last frame is $F$. The length of the last frame is $C_i - L_i \cdot F_{info} + F_{ovhd}$, which is smaller than $F$ when $K_i = L_i + 1$. Hence, the effective frame transmission time of the last frame is considered separately for this case.

To compute the token-passing overheads incurred per message, recall that the standard IEEE 802.5 protocol requires transmission of a token after every frame, even if no higher-priority message is actually ready for transmission elsewhere on the ring. Thus the cost of token circulation is incurred for each frame transmitted. The token circulating overhead may be assumed to be $\Theta/2$ on the average. Hence, the result follows by substituting the appropriate expressions for effective frame transmission times and token passing overhead in (6.8). □

**Lemma 6.3.3** *For the priority-driven protocol using the modified version of the IEEE 802.5 standard, $C_i'$, the augmented message length for a message in stream*

$S_i$, *is obtained as follows:*

$$C'_i = \begin{cases} K_i \cdot \Theta + \frac{\Theta}{2} & \text{if } F \leq \Theta, \\[2mm] L_i \cdot F + (K_i - L_i) \cdot \max\left(C_i - L_i \cdot F_{info} + F_{ovhd}, \Theta\right) \\ + \frac{\Theta}{2} & \text{otherwise.} \end{cases} \tag{6.9}$$

**Proof:** Once again, the computation of $C'_i$ is based on (6.8). Note that the expressions for $C'_i$ in (6.9) differ from those in (6.7) only in the token-passing overhead term. We show that the token circulation overhead is incurred only once per message with the modified version of the IEEE 802.5 protocol. Hence the last term in (6.9) is $\frac{\Theta}{2}$, as against $K_i \cdot \frac{\Theta}{2}$ in (6.7).

Recall from Section 6.3.2 that with the modified version of the protocol, the transmitting station does not release the token as long as it has the highest-priority messages among all the pending messages in the network. In other words, the token is released for every instance of preemption. We will show that a message will preempt transmission of lower-priority messages at most once.

Let $p_c$ be the channel service priority (that is, the priority of the circulating free token or the frame being transmitted) when message $m$ from stream $S_i$ arrives. Let $p_m$ denote the priority of $m$. If $p_m \leq p_c$, then $m$ will begin transmission only after the higher-priority nodes finish their transmission and one of these nodes lowers the channel service priority level to $p_m$ in response to the claim by $m$. If $p_m > p_c$, then $m$ will attempt to preempt the transmission of the current lower-priority message being transmitted. It will do so by staking its claim for the next free token. However, in either case, once the transmission of $m$ begins, the channel service priority cannot fall below $p_m$ until the transmission of $m$ is over. Hence, message $m$ will preempt transmission of lower-priority messages at most once (just after its arrival) during its active interval. If we charge the token-passing overheads to the messages causing the preemptions, we need to consider the token-passing overhead only once per period for each message stream.                                                      □

Having obtained the augmented message lengths, we now derive $B_i$ in (6.6), i.e., the maximum blocking interval for the $i$ highest-priority messages. A high-priority message may be blocked by a message of lower priority due to the decentralized mechanism of priority arbitration.[4] The following lemma bounds the *total* blocking period that needs to be considered.

**Lemma 6.3.4** *With the priority-driven protocol, messages from streams $S_1, \ldots, S_i$ (ordered in decreasing priority sequence) may be blocked by some lower-priority message for at most a duration of $2 \cdot \max(F, \Theta)$ during the entire active interval of one message from stream $S_i$.*

**Proof:** Note that once the transmission of a message begins, no lower-priority message can get access to the transmission medium until the transmission of this

---

[4]Priority inversions may also be caused due to insufficient levels of priorities in the system. In this study, we assume that there are sufficient levels of priorities.

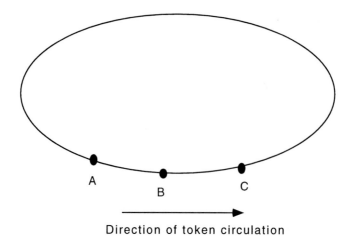

Direction of token circulation

**Figure 6.1**  Blocking in Priority-Driven Protocol

message is over. Hence, a message may be blocked only once during its active interval, upon its arrival.

Consider the blocking interval of message $m$, which arrives at station $S$ at time $t_0$. Let $t_1$ denote the first time instance after $t_0$ when station $S$ gets an opportunity to claim the next token. Let $t_2$ denote the time when $m$ gets unblocked, i.e., either $m$ or a higher-priority message begins transmission. The blocking of $m$ during the interval $[t_0, t_1]$ is because of the ongoing transmission of a lower-priority message frame at time $t_0$. Clearly, $t_1 - t_0$ cannot exceed the effective transmission time of one frame. The blocking of $m$ during $[t_1, t_2]$ is due to the priority arbitration done before $S$ claims the next token at $t_1$. A station having a message of priority lower than that of $m$ could have claimed the token before $t_1$ and hence may get the token before $S$. Again, $t_2 - t_1$ cannot exceed the effective transmission time of one frame as either $S$ or some other node having a higher-priority message will get the subsequent token at $t_2$. Hence, the total blocking time for $m$ is $t_2 - t_0$, which cannot exceed the time needed to complete transmission of two frames, i.e., $2 \cdot \max(F, \Theta)$.

Thus, $2 \cdot \max(F, \Theta)$ is an upper bound for the blocking interval. This upper bound is tight, as shown by the following example illustrated by Figure 6.1. In Figure 6.1, periodic messages with priorities $p_a$, $p_b$, and $p_c$ are assumed to arrive at nodes $A$, $B$, and $C$, respectively. Let $p_a < p_b < p_c$. Consider the following scenario. Node $A$ is currently transmitting its message frame. Node $B$ updates the reservation field in the frame header to claim the next token. Message $m$ arrives at node $C$ just after the reservation bits of the token have been relayed by node $C$. Thus, node $C$ does not claim the next token. Note that $m$ is the highest-priority message. However, it remains blocked for the remaining portion of the current frame transmission interval. Further, it is blocked for one more frame transmission interval because the token released by node $A$ is captured by node $B$.

When considering the schedulability of $S_i$, we need to account for possible priority inversions caused by messages lower in priority than $S_i$. The impact of messages with priorities lower than that of $S_i$ on the schedulability of $S_i$ is through the blocking they might cause for $S_i$ or higher-priority messages. From the preceding discussion, it follows that if a message from stream $S_i$ is blocked on arrival, then it will be never blocked again. If some higher-priority message was blocked on arrival by a message with priority lower than that of $S_i$, then the delay in its completion will be reflected in the initial delay for the message from $S_i$ to begin its transmission. However, any instance of blocking of messages from streams $S_1, S_2, \ldots, S_{i-1}$ that is not caused by a message with lower priority than $S_i$ is an *internal* blocking for the set of $i$ highest-priority messages. Such internal blockings do not contribute to the media demand to be considered for testing the schedulability of $S_i$. Hence, only one blocking interval needs to be considered for the schedulability test of $S_i$.                                                                       □

The schedulability conditions for this protocol are now given by the following theorem.

**Theorem 6.3.1** *For the priority-driven protocol, the criteria for schedulability of a synchronous message set are given by*

$$\forall i \ 1 \leq i \leq n, \quad \min_{(k,l)\in R_i} \left[ \sum_{j=1}^{i-1} \frac{C'_j}{lP_k} \left\lceil \frac{lP_k}{P_j} \right\rceil + \frac{C'_i}{lP_k} + \frac{2\cdot\max(F,\Theta)}{lP_k} \right] \leq 1 \quad (6.10)$$

*where $R_i$ is defined as*

$$R_i \quad = \quad \{(k,l)|1\leq k \leq i, \ l=1,\ldots, \lfloor P_i/P_k\rfloor\}$$

*and $C'_i$, the augmented message length, is as defined in Lemma 6.3.2 for the standard IEEE 802.5 protocol and in Lemma 6.3.3 for the modified version.*

**Proof:** The proof follows from the schedulability conditions specified in (6.6) for the rate monotonic scheduling algorithm, by substituting the augmented message transmission times for $C_i$'s and the expression for the maximum blocking interval obtained in Lemma 6.3.4 for $B_i$.                                                     □

Thus, we have obtained schedulability conditions which can be used to test whether a synchronous message set can be guaranteed using the priority-driven protocol. We note that similar schedulability criteria for the priority-driven protocol have been developed concurrently and independently in [21], where the emphasis has been on the worst-case performance rather than on the average-case performance. Consequently, the token circulation overhead is taken as $\Theta$. The specific frame layout used by the IEEE 802.5 standard has also been taken into account. Further, in [21] the IEEE 802.5 protocol with an early token release option is also considered. The early token release option allows a station to release the token as soon as it completes the transmission of its frame. This reduces the token circulation overhead at the expense of the worst-case blocking time of high-priority messages. Our extension to the protocol, on the other hand, allows a station to retain the token if it is still the highest-priority active station on the ring.

# 6.4 Schedulability of the Timed Token Protocol

In this section, we discuss the timed token protocol. We will derive the schedulability conditions for this protocol with suitable parameter settings.

## 6.4.1 Protocol Description

The access arbitration policy and the capacity control policy implemented by this protocol are described below.

- *Access arbitration policy*
  This protocol employs a simple access arbitration policy. The access to the transmission medium is controlled by passing a token. As opposed to the priority-driven protocol, the token in the timed token protocol does not have a priority field. The token is passed from node to node around the ring, allowing the stations to transmit in a round-robin fashion.

- *Capacity control policy*
  At ring initialization time, a network parameter called the *Target Token Rotation Time (TTRT)* is determined by a bidding process among the stations on the ring. This parameter indicates the expected token rotation time, i.e., the interval between two successive token arrivals at a station. The token is usually expected to visit a station within *TTRT* time units after its previous visit.

  Each station is allocated a portion of *TTRT*, known as its synchronous bandwidth[5] ($H_i$). After receiving the token, a station transmits its synchronous messages, if any, for a maximum interval given by its synchronous bandwidth. It can then transmit asynchronous frames only if the token arrived earlier than expected. The number of asynchronous frames transmitted is limited by the duration by which the token is early. Transmission of an asynchronous frame, once begun, will *always* be completed. The time needed to transmit one asynchronous frame is known as the *asynchronous overrun* and reduces the effective bandwidth available for transmission of synchronous messages [22].

## 6.4.2 Parameter Settings

The performance of this protocol depends on the selection of appropriate values for the following parameters: the *TTRT*, the synchronous bandwidths of individual stations, the synchronous message frame length, and the asynchronous message frame length.

- *TTRT selection*
  Previous studies [9] on choosing an appropriate *TTRT* value have considered

---

[5]Also referred as *synchronous capacity* in the literature [2–4]. We use the term *synchronous bandwidth*, in accordance with the most recent version of the FDDI standard.

network models with purely asynchronous loading. The issue of selecting
$TTRT$ for a real-time environment has not been addressed in the literature
so far. As shown in [22], the time between two successive token visits to a
station can be at most $2 \cdot TTRT$. Hence, $TTRT$ should be less than half of
the minimum period. Our investigations have shown that the performance of
the timed token protocol in a real-time environment is sensitive to the $TTRT$
value. Often a value much lower than half of the minimum period produces
better results.

A small value of $TTRT$ gives a better response time to synchronous messages because the nodes are served more frequently. However, in each token rotation, there are fixed overheads. Thus, a smaller value of $TTRT$
means less synchronous bandwidth to individual nodes and a higher overhead. In particular, it can be shown that for the case where all messages have
the same period $P$, the optimal value of $TTRT$ is close to $\sqrt{\tau' \cdot P}$, where
$\tau' = \Theta +$ Asynchronous message frame length $+ n \cdot F_{ovhd}$. For our study, we
chose $TTRT$ according to the following rule:

$$
TTRT = \begin{cases} \min \left( \frac{P_{min}}{\lfloor \sqrt{\frac{P_{min}}{\tau'}} \rfloor}, \frac{P_{min}}{2} \right) & \text{if } g \left( \lfloor \sqrt{\frac{P_{min}}{\tau'}} \rfloor \right) \geq g \left( \lceil \sqrt{\frac{P_{min}}{\tau'}} \rceil \right) \\[3ex] \min \left( \frac{P_{min}}{\lceil \sqrt{\frac{P_{min}}{\tau'}} \rceil}, \frac{P_{min}}{2} \right) & \text{otherwise,} \end{cases} \tag{6.11}
$$

where

$$
g(x) = \frac{x-1}{P_{min}} \cdot \left( \frac{P_{min}}{x} - \tau' \right). \tag{6.12}
$$

The justification for this choice of $TTRT$ is provided in the appendix.

- *Synchronous bandwidth allocation*
  In our study of the timed token protocol, we assign synchronous bandwidths to
  individual stations according to a *local bandwidth allocation* scheme proposed
  in [3]. According to this scheme, the synchronous bandwidth assigned to a
  station is given as follows:

$$
H_i = \frac{C_i'}{q_i - 1} \tag{6.13}
$$

where $q_i$ is defined as

$$
q_i = \left\lfloor \frac{P_i}{TTRT} \right\rfloor \tag{6.14}
$$

and $C_i'$ is the augmented message length, which takes into account the time
needed to transmit the frame headers. The method for computing $C_i'$ will be
given shortly.

The rationale behind this scheme is as follows. In [3] it was shown that a
station will receive the token at least $q_i - 1$ times in an interval of duration

$P_i$. Since $C'_i$ denotes the time needed to complete the transmission of a message from stream $S_i$ during this interval, the corresponding node must be allowed to transmit for $\frac{C'_i}{q_i-1}$ duration each time it receives the token.

This scheme was shown to have a minimum breakdown utilization of 33%. In a local scheme, the allocation of bandwidths is done purely on the basis of local information at individual nodes. Hence, local schemes are easy to implement and do not cause disruption of service when the message parameters at some nodes change at run time.

- *Synchronous message frame length*
  As in the case of the priority-driven protocol, synchronous messages are divided into frames. Since a station can transmit synchronous messages for at most $H_i$ time units after receiving a token, the synchronous frame length for a station is simply the synchronous bandwidth allocated for that station.

- *Asynchronous frame length*
  In this chapter we present the results of experiments for payload lengths of asynchronous frames chosen as 512 bytes.

Throughout this chapter, we will assume that the parameters for the timed token protocol are selected as discussed above.

## 6.4.3   Schedulability Conditions

For a given network, a set of synchronous messages are schedulable using the timed token protocol if and only if the following two constraints are satisfied:

1. *The Protocol Constraint*
   This constraint states that sum of the bandwidths allocated to individual stations cannot exceed the available network bandwidth. That is,

$$\sum_{i=1}^{n} H_i \;\leq\; TTRT - \tau \tag{6.15}$$

where $\tau$ denotes the sum of various protocol overheads which reduce the actual time available for transmission of data during one typical token rotation duration. The value of $\tau$ is obtained as [22]

$$\tau \;=\; \Theta + F \tag{6.16}$$

where $F$ denotes the time to transmit an asynchronous frame and is known as the asynchronous overrun [22]. This constraint must be met to ensure the proper working of the protocol.

2. *The Deadline Constraint*
   This constraint states that the synchronous messages must always be transmitted before their deadlines. If $X_i$ is the minimum amount of time available

for node $i$ to transmit a synchronous message during the entire period of the message, then this constraint can be stated as

$$X_i \geq C_i' \tag{6.17}$$

where $C_i'$ is the augmented message transmission time taking into account the transmission overheads.

The following lemma establishes the augmented message lengths for this protocol.

**Lemma 6.4.1** *For the timed token protocol, $C_i'$, the augmented message length for a message in stream $S_i$ is as follows:*

$$C_i' = C_i + (q_i - 1) \cdot F_{ovhd} \tag{6.18}$$

*where $q_i = \lfloor \frac{P_i}{TTRT} \rfloor$.*

**Proof:** Since overhead bits need to be transmitted along with the payload data in each frame of length $H_i$, the augmented message length must satisfy the following equation:

$$C_i' = C_i + \left\lceil \frac{C_i'}{H_i} \right\rceil \cdot F_{ovhd}. \tag{6.19}$$

Substituting (6.13) into (6.19), we get the desired result.    □

Substituting (6.18) into (6.13), the bandwidth assignment rule can be rewritten as

$$H_i = \frac{C_i}{q_i - 1} + F_{ovhd}. \tag{6.20}$$

The schedulability conditions for this protocol have to account for both of these constraints. The following theorem establishes the schedulability condition for the timed token protocol.

**Theorem 6.4.1** *For the timed token protocol, the criterion for schedulability of a synchronous message set is given by*

$$\sum_{i=1}^{n} \frac{C_i}{\lfloor \frac{P_i}{TTRT} \rfloor - 1} + n \cdot F_{ovhd} \leq TTRT - \tau. \tag{6.21}$$

**Proof:** An expression for $X_i$ in terms of various network and protocol parameters is given in [4]. It is as follows:

$$X_i = (q_i - 1) \cdot H_i + max\left(0, min\left(r_i - \left(\sum_{j=1,\dots,n, j \neq i} H_j + \tau\right), H_i\right)\right) \tag{6.22}$$

where $q_i = \lfloor \frac{P_i}{TTRT} \rfloor$ and $r_i = P_i - TTRT \cdot q_i$. This expression for $X_i$ is valid as long as (1) $TTRT$ is less than half of the smallest period, and (2) the protocol constraint specified by (6.15) is met.

The expression for $X_i$ given by (6.22) implies that $X_i \geq (q_i - 1) \cdot H_i$. Hence, if $H_i$ is chosen as $C_i'/(q_i - 1)$, the deadline constraint specified by equation (6.17) is always satisfied as long as the protocol constraint is satisfied and $TTRT$ does not exceed half of the minimum period. Consequently, the protocol constraint given by equation (6.15) is a necessary and sufficient condition for schedulability with the timed token protocol. By substituting (6.14) and (6.20) into (6.15), we obtain (6.21) as the schedulability criterion for the timed token protocol.          □

Thus, only a single inequality needs to be tested to check if a given synchronous message set is guaranteed by the timed token protocol.

## 6.5  Performance Metrics and Their Computation

In this section, we will formalize the notions of the *average breakdown utilization* and the *guarantee probability* metrics introduced earlier. We will present a geometric representation of synchronous message sets. This model will be used in conjunction with the schedulability conditions for a protocol to compute its average breakdown utilization and guarantee probability.

### 6.5.1  Metrics Definition

To better appreciate the definitions of the metrics, consider a classification of all message sets with respect to a given protocol. We partition the entire population of synchronous message sets into three classes based on the schedulability offered by a given protocol.

1. *Unsaturated Schedulable Class* ($C_1$): The message sets in this class are schedulable and remain so even if any of the message lengths are slightly increased.

2. *Saturated Schedulable Class* ($C_2$): These message sets are schedulable but an increase in the message length of some message in the set will lead to the violation of schedulability. In other words, these message sets represent the breakdown loads on the system.

3. *Unschedulable Class* ($C_3$): This class consists of message sets that are not schedulable.

The above concepts are illustrated in Figure 6.2. The saturated schedulable class is at the boundary of the schedulable region.

We define the average breakdown utilization of a protocol as the expected value of the utilization of message sets belonging to the saturated class for that protocol. That is,

$$ABU \quad = \quad E[U(M) \mid M \in C_2].  \tag{6.23}$$

To study the average performance of a protocol in further detail, we define the guarantee probability, $GP(U)$, as the probability that a randomly chosen message

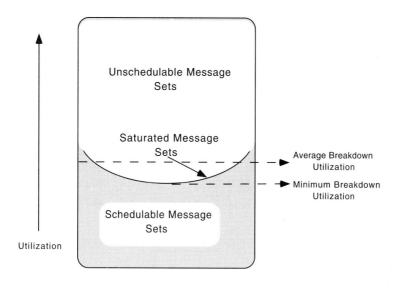

**Figure 6.2** Minimum and Average Breakdown Utilizations

set with utilization $U$ is guaranteed by the protocol. Formally,

$$GP(U) \quad = \quad Prob\,(M \in \mathcal{C}_1 \cup \mathcal{C}_2 \mid U(M) = U). \tag{6.24}$$

We would expect $GP(U)$ to be close to 1 for utilizations lower than $ABU$ and to approach zero as the utilization is increased beyond $ABU$.

## 6.5.2 Computation Methods

Recall that the deadline of a synchronous message is assumed to be the end of its period. Thus, a synchronous message stream $S_i$ can be characterized by its parameters $C_i$ and $P_i$. Since $U_i$ is defined as $\frac{C_i}{P_i}$, we may also represent $S_i$ as $S_i = (U_i, P_i)$. A message set $M$ can be defined by two $n-$dimensional vectors $\vec{U}$ and $\vec{P}$:

$$\vec{U} \quad = \quad (U_1, U_2, \ldots, U_n) \tag{6.25}$$

and

$$\vec{P} \quad = \quad (P_1, P_2, \ldots, P_n) \tag{6.26}$$

where $U_i$ and $P_i$ denote the utilization and the period of synchronous message stream $S_i$.

Thus, a random message set can be obtained by choosing two random vectors $\vec{U}$ and $\vec{P}$. It is reasonable to assume that $\vec{U}$ and $\vec{P}$ are independent. Further, when the overall utilization is given as $U$, we will assume that all the $U_i$'s are identically and uniformly distributed in $[0, U)$ subject to the constraint that $\sum_{i=1}^{n} U_i = U$.[6]

---

[6] This is a common practice in average-case analysis. For example, most average-case

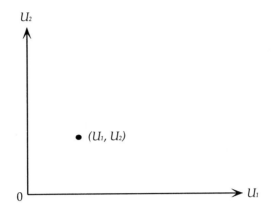

**Figure 6.3** Geometric Representation of a Message Set

**Conditional Measures.** First, we derive the conditional average breakdown utilization and the conditional guarantee probability for a given (i.e., fixed) $\vec{P}$; that is,

$$ABU_{\vec{P}} \;=\; E[U(M) \mid \vec{P}, M \in C_2] \tag{6.27}$$

and

$$GP_{\vec{P}}(U) \;=\; Prob\left(M \in C_1 \cup C_2 \mid \vec{P}, U(M) = U\right). \tag{6.28}$$

To facilitate the discussion of computational methods for obtaining these metrics, we introduce a geometric model for representing message sets. To simplify our discussion, we will focus on the timed token protocol. The same methodology applies to the priority-driven protocol.

To begin with, consider the simple case of message sets of size 2. For a given $\vec{P} = (P_1, P_2)$, any message set can be represented as single point $(U_1, U_2)$ in the $U_1$-$U_2$ plane, as shown in Figure 6.3. All message sets with a given utilization $U$ constitute the locus of points defined by the equation $U_1 + U_2 = U$. Geometrically, this equation denotes a line segment in the positive quadrant of the $U_1$-$U_2$ plane. Let the locus of points defined by $U_1 + U_2 = U$ be denoted by $W_1$. In Figure 6.4, we show $W_1$ as the line segment $\overline{EF}$.

Now consider (6.21), the schedulability condition for the timed token protocol. Writing $C_i$ as $U_i \cdot P_i$, this condition can be written as

$$U_1 \cdot \frac{P_1}{\left\lfloor \frac{P_1}{TTRT} \right\rfloor - 1} + U_2 \cdot \frac{P_2}{\left\lfloor \frac{P_2}{TTRT} \right\rfloor - 1} \;\leq\; TTRT - \tau - n \cdot F_{ovhd}. \tag{6.29}$$

With $P_1$ and $P_2$ fixed, the left-hand side of the above inequality represents a linear combination of $U_1$ and $U_2$. This inequality defines all message sets (with $n = 2$

---

analyses of sorting algorithms assume that all permutations of input sequence are equally likely.

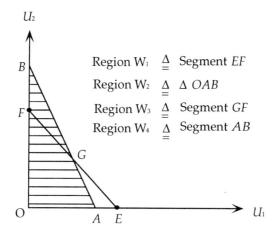

**Figure 6.4** Representation of Message Sets with Specific Characteristics

and $\vec{P} = (P_1, P_2))$ that are guaranteed by the timed token protocol, and can be represented as a right triangle (denoted by $W_2 = \triangle AOB$ in Figure 6.4). Further, we define two more regions $W_3$ and $W_4$ as follows:

- Let $W_3 = W_1 \cap W_2$. $W_3$ is given by the line segment $\overline{GF}$ in Figure 6.4. This region consists of all points (i.e., message sets) that satisfy both $U_1 + U_2 = U$ and the schedulability condition (6.29).

- Let $W_4$ denote the outer boundary of region $W_2$. $W_4$ is given by segment $\overline{AB}$ in Figure 6.4. This region is the locus of points representing message sets that are just schedulable. These message sets are the saturated message sets. This region is obtained by rewriting (6.29) as a strict equality.

It is obvious that $W_4$ denotes $C_2$ and $W_2$ denotes $C_1 \cup C_2$ for the case when periods are fixed. Since $W_4$ denotes the class of saturated message sets, the conditional average breakdown utilization is obtained as the ratio of two surface integrals as

$$ABU_{\vec{P}} \;=\; \frac{\int_{W_4} U\,dS}{\int_{W_4} dS}. \tag{6.30}$$

The conditional guarantee probability at utilization $U$ for a given $\vec{P}$ can be obtained as

$$GP_{\vec{P}}(U) = \frac{\|W_3\|}{\|W_1\|} = \frac{\|W_1 \cap W_2\|}{\|W_1\|} \tag{6.31}$$

where $\|W_i\|$ denotes the standard *Lebesgue measure* of region $W_i$. For the two-dimensional case, these two regions are line segments as shown in Figure 6.4. Thus, their *Lebesgue measures* are simply their lengths. Hence, for the case illustrated by Figure 6.4, the conditional guarantee probability obtained in (6.31) is

$$GP_{\vec{P}}(U) \;=\; \frac{\text{length}\left(\overline{FG}\right)}{\text{length}\left(\overline{EF}\right)}. \tag{6.32}$$

Expressions (6.30) and (6.31) can be generalized to message sets of size $n$. Region $W_1$ defined by equation $\sum_{i=1}^{n} U_i = U$ is generalized to a hyper-plane representing the outer face of a regular simplex in $n$ dimensions. The $n$ corners of $W_1$ are $(U, 0, 0, \ldots, 0), (0, U, 0, \ldots, 0), \cdots, (0, 0, 0, \ldots, U)$. $W_2$ is similarly generalized to a (possibly irregular) simplex region. Region $W_3$ is still defined as the intersection of $W_1$ and $W_2$. $W_4$ denotes the outer face of the simplex region $W_2$. Further, the respective *Lebesgue measures* of $W_1$ and $W_3$ are obtained as the $(n-1)$-dimensional surface areas of the corresponding regions.

Hence, with the generalized definitions of $W_1, W_2, W_3$, and $W_4$, (6.30) still defines the conditional breakdown utilization for the general case of message sets of size $n$. Similarly, the conditional guarantee probability for the timed token protocol is defined in general as

$$GP_{\vec{P}}(U) = \frac{\int_{W_3} dS}{\int_{W_1} dS} = \frac{\int_{W_1 \cap W_2} dS}{\int_{W_1} dS}. \tag{6.33}$$

As mentioned earlier, the above methodology can also be applied to the priority-driven protocol. However, regions $W_2$, $W_3$, and $W_4$ are more complex in this case. Region $W_2$ for this protocol is defined by the locus of points satisfying (6.10). Region $W_3$ is defined as $W_1 \cap W_2$ as before, and region $W_4$, comprising saturated message sets, is the locus of points satisfying the inequalities in (6.10) with the condition that at least one of them is an equality.

**Removing the Conditionality.**    The measures defined above assumed that the period vector $(\vec{P})$ was given. This conditionality can be removed if the distribution of $\vec{P}$ is known. The unconditional measures can be obtained as

$$ABU = \int ABU_{\vec{P}} \cdot dF_{\vec{P}}(\vec{P}) \tag{6.34}$$

and

$$GP(U) = \int GP_{\vec{P}}(U) \cdot dF_{\vec{P}}(\vec{P}) \tag{6.35}$$

where $F_{\vec{P}}$ denotes the distribution function of the period vector $\vec{P}$. If the individual message periods are assumed to be independent and identically distributed (i.i.d.), then $F_{\vec{P}}$ is simply the $n$-fold product of the period distribution function.

## 6.5.3   Efficient Estimation Methods

In the preceding subsection we obtained exact expressions for the average breakdown utilization and the guarantee probability. We note that (6.34) and (6.35) do not lead to closed-form expressions for these quantities. Exact values for these integrals are difficult to obtain. An approximate analysis of the average breakdown utilization for the rate monotonic scheduling algorithm without overheads or blocking is presented in [13]. An approximate analysis of the guarantee probability for the timed token protocol is presented in [11, 12]. In general, these quantities can be computed by numerical methods using Monte Carlo procedures based on the geometric model presented here.

The conditional measures (for a given period set) can be obtained as follows [13].

- To compute the conditional average breakdown utilization, one needs to generate random points in region $W_4$. This is difficult for protocols like the priority-driven protocol, due to the complexity of the $W_4$ region. An approximate method described in [13] can be employed. First, a random message set is generated with a small utilization value. The individual message utilizations are then uniformly scaled up until some message in the set just misses its deadline. An average of utilization values of a large sample of such saturated message sets is taken as an estimate of the conditional average breakdown utilization.

- To compute the conditional guarantee probability for a given period set, a large number of points are generated at random in region $W_1$ and tested for membership in region $W_2$ by checking whether the corresponding schedulability condition is met. The fraction of the points generated that also belong to $W_2$ is taken to be an estimate of the conditional guarantee probability.

Once the conditional measures are obtained, the unconditional ones can be computed numerically from (6.34) and (6.35).

## 6.6  Performance Comparison

We now discuss the results of comparison tests carried out for the two protocols under different operating conditions. These operating conditions are specified by the following choice of parameters.

- $n$ = Number of stations = 100.

- $d$ = Distance between neighboring stations = 100 meters.

- The average bit delay per station was taken as 4 bits for the priority driven protocol and 75 bits for the timed token protocol. These values are characteristic of the IEEE 802.5 and FDDI standards.

- Message periods were assumed to be independent and identically distributed. Results presented here are for uniformly distributed periods. The uniform distribution is specified by an average period of 100 msec and the maximum-to-minimum period ratio of 10.

- The signal propagation speed through the medium was assumed to be 75% of the speed of light.

- $F_{ovhd}^b$ = 112 bits.

- $F_{info}^b$ = 512 bytes.

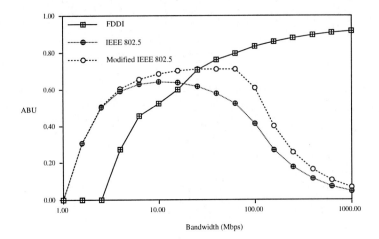

**Figure 6.5** Average Breakdown Utilization Comparison

The results obtained for other choice of parameter values were similar to those reported here.

Figure 6.5 shows the variation in the average breakdown utilization of the priority-driven protocol and the timed token protocol as the bandwidth is increased. We can make following observations from this figure.

- The performance of the priority-driven protocol initially improves as the bandwidth is increased but starts to drop beyond a certain point. This is against the intuition that performance of a protocol should improve as the bandwidth is increased. The explanation for this behavior lies in the impact of the overheads incurred by the protocol in transmitting each frame.

  When the bandwidth is increased beyond a certain value, the decrease in transmission time causes the frame transmission time $F$ to be less than the token circulation time $\Theta$. In this case, before releasing a new token,[7] the transmitting node has to wait for the token to return even after the transmission of a frame is complete. Thus, the effective frame transmission time in this case is $\Theta$ and the fraction of wasted bandwidth is $\frac{\Theta - F_{info}}{F_{info}}$. Note that $\Theta$ consists of the signal propagation delay, the ring latency, and the token transmission time. The propagation delay is independent of the bandwidth and hence can be considered as constant (denoted by $R$). The ring latency and token transmission time decrease with increasing bandwidth. Their sum can be written as $\frac{Q}{BW}$, where $Q$ is the sum of token size and the ring latency in bits. Hence, the fraction of the bandwidth that is wasted becomes

$$\frac{\Theta - F_{info}}{F_{info}} = \frac{R + Q/BW - F_{info}}{F_{info}}$$

---

[7]Or transmitting another frame, as in case of the modified IEEE 802.5 protocol.

$$= \frac{R}{F_{info}^b} \cdot BW + \frac{Q - F_{info}^b}{F_{info}^b} \quad (\text{since } F_{info} = F_{info}^b / BW). \quad (6.36)$$

Thus, the percentage of wasted bandwidth increases with an increase in bandwidth, thereby lowering the performance of the priority-driven protocol.

- The timed token protocol does not exhibit this anomaly because it allows a station to release the token immediately after transmitting its message frame. As a result, the performance of the timed token protocol improves as the bandwidth is increased.

- It is also clear that the modified version of the IEEE 802.5 protocol performs better than the implementation based on the standard. This is because the token-passing overhead is incurred once for every frame in the implementation based on the IEEE 802.5 standard, while it is incurred only once for every message in the modified version.

- It is observed that the priority-driven protocol performs better than the timed token protocol for bandwidths in the range of 1-10 Mbit/s. For these operating conditions, the overheads inherent in the implementation of the rate monotonic scheduling are not predominant. The superior performance is due to the optimality of the scheduling strategy being used.

- On the other hand, the timed token protocol performs better than the priority-driven protocol at high bandwidths. Though the scheduling strategy of the timed token protocol is not optimal, it incurs little cost (token-passing overhead). In a system with high bandwidth, the heavy priority arbitration overheads inherent in the priority-driven protocol degrade its performance, resulting in the relatively poor performance of the priority-driven protocol.

Figures 6.6(a) and 6.6(b) show the guarantee probability results for the two protocols at bandwidths 10 Mbit/s and 100 Mbit/s, respectively. We can make following observations from these figures.

- As expected, the guarantee probability decreases as the synchronous traffic utilization increases. The higher the utilization of a message set, the more difficult it is to meet its deadlines.

- In all cases it is seen that the guarantee probability remains close to 1 as long as the utilization is less than the average breakdown utilization of the protocol. There is a sharp drop in the guarantee probability at utilization values close to the average breakdown utilization. This demonstrates that the average breakdown utilization is a robust measure of average performance for real-time systems.

- These figures corroborate the previous observation that at a bandwidth of 10 Mbit/s, the priority-driven protocol performs better than the timed token protocol, while at 100 Mbit/s the reverse is true. In both cases, it is also seen that the modified priority-driven protocol performs better than the standard one.

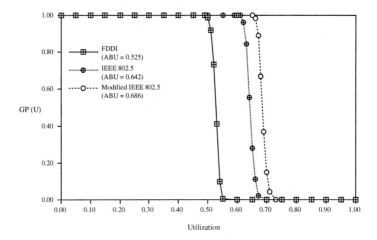

**Figure 6.6** (a) Guarantee Probability Comparison at 10 Mbit/s

## 6.7 Conclusions

The schedulability conditions for the timed token protocol and the priority-driven protocol (implementing a rate monotonic scheduling policy) were developed. These criteria were then used to study the average real-time performance of the two protocols. The average breakdown utilization, a point measure which signifies the average utilization value that a protocol can sustain without missing any deadlines, was used to study the performance as the network bandwidth is varied. The guarantee probability, which measures the ability of a protocol to guarantee all the deadlines of a message set as a function of the message set utilization, provided a more detailed picture of protocol performance.

     Our studies have shown that each protocol has its own domain of superior performance. The priority-driven protocol can be used to implement an optimal scheduling policy such as the rate monotonic scheduling algorithm. At low transmission rates (1-10 Mbit/s), this implementation is very efficient. The timed token protocol essentially implements a round-robin scheduling policy without any priority arbitration mechanism. At low transmission speeds, the priority inversions caused by such a round-robin scheduling approach tend to adversely affect the messages with short deadlines. Thus, at low transmission speeds the priority-driven protocol is better suited than the timed token protocol for real-time applications. The priority arbitration overheads incurred by the priority-driven protocol increase with network bandwidth, thereby lowering the performance of the priority-driven protocol for high-speed networks. The timed token protocol, which does not incur priority arbitration overheads and allows multiple frames to be on the ring at the same time, is found to perform better at high bandwidths such as 100 Mbit/s and above.

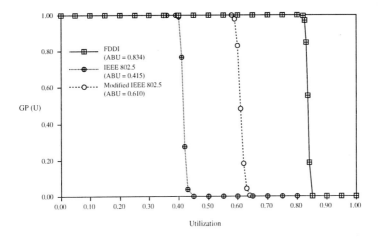

**Figure 6.6** (b) Guarantee Probability Comparison at 100 Mbit/s

## Acknowledgments

The work reported in this chapter was supported in part by the National Science Foundation under Grant NCR-9210583, the Office of Naval Research under Grant N00014-92-J-4031, and an Engineering Excellence Grant from Texas A&M University.

## References

[1] ANSI Standard X3T9.5, *Fiber Distributed Data Interface (FDDI): Token Ring Medium Access Control (MAC)*, May 1987.

[2] G. Agrawal, B. Chen, W. Zhao, and S. Davari. "Guaranteeing Synchronous Message Deadlines with Timed Token Protocol." *Proc. of the 12th IEEE International Conf. on Distributed Computing Systems*, June 1992.

[3] G. Agrawal, B. Chen, and W. Zhao. "Local Synchronous Capacity Allocation Schemes for Hard Real-Time Communications with the Timed Token Media Access Control Protocol." *Proc. of the IEEE INFOCOM'93*, 1993.

[4] B. Chen, G. Agrawal, and W. Zhao. "Optimal Synchronous Capacity Allocation for Hard Real-Time Communications with the Timed Token Media Access Control Protocol." *Proc. of the IEEE Real-Time Systems Symp.*, Dec. 1992.

[5] D. Ferrari and D. C. Verma. "A Scheme for Real-Time Channel Establishment in Wide-Area Networks." *IEEE Journal on Selected Areas in Communications*, SAC-8: 368–379, Apr. 1990.

[6] D. T. Green and D. T. Marlow. "SAFENET: A LAN for Navy Mission Critical Systems." *Proc. of the Conf. on Local Computer Networks*, Oct. 1989.

[7] R. M. Grow. "A Timed Token Protocol for Local Area Networks." *Proc. of Electro/82, Token Access Protocols*, May 1982.

[8] IEEE Standard 802.5-1989, *Token Ring Access Method and Physical Layer Specifications*. Institute of Electrical and Electronic Engineers, New York, 1989.

[9] R. Jain. "Performance Analysis of FDDI Token Ring Networks: Effect of Parameters and Guidelines for Setting *TTRT*." *IEEE LTS*, May 1991.

[10] S. Kamat and W. Zhao. "Real-Time Schedulability of two Token Ring Protocols." *Proc. of the 13th IEEE International Conf. on Distributed Computing Systems*, June 1993.

[11] S. Kamat and W. Zhao. "On Probability of Guaranteeing Synchronous Real-Time Messages in an FDDI Network." *Proc. of the International Conf. on Computer Communications and Networks*, June 1993.

[12] S. Kamat, N. Malcolm, and W. Zhao. "The Probability of Guaranteeing Synchronous Real-Time Messages with Arbitrary Deadlines in an FDDI Network." *Proc. of the IEEE Real-Time Systems Symp.*, Dec., 1993.

[13] J. Lehoczky, L. Sha, and Y. Ding. "The Rate Monotonic Scheduling Algorithm: Exact Characterization and Average Case Behavior." *Proc. of the IEEE Real-Time Systems Symp.*, 1989.

[14] C. C. Lim, L. Yao, and W. Zhao. "A Comparative Study of Three Token Ring Protocols for Real-Time Communications." *Proc. of the 11th IEEE International Conf. on Distributed Computing Systems*, May 1991.

[15] C. L. Liu and J. W. Layland. "Scheduling Algorithms for Multiprogramming in a Hard-Real-Time Environment." *Journal of the ACM*, 20(1):46–61, Jan. 1973.

[16] N. Malcolm and W. Zhao. "Hard Real-Time Communication in Multiple-Access Networks." To appear in *Journal of Real-Time Systems*.

[17] U.S. Department of Defense. *Survivable Adaptable Fiber Optic Embedded Network*. MIL-STD-2204A. Jan. 1994.

[18] J. Ng and J. Liu. "Performance of Local Area Network Protocols for Hard-Real-Time Applications." *Proc. of the 11th IEEE International Conf. on Distributed Computing Systems*, May 1991.

[19] SAE, Aerospace Systems Division, Committee AS-2. *Linear Token-passing Multiple Data Bus*. AS4074.1, Version 4.0, Jan. 1988.

[20] SAE, Aerospace Systems Division, Committee AS-2. *High Speed Ring Bus (HSRB)*. AS4074.2, Jan. 1988.

[21] S. S. Sathaye and J. K. Strosnider. "Conventional and Early Token Release Scheduling Models for the IEEE 802.5 Token Ring." Submitted for publication.

[22] K. C. Sevcik and M. J. Johnson. "Cycle Time Properties of the FDDI Token Ring Protocol." *IEEE Transactions on Software Engineering*, SE-13(3):376–385, Mar. 1987.

[23] L. Sha, R. Rajkumar, and J. Lehoczky. "Priority Inheritance Protocols: An Approach to Real-Time Synchronization." *IEEE Transactions on Computers*, 39(9):1175–1185, Sept. 1990.

[24] L. Sha and S. S. Sathaye. "A Systematic Approach to Designing Distributed Real-Time Systems." *IEEE Computer*, 26(9):68–78, Sept. 1993.

[25] K. G. Shin and C. Hou. "Analysis of Three Contention Protocols in Distributed Real-Time Systems." *Proc. of the IEEE Real-Time Systems Symp.*, Dec. 1990.

[26] W. Stallings. *Computer Communication Standards, Vol. 2: Local Area Network Standards.* Howard W. Sams & Co., Carmel, Ind., 1987.

[27] J. A. Stankovic and K. Ramamritham. *Hard Real-Time Systems.* IEEE Press, New York, 1988.

[28] J. A. Stankovic and K. Ramamritham. *Advances in Real-Time Systems.* IEEE Press, New York, 1993.

[29] J. K. Strosnider, J. Lehoczky, and L. Sha. "Advanced Real-Time Scheduling Using the IEEE 802.5 Token Ring." *Proc. of the IEEE Real-Time Systems Symp.*, Dec. 1988.

[30] A. M. van Tilborg and G. M. Koob. *Foundations of Real-Time Computing: Formal Specifications and Methods.* Kluwer Academic Publishers, Norwell, Mass., 1991.

[31] A. M. van Tilborg and G. M. Koob. *Foundations of Real-Time Computing: Scheduling and Resource Management.* Kluwer Academic Publishers, Norwell, Mass., 1991.

[32] R. W. Uhlhorn. "The Fiber-Optic High-Speed Data Bus for a New Generation of Military Aircraft." *IEEE LCS*, 2(1), Feb. 1991.

[33] L. Yao and W. Zhao. "Performance of an Extended IEEE 802.5 Protocol in Hard-Real-Time Systems." *Proc. of the IEEE INFOCOM'91*, Apr. 1991.

# 6.A   $TTRT$ Selection for the Timed Token Protocol

We now present the results concerning the choice of $TTRT$ for the timed token protocol.

**Theorem 6.A.1** *When all periods are equal to $P$, the average breakdown utilization of the timed token protocol is maximized by the following choice of* $TTRT$:

$$TTRT = \begin{cases} \dfrac{P}{\lfloor \sqrt{\frac{P}{\tau'}} \rfloor} & \text{if } g(\lfloor \sqrt{\tfrac{P}{\tau'}} \rfloor) \geq g(\lceil \sqrt{\tfrac{P}{\tau'}} \rceil), \\[2em] \dfrac{P}{\lceil \sqrt{\frac{P}{\tau'}} \rceil} & \text{otherwise} \end{cases} \qquad (6.37)$$

*where $\tau'$ equals $\tau + n \cdot F_{ovhd}$ and*

$$g(x) = \frac{x-1}{P} \cdot \left( \frac{P}{x} - \tau' \right). \qquad (6.38)$$

**Proof:** The schedulability condition given in Theorem 6.4.1 can be rewritten for the case of equal periods as:

$$\sum_{i=1}^{n} \frac{C_i}{\lfloor \frac{P}{TTRT} \rfloor - 1} \;\leq\; TTRT - \tau - n \cdot F_{ovhd} \;=\; TTRT - \tau'. \qquad (6.39)$$

Multiplying both the sides by $\frac{1}{P}(\lfloor \frac{P}{TTRT} \rfloor - 1)$ yields

$$\sum_{i=1}^{n} \frac{C_i}{P} \;\leq\; \frac{\lfloor \frac{P}{TTRT} \rfloor - 1}{P} \cdot (TTRT - \tau'). \qquad (6.40)$$

That is,

$$U \;\leq\; f(TTRT) \qquad \left(\text{since } U = \sum_{i=1}^{n} U_i = \sum_{i=1}^{n} \tfrac{C_i}{P}\right) \quad (6.41)$$

where

$$f(TTRT) \;=\; \frac{\lfloor \frac{P}{TTRT} \rfloor - 1}{P} \cdot (TTRT - \tau'). \qquad (6.42)$$

Hence, for the case when all periods are equal, the breakdown (missing of deadlines) occurs at a unique utilization value given by the value of $f(TTRT)$. Note that $f(TTRT)$ is an increasing function of $TTRT$ over any interval $\left( \frac{P}{q+1}, \frac{P}{q} \right]$ where $q = \lfloor \frac{P}{TTRT} \rfloor$ is an integer greater than 2. Hence, within this interval, the maximum value of $f$ occurs at $TTRT = \frac{P}{q}$ and such a local maximum is given by

$$f\left( \frac{P}{q} \right) = \frac{q-1}{P} \cdot \left( \frac{P}{q} - \tau' \right) = g(q). \qquad (6.43)$$

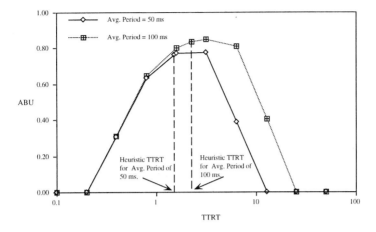

**Figure 6.7** Impact of *TTRT* on Average Breakdown Utilization

Hence, choosing a *TTRT* value to maximize $f$ is equivalent to choosing an integer $q$ which maximizes the function $g$ defined above.

We can find $q$ by first treating it as a real variable and solving $g'(q) = 0$. Let $q^*$ be the solution of the equation $g'(q) = 0$. The desired integral solution is then either $\lfloor q^* \rfloor$ or $\lceil q^* \rceil$, depending on the corresponding value of $g(q)$. It can readily be verified that $q^* = \sqrt{\frac{P}{\tau'}}$ is the solution for $g'(q) = 0$. Hence the result follows. $\square$

It is desirable to choose *TTRT* to maximize the average breakdown utilization. We note that Theorem 6.A.1 does not provide a solution for the general case where all periods can have arbitrary values. However, our studies indicate that (6.37), with $P$ replaced by $P_{min}$, is a good heuristic for selecting *TTRT* in the general case. Specifically, we adopt the following heuristic for selecting *TTRT*.

$$TTRT = \begin{cases} \min\left(\dfrac{P_{min}}{\lfloor \sqrt{\frac{P_{min}}{\tau'}} \rfloor}, \dfrac{P_{min}}{2}\right) & \text{if } g\left(\lfloor \sqrt{\tfrac{P_{min}}{\tau'}} \rfloor\right) \geq g\left(\lceil \sqrt{\tfrac{P_{min}}{\tau'}} \rceil\right) \\[4mm] \min\left(\dfrac{P_{min}}{\lceil \sqrt{\frac{P_{min}}{\tau'}} \rceil}, \dfrac{P_{min}}{2}\right) & \text{otherwise.} \end{cases}$$

(6.44)

Figure 6.7 shows the impact of *TTRT* selection on the average breakdown utilization of the FDDI network. The performance results in Figure 6.7 are for average periods of 50 ms and 100 ms, respectively. The values of other network parameters are the same as those specified in Section 6.6. It is evident from this figure that a too small or too large value of *TTRT* leads to poor system performance. As seen from the figure, a choice of *TTRT* based on the heuristic defined by equation (6.44) leads to a near optimal performance. This justifies the use of this heuristic for choosing *TTRT*.

# Chapter 7

# A Systematic Approach to Designing Distributed Real-Time Systems[1]

## Lui Sha and Shirish S. Sathaye

Distributed real-time system design raises new theoretical issues and application challenges beyond those in centralized systems. Rate monotonic scheduling (RMS) theory has been applied successfully in the scheduling of centralized systems. RMS and its generalizations have been adopted by national high-technology projects such as the Space Station and has recently been supported by major open standards such as the IEEE Futurebus+ and POSIX.4. In this chapter, we describe the use of generalized rate monotonic scheduling theory for the design and analysis of a distributed real-time system. We review the recent extensions of the theory to distributed system scheduling, examine the architectural requirements for use of the theory, and provide an application example.

## 7.1  Introduction

Real-time computing systems are critical to an industrialized nation's technological infrastructure. Modern telecommunication systems, factories, defense systems, aircraft and airports, space stations, and high-energy physics experiments cannot operate without them. Indeed, real-time computing systems control the very systems that keep us productive, safeguard our liberty, and enable us to explore new frontiers of science and engineering.

In real-time applications, the correctness of a computation depends not only

---

[1]This chapter is based on "A Systematic Approach to Designing Distributed Real-Time Systems," by Lui Sha and Shirish Sathaye, that appeared in *IEEE Computer*, vol. 26, no. 9, pp. 68–78, September 1993, ©1993 IEEE.

upon its results but also upon the time at which outputs are generated. The measures of merit in a real-time system include:

- Predictably fast response to urgent events.

- High degree of schedulability. Schedulability is the degree of resource utilization at or below which the timing requirements of tasks can be ensured. It can be thought as a measure of the number of timely transactions per second.

- Stability under transient overload. When the system is overloaded by events and it is impossible to meet all the deadlines, we must still guarantee the deadlines of selected critical tasks.

Real-time scheduling is a vibrant field. Several important research efforts are summarized in [15]. Among them, generalized rate monotonic (GRMS) theory is a useful tool that allows system developers to meet the above requirements by managing system concurrency and timing constraints at the level of tasking and message passing. In essence, this theory ensures that as long as the system utilization of all tasks lies below a certain bound, and appropriate scheduling algorithms are used, all tasks meet their deadlines. This puts the development and maintenance of real-time systems on an analytic, engineering basis, making these systems easier to develop and maintain.

DoD's 1991 Software Technology Strategy refers to rate monotonic scheduling (RMS) as a "major payoff" and states that "system designers can use this theory to predict whether task deadlines will be met long before the costly implementation phase of a project begins. It also eases the process of making modifications to application software." The Acting Deputy Administrator of NASA, Aaron Cohen, stated in a 1992 speech titled *Charting The Future*, "Through the development of Rate Monotonic Scheduling, we now have a system that will allow (Space Station) Freedom's computers to budget their time, to choose between a variety of tasks, and decide not only which one to do first but how much time to spend in the process." The RMS approach is also cited in the Selected Accomplishments section of the National Research Council's 1992 report, A Broader Agenda for Computer Science and Engineering.

Application of this theory to centralized system scheduling is well known and is discussed in several papers, including the April 1990 issue of *IEEE Computer* [9]. The focus of this chapter is on recent generalization of this theory to schedule large-scale distributed real-time systems. A more detailed discussion of the concepts discussed in this chapter may be found in [7]. In addition, we provide an example that illustrates some of the practical development problems in the application of this approach in actual system development. For example, to address the increasing trend toward open system components and to control costs, system designers have to use standardized subsystem components, which may or may not support real-time computing needs. To reduce the number of processors in a system, sometimes both real-time and non-real-time applications must co-exist in some processor and share the network with real-time traffic.

The following is a high-level view of our example application, which will be presented and solved in detail later in this chapter. Since there does not currently

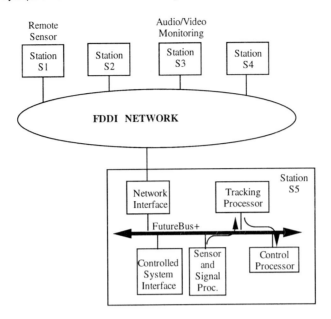

**Figure 7.1**  Block Diagram of Distributed Real-Time System

exist a widely available standard network that supports GRMS, we build our example system around the ANSI X3T9.5 FDDI network, as shown in Figure 7.1. Since IEEE Futurebus+ (896) and POSIX.4a support the use of GRMS for real-time applications, we use them in our example as the station backplane and operating system, respectively. From the application viewpoint, our example consists of both classical real-time surveillance and control applications, and multimedia applications.

The rest of the chapter is organized as follows. Section 7.2 presents a synopsis of generalized rate monotonic theory for centralized systems. Section 7.3 describes the theoretical extensions necessary for applying GRMS to a distributed system. Section 7.4 introduces the notion of scheduling abstractions, which is a technique to use and analyze existing subsystems that are not designed to support GRMS. This is a very important aspect in the application of this theory to real-world systems. Section 7.5 describes a comprehensive example that illustrates task scheduling within subsystems as well as end-to-end scheduling in a large real-time system. We make concluding remarks in Section 7.6.

## 7.2  Synopsis: GRMS in Centralized Systems

A real-time system typically consists of both periodic and aperiodic tasks. A periodic task $\tau_i$ is characterized by a worst-case computation time $C_i$ and a period $T_i$. Unless mentioned otherwise we assume that a periodic task must finish by the end of its period. Tasks are *independent* if they do not need to synchronize with each other. By using either a simple polling procedure or a more advanced technique such as a sporadic server [14], the scheduling of aperiodic tasks can be treated within the rate monotonic framework. In each case C units of computation is allocated in a period of T for aperiodic activity. However, the management and replenishment of the capacity is different in each case.

The scheduling of independent periodic tasks was originally considered by Liu and Layland [6]. The scheduling of periodic tasks with synchronization requirements can be addressed by a simple extension to the original formula as follows [10].

**Theorem 7.2.1** *A set of n periodic tasks scheduled by the rate monotonic algorithm will always meet its deadlines, for all task phasings, if*

$$\forall\, i\; 1 \le i \le n \quad \sum_{j=1}^{i} \frac{C_j}{T_j} + \frac{B_i}{T_i} \le i(2^{1/i} - 1) \tag{7.1}$$

*where $B_i$ is the duration in which task $\tau_i$ is blocked by lower-priority tasks.*

This blocking is also known as *priority inversion*. The effect of this blocking can be modeled as though task $\tau_i$'s utilization is increased by an amount $B_i/T_i$. Theorem 7.2.1 shows that the duration of priority inversion reduces *schedulability*, the degree of processor utilization at or below which all deadlines can be met. Priority inversion in a centralized system can occur when tasks have to synchronize and have common critical sections. This inversion can be controlled by a *priority ceiling protocol*. The priority ceiling protocol is a real-time synchronization protocol described in detail in [10]. Under this protocol there are no mutual deadlocks, and a higher-priority task can be blocked by lower-priority tasks at most once. As a result the worst-case duration of blocking is the longest critical section that may block a task.

A tutorial on GRMS that contains further details on these issues is given in [9].

## 7.3   Distributed System Extensions for GRMS

Scheduling in a network is different from scheduling in a centralized environment. In a centralized system, all resource requests are immediately known to the centralized scheduler. In some networks distributed scheduling decisions must be made with incomplete information. From the perspective of any particular station, some requests could be delayed and some may never be seen, depending on the relative position of the station in the network. The challenge is to achieve predictability under these circumstances.

To address this challenge GRMS theory has to be extended. Certain basic concepts such as schedulability and preemption need to be revisited, and some concepts such as system consistency need to be developed.

## 7.3.1    Extensions to Schedulability Concept

In a real-time system a particular activity is said to have "met its deadline" if the activity completes by its deadline. In scheduling tasks on a processor each task is said to have met its deadline if it completes execution by a certain time before the end of its period. In a communication network, the delay incurred by a message in reaching its destination is the sum of the transmission delay and the propagation delay. The transmission delay is the time between message arrival at a station and the time at which it is transmitted. The transmission delay can be treated analogously to task execution on a processor. However, the propagation delay can be longer than packet transmission times, causing the transmission of the next message to begin before a particular message reaches its destination. This occurs in networks such as FDDI, IEEE 802.6 distributed-queue dual-bus (DQDB), and even IEEE 802.5 token rings when early token release is used. It is therefore useful to separate transmission delay and propagation delay and consider the notion of *transmission schedulability* [11]. A set of messages is said to be *transmission schedulable* (t-schedulable) if each message can be transmitted before its deadline. Satisfaction of the end-to-end deadline of the message can be found using the relation:

$$\text{End-to-End Deadline} \geq \text{Transmission Deadline} + \text{Propagation Delay.} \qquad (7.2)$$

For example, in an FDDI network, the worst case propagation delay is the *walk time*, defined as the time taken by a single bit to traverse the ring if no station on the ring wanted to transmit.

## 7.3.2    Preemption Control

From the user's viewpoint, a certain initial delay in setting up a periodic connection is acceptable. However, once the connection is set up, users expect a steady flow of information, and hence require that C packets be delivered every period T. We will discuss the need for preemption control to achieve the above property.

*Preemption* is the most basic concept in priority scheduling. Tasks are assigned priorities according to some algorithm to maximize resource (e.g., processor) utilization. It has been a long held belief that the idealized form of priority scheduling is to achieve instantaneous preemption; i.e., whenever a high-priority task becomes ready, the resource is immediately taken away from any lower-priority task and given to the high-priority task.

It has been assumed that increasing preemptability always leads to a minimization of priority inversion, and that priority inversion is eliminated if a higher-priority task can always preempt a lower-priority task. However, this is not true in a distributed system. In a distributed system there can be special situations when a particular preemption increases the delay experienced by lower-priority connections, but does not reduce the worst-case duration of priority inversion. We call such situations *over-preemption*, whose effect is to reduce the schedulable utilization of the network. To overcome the undesirable effect of over-preemption, a *preemption control* protocol is needed. In the following, we use a dual-link network based on the IEEE 802.6 DQDB [12] as an example to introduce the two aspects of our pre-

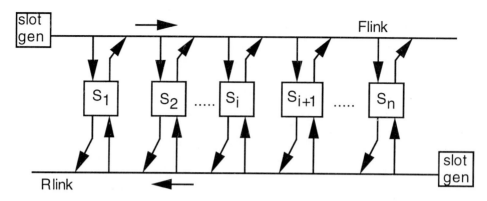

**Figure 7.2**  IEEE 802.6 DQDB Network

emption control protocol, namely *phase control* and *rate control*. Finally, we will address the logical relation between preemption control and the priority inversion.

We briefly discuss the operation of the dual-link network, the IEEE 802.6 DQDB MAC [2] operating in opposite directions. The links may be referred to as Flink and Rlink, respectively, as shown in Figure 7.2.

Fixed-length slots are generated by slot generators of the corresponding links. Although the figure shows slot generators as separate functional units, the slot generation function can be embedded in stations at the end of the links. Each station is able to transmit and receive messages on both links. The selection of the link to be used for transmission depends on the physical location of the destination. Reservation for a slot on the Flink is made on the Rlink via a **request**, and vice versa.

The operation of the protocol is based on a single busy bit, indicating whether the slot is used or free, and a request bit per slot for each priority level. Four priority levels are supported. Each priority level represents a separate access queue. A station wishing to transmit at a certain priority on Flink issues a request in a slot on Rlink by setting the proper request bit. It also places its own request into its access queue at the correct priority. On seeing a request, each station enqueues it in its access queue at the correct priority. On seeing a free slot, every station discards the top request from its highest-priority non-empty access queue, because the slot has previously been reserved by another station. If the top request is the station's request then it transmits in the slot on the Flink in addition to removing the request from its access queue. The access queues are implemented using a set of two counters for each priority level. Details may be found in [2].

The current IEEE 802.6 protocol does not have adequate mechanisms to ensure correct operation in a real-time distributed scheduling environment [13]. As a result, it exhibits unpredictable behavior under certain conditions [13, 16]. The distributed scheduling extension to GRMS reported in this chapter has been the result of studying these problems. Finally, IEEE 802.6 implements only four priority levels. As we will see in Section 7.4, this also results in a reduction of schedulability. However, IEEE 802.6 deficiencies mentioned here can be solved by extensions to

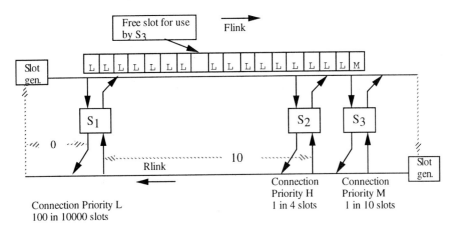

**Figure 7.3**  Preemption Control Example

the standard or by the development appropriate scheduling abstractions.

The following example shows the effects of over-preemption in a dual-link network.

**Example 7.3.1**  *Consider a dual-link network with three stations, as shown in Figure 7.3. Let the delay between $S_1$ and $S_2$ be 10 slots and between $S_2$ and $S_3$ be 1 slot, as shown. Let $S_1$ and $S_3$ be transmitting as follows: $S_1$ has a low-priority connection that uses 100 slots every 10,000 slots. $S_3$ has a medium-priority connection that wants to transmit in 1 slot every 10 slots. This leads to a slot usage pattern as shown. Slots labeled* **L** *are used by $S_1$, and the slot labeled* **M** *is used by $S_3$. Notice that $S_1$ has released an empty slot so that $S_3$ may transmit once every 10 slots as it requires. Now let $S_2$ start a new high-priority connection that needs to transmit in 1 slot every 4 slots. Since $S_2$'s request has higher priority, it preempts $S_3$'s request in $S_2$'s queue and $S_2$ will transmit in the unused slots that were meant for $S_3$. The first of the slots released by $S_1$ for $S_2$ will take 20 units of time after $S_2$'s first request to reach $S_2$. Until this time, since $S_2$ can only transmit in slots meant for $S_3$, $S_2$ can transmit only one slot in 10, which is less than it needs. As a result, even though $S_3$'s connection is interrupted, $S_2$ is not t-schedulable, resulting in an erratic connection. Therefore, the preemption of $S_3$'s request is a form of over-preemption.*

To correct the problem in the above example we need to prevent station $S_2$ from using slots released for station $S_3$. This means that $S_2$ should delay its slot use for 20 slot times after its first request, which is the round-trip delay between $S_2$ and the slot generator for the Flink. After this time, slots released by S1 in response to S2's request will reach S2. This is the phase control aspect of preemption control.

However, phase control by itself is insufficient. During the 20-unit delay, 5 cells are buffered at $S_2$. After the 20-unit delay, only 1 slot in 4 will be released for use by $S_2$. Hence $S_2$ attempts to transmit all 5 slots as soon as possible; then connection from $S_3$ will again be disrupted without improving $S_2$'s worst-case

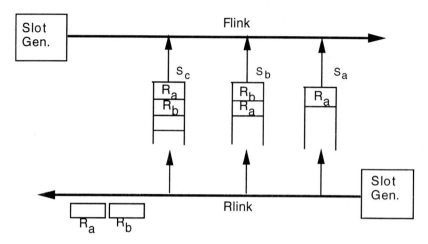

**Figure 7.4** Inconsistent Station Queues in an IEEE 802.6 DQDB Network

end-to-end latency. Observe that the 20-unit delay will add to $S_2$'s worst-case delay irrecoverably. After the connection is set up, the destination expects 1 cell every 4 slots. Hence attempting transmission of all 5 cells as soon as possible does not improve $S_2$'s worst-case performance. Hence $S_2$ should only transmit one slot every 4, after the round-trip delay of 20 slot times. This is the rate control aspect of preemption control. With phase and rate control both $S_2$ and $S_3$'s connections will be *transmission schedulable.*

Finally, we want to point out that from an implementation viewpoint, the preemption control occurs at a layer higher than the priority queueing mechanism. Prioritized packets released by preemption control protocol into the MAC layer will follow the usual priority queueing rules as in a centralized system.

### 7.3.3   System Consistency

As discussed before, stations in a distributed system may have incomplete or delayed information of the system state. This may lead to inconsistent views of the system state as illustrated by the following example.

**Example 7.3.2** *Consider three stations $S_c$ and $S_b$ and $S_a$ in a dual-link network as shown in Figure 7.4. Suppose that $S_b$ enters its own request $R_b$ in its transmission queue and then attempts to make a request on the Rlink. Let $S_b$ be prevented by making a request on Rlink by higher-priority requests until request $R_a$ by station $S_a$ passes by. On the request stream $R_a$ precedes $R_b$, while in $S_b$'s transmission queue $R_b$ precedes $R_a$. After the requests are registered in station $S_c$, the transmission queue of $S_c$ will have $R_a$ preceding $R_b$, which is inconsistent with the queue of station $S_b$.*

To address this problem we introduce the concept of system consistency. System consistency can be defined as follows: In a distributed system it is possible for two request entries to exist in multiple queues. For example, in a dual-link network two requests can exist simultaneously in multiple station queues [2]. A system is said to be *consistent* if and only if the order of the same entries in different station queues is consistent with each other. For example, in a dual-link network, if request $R_1$ and request $R_2$ both exist in queue $Q_a$ and queue $Q_b$, and if $R_1$ is ahead of $R_2$ in $Q_a$, then $R_1$ must also be ahead of $R_2$ in $Q_b$.

The inconsistency problem can lead to conflicts between distributed scheduling actions. Inconsistency can be avoided by the following rule: A station is not permitted to enter its request in its own queue until it has successfully made the request on the link. This makes the entries in each queue consistent with the ordering of requests on the link. Therefore, all the queues will be consistent with each other. In the above example, station $S_b$ cannot enter its request in its queue until it can make a request on the link. Hence $S_b$'s request will be after $S_a$'s request, both on the link and in $S_b$'s queue.

In the preceding paragraphs we have highlighted fundamental new issues in distributed real-time system design. These issues are intrinsic to a wide area network where communication delays are long and scheduling has to be carried out in parallel by distributed stations with partial or delayed information. Any distributed real-time system protocol must address at least some of these issues.

A formal description of the above concepts is described as a coherent reservation protocol (CRP) and a preemption-control protocol [12]. The important theoretical result of this work is summarized by the following theorem.

**Theorem 7.3.1** *For a given a set of periodic connections in a dual-link network that follows CRP, if the set of connections is schedulable in a centralized preemptive priority-driven system with zero (negligible) propagation delay, then the set of connections is transmission schedulable in a dual-link network.*

The importance of this theorem is that even in a wide area network with incomplete information scheduling decisions can be made as though it is a centralized system. This allows us to use GRMS seamlessly in the analysis of such systems.

## 7.4    Scheduling Abstractions

GRMS assumes preemptive, priority scheduling. Ideally, each distinct period corresponds to a distinct priority level. However, only a limited number of priorities can be supported by hardware. The effect of limited priority levels is reduced schedulability, as illustrated by the following diagram [11]

Figure 7.5 plots the schedulability as a function of priority bits, relative to the schedulability with as many priority levels as needed under the condition that the ratio between the largest and the shortest period is 100,000 [11]. As can be seen, the schedulability loss is negligible with 8 encoded priority bits, which corresponds to 256 priority levels. In other words, the worst-case schedulability obtained with 8 priority bits is close to that obtained with an unlimited number of priority levels.

To use GRMS for the development of real-time computing systems, we would like to use subsystems that support the use of GRMS, such as Futurebus+, POSIX.4,

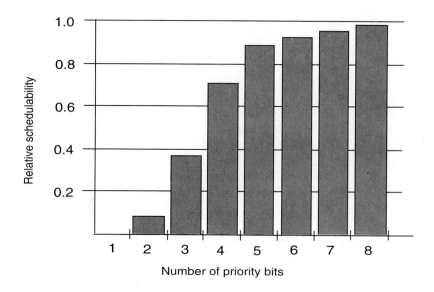

**Figure 7.5** Schedulability Loss vs. the Number of Priority Bits

and Ada 9x. However, we may have to use some components that do not support GRMS. In this case, we need to develop a *scheduling abstraction* for the sub-system so that it can be treated as if it supports GRMS. Although the scheduling abstraction allows the use of GRMS, it comes at a cost of reduced schedulability, due to the lack of direct support. With scheduling abstractions, we can provide application developers a consistent scheduling interface that allows them to develop applications as if every sub-system supports GRMS. In the following, we demonstrate the creation of scheduling abstractions by using the FDDI timed token protocol as an example.

FDDI is a 100-Mbit/s local/metropolitan area network that has gained recent popularity. FDDI is a token ring protocol that uses a timed token access method [1]. In a token rotation media access protocol, stations are connected to form a ring. All messages move around the ring and are repeated by each station through which they pass. A station reading its own address as the destination copies the packet and then passes the packet to the next station in the ring. Once the frame reaches the source station, it is removed from the ring. The permission to transmit is granted to a station that is in possession of a special type of frame called a *token*. The time for a token to traverse an idle ring is called the *walk time*, denoted here as $W_T$.

Under this protocol, stations on the network choose a *target token rotation time* (TTRT). A station in the FDDI protocol can transmit in either synchronous or asynchronous mode. Each station is allocated a *synchronous capacity*, which is the maximum time a station is permitted to transmit in synchronous mode every time it receives the token. Synchronous capacities of each station are restricted to a pre-allocated fraction of $(TTRT - W_T)$, such that the cumulative synchronous capacity of the entire network is bounded by $(TTRT - W_T)$. When a station receives a token it first transmits its synchronous traffic for an amount of time bounded by its synchronous capacity. Then it may transmit asynchronous traffic only if the the time since the previous token departure from the same station is less than TTRT. This protocol forces the token to rotate at a speed such that the time between two consecutive token visits is bounded by 2*TTRT [8]. In a network that uses only synchronous mode, time between consecutive token arrivals is bounded by one TTRT.

Real-time scheduling analysis of FDDI for the case of one periodic connection per station has been developed [3]. In this chapter, using the normalized proportional allocation scheme in [3] we create a scheduling abstraction when there is more than one periodic connection per station. In the development of this abstraction we need to consider priority granularity, priority inversion, system consistency, pre-emption control, and transmission schedulability. We will now develop the abstraction and describe how we address each of the above issues.

In an FDDI network that uses only synchronous mode, each station $S_i$ can transmit once every TTRT for an amount equal to an assigned synchronous capacity $H_i$. Therefore, the resource (network) is allocated to stations in a time-division multiplexed fashion, with no priority between stations. As an example, Figure 7.6 shows the transmission sequence from three stations, $S_1$, $S_2$, and $S_3$, allocated bandwidths of $H_1$, $H_2$, and $H_3$, respectively. Hence it may appear from Figure 7.5 that the schedulable utilization is zero. However, the order of message transmissions from each station may be prioritized. Furthermore, if since each station implements sufficient priorities to use its dedicated portion of the bandwidth, there is no schedulability loss within stations. However, since there is no priority arbitration between stations, a station with the token can transmit lower-priority messages even when high-priority messages are waiting. In this sense, it is a bounded priority inversion and limits the schedulable utilization of the network.

The conditions that a message must satisfy, for it to be schedulable in an FDDI network that operates in synchronous mode are as follows:

- Each connection's period $T_i$ must satisfy the relation $T_i \geq TTRT$.

- Each station $S_i$ must be allocated enough synchronous capacity $H_i$ so that each connection in the station is t-schedulable.

A simple scheme for synchronous bandwidth allocation is the normalized proportional scheme suggested by [3]. The total available bandwidth on each token rotation is given by $(TTRT - W_T)$. The normalized proportional allocation scheme gives each station a fraction of this bandwidth, consistent with that station's contribution to the total network utilization. Therefore, the bandwidth $H_i$ allocated to station $S_i$ is given by:

$$H_i = \frac{U_i}{U}(TTRT - W_T). \tag{7.3}$$

$U_i$ is the network bandwidth utilized by station $S_i$ and $U = U_1 + \ldots + U_n$. $TTRT$ is the target token rotation time and $W_T$ is the walk time. The following example demonstrates this formula:

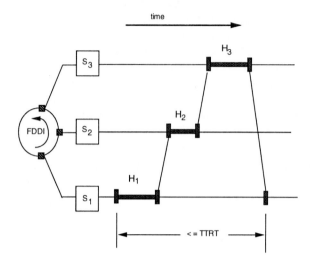

**Figure 7.6** Transmission Sequence from Three Stations in Synchronous Mode

**Example 7.4.1** *Suppose that we have three periodic messages* $\tau_1$, $\tau_2$ *and* $\tau_3$, *to be transmitted from three stations,* $S_1$, $S_2$, *and* $S_3$, *respectively, on an FDDI network. Let the TTRT be 8 and the walk time* $W_T$ *be 1.*

- *Message* $\tau_1$: $C_1 = 7$; $T_1 = 100$;

- *Message* $\tau_2$: $C_2 = 10$; $T_2 = 145$;

- *Message* $\tau_2$: $C_3 = 15$; $T_2 = 150$;

*where* $C_i$ *is the transmission time and* $T_i$ *is the period of message* $\tau_i$. *The utilization of the above message set,* $U = 0.239$. *Applying the above formula,* $H_1 = 2.05$, $H_2 = 2.02$, $H_3 = 2.93$.

Consider the application of GRMS to an FDDI network that transmits only in synchronous mode. Let synchronous bandwidths be allocated to stations by some technique such as the above formula. Notice that if each station uses its allocated synchronous bandwidth, the actual token rotation time (TRT) (time between consecutive token arrivals at the station) attains its maximum possible value TTRT. However, if any station does not use its allotted bandwidth, then the token rotates faster than TTRT.

Consider any station $S_i$ in the network. Let the capacity allocated to the station be $H_i$. Let the station be a source of periodic messages $\tau_{1i} = (C_{1i}, T_{1i}), (\tau_{2i} = C_{2i}, T_{2i}), \ldots, (\tau_{ni} = C_{ni}, T_{ni})$. The station can transmit for up to $H_i$ units of time, every TTRT.

GRMS can be applied to scheduling messages in this station as follows: In addition to the message set that must be transmitted, the station can be considered to have another 'message' to transmit. The period of this message is the actual token rotation time TRT. The 'transmission time' of this message is given by $(TRT - H_i)$. We refer to this task as Token Rotation Message $\tau_{tr}$. The token rotation message represents the time that the station is prevented from transmitting every token rotation. The longest period of the token rotation task is TTRT. A necessary condition for schedulability is that the period of the highest-frequency message must be longer than TTRT. Note that the actual token rotation time can be shorter than TTRT if other stations do not completely use their synchronous allocations. However, station $S_i$ is guaranteed $H_i$ amount of bandwidth in every token rotation cycle. Hence if connections in $S_i$ are schedulable in the longest cycle (TTRT), they are also schedulable in any shorter cycle.

The FDDI scheduling abstraction described above has two levels of scheduling. At the higher level, the resource capacity is allocated between applications in a time-division-multiplexed (TDM) manner. Within each allocation, the resource schedules activities using GRMS. This abstraction can be used directly for sharing a processor between real-time and non-real-time applications. In this case, we create a cycle and allocate portions of the cycle to real-time and non-real-time activities, respectively. Observe that similar to FDDI, the cycle has to be no greater in length than the period of the highest-frequency real-time task. The TDM switching overhead can be treated similar to the walk time in the FDDI case.

Finally, consistency between station queues is not an issue since each station has its own dedicated bandwidth. Preemption control is still necessary when a new connection has to be established and synchronous bandwidth has to be reallocated. In this case, the connection should first exercise phase control and avoid transmitting until bandwidth is allocated for the new connection. Furthermore, the new allocation should exercise rate control and not transmit all its accumulated packets. Finally, the concept of transmission schedulability is directly applicable in this abstraction, as will be discussed in Section 7.5.

# 7.5    Example Application

We have reviewed the theory for applying GRMS to a distributed system and developed a scheduling abstraction for FDDI, the only component in our system that does not directly support GRMS. This example illustrates how to apply GRMS extensions to schedule a distributed system that consists of both real-time control activities and multimedia communication. This example will illustrate the following concepts:

- Management of end-to-end deadline by partitioning into subsystem deadlines.

- Sharing of a processor by both real-time and non-real-time activities.

- Application of the FDDI scheduling abstraction.

- Management of propagation delay and jitter.

## 7.5.1    Description of Example

Consider the system in Figure 7.1. It is built around an FDDI network. Station $S_5$ is a multiprocessor built around a Futurebus+ backplane. The control processor in station $S_5$ receives a variety of sensor, audio, and video information, from both local and remote sources. There exists an end-to-end deadline from each source to the control processor. The end-to-end deadline is the permissible delay between the instant the information is captured at the sensor, to the instant the system outputs its response to the information. We assume that the priority ceiling protocol is used for task synchronization. A high-level description of the data flow in this example system is as follows. All time units in the following example are milliseconds.

### Traffic Across Network

- *Station $S_1$:* Remote sensor information is captured and transmitted across the network to the control processor in Station $S_5$. The station transmits 1.0 Mbits of data every 150. Also sends 5 Mbits of data every 100 to stations $S_2$ and $S_4$.

- *Station $S_3$:* Video monitoring station captures audio and video information and transmits it over the network to the control processor in $S_5$. The required end-to-end deadline is 100 . The video source is $1024 \times 768$ pixels per frame at 24 bits/pixel and 30 frames/sec. Three CD-quality audio channels sampled at 44.1 kHz with 32 bits/sample are also transmitted.

### Workload in Station $S_5$.

- *Signal Processor Tasks:* The local sensor takes an observation every 40. To reduce unnecessary bus traffic the signal processing task processes the signal and averages it every 4 cycles before sending it to the tracking processor.

- *Tracking Processor Tasks:* After the task executes it sends the result to the control processor with a period of 160. Task $\tau_3$ on the control processor uses this tracking information. In addition, the end-to-end latency of the pipeline of data flow from the sensor to the control processor should be no more than 785.

- *Control Processor Tasks:* The control processor has additional periodic and aperiodic tasks which must be scheduled.

  - Aperiodic event handling with an execution time of 5 and an average inter-arrival time of 100;
  - A periodic task for handling local feedback control with a computation requirement and a given period. Task $\tau_2 : C_2 = 78; T_2 = 150$;
  - A periodic task that utilizes the tracking information received. Task $\tau_3 : C_3 = 30; T_3 = 160$;
  - A periodic task responsible for reporting status across the network with a given computation time and period. Task $\tau_4 : C_4 = 10; T_4 = 300$;
  - In addition, there is an existing non-real-time application which requires 9% of the CPU cycles to meet its performance goals.

**Partitioning of End-to-End Deadlines.**    We now discuss the assignment of deadlines. When a message is sent within a station, it can be implemented by passing a message pointer to the receiving task and hence can be treated as any other OS overhead. However, when a message is sent outside the processor boundary, an integrated approach to assign message and task deadlines needs to be developed. Consider the situation in Figure 7.1.

- The sensor takes an observation every 40.

- The signal processing task processes the signal and every 4 cycles it averages the result and sends it to the tracking processor every 160.

- The tracking processor task executes with a period of 160. It then sends a message to the control processor.

- Task $\tau_3$ on the control processor that uses the tracking information has a computational requirement of 30, and period of 160 as given above. Recall that the end-to-end latency for the control processor to respond to a new observation by the sensor needs to be less than 785.

A guiding principle in partitioning the deadline is to try and minimize the impact of workload changes in a subsystem and to contain the impact within the subsystem. If each resource is allowed a full period delay, each subsystem can be analyzed as if it is an independent resource. An alternate approach is to determine the completion time at each resource and the end-end delay is the sum of the completion times. This approach is more sensitive to workload changes.

Finally, when a task is scheduled on multiple resources in series, it may arrive at the next resource well before its deadline on the current resource. If we schedule the task immediately upon its arrival, it will create a *jitter* problem, as illustrated below.

**Example 7.5.1**  *Consider two resources $R_1$ and $R_2$ connected in series. Assume that task $\tau_1$ has a period of 10. Furthermore $\tau_1$ is allocated a full period on each resource, and it uses each of the two resources for 5 units. Let task $\tau_2$ only use the second resource for 3 units, with a period of 12 units. Let the first instance of $\tau_1$ arrive at $R_1$ at $t = 0$, and let the first instance of $\tau_2$ arrive at $R_2$ at $t = 10$.*

*Suppose the first instance of $\tau_1$ at resource $R_1$ completes its execution and arrives at $R_2$ at $t = 10$. Since $\tau_1$ has higher priority than that of $\tau_2$, it will immediately use $R_2$, preempting $\tau_2$. Observe that the second instance of $\tau_1$ arrives at $R_1$ at $t = 10$. Suppose this instance is not delayed at $R_1$. Then at $t = 15$ the second instance of $\tau_1$ will begin to use $R_2$, further preempting $\tau_2$'s starting time to $t = 10$. As a result $\tau_2$ will miss its deadline at $t = 12$.*

The jitter effect can easily be controlled by a simple rule: A task becomes ready to use a resource at the beginning of a new period. Using this rule in the above example, the second instance of $\tau_1$ will be buffered and will become ready to use $R_2$ only at $t = 20$. In the following discussion we assume that this rule is enforced. It should be noted that jitter control is a special case of the phase control aspect of preemption control.

The steps involved in deadline partitioning are as follows: First we try to use the rate monotonic priority assignment. Since rate monotonic analysis guarantees end-of-period deadlines, we assume that the end-to-end delay is the sum of the period for each resource. Since the signal processor averages four cycles, each 40 units long, its delay is up to 160. Each of the other resources has a delay up to one period, which is 160. That is, the total delay using rate monotonic scheduling is bound by $4 \times 40 + 160 + 160 + 160 + 160 = 800$. If it were less than the allowable delay, then rate monotonic priority assignment could be used for all the resources. However, the specified maximum allowable latency is 785. Hence we may need to use deadline monotonic scheduling [5] for at least some of the resources in the path.

The deadline monotonic scheduling algorithm is a generalization of the rate monotonic scheduling algorithm. Rate monotonic scheduling assumes that the deadline of a periodic task is at the end of each period. Liu and Layland proved that it is optimal to give higher priorities to tasks with shorter periods. They referred to this priority assignment as the rate monotonic scheduling algorithm [6]. Leung and Whitehead [5] proved that it is optimal to assign higher priorities to tasks with shorter deadlines when deadlines are smaller than periods. They referred to this priority assignment method as the deadline monotonic scheduling algorithm [5].

From a software engineering viewpoint, it is advisable to give a full period delay for global resources such as the bus or the network since their workload is more susceptible to frequent changes. Since there are two bus transfers involved, we attempt to assign a full period to each. We also attempt to assign a full period to the signal and tracking processors. Hence the required completion time of the control processor task $\tau_3$ should be no greater than $785 - 4 \times 160 = 145$. We therefore assign a deadline of 145 to control processor task $\tau_3$.

**Scheduling Tasks on the Control Processor.**    We will concentrate on scheduling analysis of tasks in the control processor using the completion time test described below. Scheduling the backplane and other processors is similar. First, we need to create two virtual processors to separate the real-time and non-real-time applications. We select the length of the TDM cycle to be the same as the shortest period among the real-time tasks, that is, 100. Let the virtual processor switching overhead be 0.5. Out of 100, 9 will be allocated to non-real-time activities and 90 to real-time virtual processor, and one unit is lost in switching overhead.

**Completion Time Test.**    The completion time test is a faster algorithm to test the schedulability of a task set than the scheduling point test that is usually used. It is based on the *critical zone* theorem [6], which states that if a task meets its first deadline even when all higher-priority tasks become ready at the same time, then it can meet all future deadlines. Consider any task $\tau_n$ with a period $T_n$, deadline $D_n \leq T_n$, and computation $C_n$. Let tasks $\tau_1$ to $\tau_{n-1}$ have higher priorities than $\tau_n$. Note that at any time $t$, the total cumulative demand on CPU time by these $n$ tasks is:

$$W_n(t) = \sum_{j=1}^{n} C_j \left\lceil \frac{t}{T_j} \right\rceil. \tag{7.4}$$

$$\text{Set } t_0 \leftarrow W_i(t = 0)$$
$$t_1 \leftarrow W_i(t_0)$$
$$t_2 \leftarrow W_i(t_1)$$
$$\vdots$$
$$t_k \leftarrow W_i(t_{k-1})$$
$$\text{Stop when } (W_i(t_k) = t_k)$$

**Figure 7.7**  Finding Minimum $t$, Where $W_i(t) = t$

The term $\lceil t/T_j \rceil$ represents the number of times task $\tau_j$ arrives in time $t$, and therefore $C_j \lceil t/T_j \rceil$ represents its demand in time $t$. For example, let $T_1 = 10, C_1 = 5$, and $t = 9$. Task $\tau_1$ demands 5 units of execution time. When $t = 11$, task $\tau_1$ has arrived again and has a cumulative demand of 10 units of execution. Suppose that task $\tau_n$ completes its execution exactly at time $t$ before its deadline $D_n$. This means that the total cumulative demand from the $n$ tasks up to time $t$, $W_n(t)$, is exactly equal to $t$; that is, $W_n(t) = t$. A technique for finding this time is given in Figure 7.7.

Consider the following as an example of the completion time test.

**Example 7.5.2** *Consider a task set with the following independent periodic tasks:*

- *Task $\tau_1 : C_1 = 20; T_1 = 100; D_1 = 100;$*

- *Task $\tau_2 : C_2 = 90; T_2 = 145; D_2 = 145;$*

  *Task $\tau_1$ is clearly schedulable. The schedulability of $\tau_2$ can be tested as follows:*
  $t_0 = C_1 + C_2 = 20 + 90 = 110$
  $t_1 = W_2(t_0) = 2C_1 + C_2 = 40 + 90 = 130$
  $t_2 = W_2(t_1) = 2C_1 + C_2 = 40 + 90 = 130 = t_1$
  *Hence task $\tau_2$ finishes at 130 and is schedulable.*

Let the real-time task set in control processor execute on the real-time virtual processor. The effect of the TDM cycle spent in non-real-time and overhead processing can be modeled as a high-priority task with a period of 100 and execution of 10. Consider the requirement for aperiodic event handling with an execution time of 5 and an average inter-arrival time of 100. We create an equivalent sporadic server task with 10 units execution and a duration of 100, which has the highest priority. A simple approximate analysis consists of two parts.

- First, with 90% probability the aperiodic arrives during the real-time virtual processor operation. Since we have allocated twice the average required bandwidth, we assume that the probability of an aperiodic task arriving when there is no server capacity is negligibly small. Together with the fact that the aperiodic task has the highest priority, we can use a a simple M/D/1 queueing formula. We have the following result [4]:

**166**     A Systematic Approach to Designing Distributed Real-Time Systems     Chap. 7

**Table 7.1  Tasks on the Control Processor**

| Task | C | T | D |
|------|----|-----|-----|
| $\tau_1$ | 20 | 100 | 100 |
| $\tau_2$ | 78 | 150 | 150 |
| $\tau_3$ | 30 | 160 | 145 |
| $\tau_4$ | 10 | 300 | 300 |

$$W = \frac{\rho C}{2(1-\rho)} + C = 5.132, \tag{7.5}$$

where $\rho = 5/100$, the utilization by the aperiodic task, and $C = 5$.

- Second, with 10% probability the aperiodic arrives during the non-real-time virtual processor operation. Since the average aperiodic inter-arrival time is ten times longer than the duration of the non-real-time virtual processor, we assume that at most one aperiodic message can arrive when the virtual processor is executing. In this case the aperiodic must wait on average for half the duration of the non-real-time processor, including switching overhead. In this case the response time of the aperiodic message is $5 + 5.132 = 10.132$.

Finally, considering both cases the response time of the aperiodic task is: $0.9 \times 5.132 + 0.1 \times 10.132 = 5.632$. It is important to note that the analysis of aperiodic tasks is in general complex and may require simulation.

Since the TDM cycle and sporadic server have the same period, they may be considered as a single task: Task $\tau_1 : C_1 = 20; T_1 = 100$. Therefore, tasks on the control processor are as shown in Table 7.1.

Let tasks $\tau_1$, $\tau_2$, and $\tau_3$ share several data structures guarded by semaphores. Suppose the duration of critical sections accessing shared data structures is bounded by 10 units. Suppose the priority ceiling protocol is used. Since the priority ceiling protocol is assumed to be implemented, higher-priority tasks are blocked at most once for 10 by lower-priority tasks.

We now check whether or not $\tau_3$ completes within 145 under rate monotonic priority assignment. Under rate monotonic assignment, $\tau_1$ and $\tau_2$, have higher priority than $\tau_3$. Hence the completion of $\tau_3$ can be calculated using the completion time test as follows:

$$t_0 = C_1 + C_2 + C_3 = 20 + 78 + 30 = 128$$

$$t_1 = W_3(t_0) = 2C_1 + C_2 + C_3 = 40 + 78 + 30 = 148$$

$$W_3(t_1) = 2C_1 + C_2 + C_3 = 148 = t_1.$$

Therefore, the completion time of $\tau_3$ is 148, which is later than the required completion time of 145. In order to meet the deadline of 145 imposed by the maximum allowable latency requirement of the preceding section, we use the deadline monotonic priority assignment. This makes task $\tau_3$'s priority higher than task $\tau_2$'s priority, since $\tau_3$ has the shorter deadline.

Under this priority assignment, the schedulability of each task can be checked as follows: Task $\tau_1$ can be blocked by lower-priority tasks for 10, i.e., $B_1 = 10$. The schedulability test for task $\tau_1$ is a direct application of Theorem 7.2.1.

$$\frac{C_1}{T_1} + \frac{B_1}{T_1} = 0.2 + 0.1 = 0.3 \leq 1(2^{1/1} - 1) = 1.0 \tag{7.6}$$

Therefore, task $\tau_1$ is schedulable. Task $\tau_3$ is the second-highest-priority task. Since $\tau_3$ has a deadline shorter than its period, the schedulability test for $\tau_3$ can be checked as follows. Let $E_3 = (T_3 - D_3)$. In the schedulability test of $\tau_3$, the utilization of task $\tau_2$ does not appear, since $\tau_2$ has a lower priority and does not preempt $\tau_3$. Because of $\tau_2$ has a lower priority, its critical section can delay $\tau_3$ by 10 . Therefore, $B_3 = 10$.

$$\frac{C_1}{T_1} + \frac{C_3}{T_3} + \frac{E_3}{T_3} + \frac{B_3}{T_3} = 0.2 + 0.188 + 0.094 + 0.0625 = 0.545 \leq 2(2^{1/2} - 1) = 0.828 \tag{7.7}$$

Now consider the third-highest-priority task, $\tau_2$. From the viewpoint of the rate monotonic assignment, the deadline monotonic assignment is a 'priority inversion'. Therefore, in the schedulability test for task $\tau_2$, the effect of blocking has to include $\tau_3$'s execution time. The blocking time is $B_2 = (C_3 + 0)$. The zero indicates that there can be no lower-priority task blocking $\tau_2$.

$$\frac{C_1}{T_1} + \frac{C_2}{T_2} + \frac{B_2}{T_2} = 0.2 + 0.52 + 0.2 = 0.92 > 2(2^{1/2} - 1) = 0.828 \tag{7.8}$$

The schedulability test of Theorem 7.2.1 fails for $\tau_2$. The schedulability of $\tau_4$ can be checked by the following simple test since there is neither blocking or deadline before its end of period.

$$\frac{C_1}{T_1} + \frac{C_2}{T_2} + \frac{C_3}{T_3} + \frac{C_4}{T_4} = 0.2 + 0.52 + 0.188 + 0.033 = 0.941 > 4(2^{1/4} - 1) = 0.757 \tag{7.9}$$

Note that the schedulability test of Theorem 7.2.1 fails for both tasks $\tau_2$ and $\tau_4$. To determine their schedulability we use the completion time test. Since $\tau_1$ and $\tau_3$ must execute at least once before $\tau_2$ can begin executing, the completion time of $\tau_2$ can be no less than 128.

$$t_0 = C_1 + C_2 + B_2 = 20 + 78 + 30 = 128$$

However, $\tau_1$ is initiated one additional time in the interval $(0,128)$. Taking this additional execution into consideration, $W_2(128) = 148$.

$$t_1 = W_2(t_0) = 2C_1 + C_2 + B_2 = 40 + 78 + 30 = 148$$

Finally, we find that $W_2(148) = 148$ and thus the minimum time at which $W_2(t) = t$ is 148. This is the completion time for $\tau_2$. Therefore $\tau_2$ completes its first execution at time 148 and meets its deadline of 150.

$$W_2(t_1) = 2C_1 + C_2 + B_2 = 40 + 78 + 30 = 148 = t_1$$

Similarly, we can check the schedulability of task $\tau_4$ using the completion time test. It turns out to be schedulable.

### 7.5.2   Scheduling Messages on FDDI

The messages that exist on the FDDI network are as follows:

*Station $S_1$:* Sensor data is collected and stored. Every 150, the station transmits 1.0 Mbits of data. Let the station also transmit 5 Mbits of data every 100 to stations $S_2$ and $S_4$.

*Station 3:* Video information: The required end-to-end deadline is assumed to be 100. As an example we assume a video source of $1024 \times 768$ pixels per frame with 24 bits/pixel at 30 frames/second, compressed with a ratio of 16:1. There also exist 3 channels of CD-quality audio. Each channel is sampled at 44.1 kHz with 32 bits/sample. The end-to-end deadline for audio is also 100.

Consider scheduling of messages at station 3. We need to partition the end-to-end deadlines into subsystem deadlines. The resources that need to be scheduled along the path between the source and the control processor are as follows: the source interface processor, the network, the destination network interface, the backplane, and the control processor itself. As discussed in Section 7.5.1, the simplest way to partition the end-to-end deadline is to allow a delay up to a period on each resource.

First consider the video task. Its natural period at 30 frames/sec is 33. If we spend an entire period on each of the five resources, the end-to-end delay will exceed the limit of 100. Hence we transform the sending period to 60 Hz; i.e., we send half a frame every 16.5. For the resolution given above, this works out to no more than 6 of transmission time every period of 16.5.

Now consider the audio task. Its natural period is roughly one sample every 22 microseconds. This period is too short for the network as well as the packetization processing. Hence we transform the transmission period to 11. That is we accumulate 500 samples every 11 units for each of the three sources. This bundling results in efficient network utilization, but requires the destination to buffer and regulate the delivery of the voice packets at the source frequency. This yields no more than 0.5 of transmission time every period. The end-to-end delay over 5 resources will be no more than 55.

Each source of traffic first has to packetize the information. The schedulability analysis of the tasks running on the source network interface processor is simpler than the analysis of the control processor tasks since there is no complex data sharing between tasks. Hence we will omit the analysis and assume that it is schedulable.

Let the TTRT be 8 and let the walk time $W_T$ be 1. The approach to scheduling traffic on FDDI is as follows. Consider the scheduling of messages in a particular station $S_i$ with allotted synchronous bandwidth $H_i$. Therefore, the station can transmit for up to $H_i$ every TTRT. As discussed in Section 7.4, this can be treated as having another high-priority task with message transmission time $(TTRT - H_i)$ and period TTRT. We refer to this task as token rotation task $\tau_{tr}$. Using this framework, schedulability of traffic at each station can be independently analyzed.

Let us apply the above technique to messages at $S_3$. Let $H_3 = 4$; then $\tau_{tr} = C_{tr} = 8 - 4 = 4, T_{tr} = 8$. The message set for $S_3$ is then

- Token Rotation Message $\tau_{tr3} : C_{tr3} = 4; T_{tr3} = 8$;

- Audio Message $\tau_{13} : C_{13} = 0.5; T_{13} = 11$;

- Video Message $\tau_{23} : C_{23} = 6; T_{23} = 16.5$.

The schedulability of this message set can be checked using the completion time test. The token rotation message is obviously schedulable. Consider completion of message $\tau_1$:

$$t_0 = C_{tr3} + C_{13} = 4 + 0.5 = 4.5$$

$$t_1 = W_{13}(t_0) = C_{tr3} + C_{13} = 4 + 0.5 = 4.5$$

Hence $\tau_{13}$ is schedulable: Consider completion of message $\tau_{23}$:

$$t_0 = C_{tr3} + C_{13} + C_{23} = 4 + 0.5 + 6 = 10.5$$

$$t_1 = W_{23}(t_0) = 2C_{tr3} + C_{13} = 8 + 0.5 + 6 = 14.5$$

$$t_2 = W_{23}(t_1) = 2C_{tr3} + 2C_{13} = 8 + 1.0 + 6 = 15.0$$

$$t_3 = W_{23}(t_2) = 2C_{tr3} + 2C_{13} = 8 + 1.0 + 6 = 15.0 = t_2.$$

Hence $\tau_{23}$ is schedulable.

Similarly, we can test the schedulability of messages at station 1. If $S_1$ is allotted a synchronous bandwidth of $H_1 = 3$, the message set at $S_1$ can be written as:

- Token Rotation Message $\tau_{tr1} : C_{tr3} = 5; T_{tr3} = 8$;

- $\tau_{11} : C_{11} = 10; T_{11} = 100$;

- $\tau_{21} : C_{21} = 15; T_{21} = 150$.

Note that this message set is also schedulable. The utilization of the network is 60%.

## 7.6    Conclusions

The rate monotonic theory and its generalizations have been adopted by national high-technology projects such as the Space Station and have recently been supported by major open standards such as the IEEE Futurebus+. In this chapter, we have given a synopsis of GRMS for centralized systems. Furthermore, we have described the basic concepts in the extensions of GRMS for distributed system scheduling, namely transmission schedulability, system scheduling consistency, and preemption control. We also introduced the notion of scheduling abstractions as a technique for analysis of systems that do not directly support GRMS. Finally, we have provided an application example to illustrate the assignment of message and task deadlines, task scheduling, and message scheduling.

## Acknowledgments

The Software Engineering Institute is sponsored by the U.S. Department of Defense (DoD). This work is funded in part by the Office of Naval Research.

This work is part of Shirish S. Sathaye's doctoral dissertation at Carnegie-Mellon University, which was supported by Digital Equipment Corporation.

## References

[1] *FDDI Token Ring Media Access Control*, ANSI Standard X3.139, 1987.

[2] IEEE 802.6, *Distributed Queue Dual Bus: Metropolitan Area Network*, Draft Standard, Version P802.6/D15, October 1990.

[3] G. Agrawal, B. Chen, W. Zhao, and S. Davari. Guaranteeing synchronous message deadlines in high speed token ring networks with timed token protocol. *Proceedings of the IEEE International Conference on Distributed Computing Systems*, 1992.

[4] L. Kleinrock. *Queueing Systems*, vol. 1 John Wiley & Sons, New York, 1975.

[5] J. Leung and J. Whitehead. On the complexity of fixed-priority scheduling of periodic, real-time tasks. *Performance Evaluation*, 2:237–250, 1982.

[6] C. Liu and J. Layland. Scheduling algorithms for multiprogramming in a hard real-time environment. *Journal of the ACM*, 30(1):46–61, January 1973.

[7] S. Sathaye. *Scheduling Real-Time Traffic in Packet-Switched Networks*. Ph.D. thesis, Carnegie Mellon University, Pittsburgh, PA, June 1993.

[8] K. Sevcik and M. Johnson. Cycle time properties of the fddi token ring protocol. *IEEE Transactions on Software Engineering*, SE-13(3):376—385, 1987.

[9] L. Sha and J. Goodenough. Real-time scheduling theory and Ada. *IEEE Computer*, 23(4):53–62, April 1990.

[10] L. Sha, R. Rajkumar, and J. Lehoczky. Priority inheritance protocols: An approach to real-time synchronization. *IEEE Transactions on Computers*, 39(9):1175–1185, September 1990.

[11] L. Sha, R. Rajkumar, and J. Lehoczky. Real-time computing using Future-bus+. *IEEE Micro*, June 1991.

[12] L. Sha, S. Sathaye, and J. Strosnider. Analysis of reservation based dual link networks for real-time applications. Technical Report CMU/SEI-92-TR-10, Software Engineering Institute, Pittsburgh, PA, April 1992.

[13] L. Sha, S. Sathaye, and J.K. Strosnider. Scheduling real-time communication on dual link networks. *13th IEEE Real-Time Systems Symposium*, pages 188–197, December 1992.

[14] B. Sprunt. *Aperiodic Task Scheduling for Real-Time Systems*. Ph.D. thesis, Carnegie Mellon University, Pittsburgh, PA 15213, August 1990.

[15] J. Stankovic. Real-time computing systems: The next generation. *IEEE Tutorial on Hard Real Time Systems*, 1988.

[16] H.R. van As, J.W. Wong, and P. Zafiropulo. Fairness, priority and predictability of the DQDB MAC protocol under heavy load. *Proceedings of the International Zurich Seminar*, pages 410–417, March 1990.

# Part III

# Scheduling and Resource Management

# Chapter 8

# Scheduling Periodic and Aperiodic Tasks Using the Slack Stealing Algorithm

## John P. Lehoczky and Sandra R. Thuel

This chapter discusses the problem of jointly scheduling hard deadline periodic tasks and both hard and soft deadline aperiodic tasks using fixed-priority methods. A recently developed algorithm, the *slack stealing algorithm* developed by the authors, is introduced and its properties are discussed. The methods introduced provide a unified framework for dealing with several related problems, including reclaiming unused periodic and aperiodic execution time, load shedding, balancing hard and soft aperiodic execution time, and coping with transient overloads.

## 8.1 Introduction

Over the last decade, scheduling methods have been introduced which allow for the design of real-time systems with predictable timing correctness. Moreover, these methods have become sufficiently advanced so that many practical problems associated with these systems have been addressed successfully. The most complete theoretical results have been for the situation in which the system must process a significant number of periodic tasks, for example, tasks associated with monitoring in control systems. For this case, there are two popular approaches: (1) static or fixed-priority algorithms, including the rate monotonic and deadline monotonic algorithms [10, 11] and (2) dynamic priority algorithms, including the earliest deadline algorithm [11]. Both approaches are becoming increasingly well developed, although at the present time the static priority theory is much more complete. For example, static priority methods can:

- handle transient overloads in a predictable fashion,

- be combined with priority inheritance and the priority ceiling algorithm to prevent the unbounded priority inversions that can occur with task synchronization,

- permit the efficient joint scheduling of hard deadline periodic tasks and soft deadline aperiodic tasks,

- be analyzed to include the effects of the operating system and hardware architecture on the timing behavior of the workload.

The interested reader should consult a review article such as that by Burns [1] or Lehoczky [9] for a summary of the results available on fixed-priority scheduling.

Given the success of fixed priority scheduling methods, it is natural to attempt to extend this theory to solve other important problems that arise in real-time systems. This includes problems such as simultaneously scheduling hard deadline periodic tasks along with both hard and soft deadline aperiodic tasks. Hard deadline aperiodic tasks are of special importance. They arise in a number of ways, for example, from alert conditions or from failures of hard deadline periodic tasks which fail the reasonability checks to validate their results and must be retried and completed before the original deadline elapses. Thus another potential use of real-time scheduling theory is to help in identifying feasible ways to exploit time redundancy as a method for increasing fault tolerance.

In this chapter, we review recent developments in scheduling theory designed to determine a fixed-priority-based method to jointly schedule hard deadline periodic tasks and hard or soft deadline aperiodic tasks. The approach we discuss, called the *slack stealing algorithm*, is based on the exact schedulability analysis for fixed-priority algorithms used to schedule periodic task sets originated by Joseph and Pandya [7] and subsequently expanded upon by many other authors. The slack stealing algorithm, introduced by Lehoczky and Ramos-Thuel [8], was shown to be the optimal algorithm in the sense of uniformly minimizing the response times of soft aperiodic tasks among all algorithms which (1) use the same priority assignment for the periodic tasks, (2) meet all periodic task deadlines, and (3) process the aperiodic tasks in FIFO order. The slack stealing algorithm was further developed by Ramos-Thuel and Lehoczky [14], who applied it to the problem of scheduling hard aperiodic tasks while guaranteeing to meet all deadlines of the periodic tasks. Davis, Tindell, and Burns [4] generalized [8] to a broader class of scheduling problems and presented an algorithm to calculate the slack quantities required by the algorithm. They also introduced an approximation to the full slack stealing algorithm, which was less computationally intensive. Ramos-Thuel [17] developed the *myopic slack manager*, an approximation to the slack stealing algorithm designed to schedule periodic task retries due to the detection of faults. The development of algorithms which approximate the performance of the slack stealing algorithm while offering computational simplicity is likely to be an active area of research for years to come.

There is a significant difference between the soft deadline aperiodic scheduling problem and the hard deadline aperiodic scheduling problem. If the long-run traffic intensity of periodic and aperiodic tasks combined is less than 1 and the periodic deadlines can all be met by the scheduling algorithm, then all soft deadline aperiodic tasks will eventually be completed. There is no need to perform an acceptance test on the soft aperiodic arrivals to determine whether or not they should be serviced unless there is an aperiodic response-time requirement. If such is the case, some aperiodics might have to be rejected, or denied service, if the required response time cannot be guaranteed. This is the situation with scheduling any hard aperiodic task. Unless the arrival times between hard aperiodics are bounded below by a constant (in which case they can be modeled as *sporadic* tasks [13]), it is possible that not all of the hard deadlines of the periodic and aperiodic tasks can be met.

When not all of the timing requirements of the periodic and aperiodic tasks can be met simultaneously, the system designer is faced with a choice as to which tasks to accept for processing. This accept-reject decision is referred to as an *acceptance test*. The acceptance test must be executed on-line, since the arrival times and processing requirements of the aperiodic tasks are not known before run time, although the periodic task arrival times and processing requirements are known. There are a number of different possible approaches to deciding which tasks to accept for processing. The approach we follow is to require that all deadlines of all periodic tasks must be met. Subject to this constraint, for each hard aperiodic task, we perform an on-line acceptance test to determine whether the timing requirements of the arriving aperiodic task can be guaranteed, subject to maintaining the guarantee given to periodic tasks and any already accepted but not yet completed aperiodic tasks. If the aperiodic task cannot be guaranteed, it is rejected. The performance criterion for an algorithm of this sort would be based upon the fraction of aperiodic arrivals which can be guaranteed, the amount of aperiodic processing that is completed, or some combination of these.

There are other possible factors which would require that a different approach be taken. For example, the hard aperiodics might have importance values attached to them [12] which should be considered in the acceptance test. If a relatively important aperiodic arrival cannot be guaranteed, rather than rejecting it, it may be preferable to drop other tasks, either periodic or aperiodic, in order to accommodate the new arrival. If task execution times are stochastic, then there might be an incentive to accept tasks whose worst-case computation time cannot be guaranteed [19], because other tasks may complete early or the execution of the aperiodic task in question may be completed in less than its worst-case time. Finally, it is rarely the case that all periodic deadlines must be met [6]. If a periodic deadline is missed, a timing fault occurs, but in most systems, an occasional timing fault is of little consequence. It is important only to ensure that the timing faults associated with any periodic task are sufficiently widely spaced to maintain system integrity.

One can see that there are many valid approaches to the problem of jointly scheduling periodic and aperiodic tasks. In Section 8.4 we will discuss the optimality that can be achieved in this problem. We will find that in the soft aperiodic scheduling case, the slack stealing algorithm possesses a very strong optimality property. On the other hand, for the hard aperiodic scheduling problem, only a weak form of optimality can be achieved by any algorithm. Consequently, the choice of an appropriate scheduling algorithm depends strongly upon the nature of the real-time application workload being considered.

It is important to note that the slack stealing algorithm associated with fixed-priority scheduling algorithms discussed in this chapter can be extended to dynamic priority algorithms such as the earliest deadline algorithm. There are recent papers in the literature on the on-line scheduling of hard aperiodic tasks, including Chetto and Chetto [2] and Schwan and Zhou [15], based on the earliest deadline algorithm. Although these dynamic priority algorithms are not expressed within the context of slack stealing, it is possible to design slack stealing algorithms which are functionally and conceptually equivalent. Slack stealing algorithms which are based on dynamic priority algorithms offer potential improvements over slack stealing based on fixed priority algorithms in the sense that at least as much or more aperiodic processing can be done in any window of time. Nevertheless, in this chapter, we focus exclusively on fixed-priority scheduling methods.

This chapter is organized as follows. In Section 8.2, we present the model and notation. Section 8.3 presents the slack stealing algorithms for scheduling soft and hard aperiodic tasks. Section 8.4 addresses the question of the optimality of any such algorithm. Finally, we note that the slack stealing approach offers a unified framework for dealing with several related problems, including reclaiming unused periodic and aperiodic execution times, load shedding, balancing hard and soft aperiodic execution time, and coping with transient overloads. These generalizations are discussed in Section 8.5. Section 8.6 concludes the chapter.

## 8.2   Model

Consider a real-time system with $n$ periodic tasks, $\tau_1, \ldots, \tau_n$. Each task, $\tau_i$, has a worst-case computation requirement $C_i$, a period $T_i$, an initiation time or offset relative to some time origin $\phi_i$ where $0 \leq \phi_i < T_i$, and a hard deadline (relative to the initiation time) $d_i$. The parameters $C_i$, $T_i$, $\phi_i$, and $d_i$ are assumed to be known deterministic quantities. We require that these tasks be scheduled according to a fixed-priority algorithm, and we assume that the tasks are ordered by priority, with $\tau_1$ having highest priority, 1, and $\tau_n$ having lowest priority, $n$. For convenience, we assume that each periodic task has a distinct priority. Ordinarily these priorities would be assigned using the deadline monotonic scheduling algorithm. This fixed-priority assignment was proved to be optimal for the special case in which $d_i \leq T_i$ [10]; however, we do not require this priority assignment to hold, but we do assume that $d_i \leq T_i$. (A summary of the notation used in this section is provided in Table 8.1.)

A periodic task, say $\tau_i$, gives rise to an infinite sequence of jobs. The $k$th such job, $\tau_{ik}$, is ready at time $R_{ik} = \phi_i + (k-1)T_i$ and its $C_i$ units of required execution must be completed by time $d_{ik} = \phi_i + (k-1)T_i + d_i$ or else a *timing fault* will occur. We assume a fully preemptive system and assume that all task overheads due to scheduling or operating system functions are negligible. Finally, once tasks have been activated, they cannot suspend themselves until they have been completed.

We next introduce the aperiodic tasks, $\{J_k, k \geq 1\}$. Each aperiodic job, $J_k$, has an associated arrival time, $\alpha_k$, a processing requirement, $p_k$, and a hard deadline, $D_k$. If the aperiodic task does not have a hard deadline, we set $D_k = \infty$

**Table 8.1  Notation Used to Model Workload Requirements**

| Notation | Description |
|---|---|
| $n$ | Number of periodic tasks in the real-time workload |
| $C_i, T_i, d_i$ | Execution time, period, and deadline for periodic task $\tau_i$ |
| $R_{ij}, d_{ij}$ | Absolute arrival time and deadline for periodic job $\tau_{ij}$ |
| $\alpha_k, p_k$ | Absolute arrival time and processing requirement for aperiodic job $J_k$ |
| $D_k$ | Deadline of aperiodic job $J_k$ relative to its arrival time |

and seek to minimize its response time. If $D_k < \infty$, then we seek to complete processing of $J_k$ by $D_k$. We assume that there is no additional value for finishing the processing of $J_k$ earlier than $D_k$. The aperiodic tasks are indexed such that $0 \le \alpha_k \le \alpha_{k+1}, k \ge 1$. We assume that the aperiodic task sequence is not known in advance; however, when an aperiodic task arrives, its worst-case computation requirement and deadline are known.  When a hard aperiodic task arrives, an acceptance test is performed to determine whether the task can meet its deadline without causing any of the periodic tasks or any prior guaranteed aperiodic tasks to miss their deadlines. In addition, an accepted hard aperiodic task is assigned a priority level, and that task is enqueued in deadline order within the assigned execution priority level. A slack value is associated with any enqueued aperiodic task to denote how much additional execution time can be dedicated to processing it while still meeting its deadline.  This value is used to ensure that any new aperiodics will not cause its deadline guarantee to be violated. The acceptance test is run immediately upon a hard aperiodic task arrival, and the task is discarded immediately if it fails the test. Any soft aperiodic task can be kept for processing; however, the long-run traffic intensity of accepted work, including hard periodic, accepted hard aperiodic, and soft aperiodic tasks, must be less than 1. Thus, since all periodic deadlines are guaranteed, the hard and soft aperiodics will compete with each other for the remaining processing time. Indeed, the hard aperiodics compete with each other, because accepting one hard aperiodic task reduces the processing capacity available to other hard aperiodic tasks.

There are a number of different possible approaches to deciding which aperiodic tasks to process and which to reject. For example, it is possible to remove guaranteed aperiodic or periodic tasks to provide sufficient time to process an arriving aperiodic request, because the request has greater semantic importance. Instead of requiring that every periodic task meets its deadline, the frequency of missed deadlines can be limited. An alternative to discarding rejected tasks is to keep them available in case spare execution time becomes available from tasks completing earlier than their worst-case execution times. We discuss some of these possibilities in Section 8.5, and the methods presented in this chapter can be used to support systems in which widely differing acceptance strategies are used.

To simplify our ensuing presentation of the slack stealing framework, we assume that all periodic tasks must be guaranteed and we do not consider importance values in our scheduling criteria. Each hard deadline aperiodic task can be assigned to execute at any fixed-priority level. We assume that if an aperiodic task executes at priority level $k$, then it has lower priority than any periodic task with priority $1, \ldots, k-1$ and higher priority than any periodic task with priority $k, k+1, \ldots, n$. Aperiodic task execution at priority level 1 has the highest priority, while execution at priority level $n+1$ is equivalent to background execution.

In addition to an aperiodic task acceptance test, the scheduling algorithm must select a fixed-priority level at which to process each accepted aperiodic task. If all aperiodic tasks are soft, then the solution is straightforward. Lehoczky and Ramos-Thuel [8] showed that it is optimal to process all aperiodic tasks at the highest-priority level because this minimizes all aperiodic response times. Furthermore, it was shown that if soft aperiodic tasks are processed according to the shortest remaining processing time queue discipline, the average aperiodic response time is minimized. When aperiodic tasks have hard deadlines, the situation is different and more complicated. This difference arises because the aperiodic tasks can compete with each other. If an aperiodic task is processed at priority level $i$, then this reduces aperiodic processing capacity at all levels $i$ to $n$. Clearly, an accepted aperiodic task must be processed at a sufficiently high priority to meet its deadline; however, as low a priority level as possible should be chosen to minimize the impact on other aperiodic tasks. Hard aperiodics which are processed at any given priority level should be processed in earliest deadline order. This can be achieved simply by enqueueing the hard aperiodic tasks in deadline order within each priority level.

The above discussion should help to illustrate the fundamental difficulty in developing effective algorithms which can simultaneously schedule hard and soft aperiodics. Soft aperiodics must be run at a relatively high priority level to attain short response times. As such, they reduce the capacity for hard aperiodics at all priority levels. Furthermore, accepting hard aperiodics reduces the capacity available for soft aperiodics and increases their response time. These tradeoffs should make it clear that there will be no optimal approach to the general joint scheduling problem. The best approach will vary with the specific timing characteristics of the real-time workload, and this topic is likely to be an active area for research in the coming years. In this chapter, we focus instead on the valuable property of the slack stealing approach, its ability to provide the largest possible amount of processing time to aperiodic tasks, either hard or soft, subject to meeting all periodic deadlines. The next section develops the required calculations.

## 8.3   The Slack Stealing Algorithm

In this section, we derive functions for each priority level $i$ which give the largest amount of aperiodic processing that can be performed during any time interval $[t_0, t_1]$ and still ensure that all deadlines of all periodic tasks are met. We need to find an on-line algorithm, and the calculation of the largest possible amount of aperiodic processing that can be carried out is inherently computationally intensive, although only a polynomial function of $n$, the number of tasks. For this reason, we precompute some slack values for the various task instantiations or jobs and store them in a table. This can dramatically reduce the run-time computational

## Table 8.2  Summary of Important Terms

| Notation | Description |
|---|---|
| $\gamma_i(t)$ | Number of jobs of periodic task $\tau_i$ completed during $[0, t]$ |
| $F_{ij}$ | Latest completion time for periodic job $\tau_{ij}$ ($j$th job of $\tau_i$) |
| $A_{ij}$ | Largest amount of aperiodic processing that can be done from time 0 to the completion of $\tau_{ij}$ while meeting all deadlines for $\tau_1, \ldots, \tau_i$ |
| $L_{ij}$ | Total level $i - 1$ inactivity present in the interval $[0, d_{ij}]$ |
| $\mathcal{A}_i(t)$ | Total aperiodic processing time used during $[0, t]$ at priority level $i$ or higher |
| $\mathcal{I}_i(t)$ | Total level $i$ inactivity observed during $[0, t]$ |
| $S_i(t)$ | Slack available at priority level $i$ or higher at time $t$ while meeting all deadlines for $\tau_1, \ldots, \tau_i$ |
| $S_k^\star(t)$ | Largest aperiodic task that can be added at time $t$ with priority $k$ while meeting all deadlines for $\tau_1, \ldots, \tau_n$ |

requirement and make the slack stealing approach viable for hard real-time systems. This is done at the expense of requiring the storage of a potentially large number of constants, and the table would have to be modified if any of the tasks is modified or the system undergoes a mode change. The challenge is to find a relatively small set of constants that will bound the size of the table and still permit the calculation of the maximum available aperiodic processing time to be done at run time. This is done in the next subsections.

## 8.3.1   Slack Calculations

The approach presented in this subsection is based on the slack stealing analysis introduced by Ramos-Thuel and Lehoczky [8, 14]. Davis, Tindell, and Burns [4] presented an algorithm to compute the slack values on-line. The algorithm presented later in this subsection is a variation of the Davis, Tindell, and Burns algorithm. Unlike Davis, Tindell, and Burns, we assume that the algorithm for computing the slack values is executed before run time and that the precomputed slack values are stored in a table. This approach is particularly useful in situations in which the memory overhead associated with storing the table is preferred over the overhead of computing the slack values on-line. (Table 8.2 is a quick reference of important terms that will be introduced in the following discussion.)

Our approach is to compute the largest amount of aperiodic processing that can be done at any priority level during an interval $[0,t]$, $t \geq 0$, so that all periodic task deadlines are met. We do this by focusing on a particular priority level, say $i$, $1 \leq i \leq n$, and ignoring all periodic tasks and aperiodic processing with priority lower than $i$. Using standard methods in priority queueing theory (see, for example, Conway, Maxwell, and Miller [3]), we recognize that any time interval $[0,t]$ will consist of an alternating sequence of *level $i - 1$ busy periods* (periods during which the processor is busy with tasks having priorities higher than $i$) and *level $i - 1$ inactivity periods* (during which the processor is not processing any tasks with priority $i - 1$ or higher). The total length of the level $i - 1$ inactivity periods during $[0,t]$ is available for periodic tasks with priority $i$ or lower and aperiodic tasks at any priority level. This time cannot be allocated arbitrarily, and sufficient time must be available for each of the jobs of the lower-priority tasks to meet their deadlines. We temporarily ignore all periodic tasks with priority below $i$. This means that $C_i$ units of processing time must be available to $\tau_{ij}$ during $[R_{ij}, d_{ij}]$, until it completes its execution. These constraints can be handled by focusing attention on time intervals of the form $[0, d_{ij}]$. Let $L_{ij}$ represent the total level $i - 1$ inactivity during $[0, d_{ij}]$. We define $A_{ij}$ as the largest amount of time available for aperiodic processing between 0 and the completion time of $\tau_{ij}$ and still ensure that all deadlines associated with tasks $\tau_1, \ldots, \tau_i$ are met. $A_{ij}$ is given by

$$A_{ij} = L_{ij} - j \cdot C_i.$$

We next focus on the calculation of $L_{ij}$. As discussed above, the interval $[0, d_{ij}]$ is subdivided into alternating level $i-1$ busy periods and level $i-1$ inactivity periods. We must compute the total length of the idle periods, $L_{ij}$. This is done by starting at time 0, computing the length of the initial busy period, if any, then the length of the idle period, then the length of the next busy period, and so on. These alternating calculations continue until $d_{ij}$ is reached, and the sum of the lengths of the idle periods gives $L_{ij}$. A similar approach was described by Schwan and Zhou [15] for the case of dynamic scheduling, and an algorithm for the fixed-priority periodic case was presented by Davis, Tindell, and Burns [4]. Here we present a slightly different algorithm.

The standard method for computing the completion time of a task using a fixed-priority scheduling algorithm is to compute a work function giving the total amount of work that has arrived at any point in time. Then using a forward iterative search, the smallest time is found at which the total work arrived equals the total time elapsed. This gives the completion time of the required work and is also the first *idle instant* in the terminology of Gonzalez Harbour, Klein, and Lehoczky [5]. Typically, the work function uses a weighted summation of ceiling functions to determine the total arrived work. In fact, the ceiling function is a left-continuous function, meaning that at an instant, $t$, at which work arrives, the work function does not jump until after $t$. That is, the arrived work is not included in the work function until the instant after it arrives. This unfortunate feature of the ceiling function leads to a problem with having to force the algorithm to make a calculation an arbitrarily small instant after the time being considered. This problem can easily be avoided by using the right-continuous floor function, which will jump at the instant that work arrives.

The algorithm consists of two alternating parts, computation of the length of the level $i - 1$ idle period initiated at some time $t'$ and computation of the following level $i - 1$ busy period. At a time $t$ at which a level $i - 1$ busy period begins, all previously arrived periodic work at levels $i - 1$ or higher will be completed and a certain amount of cumulative level $i - 1$ inactivity or idleness in $[0, t]$, call it $x$, will have elapsed. The appropriate work function for initiating a level $i - 1$ busy period is given by:

$$W_{i-1}(t, x) = \sum_{j=1}^{i-1} C_j \cdot h_j(t) + x,$$

where $h_j(t) = \max(\lfloor (t - \phi_j)/T_j \rfloor + 1, 0)$, or the number of arrivals of $\tau_j$ in $[0, t]$.

One initializes a counter with the initial time $t_0$, then computes a new, later time $t_1 = W_{i-1}(t_0, x)$ at which this work will be completed. The iteration $t_{m+1} = W_{i-1}(t_m, x)$ continues until either $t_{m+1} \geq d_{ij}$, in which case the end of the interval has been reached, or $t_{m+1} = t_m$, in which case the end of the busy period has been reached. In the latter case, an idle interval with positive length will be initiated at time $t_{m+1}$, rather than merely an idle instant, because we are using the right-continuous floor function.

The idleness phase of the algorithm requires computation of the length of the idle interval, starting at some time $t$. This computation is straightforward, requiring that we find the next time that a job of any of the tasks $\tau_1, \ldots, \tau_{i-1}$ arrives. If the idle instant begins at time $t_a$, then the length of the idle interval is given by

$$I = \min_{(1 \leq j \leq i-1)} \{\phi_j + T_j \cdot h_j(t_a) - t_a\}.$$

If $(t_a + I) \geq d_{ij}$, then $d_{ij} - t_a$ is added to the level $i - 1$ accumulation and the algorithm stops. If $(t_a + I) < d_{ij}$, then I is added to the level $i-1$ accumulation, time is advanced to $(t_a + I)$, and a busy period calculation is initiated. This alternation continues until $d_{ij}$ is reached. We summarize this process in the algorithm shown in Figure 8.1. At the completion of this algorithm, $L_{ij+1}$ will contain the total level $i - 1$ inactivity during $[0, d_{ij+1}]$.

It is useful to compute the latest possible completion time of $\tau_{ij}$, denoted by $F_{ij}$. The latest completion time occurs when the $A_{ij}$ permissible units of aperiodic execution are used prior to the completion of $\tau_{ij}$. We note that $F_{ij}$ is computed without any regard to $\tau_{i+1}, \ldots, \tau_n$. In fact, the aperiodic time available often will be reduced by periodic task constraints at lower priority levels. Consequently, $\tau_{ij}$ will often finish before $F_{ij}$ even if the maximum aperiodic time is used.

This computation can be made in a straightforward manner using methods originally introduced by Joseph and Pandya [7] and subsequently generalized by other authors; however, we again present a slight variation. One is trying to compute the time at which $L_{ij+1}$ units of priority $i$ work will be completed. The computation is made by an iterative procedure, and at the starting time, 0, we use the floor function to include all work that has arrived at 0. However, once the iteration has been initiated, we use the ceiling function, so that high-priority work that arrives is not recognized until the instant after it arrives. This permits the lower-priority work to complete at an instant of level $i - 1$ idleness. To compute the latest completion times, we define several functions:

$$h_j(t) = \max\{\lfloor (t - \phi_j)/T_j \rfloor + 1, 0\}$$

$$H_j(t) = \max\{\lceil (t - \phi_j)/T_j \rceil, 0\}$$

```
/* Set initial conditions */
L_{ij+1} = L_{ij} (= 0, if j = 0)
X = d_{ij} (= 0, if j = 0)
Y = d_{ij+1}
/* Check if d_{ij} is in level i − 1 busy period (BZP) and set flag accordingly */
If (W_{i−1}(d_{ij}, L_{ij}) > d_{ij}) then (IN_BZP = TRUE) else (IN_BZP = FALSE)

Do while X < d_{ij+1}   /* Iterate until deadline is reached */
     If ( IN_BZP = TRUE ) then
          /* Compute size of the level i − 1 BZP that starts at time X */
          Z = Y − X
          Do while Z > 0 and X < d_{ij+1} /* Iterate until end of BZP */
               Y = W_{i−1}(X, L_{ij+1})
               Z = Y − X
               X = Y
               /* When Z = 0, end of BZP has been reached and *
                * X contains the time at which the BZP ended   */
          End while Z > 0 and X < d_{ij+1}
          IN_BZP = FALSE
     Else /* IN_BZP = FALSE */
          /* Compute I = length of idle interval before a level i − 1 BZP */
          I = min_{(1≤j≤i−1)} {φ_j + T_j · h_j(X) − X }
          L_{ij+1} = L_{ij+1} + min{I, d_{ij+1} − X}
          /* Set X to the start of the next level i − 1 BZP */
          X = X + min{I, d_{ij+1} − X}
          Y = d_{ij+1}
          IN_BZP = TRUE
     Endif
End while X < d_{ij+1}
```

**Figure 8.1** Algorithm for Computing $L_{ij+1}$, the Total Level $i − 1$ Inactivity in $[0, d_{ij+1}]$

$$U_{i−1}(t, x) = \sum_{j=1}^{i−1} C_j \cdot H_j(t) + x$$

$$W_{i−1}(t, x) = \sum_{j=1}^{i−1} C_j \cdot h_j(t) + x.$$

In the algorithm shown in Figure 8.2, the second argument of the functions $U$ and $W$ give the largest amount of level $i$ or lower-priority work that can be done in $[0, t]$.

Now that the slack computations have been discussed, we turn to defining the slack stealing algorithm, first for soft aperiodic tasks, then for hard periodic tasks.

```
/* Set initial conditions */
X = d_ij (= 0, if j = 0)
Y = W_{i-1}(X, L_{ij+1}) /* Initialize Y to the time required to      *
                         * complete all the periodic work in [0, X] *
                         * plus the L_{ij+1} units of inactivity     */
Z = Y - X
Do while Z > 0 /* Iterate until end of BZP is reached */
     Y = U_{i-1}(X, L_{ij+1})
     Z = Y - X
     X = Y
     /* When Z = 0, end of BZP has been reached and *
      * X contains the time at which the BZP ended   */
End while Z > 0

F_{ij+1} = X /* F_{ij+1} = latest completion time for job τ_{ij+1} */
```

**Figure 8.2** Algorithm for Computing Latest Completion Times, $F_{ij}$

## 8.3.2    The Slack Stealing Algorithm for Soft Aperiodics

We first consider the problem of scheduling soft aperiodic tasks. At any time $t$ at which there is aperiodic work to be processed, we must determine the largest amount of aperiodic processing at priority level $k$ which can be added to the system workload at time $t$ without causing any deadlines of any periodic tasks to be missed. If priority level 1 is chosen, the processing will be done immediately. If a lower priority level is chosen, then the work may be delayed by higher-priority periodic processing. Aperiodic processing at priority level $k$ does not have any impact on periodic tasks with priority levels $k - 1$ or higher, so we need only check its impact on periodic tasks of priority $k$ through $n$. Consider priority level $i$, $k \leq i \leq n$. We must both determine the amount of permissible processing and adjust for the different types of processing that were done during $[0, t]$. This requires that we keep track of certain quantities. We define:

$\mathcal{A}_i(t) =$ cumulative aperiodic processing consumed during $[0, t]$ at level $i$ or higher,

$\mathcal{I}_i(t) =$ level $i$ inactivity during $[0, t]$, for $1 \leq i \leq n$ and $t \geq 0$,

$\gamma_i(t) =$ number of jobs of $\tau_i$ completed by time $t$.

Note that $A_{ij}$, introduced in the previous subsection, denotes the total aperiodic processing available in an interval, whereas $\mathcal{A}_i$ denotes aperiodic processing time already consumed. Similarly, $L_{i+1j}$ is the total level $i$ inactivity present in an interval, while $\mathcal{I}_i$ is the amount of that level $i$ inactivity which has already been observed.

   At time $t$ the task $\tau_{i\gamma_i(t)}$ has been completed, but task $\tau_{i(\gamma_i(t)+1)}$ has not. Consequently, $A_{i(\gamma_i(t)+1)}$ units of aperiodic processing can be done at level $k$ and not cause any deadlines at level $i$ to be missed. However, some of this available time may already have been used for aperiodic processing at any priority level or for processing periodic tasks of priority lower than $i$. The aperiodic processing done during $[0,t]$ at level $i$ or higher is given by $A_i(t)$ and the level $i$ inactivity (including processor idleness) is given by $\mathcal{I}_i(t)$. Consequently, at time $t$, an aperiodic task with priority $i$ of size $S_i(t)$ can be added to the system without causing any deadlines of $\tau_i$ to be missed. Thus, $S_i(t)$ represents the amount of slack available for aperiodic processing at time $t$ at priority level $i$ or higher. It is given by:

$$S_i(t) = A_{i(\gamma_i(t)+1)} - A_i(t) - \mathcal{I}_i(t).  \tag{8.1}$$

Now, we must ensure that all deadlines of periodic tasks with priority level $k$ or lower are met, thus we must minimize $S_i$ over $k \leq i \leq n$ to ensure that all lower-priority periodic deadlines are met. Thus, the largest aperiodic task with priority $k$ that can be added to the system at time $t$ is given by $S_k^\star$, where

$$S_k^\star(t) = \min_{\{k \leq i \leq n\}} S_i(t).  \tag{8.2}$$

It was shown by Lehoczky and Ramos-Thuel that for soft deadline aperiodic processing, it is optimal to process all aperiodic tasks at priority level 1. As stated previously, processing at level 1 will be done immediately, whereas processing at lower priority levels may be delayed by higher-priority periodics. Even though the quantity of level 1 aperiodic processing that can be done continuously may be smaller, the cumulative amount of level 1 aperiodic processing that can be done in any interval will be at least as large as the cumulative amount of aperiodic processing that could be done at a lower priority level. The slack stealing algorithm services pending aperiodic tasks while $S_k^\star$ is positive. Otherwise, it services any pending periodic tasks in fixed-priority order.

### 8.3.3    The Slack Stealing Algorithm for Hard Aperiodics

Suppose that an aperiodic task, $J_k$, arrives at some time $t = \alpha_k$ with a processing requirement, $p_k$, and a deadline, $D_k$. We must determine whether there is sufficient time available during the interval between the arrival time and the deadline to complete the processing while ensuring that all the guaranteed tasks (periodics and previously guaranteed but not yet completed aperiodics) meet their deadlines. Furthermore, we must determine an appropriate priority level at which to process the task. The calculation is more difficult than the calculation for the soft deadline aperiodics, for two reasons. First, we must account for the previously guaranteed aperiodics. Second, the processing of the aperiodic may be done in a series of intervals rather than during a single interval. When the processing cannot be completed immediately, a large amount of detailed accounting is required.

We must first calculate the total aperiodic processing available at priority level $i$ during $[\alpha_k, \alpha_k + D_k]$ assuming that the new aperiodic task arrives at a time in which there are no pending aperiodic tasks which have been guaranteed but have not yet completed; that is, we address the problem of scheduling a hard aperiodic task when it arrives at an empty *aperiodic queue*. Because the calculations are complicated, we present them only for the special case when $i = 1$. We then show for any priority level $i$ how to use the calculated aperiodic processing time available to determine if the arriving aperiodic can be scheduled when there may be other pending aperiodic tasks.

We wish to compute the maximum amount of slack available for aperiodic processing at the highest priority level in the interval $[t_a, t_b]$, where $t_a = \alpha_k$ and $t_b = \alpha_k + D_k$. Before computing the slack available in $[t_a, t_b]$, we describe the general approach. We define an aperiodic processing time accumulator, $Q$, and initialize it to 0. At time $t_a$, we compute the slack which is immediately available, say $Q^\star$, using the methods described in the preceding section. We then add $\min\{Q^\star, t_b - t_a\}$ to $Q$. The minimization is needed because the aperiodic processing time $Q^\star$ can never exceed the time available to execute that processing. This slack is put to immediate use because we assume that aperiodic tasks are serviced at the highest priority. Then the clock is advanced to $t_a + Q^\star$. At this point, no further aperiodic processing can occur until the job at the lowest priority level with no slack at time $t_a + Q^\star$, say $\tau_{LJ}$, at priority level $L$, completes. Furthermore, this task will complete at its worst-case finishing time, $F_{LJ} = t_\beta$. Since there can be no slack available for aperiodic processing in the interval $[t_a + Q^\star, t_\beta]$, there is no need to recompute the slack $Q^\star$ at any other time $t$ in $[t_a, t_\beta]$. However, to correctly compute the slack available at time $t_\beta$, some variables need to be updated to reflect changes in task slack values and level $i$ inactivity due to processing activity in the interval $[t_a, t_\beta]$. To do so, we must consider every task with priority $L$ or higher which is either active at time $t_a$ or arrives during $[t_a, t_\beta]$. Each of these tasks must be completed along with $\tau_{LJ}$ by a time no later than $t_\beta$. The execution of any of these tasks $\tau_k$, $1 \le k \le L$, may constitute level $i$ inactivity being accumulated at higher priority levels for $i < k$. To account correctly for level $i$ inactivity in $[t_a, t_\beta]$, we must determine the total execution time spent in each priority level separately. Because there may be several jobs of one task that executes during the interval and the slack gained when each task finishes must be added to the slack for its corresponding priority level, we choose to consider each of these tasks separately. It is, however, straightforward to group together all tasks that complete at a single priority level during $[t_a, t_\beta]$. Once the appropriate accounting for the slack and level $i$ inactivity at each level $i$ for $1 \le i \le L$ have been done, the clock is advanced to $t_\beta$ and the same algorithm is applied to the interval $[t_\beta, t_b]$. This process is continued until $t_\beta \ge t_b$, and then $Q$ will contain the available aperiodic processing time in $[t_a, t_b]$. We now describe this in somewhat more detail.

Suppose we have an array of ordered pairs $\{F_{ij}, s(F_{ij})\}$, where $F_{ij}$ is the latest completion time for periodic job $\tau_{ij}$ and $s(F_{ij}) = (A_{ij+1} - A_{ij})$ is the amount by which $\tau_i$'s slack is increased upon the completion of its job at time $F_{ij}$. Recall that the $A_{ij}$ and $F_{ij}$ values are computed according to the algorithms presented in Section 8.3.1. The array is ordered by priority level $i$, $1 \le i \le n$, so that each row contains all the ordered pairs for a given task $\tau_i$, for all jobs of $\tau_i$ in a hyperperiod (the least common multiple of all task periods). In addition, we assume the existence of $C_i(t)$, which is the amount of periodic processing completed on the current job of $\tau_i$; $C_i(t)$ is 0 if $\tau_i$ has no pending job at time $t$. This is not a restrictive assumption in that such information is usually required by the operating system to support periodic scheduling.

We also require $(n+1)$ counters: $n$ counters of the form $S_i(t)$ to indicate the slack available for each task $\tau_i$ at time $t$ and one counter containing the aperiodic processing time available at the highest priority level at time $t$, or $S^\star(t)$. The $S_i(t)$ counters are essentially scratch variables to hold the $S_i(t)$ values defined by Equation (8.1). Recall that $S_i(t)$ gives us the maximum amount of aperiodic processing time available at time $t$, at priority level $i$ or higher. Similarly, $S^\star(t)$ is a scratch variable for $S_k^\star(t)$ given by Equation (8.2). Finally, we recall that $Q$ is an aperiodic processing accumulator which is initialized to 0 at time $t_a$ and accumulates slack as it becomes available at certain latest completion times in $[t_a, t_b]$.

Using these variables, we now describe our approach. Starting at time $t_a = t_0$, initialize all slack counters $S_i(t_0)$ to the values $S_i(t_0)$ computed according to Equation (8.1). Likewise, we determine $S^\star(t_0) = S_1^\star(t_0) = \min_{\{1 \le i \le n\}} S_i(t_0)$. The quantity $S^\star(t_0)$ is the time available for aperiodic processing at time $t_0$ and is added to $Q$. In addition, $S^\star(t_0)$ is subtracted from $S_i(t_0), 1 \le i \le n$, because it represents slack consumed for aperiodic processing at all priority levels. Refer to these updated $S_i(t_0)$ values as $S_i'(t_0)$. Now let $L$ be the lowest priority level for which $S_i'(t_0) = 0$, and let $\{t_\beta, s(t_\beta)\}$ be the first entry in the array described above corresponding to this priority level. Note that this should be the ordered pair containing the worst-case completion time for the lowest-priority job constraining the slack to 0 until time $t_\beta = F_{LJ}$, or job $\tau_{LJ}$. Now one must identify all entries in the array corresponding to jobs of priority higher than or equal to $L$ with a worst-case completion time $F_{ij} \le t_\beta$, or an arrival time $t$ before $t_\beta$, satisfying $t_0 < t < t_\beta$, even though its worst-case completion time may exceed $t_\beta$. All such jobs must execute during $[t_0, t_\beta]$, so each corresponding array entry calls for an adjustment to certain slack counters, described as follows. Consider such an entry, say $\{F_{ij}, s(F_{ij})\}$, where $i$ is the priority of the task and $i \le L$. This task will consume $C_i$ units of priority level $i$ processing, reduced possibly by any processing which had already been completed on this task at time $t_0$, $C_i(t_0)$, described earlier. For simplicity, let us refer to this time as $C_i^\star$, so that $[C_i - C_i(t_0)] = C_i^\star$. Note that $C_i^\star$ constitutes level $i$ inactivity for every priority level $k$ higher than $i$ and must, therefore, be subtracted from $S_k'(t_0)$ for all $k < i$. Finally, the completion of job $\tau_{ij}$ causes $s(F_{ij})$ units of slack to become available, which must be added to $S_i'(t_0)$. Note that there are various ways to determine task arrival times, such as storing these values in a pre-computed table or computing them on-line, which requires a simple and straightforward calculation. While many approaches are possible, care must be exercised to ensure that all higher-priority jobs present or arriving during $[t_0, t_\beta]$ are accounted for exactly once.

In summary, in moving from time $t_0$ to time $t_\beta$, first initialize all counters $S_k(t_\beta) = S_k'(t_0)$, for $k = 1, \ldots, n$. Then, for all tasks $\tau_k$ of priority $L$ or higher and a set of jobs $\tau_{ij}$ of priority $i \le L$ present at $t_0$ or arriving during $[t_0, t_\beta]$ with table entry $\{F_{ij}, s(F_{ij})\}$, we make the following adjustments:

$$S_k(t_\beta) = \begin{cases} S_k(t_\beta) - C_i^\star, & \text{if } k < i, \\ S_k(t_\beta) + s(F_{ij}), & \text{if } k = i. \end{cases}$$

We now advance the clock to $t_\beta$ and repeat the above procedure with $t_0$ replaced by $t_\beta$. The aperiodic processing immediately available at $t_\beta$, $S^\star(t_\beta)$, is computed and the aperiodic accumulator, $\mathcal{Q}$, is incremented by

$$\mathcal{Q} = \mathcal{Q} + \min\{S^\star(t_\beta), t_b - t_\beta\}$$

The algorithm continues until the worst-case completion time of the lowest-priority task with 0 current slack equals or exceeds $t_b$.

The previous analysis assumed that the aperiodic queue was empty when the $k$th aperiodic task $J_k$ arrived at time $\alpha_k$. If this is not true, then $J_k$ may be delayed by the execution of higher-priority aperiodics in the queue. Similarly, the acceptance of $J_k$ may cause lower-priority pending aperiodics to be delayed. Consequently, we must ensure that: (a) $J_k$ does not miss its deadline due to higher-priority aperiodic work, and (b) $J_k$ does not cause the deadlines of pending lower-priority aperiodic tasks to be missed.

To address this problem, we propose a two-step acceptance check for scheduling a new hard aperiodic job, $J_k$, which is described as follows:

**Step 1**: Ignore all previously guaranteed but uncompleted aperiodic tasks pending in the aperiodic queues. Select a priority level at which to attempt to service $J_k$. Compute the maximum amount of slack available for aperiodic processing at that level prior to the aperiodic deadline, $\mathcal{Q}$, as described earlier in this section for the case of highest priority service. If the slack available is less than the execution time required by $J_k$, then we reject the task. Otherwise, we compute a slack value to associate with $J_k$ equal to the difference between its execution time $p_k$ and the slack available and then we go to step 2. Note that the slack value associated with $J_k$ represents the maximum amount of time it can be delayed before it misses its deadline.

**Step 2**: Now we must consider all tasks pending in the aperiodic queue. We must check whether accepting $J_k$ will cause any other aperiodic deadlines to be missed or if any pending aperiodic jobs will cause $J_k$'s deadline to be missed. We assume that aperiodics within a priority level are processed in deadline order, so that the processing associated with earlier deadline tasks is done first. Each task in the aperiodic queue contains four attributes, namely, $l$, the priority level at which that task is being processed, $p$, its *remaining* processing time, $d$, its absolute deadline, and $s$, its slack value. This information is used to determine if $J_k$ can be scheduled, according to the following criteria:

- If an aperiodic task in the queue, call it $J_l$, has a higher priority than $J_k$, either because its priority is strictly higher or its priority is the same but its deadline is earlier, then we must subtract the remaining processing time $p$ for $J_l$ from the slack value computed in step 1 for $J_k$. If $J_k$'s slack value stays non-negative, we continue; if it becomes negative, we reject $J_k$. This process is repeated for every higher-priority aperiodic task in the queue. If the slack is still non-negative, then we know that $J_k$ will complete by its deadline. This reduced slack value will be its correct slack value if $J_k$ is eventually guaranteed. Now we must determine if $J_k$ will cause any lower-priority aperiodics to miss their deadlines.

- If an aperiodic task in the queue, call it $J_m$, has a lower priority than $J_k$, either because its priority is lower or its priority is the same but its deadline is later, then $J_k$ will run before $J_m$. Consequently, each of the lower-priority tasks in the table must have sufficient slack to tolerate the delay imposed by servicing $J_k$. We check if each lower-priority aperiodic has a slack value at least as large as $J_k$'s processing time. If not, then we reject $J_k$. If so, then we subtract $J_k$'s processing time from the slack values of the lower-priority tasks. Then we add $J_k$ to the aperiodic queue and resume processing.

This two-step process is summarized as follows. We define $\mathcal{P}(t_a)$ as the total higher-priority aperiodic work pending at the arrival of the aperiodic $J_k$. Thus $\mathcal{P}(t_a)$ is the sum of the remaining execution times of higher-priority aperiodics pending at time $t_a$ and it corresponds to aperiodic processing time which must be consumed prior to servicing $J_k$. We also define $\mathcal{M}(t_a)$ as the minimum slack of any lower-priority aperiodic tasks pending at time $t_a$. If no lower-priority aperiodics are pending at $t_a$, then $\mathcal{M}(t_a) = \infty$. To compute the actual slack available for servicing $J_k$ in $[t_a, t_b]$, call it $\mathcal{Q}'$, we must adjust the total slack available in $[t_a, t_b]$, or $\mathcal{Q}$, as follows:

$$\mathcal{Q}' \;=\; \min\{\, \mathcal{Q} - \mathcal{P}(t_a)\,,\; \mathcal{M}(t_a)\,\} \tag{8.3}$$

For a discussion of the implementation requirements associated with supporting the slack stealing algorithms presented for soft and hard aperiodic scheduling and their computational complexity, the reader is referred to [8, 14].


# 8.4   Optimality

Any algorithm designed to schedule hard deadline periodic tasks and aperiodic tasks jointly consists of two distinct parts: (1) determination of time intervals during which aperiodic tasks are processed or during which periodic tasks are processed and (2) within each interval deciding which periodic or aperiodic tasks to process. We assume that the processing of periodic tasks is done in accordance with the fixed priorities assigned. Ordinarily, these priorities are assigned by the deadline monotonic algorithm; however, alternative periodic priority assignments can change the amount of slack available, which can alter the performance of the aperiodic tasks. The slack stealing algorithm is the optimal algorithm in the sense that given any priority assignment for the periodic tasks, this algorithm will provide the largest cumulative amount of time to process aperiodic tasks. To provide any additional time to the aperiodics would cause a periodic deadline to be missed. In spite of this, optimality of a joint scheduling algorithm is most often defined in terms of some measure of performance observed by the aperiodic tasks, for example, the number of tasks accepted for processing in the hard deadline case or aperiodic response times in the case of soft aperiodic tasks. Such performance is determined not only by the time that can be devoted to the aperiodics (which is maximized by the slack stealing algorithm) but also the way in which this time is allocated to the individual aperiodic tasks. Since allocating time to one task either delays or eliminates the time that can be allocated to other tasks, it is rarely possible to find a truly optimal algorithm without severely limiting the way in which the time allocation can be done.

## 8.4.1   Optimality for Soft Aperiodic Scheduling

Let us consider the notion of optimality more formally, first in the case of soft deadline aperiodic tasks, where the performance that a joint scheduling algorithm achieves is defined in terms of the response times of all the aperiodic tasks.

Suppose that the periodic task is set and its phasing and priority assignment are fixed. Consider any sequence of aperiodic jobs $\mathcal{J} = \{J_k, k \geq 1\}$. We consider all joint scheduling algorithms in a class of algorithms $\mathcal{C}$, for example, all algorithms that process the aperiodic tasks in FIFO order. Any scheduling algorithm in the class $\mathcal{C}$, call it $\mathcal{X}$, will result in a set of aperiodic task response times given by the vector $\mathbf{R}(\mathcal{X})$, where $\mathbf{R}(\mathcal{X}) = (R_1(\mathcal{X}), R_2(\mathcal{X}), \ldots)$, where $R_i(\mathcal{X})$ is the response time of the $i$th aperiodic arrival. We now define optimality for the soft aperiodic case.

**Definition 1**: A scheduling algorithm $\mathcal{X}$ in class $\mathcal{C}$ *dominates* a scheduling algo-
rithm $\mathcal{Y}$ in class $\mathcal{C}$ on an aperiodic task set $\mathcal{J}$ if and only if $R_i(\mathcal{X}) \leq R_i(\mathcal{Y}), 1 \leq i$.

**Definition 2**: A scheduling algorithm $\mathcal{X}$ in $\mathcal{C}$ *dominates* a scheduling algorithm $\mathcal{Y}$
in $\mathcal{C}$ if and only if $\mathcal{X}$ dominates $\mathcal{Y}$ on every aperiodic task set $\mathcal{J}$.

**Definition 3**: A scheduling algorithm $\mathcal{X}$ in $\mathcal{C}$ is *strongly optimal* in $\mathcal{C}$ if and only
if $\mathcal{X}$ dominates every other scheduling algorithm in $\mathcal{C}$.

According to the above definitions, a scheduling algorithm belonging to a particular class of algorithms, $\mathcal{C}$, is strongly optimal if and only if that algorithm minimizes the response time of every aperiodic task among all algorithms in $\mathcal{C}$. The property of strong optimality is very difficult to achieve except with relatively small classes of algorithms, $\mathcal{C}$, hence it can be useful to weaken this notion of optimality. To do this we focus on some univariate performance measure computed from the response vector, such as the average response time. We consider performance measures which are a real-valued function of the aperiodic response vector, $\mathbf{R}(\mathcal{X})$, such as the average response time. This leads to the following definition of optimality (as opposed to strong optimality).

**Definition 4**: A scheduling algorithm $\mathcal{X}$ is *optimal* with respect to the performance measure $\mathcal{M}$ within the class of scheduling algorithms $\mathcal{C}$ if and only if
$\mathcal{M}$ is uniformly minimized over all aperiodic task sets among all scheduling
algorithms in $\mathcal{C}$.

Using the above terminology, Lehoczky and Ramos-Thuel [8] proved the following theorem:

**Theorem 8.4.1** *The slack stealing algorithm is strongly optimal within the class of all scheduling algorithms which use the same fixed-priority assignment for the periodic tasks and schedule aperiodic tasks in FIFO order.*

Throughout this chapter, we restrict attention to on-line scheduling algorithms. Furthermore, we also consider only *work-conserving* algorithms. This means that the processor will never be idle if there are periodic or aperiodic tasks ready for processing. Under the assumptions that periodic tasks are processed according to a given priority order and the aperiodic tasks are processed in FIFO order, then we conjecture that the slack stealing algorithm remains strongly optimal in the larger class of algorithms, which can be *clairvoyant* and need not be work conserving. The reasons underlying this conjecture are:

- Given that all algorithms under consideration must process the periodic tasks according to the same fixed-priority order, the slack stealing algorithm will provide at least as much time to the aperiodic tasks as will any other algorithm.

- Given that aperiodic tasks must be processed in FIFO order, knowledge of their arrival times is of no use. Furthermore, to minimize aperiodic response time, aperiodic tasks should be processed immediately upon their arrival for as long as possible subject to meeting all periodic deadlines. If no aperiodic tasks are ready, periodic tasks should be processed to create additional future processing time for the future aperiodic arrivals. Hence, non-work conserving processing strategies will be dominated by the slack stealing algorithm. These observations assume that the overhead of scheduling and task context switching is ignored.

The above conjecture applies only to soft aperiodic tasks and FIFO processing order. If one were to broaden the class $\mathcal{C}$ to permit an arbitrary processing order of the aperiodic tasks, then the strong optimality property of the slack stealing algorithm is lost. Indeed, information about future aperiodic arrivals and non-work-conserving processing disciplines can lead to a reduction in the response times of some aperiodic tasks. For example, if one unit of processing were available and an aperiodic task with a very long processing requirement is ready, the FIFO processing requirement implies that it is strongly optimal to use the one unit of aperiodic processing capacity on the long aperiodic task, even though it will be completed far in the future. However, if one were to know that a new aperiodic task will arrive one time unit in the future and require one unit of processing, the processor could be idled (if no periodic tasks are ready) for the next time unit, and the new arrival could be serviced to completion when it arrives one time unit in the future, leading to a large reduction in its response time, and possibly negligible increase in the response time of the long aperiodic task. Similar observations hold when one deals with the hard aperiodic scheduling problem.

Even though strong optimality is lost without the assumptions of a given fixed-priority order for the periodic tasks and FIFO processing of the aperiodic tasks, a weaker optimality result is possible. For example, suppose we consider the class of on-line and work-conserving algorithms which use the same fixed-priority assignment for the periodic tasks, but which may process the aperiodic tasks in any order. It is well known that the SRPT (shortest remaining processing time) queue discipline will result in the smallest mean task response time. Consequently, if the class of algorithms is enlarged to permit the SRPT queue discipline, the slack stealing algorithm with FIFO processing is no longer even optimal. If we define the performance measure $\mathcal{M}$ to be the mean aperiodic response time, then the slack stealing algorithm with SRPT aperiodic task processing would be optimal within the class of algorithms having the same priority assignment for the periodic tasks. This is a much larger class of algorithms, and as a consequence the strong optimality property has been lost. We summarize this in the following theorem:

**Theorem 8.4.2** *The slack stealing algorithm with SRPT processing of aperiodic tasks is optimal with respect to the minimum mean aperiodic response time performance measure among algorithms in the class $\mathcal{C}$ of all on-line, work-conserving algorithms which process the periodic tasks in the same fixed-priority order.*

## 8.4.2    Optimality for Hard Aperiodic Scheduling

Lehoczky and Ramos-Thuel [8] proved that the slack stealing algorithm can be the basis for constructing some strongly optimal scheduling algorithms for jointly scheduling hard periodics and soft aperiodics. Ramos-Thuel and Lehoczky [14] showed that, unfortunately, no such strong optimality is possible for the hard aperiodic case unless the sets of aperiodic tasks under consideration permit some algorithm to meet successfully all of the deadlines in each of the aperiodic task sets. Otherwise, any algorithm will be faced with a situation in which it will not be able to do all offered work. Such a situation requires that a choice be made as to which tasks to process. This choice implies that no scheduling algorithm will be able to dominate all other algorithms on the task sets under consideration, and this, in turn, prevents any algorithm from being strongly optimal.

   The conventional view of optimality for hard aperiodic scheduling is that a hard aperiodic scheduling algorithm is optimal if it is guaranteed to schedule any aperiodic task set which can be feasibly scheduled by some other scheduling algorithm; that is, if a hard aperiodic task set is feasible by a hard aperiodic scheduling algorithm, it is also feasible if scheduled by the optimal algorithm. This defines a strong sense of optimality which is very narrowly applicable, because it is limited to the class of hard aperiodic task sets which are schedulable. There are many hard aperiodic task sets which fall outside this very restricted class (e.g., fault recovery operations), and we are interested in hard aperiodic scheduling problems in which it may be impossible feasibly to schedule the aperiodic tasks by any algorithm. We next provide definitions of strong optimality for the hard aperiodic case.

   In addition to the given set of periodic tasks, consider any sequence of aperiodic jobs $\mathcal{J} = \{J_k, k \geq 1\}$. Any scheduling algorithm, call it $\mathcal{X}$, will result in a subset of the aperiodic tasks, $\mathcal{C}^{\mathcal{X}}(\mathcal{J})$, whose deadlines are met.

**Definition 1′:** A scheduling algorithm $\mathcal{X}$ *dominates* a scheduling algorithm $\mathcal{Y}$ on an aperiodic task set $\mathcal{J}$ if and only if $\mathcal{C}^{\mathcal{Y}}(\mathcal{J}) \subset \mathcal{C}^{\mathcal{X}}(\mathcal{J})$.

**Definition** 2′: A scheduling algorithm $\mathcal{X}$ dominates a scheduling algorithm $\mathcal{Y}$ on a collection of aperiodic tasks sets $\mathcal{P}$ if and only if $\mathcal{X}$ dominates $\mathcal{Y}$ on every aperiodic task set $\mathcal{J} \in \mathcal{P}$.

**Definition** 3′: A scheduling algorithm $\mathcal{X}$ is *strongly optimal* within a class of scheduling algorithms $\mathcal{C}$ on a collection of aperiodic tasks $\mathcal{P}$ if and only if it dominates every other scheduling algorithm in $\mathcal{C}$ on every $\mathcal{J} \in \mathcal{P}$.

**Definition** 4′: A scheduling algorithm $\mathcal{X}$ is *strongly optimal* within a class of algorithms $\mathcal{C}$ if and only if $\mathcal{X}$ dominates every other algorithm in $\mathcal{C}$ for all aperiodic task sets.

As discussed above and by Ramos-Thuel and Lehoczky [14], no algorithm will be strongly optimal unless the class of algorithms, $\mathcal{C}$, is very severely restricted or the collection of aperiodic task sets, $\mathcal{P}$, is very small, and includes only task sets which can be completely scheduled by a single algorithm. As soon as an aperiodic task set is included which cannot be completely scheduled by any algorithm, strong optimality is lost. As long as no algorithm can schedule every periodic and aperiodic task that arrives, there can be no strong optimality.

Given that strong optimality is rarely achievable, it is natural to weaken the concept in the way that was done in the soft aperiodic scheduling case, that is by computing a univariate performance measure, $\mathcal{M}$, and finding an algorithm that minimizes this measure over all aperiodic task sets, as discussed in Definition 4. For example, we might consider performance measures such as the long-run fraction of aperiodic tasks that are scheduled unsuccessfully, the amount of aperiodic work for which the deadlines are not met relative to the amount of work offered, or some weighted average of the uncompleted work where the weights are chosen to reflect the importance of each task. Much research remains to be done to find optimal scheduling algorithms for useful classes of algorithms with respect to interesting performance measures.

## 8.5    Extensions

In this section, we mention a series of extensions that are possible with the slack stealing approach presented in this chapter. These extensions include many important issues in real-time systems, such as the reclamation of unused task execution time, simultaneous service of soft and hard aperiodic tasks, transient overload, and the management of periodic and aperiodic deadlines.

### 8.5.1    Reclaiming Unused Periodic and Aperiodic Execution Time

It is well known that actual task execution times exhibit large variability and may be much less than their worst-case execution times [18, 19]. The slack stealing method is based on worst-case execution times in order to ensure that all deadlines are met under worst-case conditions; however, we must have a method of reclaiming any unused execution time.

The slack stealing approach offers an especially easy method of reclaiming any unused time. Since every task, whether periodic or aperiodic, is executed at a fixed priority level, its execution represents a claim on the slack available at that level. If it does not utilize all of the time claimed, then the excess should be returned to the slack available at that level, say $i$. A simple way to reclaim unused periodic execution time at priority level $i$ is to subtract the unused time from the level $k$ inactivity counters, $\mathcal{I}_k$, $i \leq k \leq n$. This will make the unused time available to those priority levels. If unused aperiodic execution time becomes available because an aperiodic job ends early, then we must adjust the slack values for any pending aperiodics. Since the aperiodic job that finished early was the highest-priority aperiodic task pending, all other pending aperiodics have lower priority. Hence, we add the unused aperiodic execution time to the slack variable associated with each of the pending aperiodic jobs.

## 8.5.2    Simultaneous Service of Hard and Soft Aperiodics

This chapter has presented the use of slack stealing for servicing either hard aperiodics or soft aperiodics, but not both. Clearly, the method can be extended to service both types of aperiodics simultaneously. One can partition the slack available into two parts, one for hard periodics and the other for soft periodics. A better solution would be to allow the two classes of tasks to draw on the same large pool of slack, thus offering the benefits of resource sharing. The soft aperiodics should be scheduled at the highest priority level, while the hard aperiodics should be scheduled at as low a priority as possible, subject to meeting their deadlines. One should consider putting bounds on the amount of slack that either class can draw over certain periods of time in order to prevent one class from gaining too large a proportion of the available capacity. Such bounds could be adjusted depending on application-related objectives and context-dependent information.

## 8.5.3    Transient Overload

In real-time systems, it is possible that some tasks will exceed their worst-case execution times, and a transient overload condition may occur. The slack stealer gives us information at each priority level as to the amount of slack available. Thus one can determine exactly the amount of time a task can overrun its deadline and still not have any other task miss its deadline. Hence, slack stealing can provide a new approach to transient overloads, an approach which is far more flexible than period transformations [16].

## 8.5.4    Modifying Periodic Deadlines

This chapter has assumed that no periodic deadlines may be missed. This requirement can often be weakened; for example, in certain applications the requirement might be that two consecutive task deadlines should never be missed. For this and similar relaxations of the periodic task deadline requirements, if a hard aperiodic task cannot pass its acceptance test, one can check whether additional slack can be claimed at the desired priority level. This will possibly cause a periodic task to miss a deadline, but this may be preferable to rejecting the aperiodic task.

The above examples of extensions to the slack stealing algorithm are intended to illustrate the point that the slack stealing approach provides a flexible framework within which a wide range of possible policies for managing periodic and aperiodic deadlines and soft aperiodic response times can be formulated and implemented.

## 8.6   Summary

This chapter has reviewed the recent developments concerning the slack stealing algorithm, a flexible approach for jointly servicing hard deadline periodic tasks with soft and/or hard deadline periodic tasks. A new algorithm, which is a slight variation of the algorithm introduced by Davis, Tindell, and Burns [4], is introduced for calculating both the slack available at all times and the worst-case completion time of each instantiation of each periodic task. Algorithms are given for using the slack stealing method to service soft aperiodic tasks or hard aperiodics tasks. An extensive discussion of optimality is presented. We show that some strong optimality results are possible for the soft aperiodic scheduling problem, whereas no strong optimality results are possible for the hard aperiodic scheduling case unless the aperiodic tasks sets being considered are severely restricted so that every task can be scheduled by some algorithm. Extensions are mentioned which highlight the flexibility and generality of the slack stealing method.

## Acknowledgments

The research presented in this chapter is supported in part by a grant from the Office of Naval Research under contract N00014-92-J-1524 and by the Federal Systems Company of IBM under University Agreement Y-278067. It was also supported by AT&T Bell Laboratories under the College Research Fellowship Program. The slack stealing algorithm for soft aperiodics and for hard aperiodics was originally presented in [8, 14], respectively. This chapter draws heavily on those two papers, but also corrects an error in the guarantee algorithm proposed in [14] which was brought to our attention by R.I. Davis and A. Burns of York University.

## References

[1] A. Burns. Scheduling hard real-time systems: A review. *Software Engineering Journal*, 6(3):116–128, 1991.

[2] H. Chetto and M. Chetto. Some results of the earliest deadline scheduling algorithm. *IEEE Transactions on Software Engineering*, 15(10):466–473, 1989.

[3] R. Conway, W. Maxwell, and L. Miller. *Theory of Scheduling.* Addison-Wesley, 1967.

[4] R. I. Davis, K. W. Tindell, and A. Burns. Scheduling slack time in fixed priority pre-emptive systems. In *Proceedings of the 14th IEEE Real-Time Systems Symposium*, pages 222–231, December 1993.

[5] M. Gonzalez Harbour, M. Klein, and J. P. Lehoczky. Fixed priority scheduling of periodic tasks with varying execution priority. In *Real-Time Systems Symposium*, pages 116–128, December 1991.

[6] H. Hecht. Fault-tolerant software for real-time applications. *ACM Computing Surveys*, 8(4):391–407, December 1976.

[7] M. Joseph and P. Pandya. Finding response times in a real-time system. *BCS Computer Journal*, 29(5):390–395, 1986.

[8] John P. Lehoczky and Sandra Ramos-Thuel. An optimal algorithm for scheduling soft-aperiodic tasks in fixed-priority preemptive systems. In *Real-Time Systems Symposium*, pages 110–123, December 1992.

[9] J. P. Lehoczky. Real-time resource management techniques. In J.J. Marciniak, editor, *Encyclopedia of Software Engineering*, pages 1011–1020. John Wiley and Sons, New York, 1994.

[10] J. Y.-T. Leung and J. Whitehead. On the complexity of fixed-priority scheduling of periodic real-time tasks. *Performance Evaluation*, 2:237–250, 1982.

[11] C. L. Liu and J. W. Layland. Scheduling algorithms for multiprogramming in a hard real-time environment. *Journal of the ACM*, 20(1):46–61, 1973.

[12] C. Douglass Locke. *Best-Effort Decision Making for Real-Time Scheduling.* Ph.D. thesis, Carnegie Mellon University, May 1986.

[13] A.K. Mok. *Fundamental Design Problems of Distributed Systems for the Hard Real-Time Environment.* Ph.D. thesis, M.I.T., 1983.

[14] Sandra Ramos-Thuel and John P. Lehoczky. On-line scheduling of hard deadline aperiodic tasks in fixed-priority systems. In *Proceedings of the Real-Time Systems Symposium*, December 1993.

[15] K. Schwan and H. Zhou. Dynamic scheduling of hard real-time tasks and real-time threads. *IEEE Transactions on Software Engineering*, 18(8):736–748, 1992.

[16] Lui Sha, John Lehoczky, and Ragunathan Rajkumar. Solutions for some practical problems in prioritized preemptive scheduling. In *Real-Time Systems Symposium*, pages 181–191, May 1986.

[17] Sandra Ramos-Thuel. *Enhancing Fault Tolerance of Real-Time Systems through Time Redundancy.* Ph.D. thesis, Carnegie Mellon University, May 1993.

[18] Michael Woodbury. Analysis of the execution time of real-time tasks. In *Real-Time Systems Symposium*, pages 89–96, May 1986.

[19] Michael H. Woodbury and Kang G. Shin. Evaluation of the probability of dynamic failure and processor utilization for real-time systems. In *Real-Time Systems Symposium*, December 1988.

# Chapter 9

# Efficient Methods of Validating Timing Constraints

## Jane W. S. Liu and Rhan Ha

Analytical and efficient validation methods to determine whether all jobs always complete by their deadlines are not yet available for systems using modern dynamic scheduling strategies. Exhaustive methods are often infeasible or unreliable since the execution time and release time of each job may vary. This chapter presents several worst-case bounds and efficient algorithms for determining how late the completion times of independent jobs with arbitrary release times can be in a dynamic multiprocessor or distributed system when their release times and execution times may vary from one instance to another. The special cases considered here are when the jobs are (1) preemptable and migratable, or (2) preemptable and nonmigratable, or (3) nonpreemptable.

## 9.1   Introduction

In a real-time system, many jobs are time-critical. Here, by *job*, we mean a unit of work to be scheduled and executed. A job may be the computation of a control law, the transmission of an operator command, the retrieval of a file, and so on. To execute, it requires a computer, a data link, a console, and a disk; we refer to them all as *processors*. The processors are identical if they can be used interchangeably. Otherwise they are functionally dedicated, as exemplified by the processors listed above. The length of time a job requires to complete if it were to execute alone is called its *execution time*. The execution of a time-critical job cannot begin until its *release time* and must complete by its *deadline*. To validate a real-time system, its builder must demonstrate convincingly that all time-critical jobs will always complete by their deadlines, after making sure that the scheduler works correctly; that is, it never schedules any job before its release time. Hereafter, we assume that the scheduler works correctly and focus on the problem of how to demonstrate that all jobs always complete by their deadlines.

Traditionally, real-time systems have been validated by exhaustive simulation and testing. Because the execution time and release time of each job may vary, exhaustive methods are often infeasible or unreliable. This is especially true when the algorithm used to schedule the jobs is priority-driven. A scheduling algorithm is *priority-driven* if it does not leave any processor idle intentionally. Such an algorithm can be implemented by assigning priorities to jobs and placing all jobs that have been released and, therefore, are ready for execution in a queue ordered by their priorities. The available processor(s) is (are) used to execute the job(s) at the head of this queue. Priority-driven algorithms differ from each other in the rules they use to assign priorities to jobs. Almost all commonly used event-driven scheduling algorithms, such as FIFO, shortest-processing-time-first, earliest-deadline-first, and rate-monotonic algorithms [1–6], are priority-driven.

Figure 9.1 shows an illustrative example. The simple system in this figure contains 6 independent jobs and 2 identical processors. The release time, deadline, and execution time of job $J_i$ are denoted by $r_i$, $d_i$, and $e_i$, respectively. These job parameters are listed in the table. In this example, the execution times of all the jobs are known except for $J_2$. Its execution time can be any value in the range [2, 6]. The scheduling algorithm in this example is preemptive and priority-driven; the priority order is $J_1, J_2, J_3, J_4, J_5$, and $J_6$, with $J_1$ having the highest priority. A constraint is that jobs are *not migratable*. In other words, once a job begins execution on a processor, it is constrained to execute on that processor until completion. We want to validate that all deadlines can be met by simulating the system. A naive way is to simulate the system twice: when the execution time of $J_2$ has the maximum value 6 and when it has the minimum value 2. The results are the schedules shown in parts (a) and (b) of Figure 9.1. By examining these schedules, we would conclude that all jobs can complete by their deadlines. This conclusion is incorrect because the simulation test does not give us full coverage. This fact is illustrated by the schedules in parts (c) and (d). The worst-case schedule is shown in (c); the completion times of $J_4$ and $J_6$ are 21 and 23, respectively, when the execution time of $J_2$ is 3. The best-case schedule is shown in (d); $J_4$ completes at time 15 and $J_6$ completes at 17 when the execution time of $J_2$ is 5. To find the schedules in (c) and (d) by simulating the system, we need to try exhaustively all possible execution times of $J_2$.

The phenomenon illustrated by Figure 9.1 is known as a *scheduling anomaly*, an unexpected behavior exhibited by priority-driven scheduling algorithms. Graham has shown that the completion time of a set of nonpreemptive jobs with identical release times can be later when more processors are used to execute them and when they have shorter execution times and fewer dependencies [7]. When jobs have arbitrary release times and share nonpreemptable resources, scheduling anomalies can occur even when there is only one processor and the jobs are preemptable. These anomalies make ensuring full coverage in simulation difficult whenever there are variations in job execution time and resource requirements or jitters in job release times. Unfortunately, these variations are often unavoidable. Given an arbitrary scheduling algorithm, it is impractical to find the worst-case completion times of all jobs in large and dynamic systems by exhaustive simulation. Because

| job | $r_i$ | $d_i$ | $e_i$ |
|-----|-------|-------|-------|
| $J_1$ | 0 | 10 | 5 |
| $J_2$ | 0 | 10 | [2,6] |
| $J_3$ | 4 | 15 | 8 |
| $J_4$ | 0 | 20 | 10 |
| $J_5$ | 5 | 200 | 100 |
| $J_6$ | 7 | 22 | 2 |

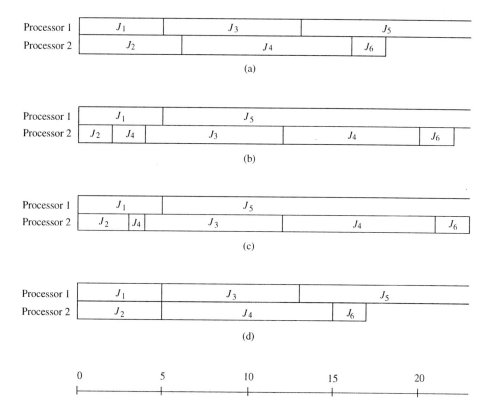

**Figure 9.1**  An Example Illustrating Unpredictable Start Times and Completion Times

of the difficulties in validation and certification, event-driven scheduling algorithms have not been used in safety-critical real-time systems until recently. Such systems have traditionally being built on the clock-driven, cyclic scheduling paradigm. As a result, they can be validated by exhaustive methods but are difficult to extend and maintain.

There are now rigorous analytical and efficient methods for bounding the worst-case completion times of jobs in a class of systems which will be referred to here as static systems. In a *static system*, jobs are statically assigned and bound to processors and are migrated among processors on a relatively infrequent basis, for example, during mode changes or processor outages. Jobs on each processor are scheduled according to a uniprocessor scheduling algorithm and synchronized according to a resource access-control protocol that leads to bounded durations of priority inversion (for example, the ones in [5, 6]). (A *priority inversion* is said to occur when a lower-priority job executes or a processor is left idle while some higher-priority job is waiting for execution. In Figure 9.1(b) and (c), priority inversion occurs after the completion of $J_1$; $J_5$ executes while $J_4$ is waiting.)

In contrast, efficient methods for validating dynamic multiprocessor and distributed systems are not yet available. The term *dynamic system* refers to a system where jobs ready for execution are placed in a common queue and are dispatched and scheduled on available processors on a priority-driven manner. Many worst-case performance bounds of priority-driven algorithms are known [7–10]. These bounds are often too pessimistic to be of practical use. More seriously, they cannot be extended readily to handle the case where jobs have arbitrary release times.

This chapter presents several worst-case bounds and efficient algorithms for determining how late the completion times of independent jobs with arbitrary release times can be in a dynamic multiprocessor or distributed system when their release times and execution times may vary from one instance to another. Specifically, the algorithms presented here deal with independent jobs that are (1) preemptable and migratable, or (2) preemptable and nonmigratable, or (3) nonpreemptable. As much as possible, these algorithms make use of the properties of the given jobs and scheduling algorithm. Consequently, the bounds found by them are typically much tighter than the known general worst-case bounds.

We refer to the problem of bounding the completion times of all jobs addressed in this chapter as the validation problem.[1] Following this introduction, Section 9.2 gives a formal definition of this problem. Section 9.3 gives an overview of methods for validating static systems. We then focus on the case when jobs are independent and the processors are identical. Sections 9.4, 9.5, and 9.6 present several efficient algorithms for bounding the completion times of independent jobs that are preemptable and migratable, preemptable but not migratable, and nonpreemptable, respectively. The results presented here are a small portion of all that are needed

---

[1]This problem has been called the schedulability analysis problem. Schedulability analysis is an overloaded term and has many aspects: making sure that timing constraints of individual jobs and the systems are consistent and that the constraints can be met by the programs, for example. To avoid confusion, we call the particular aspect of schedulability analysis addressed in works on real-time scheduling the validation problem.

to build a comprehensive strategy for validating dynamic systems. The work that remains to be done is discussed in Section 9.7. The Appendix contains the proofs that are lengthy.

## 9.2    Validation Problem

The validation problem addressed here can be stated as follows: given a set of jobs, the set of resources available to the jobs, and the scheduling (and resource access-control) algorithm to allocate processors and resources to jobs, determine whether all the jobs meet their deadlines. Because jobs have different properties and there are different rules governing resource usage, this problem has many variants. The periodic-task schedulability analysis problem that has by and large been solved is a variant [1–6]. This section describes other variants of this problem that remain to be solved, as well as the variant solved by the results presented in subsequent sections. It also introduces the notations that will be used later.

### 9.2.1    Jobs and Scheduling Algorithms

We characterize the workload to be scheduled and, hence, analyzed as a set $J = \{J_1, J_2, \ldots, J_n\}$ of jobs. Each job is defined by the following parameters, which are rational numbers. $J_i$'s release time $r_i$, deadline $d_i$, and execution time $e_i$ were defined in Section 9.1. When there is jitter in the release time of $J_i$, $r_i$ can have any value in the range $[r_i^-, r_i^+]$ where $r_i^-$ and $r_i^+$ are the *earliest release time* and the *latest release time* of $J_i$, respectively. While $r_i^-$ and $r_i^+$ are known a priori, the actual release time $r_i$ is unknown until the job is released. Without loss of generality, we assume that $r_i^- \geq 0$ for all $i$; that is, no job is released before $t = 0$. Similarly, the actual execution time $e_i$ is in the range $[e_i^-, e_i^+]$ and therefore can be as small as its *minimum execution time* $e_i^-$ and as large as its *maximum execution time* $e_i^+$. $e_i^-$ and $e_i^+$ are given parameters of $J_i$. $J_i$'s actual execution time $e_i$ may depend on its input data as well as the underlying hardware configuration and run-time environment, and may be unknown until the job's execution completes.

The jobs in $J$ may be dependent; data and control dependencies between them impose *precedence constraints* in the order of their execution. A job $J_i$ is a *predecessor* of another job $J_j$ (and $J_j$ is a *successor* of $J_i$) if $J_j$ cannot begin execution until the execution of $J_i$ completes. Two jobs $J_i$ and $J_j$ are *independent* if they can be executed in any order.

We confine our attention here to off-line scheduling. In other words, the scheduler knows before any job begins execution, the parameters $[r_i^-, r_i^+]$, $[e_i^-, e_i^+]$, and $d_i$ of every job $J_i$. The scheduling algorithm is priority-driven. It assigns fixed priorities to jobs. It may assign priorities to jobs based on the known job parameters. Some algorithms, such as the FIFO algorithm, assign priorities to jobs according to their actual release times. However, none of the algorithms considered here assign priorities to jobs based on their actual execution times.

Therefore, the given scheduling algorithm is defined completely by the list of priorities it assigns to the jobs. Without loss of generality, we assume that the priorities of jobs are distinct. We will use the list $(J_1, J_2, \ldots, J_n)$ in decreasing priority order except where it is stated to be otherwise. In other words, we always index the jobs so that $J_i$ has a higher-priority than $J_j$ according to the given scheduling algorithm if $i < j$. $\boldsymbol{J_i} = \{J_1, J_2, \ldots, J_i\}$ denotes the subset of jobs with priorities equal to or higher than the priority of $J_i$.

In a dynamic system containing $m$ identical processors, the scheduler maintains a common priority queue and places all jobs ready for execution in the queue. There are the following three cases:

(1) preemptable and migratable: In this case, a job can be scheduled on any processor. It may be preempted when a higher-priority job becomes ready. Its execution may resume on any processor.

(2) preemptable and nonmigratable: As in case (1), each job can begin its execution on any processor and is preemptable. However, it is constrained to execute to completion on the same processor. Figure 9.1 gives an example of this case.

(3) nonpreemptable: Each job can be scheduled on any processor. Some or all of the jobs are nonpreemptable.

In addition to processors, the system may also have a set of serially reusable resources. A job may require some of these resources, as well as a processor, in order to execute. When some of the resources required by two or more jobs are the same, the jobs are said to be in *resource conflict*. We assume that a resource access-control protocol is used to resolve resource conflicts among jobs, and this protocol controls priority inversion and prevents deadlock. Therefore, the length of time any job $J_i$ may be blocked from execution due to resource conflict is bounded from above. This bound is called the *worst-case blocking time* of $J_i$ and is denoted by $b_i$. For a given resource access-control protocol, $b_i$ is given for every job $J_i$.

## 9.2.2   Variants of the Schedulability Analysis Problem

Again, the objective of validation is to determine, analytically or by using an efficient algorithm, whether every job can meet its deadline. This is equivalent to finding the worst-case (the largest) completion time of each job. In trying to achieve this objective, we will take into account variations in execution times and release times. We say that the jobs have fixed release times, or there are no jitters, when $r_i^- = r_i = r_i^+$ and that they have identical, or zero, release times when $r_i^- = r_i^+ = 0$ for all $i$.

The validation problem has four dimensions. Two dimensions are whether jobs are dependent and whether they share any resource. Sections 9.4-9.6 are concerned only with independent jobs that do not share any resources. The other two dimensions of the problem are the release-time characteristics of jobs and rules in scheduling. Each special case based on these two dimensions is referred to by three capital letters separated by "/". The first letter denotes preemptability. It can be either "P", for preemptable, or "N", for nonpreemptable. The second letter defines the migratability of jobs. It can be either "M", for migratable, or "N", for nonmigratable. The third letter describes the release-time characteristics. It can be either "Z", for zero release times, or "F", for fixed arbitrary release times, or "J", for jittered release times. For example, by *P/M/F jobs*, we mean jobs that are preemptable and migratable and have fixed arbitrary release times. N/N/Z jobs are nonpreemptable and have zero, or identical, release times.

### 9.2.3   Definitions and Notations

In subsequent sections, we will use $J_i^+$ to denote the set $\{J_1^+, J_2^+, \dots, J_i^+\}$ of jobs in which every job has its maximum execution time. Similarly, $J_i^-$ denotes the set $\{J_1^-, J_2^-, \dots, J_i^-\}$ in which every job has its minimum execution time. We refer to the schedule of $J_i$ produced by the given algorithm as the *actual schedule* $A_i$ and the schedule of $J_i^+$ (or $J_i^-$) produced by the same algorithm as the *maximal* (or the *minimal*) *schedule* $A_i^+$ (or $A_i^-$) of $J_i$.

Let $S(J_i)$ be the instant of time at which the execution of $J_i$ begins according to the actual schedule $A_n$. $S(J_i)$ is the (actual) *start time* of $J_i$. Let $S^+(J_i)$ and $S^-(J_i)$ be the *observable start times* of $J_i$ in the schedules $A_n^+$ and $A_n^-$, respectively. $S^+(J_i)$ and $S^-(J_i)$ can easily be found by constructing the maximal and minimal schedules and observing when $J_i$ starts according to these schedules. We say that the start time of $J_i$ is *predictable* if $S^+(J_i) \geq S(J_i) \geq S^-(J_i)$.

Similarly, let $F(J_i)$ be the instant at which $J_i$ completes execution according to the actual schedule $A_n$. $F(J_i)$ is the *completion time* of $J_i$. The *response time* of a job is the length of time between its release time and its completion time. Let $F^+(J_i)$ and $F^-(J_i)$ be the *observable completion times* of $J_i$ according to the schedules $A_n^+$ and $A_n^-$, respectively. The completion times of $J_i$ is said to be predictable if $F^+(J_i) \geq F(J_i) \geq F^-(J_i)$.

We say that *the execution of $J_i$ is predictable* if both its start time and completion time are predictable. In this case, the completion time $F^+(J_i)$ in the schedule $A_n^+$ minus the minimum release time $r_i^-$ of $J_i$ gives $J_i$'s worst-case response time. $J_i$ meets its deadline if $F^+(J_i) \leq d_i$.

Let $w_i(t, t')$, for time instants $t < t'$, denote the sum of execution times of all the jobs in the set $J_i$ whose release times are in the interval $[t, t']$. $w_i(t) = w_i(0, t)$ is, therefore, the *total (processor) time demand* of $J_i$ before $t$. It is equal to the amount of processor time required by all jobs that are in $J_i$ and have release times at or earlier than $t$. Similarly, let $w_i^+(t, t')$ (or $w_i^-(t, t')$ ) be the sum of the maximum (or minimum) execution times of all jobs that are in $J_i$ and have release times in $[t, t']$. Let $w_i^+(t) = w_i^+(0, t)$. $w_i^+(t)$ is the *maximum time demand* of $J_i$ before $t$. Clearly, $w_i(t) \leq w_i^+(t)$ for all $i$ and $t$.

## 9.3   Methods for Validating Static Systems

Again, almost all existing analytical and efficient methods for bounding the worst-case completion times are for static systems. In this case, a general strategy is to first determine how late each job $J_i$ can be delayed from start and completion by jobs that are assigned on the same processor with it and, then, take into account additional delays due to synchronization with jobs on all processors.

The best known and the most comprehensive set of bounds and algorithms are those based on the periodic-task model [1–6]. In this model, the set of jobs assigned and executed on each processor is partitioned into $n$ subsets, each called a task. Some tasks are periodic; each periodic task $T_i$ is a sequence of jobs whose release times are spaced nominally at regular intervals. The lengths of these intervals are never less than $p_i$, called the period of the task. The release time $f_i$ of the first job in a task $T_i$ is called its phase. The length of time $\delta_i$ between the release time of every job in $T_i$ and its deadline is called the relative deadline of $T_i$. $\delta_i$ is usually equal to or less than $p_i$. With a slight abuse of the notation, we use $e_i^+$ to denote the maximum execution time of each job in $T_i$. $u_i = e_i^+/p_i$ is called the utilization of the task $T_i$.

Some tasks are (periodic) servers [5]. A periodic server is created to handle the execution of a stream of jobs whose release times and execution times are random variables. Each server $T_s$ is characterized by its period $p_s$, execution time $e_s^+$, and relative deadline $\delta_s$. The scheduler treats each server as a periodic task with these parameters. Therefore, when we try to bound the completion times of jobs in periodic tasks, there is no need to treat the servers differently.

We note that the precedence constraints between jobs in the same task are naturally taken care of by making the release time of every predecessor job equal to or earlier than its successor jobs and by executing jobs in the task in the FIFO order. We can take into account precedence constraints between jobs in different tasks by adjusting the phases of the tasks so that the deadline of every predecessor job is earlier than the release times of its successor jobs. In this way, we can ignore precedence constraints and treat all jobs as if they are independent.

In our notation, most of the jobs are P/N/J jobs; they are scheduled preemptively (and are not migratable). Their resource accesses are controlled by a protocol (such as the ones in [3, 4]) which ensures that the blocking time of every job in $T_i$ due to resource conflicts with all jobs in the system is never more than $b_i$. For such systems, there are several sufficient conditions, which, when satisfied by a task, allow us to conclude that all jobs in it always complete by their deadlines. For example, if the jobs are scheduled on the rate-monotonic basis (that is, the shorter the period, the higher the priority) and synchronized according to the priority-ceiling protocol [1, 3], all jobs in $T_i$ always complete by their deadlines if

$$\sum_{k=1}^{i} u_k + b_i/p_i \le i(2^{1/i} - 1) \qquad (9.1)$$

when $\delta_i = p_i$. Here we index the tasks so that $p_1 < p_2 < \cdots < p_n$. Similar conditions are known for many fixed-priority algorithms and for arbitrary values of $\delta_i$ less than or equal to $p_i$. It is straightforward to generalize the conditions to account for the effects of nonpreemption if some jobs are not preemptable [11, 12]. It is also straightforward to use these conditions to bound the worst-case completion times of jobs in periodic job-shops and flow-shops where each job consists of subjobs which execute in turn on two or more processors and have end-to-end deadlines

[12, 13].

The known sufficient conditions, such as (9.1), are particularly robust. For example, the values of the periods and worst-case execution times of jobs in tasks $T_1, T_2, \ldots, T_i$ do not appear on the left-hand side of (9.1), only their utilizations. Moreover, (9.1) is derived assuming that each job is released at an instant between which and the deadline of the job the total processor time demand of all higher-priority jobs is the largest. Therefore, if the job were actually released at this instant, it would have the largest response time. Because of this assumption, the conclusion that a job can complete before its deadline based on such a sufficient condition remains true no matter what its actual release time is.

However, a test based on a sufficient condition like (9.1) is sometimes pessimistic. If the condition (9.1) fails to hold for $T_i$, for example, its jobs may nevertheless always complete in time. An algorithm that makes use of the known parameters $p_i$ and $e_i^+$ can give a more accurate prediction of the worst-case response times. Such algorithms are used in PERTS [14]. To determine whether any job in a task $T_i$ can meet its deadline, the algorithm takes the release time of the job as the time origin 0 and computes the maximum time demand $w_i^+(t)$ between 0 and its deadline at $\delta_i$. To compute $w_i^+(t)$, the algorithm uses as phases of the other tasks the values that maximize $w_i^+(t)$ for all $t$. The worst-case completion time of the job is $w_i^+(t) + b_i$ after its release time.

This approach of checking when the supply of time meets the demand for time can be generalized and applied to validate most static systems. Many systems do not fit the periodic-task model; jobs have arbitrary release times and precedence constraints. A way to ensure that the scheduler can always enforce the given precedence constraints is to work with the effective deadlines and release times of jobs rather than their given deadlines and release times. A job with successors must be completed before them. Consequently, the effective deadline of the job is the earliest deadline among its deadline and the deadlines of its successors. Similarly, its effective release time is the latest time among its release time and the release times of its successors. Working with effective release times and deadlines allows the scheduler to ignore temporarily the precedence constraints between jobs and to make scheduling decisions as if the jobs are independent [15]. Similarly, to validate whether every job completes before its deadline, we can use the algorithms for validating independent jobs. Unfortunately, this method does not work when the system is dynamic. For this reason, the results on independent jobs presented in subsequent sections cannot readily be extended to deal with dependent jobs in dynamic systems.

## 9.4    Preemptable and Migratable Case

We now focus our attention on dynamic systems. It is easy to find the worst-case and best-case completion times of preemptable, migratable, independent jobs. This is especially true when their release times are fixed.

## 9.4.1   Fixed-Release-Time Case

The following theorem and corollary allow us to conclude that the execution of independent P/M/F jobs is predictable. To find the worst-case (or best-case) response time of a job $J_i$ in a set $\boldsymbol{J}_n$ of independent P/M/F jobs with arbitrary and fixed release times, we apply the given scheduling algorithm on the set $\boldsymbol{J}_n^+$ (or $\boldsymbol{J}_n^-$) where all jobs have their maximum (or minimum) execution times. The response times of $J_i$ according to the resultant schedule $\boldsymbol{A}_n^+$ (or $\boldsymbol{A}_n^-$) is its largest (or smallest) possible response time. We are sure that $J_i$ always meets its deadline if it meets its deadline in the maximal schedule $\boldsymbol{A}_n^+$.

**Theorem 9.4.1**   *The start time of every job in a set of independent P/M/F jobs is predictable; that is, $S^+(J_i) \geq S(J_i) \geq S^-(J_i)$.*

**Proof:**   Clearly, $S^+(J_1) \geq S(J_1)$ is true for the highest-priority job $J_1$. Assuming that $S^+(J_k) \geq S(J_k)$ for $k = 1, 2, \ldots, i-1$, we now prove $S^+(J_i) \geq S(J_i)$ by contradiction. Suppose that $S(J_i) > S^+(J_i)$. Because the scheduling algorithm is priority driven, every job whose release time is at or earlier than $S^+(J_i)$ and whose priority is higher than $J_i$ has started by $S^+(J_i)$ according to the maximal schedule $\boldsymbol{A}_n^+$. From the induction hypothesis, we can conclude that every such job has started by $S^+(J_i)$ in the actual schedule $\boldsymbol{A}_n$. Because $e_k \leq e_k^+$ for all $k$, $w_i^+(S^+(J_i)) \geq w_i(S^+(J_i))$. In $\boldsymbol{A}_n^+$, a processor is available at $S^+(J_i)$ for $J_i$ to start; a processor must also be available in $\boldsymbol{A}_n$ at or before $S^+(J_i)$ on which $J_i$ or a lower-priority job can be scheduled. Therefore, the start time $S(J_i)$ of $J_i$ in the actual schedule $\boldsymbol{A}_n$ being later than the observable start time $S^+(J_i)$ implies that in $\boldsymbol{A}_n$ either some job(s) whose priority is lower than $J_i$ is scheduled in $(S^+(J_i), S(J_i))$ or at least one processor is left idle in this interval. This contradicts the fact that $\boldsymbol{A}_n$ is a priority-driven schedule.

$S(J_i) \geq S^-(J_i)$ can be proved similarly as $S^+(J_i) \geq S(J_i)$.   □

**Corollary 9.4.1**   *The completion time of every job in a set of independent P/M/F jobs is predictable; that is, $F^+(J_i) \geq F(J_i) \geq F^-(J_i)$.*

**Proof:**   The fact that $F^+(J_i) \geq F(J_i)$ follows straightforwardly from Theorem 9.4.1 and that $e_k \leq e_k^+$ for all $k$. Similarly, we have $F(J_i) \geq F^-(J_i)$.   □

## 9.4.2   Jittered-Release-Time Case

When there are jitters in release times, whether $J_i$ is schedulable depends not only on its own release time and execution time but also on the release times and execution times of all the higher-priority jobs. In trying to find the worst-case completion time of a job, we cannot simply choose the earliest or latest release times of higher-priority jobs. The algorithm described below is based on this observation. It tries to find bounds of start times and completion times of independent P/M/J jobs.

The algorithm, called Algorithm $\mathcal{IPMJ}$, considers one job at a time, from the job with the highest priority to the job with the lowest priority. In order to find the worst-case completion time of $J_i$, it transforms $J_i$ and the jobs that have priorities higher than $J_i$ into jobs with fixed release times as follows. Let $K_k$ denote the job transformed from $J_k$ and $\boldsymbol{K}_i$ denote the set of transformed jobs $\{K_1, K_2, \ldots, K_i\}$. In step 1, the parameters of the transformed job $K_i$ are computed from the parameters of $J_i$. Specifically, $K_i$'s execution time is equal to $J_i$'s maximum execution time, $e_i^+$, plus the length of its jitter interval, $(r_i^+ - r_i^-)$. $K_i$'s release time is $J_i$'s earliest release time, $r_i^-$, and hence $K_i$'s feasible interval is $(r_i^-, d_i)$. Step 2 computes the parameters of $K_k$ for each of $k = 1, \ldots, i - 1$. $K_k$'s execution time is $e_k^+$, that is, the maximum execution time of $J_k$. $K_k$'s release time is chosen according to the following rule: (1) if $r_k^- < r_i^- < r_k^+$, $K_k$'s release time is $r_i^-$, (2) if $r_k^+ \le r_i^-$, $K_k$'s release time is $r_k^+$ (as late as possible), and (3) if $r_k^- \ge r_i^-$, $K_k$'s release time is $r_k^-$ (as early as possible). In other words, $K_k$'s release time is chosen among $r_i^-, r_k^+$, and $r_k^-$ so that the overlap between the feasible intervals of $K_i$ and $K_k$ is as large as possible. In step 3, we schedule $\boldsymbol{K}_i$ according to the given preemptable, migratable, priority-driven algorithm. An upper bound of the completion time $F(J_i)$ of $J_i$ is equal to the completion time of $K_i$ in the resultant schedule $\boldsymbol{A}_i'$. Because $\boldsymbol{K}_{i-1}$ is not a subset of $\boldsymbol{K}_i$, $\boldsymbol{K}_i$ needs to be constructed for every job $J_i$. Consequently, the complexity of Algorithm $\mathcal{IPMJ}$ is $O(n^2)$.

The following theorem allows us to conclude that if $K_i$ can complete by the deadline $d_i$ of $J_i$ in the schedule $\boldsymbol{A}_i'$ generated by the $\mathcal{IPMJ}$ algorithm, then $J_i$ is schedulable for all possible combinations of release times and execution times. The proof of the theorem is straightforward and hence is omitted.

**Theorem 9.4.2**    *The completion time $F(J_i)$ of $J_i$ is no later than the completion time of the transformed job $K_i$ in the observable schedule $\boldsymbol{A}_i'$ of $\boldsymbol{K}_i$ generated by Algorithm $\mathcal{IPMJ}$.*

## 9.5    Preemptable, Nonmigratable, Fixed-Release-Time Case

It is often too costly to migrate jobs among processors in a distributed system. Consequently, jobs are not migrated.

### 9.5.1    Conditions for Predictable Execution

In the special case when independent jobs have zero, or identical, release times and jobs have fixed priorities, preemption and migration can never occur. Therefore, it does not matter whether or not preemption and migration are allowed. The following theorem follows straightforwardly from this observation.

**Theorem 9.5.1**    *The execution of the independent $N(P)/N/Z$ jobs is predictable.*

**Proof:**    That the start time and completion time of every job are predictable follows straightforwardly from the fact that there is no preemption before the start time of every job and during the execution of the job and jobs always start in the same order.    □

When jobs have arbitrary release times and are not migratable, their execution behavior is no longer predictable. This fact was illustrated by the example in Figure 9.1. As discussed earlier, the completion times of jobs $J_4$ and $J_6$ are not predictable. The start time of $J_6$ is 16, 20, 21, and 15 when the execution time of $J_2$ is 6, 2, 3, and 5, respectively, and therefore is also unpredictable. In general, because of the constraint that jobs cannot migrate, priority inversion can occur. For example, in the schedules in Figure 9.1(b) and (c), $J_5$ executes before $J_4$. The existence of priority inversion makes predicting completion times more difficult.

While the execution of independent P/N/F jobs is not predictable for arbitrary priority assignments, it is predictable when the jobs are scheduled in the order in which they are released. Figure 9.2 illustrates this fact, which is stated formally in the following theorem. The job set in this figure is the same as the one in Figure 9.1 except that the priority list is $(J_1, J_2, J_4, J_3, J_5, J_6)$. $J_2$'s execution time in parts (a), (b), and (c) is 6, 2, and 5, respectively.

**Theorem 9.5.2**    *When the priorities of independent P/N/F jobs are assigned on the FIFO basis (that is, the earlier the release time, the higher the priority), the execution of the jobs is predictable.*

**Proof:**    Because jobs that are released later have lower priorities, preemption and priority inversion can never occur. That the start time and completion time of every job are predictable follows from the fact that jobs start execution in the same order in all three schedules $A_n^-$, $A_n$, and $A_n^+$ and are never preempted.    $\square$

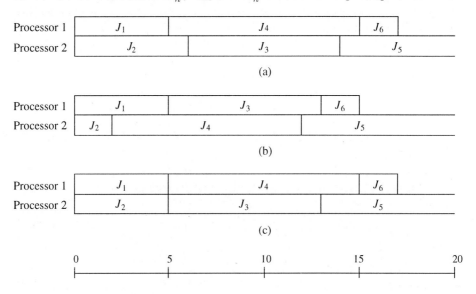

**Figure 9.2**  Predictable Execution of P/N/F Jobs Scheduled on the FIFO Basis

## 9.5.2    A General Upper Bound

When independent P/N/F jobs are not scheduled on the FIFO basis and their execution is no longer predictable, we can bound their start times and completion times according to the following theorem. The theorem is stated in terms of the set $D_i$; $D_i$ is a subset of $J_i$ in which each job $J_k$ is released after some job in $J_i$ with a priority lower than itself (that is, $J_k$) and is not scheduled to start and complete before $J_i$ on the same processor as $J_i$ in the maximal schedule. In the example in Figure 9.1, $D_1$, $D_2$, and $D_3$ are null, and so is $D_5$. $D_4$ and $D_6$ are $\{J_3\}$.

**Theorem 9.5.3**    $S(J_i) \leq S^+(J_i) + \displaystyle\sum_{J_k \in D_i} e_k^+$, and $F(J_i) \leq F^+(J_i) + \displaystyle\sum_{J_k \in D_i} e_k^+ - (e_i^+ - e_i)$.

**Proof:**    The start time and completion time of $J_i$ can be postponed beyond $S^+(J_i)$ and $F^+(J_i)$, respectively, if any job $J_k$ in $D_i$ is scheduled on the same processor as $J_i$ in the actual schedule $A_n$. In particular, $J_k$ can start before $J_i$ or preempt $J_i$ because it has a priority higher than $J_i$. When this happens, the start time and/or the completion time of $J_i$ is further delayed by at most an amount equal to the maximum execution time of $J_k$. To see why we need not be concerned with jobs not in $D_i$, we note that a job not in $D_i$ may have a release time equal to or earlier than the release times of all the jobs in $J_i$ with priorities lower than itself. Such a job never preempts jobs in $J_i$ in both the maximal schedule and the actual schedule. We can, therefore, ignore them when computing $S(J_i)$ and $F(J_i)$ from the observable start time $S^+(J_i)$ and completion time $F^+(J_i)$. The values of $S^+(J_i)$ and $F^+(J_i)$ already include the delays due to the execution of jobs that are scheduled on the same processor as $J_i$ and start and complete before $J_i$ in $A_n^+$. $\square$

The worst-case bound of completion time given by this theorem is sometimes too pessimistic. For example, this theorem tells us that the completion times of the jobs in Figure 9.1 are no greater than 5, 6, 13, 24, 113, and 26, respectively. The bounds for $F(J_4)$ and $F(J_6)$ are pessimistic. As another example, we consider a simple system containing $m$ independent jobs and $m$ identical processors. The release times of the jobs $J_1, J_2, \ldots, J_m$ are such that $r_m < r_{m-1} < \cdots < r_1$. The priority order is $J_1, J_2, \ldots, J_m$, with $J_1$ having the highest priority. Obviously, every job $J_i$ can be scheduled immediately after its release time and can always complete at or before its observable worst-case completion time $F^+(J_i)$. The bound of the worst-case completion time of $J_m$ computed from Theorem 9.5.3 can be as large as $m$ times the actual completion time of $J_m$, and is therefore not useful.

The remainder of this section discusses whether other information provided by the two observable schedules can be used to derive more accurate predictions of job completion times. Specifically, we consider tests that begin by examining the sequences in which the jobs start execution according to the minimal and maximal schedules and whether there is preemption in these observable schedules.

### 9.5.3 A Tight Upper Bound

Let $\wp_i^+(t)$ (or $\wp_i^-(t)$) be the sequence of jobs whose observable start times are at or before $t$ according to the maximal schedule $\boldsymbol{A}_i^+$ (or minimal schedule $\boldsymbol{A}_i^-$) of $\boldsymbol{J}_i$; the jobs in the sequence appear in order of increasing start times. For example, in Figure 9.1, $\wp_4^+(S^+(J_4))$ is $(J_1, J_2, J_3, J_4)$ and $\wp_4^-(S^-(J_4))$ is $(J_1, J_2, J_4)$. Similarly, let $\wp_i(t)$ be the corresponding sequence of jobs in increasing order of their actual start times according to the actual schedule $\boldsymbol{A}_i$, including all jobs whose actual start times are at or before $t$. We call $\wp_i(t)$ the *actual starting sequence*, and $\wp_i^+(t)$ and $\wp_i^-(t)$ the *maximal* and *minimal observable starting sequences* according to $\boldsymbol{A}_i^+$ and $\boldsymbol{A}_i^-$, respectively. We say that a sequence $X$ is a *subsequence* of a sequence $Y$ if $Y$ contains $X$ and the elements in both $X$ and $Y$ appear in $X$ and $Y$ in the same order. For example, in Figure 9.1, $\wp_4^-(S^-(J_4)) = (J_1, J_2, J_4)$ is a subsequence of $\wp_4^+(S^+(J_4)) = (J_1, J_2, J_3, J_4)$. Similarly, $\wp_4^+(S^+(J_3)) = (J_1, J_2, J_3)$ is a subsequence of $\wp_4^-(S^-(J_3)) = (J_1, J_2, J_4, J_3)$.

When we want to determine whether $J_i$ is schedulable, we first examine whether there is preemption in the maximal schedule. In the simpler case; no job in $\boldsymbol{J}_i$ is preempted in the maximal schedule $\boldsymbol{A}_i^+$. Then, we examine whether the two observable starting sequences $\wp_i^+(S^+(J_i))$ and $\wp_i^-(S^-(J_i))$ are identical. If the two sequences are identical, we can conclude that no job in $\boldsymbol{J}_i$ is preempted and the orders in which jobs start execution are the same, according to all the schedules of $\boldsymbol{J}_i$ for all combinations of execution times of jobs in $\boldsymbol{J}_i$. Therefore, the latest completion time of $J_i$ is $F^+(J_i)$. This fact is stated in Theorem 9.5.4 whose proof requires the following seven lemmas and their corollaries. Their proofs can be found in the appendix.

**Lemma 9.5.1** *If no job in $\boldsymbol{J}_i$ is preempted according to $\boldsymbol{A}_i^+$ and $\boldsymbol{A}_i^-$ in the time interval $[0,t)$ and in $\boldsymbol{A}_i^+$, at most $(m-1)$ processors are busy at time $t$, then in $\boldsymbol{A}_i^-$, at most $(m-1)$ processors are busy at time $t$.*

**Corollary 9.5.1** *If no job in $\boldsymbol{J}_i$ is preempted in the interval $[0,t)$ according to $\boldsymbol{A}_i^+$ and $\boldsymbol{A}_i$, and in $\boldsymbol{A}_i^+$, at most $(m-1)$ processors are busy at $t$, then in $\boldsymbol{A}_i$, at most $(m-1)$ processors are busy at $t$.*

The proof of of this corollary is same as the proof of Lemma 9.5.1.

**Lemma 9.5.2** *If no job in $\boldsymbol{J}_{i-1}$ is preempted according to $\boldsymbol{A}_{i-1}^+$ and $\boldsymbol{A}_{i-1}^-$, then $S^-(J_i) \leq S^+(J_i)$.*

**Corollary 9.5.2** *If no job in $\boldsymbol{J}_{i-1}$ is preempted according to $\boldsymbol{A}_{i-1}^+$ and $\boldsymbol{A}_{i-1}$, then $S(J_i) \leq S^+(J_i)$.*

**Corollary 9.5.3** *If no job in $\boldsymbol{J}_{i-1}$ is preempted according to $\boldsymbol{A}_{i-1}$ and $\boldsymbol{A}_{i-1}^-$, then $S^-(J_i) \leq S(J_i)$.*

The proofs of these corollaries, being same as the proof of Lemma 9.5.2, are omitted.

**Lemma 9.5.3**  *If no job in $\boldsymbol{J}_i$ is preempted according to $\boldsymbol{A}_i^+$ and $\wp_i^+(S^+(J_i))$ is a subsequence of $\wp_i^-(S^-(J_i))$, then no job in $\boldsymbol{J}_i$ is preempted according to the minimal schedule $\boldsymbol{A}_i^-$.*

**Lemma 9.5.4**  *If no job in $\boldsymbol{J}_i$ is preempted according to $\boldsymbol{A}_i^+$ and $\wp_i^+(S^+(J_i))$ is a subsequence of $\wp_i^-(S^-(J_i))$, then no job in $\boldsymbol{J}_i$ is preempted according to the actual schedule $\boldsymbol{A}_i$.*

In fact, we can restate Lemmas 9.5.3 and 9.5.4 more precisely. Instead of $\wp_i^+(S^+(J_i))$ being a subsequence of $\wp_i^-(S^-(J_i))$, we say "if $\wp_i^+(S^+(J_i))$ and $\wp_i^-(S^-(J_i))$ are identical." The following lemma says that this seemingly more restrictive condition is in fact not more restrictive.

**Lemma 9.5.5**  *If no job in $\boldsymbol{J}_i$ is preempted according to $\boldsymbol{A}_i^+$ and $\wp_i^+(S^+(J_i))$ is a subsequence of $\wp_i^-(S^-(J_i))$, then $\wp_i^+(S^+(J_i))$ is identical to $\wp_i^-(S^-(J_i))$.*

**Lemma 9.5.6**  *If no job in $\boldsymbol{J}_i$ is preempted according to $\boldsymbol{A}_i^+$ and the two observable starting sequences $\wp_i^+(S^+(J_i))$ and $\wp_i^-(S^-(J_i))$ are identical, then the actual starting sequence $\wp_i(S(J_i))$ is identical to $\wp_i^+(S^+(J_i))$ (or $\wp_i^-(S^-(J_i))$).*

**Lemma 9.5.7**  *If no job in $\boldsymbol{J}_i$ is preempted according to $\boldsymbol{A}_i^+$ and the two observable starting sequences $\wp_i^+(S^+(J_i))$ and $\wp_i^-(S^-(J_i))$ are identical, then $S^-(J_i) \leq S(J_i) \leq S^+(J_i)$.*

**Theorem 9.5.4**  *If no job in $\boldsymbol{J}_i$ is preempted according to $\boldsymbol{A}_i^+$ and the two observable starting sequences $\wp_i^+(S^+(J_i))$ and $\wp_i^-(S^-(J_i))$ are identical, then $F^-(J_i) \leq F(J_i) \leq F^+(J_i)$.*

**Proof:**  From Lemma 9.5.4, no job in $\boldsymbol{J}_i$ is preempted according to the actual schedule $\boldsymbol{A}_i$. From Lemma 9.5.7, we know that $S(J_i) \leq S^+(J_i)$. Moreover, $e_i \leq e_i^+$. $F(J_i) \leq F^+(J_i)$ follows directly. Similarly, because $S^-(J_i) \leq S(J_i)$ (by Lemma 9.5.7), $e_i^- \leq e_i$, and $J_i$ is not preempted in all schedules, $F^-(J_i) \leq F(J_i)$.  □

Obviously, the upper bound of $F(J_i)$ given by this theorem is tight. For example, for the system in Figure 9.1, no job in $\boldsymbol{J}_3$ is preempted according to the maximal schedule $\boldsymbol{A}_3^+$, and $\wp_3^+(S^+(J_3))$ is identical to $\wp_3^-(S^-(J_3))$. Consequently, we can conclude that the completion time of $J_3$ is never later than $F^+(J_3)$, which is 13 according to Figure 9.1 (a). Similarly, for the system consisting of $m$ jobs that is mentioned earlier, no job in $\boldsymbol{J}_m$ is preempted according to the maximal schedule $\boldsymbol{A}_m^+$, and $\wp_m^+(S^+(J_m))$ is identical to $\wp_m^-(S^-(J_m))$. Hence the completion time of each job $J_i$ is at most equal to $F^+(J_i)$.

## 9.5.4    Conditions for Unpredictable Executions

A natural question to ask at this point is whether a tight bound can be derived in a similar manner for the case when there is no preemption in the maximal schedule and $\wp_i^-(S^-(J_i))$ is a subsequence of $\wp_i^+(S^+(J_i))$. Figure 9.3 illustrates the impossibility. Parts (a) and (b) show the maximal and minimal schedules, respectively. Part (c) shows a possible actual schedule. $J_1, J_2, J_3$, and $J_4$ have the

| job | $r_i$ | $d_i$ | $e_i$ |
|-----|-------|-------|-------|
| $J_1$ | 0 | 10 | 5 |
| $J_2$ | 0 | 10 | $[1,6]$ |
| $J_3$ | 4 | 15 | 8 |
| $J_4$ | 2 | 20 | 10 |
| $J_5$ | 18 | 25 | 3 |
| $J_6$ | 5 | 200 | 100 |
| $J_7$ | 0 | 22 | 2 |

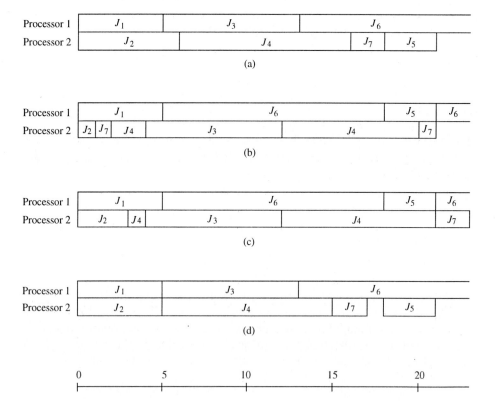

**Figure 9.3** An Example Illustrating Unpredictable Start Times and Completion Times

same parameters as the ones in Figure 9.1 except that the execution time of $J_2$ is in the range $[1, 6]$ and the release times of $J_4$ is 2. The parameters of $J_5, J_6,$ and $J_7$ are listed in the table in Figure 9.3. As shown in Figure 9.3, $\wp_7^-(S^-(J_7)) = (J_1, J_2, J_7)$ is a subsequence of $\wp_7^+(S^+(J_7)) = (J_1, J_2, J_3, J_4, J_6, J_7)$, but the actual starting sequence $\wp_7(S(J_7)) = (J_1, J_2, J_4, J_3, J_6, J_5, J_7)$, according to the actual schedule in part (c), is not. The actual start time of $J_7$ is larger than the maximal start time $S^+(J_7)$, illustrating that the start time is not predictable in this case. Moreover, according to both $\boldsymbol{A}_7^+$ and $\boldsymbol{A}_7^-$, no job is preempted before the start time of $J_7$, but $J_4$ and $J_6$ are preempted before $S(J_7)$ according to the actual schedule in Figure 9.3(c).

Similarly, when some job(s) in $\boldsymbol{J}_i$ is preempted before the completion time of $J_i$ in the maximal schedule, the start time and completion time of $J_i$ may be unpredictable, even though all the starting sequences are same. Furthermore, the actual starting sequence may be different from the observable starting sequences, even though the two observable starting sequences are same. Sometimes in the actual schedule, a job may be preempted by a different job from the one in the maximal schedule, even though all the starting sequences are same. Examples illustrating these facts can be found in [16]. We note from these examples that the completion times of the jobs are in fact accurately predicted by the upper bounds given by Theorem 9.5.3. These examples cause us to ask whether the bounds in Theorem 9.5.3 are tight in some sense when there is preemption in the maximal schedule. This question remains to be addressed in the future.

## 9.6     Some Jobs Are Nonpreemptable

In this section we present two algorithms for finding upper bounds of start times and completion times of independent N/N/F jobs, where some of the jobs are nonpreemptable. The algorithms deal with three cases: when all jobs are nonpreemptable, when preemptable jobs are migratable, and when preemptable jobs are not migratable. For all three cases, the release times of all jobs are assumed to be arbitrary but fixed.

### 9.6.1     Totally Nonpreemptable Case

A lower-priority nonpreemptable job whose release time is earlier than $J_i$ may be executed to completion after $J_i$ in the observable schedules but before $J_i$ in the actual schedule. Consequently, we cannot ignore such lower-priority jobs when trying to find the start time and the completion time of $J_i$. Let $\boldsymbol{N}$ denote the set of nonpreemptable jobs and $\boldsymbol{N}_i$ denote the subset of nonpreemptable jobs that have release times earlier than $J_i$ and priorities lower than $J_i$. Let $\boldsymbol{P}_n^-$ be a schedule of $\boldsymbol{J}_n^-$ constructed by assuming that all the jobs are preemptable and migratable. Let $\boldsymbol{B}_i$ denote the set of jobs in $\boldsymbol{N}_i$ which start before $J_i$ in $\boldsymbol{P}_n^-$. The following lemmas give us the basis of an algorithm that can be used to find upper bounds of the start times and completion times of independent N/N/F jobs.

**Lemma 9.6.1**   *Every job $J_i$ is blocked at most once by a lower-priority job with release time earlier than $r_i$.*

**Proof:**   Let $J_k$ be the job with the earliest release time among all the jobs in $\boldsymbol{J}_i$. Clearly, $J_k$ is blocked at most once. We now suppose that every job in $\boldsymbol{J}_i$ starting before $J_i$ is blocked at most once. Let $J_l$ be the job in $\boldsymbol{J}_i$ that is in the starting sequence $\wp_i(S(J_i))$ and completes last among the $m$ jobs in $\boldsymbol{J}_i$ which are scheduled last on the $m$ processors before $S(J_i)$. If $J_l$ completes after $r_i$, $J_i$ will not be blocked further. If $J_l$ completes before $r_i$, $J_i$ is blocked at most once; the effect of blocking suffered by $J_l$ has no influence on $J_i$.                                       □

**Lemma 9.6.2**   *A job $J_l$ in $\boldsymbol{N}_i$ but not in $\boldsymbol{B}_i$ cannot start before $J_i$ in the actual schedule $\boldsymbol{A}_n$.*

**Proof:**   Let $J_l$ be a job in $\boldsymbol{N}_i$ which does not start before $J_i$ according to $\boldsymbol{P}_n^-$. Suppose that $J_l$ starts before $J_i$ in $\boldsymbol{A}_n$. In other words, according to $\boldsymbol{A}_n$, at $S(J_l)$ all the jobs with higher priorities than $J_l$ have already started and there is a free processor on which $J_l$ can start. In $\boldsymbol{P}_n^-$ all jobs have minimum execution times, and all jobs are treated as preemptable and migratable. $J_l$ must also start at or before $S(J_l)$. This conclusion contradicts our supposition that $J_l$ does not start before $J_i$ in $\boldsymbol{P}_n^-$.                                       □

Lemma 9.6.2 allows us to identify the lower-priority jobs among all the jobs in $\boldsymbol{N}_i$ that have a chance to start before $J_i$ in the actual schedule. We only need to consider the subset $\boldsymbol{B}_i$ when trying to bound the completion time of $J_i$.

We note that Lemma 9.6.1 does not mean that we can simply bound the start time of $J_i$ by $S^+(J_i)$ plus the largest of the maximum execution times of jobs in $\boldsymbol{B}_i$. During the time when $J_i$ is blocked, higher-priority jobs with release times later than $r_i$ may become ready. These higher-priority jobs may be scheduled before $J_i$, further delaying its start time.

Algorithm $\mathcal{INNF}$ takes these considerations into account when trying to bound the worst-case completion times. It considers one job at a time, from the job with the highest priority to the job with the lowest priority. In order to find the worst-case completion time of $J_i$, Algorithm $\mathcal{INNF}$ transforms $J_i$ and jobs in $\boldsymbol{J}_{i-1}$ as follows. In this transformation, every job is transformed into two jobs. Let $G_k$ and $H_k$ denote the two jobs transformed from $J_k$ in steps 1 and 2.

In step 1 the parameters of the transformed jobs $G_i$ and $H_i$ are computed from those of $J_i$. $G_i$'s execution time is equal to the largest of the maximum execution times of jobs in $\boldsymbol{B}_i$ if $\boldsymbol{B}_i$ is nonempty and is equal to zero if $\boldsymbol{B}_i$ is empty, and $G_i$'s release time is release time $r_i$ of $J_i$. $H_i$'s execution time is equal to $J_i$'s maximum execution time $e_i^+$ and $H_i$'s release time $h_i$ is $r_i$ plus $G_i$'s execution time. Let 0 be a priority that is higher than the priority of $J_1$. The priority of $G_i$ is 0 and the priority of $H_i$ is equal to that of $J_i$. $G_i$ simulates the job that blocks $J_i$, and $H_i$ simulates $J_i$ blocked by $G_i$. Step 1 also computes the parameters of $G_k$ and $H_k$ for each $J_k$ for $k = 1, \ldots, i-1$. $G_k$ has release time $r_k$. Its execution time is equal to the largest of the maximum execution times of jobs in $\boldsymbol{B}_k$ if $\boldsymbol{B}_k$ is nonempty and is equal to zero if $\boldsymbol{B}_k$ is empty. $G_k$'s priority is equal to 0. $H_k$ is a job with jittered release time $[h_k^-, h_k^+] = [r_k, r_k + \text{execution time of } G_k]$, execution time equal to $e_k^+$, and priority equal to that of $J_k$. Step 2 uses Algorithm $\mathcal{IPMJ}$ presented earlier and transforms each job $H_k$ into a job $L_k$ with a fixed release time, for $k = 1, \ldots, i-1$. Let $\boldsymbol{G}_i$ and $\boldsymbol{L}_{i-1}$ denote the sets of jobs $\{G_1, \ldots, G_i\}$ and $\{L_1, \ldots, L_{i-1}\}$, respectively. In step 3 of Algorithm $\mathcal{INNF}$, $\boldsymbol{G}_i$, $\boldsymbol{L}_{i-1}$, and $H_i$ are scheduled according to the given nonpreemptable, priority-driven algorithm. An upper bound of the completion time $F(J_i)$ of $J_i$ is equal to the completion time of $H_i$ in the resultant schedule.

$\boldsymbol{L}_{i-1}$ is not a subset of $\boldsymbol{L}_i$; $\boldsymbol{L}_i$ needs to be constructed for every job $J_i$. Consequently, the complexity of Algorithm $\mathcal{INNF}$ is $O(n^2)$. Figure 9.4 illustrates how Algorithm $\mathcal{INNF}$ predicts the worst-case completion time of the job $J_5$. The schedules in parts (a), (b), and (c) are the maximal schedule, the actual schedule, and the resultant schedule generated by Algorithm $\mathcal{INNF}$, respectively. In the actual schedule, $J_4$ blocks $J_3$, and $J_3$ delays $J_5$ since it has a higher-priority than $J_5$. In the schedule generated by Algorithm $\mathcal{INNF}$, the blocking of $J_3$ by $J_4$ is accounted for by its blocking job $G_3$, which has release time $r_3$ and execution time $e_4^+$.

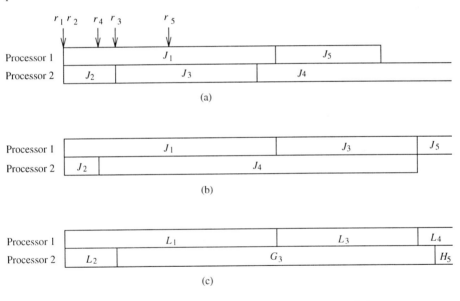

(a)

(b)

(c)

**Figure 9.4**  An Example Illustrating Algorithm $\mathcal{INNF}$

The following theorem allows us to conclude that if $H_i$ can complete by the deadline $d_i$ of $J_i$ in the schedule generated by algorithm $\mathcal{INNF}$, then $J_i$ always completes by $d_i$. The proof of the theorem can be found in [16].

**Theorem 9.6.1**   *The completion time $F(J_i)$ of $J_i$ is no later than the completion time of the transformed job $H_i$ in the schedule of $\boldsymbol{G}_i$, $\boldsymbol{L}_{i-1}$, and $H_i$ generated by algorithm $\mathcal{INNF}$.*

Because lower-priority preemptable jobs do not block any job, we can use Algorithm $\mathcal{INNF}$ with very little change to find the completion times of all jobs when some jobs are preemptable and migratable. Specifically, step 3 of Algorithm $\mathcal{INNF}$ treats (1) all the jobs in $\boldsymbol{G}_i$ as nonpreemptable, (2) $L_k$ in $\boldsymbol{L}_{i-1}$ as preemptable (nonpreemptable) if $J_k$ is preemptable (nonpreemptable), and (3) $H_i$ as preemptable (nonpreemptable) if $J_i$ is preemptable (nonpreemptable).

### 9.6.2   Nonpreemptable and Nonmigratable Case

In the case where some jobs are nonpreemptable and some jobs are preemptable but not migratable, the actual start time and completion time of $J_i$ may be postponed beyond $S^+(J_i)$ and $F^+(J_i)$ by two kinds of jobs. A nonpreemptable lower-priority job may block some jobs in the actual schedule but not in the maximal schedule. Some higher-priority jobs may preempt some jobs in the actual schedule but not in the maximal schedule.

When preemptable jobs are not migratable, Lemma 9.6.2 no longer holds. Similarly, the schedule of $\boldsymbol{J}_n^-$ constructed by assuming all the jobs are preemptable and nonmigratable gives us no information on which lower-priority jobs can actually start before $J_i$. Examples illustrating these facts can be found in [16].

Algorithm $\mathcal{INNF} - \mathcal{N}$ can be used to bound the completion times in this case. It consists of two steps. Step 1 considers the delays in the start time of each job $J_i$ by nonpreemptable lower-priority jobs. It uses Algorithm $\mathcal{INNF}$ to construct a schedule for each $J_i$, using the set $\boldsymbol{N}_i$ instead of $\boldsymbol{B}_i$ in step 1 of Algorithm $\mathcal{INNF}$. Let $F_*^+(J_i)$ denote the completion time of $H_i$ in this schedule. In step 2 it computes the delays in the completion time of $J_i$ due to higher-priority jobs which may preempt $J_i$, or some job starting before $J_i$, in the actual schedule. Step 2 makes use of the following theorem. This theorem is stated in terms of the set $\boldsymbol{E}_i$; $\boldsymbol{E}_i$ contains the subset of $\boldsymbol{J}_i$ in which each job $J_k$ is released after some preemptable job in $\boldsymbol{J}_i$ with a priority lower than itself (that is, $J_k$), as well as every job $L_k$ (the job created in step 2 of Algorithm $\mathcal{INNF}$) that is not scheduled on the same processor as $H_i$ to complete before $H_i$ in the schedule constructed by Algorithm $\mathcal{INNF}$. The complexity of Algorithm $\mathcal{INNF} - \mathcal{N}$ is $O(n^2)$.

**Theorem 9.6.2**   $F(J_i) \leq F_*^+(J_i) + \displaystyle\sum_{J_k, L_k \in \boldsymbol{E}_i} e_k^+ - (e_i^+ - e_i).$

## 9.7   Summary and Future Work

In this chapter, we have presented several worst-case upper bounds and efficient algorithms. They can predict reliably the worst-case completion times of independent jobs in homogeneous distributed systems in which jobs are dynamically dispatched and scheduled on available processors in an event-driven manner. One of the algorithms allows us to take into account release times jitters. The others assume fixed arbitrary release times but take into account the effects of nonpreemptability and nonmigratability.

In a heterogeneous distributed system, processors are divided into $c$ different types. Let $m_j$ be the number of type $j$ processors and $m = \sum_{j=1}^{c} m_j$. There are two cases: when a job can execute on only one type of processors and when a job can execute on several types of processors. The upper bounds and algorithms presented in earlier sections can be modified easily and applied to find upper bounds of completion times of jobs when each job can execute on only one type of processor. A job $J_i$ is of type $j$ if it can be executed on a type $j$ processor. Because a type $j$ job can be scheduled only on type $j$ processors, the job set $\boldsymbol{J}$ is divided into disjoint subsets according to the processor types of jobs. We can find the worst-case completion times of type $j$ jobs by applying the algorithms described in the previous sections to the subset of type $j$ jobs on $m_j$ identical processors. An algorithm for determining the worst-case completion times for the case where each job can execute on several types of processors can be found in [16].

The results presented here constitute a small part of the theoretical basis needed for a comprehensive validation strategy that is capable of dealing with dynamic distributed real-time systems. Much of the work on schedulability analysis remains to be done. For example, we must be able to deal with dependencies between jobs. Ways to reliably predict the worst-case completion times of jobs that have precedence constraints and/or share resources are yet not available. This is a part of our future work.

## Acknowledgments

This work has been partially supported by ONR Contracts N00014-89-J-1181 and N000-92-J-1815 and NASA Grant NAG 1-1613. The authors wish to thank Drs C. L. Liu and W. K. Shih for their comments and suggestions.

## References

[1] C. L. Liu and J. W. Layland. Scheduling algorithms for multiprogramming in a hard-real-time environment. *Journal of the Association for Computing Machinery*, 20(1):46–61, January 1973.

[2] J. Leung and J. Whitehead. On the complexity of fixed-priority scheduling of periodic, real-time tasks. *Performance Evaluation*, 2:237–250, 1982.

[3] L. Sha, R. Rajkumar, and J. P. Lehoczky. Priority inheritance protocols: An approach to real-time synchronization. *IEEE Transactions on Computers*, 39(9):1175–1185, September 1990.

[4] T. P. Baker. A stack-based allocation policy for realtime processes. In *Proceedings of IEEE 11th Real-Time Systems Symposium*, pages 191–200, December 1990.

[5] B. Sprunt, L. Sha, and J. P. Lehoczky. Aperiodic task scheduling for hard-real-time systems. *Journal of Real-Time Systems*, 1:27–60, 1989.

[6] J. P. Lehoczky, L. Sha, and Y. Ding. The rate monotone scheduling algorithm: Exact characterization and average case behavior. In *Proceedings of IEEE 10th Real-Time Systems Symposium*, pages 166–171, December 1989.

[7] R. L. Graham. Bounds on multiprocessing timing anomalies. *SIAM Journal of Applied Mathematics*, 17(2):416–429, March 1969.

[8] J. Blazewicz. Selected topics in scheduling theory. *Annals of Discrete Mathematics*, 31:1–60, 1987.

[9] C. Shen, K. Ramamritham, and J. A. Stankovic. Resource reclaiming in real-time. In *Proceedings of IEEE 11th Real-Time Systems Symposium*, pages 41–50, December 1990.

[10] D. W. Gillies and J. W. S. Liu. Greed in resource scheduling. *Acta Informatica*, 28:755–775, 1991.

[11] M. H. Klein, T. Ralya, B. Pollak, R. Obenza, and M. G. Harbour. *A Practitioner's Handbook for Real-Time Analysis: Guide to Rate Monotonic Analysis for Real-Time Systems*. Kluwer Academic Publishers, Dordrecht, The Netherlands, 1993.

[12] L. Sha and S. S. Sathaye. A systematic approach to designing distributed real-time systems. *IEEE Computer*, 26(9):68–78, September 1993.

[13] R. Bettati. *End-to-End Scheduling to Meet Deadlines*. Ph.D. thesis, University of Illinois at Urbana-Champaign, 1994.

[14] J. W. S. Liu, J. Redondo, Z. Deng, T. Tia, R. Bettati, A. Silberman, M. Storch, R. Ha, and W. Shih. PERTS: A prototyping environment for real-time systems. Technical Report UIUCDCS-R-93-1802, University of Illinois at Urbana-Champaign, 1993.

[15] E. L. Lawler and J. M. Moore. A functional equation and its application to resource allocation and scheduling problem. *Management Science*, 16:77–84, 1969.

[16] R. Ha and J. W. S. Liu. Validating timing constraints in multiprocessor and distributed real-time systems. Technical Report UIUCDCS-R-93-1833, University of Illinois at Urbana-Champaign, 1993.

# 9.A   Appendix

## Proof of Lemma 9.5.1

Because no job is preempted in $A_i^+$, at most $(m-1)$ jobs with release times at or before $t$ are not completed according to the schedule $A_i^+$. This fact and the facts that $e_j^- \leq e_j^+$ for all jobs, no job can be scheduled before its release time, and no job is preempted according to $A_i^-$ before $t$ allow us to conclude that there are at most $(m-1)$ jobs with release times at or before $t$ yet to be completed, keeping at most $(m-1)$ processors busy.                                                            $\square$

## Proof of Lemma 9.5.2

According to $A_i^+$, at $S^+(J_i)$, a processor is available to execute the lowest-priority job in the set $J_i$. In other words, at $S^+(J_i)$, at most $(m-1)$ of all the higher-priority jobs with release times at or earlier than $S^+(J_i)$ have not yet completed. Therefore, in $A_{i-1}^+$, at most $(m-1)$ processors are busy at $S^+(J_i)$. It follows from Lemma 9.5.1, in $A_{i-1}^-$, that at most $(m-1)$ processors are busy at $S^+(J_i)$. Consequently, there is a processor available to execute $J_i$ at $S^+(J_i)$ in $A_i^-$. This fact allows us to conclude that $S^-(J_i) \leq S^+(J_i)$.                                    $\square$

## Proof of Lemma 9.5.3

The lemma is trivially true for the highest-priority job $J_1$. Assuming that no job in $J_{i-1}$ is preempted according to $A_{i-1}^-$ (and hence $A_i^-$), we prove below by contradiction that $J_i$ is also not preempted according to $A_i^-$.

Suppose that $J_i$ is preempted in the minimal schedule $A_i^-$; let $J_l$ be the first job in $J_{i-1}$ to preempt $J_i$. We note that $S^-(J_l)$ must be the release time $r_l$ of $J_l$. Moreover, because $J_l$ starts after $J_i$ in $A_i^-$ and hence is not in $\wp_i^-(S^-(J_i))$ and because $\wp_i^+(S^+(J_i))$ is a subsequence of $\wp_i^-(S^-(J_i))$, $J_l$ is not in $\wp_i^+(S^+(J_i))$, that is, $J_l$ starts after $J_i$ in $A_i^+$ also.

Lemma 9.5.2 tells us that $S^-(J_i) \leq S^+(J_i)$. This fact and the fact that $J_l$ preempts $J_i$ at $r_l$ in $A_i^-$ allow us to conclude that $J_i$ is not completed at $r_l$ in the maximal schedule $A_i^+$. That $J_i$ is not preempted at $r_l$ in $A_i^+$ means that among all the jobs that are in $J_i - \{J_l\}$ and have release times at or earlier than $r_l$, at most $(m-1)$ are not yet completed. In other words, according to $A_i^+$, at $r_l$, at most $(m-1)$ processors are busy executing jobs that are in $J_i - \{J_l\}$ and have release times at or earlier than $r_l$. There is an idle processor available on which $J_l$ can be scheduled without preempting $J_i$. In $[0, r_l)$, there is no preemption according to both $A_i^+$ and $A_i^-$. Lemma 9.5.1 allows us to conclude that an idle processor is also available at $r_l$ according to $A_i^-$, $J_l$ is scheduled on this processor, not the one executing $J_i$ at $r_l$, and $J_l$ does not preempt $J_i$ in $A_i^-$. This conclusion contradicts our supposition that $J_l$ preempts $J_i$.                                        $\square$

## Proof of Lemma 9.5.4

The lemma is trivially true for the highest-priority job $J_1$. Assuming that no job in $\boldsymbol{J}_{i-1}$ is preempted according to $\boldsymbol{A}_{i-1}$, we now prove that $J_i$ is not preempted according to $\boldsymbol{A}_i$.

Suppose that $J_i$ is preempted in the actual schedule $\boldsymbol{A}_i$ and $J_l$ is the first job to preempt $J_i$. Clearly, $J_l$ is not in $\wp_i(S(J_i))$. Moreover, because $J_l$ has a priority higher than $J_i$ and $J_l$ starts after $J_i$, $S(J_l)$ must be the release time $r_l$ of $J_l$. $J_l$ cannot start earlier than $S(J_l)$ in any schedule. We need to consider the following two cases:

(1) $J_l$ is in $\wp_i^+(S^+(J_i))$, that is, $J_l$ starts no later than $J_i$ in $\boldsymbol{A}_i^+$. From Lemma 9.5.3 and the induction hypothesis, no job in $\boldsymbol{J}_{i-1}$ is preempted according to both $\boldsymbol{A}_{i-1}^-$ and $\boldsymbol{A}_{i-1}$. Corollary 9.5.3 tells us that $S^-(J_i) \leq S(J_i)$. In other words, $J_l$ is not in $\wp_i^-(S^-(J_i))$. This contradicts the assumption that $\wp_i^+(S^+(J_i))$ is a subsequence of $\wp_i^-(S^-(J_i))$.

(2) $J_l$ is not in $\wp_i^+(S^+(J_i))$, that is, $J_i$ starts before $J_l$ in $\boldsymbol{A}_n^+$. From the induction hypothesis and assumption, no job in $\boldsymbol{J}_{i-1}$ is preempted according to both $\boldsymbol{A}_{i-1}$ and $\boldsymbol{A}_{i-1}^+$. Corollary 9.5.2 tells us that $S(J_i) \leq S^+(J_i)$.

The facts that $J_i$ is preempted at $r_l$ and $S(J_i) \leq S^+(J_i)$ tell us that $J_i$ is not completed at $r_l$ in the maximal schedule $\boldsymbol{A}_i^+$. Nevertheless, $J_i$ is not preempted at $r_l$ in $\boldsymbol{A}_i^+$. We therefore can conclude that among all the jobs that are in $\boldsymbol{J}_i - \{J_l\}$ and have release times at or earlier than $r_l$, at most $(m-1)$ are not yet completed. In other words, at $r_l$, at most $(m-1)$ processors are busy executing these jobs according to $\boldsymbol{A}_i^+$ and there is an idle processor on which $J_l$ can be scheduled without preempting $J_i$. Corollary 9.5.1 allows us to conclude that an idle processor is also available at $r_l$ according to $\boldsymbol{A}_i$; $J_l$ is scheduled on this processor, not the one executing $J_i$ at $r_l$, and $J_l$ does not preempt $J_i$ in $\boldsymbol{A}_i$. This conclusion contradicts our supposition that $J_l$ preempts $J_i$.                    □

## Proof of Lemma 9.5.5

When no job in $\boldsymbol{J}_i$ is preempted according to $\boldsymbol{A}_i^+$ and $\wp_i^+(S^+(J_i))$ is a subsequence of $\wp_i^-(S^-(J_i))$, no job in $\boldsymbol{J}_i$ is preempted according to $\boldsymbol{A}_i^-$, by Lemma 9.5.3. Lemma 9.5.2 tells us that $S^-(J_i) \leq S^+(J_i)$; that is, $J_i$ starts in $\boldsymbol{A}_i^-$ no later than in $\boldsymbol{A}_i^+$.

Every job $J_k$ in $\wp_i^-(S^-(J_i))$ has a higher-priority than $J_i$. That it starts at or before the time $S^-(J_i)$ in $\boldsymbol{A}_i^-$ means that $J_k$'s release time $r_k$ is at or before $S^-(J_i)$. Hence, $r_k$ is at or earlier than $S^+(J_i)$, $J_k$ starts at or before $S^+(J_i)$ in $\boldsymbol{A}_i^+$, and $J_k$ is in $\wp_i^+(S^+(J_i))$. In other words, there is no such job that is in $\wp_i^-(S^-(J_i))$ but not in $\wp_i^+(S^+(J_i))$.                    □

## Proof of Lemma 9.5.6

We prove the lemma by contradiction. We will need the fact that no job is preempted according to $\boldsymbol{A}_i^-$ and $\boldsymbol{A}_i$. This fact is true because of Lemmas 9.5.3, 9.5.4, and 9.5.5. Moreover, from Corollaries 9.5.2 and 9.5.3, we know that $S^-(J_i) \leq$

$S(J_i) \leq S^+(J_i)$. Suppose that $\wp_i(S(J_i))$ is different from $\wp_i^+(S^+(J_i))$ while the two observable subsequences are identical. Then, we need to consider the following three cases, each of which leads to a contradiction.

(1) Some job $J_k$ in $\boldsymbol{J}_{i-1}$ is in $\wp_i^+(S^+(J_i))$ but is not in $\wp_i(S(J_i))$. In other words, $J_k$ starts after $J_i$ in $\boldsymbol{A}_i$. Because $J_k$ has a priority higher than $J_i$ and $J_k$ starts after $J_i$ in $\boldsymbol{A}_i$, $J_k$'s release time $r_k$ is later than $S(J_i)$. We can conclude that $J_k$ cannot start at or earlier than $S^-(J_i)$, which is equal to or earlier than $S(J_i)$. Therefore, $J_k$ is not in $\wp_i^-(S^-(J_i))$, and $\wp_i^-(S^-(J_i))$ is not identical to $\wp_i^+(S^+(J_i))$.

(2) Some job $J_k$ in $\boldsymbol{J}_{i-1}$ is in $\wp_i(S(J_i))$ but is not in $\wp_i^-(S^-(J_i))$. In other words, $J_k$ starts no later than $J_i$ in $\boldsymbol{A}_i$. $J_k$'s release time $r_k$ is no later than $S(J_i)$. Because $S(J_i) \leq S^+(J_i)$ and $J_k$ has a higher-priority than $J_i$, we can conclude that $J_k$ starts no later than $J_i$ in $\boldsymbol{A}_i^+$, and $J_k$ is in $\wp_i^+(S^+(J_i))$. Hence, $\wp_i^+(S^+(J_i))$ is not identical to $\wp_i^-(S^-(J_i))$.

(3) The set of jobs in $\wp_i^+(S^+(J_i))$ (or $\wp_i^-(S^-(J_i))$) is same as the set of jobs in $\wp_i(S(J_i))$, but $\wp_i(S(J_i))$ is a permutation of $\wp_i^+(S^+(J_i))$ (or $\wp_i^-(S^-(J_i))$). Suppose that the order in which $J_k$ and $J_l$ appear in $\wp_i(S(J_i))$ is different from the order in $\wp_i^+(S^+(J_i))$ (or $\wp_i^-(S^-(J_i))$): $J_k$ starts no later than $J_l$ in $\boldsymbol{A}_i^+$ (or $\boldsymbol{A}_i^-$) but later than $J_l$ in $\boldsymbol{A}_i$. In other words, $J_k$ is in $\wp_i^+(S^+(J_l))$ but not in $\wp_i(S(J_l))$. Equivalently, $J_l$ is in $\wp_i(S(J_k))$ but not in $\wp_i^-(S^-(J_k))$. If $J_k$ has a higher-priority than $J_l$, an argument similar to the one used in case (1) allows us to conclude that $J_k$ cannot start earlier than $J_l$ in $\boldsymbol{A}_i^-$. $J_k$ is not in $\wp_i^-(S^-(J_l))$, and hence $\wp_i^-(S^-(J_i))$ is not identical to $\wp_i^+(S^+(J_i))$. Similarly, if $J_l$ has a higher-priority than $J_k$, we can use an argument similar to the one used in case (2) to show that $J_l$ is in $\wp_i^+(S^+(J_k))$ and $\wp_i^+(S^+(J_i))$ and $\wp_i^-(S^-(J_i))$ are not identical.    □

## Proof of Lemma 9.5.7

Lemma 9.5.4 tells us that when no job in $\boldsymbol{J}_i$ is preempted in $\boldsymbol{A}_i^+$ and the two observable starting subsequences $\wp_i^+(S^+(J_i))$ and $\wp_i^-(S^-(J_i))$ are identical, no job in $\boldsymbol{J}_i$ is preempted in the actual schedule $\boldsymbol{A}_i$. Because no job in $\boldsymbol{J}_i$ is preempted according to both $\boldsymbol{A}_i^+$ and $\boldsymbol{A}_i$, by Corollary 9.5.2, $S(J_i) \leq S^+(J_i)$.

$S^-(J_i) \leq S(J_i)$ can be proved similarly as $S(J_i) \leq S^+(J_i)$.    □

# Chapter 10

# Preemptive Priority-Based Scheduling: An Appropriate Engineering Approach

## Alan Burns

Scheduling theories for fixed-priority scheduling are now sufficiently mature that a genuine engineering approach to the construction of hard real-time systems is possible. In this chapter we review recent advances. A flexible computational model is adopted that can accommodate periodic and sporadic activities, different levels of criticality, process interaction and blocking, cooperative scheduling (deferred preemption), release jitter, precedence constrained processes, arbitrary deadlines, deadlines associated with specific events (rather than the end of a task's execution), and offsets. Scheduling tests for these different application characteristics are described. This model can be supported by structured, object-oriented, or formal development methods. The chapter also considers the issues involved in producing safe and predictable kernels to support this computational model.

## 10.1  Introduction

Recent developments in the analysis of fixed-priority preemptive scheduling have made significant enhancements to the models introduced by Lui and Layland in their seminal 1973 paper [33]. These developments, taken together, now represent a body of analysis that forms the basis for an engineering approach to the design, verification, and implementation of hard real-time systems. In this chapter we review much of this analysis in order to support the thesis that safety critical real-time systems can, and should, be built using these techniques.

Preemptive priority-based scheduling prescribes a run-time environment in which tasks, with a priority attribute, are dispatched in priority order. Priorities are, essentially, static. Processes are either runnable, in which case they are held on a notional (priority-ordered) run queue; delayed, in which case they are held on a notional delay queue; or suspended, in which case they are awaiting an event which may be triggered externally (via an interrupt) or internally (from some other task).

Most existing hard real-time systems are implemented using a static table-driven schedule (often called a *cyclic executive*). Priority-based scheduling has many advantages over this static approach (see Locke [35] for a detailed discussion of this issue). In essence these advantages all relate to one theme—increased flexibility. However, in order to challenge the role of static scheduling as the premier implementation model, priority-based scheduling must:

- provide the same level of predictability (of temporal behavior)

- allow a wide range of application characteristics to be accommodated

- enable dependable (safe) implementations to be supported.

All of these issues are addressed in this review, which is organized as follows. The remainder of this introduction outlines a simple model of task attributes and shows how worst-case response times can be calculated. Section 10.2 considers the necessary run-time kernel and shows how its temporal characteristics can be accommodated and its implementation can be made safe. Section 10.3 extends the simple model to include a number of important application characteristics. One criticism that is often made about scheduling work is that it is not well integrated with other aspects of software production; in Section 10.4 we outline a computational model that is amenable to timing analysis and software production. A structured, an object-oriented, and a formal instantiation of this computational model are described. Finally, in Section 10.5 we address another criticism of priority scheduling: namely that it is too static. Methods of integrating soft and best-effort scheduling into the framework provided by the static priority-based model are considered. Section 10.6 presents our conclusions.

## 10.1.1   Calculating Response Times

We restrict our considerations to single-processor systems. The techniques are, however, applicable in a distributed environment with static allocation [52]. The processor must support a bounded, fixed number of tasks, $N$. The general approach is to assign (optimally) unique priorities to these tasks and then to calculate the worst-case response time, $R$, for each task. These values can then be compared, trivially, with each task's deadline, $D$. This approach is illustrated with the derivation of appropriate analysis for a simple computational model.

Each of the $N$ tasks is assumed to consist of an infinite number of invocation requests, each separated by a minimum time $T$. For periodic tasks this value $T$ defines its period, for sporadic tasks $T$ is the minimum inter-arrival time for the event that releases the task. Each invocation of the task requires $C$ computation time (worst case). During this time the task does not suspend itself. Tasks are independent of each other apart from their use of shared protected data. To bound priority inversion a ceiling priority protocol is assumed (for access to the protected data) [10, 42]. This gives rise to a maximum blocking time of $B$ (i.e., $B_i$ is the maximum time task $i$ can be blocked waiting for a lower-priority task to complete its use of protected data). Our simple model has the restriction that each task's deadline must be less than, or equal to, its inter-arrival time (i.e. $D_i \leq T_i$ for all $i$). We also assume that context switches, and so on, take no time (this optimistic assumption is removed in Section 10.2). Each task has a unique priority, $P$.

For this simple model optimal priority assignment is easily obtained. Leung and Whitehead [32] showed that deadline monotonic assignment is optimal, i.e. the shorter a task's deadline, the higher its priority ($D_i < D_j \implies P_i > P_j$).

The worst-case response time for the highest-priority task (assuming task 1 has the highest priority) is given by:

$$R_1 = C_1 + B_1.$$

For the other tasks it is necessary to calculate the worst-case interference suffered by the task. Interference results from higher-priority tasks executing while the task of interest is preempted. It can be shown, for this simple computational model, that maximum interference occurs when all higher-priority tasks are released at the same time as the task under consideration—this time is known as the *critical instant*. This leads to the following relation:

$$R_i = B_i + C_i + \sum_{j \in hp(i)} \left\lceil \frac{R_i}{T_j} \right\rceil C_j$$

where $hp(i)$ is the set of tasks of higher priority then task $i$.

As $R_i$ appears on both sides of this equation a simple solution is not possible [27]. Rather, an iterative (recurrent) process is derived. Let $w$ be a window (time interval) into which we attempt to insert the computation time of the task. We expand $w$ until all of $C_i$ can be accommodated:

$$w_i^{n+1} = B_i + C_i + \sum_{j \in hp(i)} \left\lceil \frac{w_i^n}{T_j} \right\rceil C_j. \tag{10.1}$$

The iteration can start with $w_i^o = C_i$ (although more optimal start values can be found). It is trivial to show that $w_i^{n+1} \geq w_i^n$. If $w_i^n > D_i$, then task $i$ cannot be guaranteed to meet its deadline. However, if $w_i^n = w_i^{n+1}$, then the interaction process has terminated and $R_i = w_i^n$.

The derivation of this result together with examples of its use can be found in a number of publications [3, 4, 7, 27]. Note that $w_i$ is referred to by Lehoczky [28] as the $i - level$ busy period since the "priority" of the processor does not fall below that of task $i$ during this period. The following simple example shows how response times are calculated using Equation (10.1). Consider the simple three-task set given in Table 10.1. Let the blocking time be 2 units of computation for Task_1 and Task_2.

Task_1 has the highest priority and has a worst-case response time of 4 (i.e., its own computation time plus the blocking time). Task_2 has an earliest possible

**Table 10.1  Simple Task Set**

|         | Period T | Computation Time, C | Priority P | Deadline D | Blocking Time, B |
|---------|----------|---------------------|------------|------------|------------------|
| Task_1  | 8        | 2                   | 1          | 6          | 2                |
| Task_2  | 12       | 3                   | 2          | 10         | 2                |
| Task_3  | 20       | 7                   | 3          | 20         | 0                |

response time of 3; putting this value into Equation (10.1) gives a right-hand-side value of 7, 7 then balances the equation:

$$7 \; = \; 3 \; + \; 2 \; + \; \left\lceil \frac{7}{8} \right\rceil 2.$$

For Task_3 the initial estimate is 7; the right-hand side of Equation (10.1) is thus (note the blocking factor is zero):

$$7 \; + \; \left\lceil \frac{7}{8} \right\rceil 2 \; + \; \left\lceil \frac{7}{12} \right\rceil 3.$$

This yields 12. Hence:

$$7 \; + \; \left\lceil \frac{12}{8} \right\rceil 2 \; + \; \left\lceil \frac{12}{12} \right\rceil 3.$$

This now yields a value of 14. A further iteration produces 17. Another iteration then gives a value of 19; this value is stable (i.e., actually causes Equation (10.1) to balance) and therefore the actual worst response time of Task_3 is 19. Hence all tasks will complete before their deadlines.

In Section 10.3 we show how this simple model can be extended. But first we must consider the implementation of preemptive priority-based scheduling.

## 10.2   Safe and Predictable Kernels

It is undoubtedly true that the support needed to implement preemptive priority-based dispatching is more complicated than static scheduling—although the difference is not as large as it would first appear. It should be noted that a full operating system is not required, only a micro-kernel with efficient context switching and an ample range of priorities [9].

The production of a correct kernel necessitates the development of a formal specification of the interface to the kernel and its behavior following calls to that interface. Formal notations such as Z [45] have been used to give precise definitions to such kernels [13, 46].

The notion of a safety kernel was introduced by Rushby [36] to imply a kernel that was not only built correctly but had a positive role in ensuring that various negative behaviors (of the application) were inhibited. A prototype run-time support system for a restricted subset of Ada9X has been built along these lines [20]. It monitors all application tasks to make sure that they do not use more resources (in particular, CPU processing time) than was assigned to them during the scheduling analysis of the application. If a task attempts to run over its budget, it has an exception raised to enable it to "clear up" (the exception handler also has a budget defined).

In addition to engineering the kernel to an appropriate level of reliability, it is also critically important for the timing characteristics of the kernel to be obtainable. This is true both in terms of models of behavior and actual cost (i.e., how long each kernel routine takes to execute). The following sections address these issues.

## 10.2.1    Predicting Overheads

Simple scheduling models ignore kernel behavior. Context switch times and queue manipulations are, however, significant and cannot usually be assured to take negligible time unless a purpose-built processor is used. For example, the FASTCHART [49] processor can genuinely claim to have zero overheads.

Even if a dual processor is used to perform context switches (in parallel with the application/host processor), there will be some context switch overhead. When a software kernel is used, models of actual behavior are needed. Without these models excessively pessimistic overheads must be assumed. The interrupt handler for the clock will usually also manipulate the delay queue. For example (in one implementation [20]), when there are no tasks on the delay queue, then a cost of 16 $\mu s$ may be experienced. If an application has 20 periodic tasks that all share a critical instant, then the cost of moving all 20 tasks from the delay queue to the run queue may take 590 $\mu s$—i.e., 37 times more.

Context switch times can be accounted for by adding their cost to the task that causes the context switch. For periodic tasks, the cost of placing itself on the delay queue (and switching back to the lower-priority task it preempted) is, however, not necessarily a constant. It may depend on the potential size of the delay queue (i.e., on the number of periodic tasks in the application).

To model adequately the delay queue manipulations that occur in the clock interrupt handler (i.e., at one of the top priority levels), it is necessary to address directly the overheads caused by each periodic task. It may be possible to model the clock interrupt handler using two parameters: $C_{CLK}$ (the overheads occurring on each interrupt assuming that tasks are on the delay queue but that none are removed), and $C_{PER}$ (the cost of moving one task from the delay queue to the run queue). Each periodic task now has a v*fictitious* task with the same period $T$ but with computation time $C_{PER}$. Equation (10.1) thus becomes :

$$w_i^{n+1} = B_i + C_i + \sum_{j \in hp(i)} \left\lceil \frac{w_i^n}{T_j} \right\rceil C_j + \left\lceil \frac{w_i^n}{T_{CLK}} \right\rceil C_{CLK} + \sum_{f \in fpt} \left\lceil \frac{w_i^n}{T_f} \right\rceil C_{PER}$$

(10.2)

where $fpt$ is the set of fictitious periodic tasks.

Our analysis of kernels indicates that this model is itself overly simplistic and hence too pessimistic. There is usually a cost saving when more than one task has been transferred between the queues. A three-parameter model would hence seem to be appropriate, (see Burns, Wellings and Hutcheon for a derivation of this model).

In addition to supporting periodic behavior, the kernel will also have to accommodate interrupt handling and the release of sporadic tasks following an interrupt. This again gives rise to parameters that must be established before full scheduling analysis can be undertaken [17].

## 10.2.2   Tick-Driven Scheduling

In all the above analysis, periodic tasks are assumed to have periods which are exact multiples of the clock period. They can thus be *released* (i.e., put on the run queue) as soon as they *arrive* (i.e., are potentially runnable). If the release time is not equal to the arrival time, then the task is said to suffer from *release jitter*. Although it would usually be a poor engineering decision to have release jitter, there are situations where it might be inevitable.

Sporadic tasks are also assumed to be released as soon as the event on which they are waiting has occurred. A full tick-driven scheduler will, however, poll for these events as part of the clock interrupt-handling routine. This has the advantage of clearly defining the times at which new tasks can become runnable. It also allows safety checks to be implemented that can ensure that sporadic tasks are not released too often. With this implementation scheme, sporadic tasks are bound to suffer release jitter.

Let $J_i$ represent the worst-case release jitter suffered by task $i$ (i.e., the maximum time between task arrival and release). Two modifications of Equation (10.1) are now required. First, the calculated response time according to Equation (10.1) is from release, not arrival. The true (desired) maximum response time is measured from arrival:

$$R_i^{TRUE} \;=\; R_i \,+\, J_i.$$

Second, the interference that this task has on lower-priority tasks is increased. This is because two releases of the task can be closer together than the notional minimum $T_j$. If one arrival suffers maximum release jitter, but the next does not, then the two releases have a time gap of only $T_j - J_j$. The interference factor in Equation (10.1) must be modified to give [3]:

$$w_i^{n+1} \;=\; B_i \,+\, C_i \,+\, \sum_{j \in hp(i)} \left\lceil \frac{w_i^n + J_j}{T_j} \right\rceil C_j. \tag{10.3}$$

## 10.2.3   Cooperative Scheduling

The kernels described above have all implemented true preemptive dispatching. In this section an alternative scheme is outlined (the use of deferred preemption). This has a number of advantages but can still be analyzed by the scheduling technique embodied in Equation (10.1). In Equation (10.1) there is a blocking term $B$ that accounts for the time a lower-priority task may be executing while a higher-priority task is runnable. In the application domain this may be caused by the existence of data that is shared (under mutual exclusion) by tasks of different priority. Blocking can, however, also be caused by the kernel. Many systems will have the non-preemptable context switch as the longest blocking time (e.g., the release of a higher priority task being delayed by the time it takes to context switch to a lower priority task-even though an immediate context switch to the higher-priority task will then ensue).

One of the advantages of using the immediate ceiling priority protocol [10] (to calculate and bound $B$) is that blocking is not cumulative. A task cannot be blocked both by an application task and a kernel routine-only one could actually be happening when the higher-priority task is released.

Cooperative scheduling exploits this non-cumulative property by increasing the situations in which blocking can occur. Let $B^{MAX}$ be the maximum blocking time in the system (using a convention approach). The application code is then split into non-preemptive blocks, the execution times of which are bounded by $B^{MAX}$. At the end of each of these blocks the application code offers a "de-scheduling" request to the kernel. If a high-priority task is now runnable, then the kernel will instigate a context switch; if not, the currently running task will continue into the next non-preemptive block.

Although this method requires the careful placement of de-scheduling calls, these could be inserted automatically by the worst-case execution-time analyzer which is itself undertaking a control flow analysis of the code.

The normal execution of the application code is thus totally cooperative. A task will continue to execute until it offers to de-schedule. To give some level of protection over corrupted (or incorrect) software, a safe kernel could use an interrupt mechanism to abort the application task if any non-preemptive block lasts longer than $B^{MAX}$. The use of cooperative scheduling is illustrated by the DIA architecture [44]. Here a kernel support chip deals with all interrupts and manages the run queue. The de-scheduling call is a single instruction and has negligible cost if no context switch is due.

The use of deferred preemption has two important advantages. It increases the schedulability of the system, and it can lead to lower values of $C$. In Equation (10.1), as the value of $w$ is being extended, new releases of higher-priority tasks are possible that will further increase the value of $w$. With deferred preemption no interference can occur during the last block of execution. Let $F_i$ be the execution time of the final block, such that when the task has consumed $C_i - F_i$, the last block has (just) started. Equation (10.1) is now solved for $C_i - F_i$ rather than $C_i$:

$$w_i^{n+1} = B_i + C_i - F_i + \sum_{j \in hp(i)} \left\lceil \frac{w_i^n}{T_j} \right\rceil C_j. \qquad (10.4)$$

When this converges (i.e., $w_i^{n+1} = w_i^n$) the response time is given by:

$$R_i = w_i^n + F_i.$$

Table 10.2  Kernel Attributes

| Notation | Description |
|---|---|
| $C_{sw}^P$ | Cost of context switch away from a periodic task— may be a function of maximum size of delay queue |
| $C_{sw}^R$ | Cost of context switch to a task currently on the run queue |
| $C_{CLK}$ | Clock interrupt handler cost (no tasks being moved) |
| $T_{CLK}$ | Clock interrupt handler period |
| $C_{PER}$ | Cost of moving one task from delay queue to run queue |
| $C_{sw}^S$ | Cost of context switch away from a sporadic task— when it suspends waiting for its next release |
| $C_{SP}$ | Cost of releasing a sporadic (i.e., putting it on the run queue) |
| $C_{INT}$ | Cost of an interrupt handler that just releases a sporadic task |
| $B_K$ | Maximum length of non-preemption in the kernel |

In effect the last block of the task has executed with a higher priority (the highest) than the rest of the task. Lehoczky has shown how increases in priority during the execution of a task can lead to better schedulability [24].

The other advantage of deferred preemption comes from predicting more accurately the execution times of a task's non-preemptable basic blocks. Modern processors have caches, prefetch queues, and pipelines that all significantly reduce the execution times of straight-line code. Typically, estimations of worst-case execution time are forced to ignore these advantages and obtain very pessimistic results because preemption will invalidate caches and pipelines. Knowledge of non-preemption can, however, be used to predict the speedup that will occur in practice. Zhang, Burns, and Nicholson have shown how a 20% reduction in worst-case execution time ($C$) can be obtained by modeling the prefetch queue directly [54]; Harmon, Baker, and Whalley have shown how the pipeline on a 68020 can be analyzed at the micro-code level [25]; and cache advantages can also be predicted. If modern processors are to be used in real-time systems, then this type of analysis is necessary.

**Summary.**  A number of the parameters defined in the above discussion (for example, $J$ and $F$) are, in reality, attributes of the application's task set. Others relate to the kernel itself. Table 10.2 summarizes those that have been introduced in this discussion. Their values are of key significance in determining the feasibility of any application running on top of the kernel. It follows that any kernel used for safety critical real-time systems will not only have to be instrumented but must also allow these parameters to be verified.

If interrupt handlers differ in terms of their cost, then a single $C_{INT}$ value will not suffice.

## 10.3    An Extendible Model

Application requirements rarely (if ever) fit the simple model described in the introduction. An appropriate scheduling theory is one that can be extended to meet the particular needs of newer application requirements. In this section we consider a number of extensions to the basic model:

1. Variations in $C$ and $T$

2. Precedence Relations and Multi-Deadline Tasks

3. Arbitrary Deadlines (i.e., $D > T$)

4. Internal Deadlines (i.e., not all $C$ has to be completed by $D$)

5. Offsets and Phased Executions

We then consider how priorities can be assigned optimally when the simple rate monotonic or deadline monotonic policies do not apply.

### 10.3.1    Variation in Computation Time and Period

Where it can be shown that a task will not execute for its maximum time on each release, it is pessimistic to assume that it does. For example, a periodic task may do a small amount of data collection in each period but every, say, 10 periods analyses this data using a much more expensive algorithm. This behavior can simply be modeled, in Equation (10.1), as two tasks, one running every period (with a small $C$) and the other running every $10T$ (with a larger computation time).

Variations in period are also possible. Bursts of activity involving a number of short periods are following by inactivity. Sporadic tasks released by interrupts can behave in this manner. For example, a sporadic could have a worst-case (minimum) arrival interval of 1 ms but have the restriction that no more than 5 releases can occur within a 100 ms interval. If the worst-case arrival interval is very small, then it is acceptable to collapse the 5 releases into a single task (with period of 100 ms). However, a more accurate prediction of the interference this task will impose on lower-priority tasks, in the window $w$, can be derived [3]. Let $T$ be the outer period (e.g., 100 ms in the above example) and $t$ be the smaller period (e.g., 1 ms). Also let $n$ be the number of releases in the outer period (e.g., 5). Task $j$ will have an interference on lower-priority tasks ($I_i^j$) as follows:

$$ I_i^j = \left\lfloor \frac{w_i^n}{T_j} \right\rfloor n_j C_j + min \left\{ \left\lceil \frac{w_i^n - \left\lfloor \frac{w_i^n}{T_j} \right\rfloor T_j}{t_j} \right\rceil , n_j \right\} C_j. \qquad (10.5) $$

This can then be incorporated into Equation (10.1). The first term in Equation (10.5) gives the cost of complete cycles (outer period) contained within $w_i^n$. The second term gives the additional cost of minor cycles, this is upper bounded by the cost of a complete burst, $n_j C_j$.

**Table 10.3  An Example Task Set**

|     | C | D | T  | P |
|-----|---|---|----|---|
| $L$ | 2 | 5 | 20 | 2 |
| $Q$ | 2 | 4 | 20 | 1 |
| $S$ | 4 | 7 | 20 | 3 |

**Table 10.4  Transformed Task Set**

|       | C | D  | T  | P |
|-------|---|----|----|---|
| $L$   | 2 | 5  | 20 | 1 |
| $Q^T$ | 2 | 9  | 20 | 2 |
| $S^T$ | 4 | 16 | 20 | 3 |

## 10.3.2  Precedence Relationships and Multi-deadline Tasks

A common paradigm for structuring real-time software is as a set of tasks linked via precedence relations (i.e., task B cannot start until task A has completed). Data is often passed along these precedence links, but as the tasks involved never execute together, mutual exclusion over this data need not be enforced.

For illustration, consider a simple straight-line "transaction" involving three tasks: $L$, which must run before $Q$, which runs before $S$. Table 10.3 contains the given timing attributes for these tasks. Note that the periods of the three tasks are identical and that the overall deadline is 16.

A naive application of, say, deadline monotonic analysis will assign priorities ($P$) as given in the table. The schedulability test will then assume that all tasks are released at the same time and deem the task set to be unschedulable.

The critical instant assumption (i.e., all tasks released simultaneously) is clearly too pessimistic for precedence-constrained tasks. We know that they never wish to execute together. Both $Q$ and $S$ require an *offset*. That, is they cannot execute at the start of the period.

A simple transformation can be applied to tasks with offsets that share the same period. We relate the deadlines of all tasks not to their start times but to the start time of the transaction. This will not affect $L$ but it will mean that $Q$ and $S$ have their deadlines stretched (we refer to the new tasks as $Q^T$ and $S^T$). Table 10.4 now has the new deadlines and priorities for the task set.

The priority model will now ensure that $L$ executed first, then $Q^T$, and then $S^T$. Moreover, the new task set is schedulable and would actually allow other tasks to be given priorities interleaved with this transaction. As the tasks share the same period, only one of them will experience a block. Note, however, that task $L$ (and $Q^T$) must not undertake any external blocking, as this would free the processor to execute $Q^T$ (or $S^T$) early.

This formulation results in tasks having lower priorities for later positions down the precedence relationship (i.e., $S$ lower than $L$). As indicated earlier, Har-

bour, Klein, and Lehoczky have shown that by increasing the priority (and imposing some mechanism to stop the later tasks starting too early) can result in greater
schedulability [24].

Finally, it should be noted that precedence relations can be implemented with
real offsets (i.e., $Q$ not being released until time 5). This technique is considered in
Section 10.3.5.

The above approach for dealing with precedence-constrained tasks has a further property that will enable multi-deadline tasks to be accommodated. Processes
can exist that have more than one deadline: they are required to complete part of
their computations by one time and the remainder by a later time. This can occur
when a task must read an input value very early in the period and must produce
some output signal at a later time.

To implement multi-deadline tasks it is necessary for the run-time system interface to facilitate dynamic priority changes. The task is modeled as a precedence-
related transaction. Each part of the transaction is thus assigned a priority (as described above). The task actually executes in a number of distinct phases, each with
its own priority: for example, a high priority to start with until its first deadline is
met, then a lower priority for its next deadline.

## 10.3.3   Arbitrary Deadlines

To cater for situations where $D_i$ (and hence potentially $R_i$) can be greater than
$T_i$, we must adapt the analysis. The following outlines the approach of Tindell
[50, 53]. When deadline is less than (or equal) to period, it is only necessary to
consider a single release of each task. The critical instant, when all higher-priority
tasks are released at the same time, represents the maximum interference, and
hence the response time following a release at the critical instant must be the
worst-case. However, when deadline is greater than period, a number of releases
must be considered. We assume that the release of a task will be delayed until any
previous releases of the same task have completed. For each potentially overlapping
release we define a separate window $w(q)$, where $q$ is just an integer identifying a
particular window (i.e., $q = 0, 1, 2, ...$). Equation (10.1) can be extended to have
the following form:

$$w_i^{n+1}(q) \;=\; (q+1)C_i \;+\; B_i \;+\; \sum_{j \in hp(i)} \left\lceil \frac{w_i^n(q)}{T_j} \right\rceil C_j. \qquad (10.6)$$

For example with $q$ equal to 2, three releases of task $i$ will occur in the window.
For each value of $q$, a stable value of $w(q)$ can be found by iteration—as in Equation (10.1). The response time is then given as

$$R_i(q) \;=\; w_i^n(q) \;-\; qT_i \qquad (10.7)$$

e.g., with $q = 2$ the task started $2T_i$ into the window and hence the response time
is the size of the window minus $2T_i$.

The number of releases that need to be considered is bounded by the lowest
value of $q$ for which the following relation is true:

$$R_i(q) \leq T_i. \tag{10.8}$$

At this point the task completes before the next release, and hence subsequent windows do not overlap. The worst-case response time is then the maximum value found for each $q$:

$$R_i = \max_{q=0,1,2,\dots} R_i(q). \tag{10.9}$$

Note that for $D \leq T$ relation (10.8) is true for $q = 0$ (if the task can be guaranteed), in which case Equations (10.6) and (10.7) simplify back to the original equation.

### 10.3.4   Internal Deadlines

In a recent report, Gerber [23] argues that it is only meaningful to attach a deadline to the last observable event of a task. Moreover, this last observable event may not be at the end of the task's execution; i.e., there may be a number of internal actions after the last output event.

When the model for analysis is enhanced to include kernel overheads (as described in Section 10.2), it is necessary to "charge" to each task the cost of the context switch that allows it to preempt a lower-priority task plus the cost of the context switch back to the preempted task once the higher-priority task has completed. For realistic context switch times (i.e., not zero) it is meaningless to attach the "deadline" to the end of the context switch. Figure 10.1 gives a block representation of a task's execution (excluding preemptions for higher-priority tasks). Phase a is the initial context switch to the task, phase b is the task's actual execution time up to the last observable event, phase c represents the internal actions of the task following the last observable event, and phase d is the cost of the context switch away from the task. The real deadline of the task is at the end of phase b.

In the following we shall denote by $C^D$ the computation time required by the real internal deadline (i.e., phases a + b only), and by $C^T$ the total computation time of the task in each period (i.e., all four phases). Note that there is no requirement to complete $C^T$ by $T$ as long as $C^D$ is completed by $D$. Hence an adaptation of the arbitrary deadline model (see the previous section) is required.

If we include the two phases of computation into Equation (10.5), we get:

$$w_i^{n+1}(q) = qC_i^T + C_i^D + B_i + \sum_{j \in hp(i)} \left\lceil \frac{w_i^n(q)}{T_j} \right\rceil C_j^T. \tag{10.10}$$

This when combined with (10.7), (10.8), and (10.9) allows the worst-case response time for $C_i^D$ to be calculated (assuming maximum $C_i^T$, interference from early releases of itself). Equation (10.6) could be used directly to calculate the response time for $C_i^T$, but this value is not directly relevant to this formulation. It can be

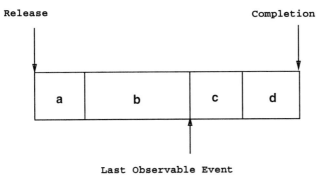

Figure 10.1  Four Phases of a Task's Execution

Table 10.5  Gerber's Task Set

| Task | $T$ | $C^D$ | $C^T$ | $D$ | $R^D$ | $R^T$ |
|------|-----|-------|-------|-----|-------|-------|
| 1 | 1000 | 400 | 400 | 1000 | 400 | 400 |
| 2 | 1600 | 400 | 400 | 1600 | 800 | 800 |
| 3 | 2500 | 493 | 653 | 2500 | 2493 | 2653 |

shown, trivially, that for utilization less than 100% there exists bounded response times for all tasks.[1] What is important is that $R_i^D$ is less than $D_i$.

The above analysis can be applied to the simple task set introduced and discussed by Gerber [23]. Table 10.5 shows the characterization of three tasks; note that $D = T$ for all entries, and that no task experiences blocking. With rate monotonic analysis, task 3 cannot be guaranteed. Gerber shows that by transforming this task, of the 653 units of computation only 493 are required to be completed by the deadline. He then shows how an implementation scheme can be used to guarantee task 3. However, the above analysis furnishes a value for $R_3^D$ of 2493, which is just before the deadline (and period). Hence standard preemptive priority-based dispatching will satisfy the timing requirements of this task set. No transformation is needed. Note, for completeness, that the worst-case response time of $R_3^T$ is 2653.

## 10.3.5    Offsets and Phased Executions

Perhaps the most extreme restriction of the basic model is that it assumes that all tasks could be released at the same time (the critical instant). This assumption simplifies the analysis but it is not applicable on many occasions. Cyclic execu-

---

[1]Consider a set of periodic tasks with 100% utilization, all of which have deadlines equal to the LCM of the task set; clearly, within the LCM no idle tick is used and no task executes for more than it needs and hence all deadlines must be met.

**Table 10.6  Three Offset Tasks**

| Task Name | Period | Computation Time | Offset | Priority | Deadline |
|---|---|---|---|---|---|
| Command actuators | 200 | 2.13 | 50 | 20 | 14 |
| Request DSS data | 200 | 1.43 | 150 | 19 | 17 |
| Request wheel speeds | 200 | 1.43 | 0 | 18 | 22 |

**Table 10.7  Combined Task**

| Task Name | Period | Computation Time | Offset | Priority | Deadline |
|---|---|---|---|---|---|
| Combined task | 50 | 2.13 | 0 | 18 | 14 |

tives (static scheduling), for example, explicitly use offsets to order executions and obtain feasible schedules. Without offsets, priority-based systems are often too pessimistic; with offsets, equivalent behavior to cyclic executives can be obtained [8]. For example, a recent case study [18, 19] of the Olympus satellite AOCS (Attitude and Orbital Control System), containing some 30 tasks, was deemed unschedulable by the standard deadline monotonic test (i.e., Equation (10.1) modified to include kernel overheads). On inspection it contained three tasks of identical period that could not all be scheduled. Table 10.6 gives the details of these tasks.

The only requirements on these tasks were their periods (and deadlines); they did not have to be released together. By giving "Command Actuators" an offset of 50 ms and "Request DSS Data" an offset of 150 ms, their work was spread out. From an analysis point of view it was possible to replace these three tasks by just one (see Table 10.7). This task has a computation time requirement equal to the greatest of the original three, and a deadline which is the shortest. The task set (including this new one but not the originals) now passed the schedulability test.

Hence a simple transformation, that actually increases the overall load on the system (as it notionally executes every 50 ms) can increase schedulability by incorporating offsets.

In the more general case of arbitrary offset relationships it would be desirable to have an exact feasibility test. One way of testing feasibility is just to simulate the behavior of the system. Leung shows that the length of interval that should be examined is twice the LCM of the task set plus the largest offset (assuming tasks have been normalized to have offsets less than period) [31]. For task sets with periods that are relative primes this implies a computationally infeasible test.

Recently, Tindell [8, 51] has developed a feasible but inexact test, using the window approach outlined earlier for arbitrary deadlines. The resulting maximum window size is only marginally greater than the one that would be obtained for the full necessary and sufficient analysis. The derivation of this result is, however, beyond the scope of this review.

## 10.3.6   Priority Assignment

The formulations given in the last three sections (i.e., arbitrary deadlines, internal deadlines, and offsets) have the common property that no simple algorithms (such as rate or deadline monotonic) gives the optimal priority ordering. In this section we reproduce Audsley's algorithm for assigning priorities in these situations. Audsley [1] proves the following theorem:

**Theorem 10.3.1** *If task $\tau$ is assigned the lowest priority and is feasible, then if a feasible priority ordering exists for the complete task set, an ordering exists with $\tau$ assigned the lowest priority.*

If a $\tau$ is found then a corollary of the theorem can be applied to the lowest-but-one priority, and so on; hence a complete priority ordering is obtained (if one exists).
    The following code in Ada implements the priority assignment algorithm; set is an array of tasks that is notionally ordered by priority, set(1) being the highest priority, set(N) being the lowest. The procedure task_test tests to see whether task K is feasible at that place in the array. The double loop works by first swapping tasks into the lowest position until a feasible result is found; this task is then fixed at that position. The next priority position is then considered. If at any time the inner loop fails to find a feasible task, the whole procedure is abandoned. Note that a concise algorithm is possible if an extra swap is undertaken.

```
procedure assign_pri (set : in out process_set; N : natural;
                      OK : in out boolean) is
begin
  for K in reverse 1..N loop
    for next in reverse 1..K loop
      swap(set,K,next);
      task_test(set,K,OK);
      set(K).P := K;
      exit when OK;
    end loop;
    exit when not OK;
  end loop;
end;
```

If the test of feasibility is exact (necessary and sufficient), then the priority ordering is optimal. Thus for arbitrary deadlines and internal deadlines (without blocking), an optimal ordering is found. Where a non-exact test is used (for example, with the offset test), the priority ordering reflects the quality of the test.

## 10.3.7   Summary

This section has reviewed a number of recent results that have taken simple schedulability equations and extended them to cover a range of realistic and necessary application features. Many variations of the basic equations have been given, but

Table 10.8  Task Attributes

| Notation | Description | Default |
|---|---|---|
| $T$ | Minimum time between task releases (or burst releases) | |
| $D$ | Deadline relative to start of any precedence relation | $T$ |
| $O$ | Release offset relative to start of a precedence relationship | $0$ |
| $J$ | Release jitter | $0$ |
| $n, T, t$ | Characteristics of a bursty task, $n$ in time $T$ with a minimum gap between inner cycles of $t$ | $1, T, 0$ |
| $B$ | Blocking time | $B_K$ |
| $C$ or $C^T$ | Computation time | |
| $C^D$ | Computation time before last observable event | $C$ |
| $F$ | Final non-preemptive section of computation time | $0$ |
| $P$ | Priority (calculated) | |
| $R$ | Response time (calculated) | |

they can all be integrated together and implemented within some appropriate software tool. Table 10.8 gives the attributes that are needed for each task if the full analysis described in this review is to be applied; those attributes with a default value can be omitted (i.e., the default can be assumed).

The overheads due to implementing fixed-priority scheduling do reduce processor utilization, but the use of internal deadlines and offsets can move utilization close to 100%. A final technique is worth noting for some tasks sets that still cannot be scheduled by the fixed-priority approach. Even when 100% utilization is needed it is not necessary to move to a fully earliest deadline approach [21, 33]. It has been shown that a dual-priority scheme is adequate [15]. Here some low-priority tasks are given an intermediate deadline at which their priority is raised (if they still have work to do). This minimally dynamic scheme provides for optimal schedulability.

## 10.4    Computational Model

Scheduling work is often criticized for not addressing the broader problems of engineering real-time systems. It is clear that attempting to apply scheduling analysis to arbitrary software is doomed to failure. The interface between software development and scheduling is the computational model. This model must be amenable to analysis but also be a natural end product of the development process. Moreover, the computational model must be applicable to implementations on multi-processors and distributed systems.

The computational model implicit in the scheduling analysis reviewed in this chapter has the following properties:

- It consists of active entities (tasks) and protected shared data areas.

- The only communication between active entities is via the shared data areas; the only exception to this is when one active entity releases another for execution.

- Precedence relationships between active entities are allowed.

- Active entities have temporal attributes defined (such as deadline, offset, period, minimal arrival rate, etc.).

- Shared data areas provide mutual exclusion but do not arbitrarily block clients.

- Entities are allocated to single processing units.

- The allowable remote actions (in a distributed system) are a remote write to a shared data area and the releasing of a remote active entity.

This simple model has sufficiently expressive power to allow systems to be designed, allocated to distributed hardware, and analyzed for realistic worst-case behavior. To support the view that it is sufficient for design work, three development methods will be reviewed briefly.

(a) A traditional approach — MASCOT

(b) A formal method — TAM

(c) An object-oriented approach — HRT-HOOD

It should be clear how the computational model leads to programs/systems that can be analyzed. Note that the desire to reduce blocking will dictate the use of simple shared data areas. The granularity of the active entities is also significant. All three design methods encourage the use of decomposition rules that lead to activities (modules) that are temporarily, as well as functionally, decoupled.

## 10.4.1   MASCOT

The MASCOT [11] method involves the production of a *real-time network*. Within this network there are activities and IDAs (intercommunication data areas). For hard real-time systems two forms of IDA are used : *pools* and *signals*. Pools provide non-destructive non-blocking read and destructive non-blocking write; signals have the same write characteristics, but the read is destructive and blocking. Hence pools are used for simple mutual exclusion, while signals are employed to release an activity that is waiting for data.

Recently, MASCOT has been extended to give full life-cycle support to the production of real-time systems. An interesting feature of this DORIS (Data-Oriented Requirements Implementation Scheme) technology is the use of algorithms that provide non-blocking mutual exclusion. If pools are single-writer, then pool I/O operations never block (for example, a read event will always return the most recent completely written data-even if a write-to operation is concurrently updating it). DORIS also advocates the use of the deferred preemption method described in Section 10.2.2. However, the main use of MASCOT is as a design method. It is used primarily in the safety-critical aerospace industry.

### 10.4.2   TAM

Many formal development methods have a very synchronous computational model that leads to difficult timing analysis. They often had to incorporate the extreme assumption of maximum parallelism and zero cost for many activities. By comparison, TAM (Temporal Agent Model) [39–41] is defined to support the development (via refinement) of systems that can be analyzed accurately.

TAM is a wide-spectrum language consisting of specification statements and concrete executable statements. As a system is being developed, specifications are refined into more concrete forms (a refinement calculus is defined for TAM). An executable program (i.e., one with no remaining specifications) consists of *agents* and *shunts*. Shunts are single-writer multiple-reader shared data areas. Agents can communicate only via shunts. All computations and communications take time, and data passing through a shunt is time stamped. Agents can also be released by the event of writing to a shunt.

First-order predicate logic has been extended (conservatively) to give the formal basis to TAM. A simple form of temporal logic (and the introduction of *timed variables*) is used to define period activities, deadlines and so on.

A number of case studies [2, 37, 38] have been written that indicate that real-time systems can be specified, refined, and analyzed using the TAM formulation.

### 10.4.3   HRT-HOOD

HRT-HOOD [14, 16] (Hard Real-Time HOOD) is an adaptation of HOOD (Hierarchical Object-Oriented Design). A system is decomposed into terminal objects that must be either cyclic, sporadic, or protected. Cyclic and sporadic objects contain a single thread of control. Protected objects are required to provide mutual exclusion (e.g., by ceiling priorities). Sporadic objects also have a single method used to release them for execution. Rules of decomposition and usage force the terminal system to match the computational model described earlier. Object attributes are used to hold the timing characteristics and derived properties such as priority and response time. HRT-HOOD is a structured method supporting a graphical representation and a textual equivalent syntactical form. It has been used, together with some of the scheduling analysis discussed in this chapter, on an extensive case study [18].

One of the interesting features of the HRT-HOOD method is that it contains systematic mapping from the object system to Ada 9X. This indicates that the computational model is realizable in that language.

## 10.5   Slack Scheduling

It is possible to compare scheduling approaches by considering the range of techniques that has at one extreme static scheduling (cyclic executives), and at the other, best-effort scheduling [12]. Fixed-priority scheduling falls in the middle of these extremes; and indeed is often criticized as being too static by the best-effort lobby, and too dynamic by the cyclic executive supporters. The value of fixed-priority scheduling is that it does allow hard guarantees to be given, while allowing flexibility and various levels of non-determinism to be accommodated. This short section reviews the techniques that are available for allowing soft (non-guaranteed tasks) to be combined with the hard tasks that make up the safety critical subsystem being executed. The motivation of this section is to show that fixed priority scheduling can be extended into the realms of best-effort scheduling.

When there is no need for a hard task to be executing, the system is said to have *slack* available. This slack can be used to satisfy a number of application needs:

- The execution of soft aperiodic tasks

- The execution of background tasks

- The early completion of sporadic tasks

- The execution of components that enhance the utility of the hard task set.

The last entry can itself be subdivided into a number of techniques that are collectively known as *imprecise computation* [5, 6, 34, 43].

In general, best-effort scheduling [26] can be applied to collections of tasks running in slack time. The amount of slack available is, of course, dependent on the load exerted by the hard task set. This may vary in different modes of operation; so that, for example, a system that has lost processing resources may reduce its hard load (and increase its soft) so as to switch over to best-effort scheduling. In the extreme, a system could move to pure best-effort scheduling when the processing resource level is below that assumed for the static analysis undertaken as part of the fixed-priority approach.

More usually, there will be a mixture of hard and soft tasks to execute. Three implementation approaches can be identified:

- execute soft tasks at low priorities

- execute soft tasks using a hard server

- execute soft tasks using optimal slack scheduling

The motivation behind all three schemes is to execute soft tasks as early as possible (commensurate with all hard tasks meeting their deadlines by some appropriate safety margin). However, the schemes can also be compared by considering their overheads and the added complexity they impose on the kernel's design and behavior.

If all soft tasks are given priorities lower than any hard tasks, then no changes are needed in the kernel. Soft tasks are, however, executed only when the processor would otherwise be idle.

A number of different server schemes have been published [30, 47, 48] (e.g., polling server, priority exchange, deferrable server, extended priority exchange, and sporadic server). Each attempts to define a capacity of work that can be assigned to soft tasks (even when there are runnable hard tasks) without jeopardizing the hard deadlines. As the servers all reserve enough capacity for the hard tasks, they are often called *bandwidth preserving*. They make differing demands on the kernel; all need task monitoring (i.e., CPU usage) and most require soft tasks to have quotas defined and enforced.

Optimal slack scheduling takes into account the phasing, and actual execution times, of tasks to calculate the maximum slack that can be made available at any moment in time (and at each priority level). For purely periodic ($D = T$) hard task sets, Lehoczky and Ramos-Thuel give an optimal scheme that can be calculated statically (i.e., off-line) [29]. For mixed periodic and sporadic task sets (and tasks with arbitrary deadlines, release jitter, etc.) Davis *et al.* have defined an optimal scheme that requires on-line analysis. The scheme would be optimal if it had zero cost and is executed frequently [22]. With realistic costs it is possible to define the frequency of execution for maximum effect.

## 10.6    Conclusions

In this chapter simple scheduling models have been extended to include realistic kernel features and necessary application requirements. The result is a flexible computational model supported by a rich set of analysis techniques. We can conclude that fixed-priority scheduling now represents an appropriate (and arguably, a mature) engineering approach. Although the many equations and relationships must be embedded in trusted tools, this is no different from many other engineering disciplines. The real-time systems designer now has the techniques available to engineer systems rather than just build them and then see if they meet their timing requirements during extensive (and expensive) testing.

## Acknowledgments

The results presented in this chapter represent the work of many individuals within the Real-Time Systems Research Group at the University of York, UK. Thanks must particularly be given to Neil Audsley, Ken Tindell, and Andy Wellings.

## References

[1] N.C. Audsley. Optimal Priority Assignment and Feasibility of Static Priority Tasks with Arbitrary Start Times. Technical Report YCS 164, Department of Computer Science, University of York, December 1991.

[2] N.C. Audsley, A. Burns, M.F. Richardson, D.J Scholefield, A.J. Wellings, and H.S.M. Zedan. Bridging the Gap between Formal Methods and Scheduling

Theory. Technical Report YCS 195, Department of Computer Science, University of York, March 1993.

[3] N.C. Audsley, A. Burns, M.F. Richardson, K. Tindell, and A.J. Wellings. Applying New Scheduling Theory to Static Priority Pre-emptive Scheduling. *Software Enginnering Journal*, September 1993.

[4] N.C. Audsley, A. Burns, M.F. Richardson, and A.J. Wellings. Hard Real-Time Scheduling: The Deadline Monotonic Approach. In *Proceedings of the 8th IEEE Workshop on Real-Time Operating Systems and Software*, Atlanta, GA, May 1991.

[5] N.C. Audsley, A. Burns, M.F. Richardson, and A.J. Wellings. Incorporating Unbounded Algorithms into Predictable Real-Time Systems. *Computer Systems Science and Engineering*, 8(3):80–89, April 1993.

[6] N.C. Audsley, A. Burns, and A.J. Wellings. Unbounded Algorithms, Predictable Real-Time Systems and Ada 9X . In *Proceedings of the IEEE Workshop on Imprecise and Approximate Computation*, pages 11–15, Phoenix, AZ, December 1992.

[7] N.C. Audsley, A. Burns, and A.J. Wellings. Deadline Monotonic Scheduling Theory and Application. *Control Engineering Practice*, 1(1), 1993.

[8] N.C. Audsley, K. Tindell, and A. Burns. The End of the Line for Static Cyclic Scheduling. In *Proceedings of the 5th Euromicro Workshop on Real-Time Systems*, pages 36–41, Oulu, Finland, June 1993. IEEE Computer Society Press, New York.

[9] N.C. Audsley, K. Tindell, A. Burns, M.F. Richardson, and A.J. Wellings. The DrTee Architecture for Distributed Hard Real-Time Systems. In *Proceedings of the 10th IFAC Workshop on Distributed Control Systems*, Semmering, Austria, September 1991.

[10] T.P. Baker. Stack-Based Scheduling of Realtime Processes. *Journal of Real-Time Systems*, 3(1), March 1991.

[11] G. Bate. Mascot3: An Informal Introductory Tutorial. *Software Engineering Journal*, 1(3):95–102, 1986.

[12] A. Burns. Scheduling Hard Real-Time Systems: A Review. *Software Engineering Journal*, 6(3):116–128, 1991.

[13] A. Burns and A.J. Wellings. Specifying an Ada Tasking Run-Time Support System. *Ada User*, 12(4):160–186, December 1991.

[14] A. Burns and A.J. Wellings. Designing Hard Real-time Systems. In *Ada: Moving Towards 2000, Proceedings of the 11th Ada-Europe Conference, LNCS 603*, pages 116–127. Springer-Verlag, New York, 1992.

[15] A. Burns and A.J. Wellings. Dual Priority Assignment: A Practical Method for Increasing Processor Utilization. In *Proceedings of the 5th Euromicro Workshop on Real-Time Systems*, pages 48–55, Oulu, Finland, June 1993. IEEE Computer Society Press, New York.

[16] A. Burns and A.J. Wellings. HRT-HOOD: A Design Method for Hard Real-Time Ada. *Real-Time Systems*, 6(1):73–114, 1994.

[17] A. Burns and A.J. Wellings. Implementing Analysable Hard Real-Time Sporadic Tasks in Ada 9X. *Ada Letters*, 14(1):38–49, 1994.

[18] A. Burns, A.J. Wellings, C.M. Bailey, and E. Fyfe. The Olympus Attitude and Orbital Control System: A Case Study in Hard Real-Time System Design and Implementation. Technical Report YCS 190, Department of Computer Science, University of York, 1993.

[19] A. Burns, A.J. Wellings, C.M. Bailey, and E. Fyfe. The Olympus Attitude and Orbital Control System: A Case Study in Hard Real-Time System Design and Implementation. In *Ada sans frontieres, Proceedings of the 12th Ada-Europe Conference, Lecture Notes in Computer Science*. Springer-Verlag, New York, 1993.

[20] A. Burns, A.J. Wellings, and A.D. Hutcheon. The Impact of an Ada Runtime System's Performance Characteristics on Scheduling Models. In *Ada sans frontieres Proceedings of the 12th Ada-Europe Conference, Lecture Notes in Computer Science 688*, pages 240–248. Springer-Verlag, New York, 1993.

[21] H. Chetto and M. Chetto. Some Results of the Earliest Deadline Scheduling Algorithm. *IEEE Transactions on Software Engineering*, 15(10):1261–1269, October 1989.

[22] R.I. Davis, K.W. Tindell, and A. Burns. Scheduling Slack Time in Fixed Priority Pre-emptive Systems. In *Proceedings of the Real-Time Systems Symposium*, pages 222–231, December 1993.

[23] R. Gerber and S. Hong. Semantic-Based Compiler Transformations for Enhanced Schedulability. In *Proceedings of the Real-Time Systems Symposium*, pages 232–243, December 1993.

[24] M. G. Harbour, M. H. Klein, and J. P. Lehoczky. Fixed Priority Scheduling of Periodic Tasks with Varying Execution Priority. In *Proceedings of the 12th IEEE Real-Time Systems Symposium*, San Antonio, TX, December 1991.

[25] M.G. Harmon, T.P. Baker, and D.B. Whalley. A Retargetable Technique for Predicting Execution Time. In *Proceedings of the 13th Real-Time Systems Symposium*, pages 68–77. IEEE Press, New York, December 1992.

[26] E.D. Jenson, C.D. Locke, and H. Tokuda. A Time-Driven Scheduling Model for Real-Time Operating Systems. In *Proceedings of the 6th IEEE Real-Time Systems Symposium*, December 1985.

[27] M. Joseph and P. Pandya. Finding Response Times in a Real-Time System. *BCS Computer Journal*, 29(5):390–395, October 1986.

[28] J. P. Lehoczky. Fixed Priority Scheduling of Periodic Task Sets With Arbitrary Deadlines. In *Proceedings of the 11th IEEE Real-Time Systems Symposium*, pages 201–209, Lake Buena Vista, FL, December 1990.

[29] J. P. Lehoczky and S. Ramos-Thuel. An Optimal Algorithm for Scheduling Soft-Aperiodic Tasks Fixed-Priority. In *Proceedings of the Real-Time Systems Symposium*, pages 110–123, December 1992.

[30] J.P. Lehoczky, L. Sha, and J.K. Strosnider. Enhancing Aperiodic Responsiveness in Hard Real-Time Environment. In *Proceedings of the 8th IEEE Real-Time Systems Symposium*, San Jose, CA, December 1987.

[31] J.Y.T. Leung and M.L. Merrill. A Note on Preemptive Scheduling of Periodic Real-Time Tasks. *Information Processing Letters*, 11(3):115–118, 1980.

[32] J.Y.T. Leung and J. Whitehead. On the Complexity of Fixed-Priority Scheduling of Periodic, Real-Time Tasks. *Performance Evaluation (Netherlands)*, 2(4):237–250, December 1982.

[33] C.L. Liu and J.W. Layland. Scheduling Algorithms for Multiprogramming in a Hard Real-Time Environment. *Journal of the ACM*, 20(1):46–61, 1973.

[34] J.W.S. Liu, K.J. Lin, W.K. Shih, A.C.S. Yu, J.Y. Chung, and W. Zhao. Algorithms for Scheduling Imprecise Computations. *IEEE Computer*, pages 58–68, May 1991.

[35] C.D. Locke. Software Architecture for Hard Real-Time Applications: Cyclic Executives vs. Fixed Priority Executives. *Journal of Real-Time Systems*, 4(1):37–53, March 1992.

[36] J. Rushby. Kernels for Safety? In *Safe and Secure Computing Systems*, pages 310–320. Blackwell Scientific, Cambridge, MA, 1987.

[37] D. J. Scholefield. *A Refinement Calculus for Real-Time Systems*. Department of Computer Science, University of York, 1992.

[38] D. J. Scholefield and H.S.M. Zedan. The Temporal Agent Model: Theory and Practice. Technical Report YCS 163, Department of Computer Science, University of York, 1991.

[39] D. J. Scholefield and H.S.M. Zedan. A Standard for Finite TAM. Technical Report YCS 206, Department of Computer Science, University of York, September 1993.

[40] D. J. Scholefield and H.S.M. Zedan. Real-Time Refinement: Semantics and Application. In *Proceedings of MFCS '93*, Gdansk (*LNCS 711*). Springer-Verlag, New York, 1993.

[41] D. J. Scholefield and H.S.M. Zedan. A Specification Oriented Semantics for Refinement of Rea-Time Systems. *Theoretical Computer Science*, 130, 1994.

[42] L. Sha, R. Rajkumar, and J. P. Lehoczky. Priority Inheritance Protocols: An Approach to Real-Time Synchronisation. *IEEE Transactions on Computers*, 39(9):1175–1185, September 1990.

[43] W.K. Shih, J.W.S. Liu, and J.Y. Chung. Algorithms for Scheduling Imprecise Computations with Timing Constraints. In *Proceedings of the 10th IEEE Real-Time Systems Symposium*, December 1989.

[44] H.R. Simpson. A Data Interactive Architecture (DIA) for Real-Time Embedded Multi-processor Systems. In *Computing Techniques in Guided Flight RAe Conference*, April 1990.

[45] M. Spivey. *The Z Notation: A Reference Manual*, 1989.

[46] M. Spivey. Specifying a Real-time Kernel. *IEEE Software*, 7(5):21–28, September 1990.

[47] B. Sprunt, J. P. Lehoczky, and L. Sha. Exploiting Unused Periodic Time for Aperiodic Service Using the Extended Priority Exchange Algorithm. In *Proceedings of the 9th IEEE Real-Time Systems Symposium*, pages 251–258, December 1988.

[48] B. Sprunt, L. Sha, and J. P. Lehoczky. Aperiodic Task Scheduling for Hard Real-Time Systems. *Journal of Real-Time Systems*, 1:27–69, 1989.

[49] F. Stanischewski. FASTCHART: Performance, Benefits and Disadvantages of the Architecture. In *Proceedings of the 5th Euromicro Workshop on Real-Time Systems*, pages 246–250, Oulu, Finland, June 1993. IEEE Computer Society Press, New York.

[50] K. Tindell. An Extendible Approach for Analysing Fixed Priority Hard Real-Time Tasks. Technical Report YCS189, Department of Computer Science, University of York, December 1992.

[51] K. Tindell. Adding Time-Offsets to Schedulability Analysis. Technical Report YCS 221, Department of Computer Science, University of York, January 1994.

[52] K. Tindell, A. Burns, and A. Wellings. Allocating Real-Time Tasks (An NP-Hard Problem Made Easy). *Journal of Real-Time Systems*, 4(2):145–165, June 1992.

[53] K. Tindell, A. Burns, and A.J. Wellings. An Extendible Approach for Analysing Fixed Priority Hard Real-Time Tasks. *Real-Time Systems*, 6(2):133–151, 1994.

[54] N. Zhang, A. Burns, and M. Nicholson. Pipelined Processors and Worst Case Execution Time. *Real-Time Systems*, 5(4):319–343, 1993.

# Chapter 11

# An Optimal Priority Inheritance Policy For Synchronization in Real-Time Systems

Ragunathan Rajkumar, Lui Sha,
John P. Lehoczky, and Krithi Ramamritham

Hard real-time systems require predictable timing behavior, and priority-driven preemptive scheduling is increasingly being used in these systems. Resources in these enviroiments should ideally be allocated to the highest-priority task. Priority inversion is a situation in which a higher-priority job is forced to wait for a lower-priority job. Priority inversion degrades system schedulability. Hence, priority inversion should be minimized in a hard real-time environment. Unfortunately, a direct application of synchronization primitives such as semaphores, monitors, and Ada rendezvous can cause uncontrolled priority inversion, a situation in which a low-priority job blocks a higher-priority job for an indefinite period of time. In this chapter we investigate policies belonging to the class of *priority inheritance policies* that minimize priority inversion. We develop a priority inheritance policy called the *Optimal Mutex Policy* (OMP) which has two desirable properties: deadlocks are avoided and the worst-case blocking duration of a job is bounded by the duration of execution of a single critical section of a lower-priority job.

## 11.1 Introduction

### 11.1.1 Real-Time Systems

Real-time systems operate under strict timing constraints and include applications such as avionics systems, space-related systems like the Space Shuttle and Space Station, production control, robotics, and defense systems. Timing constraints of different tasks in real-time systems can be either hard, soft, or non-existent.

A timing constraint is considered to be *hard* if it must be met at all times, or is considered to be *soft* if it must be met only most of the time. For example, the processing of a reactor temperature reading can have a hard deadline if it must be completed before the next reading becomes available. An operator query typically has a soft deadline with a desired average-case response time. In addition, background tasks such as on-line testing may have no associated timing constraints at all. The failure to meet hard deadlines in these systems can potentially lead to catastrophic results such as loss of life and/or property.

Real-time systems tend to be embedded systems which are not generally programmed by the end-user. Unlike traditional time-shared systems, tasks in hard real-time systems are known *a priori*. In particular, the worst-case behavior of tasks with hard deadlines and the average-case behavior of tasks with soft deadlines are reasonably well-tested and understood. Given a set of tasks and their associated timing constraints, two distinct approaches to the implementation of real-time systems are possible. One, called the *time-line* approach, is typified by the *cyclical executive*, where each segment of code to be executed is assigned a time slot for execution. The time-line is typically handcrafted such that the timing and logical constraints of the task set are met, and is repeatedly executed in cyclical fashion. However, this approach is very *ad hoc* in nature, and leads to very inflexible systems that are difficult to maintain and modify [18]. The other approach is the use of algorithmic techniques to schedule tasks using scheduling algorithms which can be mathematically modeled and analyzed [10]. In this chapter, we focus on this more powerful algorithmic approach to schedule real-time tasks to meet their timing constraints.

Real-time systems are becoming increasingly popular with the advent of faster and cheaper hardware which opens up newer application domains where automation is more reliable and cheaper. Task scheduling is a significant area of research in real-time computer systems. Both non-preemptive and preemptive scheduling algorithms have been studied [6, 8, 9, 14, 15, 16]. An important performance metric of many scheduling algorithms is the processor utilization below which tasks are guaranteed to meet their deadlines. For example, consider the rate-monotonic scheduling algorithm, which assigns a higher fixed priority to a task with a higher frequency [10] and is the optimal static priority algorithm for independent periodic tasks. A job (instance) of a periodic task must complete execution before the next job of the task arrives. The utilization of a task set is defined as the sum of all $C_i/T_i$, where $C_i$ is the worst-case execution time of a task $\tau_i$ and $T_i$ is its period. The rate-monotonic algorithm guarantees that it can schedule any periodic task set if its total utilization is less than $\ln 2$ (69%). If the periods of the tasks are harmonic, the utilization bound is 100%. It has also been shown that the rate-monotonic algorithm can schedule randomly generated periodic task sets up to 88% on the average [7].

## 11.1.2   The Resource-Sharing Problem

An important problem that arises in the context of priority-based real-time systems is the effect of blocking caused by the need for the synchronization of jobs that share logical or physical resources. Mok [11] showed that the problem of deciding whether it is possible to schedule a set of periodic processes is NP-hard when periodic processes use semaphores to enforce mutual exclusion. One approach to the scheduling of real-time jobs when synchronization primitives are used is to try to dynamically construct a feasible schedule at runtime. Mok [11] developed a procedure to generate feasible schedules with a kernelized monitor, which does not permit the preemption of jobs in critical sections. It is an effective technique for the case where the critical sections are short.

In this chapter, we investigate the synchronization problem in the context of priority-driven preemptive scheduling. Unfortunately, a direct application of synchronization mechanisms like the Ada rendezvous, semaphores, or monitors can lead to uncontrolled priority inversion: a high-priority job being blocked by a lower-priority job for an indefinite period of time. Priority inversion in real-time systems cannot only cause deadlines to be missed at low levels of resource utilization but, perhaps more important, render these systems less predictable. In this chapter, we present an extension to the *priority inheritance policies* [17] and prove the properties of an optimal policy belonging to this family of policies. The priority inheritance policies, defined in the context of a uniprocessor, rectify the uncontrolled priority inversion problem that can result from an injudicious use of traditional synchronization primitives. The reader is encouraged to study related work in the context of earliest deadline scheduling by Chen and Lin [2], Baker [1], and Jeffay [4].

## 11.1.3    Organization of the Chapter

The chapter is organized as follows. We describe the priority inversion problem and review the basic concepts underlying the priority inheritance policies in Section 11.1.4. In Section 11.2, we define the *Optimal Mutex Policy* (OMP) and investigate its properties. We show that under the policy, the system becomes deadlock-free, and a job can be blocked for the duration of at most one critical section of a lower-priority job. We also present the impact of these policies on schedulability analysis when the rate-monotonic algorithm is used. Finally, Section 11.3 presents some concluding remarks.

## 11.1.4    The Concept of Priority Inheritance

*Priority inversion* is said to occur when a higher-priority job is forced to wait for the execution of a lower-priority job. A common situation arises when two jobs attempt to access shared data. If the higher-priority job gains access to the shared data first, the appropriate priority order is maintained. However, if the lower-priority data gains access first and then the higher priority job requests access to the shared data, the higher-priority job is blocked until the lower-priority job completes its access to the data.

**Example 1:** Let $J_1$, $J_2$, and $J_3$ be jobs listed in descending order of priority. Assume that $J_1$ and $J_3$ share data guarded by a mutex $S$. Suppose that at time $t_1$, job $J_3$ locks $S$ and enters its critical section. During $J_3$'s execution of its critical section, $J_1$ arrives at time $t_2$ and preempts $J_3$ and begins execution. At time $t_3$, $J_1$ attempts to use the shared data and gets blocked. We might expect that $J_1$, being the highest-priority job, will be blocked no longer than the time for job $J_3$ to exit its critical section. However, the duration of blocking can, in fact, be unpredictable. This is because job $J_3$ can be preempted by the intermediate-priority job $J_2$. The blocking of $J_3$, and hence that of $J_1$, will continue until $J_2$ and any other pending intermediate jobs are completed.

The blocking duration in Example 1 can be unacceptably long. This situation can be partially remedied if a job is not allowed to be preempted within a critical section. However, this solution is appropriate only for short critical sections. For instance, once a low-priority job enters a long critical section, a higher-priority job which does not access the shared data structure may be needlessly blocked. Analogous problems exist with monitors and the Ada rendezvous. The priority inversion problem was first discussed by Lampson and Redell [5] in the context of monitors. They suggest that each monitor always be executed at a priority level higher than all tasks that would ever call the monitor. This solution has the same problem as the one discussed: a higher-priority job that does not share data may be unnecessarily blocked by a lower-priority job. The priority inversion problem in the context of earliest deadline scheduling has also been discussed by Clark [3]. The proposed solution is that a task with a longer deadline blocking a task with a shorter deadline promotes its deadline to that of the latter. This technique is referred to as *deadline promotion* and is analogous to the *basic priority inheritance policy* described in [17].

The use of priority inheritance policies is one approach to rectify the priority inversion problem inherent in existing synchronization primitives. The basic idea of priority inheritance policies is that when a job $J$ blocks higher-priority jobs, it executes its critical section at the highest-priority level of all of the jobs it blocks. After exiting its critical section, job $J$ returns to its original priority level. To illustrate this idea, we apply this policy to Example 1. Suppose that job $J_1$ is blocked by $J_3$. The priority inheritance policies stipulate that job $J_3$ execute its critical section at $J_1$'s priority. As a result, job $J_2$ will be unable to preempt $J_3$ and will itself be blocked. When $J_3$ exits its critical section, it regains its original priority and will immediately be preempted by $J_1$. Thus, $J_1$ will be blocked only for the duration of $J_3$'s critical section.

The concept of priority inheritance, as defined, allows us to develop a family of real-time synchronization policies based on when a job is defined to be blocked by a lower-priority job. For instance, the simplest priority inheritance policy stipulates that a lower-priority job inherit the priority of a higher-priority job when the latter tries to lock a mutex already locked by the lower-priority job. Such a policy is called the *basic priority inheritance policy* [17]. However, as we shall see, the basic priority inheritance policy can still lead to avoidable priority inversion and/or deadlocks. Our goal in this chapter is to develop a priority inheritance policy which leads to the minimum blocking duration for each job.

In all subsequent discussions, when a lower-priority job $J_L$ prevents a higher-priority job $J_H$ from executing, $J_L$ is said to *block* $J_H$. When a higher-priority job

$J_H$ preempts a lower-priority job $J_L$, $J_H$ is *not* considered to be blocking $J_L$.

## 11.1.5    Assumptions and Notation

Before we investigate other priority inheritance policies, we define our terminology, introduce the notation used, and state the assumptions which apply in the following sections.

We assume a uniprocessor executing a fixed set of tasks. The highest-priority job eligible to execute is scheduled to run on the processor. A currently executing job is preempted by a higher-priority job that becomes eligible to execute. A *job* is a sequence of instructions that will continuously use the processor until its completion if it is executing alone on the processor. A *periodic task* is a sequence of the same type of job initiated at regular intervals. Each task is assigned a fixed priority, and every job of the same task is assigned that task's priority. If two jobs are eligible to run, the higher-priority job will be run. Jobs with the same priority are executed according to a FCFS discipline by order of job arrival time.

Notation: $J_i$ denotes a job, namely an instance of a periodic task $\tau_i$. $P_i$, $T_i$, and $C_i$ denote the current executing priority, period and the worst-case execution time of task $\tau_i$, respectively. The assigned priority of a job $J_i$ is the same as that of task $\tau_i$ and is denoted by $p(J_i)$.

We also assume that jobs $J_1$, $J_2$, ..., $J_n$ are listed in descending order of assigned priority, with $J_1$ having the highest priority.

In this chapter, we develop policies assuming that each data structure shared among jobs is guarded by a mutex. However, the principle underlying the policies is also applicable when monitors or rendezvous are used for the synchronization of jobs.

Similar to the common assumption in real-time systems that there exists a worst-case execution time of a job, we assume that there is a worst-case execution time within a critical section. We also assume that the mutexes that can be locked by a critical section are known *a priori*. This assumption can be relaxed to obtain policies which approximate the policy developed in this chapter. A critical section of a task need not always be entered by any given job of the task. However, if a job is already within a critical section, the locking policy developed in this chapter assumes the worst case that all mutexes that may be potentially locked within the critical section *will* be locked by the job.

Notation: A mutex guarding shared data and/or a shared resource is denoted by $S_i$. $Lock(S_i)$ and $Unlock(S_i)$ denote the indivisible operations *lock* (wait) and *unlock* (signal), respectively, on the mutex $S_i$. The section of code beginning with the locking of a mutex and ending with the unlocking of the mutex is termed a *critical section*.

A job can have multiple critical sections that do not overlap, e.g., $\cdots Lock(S_1)$ $\cdots Unlock(S_1) \cdots Lock(S_2) \cdots Unlock(S_2) \cdots$. A critical section can be nested, i.e., a job $J_i$ may make nested requests for mutex locks, e.g., $\cdots, Lock(S_1) \cdots Lock(S_2)$

$\cdots$ *Unlock*($S_2$) $\cdots$ *Unlock*($S_1$) $\cdots$. In this case, critical section $z_{i,1}$ is bounded by *Lock*($S_1$) and *Unlock*($S_1$) and nests the critical section $z_{i,2}$. The phrase "the duration of an (outermost) critical section" refers to the execution time bounded by the outermost pair of *lock* and *unlock* operations, e.g.,, the execution time of the outermost critical section starting with *Lock*($S_1$) and ending with *Unlock*($S_1$). We shall use the terms "critical section" and "outermost critical section" interchangeably.

The $j$th critical section in job $J_i$ is denoted by $z_{i,j}$ and corresponds to the code segment of job $J_i$ between the $j$th *Lock* operation and its corresponding *Unlock* operation. The mutex that is locked and released by critical section $z_{i,j}$ is denoted by $S_{i,j}$. We write $z_{i,j} \subset z_{i,k}$ if the critical section $z_{i,j}$ is entirely contained in $z_{i,k}$. The worst-case duration of the execution of the critical section $z_{i,j}$, denoted by $d_{i,j}$, is the time required to execute $z_{i,j}$ when $J_i$ executes on the processor alone.

We assume that critical sections are properly nested. That is, given any pair of critical sections $z_{i,j}$ and $z_{i,k}$, then either $z_{i,j} \subset z_{i,k}$, $z_{i,k} \subset z_{i,j}$, or $z_{i,j} \cap z_{i,k} = \emptyset$. In addition, we assume that a mutex may be locked at most once in a single nested critical section. This implies that a job will not attempt to lock a mutex that it has already locked and thus deadlock with itself. In addition, we assume that locks on mutexes will be released before or at the end of a job.

Definition: A job $J$ is said to be blocked by the critical section $z_{i,j}$ of job $J_i$ if $J_i$ has a lower-priority than $J$ but $J$ has to wait for $J_i$ to exit $z_{i,j}$ in order to continue execution.

Definition: A job $J$ is said to be blocked by job $J_i$ through mutex $S$ if the critical section $z_{i,j}$ blocks $J$ and $S_{i,j} = S$.

An important feature of the policy that we propose is that it is possible to determine the *schedulability bound* for a given task set when this policy is used. If the utilization of the task set stays below this bound, then the deadlines of all the tasks can be guaranteed. To develop such a bound, it becomes necessary to determine the worst-case duration of blocking that any task can encounter. This worst-case blocking duration will depend upon the particular policy in use, but the following approach will always be taken.

Notation: $\beta_{i,j}$ denotes the set of all critical sections of the lower-priority job $J_j$ which can block $J_i$. That is, $\beta_{i,j} = \{z_{j,k} \mid j > i$ and $z_{j,k}$ can block $J_i\}$.[1] Since we consider only properly nested critical sections, the set of blocking critical sections is partially ordered by set inclusion. Using this partial ordering, we can focus our attention on the set of maximal elements of $\beta_{i,j}$, $\beta_{i,j}^*$. Specifically, we have $\beta_{i,j}^* = \{z_{j,k} \mid (z_{j,k} \in \beta_{i,j}) \wedge (\not\exists z_{j,m} \in \beta_{i,j}$ such that $z_{j,k} \subset z_{j,m})\}$. The set $\beta_{i,j}^*$ contains the outermost critical sections of $J_j$ which can block $J_i$ and eliminates redundant inner critical sections. For purposes of schedulability analysis, we will restrict attention to $\beta_i^* = \{\cup_{j>i} \beta_{i,j}^*\}$, the set of all outermost critical sections that can block $J_i$.

---

[1] Note that the second suffix of $\beta_{i,j}$ and the first suffix of $z_{j,k}$ correspond to job $J_j$.

# 11.2    The Optimal Mutex Policy

The basic priority inheritance policy [17] stipulates that when a job $J$ attempts to lock a mutex $S$ already locked by a lower-priority job $J_L$, $J_L$ inherits $J$'s priority until $J_L$ releases the lock on $S$. However, this policy suffers from two problems. First, a job $J$ could be blocked for the duration of $min(m, n)$ critical sections [17], where $n$ is the number of lower-priority jobs that attempt to lock a mutex also accessed by tasks with a priority higher than or equal to $p(J)$ and $m$ is the number of distinct mutexes that can be locked by lower-priority jobs. For instance, consider the following example.

**Example 2**: Suppose that $J_1$ needs to sequentially lock $S_1$ and $S_2$. Also suppose that $J_2$ preempts $J_3$ after $J_3$ has locked $S_1$. Later, $J_2$ locks $S_2$. Job $J_1$ arrives at this instant and finds that the mutexes $S_1$ and $S_2$ have been locked by the lower-priority jobs $J_3$ and $J_2$, respectively. As a result, $J_1$ would be blocked for the duration of two critical sections, once to wait for $J_3$ to release $S_1$ and again to wait for $J_2$ to release $S_2$. Thus, a job can be blocked for the duration of more than one critical section. We refer to this as *multiple blocking*.

Second, the policy does not avoid deadlocks. For instance, consider jobs $J_1$ and $J_2$. $J_1$ will make nested requests to lock mutexes $S_1$ and $S_2$ in that order. Conversely, $J_2$ will lock $S_2$ first and then $S_1$. Suppose that $J_2$ arrives first and locks $S_2$. However, before it locks $S_1$, $J_1$ arrives and preempts $J_2$. Then, $J_1$ locks unlocked mutex $S_1$. When $J_1$ attempts to lock $S_2$, it gets blocked and $J_2$ inherits $J_1$'s priority. But a deadlock situation occurs when $J_2$ tries to lock $S_1$. Hence, explicit deadlock avoidance techniques like total ordering of mutex requests may have to be employed if the basic priority inheritance policy is used.

Intuitively, it can be seen that the basic priority inheritance policy runs into its problems for the following reason. An unlocked mutex is allowed to be locked at any instant irrespective of its relationship to the mutexes that have already been locked. Hence, when a higher-priority job arrives, it can find that several mutexes that it needs have been locked by lower-priority jobs. Furthermore, such uncontrolled locking can potentially cause a deadlock as well. This situation can be remedied by allowing mutexes to be locked only under selective conditions. In other words, if the locking of a mutex may cause multiple blocking to a higher-priority job, we should not allow the mutex to be locked. We use the information about the mutex needs of each job and the job priorities to decide whether the locking of a mutex can lead to multiple blocking and/or deadlock. Imposing conditions on the locking of a mutex is the essence of the proposed policy.

In this section, we develop the Optimal Mutex Policy (OMP). The policy not only minimizes the blocking encountered by a job to the duration of execution of a single critical section but also avoids deadlocks. In this section, we shall present the policy and prove its properties. We shall show that the locking conditions used by OMP are both necessary and sufficient to limit the worst-case blocking duration to a single critical section for any job. However, an implementation of this policy may be expensive. Suboptimal but computationally simpler policies are discussed in [13].

## 11.2.1   The Concept of the Optimal Mutex Policy

<u>Definition</u>: The *priority ceiling* of a mutex $S$ is defined as the assigned priority of the highest-priority task that may lock $S$. The priority ceiling of a mutex $S$ represents the highest-priority that a critical section guarded by $S$ can inherit from a higher-priority job. In other words, if a job $J$ locks the mutex $S$, the corresponding critical section of $J$ can inherit at most a priority equal to the priority ceiling of $S$.

<u>Notation</u>: The priority ceiling of a mutex $S_j$ is denoted by $c(S_j)$.

<u>Definition</u>: The *current critical section* of a job $J$ refers to the outermost critical section that $J$ has already entered.

<u>Notation</u>: When a job $J$ requests the lock on an unlocked mutex $S$,

- $S^*$ is a mutex with the highest-priority ceiling locked by jobs other than $J$. If there is no mutex currently locked, $S^*$ is defined to be a dummy mutex $S_{dummy}$ whose priority ceiling is less than the priorities of all jobs in the system. If there is more than one mutex in the system with the same priority ceiling, any one of them may be chosen. We shall later show that this choice is immaterial, and that there can be at most two such mutexes with the highest-priority ceiling.

- $J^*$ is the job holding the lock on $S^*$. If $S^*$ is the dummy mutex $S_{dummy}$, $J^*$ can be represented by the *idle* process that runs when there is no active process ready to run.

- $SL^*$ is the set of mutexes already locked by the current critical section of job $J^*$.[2]

- $SR$ is the set of mutexes that the current critical section of $J$ may lock later.[3] For convenience, both $SL$ and $SR$ are defined to be the empty sets when $J$ is not inside a critical section. Also, once $J$ is successful in obtaining the lock, $SL$ includes $S$. Otherwise, $J$ will be blocked and $S \in SR$.

- $SR^*$ is the set of mutexes that will be locked by the current critical section of job $J^*$. If the current critical section of job $J^*$ does not request any more nested mutex locks, $SR^* = \emptyset$.

- $z$ is the (outermost) critical section that $J$ has already entered, else the critical section that $J$ is trying to enter.

<u>Remark</u>: For any given job $J$, $SL \cap SR = \emptyset$ and $SL \cup SR =$ set of mutexes that can be locked by the current critical section of $J$.

As already mentioned, OMP selectively grants locks on unlocked mutexes to requesting jobs. Suppose that job $J$ requests the lock on an unlocked mutex $S$.

---

[2] $SL$ stands for "mutexes locked."
[3] $SR$ stands for "mutexes required" for completion of the current critical section.

OMP allows $J$ to lock $S$ if and only if at least one of the following conditions is true.

1. <u>Condition C1</u>: The priority of job $J$ is greater than the priority ceiling of $S^*$, i.e., $p(J) > c(S^*)$.

2. <u>Condition C2</u>: The priority of job $J$ is equal to the priority ceiling of $S^*$ and the current critical section of $J$ will not attempt to lock any mutex already locked by $J^*$, i.e., $(p(J) = c(S^*)) \wedge (SR \cap SL^* = \emptyset)$.

3. <u>Condition C3</u>: The priority of job $J$ is equal to the priority ceiling of $S$ and the lock on mutex $S$ will not be requested by $J^*$'s preempted critical section, i.e., $(p(J) = c(S)) \wedge (S \notin SR^*)$.

If none of these conditions is true, job $J$ is blocked and $J^*$ inherits $J$'s current executing priority. We refer to conditions C1, C2, and C3 as the *locking conditions*.

Under OMP, a job can be blocked for the duration of at most a single critical section, and deadlocks cannot occur. Before we prove these properties, we illustrate the policy with a few examples. We shall first apply OMP to the examples in the preceding section, where multiple blocking occurs for a job.

**Example 3**: A job $J_1$ needs to lock $S_1$ and $S_2$ sequentially, while $J_2$ needs to lock $S_1$, and $J_3$ needs to lock $S_2$. Hence, $c(S_1) = c(S_2) = p(J_1)$. At time $t_0$, $J_3$ locks $S_2$. At time $t_1$, $J_2$ preempts $J_3$ and later attempts to lock $S_1$. Now, $J^* = J_3$ and $S^* = S_2$. However, $p(J) < c(S_2)$ and $p(J) < c(S_1)$, so all three locking conditions are false. Hence, $J_2$ is blocked and $J_3$ inherits $J_2$'s priority. When $J_1$ arrives and attempts to lock $S_1$, condition C2 is true (since $J_1$ does not make any nested requests for mutex locks and $SR = \emptyset$). Hence $J_1$ can obtain the lock on $S_1$. Later, when $J_1$ attempts to lock the locked mutex $S_1$, $J_3$ inherits $J_1$'s priority. When $J_3$ releases $S_2$, it resumes its priority before acquiring $S_2$ (its original priority in this case). Then, $J_1$ preempts $J_3$ and locks $S_2$. $J_1$ now runs to completion followed by $J_2$ and $J_3$, respectively.

It can be seen that both jobs $J_1$ and $J_2$ had to wait for a lower-priority job $J_3$ for at most the duration a single critical section guarded by $S_2$. Since $J_1$ was blocked because it needed a mutex locked by another job, the blocking encountered by $J_1$ is called *direct blocking*. Direct blocking is necessary to guarantee the consistency of shared data. However, $J_2$ is blocked when $J_3$ inherits a priority higher than $J_2$. This type of blocking is referred to as *push-through blocking*. Push-through blocking is essential to avoid multiple blocking as illustrated in Example 3, and to avoid the uncontrolled priority inversion problem exhibited in Example 1.

**Example 4**: Consider the preceding example, where deadlocks could occur under the basic priority inheritance policy. Job $J_2$ locks the mutex $S_2$, and before it makes a nested request for mutex $S_1$, $J_1$ arrives and preempts $J_2$. We again have $c(S_1) = c(S_2) = p(J_1)$. However, when $J_1$ attempts to lock $S_1$, $p(J) = c(S^*) = c(S)$, but $SR = \{S_2\}$, $SL^* = \{S_2\}$, $SR^* = \{S_1\}$, and $S = S_1$, so that all locking conditions are false. Hence, the lock on $S_1$ is denied to $J_1$ and $J_2$ inherits $J_1$'s priority. Thus, the deadlock is avoided.

We now provide an example that illustrates each of the locking conditions of OMP.

**Example 5**: Consider 5 jobs $J_0$, $J_{1a}$, $J_{1b}$, $J_2$, and $J_3$ in descending order of priority except that jobs $J_{1a}$ and $J_{1b}$ have equal priorities. There are three mutexes $S_1$, $S_2$, and $S_3$ in the system. Suppose the sequence of processing steps for each job is as follows:

$$
\begin{aligned}
J_0 &= \{\cdots Lock(S_0) \cdots Unlock(S_0) \cdots\} \\
J_{1a} &= \{\cdots Lock(S_0) \cdots Unlock(S_0) \cdots\} \\
J_{1b} &= \{\cdots Lock(S_1) \cdots Unlock(S_1) \cdots\} \\
J_2 &= \{\cdots Lock(S_2) \cdots Lock(S_1) \cdots Unlock(S_1) \cdots Unlock(S_2) \cdots\} \\
J_3 &= \{\cdots Lock(S_1) \cdots Unlock(S_1) \cdots Lock(S_2) \cdots Unlock(S_2) \cdots\}.
\end{aligned}
$$

Thus, $c(S_0) = p(J_0)$, $c(S_1) = p(J_{1b}) = p(J_{1a})$, and $c(S_2) = p(J_2)$

The sequence of events described below is depicted in Figure 11.1. A line at a low level indicates that the corresponding job is blocked or has been preempted by a higher-priority job. A line raised to a higher level indicates that the job is executing. The absence of a line indicates that the job has not yet arrived or has completed. Shaded portions indicate execution of critical sections. Suppose that:

- First, $J_3$ arrives and begins execution. At time $t_0$, it locks the unlocked mutex $S_1$ since there is no other mutex locked by another job.[4]

- At time $t_1$, $J_2$ arrives and preempts $J_3$.

- At time $t_2$, $J_2$ attempts to lock $S_2$. Since $p(J_2) < c(S_1)$, conditions C1 and C2 are false. But $p(J_2) = c(S_2)$ and $SR^* = \emptyset$. Hence, condition C3 is true and $J_2$ is allowed to lock $S_2$.

- At time $t_3$, $J_0$ arrives and preempts $J_2$.

- At time $t_4$, $J_0$ attempts to lock $S_0$. Now, $S^* = S_1$. However, $p(J_0) > c(S_1)$ and condition C1 is true. Hence, $J_0$ is granted the lock on $S_0$.

- At time $t_5$, $J_0$ releases the mutex $S_0$. $J_{1a}$ arrives now but is unable to preempt $J_0$.

- At time $t_6$, $J_0$ completes execution. $J_{1a}$, which is eligible to execute, begins execution.

- At time $t_7$, $J_{1a}$ tries to lock $S_0$. $S^* = S_1$. We have $p(J_{1a}) = c(S_1)$ and there is no nested request for mutex locks. Hence condition C2 is true, and the lock on $S_0$ is granted to $J_{1a}$.

- At time $t_8$, $J_{1a}$ releases the mutex $S_0$.

---

[4]The locking can occur because the idle process has locked the dummy mutex $S^*$ and $p(J_3) > c(S^*)$ by definition.

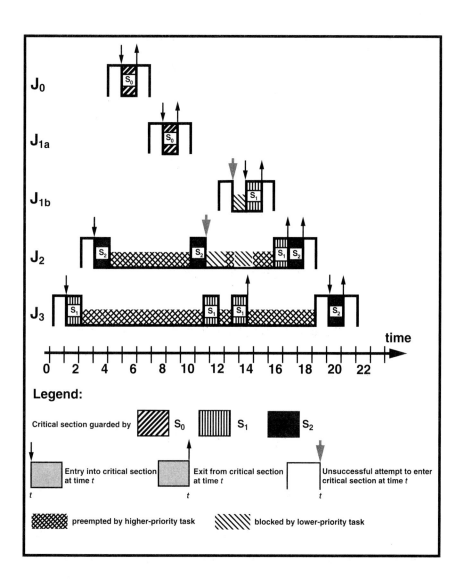

**Figure 11.1**  Sequence of Events Described in Example 5

- At time $t_9$, $J_{1a}$ completes execution and $J_2$ resumes execution.

- At time $t_{10}$, $J_2$ attempts to lock the locked mutex $S_1$ and is blocked. $J_3$, which holds the lock on $S_1$, inherits $J_2$'s priority and resumes execution.

- At time $t_{11}$, $J_{1b}$ arrives and preempts $J_3$ executing at a lower-priority of $p(J_2)$.

- At time $t_{12}$, $J_{1b}$ attempts to lock locked mutex $S_1$. $J_{1b}$ is blocked, and $J_3$ now inherits $J_{1b}$'s priority.

- At time $t_{13}$, $J_3$ releases the mutex $S_1$ and resumes its original lowest priority. $J_{1b}$ resumes execution and is now granted the lock on the mutex $S_1$, since condition C1 is satisfied w.r.t. $S_2$ locked by $J_2$.

- At time $t_{14}$, $J_{1b}$ releases the mutex $S_1$.

- At time $t_{15}$, $J_{1b}$ completes execution. $J_2$ resumes execution and locks $S_1$ since there is no mutex locked by a lower-priority job.

- At time $t_{16}$, $J_2$ releases the mutex $S_1$.

- At time $t_{17}$, $J_2$ releases the mutex $S_2$.

- At time $t_{18}$, $J_2$ completes execution and $J_3$ resumes.

- Finally, $J_3$ locks $S_2$, releases $S_2$, and completes execution at time $t_{21}$.

In the above example, jobs $J_0$ and $J_{1a}$ do not encounter any blocking due to lower-priority jobs. $J_{1b}$ is blocked by $J_3$ during the interval $t_{12}$–$t_{13}$, which corresponds to at most one critical section of $J_3$. $J_2$ is blocked by $J_3$ during the intervals $t_{10}$–$t_{11}$ and $t_{12}$–$t_{13}$, which together correspond to at most one critical section of $J_3$.

## 11.2.2   Definition of the Optimal Mutex Policy

Having illustrated OMP with examples, we now formally define the policy.

1. Let $J$ be the highest-priority job among the jobs ready to run. $J$ is assigned the processor and let $S^*$ be a mutex with the highest-priority ceiling of all mutexes currently locked by jobs other than job $J$. Let the job holding the lock on $S^*$ be $J^*$. Before job $J$ enters its critical section, it must obtain the lock on the mutex $S$ guarding the shared data structure. If the mutex $S$ is unlocked, job $J$ will be granted the lock on $S$ if and only if at least *one* of the locking conditions is true.

2. In this case, job $J$ will obtain the lock on mutex $S$ and enter its critical section. Otherwise, job $J$ is said to be blocked by $J^*$. When a job $J$ exits its critical section, the binary mutex associated with the critical section will be unlocked, and the highest-priority job, if any, blocked by job $J$ will be awakened.

3. A job $J$ uses its assigned priority unless it is in its critical section and blocks higher-priority jobs. If job $J$ blocks higher-priority jobs, $J$ *inherits* $P_H$, the executing priority of the highest-priority job blocked by $J$. When $J$ exits its critical section, it resumes its previous priority. Finally, the operations of priority inheritance and of the resumption of original priority must be indivisible.

4. A job $J$, when it does not attempt to enter a critical section, can preempt another job $J_L$ if its priority is higher than the priority, inherited or assigned, at which job $J_L$ is executing.

## 11.2.3    Properties of the Optimal Mutex Policy

In this section, we prove that under OMP, each job may be blocked for at most the duration of one critical section of a lower-priority job and, furthermore, deadlocks are avoided.

We remind the reader that when the priority of a job $J$ is being referred to, it always refers to the priority which $J$ is currently executing (unless explicitly stated otherwise to be $J$'s assigned lower-priority). Note that a job outside a critical section always executes at its own assigned priority, but a job's executing priority inside a critical section might change due to priority inheritance.

**Lemma 11.2.1** *A job $J$ can be blocked by a job $J_L$ with an assigned lower priority only if $J_L$ has entered and remains within a critical section when $J$ arrives.*

**Proof:** It follows from the definition of OMP that if $J_L$ is not in its critical section, it can be preempted by the higher-priority job $J$. Since priority inheritance is in effect and the highest-priority job that is ready will always be run, $J_L$ cannot resume execution until $J$ completes. The Lemma follows.                    □

**Lemma 11.2.2** *Once a job $J$ begins execution, a job with an equal assigned priority cannot begin until $J$ completes.*

**Proof:** This lemma follows directly from the fact that priority inheritance is in effect, the highest-priority job is always run, and equal-priority ties are broken in FCFS order.                                                                      □

**Lemma 11.2.3** *When a job $J$ executes, there can be at most one strictly lower-priority job $J_L$ that has locked a mutex $S_k$ such that $c(S_k) \geq p(J)$.*

**Proof:** Suppose that there exists another lower-priority job $J_j$ that has locked a mutex $S_j$ such that $c(S_j) \geq p(J)$. Without loss of generality, suppose that $J_j$ locked $S_j$ first. When $J_L$ attempts to lock $S_k$, it finds that $S_j$ has been locked by another job $J_j$, and that $p(J_L) < p(J) \leq min(c(S_k), c(S_j))$. Hence, locking conditions C1, C2, and C3 are false, and OMP will not permit $J_L$ to lock $S_k$, contradicting our assumption. The Lemma follows.                                                               □

Lemma 11.2.3 also leads us to the following corollary.

**Corollary 11.2.1** *Suppose that when $J$ requests $S$, condition 1 is false (i.e., $c(S^*)$ $\geq p(J)$). Then, $J^*$ must be unique.*

**Proof:** This follows directly from Lemma 11.2.3.          □

Remark: The above corollary gives us the following interesting result. When a job must be blocked, $J^*$ needs to be identified as the blocking job. Corollary 11.2.1 shows that $J^*$ is unique whenever $c(S^*) \geq p(J)$. When $c(S^*) < p(J)$, $J^*$ may not be unique, but condition 1 will be true. As a result, $J$ cannot be blocked by any of the $J^*$'s, and the non-uniqueness of $J^*$ need not be resolved! In summary, if condition 1 is true, the mutex will be granted and the non-uniqueness of $J^*$ need not be resolved. If not, $J^*$ is guaranteed to be unique.

Remark: While $J^*$ may not be unique when $c(S^*) < p(J)$, there can still be at most two jobs which have locked mutexes with the highest-priority ceiling. The following lemma proves this result.

**Lemma 11.2.4** *There can be at most two jobs which can lock mutexes with the same-priority ceiling.*

**Proof:** Let $J_L$ lock the mutex $S_L$. Let $J$ be another job that locks mutex $S$ with the same priority ceiling as $S_L$ under OMP. We first show that $p(J) = c(S_L) = c(S)$. Since $c(S_L) = c(S)$, $p(J) \leq c(S_L)$. When $J$ tries to lock $S$, there is at least one mutex ($S_L$) locked by another job. Hence $c(S^*) \geq c(S_L) \geq p(J)$. Therefore, condition C1 would evaluate to false. Since $J$ does lock $S$, at least one of condition C2 or condition C3 must be true. In either case, we have $p(J) = c(S_L) = c(S)$.

Suppose that another job $J'$ attempts to lock a mutex $S'$ such that $c(S') = c(S_L) = c(S)$. There are three cases:

Case I: $p(J') > J$. In this case, $J'$ cannot lock a mutex such that $c(S') = c(S_L)$: the definition of priority ceiling would be violated.

Case II: $p(J') = J$. However, by Lemma 11.2.2, $J'$ cannot begin execution until $J$ completes—a contradiction.

Case III: $p(J') < J$. In this case, when $J'$ requests $S'$, $S_L$ and $S$ are locked, and $c(S^*) \geq p(J)$. As a result, when $J'$ tries to lock $S'$, all three locking conditions evaluate to false. Hence, $J'$ cannot lock $S'$.

The Lemma follows.          □

We now show that the OMP avoids deadlocks and minimizes the worst-case priority inversion encountered by a job to the duration of a single critical section.

**Lemma 11.2.5** *Suppose that job $J$ enters a critical section z by obtaining the lock on mutex $S$ because condition C1 of the locking conditions is true. Then, job $J$ cannot be blocked by a lower-priority job until $J$ completes.*

**Proof:** Since condition C1 is true when $J$ requests the lock on $S$, $p(J) > c(S^*)$, whether $S^*$ is unique or not. That is, no job with equal or higher-priority than $J$ (including $J$) will lock the mutexes held by lower-priority jobs. Hence, no lower-priority job can block $J$ or any other higher-priority job, and inherit a priority $\geq$

$p(J)$. Furthermore, no arriving job with priority lower than $p(J)$ can even preempt $J$. Thus, $J$ cannot be blocked by lower-priority jobs before $J$ completes.    □

Remark: Lemma 11.2.5 provides the result that once a mutex $S$ is locked by a job $J$ because condition C1 is true, then *all* subsequent requests for mutex locks by job $J$ will also satisfy condition C1, and hence all these locks will be granted.

**Lemma 11.2.6** *Suppose that job $J$ enters a critical section $z$ by obtaining the lock on mutex $S$ because condition C2 of the locking conditions is true. Then, job $J$ cannot be blocked by a lower-priority job until $J$ exits the critical section $z$.*

**Proof:** Since condition C2 is true when $J$ requests the lock on $S$, $p(J) = c(S^*)$. By Corollary 11.2.1, $J^*$ is unique. By Lemma 11.2.3, $J^*$ is also the only job which has locked a mutex with priority ceiling $= p(J)$.

Also, no job with higher-priority than $p(J)$ will lock a mutex already locked by $J^*$ or any preempted job with lower-priority than $p(J)$. Thus, $J^*$ cannot inherit a priority higher than $p(J^*)$ unless it can lock additional mutexes. However, $J^*$ can resume execution before $J$ exits the critical section $z$ only if $J$ is blocked by $J^*$. However, the critical section $z$ will not lock any mutexes already locked by $J^*$. Let the critical section $z$ request a nested lock to mutex $S$. We again have $p(J)$ $= c(S^*)$, and still the critical section $z$ cannot lock any mutexes already locked by lower-priority jobs. Hence, OMP would allow $J$ to lock $S$. Since this is true for all requests for mutex locks nested within the critical section $z$, job $J$ will exit the critical section without being blocked by $J^*$.    □

Remark: Lemma 11.2.6 provides the result that if a job $J$ has locked the outermost mutex of a nested critical section because condition C2 is true, condition C2 will always be true for all subsequent nested requests for mutex locks within the critical section as well. Hence, no nested request to a mutex within this critical section will be blocked.

Definition: When a job $J$ is blocked by the job $J^*$, let the mutex with the highest-priority ceiling locked by $J^*$ be $S^*$. Then, $S^*$ is said to be *used* to block $J$.

**Lemma 11.2.7** *Suppose that job $J$ enters a critical section $z$ by obtaining the lock on mutex $S$, because condition 1 is false and condition C3 of the locking conditions is true. Then, the mutex $S$ cannot be used by job $J$ to block a higher-priority job.*

**Proof:** Since condition 1 is false, by Lemma 11.2.1, $J^*$ must be unique. Since condition C3 is true when $J$ requests the lock on $S$, $c(S) = p(J)$. Hence, no higher-priority job $J_H$ will lock $S$. $J^*$ is the only job that can inherit a priority higher than or equal to $J$, but $J^*$'s current critical section does not need $S$. Hence, $J$'s critical section guarded by $S$ cannot inherit a priority that is higher than or equal to $J_H$'s priority. Hence, $S$ cannot be used by job $J$ to block job $J_H$. The Lemma follows.    □

Definition: If job $J_i$ is blocked by $J_j$ and $J_j$, in turn, is blocked by $J_k$, $J_i$ is said to be *transitively blocked* by $J_k$.

**Lemma 11.2.8** *The optimal mutex policy prevents transitive blocking.*

**Proof:** Suppose that transitive blocking is possible. For some $i \geq 2$, let job $J_i$ block job $J_{i-1}$ and let job $J_{i-1}$ block job $J_{i-2}$, i.e., job $J_{i-2}$ is transitively blocked by job $J_i$. By Lemma 11.2.1, to block job $J_{i-1}$, job $J_i$ must enter and remain in its critical section when $J_{i-1}$ arrives at time $t_0$. Similarly, to block $J_{i-2}$, job $J_{i-1}$ must enter and remain in its critical section when $J_{i-2}$ arrives at time $t_1$. At time $t_1$, let the mutexes with the highest-priority ceilings locked by jobs $J_i$ and $J_{i-1}$ be $S$ and $S_n$, respectively. Since job $J_{i-1}$ is allowed to lock mutex $S_n$ when job $J_i$ has already locked $S$, one of the *locking conditions* must have been true. If one of conditions C1 and C2 were true, by Lemmas 11.2.5 and 11.2.6, job $J_i$ will be unable to block job $J_{i-1}$. Since $J_i$ does block job $J_{i-1}$ by assumption, condition C3 must have been true when $J_{i-1}$ locked $S_n$. However, according to Lemma 11.2.7, the mutex $S_n$ cannot be used by job $J_{i-1}$ to block job $J_{i-2}$, contradicting our assumption. The Lemma follows. □

**Theorem 11.2.1** *The optimal mutex policy prevents deadlocks.*

**Proof:** First, by assumption, a job cannot deadlock with itself. Thus, a deadlock can be formed only by a cycle of jobs waiting for one another. Let the $n$ jobs involved in this cycle be $J_1$, ..., $J_n$. Since a job not holding any mutexes cannot contribute to the deadlock, each of the $n$ jobs must be in its critical section. By Lemma 11.2.8, the number of jobs in the blocking cycle can only be 2, i.e., $n = 2$. Suppose that job $J_2$'s critical section was preempted by job $J_1$, which then enters its own critical section. For $J_1$ to enter its critical section, one of the *locking conditions* must be true. If conditions C1 and C2 were true, by Lemmas 11.2.5 and 11.2.6, job $J_2$ cannot block $J_1$. Hence, condition C3 must have been true and by Lemma 11.2.3, $J^* = J_2$. Since condition C3 is true, each of the critical sections of jobs $J_1$ and $J_2$ is guaranteed not to have mutually locked mutexes that are expected by the other. Hence a deadlock cannot occur. The Theorem follows. □

Remark: The above theorem leads to the useful result that programmers can write arbitrary sequences of nested requests for mutex locks when OMP is used. As long as each job does not deadlock with itself, the system is guaranteed to be deadlock-free.

We now prove that under OMP, a job can be blocked for at most the duration of one critical section of lower-priority jobs.

**Theorem 11.2.2** *A job J can be blocked for at most the duration of one critical section of lower-priority jobs.*

**Proof:** When the job $J$ arrives, by Lemma 11.2.3, there can exist at most a single job $J'$ that has locked a mutex $S_k$ such that $c(S_k) \geq p(J)$. If no such job exists, no lower-priority job can inherit a priority higher than $J$, and condition 1 will always evaluate to true when $J$ requests a mutex. As a result, $J$ will run to completion without being blocked.

If there does exist such a job, we have $J' = J^*$. That is, $J'$ is the only lower-priority job that can inherit a priority higher than that of $J$. Suppose that $J'$ does inherit a higher priority than $J$. By Lemma 11.2.8, $J^*$ will exit its critical section without being blocked by a lower-priority job. Once $J^*$ exits its critical section, by Lemma 11.2.1, $J^*$ can no longer block $J$. Since there exists no other job that can block $J$ and no arriving lower-priority job can block $J$, the Theorem follows.  □

The following corollary can be derived from Theorem 11.2.2.

**Corollary 11.2.2** *A job $J$ which voluntarily suspends itself $k$ times can be blocked for at most the duration of $k + 1$ critical sections of lower-priority jobs.*

**Proof:** The Corollary follows from Theorem 11.2.2 and the fact that a job that suspends $k$ times can be considered to be $k + 1$ jobs.  □

### 11.2.4   Necessity and Sufficiency of the *Locking Conditions*

We now prove that a worst-case blocking duration of a single critical section can be guaranteed if and only if the *locking conditions* of OMP are used.[5] In the preceding section, we have shown that the locking conditions are sufficient to avoid deadlocks and to reduce the blocking duration of a job to at most a single critical section.

We first prove that a lock on an unlocked mutex $S$ can be granted to a job $J$ only if at least one of the locking conditions is true in order to prevent deadlocks and obtain the worst-case blocking of a single critical section for each job.

**Lemma 11.2.9** *A job can be blocked for the duration of more than one critical section if a lock on an unlocked mutex $S$ is granted to a job $J$ when the following two conditions are true:*

*condition (a) $p(J) < c(S^*)$*

*condition (b) $p(J) < c(S)$*

**Proof:** When $J$ tries to lock $S$, suppose that conditions (a) and (b) are true. If $S = S^*$, $J$ is attempting to lock a locked binary mutex $S$ and has to be blocked. Hence, $J$ can possibly be granted the lock on $S$ only if $S \neq S^*$. Then, there exist jobs $J_i$ and $J_j$ with higher-priority than $J$ such that $J_i$ will lock $S^*$ and $J_j$ will lock $S$.

Only three cases arise.

Case I: $J_i = J_j = J_H$. In other words, there exists a higher-priority job $J_H$ that will lock both $S$ and $S^*$. If the lock on $S$ is granted to $J$, $J_H$ can arrive now and will find that both the mutexes $S$ and $S^*$ that it requires are locked. Hence, $J_H$ will be blocked for the duration of two critical sections, once to wait for $J$ to release $S$ and again to wait for $J^*$ to release $S^*$.

---

[5] For the worst-case blocking to be a single critical section, the system should be free from deadlocks since a deadlock contributes to prolonged blocking of two or more jobs.

<u>Case II</u>: $J_i \neq J_j$ and without loss of generality, $J_i$ has higher-priority than $J_j$. Suppose that the lock on $S$ is granted to $J$. Job $J_j$ arrives now and preempts $J$. Immediately, $J_j$ can be preempted by $J_i$. Job $J_i$ will be block for one critical section, waiting for $J^*$ to release $S^*$. However, this constitutes push-through blocking for $J_j$ as well. When $J_j$ resumes after $J_i$ completes, $J_j$ will be blocked for the duration of one more critical section, waiting for $J$ to release $S$. Thus, job $J_j$ can be blocked for the duration of two critical sections.

<u>Case III</u>: $J_i \neq J_j$, but both jobs have equal priority. Suppose that the lock on $S$ is granted to $J$. Job $J_j$ arrives now followed by $J_i$. However, $J_i$ is unable to preempt $J_j$. $J_j$ attempts to lock $S$ and is blocked by $J$, which inherits $J_j$'s priority until the release of $S$. This constitutes blocking for $J_i$ as well. After $J_j$ completes, $J_i$ begins execution and will again be blocked by $J^*$ when it attempts to lock $S^*$. Thus, $J_i$ can be blocked for the duration of two critical sections.

Thus, if both conditions (a) and (b) are true, a job can be blocked for the duration of more than one critical section. □

<u>Remark</u>: Suppose that a worst-case blocking of at most a single blocking has to be ensured. Hence, when a mutex is requested, and conditions (a) and (b) are satisfied, a job should be blocked. Thus, for a job $J$ to be granted the lock on a mutex $S$, the negation of Lemma 11.2.9 must hold. Since $p(J) > c(S)$ is not possible by definition, at least one of the following conditions must be true:

$$p(J) \geq c(S^*)$$
$$p(J) = c(S)$$

We refer to the above conditions as *necessary locking conditions*. Thus, Theorem 11.2.9 states that for a worst-case blocking duration of a single critical section, at least one of the necessary locking conditions must be true for a job to be granted the lock on a mutex. However, the necessary locking conditions are only necessary but not sufficient to guarantee a worst-case blocking of a single critical section.

<u>Remark</u>: If there are no nested requests for mutex locks at all, the *necessary locking conditions* are equivalent to the *locking conditions*. Thus, the additional checks in the *locking conditions* are needed to avoid deadlocks and to prevent a job from being blocked for multiple critical sections.

<u>Remark</u>: The *necessary locking conditions* provide us with the insight to construct policies that are computationally simpler but suboptimal. Note that if both the *necessary locking conditions* are false, then it follows that the *locking conditions* are also false.

**Lemma 11.2.10** *Suppose that job $J$ attempts to lock mutex $S$. If all three locking conditions are false, at least one of the following conditions must be true:*

(F1) $(p(J) < c(S)) \wedge (p(J) < c(S^*))$.[6]

(F2) $(p(J) < c(S)) \wedge (p(J) = c(S^*)) \wedge (SR \cap SL^* \neq \emptyset)$.

---

[6]That is, the *necessary locking conditions* are false.

(F3) $(p(J) = c(S)) \wedge (p(J) < c(S^*)) \wedge (S \in SR^*)$.

(F4) $(SR \cap SL^* \neq \emptyset) \wedge (S \in SR^*)$.

**Proof:** The Lemma follows directly from the negation of the *locking conditions*.

□

**Theorem 11.2.3** *Deadlock can occur or a job can be blocked for the duration of more than one critical section if the lock on a mutex $S$ is granted to a job $J$ when all the* locking conditions *are false, i.e., $(\neg C_1 \wedge \neg C_2 \wedge \neg C_3 \Rightarrow \exists \, J$, which can be blocked for more than one critical section$) \vee (\neg C_1 \wedge \neg C_2 \wedge \neg C_3 \Rightarrow \exists \, a \, deadlock)$.*

**Proof:** Suppose that all the locking conditions are false. By Lemma 11.2.10, one of the following cases must be true.

Case I: (F1) The *necessary locking conditions* are false. It follows from Theorem 11.2.9 that at least one job can block for the duration of more than one critical section.

Case II: (F2) $(p(J) < c(S)) \wedge (p(J) = c(S^*)) \wedge (SR \cap SL^* \neq \emptyset)$. That is, there exists a job $J_H$ with higher-priority than $J$ that will try to lock $S$. Moreover, the current critical section of $J$ will try to lock a mutex $S_i$ that has already been locked by the current critical section of $J^*$. Suppose that the lock on $S$ were granted to $J$. However, $J_H$ can arrive now and later attempt to lock $S$ already locked by $J$. In order to release $S$, $J$ would need to lock $S_i$ held by $J^*$. Consequently, $J_H$ will be blocked until $J$ releases $S$. But $J$ will be blocked until $J^*$ releases $S_i$. Effectively, $J_H$ would be blocked for the duration of two critical sections. Thus, a job can block for the duration of multiple critical sections.

Case III: (F3) $(p(J) = c(S)) \wedge (p(J) < c(S^*)) \wedge (S \in SR^*)$. That is, there exists a higher-priority job $J_H$ that will try to lock $S^*$. Moreover, the current critical section of $J^*$ will try to lock $S$. Suppose that the lock on $S$ is granted to $J$. However, $J_H$ can arrive now and later attempt to lock $S^*$ already locked by $J^*$. Consequently, $J_H$ will be blocked until $J^*$ releases $S^*$. But, $J^*$ will be blocked until $J$ releases $S$. Effectively, $J_H$ would block for the duration of two critical sections. Thus, a job can block for the duration of multiple critical sections.

Case IV: (F4) $(SR \cap SL^* \neq \emptyset) \wedge (S \in SR^*)$. Clearly, if the lock on $S$ were granted to $J$, jobs $J$ and $J^*$ will deadlock, with one waiting for the other to release a mutex. Since these jobs are deadlocked, two jobs will be blocked for an infinite duration of time.

Thus, if all the *locking conditions* were false and the lock on mutex $S$ is granted to job $J$, in the worst case, a deadlock can occur or a job can block for the duration of multiple critical sections.

□

The above theorem leads us to the necessity and sufficiency of the *locking conditions*.

**Theorem 11.2.4** *The* locking conditions *are necessary and sufficient to obtain the worst-case blocking duration of a single critical section and to avoid deadlocks.*

**Proof:** The Theorem follows from Theorems 11.2.1, 11.2.2, and 11.2.3.     □

## 11.2.5   Schedulability Analysis

OMP places an upper bound on the duration that a job can be blocked. This property makes possible the schedulability analysis of a task set using rate-monotonic priority assignment and OMP. We also show that it is possible that OMP can potentially lead to better schedulability than previously known priority inheritance policies since it is possible for a task $\tau_i$ to encounter a better worst-case blocking duration from lower-priority tasks under OMP. We quote below the following theorem due to Sha, Rajkumar, and Lehoczky [17].

**Theorem 11.2.5** *A set of $n$ periodic tasks can be scheduled by the rate-monotonic algorithm if the following conditions are satisfied [17]:*

$$\forall i, \ 1 \leq i \leq n, \quad \frac{C_1}{T_1} + \frac{C_2}{T_2} + \ldots + \frac{C_n}{T_n} + \frac{B_i}{T_i} \leq i(2^{1/i} - 1)$$

*where $C_i$, $T_i$, and $B_i$ are the worst-case execution time, period, and worst-case blocking time of a periodic task, respectively.*

Again, $C_i$ is the computation time of periodic task $\tau_i$ and $T_i$ is its period. $B_i$ is the worst-case blocking encountered by jobs belonging to $\tau_i$. Just like the priority ceiling policy, OMP also avoids deadlocks and produces a worst-case blocking of at most the duration of one critical section. Hence, the above theorems are applicable to OMP as well. The value of $B_i$ for each job $J_i$ is computed as follows.

Definition: Jobs $J_i$ and $J_j$ are said to be *active* together if $J_i$ and $J_j$ can both be ready to execute on the processor at some instant in time.

For instance, in Example 5, jobs $J_2$ and $J_3$ are said to be active together since both are ready to execute at time $t_1$. However, jobs $J_{1a}$ and $J_{1b}$, in reality, can be the execution of a single instance of task $\tau_1$ with an intervening suspension (mostly for communication or I/O activities). That is, job $J_1$ actually consists of two jobs $J_{1a}$ and $J_{1b}$. Since $J_{1a}$ always precedes the initiation of job $J_{1b}$, jobs $J_{1a}$ and $J_{1b}$ are *not* said to be active together.

A job can be *blocked* only by jobs with lower-priority. Then, a critical section $z_j$ of a lower-priority job $J_j$ guarded by a mutex $S_{j,k}$ can block $J_i$ if

- $p(J_i) < c(S_{j,k})$.

- $p(J_i) = c(S_{j,k}) \wedge J_i$ (or an equal-priority job that is active with $J_i$) may lock $S_{j,k}$.

The set of maximal elements of $\beta_{i,j}$, $\beta_{i,j}^*$, is formed by eliminating those critical sections nested inside other elements of $\beta_{i,j}$. Then, $B_i$ is equal to the length of the longest critical section in $\beta_i^* = \cup_{j>i} \beta_{i,j}^*$, the set of all outermost critical sections that can block $J_i$.

### Worst-Case Superiority of OMP over Previous Policies

If only condition 1 of the OMP *locking conditions* is used, we obtain the priority ceiling policy (PCP) defined in [17], where the use of condition 1 is shown to be a sufficient condition to obtain the deadlock prevention property and a worst-case blocking of at most one critical section of a lower-priority task.

Consider the use of the priority ceiling policy on Example 4. Both jobs $J_2$ and $J_{1a}$ would not have been allowed to enter their respective critical sections when $S_1$ is locked. This example illustrates the fact that OMP can lead to lower worst-case blocking relative to the priority ceiling policy. In particular, consider the case where each job $J_1$ of task $\tau_1$ voluntarily suspends itself once (say for I/O) such that it executes as sub-jobs $J_{1a}$ and $J_{1b}$. Under the priority ceiling policy, both of these sub-jobs can be blocked when they try to lock $S_0$ and $S_1$, respectively. Hence, each job of $\tau_1$ will be blocked for the duration of two critical sections of lower-priority tasks. However, under OMP, whenever $J_{1a}$ tries to lock $S_0$, it will always find that either condition 1 or condition 2 of OMP will be true. Thus, $J_{1a}$ is never blocked and $B_1$ under OMP will be shorter than in the case of the priority ceiling policy. As a result, it is possible for OMP to lead to a better worst-case schedulability analysis than PCP.

## 11.3   Conclusions

Synchronization primitives used in real-time systems should bound the blocking duration that a job can encounter. Unfortunately, a direct application of commonly used primitives like semaphores, monitors, and Ada rendezvous can lead to unbounded priority inversion, where a high-priority job can be blocked by a lower-priority job for an arbitrary amount of time. Priority inheritance policies solve this unbounded priority inversion problem and bound the blocking duration that a job can experience. We have presented an optimal priority inheritance policy that not only bounds the worst-case blocking duration of a job to that of a single critical section but also prevents deadlocks. It can also be shown that this policy is also optimal in the sense that no other priority inheritance policy can guarantee a better worst-case blocking duration [13]. Other approximations to the policy which can be easier to implement are also possible.

## Acknowledgments

The authors wish to thank Ted Baker for pointing out that $J^*$ may not be unique, and for his many comments on this chapter. The authors would also like to thank many reviewers, including Prashant Waknis and Joo Yong Kim, for their valuable comments. This chapter is based on work reported in [12, 13].

## References

[1] Baker, T. P. A stack-based resource allocation policy for real-time processes. *IEEE Real-Time Systems Symposium*, December 1990.

[2] Chen, M. I., and Lin, K.-J. Dynamic priority ceilings: a concurrency control protocol for real-time systems. *UIUCDCS-R89-1511, Technical Report*, Department of Computer Science, University of Illinois at Urbana-Champaign, 1989.

[3] Clark, D. D. The structuring of systems using upcalls. *The Tenth Symposium on Operating System Principles*, 1985.

[4] Jeffay, K. Scheduling sporadic tasks with shared resources in hard real-time systems. *TR90-038, Technical Report*, Department of Computer Science, University of North Carolina at Chapel Hill, November 1989.

[5] Lampson, B. W., and Redell, D. D. Experience with processes and monitors in mesa. *Communications of the ACM*, 23(2):105–117, February 1980.

[6] Lehoczky, J. P., and Sha, L. Performance of real-time bus scheduling algorithms. *ACM Performance Evaluation Review, Special Issue*, 14(1), May 1986.

[7] Lehoczky, J. P., Sha, L., and Ding, Y. The rate monotonic scheduling algorithm: exact characterization and average-case behavior. *IEEE Real-Time Systems Symposium*, December 1989.

[8] Leinbaugh, D. W. Guaranteed response time in a hard real-time environment. *IEEE Transactions on Software Engineering*, January 1980.

[9] Leung, J. Y., and Merrill, M. L. A note on preemptive scheduling of periodic, real time tasks. *Information Processing Letters*, 11(3):115–118, November 1980.

[10] Liu, C. L., and Layland, J. W. Scheduling algorithms for multiprogramming in a hard real time environment. *Journal of the ACM*, 20(1):46–61, 1973.

[11] Mok, A. K. Fundamental design problems of distributed systems for the hard real time environment. *Ph.D. thesis*, M.I.T., 1983.

[12] Rajkumar, R. Task synchronization in real-time systems. *Ph.D. thesis*, Carnegie Mellon University, August 1989.

[13] Rajkumar, R., Sha, L., Lehoczky, J. P., and Ramamritham, K. An optimal priority inheritance protocol for real-time synchronization. *Technical Report*, IBM Thomas J. Watson Research Center, 1991.

[14] Ramaritham, K., and Stankovic, J. A. Dynamic task scheduling in hard real-time distributed systems. *IEEE Software*, July 1984.

[15] Sha, L., Lehoczky J. P., and Rajkumar, R. Solutions for some practical problems in prioritized preemptive scheduling. *IEEE Real-Time Systems Symposium*, 1986.

[16] Sha, L., and Goodenough, J. B. Real-time scheduling theory and ada. *Computer*, May 1990.

[17] Sha, L., Rajkumar, R., and Lehoczky, J. P. Priority inheritance protocols: An approach to real-time synchronization. *IEEE Transactions on Computers*, pages 1175–1185, September 1990.

[18] SofTech Inc. Designing real-time systems in ada. *Final Report 1123-1*, SofTech, Inc., January 1986.

# Part IV

# Formal Methods

# Chapter 12

# The Algebra of Communicating Shared Resources and Its Toolkit

## Insup Lee, Duncan Clarke, and Hong-Liang Xie

There has been significant progress in the development of timed process algebra for the specification and analysis of real-time systems in recent years. This chapter describes a timed process algebra, called ACSR, which supports synchronous timed actions and asynchronous instantaneous events. Timed actions model the usage of shared resources and the passage of time, whereas events allow synchronization between processes. To be able to specify real-time systems accurately, ACSR supports the notion of priorities that can be used to arbitrate between timed actions competing for shared resources and between events that are ready for synchronization. This chapter also describes a set of tools that have been implemented to facilitate the use of ACSR. ACSR and the tools are illustrated through the specification and analysis of a variant of the railroad crossing problem, in which trains and cars compete for the crossing.

## 12.1 Introduction

Reliability in real-time systems can be improved through the use of formal methods for the specification and analysis of real-time systems. Formal methods treat system components as mathematical objects and provide mathematical models to describe and predict the observable properties and behaviors of these objects. There are several advantages to using formal methods for the specification and analysis of real-time systems. They are, first, the early discovery of ambiguities, inconsistencies, and incompleteness in informal requirements; second, the automatic or machine-assisted analysis of the correctness of specifications with respect to requirements; and third, the evaluation of design alternatives without expensive prototyping.

During the past several years, there has been much progress in the development of formal methods for real-time systems. Much of this work falls into the traditional categories of untimed systems, such as temporal logics, assertional methods, net-based models, automata theory, and process algebras. This chapter presents an overview of a real-time process algebra, called ACSR (the Algebra of Communicating Shared Resources), and a set of tools based on ACSR.

Process algebras, such as CCS [16], CSP [12], and ACP [3], have been developed to describe and analyze concurrent systems without the notion of time. They are based on the premises that the two most essential notions in understanding complex dynamic systems are concurrency and communication [16] and that complex processes should be constructed from simpler processes by combining them using a relatively small set of operators. The most salient aspect of process algebras is that they support the *modular* specification and verification of a system. This is due to the algebraic laws forming a compositional proof system, making it possible to verify the whole system by reasoning about its parts.

To specify and analyze real-time systems, many process algebras have been augmented to include the notion of time and a set of timed operators [1, 2, 10, 17, 19, 23, 26]. The domain of time is either discrete or dense. A time domain is discrete if each element in the domain has a unique successor; that is, events can occur only at fixed time intervals. A time domain is dense if there is an element between any two elements in the domain; that is, an event can happen at an arbitrary moment in time. Real-time algebras were first developed using discrete time and then evolved to support dense time. Although a version of ACSR with dense time is being developed, the presentation of ACSR in this chapter is restricted to the discrete time domain due to space limitations.

The timing behavior of a real-time system depends not only on delays due to process synchronization, but also on the availability of shared resources. Most current real-time process algebras adequately capture delays due to process synchronization; however, they abstract out resource-specific details. In contrast, the computation model of ACSR is based on the view that a real-time system consists of a set of communicating processes that compete for shared resources. The use of shared resources is modeled by timed actions whose executions are subject to the availability of resources. Contention for resources is arbitrated according to the priorities of competing actions. To ensure the uniform progression of time, processes execute timed actions synchronously. In addition to timed actions, ACSR supports instantaneous actions, called events, that do not consume any resource. Processes execute events asynchronously except when two processes synchronize through matching events. Priorities are also used to arbitrate the choice among multiple events that are possible at the same time.

Although mathematical formalisms for expressing processes are important in themselves, their manual application to realistic problems is time consuming and error prone. As a result, many formalisms are supported by automated tools that perform tasks such as syntax checking, state space analysis, and interactive execution. CSP [11] and CCS [16, 18] are supported by FDR [7] and CWB [5], respectively, which offer textual interfaces for process description, comparison of processes, and model checking. Modechart [13] provides a graphical formalism to express concurrent real-time systems and has been implemented in MCTool [6, 9].

Tools based on timed transition system models such as the TTM/RTTL verifier [20] and the CRSM Toolset [22, 24] have also been developed.

To facilitate the use of ACSR in the design and analysis of real-time systems, we have developed an integrated set of tools called VERSA (Verification, Execution and Rewrite System for ACSR). Since VERSA is based on ACSR, real-time systems are specified as ACSR processes. VERSA supports three types of analysis techniques. The first is to apply rewriting rules to the specification to deduce system properties. The second is to construct a state machine and explore and analyze the state space to verify safety properties and test equivalence of alternative process formulations. The third is to interactively execute the process specification to explore specific system properties and sample the execution traces of the system.

The remainder of this chapter is organized as follows: Section 12.2 provides a brief introduction to ACSR, including the syntax, semantics, laws, and prioritized bisimulation. As an illustration of the expressiveness and use of ACSR, we describe in Section 12.3 a variant of the railroad crossing problem, which involves trains and cars. Section 12.4 presents an overview of VERSA, followed by the specification and analysis of the variant railroad crossing problem using VERSA. Section 12.5 summarizes current and future work.

## 12.2   ACSR: A Real-Time Process Algebra

ACSR, like other process algebras, consists of (1) a set of operators and syntactic rules for constructing processes; (2) a semantic mapping which assigns meaning or interpretation to processes; (3) a notion of equivalence or partial order between processes; and (4) a set of algebraic laws that allows syntactic manipulation of processes. ACSR uses two distinct action types to model computation: time and resource-consuming actions, and instantaneous events.

**Timed Actions.**   We consider a system to be composed of a finite set of serially reusable resources, denoted by $\mathcal{R}$. An action that consumes one "tick" of time is drawn from the domain $\mathbb{P}(\mathcal{R} \times \mathbb{N})$, with the restriction that each resource be represented at most once. As an example, the singleton action, $\{(r, p)\}$, denotes the use of some resource $r \in \mathcal{R}$ running at the priority level $p$. The action $\emptyset$ represents idling for one time unit, since no resources are being consumed.

We use $D_R$ to denote the domain of timed actions, and we let $A, B$, and $C$ range over $D_R$. We define $\rho(A)$ to be the set of resources used by the action $A$; e.g., $\rho(\{(r_1, p_1), (r_2, p_2)\}) = \{r_1, r_2\}$. We also use $\pi_r(A)$ to denote the priority level of the resource $r$ in the action $A$; e.g., $\pi_{r_1}(\{(r_1, p_1), (r_2, p_2)\}) = p_1$. By convention, if $r$ is not in $\rho(A)$, then $\pi_r(A) = 0$.

**Instantaneous Events.**   We call instantaneous actions *events*, which provide the basis for synchronization in our process algebra. An event is denoted by a pair $(a, p)$, where $a$ is the *label* of the event, and $p$ is its *priority*. Labels are drawn from the set $\mathcal{L} \cup \overline{\mathcal{L}} \cup \{\tau\}$, where if $a$ is a given label, we say that $\bar{a}$ is its *inverse* label; i.e., $\bar{\bar{a}} = a$. As in CCS [16], the special identity label, $\tau$, arises when two events with inverse labels are synchronously executed in parallel.

We use $D_E$ to denote the domain of events, and let $e$, $f$, and $g$ range over $D_E$. We use $l(e)$ and $\pi(e)$ to represent the label and priority, respectively, of the event $e$. The entire domain of actions is represented by $D = D_R \cup D_E$, and we let $\alpha$ and $\beta$ range over D.

## 12.2.1  The Syntax and Informal Semantics

The following grammar describes the syntax of ACSR processes:

$$P \quad ::= \quad NIL \mid A : P \mid e.P \mid P_1 + P_2 \mid P_1 \| P_2 \mid$$
$$P \triangle_t^a (P_1, P_2, P_3) \mid [P]_I \mid P \setminus F \mid rec\ X.P \mid X$$

NIL is a process that executes no action (i.e., it is initially deadlocked). There are two prefix operators, corresponding to the two types of actions. The first, $A : P$, executes a timed, resource-consuming action $A$, which consumes one time unit, and proceeds to the process $P$. The second prefix operator, $e.P$, executes the instantaneous event $e$, and proceeds to $P$. The Choice operator $P_1 + P_2$ represents nondeterminism – either of the processes may be chosen to execute, subject to the event offerings and resource limitations of the environment. The operator $P_1 \| P_2$ is the concurrent execution of $P_1$ and $P_2$.

The Scope construct $P \triangle_t^a (P_1, P_2, P_3)$ binds the process $P$ by a temporal scope [15], and incorporates the features of both timeouts and interrupts. We call $t$ the *time bound*, where $t \in Z \cup \{\infty\}$. $P$ executes for a maximum of $t$ time units. The scope may be exited in a number of ways. First, if $P$ successfully terminates within time $t$ by executing an event labeled with $\bar{a}$, then control proceeds to the "success-handler" $P_1$. Here, $a$ may be any label other than $\tau$. Process $P_2$ is a timeout exception-handler; that is, if $P$ fails to terminate within time $t$, then control proceeds to $P_2$. Last, at any time while $P$ is executing, it may be interrupted by $P_3$'s execution of a timed action or instantaneous event. An interrupt occurs and control proceeds to the "interrupt-handler" $P_3$ if $P_3$ offers an event or action with a priority higher than any offered by $P$.

The Close operator, $[P]_I$, produces a process $P$ that monopolizes the resources in $I \subseteq \mathcal{R}$. The Restriction operator, $P \setminus F$, limits the behavior of $P$. Here, no events with labels in $F$ are permitted to execute. The process $rec\ X.P$ denotes standard recursion, allowing the specification of infinite behaviors.

## 12.2.2  The Structured Transition System

When specifying a process with algebraic expressions, the progress of the process is captured by the execution of discrete "actions" permitted by the transition rules for ACSR. The semantics of ACSR is defined in two steps. We first develop the *unconstrained* transition system, where a transition is denoted as $P \xrightarrow{\alpha} P'$ (for $P$ and $P'$ processes and $\alpha$ an action). Within "$\to$" no priority arbitration is made between actions; we subsequently refine "$\to$" to define our prioritized transition system, "$\to_\pi$."

The two rules for the prefix operators are *axioms*; i.e., they have premises of *true*. There is one rule for time-consuming actions, and one for events.

$$\textbf{ActT} \quad \frac{\quad-\quad}{A : P \xrightarrow{A} P} \qquad\qquad \textbf{ActI} \quad \frac{\quad-\quad}{e.P \xrightarrow{e} P}$$

For example, the process $\{(r_1, p_1), (r_2, p_2)\} : P$ simultaneously uses resources $r_1$ and $r_2$ for one time unit, and then executes $P$. Alternatively, the process $(a, p).P$ executes the event "$(a, p)$," and proceeds to $P$.

The rules for Choice are identical for both timed actions and instantaneous events (and hence we use "$\alpha$" as the label).

$$\textbf{ChoiceL} \quad \frac{P \xrightarrow{\alpha} P'}{P + Q \xrightarrow{\alpha} P'} \qquad\qquad \textbf{ChoiceR} \quad \frac{Q \xrightarrow{\alpha} Q'}{P + Q \xrightarrow{\alpha} Q'}$$

As an example, $(a, 7).P + \{(r_1, 3), (r_2, 7)\} : Q$ may choose between executing the event $(a, 7)$ or the time-consuming action $\{(r_1, 3), (r_2, 7)\}$. The former behavior is deduced from rule **ActI**, while the latter is deduced from **ActT**.

The Parallel operator provides the basic constructor for concurrency and communication. The first rule, **ParT**, is for time-consuming transitions.

$$\textbf{ParT} \quad \frac{P \xrightarrow{A_1} P', Q \xrightarrow{A_2} Q'}{P\|Q \xrightarrow{A_1 \cup A_2} P'\|Q'} \quad (\rho(A_1) \cap \rho(A_2) = \emptyset)$$

Note that timed transitions are truly synchronous, in that the resulting process advances only if both of the constituents take a step. The condition $\rho(A_1) \cap \rho(A_2) = \emptyset$ ensures that each resource is truly sequential, and that only one process may use a given resource during any time step.

The next three laws are for event transitions. As opposed to timed actions, events may occur asynchronously (as in CCS and related interleaving models).

$$\textbf{ParIL} \quad \frac{P \xrightarrow{e} P'}{P\|Q \xrightarrow{e} P'\|Q} \qquad\qquad \textbf{ParIR} \quad \frac{Q \xrightarrow{e} Q'}{P\|Q \xrightarrow{e} P\|Q'}$$

$$\textbf{ParCom} \quad \frac{P \xrightarrow{(a,n)} P', Q \xrightarrow{(\bar{a},m)} Q'}{P\|Q \xrightarrow{(\tau, n+m)} P'\|Q'}$$

The first two rules show that events may be arbitrarily interleaved. The last rule is for two synchronizing processes; that is, $P$ executes an event with the label $a$, while $Q$ executes an event with the inverse label $\bar{a}$. Note that when the two events synchronize, their resulting priority is the sum of their constituent priorities.

The Scope operator possesses a total of five transition rules describing the behaviors induced by a temporal scope. The first two rules show that as long as

$t > 0$ and $P$ does not execute an event with label $b$, the execution of $P$ continues.

$$\textbf{ScopeCT} \qquad \frac{P \xrightarrow{A} P'}{P \, \Delta_t^b \, (Q, R, S) \xrightarrow{A} P' \, \Delta_{t-1}^b \, (Q, R, S)} \qquad (t > 0)$$

$$\textbf{ScopeCI} \qquad \frac{P \xrightarrow{e} P'}{P \, \Delta_t^b \, (Q, R, S) \xrightarrow{e} P' \, \Delta_t^b \, (Q, R, S)} \qquad (l(e) \neq \bar{b}, t > 0)$$

The **ScopeE** (for "end") shows that $P$ can depart the temporal scope by executing an event labeled with $\bar{b}$. Upon exit, the label $\bar{b}$ is converted to the identity label $\tau$ with the same priority.

$$\textbf{ScopeE} \qquad \frac{P \xrightarrow{(\bar{b},n)} P'}{P \, \Delta_t^b \, (Q, R, S) \xrightarrow{(\tau,n)} Q} \qquad (t > 0)$$

The next rule, **ScopeT** (for "timeout"), is applied whenever the scope times out, that is, when $t = 0$. At this point, control proceeds to the exception-handler $R$.

$$\textbf{ScopeT} \qquad \frac{R \xrightarrow{\alpha} R'}{P \, \Delta_t^b \, (Q, R, S) \xrightarrow{\alpha} R'} \qquad (t = 0)$$

Finally, **ScopeI** (for "interrupt") shows that the process $S$ may interrupt (and kill) $P$ while the scope is still active.

$$\textbf{ScopeI} \qquad \frac{S \xrightarrow{\alpha} S'}{P \, \Delta_t^b \, (Q, R, S) \xrightarrow{\alpha} S'} \qquad (t > 0)$$

The Restriction operator defines a subset of instantaneous events that are excluded from the behavior of the system. This is done by establishing a set of labels, $F$ ($\tau \notin F$), and allowing only the behaviors that do not involve events with those labels. Time-consuming actions, on the other hand, remain unaffected.

$$\textbf{ResT} \quad \frac{P \xrightarrow{A} P'}{P \setminus F \xrightarrow{A} P' \setminus F} \qquad \textbf{ResI} \quad \frac{P \xrightarrow{(a,n)} P'}{P \setminus F \xrightarrow{(a,n)} P' \setminus F} \qquad (a, \bar{a} \notin F)$$

The effect of Restriction is to "force" synchronization between concurrent processes and to prevent restricted events from being used in synchronization with other processes. The Restriction operator can be viewed as assigning dedicated synchronization channels between processes.

The Close operator assigns dedicated resources. When a process $P$ is embedded in a closed context such as $[P]_I$, we ensure that there is no further sharing of the resources in $I$. Assume that $P$ executes a time-consuming action $A$. If $A$ utilizes less than the full resource set $I$, the action is augmented with $(r, 0)$ pairs for each unused $r \in I - \rho(A)$ to ensure that all resources in $I$ are held by $P$.

$$\textbf{CloseT} \quad \frac{P \xrightarrow{A_1} P'}{[P]_I \xrightarrow{A_1 \cup A_2} [P']_I} \qquad (A_2 = \{(r,0) \mid r \in I - \rho(A_1)\})$$

$$\textbf{CloseI} \quad \frac{P \xrightarrow{e} P'}{[P]_I \xrightarrow{e} [P']_I}$$

The operator $rec\ X.P$ denotes recursion, allowing the specification of infinite behaviors.

$$\textbf{Rec} \quad \frac{P[^{rec\ X.P}/_X] \xrightarrow{\alpha} P'}{rec\ X.P \xrightarrow{\alpha} P'}$$

where $P[^{rec\ X.P}/_X]$ is the standard notation for substitution of $rec\ X.P$ for each free occurrence of $X$ in $P$.

As an example, consider $rec\ X.(A : X)$, which executes the resource-consuming action "$A$" forever. By **ActT**, $A : (rec\ X.(A : X)) \xrightarrow{A} rec\ X.(A : X)$, so by **Rec**, $rec\ X.(A : X) \xrightarrow{A} rec\ X.(A : X)$.

## 12.2.3 Priority and Preemption

The prioritized transition system is based on *preemption*, which incorporates our treatment of synchronization, resource sharing, and priority. The notion of preemption is as follows: Let "$\prec$", called the *preemption relation*, be a transitive, irreflexive, binary relation on actions. For two actions $\alpha$ and $\beta$, if $\alpha \prec \beta$, then we say that "$\alpha$ is preempted by $\beta$." This means that in any real-time system, if there is a choice between executing either $\alpha$ or $\beta$, $\beta$ will always be executed.

**Definition 12.2.1 (Preemption Relation)** *For two actions, $\alpha, \beta$, we say that $\beta$ preempts $\alpha$ ($\alpha \prec \beta$) if one of the following cases holds:*

(1) Both $\alpha$ and $\beta$ are timed actions in $D_R$, where

$$(\rho(\beta) \subseteq \rho(\alpha)) \wedge (\forall r \in \rho(\alpha).\pi_r(\alpha) \leq \pi_r(\beta)) \wedge (\exists r \in \rho(\beta).\pi_r(\alpha) < \pi_r(\beta))$$

(2) Both $\alpha$ and $\beta$ are events in $D_E$, where $\pi(\alpha) < \pi(\beta) \wedge l(\alpha) = l(\beta)$

(3) $\alpha \in D_R$ and $\beta \in D_E$, with $l(\beta) = \tau$ and $\pi(\beta) > 0$.                           □

Here, $\alpha$ may use a superset of $\beta$'s resources. However, $\beta$ uses all the resources at the same priority level as $\alpha$ or higher (recall that $\pi_r(B)$ is, by convention, 0 when $r$ is not in $B$). Also, $\beta$ uses at least one resource at a higher level.

Case (2) shows that an event may be preempted by another event sharing the same label, but with a higher priority.

Finally, case (3) shows the single case in which an event and a timed action are comparable under "$\prec$." That is, if $n > 0$ in an event $(\tau, n)$, we let the event preempt any timed action.

**Example 12.2.1** The following examples show some comparisons made by the preemption relation, "$\prec$."

      a. $\{(r_1, 2), (r_2, 5)\} \prec \{(r_1, 7), (r_2, 5)\}$
      b. $\{(r_1, 2), (r_2, 5)\} \not\prec \{(r_1, 7), (r_2, 3)\}$
      c. $\{(r_1, 2), (r_2, 0)\} \prec \{(r_1, 7)\}$
      d. $\{(r_1, 2), (r_2, 1)\} \not\prec \{(r_1, 7)\}$
      e. $(\tau, 1) \prec (\tau, 2)$
      f. $(a, 1) \not\prec (b, 2)$ if $a \neq b$
      g. $(a, 2) \prec (a, 5)$
      h. $\{(r_1, 2), (r_2, 5)\} \prec (\tau, 2)$                □

We define the prioritized transition system "$\rightarrow_\pi$," which refines "$\rightarrow$" to account for preemption.

**Definition 12.2.2** *The labeled transition system "$\rightarrow_\pi$" is defined as follows:*
$P \xrightarrow{\;\;\alpha\;\;}_\pi P'$ *if and only if*

*(a) $P \xrightarrow{\alpha} P'$ is an unprioritized transition, and*

*(b) There is no unprioritized transition $P \xrightarrow{\beta} P''$ such that $\alpha \prec \beta$.*     □

## 12.2.4   Prioritized Strong Bisimulation and Laws

Our analysis techniques are based on process equivalence, where we attempt to prove that a process $P$ is equivalent to a process $Q$. Typically, $P$ is an abstract specification of the problem, while $Q$ is a detailed implementation with more complicated syntax. The objective is to show that the two processes are operationally equivalent. Equivalence between two ACSR processes is based on the concept of *bisimulation* [21], which compares the computation trees of the two processes.

**Definition 12.2.3** *For a given transition system "$\longrightarrow$", any binary relation $r$ is a strong bisimulation if, for $(P, Q) \in r$ and $\alpha \in D$,*

*1. if $P \xrightarrow{\alpha} P'$, then for some $Q'$, $Q \xrightarrow{\alpha} Q'$ and $(P', Q') \in r$, and*

*2. if $Q \xrightarrow{\alpha} Q'$, then for some $P'$, $P \xrightarrow{\alpha} P'$ and $(P', Q') \in r$.*     □

In other words, if $P$ (or $Q$) can take a step on $\alpha$, then $Q$ (or $P$) must also be able to take a step on $\alpha$ with both of the next states also bisimilar. There are some very obvious bisimulation relations; e.g., $\emptyset$ (which satisfies the above rules vacuously) or syntactic identity. However, using the theory found in [16], it is straightforward to show that there exists a largest such bisimulation over "$\rightarrow$," which we denote as "$\sim$." This relation is an equivalence relation, and is a congruence with respect to ACSR's operators. Similarly, "$\sim_\pi$" is the largest strong bisimulation over "$\rightarrow_\pi$," and we call it *prioritized strong equivalence*.

    The notion of bisimulation provides us with two techniques to show whether two processes are bisimulation-equivalent. One way is to show that $P$ and $Q$ are equivalent by finding a binary relation $r$ such that (1) $(P, Q) \in r$ and (2) $r$ is a bisimulation. An algorithm exists for finding such a relation $r$ for finite-state processes [14].

Another way is to formulate a set of equivalence-preserving laws which characterize bisimulation equivalence. These laws are then used to rewrite process terms in order to demonstrate their equivalence. A sound and complete set of equivalence-preserving laws for ACSR is defined in [4]. Table 12.1 shows a subset of the ACSR laws that we use in Section 12.3.2. In the sequel, wherever we use the equality symbol "=" in showing that two processes are equivalent, it means that we have used our laws to construct the proof. The bisimilarity of the processes follows from the soundness of the laws.

Note the use of the summation symbol $\sum$ in Par3. The interpretation is as follows: Let $I$ be an index set representing processes, such that for each $i \in I$, there is some corresponding process $P_i$. If $I = \{i_1, \ldots, i_n\}$, because of Choice4 we are able to neglect parentheses and use the following notation:

$$\sum_{i \in I} P_i \stackrel{\text{def}}{=} P_{i_1} + \cdots + P_{i_n}$$

and where $\sum_{i \in \emptyset} P_i \stackrel{\text{def}}{=} NIL$.

Par3 is representative of many of the laws, in that its objective is to "undo" a constructor. That is, it reduces the "||" operator to a simpler form—in this case, a process whose initial steps can be determined by the Prefix and Choice constructors.

# 12.3    A Variant of the Railroad Crossing Problem

The standard railroad crossing problem has been used to compare different formal methods for real-time systems [8]. Here, we use a variant of the railroad crossing problem that requires explicit modeling of both trains and cars. The problem is as follows: There is a crossing which is shared by trains and cars as illustrated in Figure 12.1. The correctness requirements are that trains never stop at the crossing and cars should only cross when there is no danger of being struck by a train.

As shown in Figure 12.1, a sensor is installed to detect that a train is approaching the crossing. We define the region $R$ to be the segment of track between the sensor and the crossing, and the track that passes through the crossing. Since the problem states that a train never stops at the crossing, cars have to stop in front of the gate whenever a train is approaching the crossing. Obviously, a car should never stop in the middle of the crossing. Thus, if a car is already in the crossing when a train is approaching, it should continue through the crossing.

We use the following five timing parameters: $t_1$ is the time it takes for a train to travel from entering the region $R$ to reaching the crossing. $t_2$ is the time it takes for a train to pass the crossing. $t_3$ is the time it takes for a car to pass the crossing. In addition, $\delta$ is assumed to be the minimum time from the current train exiting the crossing to the next train entering the region, and $\theta$ is the time from the current car leaving the crossing to the next car arriving at the crossing.

Table 12.1  The Set of ACSR Laws

| | |
|---|---|
| Choice1 | $P + \text{NIL} = P$ |
| Choice2 | $P + P = P$ |
| Choice3 | $P + Q = Q + P$ |
| Choice4 | $(P + Q) + R = P + (Q + R)$ |
| Choice5 | $A_1 : P_1 + A_2 : P_2 = A_2 : P_2$ if $A_1 \prec A_2$ |
| Choice6 | $(a_1, n_1).P_1 + (a_2, n_2).P_2 = (a_2, n_2).P_2$ if $(a_1, n_1) \prec (a_2, n_2)$ |
| Choice7 | $A : P + (\tau, n).Q = (\tau, n).Q$ if $n > 0$ |
| Par1 | $P \| Q = Q \| P$ |
| Par2 | $(P \| Q) \| R = P \| (Q \| R)$ |

Par3

$$\left( \sum_{i \in I} A_i : P_i + \sum_{i \in J} (a_j, n_j).Q_j \right) \parallel \left( \sum_{k \in K} B_k : R_k + \sum_{l \in L} (b_l, m_l).S_l \right)$$

$$= \left[ \begin{array}{l} \displaystyle\sum_{\substack{i \in I, k \in K, \\ \rho(A_i) \cap \rho(B_k) = \emptyset}} (A_i \cup B_k) : (P_i \| R_k) \\[2em] + \displaystyle\sum_{j \in J} (a_j, n_j). \left( Q_j \| \left( \sum_{k \in K} B_k : R_k + \sum_{l \in L} (b_l, m_l).S_l \right) \right) \\[2em] + \displaystyle\sum_{l \in L} (b_l, m_l). \left( \sum_{i \in I} A_i : P_i + \sum_{j \in J} (a_j, n_j).Q_j \right) \| S_l \\[2em] + \displaystyle\sum_{\substack{j \in J, l \in L, \\ a_j = b_l}} (\tau, n_j + m_l).(Q_j \| S_l) \end{array} \right]$$

| | |
|---|---|
| Scope1 | $A : P \triangle_t^b (Q, R, S) = A : (P \triangle_{t-1}^b (Q, R, S)) + S$ if $t > 0$ |
| Scope2 | $(a, n).P \triangle_t^b (Q, R, S) = (a, n).(P \triangle_t^b (Q, R, S)) + S$ if $t > 0 \wedge \bar{a} \neq b$ |
| Scope3 | $(a, n).P \triangle_t^b (Q, R, S) = (\tau, n).Q + S$ if $t > 0 \wedge \bar{a} = b$ |
| Scope4 | $P \triangle_0^b (Q, R, S) = R$ |
| Scope5 | $(P_1 + P_2) \triangle_t^b (Q, R, S) = P_1 \triangle_t^b (Q, R, S) + P_2 \triangle_t^b (Q, R, S)$ |
| Scope6 | $(\text{NIL}) \triangle_t^b (Q, R, S) = S$ if $t > 0$ |
| Res1 | $\text{NIL} \setminus F = \text{NIL}$ |
| Res2 | $(P + Q) \setminus F = (P \setminus F) + (Q \setminus F)$ |
| Res3 | $(A : P) \setminus F = A : (P \setminus F)$ |
| Res4 | $((a, n).P) \setminus F = (a, n).(P \setminus F)$ if $a, \bar{a} \notin F$ |
| Close1 | $[\text{NIL}]_I = \text{NIL}$ |
| Close2 | $[P + Q]_I = [P]_I + [Q]_I$ |
| Close3 | $[A_1 : P]_I = (A_1 \cup A_2) : [P]_I$ where $A_2 = \{(r, 0) | r \in I - \rho(A_1)\}$ |
| Close4 | $[(a, n).P]_I = (a, n).[P]_I$ |
| Rec1 | $recX.P = P[recX.P/X]$ |

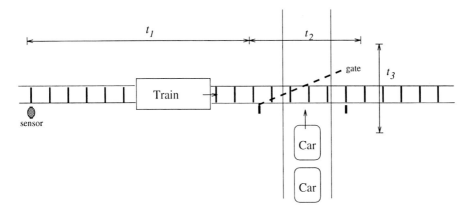

**Figure 12.1**  Railroad Crossing

We use the following notations to simplify the presentation of ACSR specifications:

$$A^0 : P \stackrel{\text{def}}{=} P$$

$$A^1 : P \stackrel{\text{def}}{=} A : P$$

$$A^n : P \stackrel{\text{def}}{=} A : A^{n-1} : P \qquad\qquad (n > 1)$$

$$A^\infty \stackrel{\text{def}}{=} \text{REC } X.\ A : X$$

$$A^{[0,\infty]} : P \stackrel{\text{def}}{=} A^\infty \triangle (\text{NIL}, \text{NIL}, P)$$

$$A^{[n,\infty]} : P \stackrel{\text{def}}{=} A^n : (A^{[0,\infty]} : P) \qquad\qquad (n \geq 1)$$

$$(A, B)^n : P \stackrel{\text{def}}{=} \Gamma_n(A, B, P) \qquad\qquad (n \geq 1)$$

$$\text{where} \begin{cases} \Gamma_1(A, B, P) \stackrel{\text{def}}{=} A : P + B : P \\ \Gamma_i(A, B, P) \stackrel{\text{def}}{=} A : \Gamma_{i-1}(A, B, P) + B^i : P \\ \qquad\qquad (1 < i \leq n) \end{cases}$$

$A^n$ means that $A$ is repeated for $n$ times, and $A^\infty$ means that $A$ is repeated forever. $A^{[n,\infty]} : P$ means that control transfers to $P$ after $A$ is repeated for $n$ or more times.

$(A, B)^n : P$ means that $A$ is repeated $m$ times, $0 \leq m \leq n$, followed by the $n - m$ repetition of $B$'s, which is followed by $P$. Here, the sum of $A$'s and $B$'s is exactly $n$. For example, the possible behaviors of $(A, B)^3 : P$ are: $A : A : A : P$, $A : A : B : P$, $A : B : B : P$, and $B : B : B : P$.

## 12.3.1   The ACSR Specification

The resources, events, and actions used in the ACSR specification are as follows:

Resources:   $train$

                     $car$

                     $crossing$

Events:       $TNear \overset{\text{def}}{=} (signal, 1)$

                   $CNear \overset{\text{def}}{=} (signal, 2)$

Actions:     $TTravel \overset{\text{def}}{=} \{(train, 1)\}$

                   $CWait \overset{\text{def}}{=} \{(car, 1)\}$

                   $TCross \overset{\text{def}}{=} \{(train, 1), (crossing, 5)\}$

                   $CCross \overset{\text{def}}{=} \{(car, 1), (crossing, 2)\}$

The events $TNear$ and $CNear$ are used to indicate that a train and a car are approaching the crossing, respectively. The action $TTravel$ represents the train that has entered the region $R$, but has not yet acquired the resource $crossing$. The action $CWait$ indicates that the car is waiting in front of the gate. The action $TCross$ represents that the train has acquired the resource $crossing$; the action $CCross$ is similarly defined for a car.

Note that both $TCross$ and $CCross$ use the resource $crossing$, but $TCross$ uses it at a higher priority than $CCross$. As we explain later, this condition is necessary for correctness. To simplify the presentation, we assign the priority of the event $CNear$ to be higher than that of $TNear$, that is, $TNear \prec CNear$. This condition, however, is not necessary for correctness.

The specification of the problem in ACSR is as follows:

$$\text{Train} \overset{\text{def}}{=} \emptyset^{[\delta,\infty]} : TNear.(TTravel, TCross)^{t_1} : TCross^{t_2} : \text{Train}$$

$$\text{Car} \overset{\text{def}}{=} \emptyset^{\theta} : CNear.CWait^{[0,\infty]} : CCross^{t_3} : \text{Car}$$

$$\text{System} \overset{\text{def}}{=} [\text{Train} \parallel \text{Car}]_{\{crossing\}}$$

We now show that this specification is safe in the sense that a train and a car never collide under certain reasonable constraints on the timing parameters. That is, under constraints to be identified, the system does not lead to deadlock caused by having $(TCross \cup CCross)$ as the only alternative. Furthermore, we show that the specification ensures that neither a train nor a car waits while the crossing is free. There are five cases to consider: (1) a train enters the region $R$ when there is no car in the crossing; (2) a train enters the region $R$ when there is a car in the crossing; (3) a train enters the region $R$ at the same time as a car arrives at the crossing; (4) a car arrives at the crossing when there is no train in the region $R$; and (5) a car arrives at the crossing when there is a train in the region $R$.

Once a train enters the region $R$, which is indicated by the event $TNear$, its subsequent behavior is specified by the ACSR term $(TTravel, TCross)^{t_1}$. If there is no car in the crossing, the train acquires the resource $crossing$ immediately since the resource $crossing$ is closed in System and $TCross$ preempts $TTravel \cup \{(crossing, 0)\}$. After this, the resource $crossing$ is unavailable to a car arriving later, until the train leaves the region $R$.

If a car is in the crossing when the train arrives, the car is executing *CCross*, which means the car possesses the resource *crossing*. The train performs *TTravel* until it acquires *crossing*. By the definition of $(TTravel, TCross)^{t_1}$, the train can perform *TTravel* for at most $t_1$ time units. Since it takes $t_3$ time units for a car to pass through the crossing, there are two cases, $t_1 < t_3$ and $t_1 \geq t_3$, to consider. If $t_1 < t_3$, then it is possible for the train to be in a situation in which *TCross* is the only possible action, but the car has not yet released the resource *crossing*. This situation means that the train reaches the crossing without acquiring the resource *crossing*, which results in deadlock. On the other hand, if $t_1 \geq t_3$, the car releases the resource *crossing* before the train reaches the crossing, and thus deadlock does not occur.

If a train enters the region $R$ at the same time as a car arrives at the crossing, then there are four possible actions from the following ACSR term:

$$(TTravel, TCross)^{t_1} : TCross^{t_2} : \text{Train} \parallel CWait^{[0,\infty]} : CCross^{t_3} : \emptyset^\theta : \text{Car} \quad (12.1)$$

The possible actions are $(TTravel \cup CWait)$, $(TTravel \cup CCross)$, $(TCross \cup CWait)$, and $(TCross \cup CCross)$.

The action $TCross \cup CCross$ is impossible since the two constituent actions have resource conflict on the resource *crossing*. Since the resource *crossing* is closed in System, $(TTravel \cup CWait)$ is preempted by $(TTravel \cup CCross)$. Furthermore, since $(TTravel \cup CCross)$ is preempted by $(TCross \cup CWait)$, the only possible action is $(TCross \cup CWait)$, which means that the train gets the right of way and the car waits, as desired.

If a car arrives at the crossing when no train is in the region, the car acquires the resource *crossing* immediately and starts the action *CCross*. Here, $(CWait^{[0,\infty]} : CCross^{t_3} : \cdots)$ does not wait for the resource *crossing* since the resource *crossing* is currently available and it is closed in System.

The above analysis is an informal justification that the specification describes a safe railroad crossing system under the condition $t_1 \geq t_3$. In the next section, we present the formal verification of correctness of a particular instance of the specification using the ACSR laws.

## 12.3.2   The Proof of an Instance Using ACSR Laws

We define a particular instance of the specification using the following timing parameters:

$$\delta \stackrel{\text{def}}{=} 4, \quad \theta \stackrel{\text{def}}{=} 0, \quad t_1 \stackrel{\text{def}}{=} 8, \quad t_2 \stackrel{\text{def}}{=} 5, \quad t_3 \stackrel{\text{def}}{=} 2.$$

The instance of the specification we consider is therefore as follows:

$$\text{Train} \stackrel{\text{def}}{=} \emptyset^{[4,\infty]} : TNear . (TTravel, TCross)^8 : TCross^5 : \text{Train}$$

$$\text{Car} \stackrel{\text{def}}{=} CNear . CWait^{[0,\infty]} : CCross^2 : \text{Car}$$

$$\text{System} \stackrel{\text{def}}{=} [\text{Train} \parallel \text{Car}]_{\{crossing\}}$$

$\theta \stackrel{\text{def}}{=} 0$ means that the next car arrives at the crossing as soon as the current car leaves the crossing.

In order to show that System is correct, we derive a sequential specification from which it is straightforward to see that the specification meets the problem requirements. Expanding and rewriting System using the definitions of Train and Car, and laws Par3 and Close4 gives:

$$\text{System} = CNear.[\text{Train} \parallel CWait^{[0,\infty]} : CCross^2 : \text{Car}]_{\{crossing\}}.$$

Let
$$\text{System}_1 \overset{\text{def}}{=} [\text{Train} \parallel CWait^{[0,\infty]} : CCross^2 : \text{Car}]_{\{crossing\}}.$$

Expand by the definition of Train and rewrite by $\emptyset^{[4,\infty]} \overset{\text{def}}{=} \emptyset^4 : \emptyset^{[0,\infty]}$:

$$\text{System}_1 = [\emptyset^4 : \emptyset^{[0,\infty]} : TNear.(TTravel, TCross)^8 : TCross^5 : \text{Train} \parallel$$
$$CWait^{[0,\infty]} : CCross^2 : \text{Car}]_{\{crossing\}}$$

by Scope1, Par3, Close2, Close3, Choice5:

$$\text{System}_1 = CCross^2 : [\emptyset^2 : \emptyset^{[0,\infty]} : TNear.(TTravel, TCross)^8 : TCross^5 : \text{Train} \parallel$$
$$\text{Car}]_{\{crossing\}}$$

by Scope1, Par3, Close2, Close3, Choice5:

$$\text{System}_1 = CCross^2 : CNear. CCross^2 :$$
$$[\emptyset^{[0,\infty]} : TNear.(TTravel, TCross)^8 : TCross^5 : \text{Train} \parallel \text{Car}]_{\{crossing\}}.$$

We let
$$\text{System}_2 \overset{\text{def}}{=} [\emptyset^{[0,\infty]} : TNear.(TTravel, TCross)^8 : TCross^5 : \text{Train} \parallel \text{Car}]_{\{crossing\}}$$

and obtain by the definition of Car, and laws Par3, Close4, and Choice6:

$$\text{System}_2 = CNear.[\emptyset^{[0,\infty]} : TNear.(TTravel, TCross)^8 : TCross^5 : \text{Train} \parallel$$
$$CWait^{[0,\infty]} : CCross^2 : \text{Car}]_{\{crossing\}}$$

and by Scope1, Par3, Close2, Close3, Close4, Choice5, Choice6:

$$\text{System}_2 = CNear.(TNear.[(TTravel, TCross)^8 : TCross^5 : \text{Train} \parallel$$
$$CWait^{[0,\infty]} : CCross^2 : \text{Car}]_{\{crossing\}}$$
$$+$$
$$CCross:[\emptyset^{[0,\infty]} : TNear.(TTravel, TCross)^8 : TCross^5 : \text{Train} \parallel$$
$$CCross:\text{Car}]_{\{crossing\}}).$$

Let
$$\text{System}_3 = [\emptyset^{[0,\infty]} : TNear.(TTravel, TCross)^8 : TCross^5 : \text{Train} \parallel$$
$$CCross:\text{Car}]_{\{crossing\}}.$$

Applying Scope1, Par3, Close2, Close3, Choice5 several times to keep ($TCross \cup CWait$) (as explained with Equation 12.1) and folding using the definition of $\mathsf{System_3}$ gives:

$$\mathsf{System_2} \;=\; CNear.\,(TNear.\,(TCross \cup CWait):$$
$$[TCross^7 : TCross^5 : \mathsf{Train} \;\|$$
$$CWait^{[0,\infty]} : CCross^2 : \mathsf{Car}]_{\{crossing\}}$$
$$+\;\; CCross: \mathsf{System_3}).$$

Expanding $\mathsf{System_2}$ similarly for 12 more times gives:

$$\mathsf{System_2} \;=\; CNear.\,(TNear.\,(TCross \cup CWait)^{13}:$$
$$[\mathsf{Train} \;\| \; CWait^{[0,\infty]} : CCross^2 : \mathsf{Car}]_{\{crossing\}}$$
$$+\;\; CCross: \mathsf{System_3}).$$

Using the definition of $\mathsf{System_1}$, we have:

$$\mathsf{System_2} = CNear.\,(TNear.\,(TCross \cup CWait)^{13}: \mathsf{System_1} \;+\;\; CCross: \mathsf{System_3}).$$

Applying the same reasoning that was used to simplify $\mathsf{System_2}$ to $\mathsf{System_3}$ gives:

$$\mathsf{System_3} \;=\; TNear.\,(TTravel \cup CCross): CNear.\,(TCross \cup CWait)^{12}: \mathsf{System_1}$$
$$+$$
$$CCross: [\emptyset^{[0,\infty]} : TNear.\,(TTravel, TCross)^{10} : TCross^5 : \mathsf{Train} \;\|$$
$$\mathsf{Car}]_{\{crossing\}}$$
$$=\; TNear.\,(TCross \cup CWait): CNear.\,(TCross \cup CWait)^{12}: \mathsf{System_1}$$
$$+$$
$$CCross: \mathsf{System_2}.$$

We simplify System by replacing the body of $\mathsf{System_1}$ with the name $\mathsf{System_1}$ and $\mathsf{System_1}$ by replacing the body of $\mathsf{System_2}$ with the name $\mathsf{System_2}$. We then rename System, $\mathsf{System_1}$, $\mathsf{System_2}$, and $\mathsf{System_3}$, by Spec, $\mathsf{Spec_1}$, $\mathsf{Spec_2}$, and $\mathsf{Spec_3}$, respectively. The resulting specifications are as follows:

$$\mathsf{Spec} \;\overset{\text{def}}{=}\; CNear.\,\mathsf{Spec_1}$$

$$\mathsf{Spec_1} \;\overset{\text{def}}{=}\; CCross^2 : CNear.\,CCross^2 : \mathsf{Spec_2}$$

$$\mathsf{Spec_2} \;\overset{\text{def}}{=}\; CNear.\,(TNear.\,(TCross \cup CWait)^{13}: \mathsf{Spec_1} \;+\; CCross: \mathsf{Spec_3})$$

$$\mathsf{Spec_3} \;\overset{\text{def}}{=}\; TNear.\,(TTravel \cup CCross): CNear.\,(TCross \cup CWait)^{12}: \mathsf{Spec_1}$$
$$+$$
$$CCross: \mathsf{Spec_2}.$$

Note that these specifications do not contain any parallel or close operators.

From these sequential specifications, we can easily see that *TCross* and *CCross* never occur simultaneously. In addition, if a train enters the region at the same time as a car arrives at the crossing, then the train acquires the resource *crossing* and performs the action *TCross* as shown in the left choice of Spec$_2$. If a train enters the region after a car has entered the crossing (modeled by the right choice of Spec$_2$ followed by the left choice of Spec$_3$), then the car continues with *CCross* while the train performs *TTravel*. After this car passes the crossing, the next car waits until the current train departs from the crossing, as indicated by the remainder of the left choice of Spec$_3$. The right choice of Spec$_3$ represents the case where there is no train in the region. Thus, Spec satisfies all the requirements of the problem described in Section 12.3.1.

Since every step of the derivation of Spec from System is based on ACSR laws, the equivalence of the original formulation of System and Spec follows from the soundness of these laws. We, therefore, conclude that System meets the requirements of the problem.

# 12.4   VERSA: A Set of Tools Based on ACSR

In experimenting with ACSR, we have found that it is difficult to use our algebra for non-trivial examples without computer assistance for syntax-checking and analysis. We thus have implemented the VERSA system that facilitates algebraic manipulation of specifications and state-space-exploration-based analysis.

The VERSA system parses input specifications into an internal representation based on abstract syntax trees. Analysis and rewriting tools operate on these trees for automatic and user-directed analysis of system specifications. At present there are three major functions implemented: rewriting, equivalence testing, and interactive execution.

The rewrite system facilitates the rewriting of ACSR process expressions according to ACSR laws that preserve prioritized strong equivalence. At the direction of the user, the rewrite system applies predefined algebraic laws to the abstract syntax tree of one or more processes, producing a new process that may be bound to a process variable. In this way algebraic proofs of the equivalence of process expressions may be developed interactively.

For state-based analysis and interactive execution, the state space generator converts abstract syntax trees of one or more processes to a labeled transition system (LTS). This generator also prunes edges made unreachable by the semantics of the prioritized transition system. We have found that this pruning significantly reduces the time required for state space explorations. Once an LTS has been generated, the user can query its size and the presence of deadlock. In addition, processes can be tested for a number of different notions of equivalence based on their LTS. These notions are syntactic equivalence, a weaker syntactic equivalence which allows renaming and simple changes in structure, prioritized strong equivalence, and prioritized weak equivalence. In the order listed, these notions of equivalence become coarser (i.e., equate more processes) and increase in computational complexity.

The interactive execution feature allows user-directed execution of process specifications. The user may interactively step through the LTS one action at a time, produce traces from random executions of the LTS, and save process configurations to a stack for later analysis while an alternate path is explored.

The remainder of this section describes the VERSA system's input conventions and automatic analysis features. We also illustrate how the instance of the railroad crossing example described in Section 12.3.2 is verified using VERSA.

## 12.4.1    Syntax

One of the primary goals of the VERSA system is to make the language in which processes are represented as readable as possible. Toward this end, ACSR's syntax for process expressions has been copied wherever possible, and syntactic conventions from mathematics and programming languages have been added. Additions to the ACSR syntax of Section 12.2 were chosen for their ability to simplify the task of describing large systems.

VERSA's syntax for processes is necessarily different from ACSR, because of ACSR's extensive use of subscripting, superscripting, and characters not available on standard ASCII keyboards. The differences between the ACSR syntax and VERSA syntax are summarized in Table 12.2. The syntax of operators not appearing in this table is identical to the original ACSR syntax.

| ACSR | VERSA |
|---|---|
| $a, \bar{a}, a', a_i$ | `a`, `'a`, `a'`, `a[i]` |
| $\tau$ | `t` or `tau` |
| $NIL$ | Any capitalization of `NIL` |
| $\|$ (composition) | `\|\|` or `\|` |
| $P\Delta_t^a(Q, R, S)$ | `scope(P,a,t,Q,R,S)` |
| $\infty$ | `inf` or `infinite` or `infinity` |
| $[P]_I$ | `[P]I` |
| $\emptyset$ | `{}` or `idle` |

**Table 12.2  ACSR vs. VERSA Syntax**

The syntax used for binding process expressions to names is a semicolon terminated assignment statement. A sample of a complete process description is shown in the following example:

$$\begin{aligned}
\text{SYS} &= (\text{OBBL}\|\text{OBBR})\backslash\{\text{sync}\}; \\
\text{OBBL} &= (\text{in}, 1).(\text{sync}, 3).\text{OBBL}; \\
\text{OBBR} &= ('\text{sync}, 3).(\text{out}, 2).\text{OBBR};
\end{aligned}$$

Here, ACSR process expressions are bound to three process variables SYS, OBBL, and OBBR to form a buffer of capacity two.

Many realistic process descriptions involve bounded counting, which is implemented as progression through a finite sequence of similar states. In mathematical contexts, it is common to use subscripts to describe such sets of similar items with a single, concise expression. The following example of a ten-place bounded buffer, presented first in ACSR as $BB_i$ and then in VERSA as BB[i], demonstrates how subscripting is expressed in VERSA:

$$
\begin{aligned}
BB_0 &= (in, 1).BB_1 \\
BB_i &= (in, 1).BB_{i+1} + (out, 2).BB_{i-1}, 1 \leq i \leq 9 \\
BB_{10} &= (out, 2).BB_9
\end{aligned}
$$

$$
\begin{aligned}
\text{BB[0]} &= \text{(in, 1).BB[1]}; \\
\text{BB[i]} &= \text{(in, 1).BB[i + 1] + (out, 2).BB[i - 1]} \ \{\text{i}, 1, 9\}; \\
\text{BB[10]} &= \text{(out, 2).BB[9]};
\end{aligned}
$$

The syntax for defining index variables is borrowed from *Mathematica* [25], and the semantics are consistent with the traditional mathematical conventions for subscripting.

A preprocessing facility that performs macro substitution and file inclusion is provided to improve the readability of VERSA descriptions. The preprocessor accepts a syntax identical to the preprocessor of the "C" programming language, and supports the #include<...> directive for including files from a standard directory and the #define... directive for defining symbolic constants. Macro definitions with parameter substitution are also supported.

## 12.4.2   The Algebraic Rewrite System

As Section 12.3.2 demonstrated, one approach to the formal analysis of systems involves rewriting terms according to a set of predefined laws. For ACSR there are approximately 30 such laws, many of which are shown in Table 12.1.

Rewriting of VERSA terms uses a function-style syntax whereby the name of the law is applied to the process being rewritten. For example, the process expression that results from applying law Choice1 to the process $(a, 1).Q + NIL$ is specified in VERSA as Choice1((a,1).Q + NIL). The result of a rewriting can be bound to process variables or embedded in larger process expression contexts.

## 12.4.3   Queries

The VERSA command language includes a query facility for displaying information about identifiers and the binding of process variables, for comparing actions using ACSR's preemption relation, and for comparing processes for equality with respect to several different definitions of equivalence.

Processes are compared using the query

$$P_1 == P_2?$$

where $P_1$ and $P_2$ are process variables. The type of equality tested by VERSA that is of interest for our example is prioritized strong equivalence, defined in Section 12.2.4. The test for prioritized strong equivalence is carried out by converting the process descriptions bound to $P_1$ and $P_2$ to state machines (LTSs, as discussed above) and applying a state minimization algorithm that preserves strong bisimulation [14] to the two machines simultaneously. If the resulting minimal state machine has a state that includes the start state of both of the original machines, the original machines are strongly bisimilar. As conversion from an algebraic expression to an LTS requires space exponential in the size of the expressions, testing of prioritized strong equivalence can be slow for systems that produce a large number of states.

The following processes, though not syntactically equivalent, can be shown to be equivalent via prioritized strong equivalence.

$$
\begin{aligned}
\text{P} \;&=\; ((\texttt{e}, 1).\texttt{NIL}||(\texttt{'e}, 2).\texttt{NIL})\backslash\{\texttt{e}\}; \\
\text{Q} \;&=\; (\texttt{tau}, 3).\texttt{NIL};
\end{aligned}
$$

## 12.4.4  Example Revisited

The concurrent specification of the railroad crossing problem and its sequential correctness specification can be formulated as a set of VERSA process definitions, and an automatic test of their equivalence can be performed by the VERSA system. Figure 12.2 is one possible formulation of such a system using VERSA's syntax.

The first half of Figure 12.2 defines symbolic constants and macros that improve the readability of the train and car specifications to follow. The symbolic constants TNear, CNear, TTravel, CWait, TCross, and CCross implement the labeling notation for resources, events, and actions used in Section 12.3.1. Constants T1, T2, T3, delta, and theta implement the timing constants specific to this instance of the railroad crossing problem. The REP_ACT macro implements the $A^n$ notation of Section 12.3 such that

$$ A^n : P \;=\; \text{REP\_ACT}(A, n, P). $$

The REP_ACT_UNBOUND macro implements the $A^{[m,\infty]}$ notation such that

$$ A^{[m,\infty]} : P \;=\; \text{REP\_ACT\_UNBOUND}(A, m, P). $$

Next, the section of Figure 12.2 labeled "System Specification" implements the System specification presented at the beginning of Section 12.3.2. The Car process represents the arrival of the car at the region (signaling CNear), followed by any waiting on the part of the car for a train to clear the crossing. Once the crossing resource becomes available, the scope within the REP_ACT_UNBOUND macro is interrupted and the car proceeds according to the Car1 process. Car1 implements the passage of the car through the crossing for a duration of T3 time units, followed by the return of the car to its initial state.

VERSA processes Train, Train1, GAMMA[1], ..., GAMMA[T1], and Train2 correspond to the Train process of the system specification. Train implements the idle phase, where the train is outside the region $R$ of interest. As the train

```
//--------------------- Events and Actions -----------------------
#define TNear   (signal,1) // Train nearing crossing
#define CNear   (signal,2) // Car nearing crossing
#define TTravel {(train,1)} // Train outside crossing
#define CWait   {(car,  1)} // Car waiting for train to clear
#define TCross  {(train,1),(crossing,5)} // Train in crossing
#define CCross  {(car,  1),(crossing,2)} // Car in crossing
#define TTCC {(train,1),(crossing,2),(car,1)} // TTravel U CCross
#define TCCW {(train,1),(crossing,5),(car,1)} //  TCross U CWait


//--------------------- Timing Parameters ----------------------
#define T1      8      // Train's delay---TNear to reaching crossing
#define T2      5      // Time for train to pass the crossing
#define T3      2      // Time for car to pass the crossing
#define delta   4      // Minimum interval between trains
#define theta   0      // Interval between cars


//---------------------------- Macros -------------------------------
#define REP_ACT(ACT,COUNT,NEXT) \
  scope(rec X.(ACT:X),dummy,(COUNT),NIL,(NEXT),NIL)

#define REP_ACT_UNBOUND(ACT,MIN,NEXT) \
  REP_ACT(ACT,MIN,scope(rec X.(ACT:X),dummy,infty,NIL,NIL,(NEXT)))


//--------------------- System Specification --------------------
Car  = CNear.REP_ACT_UNBOUND(CWait,0,Car1);    // Car Subsystem
Car1 = REP_ACT(CCross,T3,Car);


Train    = REP_ACT_UNBOUND({},delta,Train1);   // Train Subsystem
Train1   = TNear.GAMMA[T1];
GAMMA[i] = TTravel:GAMMA[i-1] + REP_ACT(TCross,i,Train2)  {i,2,T1};
GAMMA[1] = TTravel:Train2 + TCross:Train2;
Train2   = REP_ACT(TCross, T2, Train);


System = [Train || Car] {crossing};           // Complete System


//----------------- Correctness Specification --------------------
Spec  = CNear.Spec1;
Spec1 = CCross: CCross: CNear. CCross: CCross: Spec2;
Spec2 = CNear.(TNear. REP_ACT(TCCW, 13, Spec1) + (CCross : Spec3));
Spec3 = TNear.TTCC: CNear. REP_ACT(TCCW, 12, Spec1) + CCross:Spec2;
```

**Figure 12.2** VERSA Description of Railroad Problem and Correctness Specification

approaches, it signals TNear and proceeds as GAMMA[T1], where it attempts to acquire the crossing resource. Each GAMMA[i] for i in the interval [1, T1] represents the train in a state where i time units remain of the time required for the train to pass from entering the region to entering the crossing. Each GAMMA[i] attempts, in turn, to acquire the crossing resource and hold it until the interval of T1 time units has expired. If GAMMA[i] fails to obtain crossing, then TTravel is executed and the process continues as GAMMA[i-1], marking the passage of a unit of time. Once the interval of T1 time units has elapsed, the GAMMA[i] that acquired the crossing resource switches control to Train2. If GAMMA[1] fails to acquire crossing, then control automatically passes to Train2, since the parameters of the problem require that the train arrives at the crossing T1 time units after signaling TNear. Train2 implements the passage of the train through the crossing for a duration of T2 time units, and the return of the train to its initial state.

The System definition of Figure 12.2 is a translation of the ACSR System specification directly into VERSA syntax.

The Spec definition of Figure 12.2 is a translation of the Spec correctness specification of Section 12.3.2 directly into VERSA syntax. With the definitions of Figure 12.2 saved in a file called RailRoad.acsr, the task of verifying that the System shown at the beginning of Section 12.3.2 is strongly equivalent to the derived correctness specification using VERSA's equivalence testing feature proceeds as follows:

```
Ready> #include <RailRoad.acsr>
Ready> System == Spec?
true (by prioritized strong equivalence)
Ready>
```

## 12.5   Summary

We have described a timed process algebra called ACSR that supports the notions of resource and priority. ACSR employs a synchronous semantics for resource-consuming actions that take time and an asynchronous semantics for events that are instantaneous. There is a single parallel operator that can be used to express both interleaving at the event level and lock-step parallelism at the action level. ACSR's algebraic laws are derived from a term equivalence based on prioritized strong bisimulation, which incorporates a notion of preemption based on priority, synchronization and resource utilization. As illustrated with the variant railroad crossing example, these laws can be used to rewrite process terms in proving the correctness of a real-time system.

There are two areas of research that are currently being explored to extend the capabilities of ACSR. The first extension is to support dynamic priorities. ACSR supports only static priority; i.e., the priorities of actions and events cannot change during the execution of a process. Since modeling of many real-time scheduling algorithms, such as earliest deadline first, first-come-first-served, and so on, requires dynamic priorities, it would be useful to support dynamic priority in timed process algebras. This requires some method to capture the state information and then use that information in reassigning priorities. The second extension is to allow dense time so that a timed action can take an arbitrary non-zero amount of time.

We have also described a set of tools based on ACSR called VERSA. The tools include a text-based user interface, a rewrite system based on the ACSR laws, bisimulation checkers, and an interpreter for interactive process execution. We have found that these automated tools greatly facilitate the task of using ACSR for non-trivial examples through computer assistance for syntax checking and analysis. VERSA should allow us to evaluate the effectiveness of the algebraic approach for the specification and analysis of large real-time systems. It should also make ACSR more attractive to software designers discouraged by error-prone and labor-intensive paper-and-pencil formal approaches. We plan to enhance our VERSA tools further by adding a graphical user interface, a state-based formal model, and a model checker.

## Acknowledgments

The work described in this chapter has benefited significantly from discussions with the members of the Real-Time Group at the University of Pennsylvania. Patrice Brémond-Grégoire and Rich Gerber contributed significantly during the development of the theory of ACSR. We wish to thank Connie Heitmeyer for suggesting the variant railroad crossing problem and Ralph Jeffords for his helpful comments on the ACSR specifications of the variant railroad crossing problem.

This work was supported in part by ONR N00014-89-J-1131, ONR N00014-89-J-1131S1, DARPA/NSF CCR90-14621, and NSF CCR93-11622.

## References

[1] L. Aceto and D. Murphy. On the Ill-Timed but Well-Caused. In *Proc. CONCUR'93, International Conference on Concurrency Theory*. LNCS 715, Springer-Verlag, New York, August 1993.

[2] J.C.M. Baeten and J.A. Bergstra. Real Time Process Algebra. *Formal Aspects of Computing*, 3(2):142–188, 1991.

[3] J.A. Bergstra and J.W. Klop. Algebra of Communicating Processes with Abstraction. *Journal of Theoretical Computer Science*, 37:77–121, 1985.

[4] P. Brémond-Grégoire, J.Y. Choi, and I. Lee. The Soundness and Completeness of ACSR (Algebra of Communicating Shared Resources). Technical Report MS-CIS-93-59, Univ. of Pennsylvania, June 1993.

[5] R. Cleaveland, J. Parrow, and B. Steffen. The Concurrency Workbench: A Semantics-Based Tool for the Verification of Concurrent Systems. *TOPLAS*, 15:36–72, 1993.

[6] P. Clements, C. Heitmeyer, B. Labaw, and A. Rose. MT: A Toolset for Specifying and Analyzing Real-Time Systems. In *Proc. Real Time Systems Symposium*, December 1993.

[7] *Failures Divergence Refinement: User Manual and Tutorial*, Formal Systems (Europe) Ltd., Oxford, UK, April 1993.

[8] C. Heitmeyer, R. Jeffords, and B. Labaw. Comparing Different Approaches for Specifying and Verifying Real-Time Systems. In *Proc. 10th IEEE Workshop on Real-Time Operating Systems and Software*, May 1993.

[9] C. Heitmeyer, B. Labaw, P. Clements, and A. Mok. Engineering CASE Tools to Support Formal Methods for Real-Time Software Development. In *Proc. 5th International Workshop on Computer-Aided Software Engineering*, July 1992.

[10] M. Hennessy and T. Regan. A Process Algebra for Timed Systems. Technical Report 5/91, Univ. of Sussex, UK, April 1991.

[11] C.A.R. Hoare. Communicating Sequential Processes. *Communications of the ACM*, 21(8):666–676, August 1978.

[12] C.A.R. Hoare. *Communicating Sequential Processes*. Prentice Hall, Englewood Cliffs, N.J., 1985.

[13] F. Jahanian and A. Mok. Modechart: A Specification Language for Real-Time Systems. *IEEE Transactions on Software Engineering*, 1993.

[14] P.C. Kanellakis and S.A. Smolka. CCS Expressions, Finite State Processes, and Three Problems of Equivalence. *Information and Computation*, 86:43–68, 1990.

[15] I. Lee and V. Gehlot. Language Constructs for Distributed Real-Time Programming. In *Proc. IEEE Real-Time Systems Symposium*, 1985.

[16] R. Milner. *Communication and Concurrency*. Prentice Hall, Englewood Cliffs, N.J., 1989.

[17] F. Moller and C. Tofts. A Temporal Calculus of Communicating Systems. In *Proc. CONCUR '90*, pages 401–415. LNCS 458, Springer-Verlag, New York, August 1990.

[18] F. Moller and C. Tofts. A Temporal Calculus of Communicating Systems. In *Proc. CONCUR '90*, pages 401–415. LNCS 458, Springer-Verlag, New York, August 1990.

[19] X. Nicollin and J. Sifakis. The Algebra of Timed Processes ATP: Theory and Application. Technical Report RT-C26, Institut National Polytechnique de Grenoble, November 1991.

[20] J. Ostroff. A Verifier for Real-Time Properties. *Journal of Real-Time Systems*, 4:5–35, 1992.

[21] D. Park. Concurrency and Automata on Infinite Sequences. In *Proc. 5th GI Conference*. LNCS 104, Springer-Verlag, New York, 1981.

[22] S. Raju and A. Shaw. A Prototyping Environment for Specifying, Executing and Checking Communicating Real-Time State Machines. Technical Report 92-10-03, Department of Computer Science and Engineering, Univ. of Washington, 1992.

[23] G.M. Reed and A.W. Roscoe. Metric Spaces as Models for Real-Time Concurrency. In *Proc. Mathematical Foundation of Computer Science*. LNCS 298, Springer-Verlag, New York, 1987.

[24] A. Shaw. Communicating Real-Time State Machines. *IEEE Transactions on Software Engineering*, September 1992.

[25] S. Wolfram. *Mathematica: A System for Doing Mathematics by Computer*. Addison-Wesley, Reading, Mass., second edition, 1991.

[26] Wang Yi. CCS + Time = An Interleaving Model for Real Time Systems. In *Proc. International Conference on Automata, Languages and Programming*, July 1991.

# Chapter 13

# Simulation Techniques for Proving Properties of Real-Time Systems[1]

## Nancy Lynch

The method of *simulations* is an important technique for reasoning about real-time and other timing-based systems. It is adapted from an analogous method for untimed systems. This chapter presents the simulation method in the context of a very general automaton (i.e., labeled transition system) model for timing-based systems. Sketches are presented of several typical examples for which the method has been used successfully. Other complementary tools are also described, in particular, invariants for safety proofs and execution correspondences for liveness proofs.

## 13.1  Introduction

In recent years, a good deal has been learned about how to reason about real-time and other timing-based systems. In many cases, the methods that have been developed have been adaptations of methods that had previously been used for untimed systems.

In this chapter, I present a useful method for verifying properties of timing-based systems: the method of *simulations*. This method falls into the general category of *assertional techniques*, and includes refinement mappings, forward and backward simulations, and history and prophecy mapping techniques as special cases. This method has been adapted from the simulation method that has been widely used for untimed systems.

I illustrate how simulations can be used for timing-based systems by introducing them in the context of a very general timed automaton model. I present

---

[1]This chapter is based on the paper which originally appeared in the *Proceedings for the 1993 REX Summer School on Concurrency*, Springer-Verlag.

sketches of typical examples for which the method has been used successfully. These examples include proofs of ordinary safety properties and time-bound properties. Along the way, I describe other complementary tools: invariants for safety proofs and execution correspondences for liveness proofs.

The chapter proceeds as follows. In Section 13.2, I describe the very general and basic timed automaton model of Lynch and Vaandrager [15], and use it to model a simple clock system. In Section 13.3, I describe the various notions of simulations from the literature, together with their basic soundness properties, all in terms of the basic model. As an example, I describe a simple clock synchronization algorithm and show, using a refinement mapping, that it implements the bounded clock system.

Next, I impose some structure on the model and simulations, and present several examples of simulation proofs that take advantage of this structure. Specifically, in Section 13.4, I define an important special case of the general timed automaton model—the timed automaton model of Merritt, Modugno, and Tuttle [21]. I use this model to describe Fischer's timing-based mutual exclusion algorithm [3], and to verify that the algorithm in fact satisfies the mutual exclusion property. Then in Section 13.5, I illustrate how simulations, in particular, forward simulations, can be used to prove time bounds as well as ordinary safety properties. I do this using two examples: a simple counting automaton, and Fischer's algorithm. Both examples are described using the model of [21].

Section 13.6 indicates how liveness proofs can be integrated with the safety and time-bound proofs, and Section 13.7 concludes.

This chapter is an abbreviated version of a longer paper appearing in [16]; the longer version contains additional details of the results of this chapter, and additional examples.

## 13.2   The Basic Timed Automaton Model

The basic model that I use for describing timing-based systems is a slight variant of the simple and general model of Lynch and Vaandrager [15, 17, 27]. This section extracts the relevant definitions.

### 13.2.1   Timed Automata

A *timed automaton* $A$ consists of:

- a set $states(A)$ of states;

- a nonempty subset $start(A)$ of start states;

- a set $acts(A)$ of actions, including a special *time-passage* action $\nu$; the actions are partitioned into *external* and *internal* actions, where $\nu$ is considered external; the *visible* actions are the non-$\nu$ external actions; the visible actions are partitioned into *input* and *output* actions;

- a set $steps(A)$ of steps (transitions); this is a subset of $states(A) \times acts(A) \times states(A)$;

- a mapping $now_A : states \to \mathsf{R}^+$. ($\mathsf{R}^+$ denotes the nonnegative reals.)

I write $s' \xrightarrow{a}_A s$ as shorthand for $(s', \pi, s) \in steps(A)$. I usually write the $s.now_A$ in place of $now_A(s)$. I sometimes suppress the subscript or argument $A$ when no confusion seems likely. There are several simple axioms that a timed automaton is required to satisfy:

[A1] If $s \in start$, then $s.now = 0$.

[A2] If $s' \xrightarrow{\pi} s$ and $\pi \neq \nu$, then $s'.now = s.now$.

[A3] If $s' \xrightarrow{\nu} s$, then $s'.now < s.now$.

[A4] If $s' \xrightarrow{\nu} s''$ and $s'' \xrightarrow{\nu} s$, then $s' \xrightarrow{\nu} s$.

In order to state the last axiom, I need a preliminary definition of a *trajectory*, which describes restrictions on the state changes that can occur during time passage. Namely, if $I$ is any interval of $\mathsf{R}^+$, then an *$I$-trajectory* is a function $w : I \to states$, such that

1. $w(t).now = t$ for all $t \in I$, and

2. $w(t_1) \xrightarrow{\nu} w(t_2)$ for all $t_1, t_2 \in I$ with $t_1 < t_2$.

That is, $w$ assigns, to each time $t$ in interval $I$, a state having the given time $t$ as its *now* component. This assignment is done in such a way that time-passage steps can span between any pair of states in the range of $w$. If $w$ is an $I$-trajectory and $I$ is left-closed, then define $w.fstate = w(min(I))$, while if $I$ is right-closed, then define $w.lstate = w(max(I))$. The final axiom is:

[A5] If $s' \xrightarrow{\nu} s$, then there exists a trajectory from $s'$ to $s$.

Axiom [A1] says that the current time is always 0 in a start state. Axiom [A2] says that non-time-passage steps do not change the time; that is, they occur "instantaneously," at a single point in time. Axiom [A3] says that time-passage steps must cause the time to increase; this is a convenient technical restriction. Axiom [A4] allows repeated time-passage steps to be combined into one step. Axiom [A5] is a kind of converse to [A4]; it says that any time-passage step can be "filled in" with states for each intervening time, in a "consistent" way.

Note that this model is sufficiently general to allow description of systems in which some of the components (e.g., those representing real-world entities) exhibit continuous rather than discrete behavior [20].

## 13.2.2   Timed Executions

In this subsection, I define a notion of "timed execution" for a timed automaton. The most obvious formulation of a timed execution might be as a sequence of visible, internal, and time-passage actions, interspersed with their intervening states. I augment this information slightly by including the trajectories for each time-passage action.

Formally, a *timed execution fragment* is a finite or infinite alternating sequence $\alpha = w_0 \pi_1 w_1 \pi_2 w_2 \cdots$, where:

1. Each $w_j$ is a trajectory and each $\pi_j$ is a non-time-passage action.

2. If $\alpha$ is a finite sequence, then it ends with a trajectory.

3. If $w_j$ is not the last trajectory in $\alpha$, then its domain is a closed interval. If $w_j$ is the last trajectory, then its domain is left-closed (and either right-open or right-closed).

4. If $w_j$ is not the last trajectory, then $w_j.lstate \xrightarrow{\pi_{j+1}} w_{j+1}.fstate$.

The trajectories describe the changes of state during the time-passage steps. The last item says that the actions in $\alpha$ span correctly between successive trajectories.

A *timed execution* is a timed execution fragment for which the first state of the first trajectory, $w_0$, is a start state. In this chapter, I am mainly interested in a particular subclass of the set of timed executions: the *admissible* timed executions. These are defined to be the timed executions in which the supremum of the set of *now* values occurring in the states is $\infty$. A state of a timed automaton is defined to be *reachable* if it is the final state of the final trajectory in some finite timed execution of the automaton.

Note that, as I have described them so far, timed automata have no features for expressing liveness or fairness properties (with the exception of admissibility). In general, such features are less important in the timed setting than they are in the untimed setting, since they are often replaced by time-bound requirements. However, in Section 13.6, I will say more about how liveness can be added in.

Note that there exist timed automata that have *no* admissible timed executions. To rule out this case, one generally restricts attention to timed automata that are *feasible*, i.e., in which each "finite" timed execution can be extended to an admissible timed execution. I do not address issues of feasibility in this chapter, but refer the reader to [5].

## 13.2.3   Timed Traces

In order to describe the problems to be solved by timed automata, I require a definition of their visible behavior. The *timed trace* of any timed execution is defined to be the sequence of visible events that occur in the timed execution, paired with their times of occurrence. The *admissible timed traces* of the timed automaton are just the timed traces that arise from all the admissible timed executions. If a problem $P$ is formulated as a set of (finite and infinite) sequences of actions paired with times, then a timed automaton $A$ is said to *solve* $P$ if all its admissible timed traces are in $P$. Often, it is natural to express a problem $P$ as the set of admissible timed traces of another timed automaton $B$. Thus, the notion of admissible timed traces induces a preorder on timed automata: $A \leq B$ is defined to mean that the set of admissible timed traces of $A$ is a subset of the set of admissible timed traces of $B$.

## 13.2.4    Discrete Executions

Sometimes it is useful in proofs about timed automata to use another notion of execution, one that omits the trajectory information in favor of just recording time-passage steps. I define a *discrete execution fragment* of a timed automaton to be a finite or infinite alternating sequence $\alpha = s_0 \pi_1 s_1 \pi_2 s_2 \cdots$, where:

1. Each $s_j$ is a state and each $\pi_j$ is an action (possibly a time-passage action).

2. If $\alpha$ is a finite sequence, then it ends with a state.

3. If $s_j$ is not the last state, then $s_j \xrightarrow{\pi_{j+1}} s_{j+1}$.

A *discrete execution* is a discrete execution fragment whose first state is a start state. Again, I am mainly interested in the *admissible* discrete executions—those in which the supremum of the *now* values occurring in the states is $\infty$. Note that any admissible discrete execution must be an infinite sequence. The *timed trace* of an admissible discrete execution is the sequence of visible events that occur in the execution, paired with their times of occurrence, i.e., the *now* values in the preceding states.

    An admissible discrete execution $\alpha$ is said to *sample* an admissible timed execution $\alpha'$ if its sequence of actions consists of exactly the actions of $\alpha'$, occurring at the same times, interspersed with time-passage actions; several consecutive time-passage actions can be used to span a trajectory. The states appearing in $\alpha$ must be extracted in the natural way from the trajectories in $\alpha'$.

**Lemma 13.2.1**    *1. If $\alpha'$ is an admissible timed execution, then there exists an admissible discrete execution $\alpha$ that samples it. Conversely, if $\alpha$ is an admissible discrete execution, then there exists an admissible timed execution $\alpha'$ such that $\alpha$ samples $\alpha'$.*

*2. If $\alpha$ samples $\alpha'$, then the timed trace of $\alpha$ is the same as that of $\alpha'$.*

*3. A state of a timed automaton is reachable exactly if it is the final state of some finite discrete execution.*

## 13.2.5    Example: Bounded Clock System

As an example of a timed automaton, consider a clock system, consisting of a collection of "local clocks," each of whose values is always within a bound $\epsilon$ of real time. The automaton just maintains this property, while permitting real time to pass.

In the code, the state is described in a structured fashion, as a collection of values for a collection of state components. Likewise, the start state is described as a collection of initial values for the components. The actions are listed explicitly. The steps are described in a guarded command style, organized by actions (including the time-passage action), each with a "precondition" (guard) describing conditions on the state that enable the action to occur, and an "effect" describing the state changes that accompany the action. The time-passage action $\nu$ is parameterized with an incremental time $\Delta t$, describing the amount of time that passes. The *now* component appears as an explicit state component.

## Automaton $B$: Bounded Clock System

Actions:
    Output:
        $report_i(c)$, $i \in I$, where $I$ is a nonempty, finite set of node indices
    Internal:
        $tick_i(c)$, $i \in I$

State components:
    $now \in R^+$, initially 0
    $clock_i \in R^+$, $i \in I$, initially 0

$tick_i(c)$
  Precondition:
    $c \geq clock_i$
    $|c - now| \leq \epsilon$
  Effect:
    $clock_i := c$

$report_i(c)$
  Precondition:
    $c = clock_i$
  Effect:
    none

$\nu(\Delta t)$
  Precondition:
    $t = now + \Delta t$
    for all $i$, $|t - clock_i| \leq \epsilon$
  Effect:
    $now := t$

Thus, any local clock is allowed to "tick" (i.e., advance to a new specified value $c$) if the new value is at least as big as the old value, and is within $\epsilon$ of real time. Moreover, real time is allowed to pass, as long as it remains within $\epsilon$ of all the local clock values. Finally, any current local clock value can be reported at any time. The following lemma captures the key synchronization property.

**Lemma 13.2.2** *The following is true of every reachable state of B: For all i, $|clock_i - now| \leq \epsilon$.*

**Proof:** In view of Lemma 13.2.1, it suffices to prove the property for all states that occur as final states of finite discrete executions of $B$. The proof proceeds by induction on the number of events in a finite discrete execution. Correctness follows from the explicit checks performed by the *tick* and $\nu$ actions.                              □

Note that in the admissible timed executions of $B$—those in which the time components of the states approach infinity—it must be that the clocks all tick infinitely often (and by an appropriate amount) so they can stay close to real time. The *report* actions are optional.

## 13.2.6     Operations on Timed Automata

I define a simple parallel composition operator for timed automata. Let $A$ and $B$ be timed automata satisfying the following *compatibility* conditions:

1. $A$ and $B$ have no output actions in common.

2. No internal action of $A$ is an action of $B$, and vice versa.

Then the *composition* of $A$ and $B$, written as $A \times B$, is defined as follows.

- $states(A \times B) = \{(s_A, s_B) \in states(A) \times states(B) : s_A.now_A = s_B.now_B\}$;

- $start(A \times B) = start(A) \times start(B)$;

- $acts(A \times B) = acts(A) \cup acts(B)$; an action is *external* in $A \times B$ exactly if it is external in either $A$ or $B$, and likewise for *internal* actions; a visible action of $A \times B$ is an *output* in $A \times B$ exactly if it is an output in either $A$ or $B$, and is an *input* otherwise;

- $(s'_A, s'_B) \xrightarrow{\pi}_{A \times B} (s_A, s_B)$ exactly if

  1. $s'_A \xrightarrow{\pi}_A s_A$ if $\pi \in acts(A)$, else $s'_A = s_A$, and
  2. $s'_B \xrightarrow{\pi}_B s_B$ if $\pi \in acts(B)$, else $s'_B = s_B$;

- $(s_A, s_B).now_{A \times B} = s_A.now_A$.

It is not hard to show that $A \times B$ is indeed a timed automaton, and that the parallel composition operator is substitutive for the admissible timed trace inclusion ordering, $\leq$, on timed automata. That is, if $A_1 \leq A_2$, then $A_1 \times B \leq A_2 \times B$.

In [27], several other useful operations on timed automata are defined. These include standard "untimed operations" such as hiding, renaming, internal and external choice, sequential composition, and the CSP interrupt operator [6] (i.e., $A$ and $B$ are both started; if $B$ performs a visible action, then $A$ is interrupted and $B$ continues to run). They also include some "timed operations," such as the timed CSP timeout [2, 24] (i.e., $A$ is started; if $A$ does not perform a visible action by real time $d$, then $A$ is interrupted and $B$ is started), and the ATP execution delay operator [22]. The admissible timed trace inclusion relation (more precisely, a variant of it that includes certain kinds of "finite timed traces" as well) is shown to be substitutive with respect to all of these operations.

## 13.3   Simulations for Timed Automata

In this section, I introduce the basic types of simulations that can be used for proving properties of systems described as timed automata. The value of the simulation method for verifying safety properties of untimed systems is well established (see, for example, [7, 10, 14, 23, 25, 28]). The use of this method for timed systems is much newer, but appears very promising; preliminary results appear in [8, 9, 25]. The definitions are paraphrased from [15, 17].

### 13.3.1   Simulations

Suppose that $A$ and $B$ are timed automata. A *refinement* from $A$ to $B$ is a function $r : states(A) \to states(B)$ that satisfies:

1. $r(s).now = s.now$.

2. If $s \in start(A)$, then $r(s) \in start(B)$.

3. If $s' \xrightarrow{\pi}_A s$, then there is a timed execution fragment from $r(s')$ to $r(s)$ having the same sequence of timed visible actions (that is, the same sequence of visible actions, with the same associated times) as the given step.

Note that the third item includes the case where $\pi$ is the time-passage action. In the following definitions, I use the notation $r[s]$, where $r$ is a binary relation, to denote $\{u : (s, u) \in r\}$. A *forward simulation* from $A$ to $B$ is a relation $f$ over $states(A)$ and $states(B)$ that satisfies:

1. If $u \in f[s]$, then $u.now = s.now$.

2. If $s \in start(A)$, then $f[s] \cap start(B) \neq \emptyset$.

3. If $s' \xrightarrow{\pi}_A s$ and $u' \in f[s']$, then there exists $u \in f[s]$ such that there is a timed execution fragment from $u'$ to $u$ having the same sequence of timed visible actions as the given step.

A *backward simulation* from $A$ to $B$ is a total relation $b$ over $states(A)$ and $states(B)$ that satisfies:

1. If $u \in b[s]$, then $u.now = s.now$.

2. If $s \in start(A)$, then $b[s] \subseteq start(B)$.

3. If $s' \xrightarrow{\pi}_A s$ and $u \in b[s]$, then there exists $u' \in b[s']$ such that there is a timed execution fragment from $u'$ to $u$ having the same sequence of timed visible actions as the given step.

A backward simulation is said to be *image-finite* provided that $b[s]$ is a finite set for every state $s$ of $A$. Note that every refinement is a forward simulation, and is also an image-finite backward simulation.

   I write $A \leq_R B$, $A \leq_F B$, and $A \leq_B B$ to denote the existence of a refinement, forward simulation, or backward simulation from $A$ to $B$, respectively. Also, I write

$A \leq_{\text{iB}} B$ to denote the existence of an image-finite backward simulation from $A$ to $B$. The most important fact about these simulations is captured by a set of results saying that they are sound for admissible timed trace inclusion:

**Theorem 13.3.1 (Soundness)** *Each of $A \leq_{\text{R}} B$, $A \leq_{\text{F}} B$ and $A \leq_{\text{iB}} B$ implies that $A \leq B$.*

Note that $A \leq_{\text{B}} B$ does not by itself imply admissible timed trace inclusion; a weaker soundness result, involving inclusion of sets of "finite timed traces," does hold in this case. The proofs of all the soundness results are based on corresponding results for untimed automata. For untimed automata, the first two results are proved by induction on the number of steps, while the last is proved by a backward induction together with König's Lemma.

Another important fact about these simulations is a completeness result, also proved in [15, 17], for the methods used in combination: Namely, define a timed automaton to have *finite invisible nondeterminism* if, for every sequence of timed visible actions and every real time $t$, there are only finitely many states that can result from finite timed executions that generate the given sequence of timed visible actions and have $t$ as the final time.

**Theorem 13.3.2 (Completeness)** *If $A \leq B$ and $B$ has finite invisible nondeterminism, then there exists a timed automaton $C$ such that $A \leq_{\text{F}} C \leq_{\text{iB}} B$.*

## 13.3.2   Invariants and Weak Simulations

In practical uses of simulation methods, the first thing that one usually wants to do is to divide the work by first proving some invariants about either or both of the two automata involved. The use of such invariants must be justified; doing this requires augmenting the simulation definitions and soundness results to incorporate the invariants explicitly. I define an *invariant* of a timed automaton to be any property that is true of all reachable states.

A *weak refinement* from $A$ to $B$ with respect to invariants $I_A$ and $I_B$ (of $A$ and $B$, respectively) is a function $r : states(A) \rightarrow states(B)$ that satisfies:

1. $r(s).now = s.now$.

2. If $s \in start(A)$, then $r(s) \in start(B)$.

3. If $s' \xrightarrow{\pi}_A s$, $\{s', s\} \subseteq I_A$, and $r(s') \in I_B$, then there is a timed execution fragment from $r(s')$ to $r(s)$ having the same timed visible actions as the given step.

A *weak forward simulation* from $A$ to $B$ with respect to $I_A$ and $I_B$ is a relation $f$ over $states(A)$ and $states(B)$ that satisfies:

1. If $u \in f[s]$, then $u.now = s.now$.

2. If $s \in start(A)$, then $f[s] \cap start(B) \neq \emptyset$.

3. If $s' \xrightarrow{\pi}_A s$, $\{s', s\} \subseteq I_A$, and $u' \in f[s'] \cap I_B$, then there exists $u \in f[s]$ such that there is a timed execution fragment from $u'$ to $u$ having the same timed visible actions as the given step.

A *weak backward simulation* from $A$ to $B$ with respect to $I_A$ and $I_B$ is a relation $b$ over $states(A)$ and $states(B)$ that satisfies:

1. If $u \in b[s]$, then $u.now = s.now$.

2. If $s \in start(A)$, then $b[s] \cap I_B \subseteq start(B)$.

3. If $s' \xrightarrow{\pi}_A s$, $\{s', s\} \subseteq I_A$, and $u \in b[s] \cap I_B$, then there exists $u' \in b[s'] \cap I_B$ such that there is a timed execution fragment from $u'$ to $u$ having the same timed visible actions as the given step.

4. If $s \in I_A$, then $b[s] \cap I_B \neq \emptyset$.

A weak backward simulation is said to be *image-finite* provided that $b[s]$ is a finite set for every state $s$ of $A$.

Each of these three new definitions says that it is permissible to use the invariants on all the hypothesized states, in proving the existence of the required timed execution fragment. Note that in the case of a backward simulation, there is an extra proof obligation—to show that the invariant for $B$ gets preserved "in reverse." Every weak refinement is a weak forward simulation, but not necessarily a weak backward simulation.

I extend the notation defined earlier, writing $A \leq_{WR} B$, $A \leq_{WF} B$, $A \leq_{WB} B$, and $A \leq_{WiB} B$ to denote that there exists a weak refinement, weak forward simulation, weak backward simulation, or weak image-finite backward simulation, from $A$ to $B$, respectively, with respect to some invariants. The extended soundness results are:

**Theorem 13.3.3 (Soundness)** $A \leq_{WR} B$, $A \leq_{WF} B$ *and* $A \leq_{WiB} B$ *all imply that* $A \leq B$.

## 13.3.3   Example: Clock Synchronization Algorithm

I describe a very simple implementation (in the sense of the $\leq$ preorder) of the bounded clock system $B$ (where $|I| = 2$, i.e., the system has two nodes). The algorithm consists of two nodes connected by a one-way channel, with the message delay always in the range $[0, d]$. Node 1 maintains its own local clock, assumed always to be within $\delta$ of real time. Node 1 informs node 2 whenever its own clock changes, and node 2 simply adopts the maximum clock value it has seen as its own. Although it would probably be most natural to model this algorithm as the composition of three timed automata (the two nodes and the channel), for brevity, I just model it as a single timed automaton $A$.

**Automaton $A$: Clock Synchronization Algorithm**

Actions:
>    Output:
>>        $report_i(c)$, $i \in \{1,2\}$
>    Internal:
>>        $tick_1(c)$
>>        $deliver(c)$

State components:
>    $now \in R^+$, initially 0
>    $clock_i \in R^+$, $i \in \{1,2\}$, initially 0
>    $channel$, a multiset of $R^+ \times R^+$, initially empty

$tick_1(c)$
>    Precondition:
>>        $c \geq clock_1$
>>        $|c - now| \leq \delta$
>    Effect:
>>        $clock_1 := c$
>>        add $(c, now + d)$ to $channel$

$\nu(\Delta t)$
>    Precondition:
>>        $t = now + \Delta t$
>>        $|t - clock_1| \leq \delta$
>>        for all $(c, v) \in channel, t \leq v$
>    Effect:
>>        $now := t$

$deliver(c)$
>    Precondition:
>>        $(c, v) \in channel$
>    Effect:
>>        remove $(c, v)$ from $channel$
>>        $clock_2 := max(clock_2, c)$

$report_i(c)$
>    Precondition:
>>        $c = clock_i$
>    Effect:
>>        none

The *tick* action for node 1 is like the *tick* actions of $B$, except that, in addition to updating the local clock, it also puts a copy of the new clock value into the channel. The second component $v$ of the message that is put into the channel represents a real time "deadline" by which that message is supposed to get delivered to node 2. Note that this second component is not a "normal" component of the algorithm; it is only introduced in order to encode a real-time restriction on the algorithm's behavior. This strategy—representing a real-time deadline by an explicit deadline component in the state—is a frequently used technical device in defining timed automata.

The *deliver* action causes node 2 to reset its clock to the newly received value (provided that the new value is not less than the old value). Now the time-passage action is explicitly required to maintain the appropriate relationship with clock 1, but there is no direct requirement that it remain close to clock 2. However, there is a new constraint on real time: time is constrained not to pass beyond the scheduled last delivery time for any message in the channel. The *report* actions are as in $B$.

I claim that, provided that $\epsilon \geq \delta + d$, this algorithm $A$ "implements" system $B$, in the sense that $A \leq B$. To show this, I use a trivial weak refinement, $r$, defined as follows. Here, record notation is used to indicate state components.

- $r(s).now = s.now.$

- $r(s).clock_i = s.clock_i$, $i \in \{1, 2\}$.

Note that, here and elsewhere, the simulation definition gives the key insights about why the algorithm is correct. In order to show that $r$ is a weak refinement, define $I_A$ to be the set of states of $A$ in which $now - \epsilon \leq clock_2 \leq now + \delta$ and $now - \delta \leq clock_1 \leq now + \delta$. I claim that $I_A$ is an invariant of $A$; this requires two lemmas.

**Lemma 13.3.1** *The following are true of every reachable state of $A$:*

1. $|clock_1 - now| \leq \delta$.

2. *If* $(c, v) \in channel$, *then* $c \leq clock_1$.

3. $clock_2 \leq clock_1$.

4. $clock_2 \leq now + \delta$.

**Proof:**  By an easy induction on the number of actions in a discrete execution.
□

It remains to prove that $now - \epsilon \leq clock_2$, i.e., that $clock_2$ does not lag too far behind real time. This is proved in the following lemma. The first part asserts that the value of $clock_1$ is in fact communicated to node 2, while the second part says that every message in the channel is scheduled to be delivered at most time $d$ in the future. The third part is the key claim. It implies that, for $0 \leq l \leq d$, the value that $clock_2$ will have $l$ time units from now is at least $now - \delta - (d - l) \geq now - \epsilon + l$. This claim explicitly describes the smallest value that $clock_2$ can take on, in terms of the current value of $clock_2$ and the messages that are guaranteed to be delivered strictly before time $l$ from now. The fourth part is the needed inequality.

**Lemma 13.3.2** *The following are true of every reachable state of $A$:*

1. *Either* $clock_2 = clock_1$ *or there is some* $(c, v) \in channel$ *such that* $c = clock_1$.

2. *If* $(c, v) \in channel$, *then* $now \leq v \leq now + d$.

3. *For any* $l$, $0 \leq l \leq d$, *either* $clock_2 \geq now - \delta - (d - l)$ *or there is some* $(c, v) \in channel$ *such that* $c \geq now - \delta - (d - l)$ *and* $v < now + l$.

4. $now - \epsilon \leq clock_2$.

**Proof:**  By induction on the number of actions in a discrete execution. The complicated case is 3; see [16] for details.
□

**Lemma 13.3.3** *$r$ is a weak refinement from $A$ to $B$, with respect to invariant $I_A$.*

**Proof:**  The three conditions of the definition of a weak refinement are checked explicitly. The step condition is broken up into cases based on the type of action performed.
□

**Theorem 13.3.4** *Let A be the clock synchronization algorithm and B the bounded clock system. Then $A \leq_{\text{WR}} B$, and therefore $A \leq B$.*

This example showed a simple weak refinement. For an example of a weak forward simulation, consider $A'$, which is defined to be the same system as $A$, but instead of sending the full clock values, node 1 just send the "low-order bits." More precisely, in place of sending $c$, node 1 sends $c' = c \bmod \gamma$, for some fixed $\gamma$ such that $\gamma > 2\epsilon + 2\delta$. (I use the notation $c \bmod \gamma$ to denote the remainder when $c$ is divided by $\gamma$, i.e., $c/\gamma - \lfloor c/\gamma \rfloor$.) The second component, $v$, of each message, is still allowed to be an unbounded time, because it does not represent an actual component to be included in the message, but rather just a conceptual real-time deadline.

The key idea is that from any state $s$ of algorithm $A$, the range of $c$ values that might arrive at node 2 in a *deliver* step in algorithm $A$ is $[s.clock_2 - \epsilon - \delta, s.clock_2 + \epsilon + \delta]$. Thus, node 2 can correctly decode an arriving condensed clock value $c'$ into the unique clock value $c$ in the given range such that $c' = c \bmod \gamma$, and sets $clock_2$ to $max(clock_2, c)$.

There is a (multivalued) forward simulation from $A'$ to $A$, defined by $(s, u) \in f$ if and only if all state components are the same in $s$ and $u$, with the following exception. For each message $(c, v)$ in $u.channel$, the corresponding message $(c \bmod \gamma, v)$ appears in $s.channel$. Correctness of this simulation rests on first proving the invariant for $A$ that all clock values appearing in messages in the channel are in the indicated interval; this follows in turn from the claim that $clock_2$ and all the clocks in the channel are in the interval $[now - \epsilon, now + \delta]$.

This example shows a typical use for forward simulations—describing an optimized version of an algorithm in terms of a simpler, less efficient original version. In such a case, the correspondence generally needs to be multi-valued, since the original algorithm typically contains more information than the optimized version.

I do not have a related example to show here of a backward simulation. In fact, it seems hard to find practical examples where backward simulations are needed. They arise in situations where a choice is made earlier in the specification automaton than in the implementation automaton. The rest of the chapter will involve refinements and forward simulations only.

## 13.4   A Specialized Model

So far, I have presented the basic simulation definitions in terms of a very general timed automaton model. But when one carries out interesting verifications, it is often the case that the implementation and/or specification has some specialized structure that can help to organize the proofs. Here I describe a special case of the general timed automaton model that is suitable for describing most implementations, and many specifications as well. The specialized model is based on one defined by Merritt, Modugno, and Tuttle [21], hence I call it the *MMT automaton* model.

## 13.4.1   MMT Automata

An MMT automaton is an I/O automaton [13, 14] together with some upper and lower bounds on time. Formally, an I/O automaton $A$ consists of

- a set $states(A)$ of states;

- a nonempty subset $start(A)$ of start states;

- a set $acts(A)$ of actions, partitioned into *external* and *internal* actions; the external actions are further partitioned into *input* and *output* actions;

- a set $steps(A)$ of steps; this is a subset of $states(A) \times acts(A) \times states(A)$;

- a partition $part(A)$ of the locally controlled (i.e., output and internal) actions into at most countably many equivalence classes.

An action $\pi$ is said to be *enabled* in a state $s'$ provided that there exists a state $s$ such that $(s', \pi, s) \in steps(A)$, i.e., such that $s' \xrightarrow{\pi}_A s$. A set of actions is said to be *enabled* in $s'$ provided that at least one action in that set is enabled in $s'$. It is required that the automaton be *input-enabled*, by which is meant that $\pi$ is enabled in $s'$ for every input action $\pi$ and every state $s'$. There is no explicit time-passage action. The final component, *part*, is sometimes called the *fairness partition*. Each class in this partition groups together actions that are supposed to be part of the same "task." *Fair executions* are defined in such a way as to allow "fair turns" to each class of the partition. That is, for each partition class $C$, either (a) the execution is finite and ends in a state in which $C$ is not enabled, or (b) the execution is infinite and either contains infinitely many $C$ actions or infinitely many states in which $C$ is not enabled. The I/O automaton model is a simple, yet rather expressive model for asynchronous concurrent systems. Typical examples of its use in describing and reasoning about such systems appear in [11].

The I/O automaton model, however, does not have any facilities for describing timing-based systems. An MMT automaton is obtained by augmenting an I/O automaton with certain upper and lower time-bound information. In this chapter, I use a special case of the MMT model that is described formally in [9]. Namely, let $A$ be an I/O automaton with only finitely many partition classes. For each class $C$, define lower and upper time bounds, $lower(C)$ and $upper(C)$, where $0 \leq lower < \infty$ and $0 < upper(C) \leq \infty$; that is, the lower bounds cannot be infinite and the upper bounds cannot be 0.

A timed execution of an MMT automaton $A$ is defined to be an alternating sequence of the form $s_0, (\pi_1, t_1), s_1, \cdots$, where now the $\pi$'s are input, output, or internal actions. For each $j$, it must be that $s_j \xrightarrow{\pi_{j+1}} s_{j+1}$. The successive times are nondecreasing, and are required to satisfy the given *lower* and *upper* bound requirements. Specifically, define $j$ to be an *initial index* for a class $C$ provided that $C$ is enabled in $s_j$, and either $j = 0$, or else $C$ is not enabled in $s_{j-1}$, or else $\pi_j \in C$; initial indices are the points at which the bounds for $C$ begin to be measured. Then for every initial index $j$ for a class $C$, the following conditions must hold:

1. (Upper bound)

   If $upper \neq \infty$, then there exists $k > j$ with $t_k \leq t_j + upper(C)$ such that either $\pi_k \in C$ or $C$ is not enabled in $s_k$.

2. (Lower bound)

   There does not exist $k > j$ with $t_k < t_j + lower(C)$ and $\pi_k \in C$.

Note that an *upper* bound of $\infty$ does not impose any requirement that actions in the corresponding class ever occur. Finally, *admissibility* is required: if the sequence is infinite, then the times of actions approach $\infty$.

Each timed execution of an MMT automaton $A$ gives rise to a *timed trace*, which is just the subsequence of external actions and their associated times. The *admissible timed traces* of the MMT automaton $A$ are just the timed traces that arise from all the timed executions of $A$.

MMT automata can be composed in much the same way as ordinary I/O automata, using synchronization on common actions. More specifically, define two MMT automata $A$ and $B$ to be *compatible* according to the same definition of compatibility for general timed automata. Then the *composition* of the two automata is the MMT automaton consisting of the I/O automaton that is the composition of the two-component I/O automata (according to the definition of composition in [13, 14]), together with the bounds arising from the components. This composition operator is substitutive for the admissible timed trace inclusion ordering on MMT automata.

The MMT model just described is useful for describing many real-time systems. It is especially good as a low-level model for computer systems, since the class structure and associated time bounds are natural ways of modelling physical components and their speeds. However, it cannot be used for describing systems in which continuous state changes can accompany time-passage actions. Also, the MMT model does not appear to be general enough to provide a good model for arbitrary specifications or high-level system descriptions. For example, the model does not seem to be appropriate for describing the bounded clock system in Section 13.2.5.

MMT automata, as presented so far, are not exactly a special case of the general timed automata defined above. This is because the MMT model uses an "external" way of specifying the time-bound restrictions, via the added lower and upper bounds. The general model, in contrast, builds the time-bound restrictions explicitly into the time-passage steps. However, it is not hard to transform any MMT automaton $A$ into a naturally corresponding Lynch-Vaandrager timed automaton $A'$. This can be done using a construction similar to the one in Section 3 of [9], as follows.

First, the state of the MMT automaton $A$ is augmented with a *now* component, plus *first*($C$) and *last*($C$) components for each class. The *first*($C$) and *last*($C$) components represent, respectively, the earliest and latest time in the future that an action in class $C$ is allowed to occur. The rest of the state is called *basic*. The *now*, *first*, and *last* components all take on values that represent *absolute* times, not incremental times. The time-passage action $\nu$ is also added.

The *first* and *last* components get updated in the natural way by the various steps, according to the *lower* and *upper* bounds specified in the MMT automaton $A$. The time-passage action has explicit preconditions saying that time cannot pass beyond any of the $last(C)$ values, since these represent deadlines for the various tasks. Note that this usage of the $last(C)$ components as deadlines is similar to the usage of deadline components in messages in the clock synchronization algorithm above. Restrictions are also added on actions in any class $C$, saying that the current time *now* must be at least equal to $first(C)$.

In more detail, each state of $A'$ is a record consisting of a component *basic*, which is a state of $A$, a component $now \in \mathsf{R}^+$, and for each class $C$ of $A$, components $first(C)$ and $last(C)$, each in $\mathsf{R}^+ \cup \{\infty\}$. Each start state $s$ of $A'$ has $s.basic \in start(A)$, and $s.now = 0$. Also, if $C$ is enabled in $s.basic$, then $s.first(C) = lower(C)$ and $s.last(C) = upper(C)$; otherwise, $s.first(C) = 0$ and $s.last(C) = \infty$. The actions of $A'$ are the same as those of $A$, with the addition of the time-passage action $\nu$. Each non-time-passage action is classified as an input, output, or internal action, according to its classification in $A$.

The steps are defined as follows. If $\pi \in acts(A)$, then $s' \xrightarrow{\pi}_{A'} s$ exactly if all the following conditions hold:

1. $s'.now = s.now$.

2. $s'.basic \xrightarrow{\pi}_A s.basic$.

3. For each $C \in part(A)$:

    (a) If $\pi \in C$, then $s'.first(C) \leq s'.now$.

    (b) If $C$ is enabled in both $s$ and $s'$, and $\pi \notin C$, then $s.first(C) = s'.first(C)$ and $s.last(C) = s'.last(C)$.

    (c) If $C$ is enabled in $s$ and either $C$ is not enabled in $s'$ or $\pi \in C$, then $s.first(C) = s'.now + lower(C)$ and $s.last(C) = s'.now + upper(C)$.

    (d) If $C$ is not enabled in $s$, then $s.first(C) = 0$ and $s.last(C) = \infty$.

On the other hand, if $\pi = \nu$, then $s' \xrightarrow{\pi}_{A'} s$ exactly if all the following conditions hold:

1. $s'.now < s.now$.

2. $s.basic = s'.basic$.

3. For each $C \in part(A)$:

    (a) $s.now \leq s'.last(C)$.

    (b) $s.first(C) = s'.first(C)$ and $s.last(C) = s'.last(C)$.

The resulting timed automaton $A'$ has the same admissible timed traces as the MMT automaton $A$. From now on in this chapter, I will often refer to an MMT timed automaton and to its transformed version interchangeably, relying on the context to distinguish them.

Suppose that two MMT automata are given, one ($A$) describing an implementation and the other ($B$) describing a specification. Then by regarding both $A$ and $B$ as timed automata, it is possible to use the simulation techniques defined in Section 13.3 to show that $A$ implements $B$ (in the sense of admissible timed trace inclusion).

## 13.4.2    Example: Fischer's Mutual Exclusion Algorithm

Now I use MMT automata to model a simple algorithm—the well-known Fischer mutual exclusion algorithm using read-write shared memory [3]. This algorithm has become a standard example for demonstrating the power of formal methods for reasoning about real-time systems. It can be verified in several ways, but to fit it into this chapter, I express the proof as a simulation.

The most important correctness property of this algorithm is mutual exclusion. Other properties may also be of interest, for example, a time-bound property, limiting the time that it takes from when anyone requests the resource until someone gets it, and a liveness property, stating that if anyone is trying to obtain the resource, then someone succeeds. In this subsection, I will just argue mutual exclusion, but will return to this example twice later in the chapter to prove time bounds and liveness properties. Both of these proofs will also be based on simulations, but they will require a little more machinery.

The problem specification consists of a set of *users*, $U_i$, $1 \le i \le n$, each an MMT automaton, plus a *mutex object $M$*, also an MMT automaton. Let $U$ denote the composition of all the $U_i$. Each $U_i$ has a state containing its current *region*, either trying, critical, exit, or remainder. The outputs are $try_i$ and $exit_i$, while the inputs are $crit_i$ and $rem_i$. Each action moves the user to the indicated region, The input-output behavior is intended to be cyclical, in the order $try_i, crit_i, exit_i, rem_i \cdots$; the definition of the user guarantees that it will not be the first to violate the cyclic condition.

The $try_i$ and $exit_i$ actions are placed in separate singleton classes of the fairness partition. There are no special bounds on when try actions must occur, or when the critical region must be exited; therefore, the bounds are $[0, \infty]$ for each class.

**Automaton $U_i$: User**

Actions:
   Input:
          $crit_i$
          $rem_i$
   Output:
          $try_i$
          $exit_i$

State components:
   $region_i \in \{rem, try, crit, exit\}$, initially $rem$

$try_i$
  Precondition:
    $region_i = rem$
  Effect:
    $region_i := try$

$crit_i$
  Effect:
    $region_i := crit$

$exit_i$
  Precondition:
    $region_i = crit$
  Effect:
    $region_i := exit$

$rem_i$
  Effect:
    $region_i := rem$

Classes and bounds:
  $\{try_i\}$, bounds $[0, \infty]$
  $\{exit_i\}$, bounds $[0, \infty]$

The mutex object models the high-level behavior of a mutual exclusion system. It interacts with users by receiving the $try_i$ and $exit_i$ inputs and producing the $crit_i$ and $rem_i$ outputs. It keeps track of the regions for all the users, and ensures that it does not issue two $crit$ actions before the first has exited. All $crit$ actions are placed in one class, while each $rem_i$ is in a class by itself. Again, all the classes only have the trivial bounds $[0, \infty]$.

**Automaton $M$: Mutex Object**

Actions:
  Input:
    $try_i$, $1 \leq i \leq n$
    $exit_i$, $1 \leq i \leq n$
  Output:
    $crit_i$, $1 \leq i \leq n$
    $rem_i$, $1 \leq i \leq n$

State components:
  $region_i$, $1 \leq i \leq n$, each in $\{rem, try, crit, exit\}$, initially $rem$

$try_i$
  Effect:
    $region_i := try$

$crit_i$
  Precondition:
    $region_i = try$
    for all $j$, $region_j \neq crit$
  Effect:
    $region_i := crit$

$exit_i$
  Effect:
    $region_i := exit$

$rem_i$
  Precondition:
    $region_i = exit$
  Effect:
    $region_i := rem$

Classes and bounds:
  $crit = \{crit_i, 1 \leq i \leq n\}$, bounds $[0, \infty]$
  $\{rem_i\}$, $1 \leq i \leq n$, bounds $[0, \infty]$

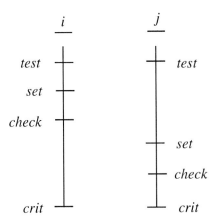

**Figure 13.1**  Bad Interleaving Prevented by Fischer Mutual Exclusion Algorithm

Fischer's algorithm is modeled formally as a single MMT automaton containing several processes sharing read-write memory. The state consists of the state of the shared memory (in this case, just the single variable $x$), plus the local states of all the processes. Each class of the fairness partition consists of the actions of one of the processes.

In this algorithm, each process $i$ that is trying to obtain the resource tests the shared variable $x$ until it finds the value equal to 0. After it finds this value, process $i$ sets $x$ to its own index $i$. Then it checks that $x$ is still equal to $i$. If so, process $i$ obtains the resource, and otherwise, it goes back to the beginning, testing for $x = 0$. When a process $i$ exits, it resets $x$ to 0.

A possible problem with the algorithm as described so far is that two processes, $i$ and $j$, might *both* test $x$ and find its value to be 0. Then $i$ might set $x := i$ and immediately check and find its own index, and then $j$ might do the same. This execution is illustrated in Figure 13.1.

In order to avoid this bad interleaving, a simple time restriction is used. Each of the actions $test_i$, $set_i$, $check_i$, $crit_i$, $reset_i$, $rem_i$, for each $i$, comprises a singleton class. The bounds assigned to all the classes are $[0, \infty]$, except that $set_i$ gets assigned $[0, a]$ and $check_i$ gets assigned $[b, \infty]$, for some constants $a$, $b$, where $a < b$.

The two bounds $a$ and $b$ prevent the bad interleaving in Figure 13.1 as follows. Any process $i$ that sets $x := i$ is made to wait long enough before checking to ensure that any other process $j$ that tested $x$ before $i$ set $x$ (and therefore might subsequently set $x$ to its own index) has already set $x$ to its index. That is, there should be no processes left at the point of setting, when $i$ finally checks.

**Automaton $F$: Fischer Mutual Exclusion Algorithm**

Actions:
    Input:

$try_i$, $1 \leq i \leq n$
$exit_i$, $1 \leq i \leq n$

Output:

$crit_i$, $1 \leq i \leq n$
$rem_i$, $1 \leq i \leq n$

Internal:

$test_i$, $1 \leq i \leq n$
$set_i$, $1 \leq i \leq n$
$check_i$, $1 \leq i \leq n$
$reset_i$, $1 \leq i \leq n$

State components:

$pc_i$, $1 \leq i \leq n$,

each in $\{rem, test, set, check, leave\text{-}try, crit, reset, leave\text{-}exit\}$, initially $rem$
$x$, an integer in $[0, n]$, initially 0

$try_i$

Effect:

$pc_i := test$

$test_i$

Precondition:

$pc_i = test$

Effect:

if $x = 0$ then $pc_i := set$

$set_i$

Precondition:

$pc_i = set$

Effect:

$x := i$
$pc_i := check$

$check_i$

Precondition:

$pc_i = check$

Effect:

if $x = i$
then $pc_i := leave\text{-}try$
else $pc_i := test$

$crit_i$

Precondition:

$pc_i = leave\text{-}try$

Effect:

$pc_i := crit$

$exit_i$

Effect:

$pc_i := reset$

$reset_i$

Precondition:

$pc_i = reset$

Effect:

$x := 0$
$pc_i := leave\text{-}exit$

$rem_i$

Precondition:

$pc_i = leave\text{-}exit$

Effect:

$pc_i := rem$

Classes and bounds:

Assume that $a < b$.

$\{test_i\}$, $1 \leq i \leq n$, bounds $[0, \infty]$
$\{set_i\}$, $[0, a]$
$\{check_i\}$, $[b, \infty]$
$\{crit_i\}$, $[0, \infty]$
$\{reset_i\}$, $[0, \infty]$
$\{rem_i\}$, $[0, \infty]$

When the composition $F \times U$ is transformed into a timed automaton, the only nontrivial state components that are added by the transformation are *now*, and *last*($set_i$) and *first*($check_i$), $1 \leq i \leq n$. (Here and elsewhere, I am using the convention of naming a singleton class by the single action contained in the class. Also, for simplicity, I ignore trivial *first* and *last* components.) Likewise, when $M \times U$ is transformed into a timed automaton, the only nontrivial added state component is *now*. Note that the external actions in each of the compositions $F \times U$ and $M \times U$ are $try_i$, $crit_i$, $exit_i$ and $rem_i$, $1 \leq i \leq n$.

I claim that the composition $F \times U$ is an implementation of $M \times U$, in the sense that $F \times U \leq M \times U$. To show the implementation, I define a mapping $r$ from $F \times U$ to $M \times U$. Here, dot notation is used to indicate component automata, as well as state components.

- $r(s).now = s.now$.

- $r(s).U.region_i = s.U.region_i$.

- $r(s).M.region_i = \begin{cases} try & \text{if } s.F.pc_i \in \{test, set, check, leave\text{-}try\}, \\ crit & \text{if } s.F.pc_i = crit, \\ exit & \text{if } s.F.pc_i \in \{reset, leave\text{-}exit\}, \\ rem & \text{if } s.F.pc_i = rem. \end{cases}$

In order to show that $r$ is a weak refinement, I first prove some invariants. The main invariant is *mutual exclusion*, i.e., that there do not exist two different users whose regions are both *crit*. Mutual exclusion is proved by means of a series of auxiliary invariants; these invariants and their proofs are due to Luchangco [8], and are based on those used by Abadi and Lamport [1]. The first property is obvious from the general definitions of the *last* functions—it says that the *last* value is no later than the current time plus the upper bound for the class.

**Lemma 13.4.1** *The following is true of every reachable state of $F \times U$:*
*If $pc_i = set$, then last($set_i$) $\leq$ now $+ a$.*

This lemma is used to prove the following key claim. It says that the earliest time a successful $check_i$ can happen is after the $set_j$ of any $j$ that has already passed the test. This lemma serves to rule out the bad interleaving in Figure 13.1, in which the sequence $set_i$, $check_i$, $set_j$, $check_j$ occurs, and both checks are successful.

**Lemma 13.4.2** *The following is true of every reachable state of $F \times U$:*
*If $pc_i = check$ and $x = i$ and $pc_j = set$, then first($check_i$) $>$ last($set_j$).*

**Proof:**  By induction. For the inductive step, consider transitions of the form $s' \xrightarrow{\pi} s$. The interesting cases are:

1. $\pi = set_i$

   Then $s.first(check_i) = s.now + b$ and $last(set_j) \leq s.now + a$, by Lemma 13.4.1. Since $a < b$, the inequality follows.

2. $\pi = test_j$ and $s'.x = 0$ (i.e., the test is successful)

   Then $s.x = 0$, making the statement true vacuously.                       $\square$

The next lemma says that if a process $i$ is in the critical region (or just before or just after it), then $x = i$ and no other process can be about to set.

**Lemma 13.4.3** *The following is true of every reachable state of $F \times U$:*
*If $pc_i \in \{leave\text{-}try, crit, reset\}$, then $x = i$ and for all $j$, $pc_j \neq set$.*

**Proof:**   By induction. The interesting cases are:

1.  $\pi = check_i$ and $s'.x = i$ (i.e., the check is successful)

    Then $s.x = s'.x = i$, and Lemma 13.4.2, together with the time requirements, imply that no $j$ has $s'.pc_j = set$ nor (therefore) $s.pc_j = set$.

2.  $\pi = set_j$, $j \neq i$

    This is impossible because the inductive hypothesis implies that there can be no $j$ with $s'.pc_j = set$.

3.  $\pi = reset_j$, $j \neq i$

    This is impossible because if it were true, the inductive hypothesis applied to both $i$ and $j$ would imply the contradictory requirements $s'.x = i$ and $s'.x = j$.

4.  $\pi = test_j$, $j \neq i$, and $s'.x = 0$ (i.e., the test is successful)

    Then the inductive hypothesis implies that $s'.pc_i \notin \{leave\text{-}try, crit, reset\}$, so $s.pc_i \notin \{leave\text{-}try, crit, reset\}$, which implies that the condition is true vacuously.   □

Now Lemma 13.4.3 implies the mutual exclusion property:

**Lemma 13.4.4 (Mutual Exclusion)** *The following is true of every reachable state of $F \times U$:*
*There do not exist $i$, $j$, $i \neq j$, such that $pc_i = pc_j = crit$.*

Using the mutual exclusion invariant, it is easy to argue that $r$ is a weak refinement. Note that this says only slightly more than just that the system satisfies the mutual exclusion *property*—it says that the system behaves as a mutual exclusion *system*, with a particular user interface, and so on.

**Lemma 13.4.5** *The function $r$ is a weak refinement from $F \times U$ to $M \times U$.*

**Theorem 13.4.1** *Let $F$ be the Fischer mutual exclusion algorithm, $U$ the composed user automaton, and $M$ the mutex object. Then $F \times U \leq_{WR} M \times U$, and therefore $F \times U \leq M \times U$.*

Note that this proof, while technically a simulation proof, does not really demonstrate the power of the method, since the key property being proved, mutual exclusion, is shown just using invariants. The remaining examples in this chapter better illustrate the power of the simulation method.

## 13.5    Using Simulations to Prove Time Bounds

In this section, I show how simulations can be used to prove time bounds, not just ordinary safety properties. In the Fischer example, the implementation automaton had upper and lower bound assumptions, which were used in proving mutual exclusion. The specification, however, did not include any time bounds. The main idea for proving time bounds via simulations is also to include lower and upper time bounds on the classes of the specification automaton.

I demonstrate the power of this method with two examples: a simple counting process and Fischer's mutual exclusion algorithm. These examples demonstrate that the power of simulation methods is greater in the real-time setting than it is in the asynchronous setting. For in the asynchronous setting there are usually *liveness conditions* rather than *time bounds* to be proved. Proofs of liveness conditions require some extra machinery, e.g., temporal logic, in addition to simulations, but time bounds can be proved just using simulations. I will say more about liveness in Section 13.6.

This method of proving timing properties and the first example are derived from [9].

### 13.5.1    Example: Counting Process

The first example involves a simple automaton that counts down from some fixed positive integer $k$ and then reports its completion. If the time between the automaton's steps is always in a limited range, say $[c_1, c_2]$, then it should be possible to prove a corresponding range of times until the report occurs.

**Automaton** *Count*: **Counting Automaton**

Actions:
>      Output:
>>           *report*
>      Internal:
>>           *decrement*

State components:
>      *count*, initially $k > 0$
>      *reported*, Boolean, initially *false*

*decrement*
>      Precondition:
>>           $count > 0$
>      Effect:
>>           $count := count - 1$

*report*
>      Precondition:
>>           $count = 0$
>>           $reported = false$
>      Effect:
>>           $reported := true$

Classes and bounds:
>      $\{report\}$, bounds $[c_1, c_2]$

{*decrement*}, each with bounds $[c_1, c_2]$

Informally, it is easy to see that the time until a *report* occurs can be any time in the interval $[(k+1)c_1, (k+1)c_2]$. In order to prove this formally, I express these time-bound assumptions using a high-level reporting automaton called *Report*.

**Automaton *Report*: Reporting Automaton**

Actions:
    Output:
        *report*

State components:
    *reported*, Boolean, initially *false*.

*report*
    Precondition:
        *reported* = *false*
    Effect:
        *reported* := *true*

Classes and bounds:
    {*report*}, bounds $[(k+1)c_1, (k+1)c_2]$.

I show that *Count* implements *Report* using a weak forward simulation. The multiple values permitted by a forward simulation are needed because the simulation is expressed in terms of inequalities. Specifically, I define $(s, u) \in f$ provided that the following hold:

- $u.now = s.now$,

- $u.reported = s.reported$,

- $u.last(report) \geq$
$\begin{cases} s.last(decrement) + s.count \cdot c_2 & \text{if } s.count > 0, \\ s.last(report) & \text{otherwise.} \end{cases}$

- $u.first(report) \leq$
$\begin{cases} s.first(decrement) + s.count \cdot c_1 & \text{if } s.count > 0, \\ s.first(report) & \text{otherwise.} \end{cases}$

As before, the simulation definition gives the key insights about why the algorithm is correct. The *now* and *reported* component definitions are straightforward. The *last(report)* component is constrained to be at least as large as a certain quantity that is calculated in terms of the state (including time components) of *Count*. This quantity is an upper bound on the latest time until a *report* action is performed by *Count*. There are two cases: If *count* > 0, then this time is bounded by the last time at which the first *decrement* can occur, plus the additional time required to do *count* − 1 *decrement* steps, followed by a *report*; since each of these *count* steps could take at most time $c_2$, this additional time is at most $count \cdot c_2$. On the other hand, if $count = 0$, then this time is just bounded by the last time at which the *report* can occur. The inequality expresses the fact that this calculated bound on the actual time until *report* is at most equal to the upper bound to be proved. The interpretation of the *first(report)* component is analogous—it should be no larger than a calculated lower bound on the earliest time until a *report* action is performed by *Count*.

In order to prove that $f$ is a weak forward simulation, I use the simple invariant "if $count > 0$, then *reported* = *false*," plus basic properties of the *Count* automaton, of the style of Lemma 13.4.1.

**Lemma 13.5.1** *The relation $f$ is a weak forward simulation from Count to Report.*

**Proof:**   I verify the three properties in the definition of a weak forward simulation. The inequalities are treated just like any other type of relationship between the states. The correspondence between *now* values is immediate.

For the correspondence between start states, let $s$ and $u$ be the unique start states of *Count* and *Report*, respectively. I show that $(s, u) \in f$. The first two parts of the definition of $f$ are immediate; consider the third part. The definition of *Report* implies that $u.last(report) = (k + 1)c_2$, while the definition of *Count* implies that $s.count > 0$ and $s.last(decrement) + s.count \cdot c_2 = c_2 + kc_2 = (k+1)c_2$. Therefore, $u.last(report) = s.last(decrement) + s.count \cdot c_2$, which shows the third part of the definition of $f$. The fourth part is analogous to the third.

Finally, for the correspondence between steps, consider cases based on the type of action. For example, consider a transition $s' \xrightarrow{decrement}_{Count} s$, where $u' \in f[s']$. Since *decrement* is enabled in $s'$, it must be that $s'.count > 0$. Suppose that also $s.count > 0$. The fact that $u' \in f[s']$ means that $u'.now = s'.now$, $u'.reported = s'.reported$, $u'.last(report) \geq s'.last(decrement) + s'.count \cdot c_2$, and $u'.first(report) \leq s'.first(decrement) + s'.count \cdot c_1$. It suffices to show that $u' \in f[s]$.

The first two conditions in the definition of $f$ carry over immediately. For the third condition, the left-hand side of the inequality, $last(report)$, does not change, while on the right-hand side, $last(decrement)$ is increased by at most $c_2$, while the second term decreases by exactly $c_2$. (The reason why $last(decrement)$ is increased by at most $c_2$ is as follows: the construction of the timed automaton from the MMT automaton for *Count*—captured in the invariants—implies that $s'.now \leq s'.last(decrement)$, but note that $s.last(decrement) = s.now + c_2$ and $s.now = s'.now$.) So the inequality still holds after the step.

Similar arguments can be made for the case of decrementing to 0, and for the lower bound.                                                                           □

**Theorem 13.5.1** *Count $\leq_{\mathrm{WF}}$ Report, and therefore Count $\leq$ Report.*

This implies that *Count* satisfies the timing requirements.

## 13.5.2   Example: Fischer Mutual Exclusion Algorithm

I return to the Fischer mutual exclusion algorithm to prove an upper bound for the time from when some process is trying to obtain the resource and no one is critical until some process is critical. There is also a corresponding bound (trivial to prove) for the remainder region.

In order to prove these time bounds, I must assume additional time bounds for process steps, besides the upper bound of $a$ on $set$ steps and lower bound of $b$ on $check$ steps already used for proving mutual exclusion. For simplicity, I assign the same upper bound of $a$ used for $set$ steps to all of the other locally controlled steps except for the $check$ steps, i.e., to the $test$, $crit$, $reset$, and $rem$ steps. (Upper bounds are not needed for $try$ or $exit$ steps.) I also assign an upper bound of $c$ to the $check$ steps, for some $c \geq b$. The result is a new MMT automaton, which I call $F'$.

I also express the time-bound requirements using an MMT automaton, $M'$. $M'$ is the same as $M$ except that the class $crit$ of $crit_i$ actions has the bounds $[0, 2c + 5a]$ and each class $rem_i$ has the bounds $[0, 2a]$.

It is possible to give a direct weak forward simulation from $F' \times U$ to $M' \times U$, but it seems useful instead to introduce an intermediate level of abstraction. The intermediate level expresses certain *milestones* toward the goal of some process reaching the critical region. Specifically, from the point when actions in the class $crit$ becomes enabled (that is, when some process enters the trying region when no process is critical, or when some process leaves the critical region), there is a later step at which some process first converts $x$ from 0 to a process index; I call this a *seize* step. Then there is a later step at which some process last sets $x$ to an index, leaving no other processes with program counters equal to $set$ (this means that no one will do another $set$, before some process reaches the critical region); I call this a *stabilize* step. The milestones I will consider are just the *seize* and *stabilize* steps.

I will argue that, from the time of enabling of $crit$, a *seize* step occurs at most time $c + 3a$ later. From the time of a *seize* step, a *stabilize* step occurs at most time $a$ later, and from the time of a *stabilize* step, a *crit* step occurs at most time $c + a$ later. The total is $2c + 5a$, as claimed. To express these milestones, I describe an intermediate MMT automaton $I'$.

**Automaton $I'$: Intermediate Automaton for Fischer Algorithm**

Actions:
  Input:
    $try_i$, $1 \leq i \leq n$
    $exit_i$, $1 \leq i \leq n$
  Output:
    $crit_i$, $1 \leq i \leq n$
    $rem_i$, $1 \leq i \leq n$
  Internal:
    $seize$, $1 \leq i \leq n$
    $stabilize$, $1 \leq i \leq n$

State components:

$region_i$, $i \in I$, an element of $\{rem, try, crit, exit\}$, initially $rem$

$status$, an element of $\{start, seized, stab\}$, initially $start$

$try_i$
  Effect:
    $region_i := try$

$seize$
  Precondition:
    $\exists i, region_i = try$
    $\forall i, region_i \neq crit$
    $status = start$
  Effect:
    $status := seized$

$stabilize$
  Precondition:
    $status = seized$
  Effect:
    $status := stab$

$crit_i$
  Precondition:
    $region_i = try$
    $status = stab$
  Effect:
    $region_i := crit$
    $status := start$

$exit_i$
  Effect:
    $region_i := exit$

$rem_i$
  Precondition:
    $region = exit$
  Effect:
    $region := rem$

Classes and bounds:

$\{seize\}$, bounds $[0, c + 3a]$

$\{stabilize\}$, bounds $[0, a]$

$crit = \{crit_i : 1 \leq i \leq n\}$, bounds $[0, c + a]$

$\{rem_i\}$, $1 \leq i \leq n$, bounds $[0, 2a]$

There is a simple weak forward simulation from $I' \times U$ to $M' \times U$. Namely, define $(s, u) \in f$ provided that the following hold.

- $u.now = s.now$.

- $u.U.region_i = s.U.region_i$ for all $i$.

- $u.M'.region_i = s.I'.region_i$ for all $i$.

- $u.last(crit) \geq \begin{cases} s.last(seize) + c + 2a & \text{if } s.status = start, \\ s.last(stabilize) + c + a & \text{if } s.status = seized, \\ s.last(crit) & \text{if } s.status = stab. \end{cases}$

- $u.last(rem_i) \geq s.last(rem_i)$.

Here, the inequality for $last(crit)$ uses a calculated upper bound on the time until $I' \times U$ performs a $crit$ action. This calculation is based on a series of cases. Working backward, in the last case, where $status = crit$, $crit$ is enabled in $I' \times U$, and a calculated upper bound is just $last(crit)$. In the next-to-last case, $stabilize$ is enabled, and after it occurs, only the worst-case time $c + a$ for $crit$ remains. In the first case, $seize$ is enabled, and after it occurs, the additional remaining time is at most the worst-case time for $stabilize$ and $crit$ to occur, in succession.

I use the following invariant of $I' \times U$: "If $region_i = crit$ for some $i$, then $status = start$." Then I show:

**Lemma 13.5.2** *The relation $f$ is a weak forward simulation from $I' \times U$ to $M' \times U$.*

**Theorem 13.5.2** *$I' \times U \leq_{\mathrm{WF}} M' \times U$, and therefore $I' \times U \leq M' \times U$.*

Now consider the simulation from $F' \times U$ to $I' \times U$. Define $(s, u) \in g$ if the following hold. (All unbound uses of process indices are implicitly universally quantified.)

- $u.now = s.now$.

- $u.U.region_i = s.U.region_i$.

- $u.I'.region_i = \begin{cases} rem & \text{if } s.F'.pc_i = rem, \\ crit & \text{if } s.F'.pc_i = crit, \\ exit & \text{if } s.F'.pc_i \in \{reset, leave\text{-}exit\}, \\ try & \text{otherwise.} \end{cases}$

- $u.status = \begin{cases} start & \text{if } s.x = 0, \text{ or } \exists i : s.pc_i \in \{crit, reset\}, \text{ else} \\ seized & \text{if } \exists i : s.pc_i = set, \text{ else} \\ stab. \end{cases}$

- $u.last(seize) \geq s.last(reset_i) + c + 2a$ if $s.pc_i = reset$.

- $u.last(seize) \geq \min_i\{h(i)\}$ if $s.x = 0$,

$$\text{where } h(i) = \begin{cases} s.last(check_i) + 2a & \text{if } s.pc_i = check, \\ s.last(test_i) + a & \text{if } s.pc_i = test, \\ s.last(set_i) & \text{if } s.pc_i = set, \\ \infty, & \text{otherwise.} \end{cases}$$

- $u.last(stabilize) \geq s.last(set_i)$ if $s.pc_i = set$.

- $u.last(crit) \geq \begin{cases} s.last(check_i) + a & \text{if } s.pc_i = check \wedge s.x = i, \\ s.last(crit_i) & \text{if } s.pc_i = leave\text{-}try. \end{cases}$

- $u.last(rem_i) \geq \begin{cases} s.last(reset_i) + a & \text{if } s.pc_i = reset, \\ s.last(rem_i) & \text{if } s.pc_i = leave\text{-}exit. \end{cases}$

The *now* and region correspondences and *status* definition are straightforward. The first inequality for *seize* says that if some process is about to *reset*, then the time until the variable is seized is at most an additional $c + 2a$ after the *reset* occurs. The second inequality for *seize* says that if $x = 0$ (which means that no process is about to *reset*), then the time until the variable is seized is determined by the minimum of a set of possible times, each corresponding to some candidate process that might set $x$. For instance, if some process $i$ is about to set $x$, then the corresponding time is only the maximum time until it does so, while if $i$ is about to test $x$, then the corresponding time is an additional $a$ after the *test* occurs. The interpretations for the remaining inequalities are similar.

Using the invariant given in Lemma 13.4.3, I show:

**Lemma 13.5.3** *The relation $g$ is a weak forward simulation from $F' \times U$ to $I' \times U$.*

**Theorem 13.5.3** *Let $F'$ be the Fischer mutual exclusion algorithm with time bounds, $U$ the composed user automata, and $I'$ the Fischer intermediate automaton with time bounds. Then $F' \times U \leq_{\text{WF}} I' \times U$, and therefore $F' \times U \leq I' \times U$.*

**Corollary 13.5.1** *Let $F'$ be the Fischer mutual exclusion algorithm with time bounds, $U$ the composed user automaton, and $M'$ the mutex object with time bounds. Then $F' \times U \leq M' \times U$.*

## 13.6    Liveness

It is sometimes desirable to prove liveness properties, e.g., properties that say that something eventually happens, even for systems with time bounds. In this section, I give a way of describing systems with liveness assumptions, and a way, based on simulations and an "Execution Correspondence Lemma," to verify that timed systems satisfy liveness properties. Thus, the liveness proof is built incrementally on top of the simulation proof. These notions are taken from [5].

### 13.6.1    Augmented Timed Automata and the Execution Correspondence Lemma

An *augmented timed automaton* consists of a timed automaton $A$, together with a subset $L$ of the admissible timed executions called the *live timed executions*. A timed automaton $A$ can be regarded as a special case of an augmented timed automaton, where the live timed executions are just the entire set of admissible executions. Define an admissible timed trace of $A$ to be a *live timed trace* of $(A, L)$ provided that it is the timed trace of some live timed execution of $(A, L)$.

  If $(A, L)$ and $(B, M)$ are augmented timed automata, and $A$ and $B$ are compatible, then I define the *composition* of $(A, L)$ and $(B, M)$ to be the augmented timed automaton $(A \times B, N)$, where $N$ is the set of admissible executions of $A \times B$ that project onto $A$ and $B$ to give timed executions in $L$ and $M$, respectively. If $(A, L)$ and $(B, M)$ are augmented timed automata, I define $(A, L) \leq (B, M)$ provided that all the live timed traces of $(A, L)$ are also live timed traces of $(B, M)$. Then composition is substitutive with respect to $\leq$.

  Suppose that $(A, L)$ is a timing-based algorithm with some additional liveness assumptions, expressed as an augmented timed automaton. To show that $(A, L)$ satisfies certain high-level liveness properties, one can express the entire specification, safety plus liveness conditions, as another augmented timed automaton $(B, M)$. Then showing that the algorithm satisfies the required liveness properties amounts to showing that $(A, L) \leq (B, M)$.

  In order to show that $(A, L) \leq (B, M)$, one can first produce a simulation from $A$ to $B$, yielding safety and timing properties as usual. But more strongly, it turns out that a simulation yields a close correspondence between *any* admissible discrete execution of $A$ and *some* admissible discrete execution of $B$, as follows.

  Let $A$ and $B$ be timed automata with the same visible actions and let $R$ be a relation over $states(A)$ and $states(B)$ that only relates states with the same *now* component. Let $\alpha = s_0 \pi_1 s_1 \pi_2 s_2 \cdots$ and $\alpha' = s'_0 \pi'_1 s'_1 \pi'_2 s_2 \cdots$ be admissible discrete executions of $A$ and $B$, respectively. Then $\alpha$ and $\alpha'$ are *related by* $R$, or $(\alpha, \alpha') \in R$, provided that there is a total nondecreasing mapping $m$ from natural numbers (i.e., indices of states in $\alpha$) to natural numbers (i.e., indices of states in $\alpha'$), such that:

1. $m(0) = 0$.

2. $(s_i, s'_{m(i)}) \in R$ for all $i$.

3. The execution fragment $s'_{m(i)} \cdots s'_{m(i+1)}$ contains the same sequence of timed visible actions as the step $s_i, \pi_{i+1}, s_{i+1}$.

That is, the initial states of $\alpha$ and $\alpha'$ correspond, corresponding states are $R$-related, and the fragment corresponding to any step has the same sequence of timed visible actions. $A$ and $B$ are *related by* $R$ (or $(A, B) \in R$) if for every admissible discrete execution of $A$, there is an $R$-related admissible discrete execution of $B$.

**Lemma 13.6.1 (Execution Correspondence)** *Suppose that $R$ is a refinement, forward simulation, or image-finite backward simulation from $A$ to $B$ (or a weak version thereof). Then $(A, B) \in R$.*

So, in order to show that $(A, L) \leq (B, M)$, one first produces a simulation from $A$ to $B$, thus obtaining an execution correspondence. Now given a live timed trace $\beta$ of $(A, L)$, one can obtain a timed execution $\alpha_1$ in $L$ that gives rise to $\beta$. Let $\alpha$ be any admissible discrete execution of $A$ that samples $\alpha_1$; Lemma 13.2.1 implies that $\alpha$ exists. Then $\alpha \in L_d$, the set of admissible discrete executions of $A$ that sample timed executions in $L$, and Lemma 13.2.1 implies that $\alpha$ also has $\beta$ as its timed trace.

Next, one uses the Execution Correspondence Lemma to obtain a corresponding admissible discrete execution $\alpha'$ of $B$, again with $\beta$ as its timed trace. Then one shows that $\alpha' \in M_d$, the set of admissible discrete executions of $B$ that sample timed executions in $M$. This is done using a case analysis on the different liveness conditions to be shown, making heavy use of the correspondence with $\alpha$ and the definition of $L_d$. Let $\alpha_2$ be a live timed execution of $(B, M)$ that is sampled by $\alpha'$; $\alpha_2$ exists by definition of $M_d$. Lemma 13.2.1 implies that $\alpha_2$ also has $\beta$ as its timed trace. This implies that $\beta$ is a live timed trace of $(B, M)$, as needed.

## 13.6.2   Example: Fischer Mutual Exclusion Algorithm

This strategy can be applied to the Fischer mutual exclusion algorithm to prove liveness properties. More precisely, consider a version $F''$ of Fischer's algorithm that is similar to the time-bounded version $F'$, but instead of the explicit upper bounds of $a$ on the steps, it just has *eventual* upper bounds for each type of step of each individual process. However, the upper bound of $a$ on each $set_i$ and the lower bound of $b$ on each $check_i$ are retained, because they are needed to guarantee mutual exclusion. $F''$ is described formally as an augmented timed automaton $(F, L_F)$, where $F$ is the Fischer algorithm in Section 13.3 and $L_F$ is a liveness condition for $F$ giving the eventual bounds for all the non-*set* steps.

For the specification, I use a version $M''$ of $M$, giving eventual bounds for the classes *crit*, and $rem_i$ for each $i$. $M''$ is described formally as an augmented timed automaton $(M, L_M)$, where $M$ is the untimed mutex object and $L_M$ is a liveness condition for $M$ giving the eventual bounds.

In order to show that the live timed traces of $F'' \times U$ are also live timed traces of $M'' \times U$, I again use an intermediate level. Here I use a version $I''$ of the intermediate algorithm $I'$, giving eventual bounds for the classes *seize*, *stabilize*, *crit* and $rem_i$ for each $i$. I carry out the liveness proof in two stages, first showing that every live timed trace of $I'' \times U$ is a live timed trace of $M'' \times U$, and then showing that every live timed trace of $F'' \times U$ is also a live timed trace of $I'' \times U$. I use the Execution Correspondence Lemma for each of these steps, with a case analysis based on the liveness properties to be shown. The details appear in [16].

## 13.7    Conclusions

In this chapter, I have given a survey of simulation methods and other related techniques for reasoning about timing-based systems. The main concepts that I have presented are:

1. The general timed automaton model.

2. Refinements, forward and backward simulations, and their weak versions.

3. The special-case MMT model.

4. Building time, in particular, the current time and timing predictions, into the state.

5. Invariants, especially those involving time predictions.

6. Milestones.

7. Execution correspondence.

I have shown several examples of proofs using these methods; additional examples appear in [16].

Future work includes applying these methods to additional timing-based algorithms chosen, for example, from the areas of telecommunications and real-time process control. Also, work is needed in systematizing and formalizing the liveness proofs. Finally, simulation proofs appear to be excellent candidates for mechanical verification using automatic theorem provers. Work in progress [26] involves using the Larch Prover [4] to carry out some simple simulation proofs for timing properties.

# Acknowledgments

Thanks go to Hagit Attiya, Rainer Gawlick, Victor Luchangco, Roberto Segala, Jorgen Søgaard-Andersen, and Frits Vaandrager for their many contributions to this chapter.

# References

[1] M. Abadi and L. Lamport. An old-fashioned recipe for real time. In *Proceedings of REX Workshop "Real-Time: Theory in Practice,"* volume 600 of *Lecture Notes in Computer Science*, pages 1–27, Mook, The Netherlands, Springer-Verlag, New York, June 1991.

[2] J. Davies and S. Schneider. An introduction to CSP, August 1989. Technical Monograph PRG-75.

[3] Michael Fischer. "Re: Where are you?" E-mail message to Leslie Lamport. Arpanet message number 8506252257.AA07636@YALE-BULLDOG.YALE.ARPA (47 lines), June 25, 1985 18:56:29EDT.

[4] Stephen J. Garland and John V. Guttag. A guide to LP, the Larch Prover. Technical report, Digital Systems Research Center, Palo Alto, Calif., December 1991. Research Report 82.

[5] R. Gawlick, R. Segala, J. Søgaard-Andersen, and N. Lynch. Liveness in timed and untimed systems. Submitted for publication.

[6] C.A.R. Hoare. *Communicating Sequential Processes*. Prentice Hall, Englewood Cliffs, N.J., 1985.

[7] Butler Lampson, William Weihl, and Eric Brewer. 6.826 Principles of computer systems, Fall 1991. MIT/LCS/RSS 19, Massachusetts Institute of Technology, Cambridge, Mass., 1992. Lecture notes and handouts.

[8] Victor Luchangco. Using simulation techiniques to prove timing properties. Master's thesis, MIT Electrical Engineering and Computer Science, Cambridge, Mass., 1993.

[9] N. Lynch and H. Attiya. Using mappings to prove timing properties. *Distributed Computing*, 6(2):121–139, 1992.

[10] N. Lynch, M. Merritt, W. Weihl, and A. Fekete. *Atomic Transactions*. Morgan Kaufmann Publishers, San Mateo, Calif., 1994.

[11] N. Lynch and B. Patt-Shamir. Distributed algorithms. MIT/LCS/RSS 20, Massachusetts Institute of Technology, Cambridge, Mass., 1992. Lecture notes for 6.852.

[12] N. Lynch and M. Tuttle. An introduction to input/output automata. Technical
     Memo MIT/LCS/TM-373, Laboratory for Computer Science, Massachusetts
     Institute Technology, Cambridge, Mass., November 1988.

[13] N. Lynch and M. Tuttle. An introduction to input/output automata. *CWI-
     Quarterly*, 2(3):219–246, September 1989. Also, appeared as Technical Memo
     [12].

[14] N. Lynch and Mark Tuttle. Hierarchical correctness proofs for distributed
     algorithms. Master's thesis, Massachusetts Institute of Technology, Dept. of
     Electrical Engineering and Computer Science, Cambridge, Mass., April 1987.

[15] N.A. Lynch and F.W. Vaandrager. Forward and backward simulations. Part
     II: Timing-based systems. Submitted for publication. Also, [19].

[16] Nancy Lynch. Simulation techniques for proving properties of real-time sys-
     tems. In *Rex Workshop '93*, Lecture Notes in Computer Science, Mook, The
     Netherlands, Springer-Verlag, New York, 1993.

[17] Nancy Lynch and Frits Vaandrager. Forward and backward simulations for
     timing-based systems. In *Proceedings of REX Workshop "Real-Time: Theory
     in Practice"*, volume 600 of *Lecture Notes in Computer Science*, pages 397–446,
     Mook, The Netherlands, June 1991. Springer-Verlag, New York, Also, [18].

[18] Nancy Lynch and Frits Vaandrager. Forward and backward simulations for
     timing-based systems. Technical Memo MIT/LCS/TM-458, Laboratory for
     Computer Science, Massachusetts Institute Technology, Cambridge, Mass.,
     November 1991.

[19] Nancy Lynch and Frits Vaandrager. Forward and backward simulations. Part
     II: Timing-based systems. Technical Memo MIT/LCS/TM-487, Laboratory
     for Computer Science, Massachusetts Institute Technology, Cambridge, Mass.,
     April 1993.

[20] O. Maler, Z. Manna, and A. Pnueli. From timed to hybrid systems. In *Pro-
     ceedings of REX Workshop "Real-Time: Theory in Practice"*, volume 600 of
     *Lecture Notes in Computer Science*, pages 447–484, Mook, The Netherlands,
     June 1991. Springer-Verlag, New York.

[21] M. Merritt, F. Modugno, and M. Tuttle. Time constrained automata. In
     *CONCUR'91 Proceedings Workshop on Theories of Concurrency: Unification
     and Extension*, Amsterdam, August 1991.

[22] X. Nicollin and J. Sifakis. The algebra of timed processes ATP: Theory and
     application, November 1991. Technical Report RT-C26, LGI-IMAG (revised
     version).

[23] Tobias Nipkow. Formal verification of data type refinement. In *Proceedings
     of REX Workshop "Stepwise Refinement of Distributed Systems: Models, For-
     malisms, Correctness"*, volume 430 of *Lecture Notes in Computer Science*,

pages 561–591, Mook, The Netherlands, June 1989. Springer-Verlag, New York.

[24] G.M. Reed and A.W. Roscoe. A timed model for communicating sequential processes. *Theoretical Computer Science*, 58:249–261, 1988.

[25] Jørgen Søgaard-Andersen, Nancy A. Lynch, and Butler Lampson. Correctness of at-most-once message delivery protocols. In *FORTE '93: Sixth International Conference on Formal Description Techniques*, pages 387–402, October 1993.

[26] Ekrem Soylemez. Automatic verification of the timing properties of MMT automata. Master's thesis, Dept. of Electrical Engineering and Computer Science, Massachusetts Institute Technology, Cambridge, Mass., 1993.

[27] F.W. Vaandrager and N.A. Lynch. Action transducers and timed automata. In *Proceedings of CONCUR '92, 3rd International Conference on Concurrency Theory*, Lecture Notes in Computer Science, Stony Brook, N.Y., August 1992. Springer-Verlag, New York.

[28] J.L. Welch, L. Lamport, and N. Lynch. A lattice-structured proof technique applied to a minimum spanning tree algorithm. In *Proceedings of the 7th Annual ACM Symposium on Principles of Distributed Computing*, pages 28–43, Toronto, Canada, August 1988. Expanded version in [29].

[29] J.L. Welch, L. Lamport, and N. Lynch. A lattice-structured proof technique applied to a minimum spanning tree algorithm. Technical Memo MIT/LCS/TM-361, Laboratory for Computer Science, Massachusetts Institute Technology, Cambridge, Mass., June 1988.

# Part V

# Programming Language and Tools

# Chapter 14

# Issues on Real-Time Systems Programming: Language, Compiler, and Object Orientation

Kwei-Jay Lin

This chapter investigates how real-time system programs can be implemented. We first review the important issues in a real-time programming language. The timing constraint constructs in various programming languages, such as *Flex*, RTC++, and RT-Euclid, are introduced and compared. We also present an implementation scheme of the timing constraint block in *Flex*. The interactions between constraints and the consistency checking mechanism are discussed. In some cases, compilers can be used be improve the real-time quality of programs; we discuss two such proposals. Finally, we show how object-orientation may be desirable in real-time systems, as it may enhance the flexibility, predictability, and schedulability of systems.

## 14.1   Introduction

Computations in real-time systems [24] have stringent timing constraints. Different from non-real-time computations, a real-time computation must satisfy both the *logical* and the *temporal* correctness criteria; failure to satisfy either makes a result unacceptable. The logical correctness concerns the values of the output generated by the computation and the internal state of the system after the computation is performed. The temporal correctness decides if a computation meets its *absolute* timing constraints, like the *ready time* and the *deadline*, and also its *relative* timing constraints, like the temporal *distance* between computations [12]. The absolute timing constraint defines the temporal relationship between a computation and real-world event, while the relative timing constraint defines the temporal relationship between a computation and other computations in the system. For a *soft* real-time computation, a slight delay in meeting the deadline will degrade the usefulness of a result; while for a *hard* real-time computation, any result produced after the deadline is considered useless or even counter-productive. For safety-critical applications, a missed deadline may even cause a system or its host environment to have a failure or a disaster. Therefore, it is desirable to provide some forms of *guarantee* on the system's capability to complete critical jobs .

Computations in real-time systems are usually triggered by both external events and interval timers. The program specification [8] includes the times at, before, or after which events and responses may occur, as well as the minimum and maximum time intervals that may elapse between events. To ensure that a program meets its specifications, a real-time programming language must allow

- programmers to express different types of timing constraints,

- compilers to check the feasibility of meeting the timing requirements,

- systems to enforce timing constraints either before or at run time.

Given a program coded and the timing constraints on it, the system must know how much time and resources the program needs in order to check if the timing constraints can be satisfied. The timing problem is non-trivial since many factors may affect the execution time of a program. For example, many processors have operation pipelines which have different execution times depending on the number of branch operations executed. Factors like data-dependent execution path make compile-time analysis impossible. In fact, in the general case, the problem of determining the program execution time is equivalent to the halting problem, which means that we may not be able to tell if a program execution will terminate. With a limited set of language and system primitives which have well-defined temporal semantics (like time-bounded loops or IPC with time-out parameters), however, one may be able to bound the execution time of a program. It is thus the goals of many research projects to design such a limited set of high-level programming constructs so that programmers can better manage the temporal behavior of their programs. With these constructs and timing constraints, intelligent compilers and powerful tools can be implemented to improve the predictability and the schedulability of real-time programs.

Even with a good set of programming constructs, a real-time program can still miss its timing constraints if the amount of computing resources available to it is insufficient. The available resource may change in systems with a dynamically changing task population or unpredictable hardware failures. For systems which must handle dynamic events, tasks may be initiated or discontinued as situations require. For systems with fault-tolerant capabilities and expected faults, the available resources in a system may change from time to time. In many applications, the program implemented must ensure that timing constraints are still met in such situations.

One possible approach to handle the above dynamic requirement is to design real-time computations with a flexible execution requirement (in terms of time and resources needed) and to implement run-time systems which can adjust the time and resources allocated to each computation so that the timing constraints of critical tasks (i.e., a subset of the tasks that are critical to the system's mission) are met. Such a flexibility can be accomplished by structuring computations as *real-time objects* and by using scheduling models such as *imprecise computation* and *performance polymorphism* to produce the best result under all situations.

In this chapter, we investigate real-time systems programming and related issues. We first discuss the design and implementation of real-time languages like *Flex*, Real-Time Euclid, RTC++, Dicon, and so on. We describe how different types of timing constraints may be expressed, and how they may be compiled or enforced by the compiler and the run-time system. We then review the object-oriented model for real-time systems, pointing out how object-orientation may be used to enhance the flexibility of real-time systems. Our objective in this chapter is to present a snapshot of the state-of-the-art on real-time systems programming. By comparing different proposed approaches, we hope to identify a promising approach in implementing future real-time systems.

## 14.2    Real-Time Language Issues

In the past, a real-time system programmer's job is to write a program with an execution time which is shorter than the time allowed in the timing constraints. Since it is difficult to predict the precise execution time of a program, it usually takes many rounds of trials and errors to build a dependable real-time system. Moreover, it takes the same level of effort to port existing real-time software to a new configuration than to build it from scratch. This is definitely undesirable since the demands for real-time software are stronger than ever, due to the ubiquity of computers in all application areas. To make matters worse, most next-generation real-time applications have very strict timing constraints and must provide very dependable services. We thus need new real-time programming languages and methodologies so that we can meet these demands.

A possible approach is not to expect a precise execution time from a computation, but to make the system so flexible that it can meet a wide range of timing constraints under different system configurations. Like a good manager, a computation can be designed to make the best use of whatever time and resources are available to it. The system scheduler decides the amount of time and resources a computation can have, and the computation then produces a result using only the time and resources allowed. In this way, the computation is guaranteed to be always *temporally* correct, although it may sacrifice its *functional* correctness by producing less desirable results. In many hard real-time systems, the requirement for functional correctness is not as strict as the requirement for temporal correctness. For these applications, the flexible performance approach is thus preferred.

To develop the next generation real-time systems using this approach, we need to have a programming language which has constructs for directly expressing timing constraints. The programmer defines the temporal constraints for (part of) the computation and provides the possible set of codes to be executed. The run-time system, together with the compiler and the system scheduler, must decide and/or generate the code to be executed so that the constraints are met.

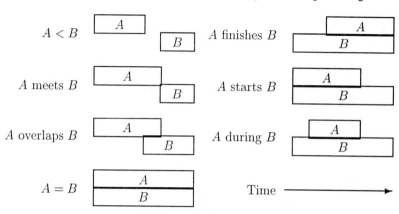

Figure 14.1  Temporal Relations between Computations

Many language features are desirable for real-time systems programming. In fact, almost all features desirable in a "good" conventional (i.e., non-real-time) programming language can be considered as essential for real-time systems programming. For example, five requirements have been suggested for real-time software in [26]: predictability, reliability, tasking, modularity, and maintainability. Of the five, only the predictability is a less familiar requirement for conventional software. The other four are highly desirable in all types of software systems. Although real-time systems may bring new meanings to these four requirements, we will not discuss them in this chapter, due to the space constraint. We will focus only on the predictability issue in this chapter.

In this section, we investigate the real-time constraint issues, including the theory, the construct, and the compilation.

## 14.2.1   Specification of Real-Time Constraints

A consistent theory of timing constraints has been presented by Allen [1] in his study of how to maintain knowledge about the temporal ordering of a set of actions using the temporal logic. He represents each action as taking place in an interval of time, and defines seven relations between intervals (see Figure 14.1) that describe the synchronization of one event with respect to another. These relations correspond to intuitive notions such as "$A$ takes place before $B$" ($A < B$), "$A$ and $B$ begin and end at the same time" ($A = B$), and "$A$ takes place during the time that $B$ does" ($A$ during $B$). Although many other temporal models have been proposed by others, Allen's work provides a good foundation for our discussion of real-time constraints.

One of the first researchers to describe timing constraints in real-time systems was Dasarathy [8]. He constructed a language, called the Real-Time Requirements Language (RTRL), for the event-action model. In his scheme, timing constraints could express the minimum or maximum time allowed between the occurrence of stimuli $S$, actions in the outside world, and responses $R$, the completion of the actions that a system takes. All four combinations $S - S$, $S - R$, $R - S$, and $R - R$ could be specified. Constraints on the time before a stimulus were constraints on the behavior of the outside world (e.g., a telephone user in Dasarathy's paper). Constraints on the time before a response were interpreted as constraints on the amount of time that the system could use to process the corresponding stimuli. Note that Dasarathy's RTRL was a specification language, and not intended for automatic processing.

A similar scheme was Jahanian's Real-Time Logic (RTL) [14]. In this scheme events and actions, corresponding roughly to Dasarathy's stimuli and responses, were identified. A mechanized inference procedure was presented to perform automatic reasoning about timing properties, and the events and responses could be associated by annotation with program constructs. A run-time monitoring system for the constraints specified in RTL has also been implemented, so that the system can adapt to a changing environment or an exception condition [7]. Like RTRL, RTL is designed to be a specification language.

## 14.2.2    Real-Time Constraint Constructs

The executions of real-time programs must meet timing constraints. As mentioned earlier, many different types of constraints may be required of a real-time computation, including *absolute* (e.g., deadline and duration) and *relative* (e.g., distance and frequency) constraints. We believe that these constraints should be explicitly defined in the program, rather than implicitly embedded in the code. This is because an implicit timing constraint may not be guaranteed whenever the normal execution flow is interrupted by unexpected events or altered by new system configurations. It is better to have timing constraints explicitly defined so that it is known by the system scheduler and other system resource managers (like network manager and I/O device manager).

Real-Time Euclid is a language extended from Euclid with real-time constructs and with provisions for "schedulability analysis," i.e. to verify that software adheres to its timing constraints at compile time. The effort, in fact, is to make real-time software as predictable as possible since it is impossible to analyze the schedulability without taking into account the actual system configuration and run-time support (like OS support, scheduling model, network protocol, etc.). In other words, some part of the schedulability analysis may need to be performed outside the compile time. In Real-Time Euclid, timing constraints are defined by the frames associated with processes. Each process must complete its task before the end of the current frame, and cannot be reactivated until the end of the current frame. To be able to verify that software can meet its timing constraints, Real-Time Euclid has no constructs that can take arbitrarily long to execute. For example, loops must have constant counts. No recursion and dynamic variables are allowed. Wait- and device-condition variables, as well as exception handlers, are all time-bounded.

RTC++ [13] is an extension of C++ with the real-time object model. In RTC++, active objects can be defined to have timing constraints like the worst-case execution time *(Bound)* and the deadline *(Within)*. Periodic tasks can also be defined by the *cycle* statement, which has the parameters for *start time, end time, period*, and *deadline*. For schedulability analysis, RTC++ adopts the rate monotonic scheduling analysis as the scheduling model. It also adopts the priority inheritance protocol to control the priority inversion problems when concurrent threads must share resources. A similar work is the Real-Time Concurrent C [2], which is an extension of the Concurrent C language. Real-time constraints such as deadline and periodicity can be defined. Another construct called *guarantee* is provided so that the run-time system will check if the statement can be guaranteed to complete before the deadline. If not, an alternate computation is executed.

More complex definition of timing constraints have been investigated by other projects. One early work is Dicon [17], which defines the *temporal scope*. Dicon is a distributed configuration language in which for each task, one can specify the deadline, the minimum and maximum delay before execution begins, the maximum execution time, and the maximum elapsed time. This is the first language where one can constrain both the upper and lower bounds of some temporal behavior.

Another timing constraint proposal which can define not only the upper and lower bounds, but also the absolute and relative constraints is the *Flex* language [15, 19], which is also an extension of C++. *Flex* reasons about time and resources by specifying *constraints* and propagating information among them. In *Flex*, constraints on time and resources are described by the *constraint block*. A constraint block identifies a constraint that must apply while a section of code is in execution. A constraint may be either a Boolean expression (which is treated as an assertion to be maintained throughout the block's lifetime) or a timing constraint, which describes a constraint on the time at which the block may begin or end its execution.

Associated with each constraint block is an interval of time representing the lifetime of the block. Another block may refer to the *start* and *finish* times of a given block by using the block's label; thus *A.start* represents the start time of block *A*, and *A.finish* represents the finish time of *A*. The boundaries of a constraint block may be designated in terms of the relative time from the start of the block. *A.duration* represents the difference between the *start* and *finish* times of *A*, and *A.interval* represents the difference between the *start* time of one execution of block *A* and the *start* of the next time it is executed. Figure 14.2 shows all four of these timing attributes.

Timing constraints in *Flex* take one of the forms shown in Table 14.1. They can be classified by the following properties:

**Start or Finish Time.** Constraints can refer either to the time that the computations represented by a constraint block begin, or to the time that they complete.

**Absolute or Relative Time.** Absolute times represent the actual time of the start or finish event. Relative times represent the elapsed time from the start event to the event described.

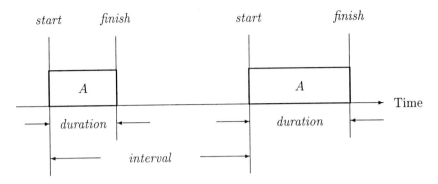

**Figure 14.2** Timing Attributes of Constraint Blocks

**Table 14.1  Timing Constraints in** *Flex*

|          | Absolute Time | | Relative Time | |
|----------|---------------|---------------|---------------|---------------|
|          | Start | Finish | Start | Finish |
| Earliest | $start \geq t$ | $finish \geq t$ | $interval \geq t$ | $duration \geq t$ |
| Latest   | $start \leq t$ | $finish \leq t$ | $interval \leq t$ | $duration \leq t$ |

**Earliest or Latest Time.** Constraints can refer either to the earliest time at which an event may occur, or to the latest time at which it is permitted to occur.

The left-hand side of a timing constraint must refer to a timing attribute of the current block. The relational operator ($\geq$ or $\leq$) can be used to specify either the earliest or the latest time for executing the block, or the upper and the lower bounds on event distances . The right-hand side of a constraint can be a constant, or an expression involving the timing attribute of another constraint block. Thus a timing constraint on a constraint block can be defined *relative* to the execution of another block, not just to the global clock. When one block refers to the attribute of another block that may be executed many times (like periodic tasks), the values always refer to the most recent activation of the block.

With the timing constructs provided in *Flex*, one can implement all the timing relations as defined in Figure 14.1. One can also easily define temporal constraint macros for *periodic* and *aperiodic* computations.

## 14.2.3   Checking Real-Time Constraints

Given the timing constraint constructs defined in a real-time language, the compiler must generate the code to enforce them. In this section, we present how the real-time constructs in *Flex* are implemented since it has one of the more complex constructs.

There are three basic temporal data types in *Flex*: `Tick` , `TickInterval`, and

```
Episode E;          // Episode describing block's execution time
{
    Context __C_n;                  // Establish context
    if (__C_n.save())
    {
        -- user's exception handler goes here --
    }
    else
    {
        -- declarations for non-temporal constraints --
        -- declarations for latest finish time --
        -- declarations for latest start time --
        -- code to delay until earliest start time --
        -- code to clean up latest start time structures --
        E.start = NOW ();       // Record the start time

        -- body of the constraint block --

        -- code to delay until earliest finish time --
        -- code to clean up latest finish time structures. --
        -- code to clean up non-temporal constraints --
    }
    E.finish = NOW (); // Record the finish time
}
```

**Figure 14.3** Structure of a Constraint Block

**Episode.** In *Flex*, time is represented as a set of discrete, quantized instants. Each instant is represented as an instance of the data type `Tick`. There is a function called `NOW()` that returns the current absolute time. A `Tick` is a precisely known instant of time. In many cases, such as an event that is to occur in the future, the time of an event is not known precisely. The `TickInterval` type represents these uncertain ranges of time. The `Episode` data type represents the period of time during which some constraint block is executed. It comprises two attributes: the *start* time, at which the process begins, and the *finish* time, at which the process is completed. Both of these times may be uncertain, and are therefore expressed as intervals. In addition, there are two values that may be determined for an activation: *interval,* the period of time between successive starts, and *duration,* the period of time between a start and a finish. With these temporal data types, the basic structure for the compiled *Flex* constraint block [20] is as shown in Figure 14.3.

Given a real-time program implemented with a set of timing constraint blocks, the system must be able to detect any constraint inconsistency. For example, two blocks may both specify that it has to be executed before the other. Some of the inconsistencies can be checked at the compile time, while others can be checked

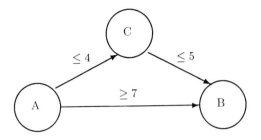

**Figure 14.4**  A Simple Program Graph

only at run time. Simple checking can be performed for the consistency between *duration* and (*finish* − *start*). For example, if *duration* is defined to be ≥ 10, but (*finish* − *start*) can only be ≤ 8, there is an inconsistency.

Given a set of constraint blocks with distance constraints [11] such as

$$A : (start \geq B.start + 5)$$

or

$$A : (start \leq B.start + 5)$$

one can check their distance consistency by propagating the relationship in a program graph like Figure 14.4. In a program graph, each constraint block is represented as a node. Each '$A \leq B$' constraint defines a '≤' edge from A to B and each '$A \geq B$' constraint defines a '≥' edge from B to A. The constant in the constraint defines the value of the edge. Algorithms have been devised to check the consistency in the graph [20].

## 14.3   Meeting Timing Constraints

Given a set of timing constraints defined in a program, the compiler and the run-time system must provide the means to meet them. One approach is to compile the program just like a non-real-time program, and then predict the performance of the computation as implemented. With the performance prediction, the system can check if the constraints can be satisfied in a specific run-time environment using a specific scheduling algorithm. Another approach in meeting the timing constraints is to compile and to transform the program so that the code generated is guaranteed or at least has a better chance to meet the constraints. This again must take into account the run-time scheduling model used.

The problem with the former approach is the performance prediction. One possible way to determine the performance of a program is to run it, either on the target hardware itself, or on some sort of simulator that models the hardware. The simulation or test run must be presented with data that are representative of the data that will be seen in actual service of the system. The problem with this method is that the testing is limited, and generally cannot include the entire set of possible inputs. The worst case for the consumption of time or some other resource may not be uncovered in testing. Moreover, if a simulator is used, there may be some uncertainty that the simulator actually reflects the performance of the underlying hardware. For this reason, many have proposed conducting analyses that examine some form of the program code and attempt to prove assertions about the program's performance behavior. Using this method, the worst-case performance can always be identified so that any guarantee made is absolute.

In this section, we review some of the work on predicting program performances and on meeting timing constraints.

## 14.3.1    Predicting Program Performances

An early research to attempt to characterize the performance of high-level programs was conducted by Leinbaugh [18]. This work characterized the time required by a higher-level construct in terms of its CPU time, time spent waiting to enter a critical section, time spent ready and waiting for a processor, time spent performing I/O, and time spent waiting at a synchronization point. Conservative bounds for all of these quantities were estimated.

Stoyenko [25] adopted Leinbaugh's ideas into a programming system for Real-Time Euclid. Among its features was the ability to verify, a priori, that all resource and timing constraints would be satisfied. Rather than using Leinbaugh's conservative time bounds, their system attempted to find tighter bounds on execution time by an exhaustive search of all possible sequences of execution of processes. However, Stoyenko made the analysis easier by forbidding many programming constructs, including **while** loops (only counted loops were allowed), recursion, and recursive data structures such as linked lists. In this way, tight time bounds could be established for all programming constructs, at the expense of increased programming effort in coping with the limitations of working with the set of constructs remaining.

Mok et al. [21] have taken another approach to this *a priori* program analysis. The performance analyzer works on an abstraction (the interval partition) of the flow graph of the program, and the programmer supplies the worst-case number of iterations of each unbounded loop using a separate timing analysis language. Other work on program performance analysis includes the static approach by Puschner [22], who has refined the calculation of time required in **if** ... **then** ... **else** constructs, and Shaw [23], who has presented some rules for formal verification of programs' timing behavior.

Kenny and Lin have presented an alternative approach based on program measurements [16]. It alleviates some of the objections to program measurements by showing how statistical confidence in the program's performance behavior can be achieved. It also allows actual behavior, and not just worst-case performance, of programs to be estimated, by allowing a performance model to contain dependencies on the input data. In their approach, the system is provided with a performance model which defines a task's execution time as a function of its input data. The model can incorporate the programmer's knowledge about the expected timings. The system then collects the performance data measured from the actual run of the task on some input data. The system then gives a measure of statistical confidence that the model accurately represents the program's actual behavior. Such an approach may be desirable since a system will be able to:

- analyze program structures that are impossible for other systems, such as unbounded loops and recursive control structures,

- provide accurate timing information even on hardware whose timing behavior is difficult to model and analyze, and

- provide confidence in the timing model, which should improve statistically as more experience on a computation is collected.

In summary, the performance prediction for real-time programs (or any type of programs) remains a difficult problem. The static analysis approach can be used to provide an estimate on the worst-case execution time. Given that real-time systems must provide guarantees on meeting timing constraints, the approach is viewed to be safer and more acceptable. However, such estimates are very pessimistic and may be too conservative for most practical applications. Moreover, program execution time often is dependent on the input data and normally is much less than the worst-case execution time. Thus if every program uses the worst-case execution time for system design, the system implemented will be largely under-utilized. Again, we believe that the flexible performance model can help to achieve a better system efficiency. One can identify a subset of the critical computations in a system to perform the worst-case scenario analysis using their worst-case execution times. In addition, one can perform a normal case analysis using the execution-time predictions from the measurement approach. In this way, the system can be designed to have a high system utilization using the normal case schedule and still is guaranteed to perform acceptably under the worst-case scenario.

## 14.3.2   Improving the Schedulability

In all the work discussed above, the compiler is used to generate real-time codes with very little consideration for performance issues, except to provide some mechanism for checking and detecting timing errors. However, as demonstrated in many parallel programming systems with optimizing compilers, compilers can be used to capture certain high-level knowledge about the program and produce a better code than that produced by simple-minded compilers. Traditionally, compilers have been used to reduce the time or space required to run a program, or to increase the parallelism in a program. For real-time systems, it may be possible to use compilers to improve the quality of real-time programs. We present two such projects in this section. One design is to increase the schedulability of codes. The other is to increase the flexibility of the system.

In [10], a technique called *Compiler-Assisted Adaptive Scheduling* is presented. In this approach, the compiler examines the application program and inserts the measurement code at appropriate boundaries so that computations can be adapted to avoid violating timing constraints. In addition, code reordering is performed to allow greater adaptability and early failure detection. In the compiler, codes are classified by their predictability and monotonicity. If possible, non-predictable codes are executed before predictable codes, and non-monotonic codes are executed before monotonic codes. This is because the non-predictable code may take an unknown amount of time: If it takes longer than originally estimated, an early execution will given it a better chance to meet the deadline. But if it takes shorter than expected, the time left can still be utilized by other tasks. Similarly, the monotonic code is executed last since they can be terminated at any time, as required.

In [9], compiler techniques are used to move codes from blocks constrained by tight deadlines into blocks with sufficient slack, and also from tasks with a tight deadline to others without. In this approach, the codes needed to produce an observable event are separated from those that do not. The compiler then moves the latter from the original control flow to after the timing constraint is satisfied by the former. The technique is further tied in with the RM scheduling model to enhance the schedulability.

Other approaches to improve the real-time quality of programs with the aid of compilers are possible. This is a promising area for producing schedulable and flexible real-time programs. Several new projects have been initiated, but more effort should be expended in this direction.

## 14.4    Adopting Object Orientation

Most real-time systems implemented in the past use the traditional process-oriented model where tasks are implemented as functions performing in a global system state. Some recent real-time systems have adopted a new software paradigm called the object-oriented model. In object-oriented systems, all entities in the system are defined as objects. An object may invoke methods defined in itself or in other objects for the services needed, which in turn may invoke methods in other objects. Each object is defined with a specific type. Types may form a hierarchy where some types inherit the definition of other types. Cardelli and Wegner [6] have therefore identified the three basic elements of object orientation as:

$$object\ oriented = data\ abstraction + object\ types + type\ inheritance. \quad (14.1)$$

With object type and type hierarchy, when an object is requested to perform a method, it must *bind* the request with the definition of a method which may be defined outside the object in the type hierarchy. Sometimes, the same method requested may be bound to different methods according to the data it needs to process, using a mechanism called *polymorphism*.

Lately, the object-oriented model has received much favorable advocacy from the software community. One of the reasons is that the object-oriented model allows one to apply the principles of hierarchical structuring and component abstraction, which are essential in building large systems. The object-oriented approach also promotes component reusability (by type inheritance), which makes systems easier to maintain and to modify.

For real-time applications, the above are very important benefits. In addition, there are many other good reasons why object orientation is attractive. Most real-time systems have physical devices which can be modeled naturally as objects. The object model may allow object designers to address the timing and performance issues in each object directly. Therefore, if designed correctly, it may be easier to port a real-time object from one configuration to another. It is also easier to optimize objects independently to improve their performances. Finally, objects can be enhanced with different capabilities using the type hierarchy, with different types corresponding to different generations of a real-time system component.

With all of the benefits, however, many believe that object orientation is counter-productive since there may be extra heavy overheads in dynamic binding and dynamic memory management. However, the overheads in these mechanisms can be minimized with a careful compiler and run-time implementation. Moreover, object-oriented real-time systems may provide more flexibility, which may result in even higher performance gains than those attained by non-object-oriented systems. To meet the strict requirement of graceful system degradation in safety-critical real-time systems, object orientation may enhance the predictability of system performance by using a flexible scheduling framework, and by integrating the performance consideration into the structures of object types and the whole system. We will discuss these benefits in this section.

In this section we investigate the issues of implementing object-oriented real-time systems. We review three such proposals: namely, RTC++, Chaos, and *Flex*. Although all of them intend to enhance the adaptability and flexibility of real-time objects, each of the languages adopts object orientation for slightly different reasons.

## 14.4.1    Real-Time Objects in RTC++

The motivation for RTC++ is to extend C++ with some real-time constructs so that programmers can use the popular language to design real-time programs. To achieve that, the notion of real-time objects have been defined. Some of the issues considered important for real-time programming include (1) timing specification, (2) priority inversion, and (3) multiple threads.

Real-time objects in RTC++ are defined to be active objects with timing constraints. The design of RTC++ places the emphasis on the schedulability of real-time objects using the rate monotonic fixed-priority scheduling model. All considerations for real-time objects are based on the scheduling theory; i.e., the language provides enough timing constructs to programmers so that the system can support the RM scheduler. In other words, objects in RTC++ do not have more capability than objects in C++, other than RM scheduling.

## 14.4.2    Dynamic Objects in Chaos

In some real-time applications, the system must be able to handle the dynamic nature of the real world to provide a dependable service. For example, avionic software must be able to handle unexpected weather conditions and bursty air traffic. In such applications, real-time software must be able to adapt to changes in the target environment and yet behave in a predictable manner.

Chaos is an object-oriented language and programming/execution system designed for dynamic real-time systems. The designers of Chaos have chosen to use object orientation in real-time software for the following reasons [3]:

- Using the process-oriented model, the problem decomposition must divide the system according to the functional aspects of the system. In other words, the mapping from software modules to real-world entities, and vice versa, is not apparent. This makes the codes difficult to understand, to maintain, and to reuse.

- The process-oriented model often implements the event-action view: i.e., events are generated by the real world and the software must produce responses. However, the discrete events are actually approximations of continuous activities in the real world. By mapping the activities into pre-defined discrete events, some aspects of the activities are lost and the software loses the flexibility to handle them in different, better ways.

- The object-oriented model is able to represent directly the structural or anatomical aspect of the real world by object definitions. Moreover, since every entity in the system is uniformly represented as objects and communicated by messages, code reuse and maintenance become easier.

Chaos objects and messages have both functional and temporal attributes. Chaos has three components: a C-based run-time library, a programming environment with an entity-relationship database, and a specification language. A programmer specifies the mapping between real-world entities and corresponding software objects. The environment then generates the configuration files, which are then compiled to create object classes and instances. The environment is also used to analyze the application's temporal behavior and to monitor its execution at run time.

Chaos has carefully investigated the predictability issues on dynamic binding, dynamic instance creation, and dynamic class creation mechanisms. Another major effort is the object's ability to negotiate temporal constraints placed on it. In general, Chaos provides very powerful and dynamic mechanisms for object-oriented real-time systems.

### 14.4.3  Performance Polymorphism in *Flex*

One approach to enhance the flexibility of real-time software so that timing constraints are always satisfied is to change the software structure so that the amount of work performed is based on the amount of time and resources available. In other words, instead of defining a fixed amount of work to be performed, we can define a set of workloads which may or may not be completely executed. During run-time or system reconfiguration, a subset of the workloads is executed using only the amount of time available. The system design and scheduling issue is then to select the optimal subset of the workloads which gives the best reward under the available time and resources.

In real-time systems, the approach can be implemented in three different ways. First, a computation may actively evaluate its timing constraints to select the execution path with the most desirable response time. Second, the run-time system, given global scheduling knowledge, may bind a real-time request dynamically to a server with appropriate time and resources available. Finally, a computation may resort to producing imprecise results if its timing constraints are so dynamic that they are beyond the control of the previous two mechanisms. The novel feature in this approach is that the execution time is modeled as a first-class object so that it can be modified if necessary.

In object-oriented systems, some methods in an object may be provided by other objects; these methods are bound based on the class hierarchy, and by the parameters of the invocation. In *Flex*, the concept is further generalized to include the execution performance as one of the binding parameters. This binding based on architectural or performance criteria is a form of polymorphism. Instead of having multiple procedures that perform the same action on objects of different types, we can define multiple procedures in *Flex* that perform similar functions based on different environmental constraints.

This model of *performance polymorphism* raises some scheduling issues relating to the binding of the polymorphic operations. When jobs are performance polymorphic computations, jobs do not have a fixed amount of execution time, but can be executed for a variable amount of time. Each version defines a reward function which specifies how much reward can be received for a given execution time. For non-real-time systems, we may want to allocate resources (especially CPU time) evenly to jobs such that all jobs have about the same reward. This is known as the *knapsack sharing* problem, where one maximizes the minimum reward for any job in the system. Brown [5] has proposed an efficient algorithm. For real-time systems the objective is concerned with the allocation of resources to maximize the total value among all reward functions. It is known as the *knapsack* problem [4], which is NP-complete in general. Heuristic algorithms can be used to solve the knapsack problem.

## 14.5    Conclusions

We have discussed the issues related to real-time systems programming. Three topics have been reviewed: real-time programming language, compiler and tool implementation, and object-oriented real-time systems. In each of the topics, we survey and compare different research proposals and implementations. We show how timing constraints can be monitored and enforced at run time using run-time servers, and discuss how real-time programs can be checked and transformed at compile time. Although much has been done, more refined design and practical experience on the general constructs and programming tools that can be used in a high-level language to enhance its real-time predictability and schedulability are still needed. We believe that such research will provide very helpful results in building next-generation real-time systems.

## Acknowledgments

This research was partially supported by the Office of Naval Research under Grant N00014-94-1-0034 and by the National Science Foundation under Grant CCR-89-11773.

## References

[1] James F. Allen. Maintaining knowledge about temporal intervals. *Communications of the ACM*, 26(11):832–843, November 1983.

[2] T. Bihari and P. Gopinath. Real-time concurrent c: A language for programming dynamic real-time systems. *Real-Time Systems*, 3(4):337–406, 1991.

[3] T. Bihari and P. Gopinath. Object-oriented real-time systems. *IEEE Computer*, 25(12):25–32, December 1992.

[4] J. R. Brown. The knapsack sharing problem. *Operations Research*, 27(2):341–355, March–April 1979.

[5] J. R. Brown. The sharing problem. *Operations Research*, 27(2):324–340, March–April 1979.

[6] Luca Cardelli and Peter Wegner. Understanding types, data abstractions, and polymorphism. *ACM Computing Surveys*, 17(4):471–522, December 1985.

[7] S.E. Chodrow, F. Jahanian, and M. Donner. Run-time monitoring of real-time systems. In *Proc. of 12th IEEE Real-Time Systems Symp.*, pages 74–83, 1991.

[8] B. Dasarathy. Timing constraints of real-time systems: Constructs for expressing them, methods for validating them. *IEEE Transactions on Software Engineering*, SE-11(1):80–86, January 1985.

[9] R. Gerber and S. Hong. Semantics-based compiler transformations for enhanced schedulability. In *Proc. of 14th Real-Time Systems Symp.*, 1993.

[10] P. Gopinath and R. Gupta. Applying compiler techniques to scheduling in real-time systems. In *Proc. of 11th IEEE Real-Time Systems Symp.*, pages 247–256, 1990.

[11] C.-C. Han and K. J. Lin. Job scheduling with temporal distance constraints. In *Proc. of 6th IEEE Workshop on Real-Time Operating Systems and Software*, May 1989.

[12] C.-C. Han and K. J. Lin. Scheduling distance-constrained real-time tasks. In *Proc. of the 13th Real-Time Systems Symp.*, pages 300–308, December 1992.

[13] Y. Ishikawa, H. Tokuda, and C.M. Mercer. An object-oriented real-time programming language. *IEEE Computer*, 25(10):66–73, October 1992.

[14] Farnam Jahanian and Aloysius Ka-Lau Mok. Safety analysis of timing properties in real-time systems. *IEEE Transactions on Software Engineering*, SE-12(9):890–904, September 1986.

[15] Kevin B. Kenny and K. J. Lin. Building flexible real-time systems using the *Flex* language. *IEEE Computer*, pages 70–78, May 1991.

[16] Kevin B. Kenny and K. J. Lin. Measuring and analyzing the performances of real-time programs. *IEEE Software*, pages 41–49, September 1991.

[17] I. Lee and V. Gehlot. Language constructs for distributed real-time systems. In *Proc. of IEEE Real-Time Systems Symp.*, pages 57–66, December 1985.

[18] Dennis W. Leinbaugh. Guaranteed response times in a hard real-time environment. *IEEE Transactions on Software Engineering*, SE–6(1):85–91, January 1980.

[19] K. J. Lin and S. Natarajan. Expressing and maintaining timing constraints in FLEX. In *Proc. of 9th Real-Time Systems Symp.*, pages 96–105, Huntsville, Ala., December 1988.

[20] K. J. Lin and Kevin B. Kenny. Implementing and checking timing constraints in real-time systems. *Microprocessing and Microprogramming*, 38:477–484, 1993.

[21] A. K. Mok, P. Amerasinghe, M. Chen, and K. Tantisirivat. Evaluating tight execution time bounds of programs by annotations. In *Proc. of 6th IEEE Workshop on Real-Time Operating Systems and Software*, pages 272–279, May 1989.

[22] P. Puschner and Ch. Koza. Calculating the maximum execution time of real–time programs. *Journal of Real–Time Systems*, 1:159–176, 1989.

[23] Alan C. Shaw. Reasoning about time in higher–level language software. *IEEE Transactions on Software Engineering*, 15(7):875–889, July 1989.

[24] John A. Stankovic. Misconceptions about real-time computing. *IEEE Computer*, October 1988.

[25] A. D. Stoyenko. A schedulability analyzer for real-time Euclid. In *Proc. of 8th Real-Time Systems Symp.*, pages 218–227, San Jose, Calif., December 1987.

[26] A. D. Stoyenko and W. A. Halang. High-integrity pearl: A language for industrial real-time applications. *IEEE Software*, 10(4):65–74, July 1993.

# Chapter 15

# Compiler Support for Real-Time Programs

## Richard Gerber and Seongsoo Hong

We present a compiler-based approach to assist automatically in constructing real-time systems. In this approach, source programs are written in TCEL (or Time-Constrained Event Language) which possesses high-level timing constructs, and whose semantics characterizes time-constrained relationships between observable events. A TCEL program infers only those timing constraints necessary to achieve real-time correctness, without over-constraining the system. We exploit this looser semantics to help transform programs to achieve schedulability automatically. In this chapter we present two such transformations. The first is trace scheduling, which we use to achieve consistency between a program's worst-case execution time and its real-time requirements. The second is program slicing, which we use to tune automatically application programs driven by rate-monotonic scheduling.

## 15.1  Introduction

One of the primary challenges of building a real-time system lies in balancing its functional requirements against its temporal requirements. Functional requirements define valid translations from inputs into outputs. As such they are realized by a set of programs, which *consume* CPU time.

Temporal requirements, on the other hand, place upper and lower bounds between *occurrences of events* [3, 14]. An example is: *the robot arm must receive a next-position update every 10 ms.* Such a constraint arises from the system's requirements, or from a detailed analysis of the application environment. Thus temporal requirements implicitly *limit* the time that can be provided by the system's resources. When a balance between the functional and temporal constraints is not achieved, the result is often a costly and arduous process of system tuning. This typically involves multiple phases of instrumentation and hand-optimization.

In this chapter we present an automated methodology to assist programmers in this process. Our approach consists of two interrelated factors: a programming language and compiler transformations. The real-time programming language, called TCEL (Time-Constrained Event Language), contains high-level timing constructs and semantics based on time-constrained relationships between observable events. As the only timing constraints are imposed by observable events, the unobservable code can be transformed to assist automatically in the low-level tuning process. As we show in this chapter, it is precisely the TCEL semantics which makes the compiler transformations possible.

**The TCEL Language.**     TCEL contains constructs quite similar to those developed in other experimental languages [13, 16, 18, 20, 23, 31]. In these approaches, however, timing constraints are established between *blocks of code*. The TCEL semantics, on the other hand, establishes constraints between the *observable events* within the code.

For example, consider a construct such as "**every** 10 ms **do** B," where the block of code "B" is executed once every 10 milliseconds. In a code-based semantics, *all* of the code in B must fit properly within each 10-ms time frame. In the TCEL event-based semantics, *only the observable events* in B must fit properly within the time frame. This looser semantics yields two immediate benefits. First, the decoupling of timing constraints from code blocks enables a more straightforward implementation of an event-based specification. But more importantly, the unobservable code can be moved to tune the program automatically to its hardware environment.

In the sequel we consider all "**send**" and "**receive**" operations to be observable. As an example, the following is a fragment of a periodic TCEL program. During each period, sensor data is read in, a new system state is updated, and an actuator command is determined, after which it is sent to the actuator.

```
A1:  every 25 ms
       {
A2:      receive(Sensor, &data);
A3:      state = nextState(state, data);
A4:      cmd = nextCmd(state, data);
A5:      send(Actuator, cmd);
       }
```

The system's only observable events are triggered instantaneously during execution of the "**send**" and "**receive**" operations. The "**every**" statement establishes timing constraints *only* between these two operations. On the other hand, the local statements A3 and A4 are simply constrained by the program's natural control and data dependencies.

Under a code-based semantics the program is interpreted in a different way; that is, statements A2–A5 must be executed within a single frame. This interpretation is in fact *much* stronger than the requirements mandate, and indeed, may result in an unnecessary fault. For example, if the system experiences a transient overload caused by higher-priority tasks, the program may not meet its deadline.

In this case there are obvious remedies, which *would have to be performed by hand*. For example, part or all of the next-state update in A3 could be relocated beyond A5. Then, in the case of transient overload, this operation could be postponed beyond the end of the period. However, the necessary corrections would include manually decomposing A4, moving part of it, and adding necessary hooks for the scheduler to postpone a deadline. The actual changes would depend heavily on the particular characteristics of the computer, and thus the very reason for using high-level timing constructs would be defeated.

The event-based semantics provides a solid foundation for a compiler to tune the system automatically. Returning to our example, a transformation can be used to decompose A3 automatically. Yet another transformation can relocate as much (or as little) code as is necessary to tolerate single-period overloads. In performing these transformations, the TCEL compiler uses the observable events as "semantic markers," which establish boundaries of code decomposition, and constrain the places where code can be moved.

**Contents of This Chapter.**   This chapter summarizes our recent results in program transformations for real-time applications (for a more comprehensive treatment, see [9] and [11]). In Section 15.2 we present an overview of the TCEL language, stressing mainly the event-based semantics.

Then, in Section 15.3 we show how we use code-motion optimizations to resolve conflicts within single tasks. These conflicts can arise when tasks have nested constraints; e.g., when deadlines are tighter than periods, or when there are inserted delay statements. Since these timing constraints may conflict with the task's execution time, it may appear to be inherently unschedulable. Hence the objective is to achieve "internal" consistency automatically between real-time requirements and elapsed execution time. Our approach is to use instruction-scheduling techniques [7], with which our compiler moves code from blocks constrained by tight deadlines into blocks with sufficient slack.

In Section 15.4 we address a more aggressive goal—inter-task transformations for schedulability. To accomplish this we apply the technique of *program slicing* [24, 29, 30], in which a single task is split into multiple threads, based on the application's real-time requirements. This method is particularly amenable to control-domain programs running under rate-monotonic scheduling [21]. Using this method, our algorithm converts an unschedulable task set into a schedulable one, by isolating the time-critical threads from each control task, and ensuring that they can be scheduled. In particular, this technique is a *safe, automatic* way to apply deadline postponement [26] to the unobservable threads.

We conclude in Section 15.5 with a discussion on the practical implications of our work.

## 15.2   Overview of TCEL

In this section we present two of TCEL's constructs to denote timing constraints within a program. Both constructs are syntactic descendants of the *temporal scope*,

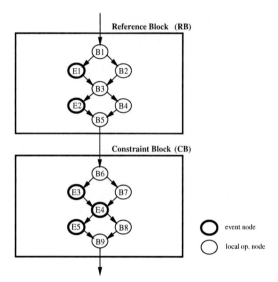

**Figure 15.1** Typical Flow Graph

introduced in [18]. However, as we have stated, our semantics is quite different, in that it relies on constrained relationships between observable events.

We use the "**do**" construct to denote a sporadic program with relative timing constraints:

> **do**
>     ⟨reference block⟩
> [**start after** $t_{min}$] [**start before** $t_{max1}$] [**finish within** $t_{max2}$]
>     ⟨constraint block⟩

The reference block (RB) and the constraint block (CB) are simply C statements, or alternatively, timing constructs themselves. The "**do**" construct induces the following timing constraints:

- **start after** $t_{min}$: There is a minimum delay of $t_{min}$ between the last event executed in the RB, and the first event executed in the CB.

- **start before** $t_{max1}$: There is a maximum delay of $t_{max1}$ between the last event executed in the RB, and the first event executed in the CB.

- **finish within** $t_{max2}$: There is a maximum delay of $t_{max2}$ between the last event executed in the RB, and the last event executed in the CB.

Since either block may contain conditionals, depending on the program's state there may be several such events executed either "first" or "last." For example, consider the fragment from a typical flow graph in Figure 15.1.

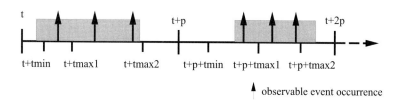

**Figure 15.2**  Behavior of Periodic Timing Construct

Depending on the path taken, the last event executed in the reference block may be either E1 or E2. Similarly, the first event in the constraint block will be E3 or E4, while the last event will be either E4 or E5. To denote such possibilities, we introduce two mappings, *First* and *Last*, from code blocks to sets of events. That is, $Last(RB) = \{E1, E2\}$, $First(CB) = \{E3, E4\}$, and $Last(CB) = \{E4, E5\}$. Thus, the "**do**" construct introduces two potential constraints between an executed event from *Last*(RB) and another from *First*(CB), as well as one constraint between two events from *Last*(RB) and *Last*(CB) each.

The second real-time construct denotes a statement with cyclic behavior of a positive periodicity:

> **every** $p$ [**while** ⟨condition⟩ ]
> [**start after** $t_{min}$] [**start before** $t_{max1}$] [**finish within** $t_{max2}$]
> ⟨constraint block⟩

As long as the "**while**" condition is true, the observable events in the constraint block execute every $p$ time units. Akin to an untimed **while**-loop, when the condition evaluates to false, the statement terminates. In its real-time behavior, the interpretation of the "**every**" construct is similar to that of "**do**." For example, assume that the statement is first scheduled at time $t$, and that the "**while**" condition is true for periods 0 through $i$. As depicted in Figure 15.2, the following constraints on events are induced for period $i$:

- **start after** $t_{min}$: The first event executed in the CB occurs after $t + ip + t_{min}$.
- **start before** $t_{max1}$: The first event executed in the CB occurs before $t + ip + t_{max1}$.
- **finish within** $t_{max2}$: The last event executed in the CB occurs before $t + ip + t_{max2}$.

As we have stated, timing constraints may be arbitrarily nested. For example, consider the two-arm robot control program in Figure 15.3, which monitors a conveyer belt and gives commands to the robot's arms. The specification is as follows:

(1) Every 10 ms, a position-sensor sends a message to the controller.

```
every 10 ms finish within 8 ms
  do
    {
    receive(Sensor, &dim);
    msg_cnt++;
    }
  start after 1.5 ms finish within 4 ms
    {
    if (!null(dim))
      {
      z1 = convert(dim, loc1);
      z2 = convert(dim, loc2);
      send(arm1, z1);
      send(arm2, z2);
      }
    }
```

**Figure 15.3**  Source Code for Robot Controller

(2) Each message contains the dimensions of an object currently approaching the robot. If no object is approaching, the message is tagged as "null."

(3) To achieve steady state, the controller delays at least 1.5 ms after receiving the message.

(4) If an object was detected, new commands are sent to arm1 and arm2.

(5) Both commands must be sent within 4.0 ms of receiving the sensor's message, and within 8.0 ms of the beginning of the period.

# 15.3  Transformation 1: Consistent Task Synthesis

While an event-based semantics makes sense at the source-program level, most real-time schedulers only accept timing constraints on the start and finish times of *tasks*. Thus, the role of the compiler is to transform event-driven source programs into constrained blocks of code. The challenge is to achieve a task set which is *feasible*, i.e., whose tasks have execution times consistent with the timing constraints.

This is done in the following three steps. First, a timing construct is decomposed into several *sections*, denoted by its control flow structure (Section 15.3.1). Next, code-based timing constraints are derived from the construct's event-based timing constraints (Section 15.3.2), and checked for their consistency with the exe-

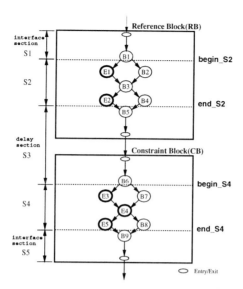

**Figure 15.4** The Flow Graph of a Timing Construct and Its Section Division

cution time. Finally, code-scheduling transformations are used to reduce the worst-case execution time of the infeasible sections (Section 15.3.3).

## 15.3.1    Section Generation

A timing construct is divided into five code sections, as portrayed in Figure 15.4. As can be seen, the reference block is decomposed into three sub-blocks. The unobservable code before the first observable statement becomes an interface section (S1). The code containing the observable statements becomes the reference section (S2). The unobservable code after the observable statements becomes the first part of the delay section (S3). Consequently, the topmost unobservable code of the constraint block becomes the second part of S3, and so on.

Recall the discussion of the *First* and *Last* functions in Section 15.2. Since a code block may contain complicated control structures, we require a convenient means of defining the boundaries of S2 and S4—the sections that contain observable events. We accomplish this by inserting "markers" in the flow graph, which consume no time and are not visible. The following marker definitions guarantee that there are unique boundaries into and out of the sections containing observable events.

- begin_S2: This marker is inserted directly after the unobservable instruction most closely dominating $Last(\text{RB}) \cup \{exit(\text{RB})\}$.

- end_S2: This marker is inserted directly before the unobservable instruction most closely post-dominating $Last(\text{RB}) \cup \{entry(\text{RB})\}$.

- begin_S4: This marker is inserted directly after the unobservable instruction most closely dominating $First(\text{CB}) \cup \{exit(\text{CB})\}$.

```
S6:   (S6.start[p]≥p×10ms,
          S6.finish[p]≤p×10ms+8ms)
S1:   { /* null */ }
S2:   { receive(Sensor, &dim); }              [0.40 ms]
S3:   {
          msg_cnt++;                           [0.02 ms]
          c = !null(dim);                      [0.20 ms]
      }
S4:   (S4.start≥S2.finish+1.5ms,
          S4.finish≤S2.finish+3.6ms)
      {
          if (c) {                             [0.02 ms]
              z1 = convert(dim, loc1);         [1.00 ms]
              z2 = convert(dim, loc2);         [1.00 ms]
              send(arm1, z1);                  [0.40 ms]
              send(arm2, z2);                  [0.40 ms]
          }
      }
S5:   { /* null */ }
      }
```

**Figure 15.5** Robot Program—After Section Generation.

- end_S4: This marker is inserted directly before the unobservable instruction most closely post-dominating $Last(CB) \cup \{entry(CB)\}$.

For example, consider the constraint block in Figure 15.4. The unobservable node B9 post-dominates $Last(CB)$ and the entry node. Thus, its logical place is in the interface section S5, which is not subject to the construct's timing constraints—Hence the need for the marker end_S4, which is the unique exit point for the constrained section S4.

Now, let the variable S2.start correspond to the actual time that the marker begin_S2 is "executed" (that is, the dispatch time of section S2), and let S2.finish correspond to the time that the section ends. Similarly, let S4.start and S4.finish represent the start and finish times of section S4. Using these variables we can represent the section decomposition of a TCEL construct in a manner similar to that found in the Flex language [15].

Recall the robot controller program from Figure 15.3. Figure 15.5 illustrates its constituent sections, where the bracketed numbers are the maximum execution times for each instruction on the given CPU. These times are generated by a timing analysis tool, such as those found in [5, 10, 25, 27, 32]. The constraint-expression for S6 corresponds to the program's outer, periodic loop.

## 15.3.2    Deriving Code-Based Timing Constraints

As seen in Figure 15.5, the code-based timing constraints can be expressed as conjunctions of linear inequalities between start times and finish times of different sections. However, note the difference between the code-based constraints and the TCEL source-level constraints: In Figure 15.3 the "**finish within**" deadline is 4 ms, while in Figure 15.5 it is tightened to 3.6 ms. There is good reason for this—the new code-based timing constraints must be strong enough to guarantee the original semantics of the event-based constraints. That is, they must take into account the program's execution-time characteristics. In general, consider a TCEL construct such as

**do RB  start after** $t_{min}$  **start before** $t_{max1}$  **finish within** $t_{max2}$  **CB**

Obviously, the TCEL parameters are not tight enough to guarantee the correctness of the code-based constraints. For example, if we wish to maintain the "$t_{max1}$" requirement, it is not sufficient simply to mandate that S4 start within a maximum delay of $t_{max1}$ after S2 ends (though this is certainly necessary). We can see in Figure 15.4 that the event actually *executed* in *Last*(S2) may be E1, while the event executed in *First*(S4) may be E4. Thus the naive strategy fails to factor in the execution times of B3 and B4.

However, the event-based semantics is clear: the time between the *executed* event in *Last*(S2) and the *executed* event in *First*(S4) is at most $t_{max1}$. To guarantee that this occurs, we must account for *all* possible execution scenarios. Specifically, we must tighten the constraints, allowing for the maximum amount of time between an event in *Last*(S2) and end_S2, as well as the maximum amount of execution time between begin_S4 and an event in *First*(S4). We must similarly adjust $t_{max2}$. To do this, we make the following definitions:

- $\Delta_{S2} \overset{\text{def}}{=} max\{wt(p) \mid e \in Last(S2),\ e \Rightarrow_+^p end\_S2\}.$

- $\Delta_{S4} \overset{\text{def}}{=} max\{wt(p) \mid e \in First(S4),\ begin\_S4 \Rightarrow_+^p e\}.$

where

- For nodes $n1$ and $n2$ in the flow graph, $n1 \Rightarrow_+^p n2$ means that there is a non-null path from $n1$ to $n2$.
- For a fragment of code $c$, $wt(c)$ is the worst-case execution time of $c$.

Note that $\Delta_{S2}$ and $\Delta_{S4}$ are sensitive not only to code's execution time characteristics, but also changes made to some paths between events and markers during program translation. For example, changes to paths between end_S2 and a node in *Last*(S2) might require re-evaluation of $\Delta_{S2}$.

Now the code-based timing constraints can be postulated as follows:

| (1) | S4.start | $\geq$ | S2.finish $+ T_{min}$ | (where $T_{min} = t_{min}$) |
|---|---|---|---|---|
| (2) | S4.start | $\leq$ | S2.finish $+ T_{max1}$ | (where $T_{max1} = t_{max1} - \Delta_{S2} - \Delta_{S4}$) |
| (3) | S4.finish | $\leq$ | S2.finish $+ T_{max2}$ | (where $T_{max2} = t_{max2} - \Delta_{S2}$) |

**Table 15.1   Timing Constraints of S3 and S4**

| Section | Duration Constraint $(DUR(S))$ |
|---------|--------------------------------|
| S3 | $min\{T_{max1}, T_{max2} - wt(S4)\}$ |
| S4 | $T_{max2} - T_{min}$ |

These timing constraints are strong enough to guarantee the original event-based timing constraints. (By convention, if the "**start after**" constraint is omitted, we consider $t_{min}$ to be 0. Similarly, when either the "**start before**" or "**finish within**" constraints are missing, we consider $t_{max1} = \infty$ or $t_{max2} = \infty$, respectively.) Returning to Figure 15.5, we can see that equation (3) indeed mandates tightening the original 4 ms to 3.6 ms.

Now we wish to determine when (1)–(3) can be met. That is, what do these equations imply about the program's allowable worst-case execution-time behavior? This can easily be derived if we add precedence constraints reflecting the natural flow of the program; i.e., that S4 executes after S3, which executes after S2:

$$\text{(4)} \qquad \text{S2.finish} + wt(\text{S3}) \;\leq\; \text{S4.start}$$
$$\text{(5)} \qquad \text{S4.start} + wt(\text{S4}) \;\leq\; \text{S4.finish}$$

Eliminating S2.finish, S4.start, and S4.finish from (1)–(5), we end up with:

$$\text{(a)} \qquad\qquad\qquad T_{min} \;\leq\; T_{max1}$$
$$\text{(b)} \qquad\qquad\quad\; wt(\text{S3}) \;\leq\; T_{max1}$$
$$\text{(c)} \qquad wt(\text{S3}) + wt(\text{S4}) \;\leq\; T_{max2}$$
$$\text{(d)} \qquad\qquad\quad\; wt(\text{S4}) \;\leq\; T_{max2} - T_{min}$$

Obviously, (a) had better be true in order for the TCEL construct to make any sense. For the purposes of our algorithm we combine (b) and (c), yielding the following two constraints on execution times:

$$\text{(*)} \qquad wt(\text{S3}) \;\leq\; min\{T_{max1}, T_{max2} - wt(\text{S4})\}$$
$$\text{(**)} \qquad wt(\text{S4}) \;\leq\; T_{max2} - T_{min}$$

These are the necessary and sufficient conditions to achieve feasibility, and they are summarized in Table 15.1. In the next subsection we discuss our code-scheduling techniques to handle the cases in which one of these conditions fails to hold.

## 15.3.3   Code Scheduling

The final step is to rearrange instructions across sections in such a way that all the sections satisfy their derived timing constraints. Such a process is similar to that of *code scheduling*, which is a well-defined problem for automatic fine-grain (instruction level) parallelization for superscalar and VLIW processors [1, 4, 7, 8, 22, 28]. However, our problem context has a different goal. In what follows, we sketch a code scheduling algorithm, which moves code from sections that violate their duration constraints into those with more lenient constraints.

```
Algorithm Code_Scheduling(T) /* T is a timing construct */
input: the ordered set of sections {S1, S2, ..., S5} in T
begin
    dur = Tmax2 - Tmin;
    compute t such that wt(t) = max{wt(path) | path in S4};
    while (wt(t) > dur)
        perform Code_Scheduling on t into S3;
        if (t is still critical) then exit("Unable to synthesize.");
        recompute t such that wt(t) = max{wt(path) | path in S4};
    end
    recompute Tmax1; /* to reflect the change in ΔS4. */
    if (wt(S3) ≤ Tmin) then exit("No scheduling needed for S3.");
    else dur = min{Tmax1, Tmax2 - wt(S4)};
    compute t such that wt(t) = max{wt(path) | path in S3};
    while (wt(t) > dur)
        perform Code_Scheduling on t into S1;
        if (t is still critical) then exit("Unable to synthesize.");
        recompute t such that wt(t) = max{wt(path) | path in S3};
    end
end
```

**Figure 15.6**  Code Scheduling Algorithm

*Code scheduling* involves copying or relocating unobservable instructions[1] to new locations, while preserving the functional semantics of the original code. In doing so, we attempt to achieve the following goal:

- Satisfy $wt(Si) \leq DUR(Si)$ for $i = 3, 4$.

The algorithm is greedy, and it attempts to attain the desired consistency of a timing construct in a section-by-section manner. It inspects sections S4 and S3 (in reverse topological order), checking if they satisfy their duration constraints. If S4 violates its duration constraint, the algorithm attempts to reduce its surplus execution time by moving instructions to section S3. In turn, it processes section S3, which may now contain newly moved code.

To actually perform greedy code motion, we have adapted the approach to trace scheduling in [7], and we use it as a component of the code scheduling algorithm (consult [11] for more details). Instructions lying on paths that exceed their section's duration constraints are considered for code motion. We distinguish such paths as *critical traces*. Formally, the critical trace $t$ of section S is defined as a path from $entry(S)$ to $exit(S)$ such that $wt(t) > DUR(S)$.

---

[1] We conservatively prohibit event-generating instructions from being moved, so that the timing relationships between events are preserved.

```
S6:  (S6.start[p]≥p×10ms, S6.finish[p]≤p×10ms+8ms)
     {
S1:     { /* null */ }
S2:     { receive(Sensor, &dim); }
S3:     {
           msg_cnt++;
           c = !null(dim);
           if (c) z1 = convert(dim, loc1);

        }
S4:     (S4.start≥S2.finish+1.5ms, S4.finish≤S2.finish+3.6ms)
        {
           if (c) {
              z2 = convert(dim, loc2);
              send(arm1, z1);
              send(arm2, z2);
           }

        }
S5:     { /* null */ }
     }
```

**Figure 15.7**  Robot Program: After Code Scheduling

Figure 15.6 sketches the algorithm. Note that $T_{max1}$ is recomputed after scheduling S4 and before scheduling S3. This is mandatory, since $\Delta_{S4}$ may be changed during the scheduling. Also observe that the code of S3 is moved into S1, while that of S4 is moved into S3. We disallow code from moving into S2 because it could potentially change the value of $\Delta_{S2}$, which would, in turn, invalidate our assumptions about $DUR(S4)$. In order to complete the procedure in a single pass, we assume that $\Delta_{S2}$ remains constant. In reality this restriction does not seriously limit the approach: from our experience, events in the RB typically lie in straight-line code (and thus S2 contains a single instruction).

Figure 15.7 illustrates the code scheduling process for our robot example. The duration constraint for section S4 is violated, since its predicted worst-case execution is 2.82 ms. However, S4 is allowed only 2.1 ms to execute its body.[2] Figure 15.7 yields the result of code scheduling: an assignment is moved into S3, and the test guarding it is copied. Now the implementation satisfies the necessary condition for feasibility, since the body of S3 requires at most 1.82 ms. In addition to such an instant benefit, the transformation converts the possibly wasteful delay into useful computation time, since the new code in S3 can be scheduled within the delay interval between S2 and S4.

---

[2]$2.1 \text{ ms} = \text{S4.finish} - \text{S4.start} = (\text{S2.finish} + 3.6 \text{ ms}) - (\text{S2.finish} + 1.5 \text{ ms})$

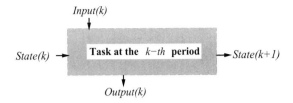

**Figure 15.8**  Task Behavior at $k$th Period

# 15.4    Transformation 2: Real-Time Schedulability

The event-based semantics of TCEL gives a clear separation between constraints based on time, and those based on data and control dependencies. In this section we present another useful application of this semantics; namely, an automated tuning tool for enhancing the schedulability of (purely) periodic task sets. Thus we are concerned with a subset of TCEL, i.e., tasks written only using the **every** construct.

Our approach is as follows: whenever a task set is found unschedulable, we identify the tasks that miss their deadlines. Each of these tasks gets split into two threads—one containing its observable events, and the other containing its unobservable instructions. While the former thread must finish by the original deadline, the latter is allowed to "slide" into the next frame. Thus the transformation effectively increases the original task's deadline, while maintaining its semantics.

This approach is particularly appropriate for programs that drive guidance, navigation, and control (GN&C) applications [17]. First, GN&C programs typically possess periodic behavior; thus they are amenable to fixed-priority, rate-driven scheduling. Second, these programs possess structure resembling that displayed in Figure 15.8: During each period, physical world measurements are sampled, a current global state is updated, and actuator commands are computed, which are then sent to a set of actuators.

Since the events (i.e., inputs and outputs) are clearly identifiable here, this type of process easily lends itself to aggressive code transformations, assuming the underlying the semantics of TCEL.

## 15.4.1    Rate-Monotonic Schedulability Analysis

Rate-monotonic scheduling is well-suited for control domain applications, not only because they possess the periodic behavior, but also because efficient schedulability tests can be applied. One of these is the exact (necessary and sufficient) test presented in [19], which is based on *critical instant* analysis.

To review, a task's critical instant occurs whenever it is initiated simultaneously with all higher-priority tasks [21]. Let $T_i$ and $C_i$ be the period and the worst-case computation time of task $\tau_i$, respectively, and assume that the $\tau_i$'s are numbered in the increasing order of their $T_i$'s. Since the rate-monotonic scheduling algorithm assigns a higher priority to a task with a smaller period, a task with a smaller number has a higher priority.

To determine if task $\tau_k$ can meet its deadline under the worst-case phasing, it is necessary to check if there is point $t$ in time in the interval $[0, T_k]$ (i.e., $\tau_k$'s critical interval), which satisfies the following inequality:

$$\sum_{i=1}^{k} \frac{C_i \lceil \frac{t}{T_i} \rceil}{t} \leq 1.$$

To do so, we need only check those points in the interval $[0, T_k]$ which are multiples of the periods of $k$ tasks $\{\tau_1, \tau_2, \ldots, \tau_k\}$. They are called *scheduling points*, and become points where the left-hand side of the above inequality achieves the local minima.

**Example 15.4.1** Consider the case of three periodic tasks, where the source code of task $\tau_3$ is given in Figure 15.9.

| Task | Execution Time | Period |
|------|----------------|--------|
| $\tau_1$ | $C_1 = 4.00$ | $T_1 = 10$ |
| $\tau_2$ | $C_2 = 4.00$ | $T_2 = 16$ |
| $\tau_3$ | $C_3 = 6.41$ | $T_3 = 25$ |

We can carry out the exact schedulability test for these tasks as follows:

| For $\tau_1$: | | $C_1$ | $=$ | $4.00$ | $<$ | $T_1 = 10$ |
|---|---|---|---|---|---|---|
| For $\tau_2$: | | $C_1 + C_2$ | $=$ | $8.00$ | $<$ | $T_1 = 10$ |
| For $\tau_3$: | $C_1 + C_2 + C_3$ | $=$ | $14.41$ | $>$ | $T_1 = 10$ |
| | $2C_1 + C_2 + C_3$ | $=$ | $18.41$ | $>$ | $T_2 = 16$ |
| | $2C_1 + 2C_2 + C_3$ | $=$ | $22.41$ | $>$ | $2T_1 = 20$ |
| | $3C_1 + 2C_2 + C_3$ | $=$ | $26.41$ | $>$ | $T_3 = 25$ |

That is, tasks $\tau_1$ and $\tau_2$ are schedulable, since they can both complete before their (shared) scheduling point $T_1$. However, the entire task set is not schedulable, because the total utilization factor exceeds 1 at all scheduling points within the critical interval of $\tau_3$.

## 15.4.2 Transformation Approach

A straightforward technique to achieve schedulability is to let some of $\tau_3$'s code "slide" into the next period. This can be done by postponing the deadline of $\tau_3$ (as suggested by Sha et al. in [26]). However, since $\tau_3$ contains critical IO operations, this technique is not always safe with respect to the event-based semantics. In this section we show how to transform the task so that the original semantics is preserved. The high-level approach is as follows:

- Given an unschedulable task $\tau$ with period $T$, decompose it into

    (1) $\tau_a$, a subtask containing all of $\tau$'s observable operations.

```
         every 25 ms
            {
L1:         receive(Sensor, &data);      [0.50 ms]
L2:         if (!null(data))             [0.06 ms]
              {
L3:             t1 = F1(state);          [1.05 ms]
L4:             t2 = F2(state);          [1.35 ms]
L5:             t3 = F3(data);           [1.35 ms]
L6:             t4 = F4(data);           [1.35 ms]
L7:             cmd = t1 * ( t3 + t4 );  [0.10 ms]
L8:             send(Actuator, cmd);     [0.50 ms]
L9:             state = t1 * ( t2 + t3 );[0.15 ms]
              }
L10:        }
```

**Figure 15.9**  TCEL Program for Task $\tau_3$

(2) $\tau_b$, a subtask containing the remaining operations.

- Ensure that $\tau_a$ followed by $\tau_b$ exhibits the same functionality of the $\tau$.

- $\tau_a$ keeps $\tau$'s original period $T$, so that the IO operations execute within their deadline.

- Two iterations of $\tau_b$ must execute within a period of $2T$.

- The precedence constraints between $\tau_a$ and $\tau_b$ must be maintained; i.e., the execution behavior will be:

$$\tau_a \to \tau_b \to \tau_a \to \tau_b \to \cdots$$

The net result is as follows: within a 2T time interval, the first iteration of $\tau_b$ can miss the original deadline. The run-time behavior is portrayed in Figure 15.10. The original task fails to tolerate single-frame overloads; i.e., its IO operations occur after the deadline (time $T$). However, the transformed task only executes internal operations after $T$, which preserves the event-based semantics.

**Automatic Task Decomposition by Program Slicing.**    Straightforward as it may look, this decomposition can in reality be a very complex compiler problem. Many factors make this the case, among which are intertwined threads of control, nested control structures, complex data dependencies between statements, procedure calls in the task code, and so on. To cope with these problems in a systematic manner, we harness a novel application of *program slicing* [24, 29, 30].

Briefly stated, a *slice* of program $P$ with respect to program point $p$ and variable $v$ consists of $P$'s statements and control predicates that may affect the value of $v$ at point $p$. To help carry out our slicing approach we use a *program*

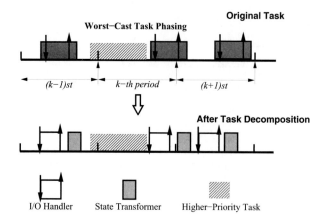

**Figure 15.10**  Scheduling of Newly Constructed Tasks

*dependence graph* [6, 12, 24], whose vertices represent a program's instructions, and whose edges represents control, data, and loop-carried dependencies between them. For example, the program dependence graph corresponding to our controller program $\tau_3$ is shown in Figure 15.11. Note that loop-carried dependencies caused by "state" exist in the program dependence graph, even if there is no inner loop in the program: they derive from a loop-like nature of periodic tasks. We use the notation "$p \Rightarrow_* q$" to mean that node $p$ can reach node $q$ via zero or more control dependence edges or data dependence edges.

The slice of program $P$ with respect to program point $p$ and variable $v$—denoted as $P/\langle p, v \rangle$—can be obtained through a traversal of $P$'s program dependence graph. A simple algorithm to compute the slice is given below.

**Algorithm 15.4.1**  *Compute the slice $P/\langle p, v \rangle$:*

   **Step 1** Compute reaching definitions $RD(p, v)$ such that for any vertex $n \in RD(p, v)$, the statement $n$ defines variable $v$, and control can reach $p$ from $n$ via an execution path along which there is no redefinition of $v$.

   **Step 2** Compute the slice by a backward traversal of the program dependence graph such that

$$P/\langle p, v \rangle = \{m \mid \exists n \in RD(p, v) \; : \; m \Rightarrow_* n\}. \qquad \square$$

The definition of the program slice can be extended for a set of slicing criteria $C$ in such a way that $P/C = \bigcup_{\langle p,v \rangle \in C} P/\langle p, v \rangle$.

Using the algorithm above, we can compute the subtasks $\tau_a$ and $\tau_b$ as follows:

**Algorithm 15.4.2**  *Decompose task $\tau$ into $\tau_a$ and $\tau_b$:*

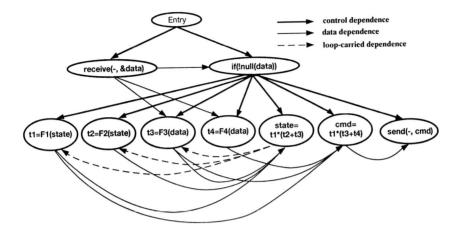

**Figure 15.11**  Program Dependence Graph for $\tau_3$

**Step 1** Compute the slice $\tau/IO$, where

$$IO = \{\langle o, var(o)\rangle \,|\, o \text{ is observable and } var(o) \text{ is a variable used in } o\}.$$

**Step 2** Compute the slice $\tau/ST$, where

$$ST = \{\langle eot, s\rangle \,|\, s \text{ is a state variable}\}$$

where $eot$ is considered a point at the end of the task, and where a state variable is any variable which causes a periodic loop-carried dependence.

**Step 3** Delete from $\tau/ST$ all non-conditional statements common to both of the slices. The remaining code becomes $\tau_b$.                                                    □

Using our original program dependence graph in Figure 15.11, the result of **Step 1** is depicted in Figure 15.12 (top), while the result of **Step 2** is depicted in Figure 15.12 (bottom). Returning to our task $\tau_3$ in Figure 15.9, we see that L1, L3, L5, L6, and L8 are included in the IO-slice. Also, the predicate on line L2 is included, since the execution of L3, L5, L6, and L8 depend on its outcome. Similarly, L1, L2, L3, L4, L5, and L9 are included in the State-update slice. Then, by **Step 3**, common statements L1, L3, and L5 are deleted from it (but not L2!).

The textual results of these operations can be seen in Figure 15.13, where the total times for each subtask are:

$$C_{3a} = 4.93 \text{ ms}, \quad C_{3b} = 1.52 \text{ ms}.$$

## 15.4.3   Scheduling and Analysis

We can now sketch a high-level procedure that uses Algorithm 15.4.2 to transform an unschedulable task set into a schedulable one. The input is a set of $n$ tasks

$$\Gamma = \{\tau_1, \tau_2, \ldots, \tau_n\}$$

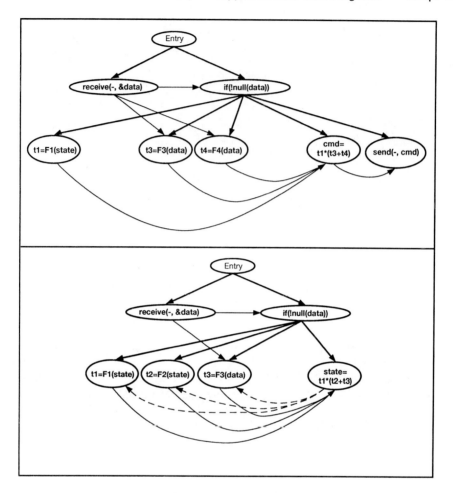

**Figure 15.12** IO-Handling Slice (Top) and State-Update Slice (Bottom)

which are processed in decreasing order, from $\tau_n$ to $\tau_1$. If the task set is found to be unschedulable, Algorithm 15.4.2 is invoked to slice $\tau_n$ into its two constituent threads, which then replace $\tau_n$ in $\Gamma$. If the updated set is still deemed unschedulable, the procedure goes to work on $\tau_{n-1}$, and so on.

In [9] we present a detailed alternative to this approach, in which tasks are processed from $\tau_1$ to $\tau_n$; i.e., the first task found unschedulable is selected for slicing. One can imagine other alternatives as well.

However, any such scheme is critically dependent on two elements:

(1) A scheduling policy that can exploit our task model; i.e., while the $\tau_b$ threads can miss their original deadlines, the precedence constraints between instances $\tau_a$ and $\tau_b$ must be maintained.

(2) An off-line schedulability analyzer for the given scheduling policy.

| /* Subtask $\tau_{3a}$ */ | | /* Subtask $\tau_{3b}$ */ | |
|---|---|---|---|
| { | | { | |
| **receive**(Sensor, &data); | [0.50 ms] | if (c) | [0.02 ms] |
| c = !null(data); | [0.06 ms] | { | |
| if (c) | [0.02 ms] | t2 = F2(state); | [1.35 ms] |
| { | | state = t1 * ( t2 + t3 ); | [0.15 ms] |
| t1 = F1(state); | [1.05 ms] | } | |
| t3 = F3(data); | [1.35 ms] | } | |
| t4 = F4(data); | [1.35 ms] | | |
| cmd = t1 * ( t3 + t4 ); | [0.10 ms] | | |
| **send**(Actuator, cmd); | [0.50 ms] | | |
| } | | | |
| } | | | |

**Figure 15.13**  Two Decomposed Subtasks

There are several methods that can be used to address (1) and (2), each of which has its relative strengths and weaknesses. In this section we outline three such approaches which are useful for many applications, and also fairly simple to implement.

**Method 1 (Slicing the lowest-priority task):**  We include this method to show that in many cases the scheduler need not be altered at all. Indeed, when only the lowest-priority task is sliced—as in our example—the original rate-monotonic priority assignment may still be used. We illustrate this by returning to the example.

*On-line Scheduler:* Now that $\tau_3$'s two subthreads have been isolated, they are "glued" back into a single task $\tau_3'$ by way of sequential composition:

$$\tau_3' = \tau_{3a}; \tau_{3b}$$

The new task $\tau_3'$ is still initiated every $T_3$ time units, and remains at the lowest priority. However, if iteration $k$ has not completed when the new period $k+1$ starts, the new instance waits for the old one to finish.

*Off-line Analyzer:* There is a simple method to determine whether the transformed task set is schedulable under this policy. First, since the higher-priority tasks remain unaltered, their schedulability can be determined using the "critical-instant" approach outlined in Example 15.4.1. As for the entire application, consider the newly constructed tasks in our example:

| Task | Execution Time | | Period |
|---|---|---|---|
| $\tau_1$ | $C_1 = 4.00$ | | $T_1 = 10$ |
| $\tau_2$ | $C_2 = 4.00$ | | $T_2 = 16$ |
| $\tau_3'$ | 4.93 | for $\tau_{3a}$ | $T_3 = 25$ |
| | + 1.52 | for $\tau_{3b}$ | |
| | $C_3' = 6.45$ | | |

In establishing schedulability, it is sufficient to check whether the following two conditions hold:

(1)  whether $\tau_{3a}$ can always run within time $T_3$, and

(2)  whether two successive instances of $\tau_3'$ can run within time $2T_3$.

An easy argument shows that this test is sound. Recall that task $\tau_3'$ is invoked at times $0$, $T_3$, $2T_3$, and so on. Let period $i$ be the first in which $\tau_{3b}$ slides past its deadline. By condition (1), the $i$th instance of $\tau_{3a}$ finishes by time $(i + 1)T_3$, and by condition (2) the $(i + 1)$st instance of $\tau_3'$ finishes by time $(i + 2)T_3$. Thus task $\tau_{3a}$ finishes by time $(i + 2)T_3$ as well, which preserves the TCEL semantics.

Returning to our example, we can verify conditions (1) and (2) by again making use of the critical-instant analysis. For condition (1), we "pretend" that $\tau_{3a}$ is autonomously invoked with a period of $T_3$, and show that it is schedulable with respect to tasks $\tau_1$ and $\tau_2$. Then, for (2), we assume another "imaginary" task $\tau_3'; \tau_3'$—with period $2T_3$ and cost $2C_3'$—and show that it too is schedulable with $\tau_1$ and $\tau_2$.

| | | | | | |
|---|---|---|---|---|---|
| For $\tau_{3a}$: | $3C_1 + 2C_2 + C_{3a}$ | $=$ | $20.93$ | $< \quad 25 \quad =$ | $T_3$ |
| For $\tau_3'; \tau_3'$: | $5C_1 + 3C_2 + 2C_3'$ | $=$ | $44.90$ | $< \quad 48 \quad =$ | $3T_2$ |

Thus both conditions (1) and (2) hold. Note that this procedure yields a *sufficiency* test for schedulability, and not a necessary one. For example, the scheduler could, in fact, force *every* instance of $\tau_{3b}$ to miss its deadline. As long as $\tau_{3a}$ is always completed within the deadline, the TCEL semantics is maintained.

**Method 2 (Slicing any number of tasks):**   Method 1 is clearly insufficient to dispatch several sliced tasks, each of which may have a different period. However, it can be generalized by slightly modifying the dispatching scheme. Briefly stated, when a task $\tau$ is sliced, it now receives *two* priorities: $p_h$, which is inversely proportional to its original period $T$, and $p_l$, which is inversely proportional to a period of $2T$. We briefly sketch the method below (details can be found in [9]).

*On-line Scheduler:* Again, when a task $\tau$ is sliced, the two subthreads $\tau_a$ and $\tau_b$ are "glued" back into a single task "$\tau' = \tau_a; \tau_b$," where we let $C_a$ and $C_b$ denote the worst-case execution times of $\tau_a$ and $\tau_b$, respectively. The scheduler uses a countdown timer for $\tau'$ to ensure that within any time frame $[i \cdot T, (i + 1) \cdot T]$, the first $C_a$ units of execution time of $\tau'$ are run at priority $p_h$, with any remaining time in the frame run at priority $p_l$. Note that since $\tau_b$ may have "slid" beyond time $i \cdot T$, it may be the case that part of $\tau_b$ runs at priority $p_h$, while part of $\tau_a$ runs at priority $p_l$.

The algorithm works as follows: task $\tau'$ is initiated at time 0 with priority $p_h$, and its countdown time is set to $C_a$. The timer decrements whenever $\tau'$ runs at priority $p_h$; when $\tau'$ gets preempted, it is temporarily stopped. When the timer expires, $\tau'$ gets demoted to priority $p_l$. Note that this will always occur before time $T$ if the IO-handler is to complete by its deadline.

As in Method 1, at time $T$ task $\tau'$ is re-invoked, and if the old iteration is not finished, the new one must wait. In either case, task $\tau'$'s priority is immediately reset to $p_h$, and the timer is reset to $C_a$ as well. When the timer expires during the frame [T,2T], the priority is again demoted to $p_l$—*regardless of which iteration is currently running.* Thus, as we stated above, the net result is that during any given frame the task is first run at priority $p_h$ for $C_a$ time, with the remainder of time in the frame run at priority $p_l$.

The implementation of this scheme requires one countdown timer for each sliced task, which can easily be managed by only one programmable hardware timer—a standard component in most systems.

*Off-line Analyzer:* We can subject task $\tau'$ to a simple schedulability test not unlike the one mentioned above. In doing so, we "pretend" that both tasks $\tau_a$ *and* $\tau_b$ are invoked autonomously every $T$ time units, without regard to any precedence constraints. (Thus we pretend that that $\tau_a$ can always preempt $\tau_b$.) The test involves checking the following two conditions:

(1) whether $\tau_a$ can always run within time $T$ at priority $p_h$, and

(2) whether two successive instances of $\tau_b$ can run within time $2T$ at priority $p_l$.

This test—which actually assumes a static-priority, fully preemptive dispatching scheme—is still sufficient for our purposes. After all, condition (1) shows that when any task with cost $C_a$ and priority $p_h$ is released at times 0 and $T$, it will finish by time $T$ and $2T$, respectively. Condition (2) shows that if another task with cost $C_b$ and priority $p_l$ is released at times 0 and and $T$, both instances can finish by time $2T$. Since our on-line scheduler always raises $\tau's$ priority at frame boundaries, and always lowers it after $C_a$ execution time, the test's underlying notion of preemption simulates the behavior of the on-line scheduler.

**Method 3 (A static-priority approach):** Method 2 enjoys a simple analysis test for its dual-priority scheme, which is certainly one of its strengths. Its principal weakness is that the on-line component lacks the simplicity found in pure, static-priority scheduling. For example, recall that Method 1 successfully uses the original rate-monotonic scheduler.

Thus the following question arises: When can a set of transformed TCEL tasks be scheduled under a fully preemptive, static-priority scheme? Burns [2] provides an answer to this question after identifying a simple, but essential fact about the TCEL task model. That is, whenever we let a task's deadline be greater than its period, this represents a relaxation of the classical rate-monotonic restrictions put forth in [21]. Thus the rate-monotonic priority assignment may not be the optimal one; indeed, perhaps another static assignment will result in a feasible schedule when the rate-monotonic ordering fails.

Given a set of transformed TCEL tasks

$$\tau_1' = \tau_{1a}; \tau_{1b}$$
$$\tau_2' = \tau_{2a}; \tau_{2b}$$
$$\vdots$$
$$\tau_n' = \tau_{na}; \tau_{nb}$$

it turns out that the appropriate priority assignment is not only dependent on the periods (as in the pure rate-monotonic model), but also on the respective execution times of each IO-handler and state-update component. In [2] Burns presents a search algorithm to generate the feasible static-priority order—or to detect when no such order exists. Thus the approach includes the following components.

*On-line Scheduler:* This is a simple, preemptive dispatching mechanism, in which priority "ties" are broken in favor of the task dispatched first. Thus, for example, a task's current iteration will finish before the next one starts.

*Off-line Analyzer:* The analyzer is *constructive*, in that it produces a feasible priority assignment if one exists. If no such assignment exists, perhaps Method 2 can be used instead. In fact, we have identified task sets in which Method 2 succeeds and Method 3 fails, as well as other task sets in which Method 3 succeeds and Method 2 fails.

## 15.5   Conclusions

Modern real-time applications are becoming more complex in both their functional and temporal requirements, as well as their scale. At the same time, there is an increasing desire to use off-the-shelf hardware and standardized run-time support, with a concomitant demand for portability and upward compatibility.

These themes should not be surprising, since they also characterize the evolution of computer systems in general. In time-independent domains, however, they are often realized through the use of a high-level language, which serves as an abstraction between a designer's intentions and the low-level operation of the system architecture. Compilers, therefore, are relied on to do much of the dirty work, and to provide a bridge between the program and the platform.

The TCEL paradigm helps incorporate this development into real-time domains. As we have shown, TCEL's event-based semantics constrains only those operations that are critical to real-time operation, i.e., the events denoted in the specification or those derived from it. As such, a source program is an appropriate abstraction of the designer's intentions, and it need not over-burden the system with unnecessary constraints. Moreover, the event-based semantics enables a compiler to transform the program to suit the characteristics of the underlying system.

In this chapter we have presented two such transformation techniques. The first, trace scheduling, helps resolve conflicts that arise when timing constraints are nested, e.g., when deadlines are tighter than periods, or when delay statements are inserted within the code. Our fine-grained synthesis procedure can be a useful tool for eliminating these conflicts. Since this is exactly the type of low-level work that compilers do best, a human programmer's time is probably better spent elsewhere.

The second technique is based on program slicing, and it helps enhance the schedulability of periodic task sets. In this chapter we have concentrated on rate-based scheduling, one of the best understood areas in the real-time literature. However, the tradition has been to consider the "task" as an uninterpreted block of execution time—perhaps with a period, a start time, and a deadline, but no other semantics to speak of. We have shown that once we "open up" the task to consider its event-based semantics, we can automatically convert an unschedulable application into a schedulable one. We believe that our approach can be used as a first-line defense in the tuning process, and is certainly preferable to measures such as hand-optimization or re-implementation in silicon—two of the more common remedies.

# Acknowledgments

This research is supported in part by ONR Grant N00014-94-10228, NSF Grant CCR-9209333, an NSF Young Investigator Award CCR-9357850, and ONR/ARPA Contract N00014-91-C-0195.

# References

[1] A. Aiken and A. Nicolau. A development environment for horizontal microcode. *IEEE Transactions on Software Engineering*, pages 584–594, May 1988.

[2] A. Burns. Fixed priority scheduling with deadlines prior to completion. Technical Report YCS 212 (1993), Department of Computer Science, University of York, England, October 1993.

[3] B. Dasarathy. Timing constraints of real-time systems: Constructs for expressing them, method for validating them. *IEEE Transactions on Software Engineering*, 11(1):80–86, January 1985.

[4] K. Ebcioglu and A. Nicolau. A global resource-constrained parallelization technique. In *International Conference on Supercomputing*, pages 154–163. ACM Press, New York, June 1989.

[5] A. Mok et al. Evaluating tight execution time bounds of programs by annotations. In *Proceedings IEEE Workshop on Real-Time Operating Systems and Software*, pages 74–80, May 1989.

[6] J. Ferrante and K. Ottenstein. The program dependence graph and its use in optimization. *ACM Transactions on Programming Languages and Systems*, 9:319–345, July 1987.

[7] J. Fisher. Trace scheduling: A technique for global microcode compaction. *IEEE Transactions on Computers*, 30:478–490, July 1981.

[8] F. Gasperoni. Compilation techniques for VLIW architectures. Technical Report RC 14915(#66741), IBM T. J. Watson Research Center, September 1989.

[9] R. Gerber and S. Hong. Semantics-based compiler transformations for enhanced schedulability. In *Proceedings IEEE Real-Time Systems Symposium*, pages 232–242. IEEE Computer Society Press, New York, December 1993.

[10] M. G. Harmon, T. P. Baker, and D. B. Whalley. A retargetable technique for predicting execution time. In *Proceedings IEEE Real-Time Systems Symposium*, pages 68–77. IEEE Computer Society Press, New York, December 1992.

[11] S. Hong and R. Gerber. Compiling real-time programs into schedulable code. In *Proceedings of the ACM SIGPLAN '93 Conference on Programming Language Design and Implementation*. ACM Press, New York, June 1993. *SIGPLAN Notices*, 28(6):166–176.

[12] S. Horwitz, T. Reps, and D. Binkley. Interprocedural slicing using dependence graph. *ACM Transactions on Programming Languages and Systems*, 12:26–60, January 1990.

[13] Y. Ishikawa, H. Tokuda, and C. Mercer. Object-oriented real-time language design: Constructs for timing constraints. In *Proceedings of OOPSLA-90*, pages 289–298, October 1990.

[14] F. Jahanian and Al Mok. Safety analysis of timing properties in real-time systems. *IEEE Transactions on Software Engineering*, 12(9):890–904, September 1986.

[15] K. Kenny and K. J. Lin. Building flexible real-time systems using the Flex language. *IEEE Computer*, pages 70–78, May 1991.

[16] E. Kligerman and A. Stoyenko. Real-time Euclid: A language for reliable real-time systems. *IEEE Transactions on Software Engineering*, 12:941–949, September 1986.

[17] J. Krause. GN&C domain modeling: Functionality requirements for fixed rate algorithms. Technical Report (DRAFT) version 0.2, Honeywell Systems and Research Center, December 1991.

[18] I. Lee and V. Gehlot. Language constructs for real-time programming. In *Proceedings IEEE Real-Time Systems Symposium*, pages 57–66. IEEE Computer Society Press, New York, 1985.

[19] J. Lehoczky, L. Sha, and Y. Ding. The rate monotonic scheduling algorithm: Exact characterization and average case behavior. In *Proceedings IEEE Real-Time Systems Symposium*, pages 166–171. IEEE Computer Society Press, New York, December 1989.

[20] K. J. Lin and S. Natarajan. Expressing and maintaining timing constraints in FLEX. In *Proceedings IEEE Real-Time Systems Symposium*. IEEE Computer Society Press, New York, December 1988.

[21] C. Liu and J. Layland. Scheduling algorithm for multiprogramming in a hard real-time environment. *Journal of the ACM*, 20(1):46–61, January 1973.

[22] A. Nicolau. *Parallelism, Memory Anti-aliasing and Correctness Issues for a Trace Scheduling Compiler*. Ph.D. thesis, Yale University, June 1984.

[23] V. Nirkhe. *Application of Partial Evaluation to Hard Real-Time Programming.* Ph.D. thesis, Department of Computer Science, University of Maryland at College Park, May 1992.

[24] K. Ottenstein and L. Ottenstein. The program dependence graph in a software development environment. In *Proceedings of the ACM SIGSOFT/SIGPLAN Software Engineering Symposium on Practical Software Development Environments*, pages 177–184, May 1984.

[25] C. Park and A. Shaw. Experimenting with a program timing tool based on source-level timing schema. In *Proceedings IEEE Real-Time Systems Symposium*, pages 72–81. IEEE Computer Society Press, New York, December 1990.

[26] L. Sha, J. Lehoczky, and R. Rajkumar. Solutions for some practical problems in prioritized preemptive scheduling. In *Proceedings IEEE Real-Time Systems Symposium*, pages 181–191. IEEE Computer Society Press, New York, December 1986.

[27] A. Shaw. Reasoning about time in higher level language software. *IEEE Transactions on Software Engineering*, pages 875–889, July 1989.

[28] M. Smith, M. Horowitz, and M. Lam. Efficient superscalar performance through boosting. In *Fifth International Conference on Architectural Support for Programming Languages and Operating Systems*, pages 248–259. ACM Press, New York, October 1992.

[29] G. Venkatesh. The semantic approach to program slicing. In *Proceedings of the ACM SIGPLAN '91 Conference on Programming Language Design and Implementation*, June 1991.

[30] M. Weiser. Program slicing. *IEEE Transactions on Software Engineering*, 10:352–357, July 1984.

[31] V. Wolfe, S. Davidson, and I. Lee. RTC: Language support for real-time concurrency. In *Proceedings IEEE Real-Time Systems Symposium*, pages 43–52. IEEE Computer Society Press, New York, December 1991.

[32] N. Zhang, A. Burns, and M. Nicholson. Pipelined processors and worst case execution times. *Journal of Real-Time Systems*, 5(4), October 1993.

# Chapter 16

# Reasoning about Time in Higher-Level Language Software[1]

## Alan Shaw

A methodology for specifying and proving assertions about time in higher-level language programs is described. The approach develops three ideas: the distinction between, and treatment of, both real time and computer times; the use of upper and lower bounds on the execution times of program elements; and a simple extension of Hoare logic to include the effects of the passage of real time. Schemas and examples of timing bounds and assertions are presented for a variety of different statement types and programs, such as conventional sequential programs, including loops, time-related statements such as delay, concurrent programs with synchronization, and software in the presence of interrupts. Examples of assertions that are proven include deadlines, timing invariants for periodic processes, and the specification of time-based events such as those needed for the recognition of single and double clicks from a mouse button.

## 16.1    Introduction

Real-time systems and many other computer applications must meet specifications and perform tasks that satisfy timing as well as logical criteria for correctness. Examples of timing properties and constraints include deadlines, the periodic execution of processes, and external event recognition based on time of occurrence (e.g., [9, 18]).

We present a scheme for reasoning with and about time and for specifying timing properties in concurrent programs. The objectives are to predict the tim-

---

[1]This chapter is based on "Reasoning about Time in Higher-Level Language Software," by Alan Shaw that appeared in *IEEE Transactions on Software Engineering*, vol. 15, no. 7, pp. 875–889, July 1989, ©1989 IEEE.

ing behavior of higher-level language programs and to prove that they meet their timing constraints, through the direct analysis of program statements. Timing is *deterministic*, not stochastic, so that our results are applicable to "hard" real-time systems.

There is a clear distinction—one that is not always recognized—between timing *predictability* on the one hand and speed or efficiency on the other. Both are important, but our work is concerned primarily with predictability. Higher-level languages are being considered and used more frequently for constructing concurrent real-time software, for all of the standard reasons—they offer facilities for structuring data and control and for modularization; programs are easier to design and code; the results are easier to understand and maintain; and software is more portable. What is missing is the ability to predict the timing behavior of these programs and methods to reason about time within programs.

Two major ideas are developed. The first is that upper and lower bounds on execution times for statements can be derived, based on given bounds for primitive statements and elements in the language and underlying system. Schemas for obtaining bounds are presented for conventional sequential statements, including loops, for timing-related statements that refer to imperfect computer clocks, and for synchronization and communications operations with timeouts. The second idea is to extend Hoare logic to include the effects of updating real time (as defined by an ideal global clock) after each statement execution. Many examples are used to illustrate the techniques. The main contributions are the development and synthesis of these two ideas, and the demonstrations of program assertions and invariants involving time.

Several works are related to or have influenced our research. A methodology that has some similarities with ours was proposed by Haase [10]. His methods assume a concurrent programming language based on guarded commands, running on a non-von Neumann architecture; a deterministic execution time is given for each simple statement, but execution times for conditional elements and iterations need not be defined. Dijkstra's weakest preconditions are employed for making and proving assertions. In our work, we assume a range of *conventional* machine architectures and develop time *bounds* to reflect execution of *control* (conditional, iteration), as well as data transforming operations. Also unlike Haase, we distinguish between computer time and real time, and analyze the timing behavior of timing-related statements and communications operations. Haase introduces real time as a (fictitious) variable in his program space that is updated to reflect exact execution times; we use the same idea initially and then derive running bounds for real time. We have also been influenced by Jahanian and Mok, who argue that the notion of a real-time or clock variable cannot be realized correctly because of concurrency problems [13], and by a presentation given by Pnueli, who argues that clock variables are indeed feasible [20].

There does not seem to be any literature on how to derive execution time for statements in higher-level programming languages. (At the machine language level, one can use Knuth's techniques for conventional sequential programs [15].) An interesting attempt at designing a language with deterministic timing predictability is the ESTEREL project [4]; in ESTEREL, instructions take zero time except for those that deal explicitly with time and external events. Other than ESTEREL, it appears that predictability has not received much attention. In fact, part of the motivation for our research has been the lack of predictability in languages and systems proposed or used for real-time applications—Ada, of course, being the most outstanding example [8].

The next section presents the basis and elements of our techniques for dealing with time. Sections 16.3, 16.4, and 16.5 then show how timing bounds and assertions can be produced for a variety of different statement types and programs. In Section 16.6, some additional practical issues related to interrupt handling and processor sharing are introduced. The concluding section discusses some undeveloped areas and next steps.

# 16.2    A Simple Logic for Handling Time

## 16.2.1    Real Time and Computer Time

Our reasoning about time refers ultimately to an idealization of real time as realized by a perfect global clock. This real time is denoted by $rt$; it may be, for example, Greenwich Mean Time.

*Computer time* is the discrete approximation to real time implemented on machines by a variety of hardware and software methods. At the hardware level, there may be fixed-interval or programmable-interval timers that produce "tick" interrupts, or absolute timers that periodically update a software-accessible counter [24]. A software clock would typically use the tick interrupts or the value of an absolute-time counter to generate a computer time.

Many versions of computer time can co-exist in a system. We will assume that each version is approximately synchronized with perfect real time as follows. If $ct$ represents a computer time, then

$$ct = rt + \delta$$

where $\mid \delta \mid \leq \varepsilon$ and $\varepsilon$ is determined by the accuracy of the hardware clock, tick interval, synchronization interval, and synchronization method (e.g., [17]). (This relation does not include the access time to obtain or compute $ct$.)

It has been assumed implicitly that our abstract real time $rt$ is represented by a real number and that each $ct$ is a computer approximation to a real number. $ct$ is normally a more complex data structure, with separate components designating, for example, the year, month, day, hour, minutes, and seconds. Updating a clock, computing with time as a variable, or even reading a computer clock can therefore consume a significant amount of time. These effects are considered in Section 16.4.

## 16.2.2    Initial Architectural Assumptions

A broad spectrum of hardware architectures is possible. There may be many processors with private or shared memory; these could communicate through a shared memory, directly over a bus, through a general communications network, or some combination of these. Programmed processes or tasks are considered static, with no dynamic creation at run time except perhaps during an initialization period.

We assume that each software process has its own dedicated processor, i.e., no timesharing of machines. This includes processes responsible for input and output. Similarly, each clock computes its version of time on a dedicated processor. While we will relax these assumptions later, they permit a simple basis for the treatment of time. Also, the one-to-one association between processes and processors is a feasible allocation scheme for systems where performance and timing predictability are critical, especially in an era of reduced hardware costs (e.g., [11]).

Thus, software interference from an operating system for such functions as dispatching, interrupt handling, and input-output will not occur. The effects of hardware sharing, for example, due to common memory or to bus contention, are factored into the execution times of program statements.

## 16.2.3    Execution Times for Statements

The aim is to analyze directly higher-level language programs. We assume a modern Algol-like language, augmented by functions for handling computer time, process synchronization and communication, input-output with the real-time external world, and standard input-output. A program consists textually of one or more statements, plus some declarative text.

A particular execution of a statement $S$ will be delimited by two events: a *start* event and an *end* event. (Events are just points in time and consume no time.) Let $t(S)$ be the real time between these two events. Ideally, one would like to know the *execution time* $t(S)$ for every execution of every statement $S$ in a given program. Unfortunately, there is no way to determine $t(S)$ *a priori* in general. The value depends on the context of $S$, the data of the program, the compiler, the run-time system, the target machine, and possibly other things.

However, it is possible to obtain *bounds* for $t(S)$. Let

$$T(S) = [t_{min}(S), t_{max}(S)]$$

where $t_{min}(S) \leq t(S) \leq t_{max}(S)$ for *all* executions of $S$ in a given program. In the worst case, $T(S) = [0, \infty]$; but one can almost always do better than this. Much of this chapter is concerned with methods for finding tight bounds in $T(S)$ for various types of statements $S$. It should be emphasized that, like $t(S)$, $T(S)$ is also in general dependent upon the particular language, context, compiler, run-time system, and target machine.

Generally, $T(S)$ will be provided for elementary statements, expressions, and control structures $S$, and $T$ is then derived or computed for more elaborate constructs. A simple example is the sequential composition of two statements $S = S_1; S_2$, yielding the bounds

$$T(S) = T(S_1) + T(S_2)$$

where we define $[a, b] + [c, d] = [a + c, b + d]$. This assumes that the end event of $S_1$ occurs simultaneously with the start event of $S_2$. It is also conceivable that sequential control might consume time in a particular realization of a programming language. Including sequencing overhead, we obtain

$$T(S) = T(S_1) + T(S_2) + T(;)$$

where $T(;)$ is the time for sequencing $S_1$ and $S_2$. We will use the first interpretation throughout the chapter (i.e., $T(;) = [0,0]$).

Similarly, consider a system with two concurrent processes and associated programs $S_1$ and $S_2$, respectively. Denote $S = S_1 \;//\; S_2$, where $//$ indicates concurrent control. The execution time bounds are typically given by

$$T(S) = max(T(S_1), T(S_2)) + T(//)$$

where $max([a,b],[c,d])$ is defined as $[max(a,c), max(b,d)]$ and $T(//)$ is the overhead corresponding to running $S_1$ and $S_2$ in parallel.

At a lower level, a conventional conditional construct

$$S = \textbf{if } B \textbf{ then } S_1 \textbf{ else } S_2$$

may have the following performance:

$$\text{Let } T_1 = T(B) + T(S_1) + 2 \times T(then/else) = [t_{11}, t_{12}], \text{and}$$

$$T_2 = T(B) + T(S_2) + T(then/else) = [t_{21}, t_{22}],$$

where $T(then/else)$ are the control flow times within $S$, e.g., the time to transfer around $S_2$ (assuming execution of $S_1$) or the time to transfer to (or not transfer to) $S_2$ after testing $B$. Then $T(S)$ may be simply

$$[min(t_{11}, t_{21}), max(t_{12}, t_{22})].$$

(We develop this further in Section 16.3.2.)

The schemas illustrated above for $T(S)$ are independent of the program context of $S$. Stronger bounds may be derivable when the context is known.

## 16.2.4   Hoare Logic with Time

Standard Hoare logic [12] uses assertions $P$ and $Q$, respectively, before and after a statement $S$, with the notation

$$\{P\}S\{Q\}.$$

The interpretation is: if $P$ is true before the execution of $S$ and $S$ is executed, then $Q$ will be true after $S$ (assuming that $S$ terminates). With perfect knowledge of timing, we would augment the above form to:

$$\{P\} < S; rt := rt + t(S) > \{Q\}$$

where $P$ and $Q$ could now include relations involving real time ($rt$) before and after execution of $S$, i.e., at the start and end events, respectively, of $S$, and the brackets ($<>$) indicate that the execution of $S$ and incrementing of $rt$ occur at the same time. (It is assumed that the statement incrementing $rt$ takes zero time.) The axiom of assignment can then be used in $P$ and $Q$ for assertions about $rt$. For example, if $P = P(rt, \ldots)$, then one can assert either

$$\{P(rt, \ldots)\} \; S \; \{P(rt - t(S), \ldots)\} \quad \text{or}$$

$$\{P(rt + t(S), \ldots)\} \; S \; \{P(rt, \ldots)\}.$$

Our approximation to this unrealizable ideal is the rule:

$$\{P\} < S; \; RT := RT + T(S) > \{Q\}$$

where $RT$ is a pair $[rt_{min}, rt_{max}]$ such that at any time, the perfect real time $rt$ is in the interval defined by $rt_{min}$ and $rt_{max}$. $P$ and $Q$ may now include assertions about the elements of $RT$. Finally, to avoid naming conflicts on $RT$ when statements are composed, we introduce a local real-time variable $RT_0$ for each statement and use

$$(*) \quad \{P\} < RT_0 := RT; \; S; \; RT := RT_0 + T(S) > \{Q\}.$$

(This trick was employed in [10].) For brevity, we shorten this to the standard Hoare form; henceforth, whenever $\{P\}S\{Q\}$ appears, it is assumed that this is an abbreviation for $(*)$. Our bounded intervals are exactly the *interval numbers* defined and analyzed in [19], and we use the same kind of arithmetic. For example, if $\phi$ is one of the operator symbols $+, \times$, or $-$, then

$$[a, b] \; \phi \; [c, d] = \{x \; \phi \; y : x \text{ in } [a, b], y \text{ in } [c, d]\}.$$

Bounded intervals, such as $RT$ and $T(S)$, will also be treated as sets of numbers. The notation $t$ in $RT$ or $t$ in $T(S)$ will be used to indicate that $t$ is in the range defined by the bounds. Bounded intervals will be denoted by uppercase names.

**Examples:**

The extended logic can express conveniently basic timing properties and constraints. Examples in later sections provide detailed reasonings and proofs for particular program instances.

    1. Performance specifications

        If $S$ starts executing in the timing interval $RT_{start}$, it will finish sometime in the interval $RT_{start} + T(S)$. i.e.,

$$\{RT = RT_{start}\} \; S \; \{RT = RT_{start} + T(S)\}.$$

        A simple variation is:

$$\{rt = t_{start}\} \; S \; \{rt = t_{start} + t, t \text{ in } T(S)\}.$$

This last assertion will sometimes be abbreviated to

$$RT = t_{start} + T(S)$$

where $t_{start}$ is itself a shortening of $[t_{start}, t_{start}]$.

2. Deadlines

Let $RT_{dl} = [t_{dlmin}, t_{dlmax}]$ be deadlines such that a program $S$ must be completed no earlier than $t_{dlmin}$ and no later than $t_{dlmax}$. This general deadline problem can be expressed (after employing the axiom of assignment):

$$\{RT + T(S) = RT_{dl}\}\ S\ \{RT = RT_{dl}\}$$

i.e., at the start event of $S$, real time must be bounded:

$$t_{dlmin} - t_{min}(S)\ \leq\ rt\ \leq\ t_{dlmax} - t_{max}(S).$$

It is impossible to meet this constraint if

$$t_{dlmin} - t_{min}(S) > t_{dlmax} - t_{max}(S).$$

From the above (letting $t_{dlmin} = -\infty$) or directly, it is easy to specify a conventional deadline constraint:

$$\{rt \leq t_{dlmax} - t_{max}(S)\}\ S\ \{rt \leq t_{dlmax}\}.$$

A similar expression is produced for the earliest finish-time constraint given by $t_{dlmin}$.

3. Control of a periodic process

Consider a program $S$ which is to be executed periodically, starting at time $rt_{start}$. An appropriate *invariant* involving the time $rt$ before and after each execution is

$$next = rt_{start} + n \times period = rt + delta,\quad |delta| \leq eps$$

where *next* is the computed start time for each cycle (*next* is usually a program variable), $n$ gives the number of executions of $S$, *period* is the time interval allocated to a cycle, and *delta* is the error, bounded by *eps*, of *next* relative to real-time. $T(S)$ is not used directly here, but it is assumed that a delay is introduced in $S$ (using a computer clock) to fill up the entire period. An implementation of the example is developed and analyzed in Section 16.4.

## 16.3    Reasoning and Execution Times for Sequential Programs

### 16.3.1    Expressions and Simple Statements

Consider straight-line programs consisting of assignment statements and procedure calls of the form, respectively,

$$v := Exp \text{ and } P\_name(e_1, \ldots, e_n)$$

where $v$ is a variable name, $Exp$ is an expression, $P\_name$ is a procedure identifier, and $e_1, \ldots, e_n, n \geq 0$, are the actual parameters of the procedure call. Assume that $Exp$ has the syntax

$$Exp ::= v \mid c \mid F\_name(e_1, \ldots, e_n) \mid (Exp \; \emptyset \; Exp)$$

where $c$ denotes a constant, $F\_name$ is a function identifier, and $\emptyset$ is a basic binary operator.

A separate analysis of the system, for example, of the compiler and target machine, is done to produce execution times $T(S)$ for primitive entities $S$ as follows:

$T(x)$ :           retrieve the value of a variable or constant $x$.
                    This may just be the time to load a register.

$T(.v)$ :          obtain the address of a variable $v$. In those cases where addresses are known at compile time, $T(.v) = [0, 0]$.

$T(:=)$ :          perform an assignment. Typically, the value is the "store" time of the target machine.

$T(\emptyset)$ :          execute the basic operation $\emptyset$.

$T(call/return)$ : call and return from a procedure or function.

$T(par)$ :          pass a parameter to a procedure or function. There may be several variations of $T(par)$ according to the type of parameter, for example, $T(par\_call\_by\_reference)$ and $T(par\_call\_by\_value)$.

Times for the higher-level constructs are computed by adding bounds in the obvious manner. The schema for an assignment statement is

$$T(v := Exp) = T(.v) + T(:=) + T(Exp).$$

A procedure call has the time property

$$T(P\_name(e_1, \ldots, e_n)) = T(call/return) + n \times T(par) + T(P\_body)$$

where *P_body* is the program text of the procedure. If a parameter $e_i$ is a general expression, then it is necessary to add a corresponding term $T(e_i)$.

These schemes, of course, do not take into account various compiler optimizations that might occur. For example, in the procedure call

$$P1((i + j) \bmod k, (i + j) \bmod k)$$

a smart compiler might choose to evaluate the common expression only once rather than twice, giving execution time bounds

$$T(call/return) + 2 \times T(par) + T((i+j)\bmod k) + T(P1\_body)$$

assuming that both parameters are "value" parameters.

Expression evaluation is handled similarly:

$$T((E_1 \oslash E_2)) = T(E_1) + T(\oslash) + T(E_2)$$

For example, $T((i + j) \bmod k) = T((i + j)) + T(\bmod) + T(k) = T(i) + T(+) + T(j) + T(\bmod) + T(k)$.

The sequential composition of statements yields execution times as discussed earlier in Section 16.2.4.

Target machine details, resource allocation strategies for fast registers, and possible compiler optimizations all increase the difficulty of obtaining good bounds manually. However, it is anticipated that machine assistance would be available for analyzing the actual compiler-produced code, especially for the straight-line cases considered in this section.

## Example:

Let us analyze the simple assignment statement:

$$c := a + b.$$

Using the schema presented here, we obtain the execution time

$$T(.c) + T(:=) + T(a) + T(+) + T(b).$$

This corresponds to a generous machine language program:

```
load a in R1
load b in R2
add R2 to R1
load .c in R2
store R1 in R2 indirect
```

But the machine architecture might permit a much tighter program:

```
load a in R1
add b to R1
store R1 in c
```

i.e., $T(.c) = T(b) = [0,0]$ for this instance.

Even better, it may be that the value of $a$ had previously been loaded in a register, reducing the above program to only two instructions. Of course, the other extreme can also happen; registers may contain valuable information which must be saved before executing the assignment statement, thus adding instructions.

For simple cases of straight-line code, it may be that the exact execution time $t(S)$ is predictable. More likely are cases where only bounds will be predictable. The compiled code, for example, may have to compute addresses of variables at run time. Hardware features, such as memory contention, instruction look-ahead, and caching of results, can also account for a range of possible execution times.

## 16.3.2   Conditional and Looping Constructs

Typical conditional constructs are the **if/then/else** and **case** statements:

(a)   **if** $B_1$ **then** $S_1$ **else if** $B_2$ **then** $S_2$ **else** ... **else if** $B_n$ **then** $S_n$.

(b)   **case** *expr* **of**
    $i_1$  :   $S_1$;
    $i_2$  :   $S_2$;
        :
    $i_n$  :   $S_n$
    **end case**    $(n \geq 1)$

Conventional realizations for these statements are:

(a)   **if/then/else**:      $< B_1 >$
                    transfer on false to 2
                    $< S_1 >$
                    transfer to $n + 1$
       2 :    $< B_2 >$
                    transfer on false to 3
                    $< S_2 >$
                    transfer to $n + 1$
       3 :    .
                    .
                    .
       $n$ :    $< B_n >$
                    transfer on false to $n + 1$
                    $< S_n >$
       $n + 1 : \{\text{start of next statement}\}$

$< X >$ means the code for construct $X$.

(b)   **case**:      $\{$assumes $expr = i_k$ for some $k \leq n\}$
                    $< x := expr >$
                    transfer to $x$
     $i_1$ :    $< S_1 >$
                    transfer to $i_{n+1}$

$$i_2: \quad < S_2 >$$
$$\text{transfer to } i_{n+1}$$

.

.

.

$$i_n: \quad < S_n >$$
$$i_{n+1}: \{\text{start of next statement}\}$$

The primitive entities for these statements are the control flow objects as realized by the transfer instructions. Let the time bounds for these objects be given by $T(then/else)$ and $T(case)$. (We assume that all transfers have the same time bounds, so that conditional and unconditional transfers take the same time and $T(then/else) = T(case)$—but, in general, they may have different values.) Bounds for execution times are then found as follows:

(a)  **if/then/else**

$$\text{Let } T_k = T(S_k) + min(k+1,n) \times T(then/else) + \sum_{i=1}^{n} T(B_i) = [t_{k1}, t_{k2}].$$

Then

$$T(\textbf{if } B_1 \textbf{ then } S_1 \textbf{ else} \ldots \textbf{ then } S_n)$$

$$= [\, \min(\min_{k<n}(t_{k1}), \; n \times T(then/else) + \sum_{i=1}^{n} T(B_i) \,), \; \max_k(t_{k2}) \,].$$

(b)  **case**

$$\text{Let } T_k = T(expr) + a_k \times T(case) + T(S_k) = [t_{k1}, t_{k2}]$$

where $a_k = 2$ for $k < n$ and $a_k = 1$ for $k = n$. Then

$$T(\textbf{case } expr \textbf{ of } i_1 : S_1 \ldots S_n \textbf{ end case}) = [\min_k(t_{k1}), \; \max_k(t_{k2})].$$

Because of the detail and tediousness of actually making the calculations, it is expected that machine aids will be available to assist in the analysis of these statements.

To illustrate the schemas and method of analysis for loops, we consider two common instances:

(a) an "infinite" loop, usually implementing a cyclic process
   **loop** $S$ **end loop**

(b) the classical while statement
   **while** $B$ **do** $S$ **end while**

The primitive loop time, designated $T(loop)$, will just correspond to the time to unconditionally branch back to the beginning of the loop after each execution of $S$. Similarly, the **while** statement has a basic object with execution time $T(while)$, corresponding to either the unconditional branch back after execution of $S$ or the conditional test and branch after evaluating $B$. Like the **if/then/else** construct, it is assumed that conditional and unconditional branches, regardless of whether or not a branch is taken, all consume the same amount of time—or at least have the same time bounds. (These times could, of course, have different values, but this would not change the methods of analysis, only some of the details.)

For analysis purposes, an auxiliary counting variable is maintained (fictitiously) in every loop as follows:

(a) $n := 0;$ **loop** $S; n := n + 1$ **end loop**

(b) $n := 0;$ **while** $B$ **do** $S; n := n + 1$ **end while**

The counting variable $n$ gives the number of executions of $S$. The statements involving $n$ take zero time to execute.

It is now straightforward to derive a basic timing *invariant* for both kinds of loops. Let $RT_{start}$ denote the real-time bounds at the beginning, i.e., the start event, of either loop. Then, for the infinite loop, we have the following invariant at the start event of $S$:

(a)  $RT = RT_{start} + n \times (T(S) + T(loop))$
     ($n \times [a, b]$ is defined as $[n \times a, n \times b]$)

The **while** statement is slightly more complex, since $B$ must be tested each time through the loop and a control decision is made whether to continue or transfer out. Taking all of this into account, we obtain the following invariant at $S$ for the while loop:

(b)  $RT = RT_{start} + (n + 1) \times (T(B) + T(while)) + n \times (T(S) + T(while))$

which simplifies to

$$RT = RT_{start} + (n + 1) \times T(B) + n \times T(S) + (2n + 1) \times T(while).$$

The same type of analysis leads to execution bounds for the **while** statement. If, somehow, the number $n$ of executions of the loop is known, then $T(\textbf{while } B \textbf{ do } S$ **end while**) is just $RT - RT_{start}$ in the invariant (b) above, giving

$$T(\textbf{while } B \textbf{ do } S \textbf{ end while}) = (n + 1) \times T(B) + n \times T(S) + (2n + 1) \times T(while).$$

We propose to obtain bounds for $n$ using Hoare logic and techniques similar to those developed for proving termination of loops. Let $N = [n_{min}, n_{max}]$ and $n$ in $N$. The timing bounds for the while construct are then

$$T(\textbf{while } B \textbf{ do } S \textbf{ end while}) = (N + 1) \times T(B) + N \times T(S) + (2N + 1) \times T(while)$$

where the notation is defined: $[a, b] \times [c, d] = [ac, bd]$.

At this point, it is worth noting that in order to be able to predict timing behavior, one simply *must* have bounds on such loop executions. There is at least one real-time programming language that explicitly includes limits on either the number of iterations or the execution time of each loop [14].

## Examples:

1. These ideas are illustrated first with a standard "toy" example, a program to compute an integer approximation to the square root of an integer. Conventional assertions appear as comments in braces.

$$\{x \geq 0\}$$
$$a := 0;$$
$$\{a^2 \leq x \text{ and } x \geq 0d\}$$
**while** $(a + 1)^2 \leq x$ **do** $a := a + 1$ **end while**
$$\{a^2 \leq x, x \geq 0, \text{ and } (a + 1)^2 > x\} \quad \{a = \lfloor \sqrt{x} \rfloor\}$$

The loop invariant is $\{a^2 \leq x \text{ and } x \geq 0\}$, which upon loop termination permits the implication $\{a = \lfloor \sqrt{x} \rfloor\}$; i.e., $a$ is the largest integer less than or equal to the square root of $x$. Here, the auxiliary counting variable $n$ would have the identical values as the program variable $a$; therefore at termination $n = \lfloor \sqrt{x} \rfloor$. Termination is proven (trivially) by noting that $a$ increases each time through the loop but is also bounded above by $\sqrt{x}$ (i.e., $a^2 \leq x$), which cannot remain true forever. If the input $x$ is restricted to the range $[0, x_{max}]$, then $N = [0, \lfloor \sqrt{x_{max}} \rfloor]$ is the tightest possible bounds. A practical one might be $N = [0, \lceil x_{max}/2 \rceil]$.

Assuming that $T(a := 0) = 1$ (i.e., $[1, 1]$), $T(while) = 1, T((a + 1)^2 \leq x) = 4$, and $T(a := a + 1) = 3$, the program has execution time bounds.

$$1 + (N + 1) \times 4 + N \times 3 + (2N + 1) \times 1 = 9N + 6$$

2. A more interesting example is the following program $S$, presented in [10], which computes $x = max(1, a, b)$ in a roundabout fashion.

$$x := a;$$
**if** $x < 1$ **then** $x := 1;$
**while** $x < b$ **do** $x := x + 1$ **end while**

Including our auxiliary loop count variable $n$, the **while** statement has the invariant

$$\{x \geq 1, n < x, b > 1 \Rightarrow n \leq b - 1, b \leq 1 \Rightarrow n = 0\}$$

This invariant provides upper and lower bounds on the number of times the loop statement is executed as a function of $b$. (Note that this particular invariant does not permit proving that $x = max(1, a, b)$).

Let input $b$ be restricted so that $b \leq bmax > 1$; therefore, the loop is executed no more than $bmax - 1$ times. Assuming that $T(x := a) = 2$, $T(x < 1) = 2$, $T(then/else) = 1$, $T(x := 1) = 1$, $T(x < b) = 2$, $T(while) = 1$, and

$T(x := x + 1) = 3$, execution times for $S$ can be bounded:

$$
\begin{aligned}
T(S) &= [2 + (2+1) + (2+1),\ 2 + (2+1+1) + (b_{max} \times 2 + (b_{max} - 1) \times 3 \\
&\quad + (2 \times (b_{max} - 1) + 1) \times 1)] \\
&= [8, 7b_{max} + 2].
\end{aligned}
$$

## 16.4  Time-Related Statements

### 16.4.1  Higher-Level Constructs for Dealing with Time

Most systems provide a clock abstraction in the form of software functions to read time and possibly also to set the time (e.g., [1, 7, 23]). Define these functions as follows:

$get\_time$     : returns the current value $ct$ of computer time
$set\_time(t)$ : sets computer time to $t$ (i.e., $ct := t$)

Another basic timing facility, one that is useful for programming real-time applications, delays a process for a specific interval of time or until time reaches some absolute value. These are defined:

$int\_delay(t)$ : wait until $ct = ct_0 + t, t \geq 0$, before proceeding, where
$ct_0$ is the time of the delay statement invocation
$abs\_delay(t)$ : wait until $ct = t$ before proceeding; proceed
immediately if $t \leq ct$

For "practical" reasons, the delay statements are usually defined more loosely to guarantee continued execution only at some future time $ct \geq ct_0 + t$ and $ct \geq t$, respectively. We give a tighter but still practical specification that permits better timing predictability in the next section.

A third class of timing facility that is commonly available in concurrent systems is the timeout. These are associated with communications and synchronization constructs, and permit the specification of a timing limit when waiting for some event to occur. Timeouts are treated in Section 16.5.

These constructs permit the implementation of more elaborate and higher-level statements and abstractions. One example is the calendar package of Ada, which allows the programmer to perform arithmetic on variables of type "time" in a straightforward manner, and to construct elements of type time from, and to decompose time into, its various components. The Pearl language provides mechanisms for directly scheduling processes based on time [25]. For example, tasks can be activated or resumed at a given time frequency, at a particular time, or after a specified time interval. A third example is the realization of different clocks on the same system, with differing granularities for tick time and even variable interval ticking [21].

## 16.4.2    Timing Analysis of *get_time* and *delay*

Given the execution times for standard statements in sequential programs, a straightforward analysis can be made to determine whether a program satisfies some performance constraints or *implicit* timing constraints. However, a principal purpose of the timing-related statements is to program these constraints directly, i.e., explicitly. In order to obtain any sort of sensible predictability, it must be possible to produce tight bounds for these statements. Most languages, even so-called real-time languages such as Ada, do not provide these timing bounds. An important but reasonable question is: Does the sequence

$$int\_delay(3); \quad int\_delay(2);$$

produce the same result as the single statement

$$int\_delay(5)$$

and what *exactly* is the result? (This particular problem is presented in [4], where it is indeed handled precisely in their interesting, but quite different, ESTEREL language.)

Consider first some possible realizations of *get_time* under our initial architectural assumptions (Section 16.2.2). Because computer time is maintained by a separate processor, its value $ct$ will be returned either through a message-passing communication or directly if it is accessible through a shared memory. There may be some computation to put $ct$ into a more suitable form. The function could be implemented in several different ways, for example, as a procedure or as an in-line macro. All of these factors must be included to yield the time bounds $T(get\_time)$, which we assume are found by a combination of measurement and analysis.

If $T(get\_time) = 0$, then the value $ct$ returned would be related to real-time $rt$ as follows:

$$CT = RT + E$$

where $ct$ in $CT$, $rt$ in $RT$, and $E = [-\varepsilon, \varepsilon]$ ($\varepsilon$ is defined in Section 16.2.1), i.e., $ct$ in $RT + E$. However, in the realistic cases, the $ct$ value used is obtained sometime after the start event of *get_time* and before its end event. At the end event of *get_time*, we will therefore be able to bound $ct$ according to the relation

$$CT = RT + [-t_{max}(get\_time), 0] + E$$

where $t_{max}(get\_time)$ is the upper bound in $T(get\_time)$. Alternatively, $ct$ can be expressed as a function of the real time at the start event of *get_time*:

$$CT = RT + [0, t_{max}(get\_time)] + E$$

Some definitions and an analysis of the *int_delay* version of the delay statement are now presented. One reasonable implementation, under our separate processor assumption, might use the *get_time* function in a busy-wait loop:

(a) *int_delay(t)*:

$Wakeup\_Time := get\_time + t;$     {Call this statement $S_1$.}
**while** $get\_time < Wakeup\_Time$ **do** {null statement} **end while**

Alternatively, a hardware interval timer, *hit*, could be employed directly. It is assumed that the timer decrements its value at each hardware tick and interrupts an applications processor when it reaches zero.

(b)     $hit := t;$  {Load hit with $t$.} {$S_1$}
**while not** $hit\_interrupt$ **do** {*null*} **end while**

To determine execution-time bounds, which also leads to a precise definition of *int_delay*, we first examine the no-overhead case. The ideal, but unrealizable, semantics and time bounds would of course be:

$$T(int\_delay(t)) = t.$$

However, since delay is implemented with some type of computer clock, we can never do better than

$$T(int\_delay(t)) = [max(0, t - \varepsilon), t + \varepsilon].$$

If $t \geq \varepsilon$, a simpler relation is obtained:

$$T(int\_delay(t)) = t + E.$$

For convenience we will assume that $t \geq \varepsilon$, but the results for the more general case should also be evident.

Next, consider the effects of various overheads in the implementations given in (a) and (b) above. We will show that in each case, one can derive useful execution time bounds for the overhead, $T_{oh}$, that are independent of the parameter $t$. The final result is

$$T(int\_delay(t)) = t + E + T_{oh}( \text{ for } t \geq \varepsilon).$$

For the code in (a), a lower bound of $T_{oh}$ is the sum of the lower bounds of $T(x < Wakeup\_Time)$ and $T(while)$, where $x$ is a simple variable or constant. This corresponds to the case where $ct$ has changed to $ct \geq Wakeup\_Time$ just prior to the retrieval of $ct$ in $get\_time$.

Analogously, if $ct$ has changed to $ct \geq Wakeup\_Time$ just after $ct$ was retrieved in the $get\_time$ call in the test, we can trace this worst-case scenario to obtain an upper bound of $T_{oh}$ equal to twice the sum of the upper bounds of $T(get\_time < Wakeup\_Time)$ and $T(while)$ plus the upper bound of $T(while)$. A competitor for the upper bound may be the case for small $t$, when $get\_time+t$ would fail the test even before the execution of $S_1$ has terminated; here the upper bound for $T_{oh}$ is the sum of the upper bounds of $T(S_1), T(get\_time < Wakeup\_Time)$, and $T(while)$. The final upper bound for $T_{oh}$ is the larger of these two possibilities.

The code in (b) admits to a much simpler analysis. The entire **while** loop would realistically be coded as a single instruction "branch to self." The **while** loop of (a) would most likely be optimized to eliminate the unconditional transfer at the end of the loop, also. The overhead bounds are

$$T_{oh} = [t_{min}(inter), t_{max}(inter) + max(t_{max}(S_1), t_{max}(while))]$$

where $[t_{min}(inter), t_{max}(inter)]$ are the execution bounds for handling the timer interrupt. The handling may be a simple transfer instruction. A "branch to self" is assumed for realizing the **while** loop. The upper bound considers two cases similar to those treated for (a).

The results of this section can now be used to compare the sequence "$int\_delay(3); int\_delay(2)$" with $int\_delay(5)$. The sequence of two delays has the execution times and meaning:

$$3 + E + T_{oh} + 2 + E + T_{oh} = 5 + 2E + 2T_{oh}$$

while

$$T(int\_delay(5)) = 5 + E + T_{oh}.$$

Thus, the two are not identical with our timing semantics. (ESTEREL produces identical results for the two in their model because they assume no overhead, instantaneous computations, and no distinction between computer time and real time.)

## 16.4.3   A Program Proof including Time

A common method for programming a periodic process $P$ is through an (apparently) simple delay loop as illustrated below. $P$ is executed approximately every "period" units of time.

```
next := get_time;
loop
        {The next execution of P starts here.}
        next := next + period;
        x := next - get_time;
        int_delay(x)
end loop
```

A variation of this code, for example, appears in the Ada Reference Manual [1].

The code for $P$ could be inserted directly after the comment, or a "start" message might be sent to a separate process implementing P. This schema could also be used to build a higher-level software clock that ticks at every "period"; for example, P might then compute the time-of-day.

Informally, we wish to show that the code does indeed compute the correct time for each cycle of $P$ provided that $x$ is always greater than zero; i.e., the variable $next$ always contains the start time of the next or current cycle. As indicated earlier in Example 3 of Section 16.2.4, this requirement can be formalized as a loop invariant $I$ that is always true just after **loop**; $I$ refers to an auxiliary counting variable $n$ (Section 16.3.2):

$$I : next = rt_{start} + n \times \ period \ \text{and} \ RT = next + EPS$$

$rt_{start}$ is approximately the program start time, and $EPS = [eps_{min}, eps_{max}]$, where $|eps_{min}|$, $|eps_{max}| \leq eps$ for some constant $eps$.

The problem is first to bound $rt_{start}$ with respect to the real time at the beginning of the program, say $rt_0$ ($rt_0$ is the time at the start event of the first statement). The second, more difficult and more interesting, problem is to find $EPS$. The program is (supposedly) written so that timing errors don't accumulate each time through the loop; that is the reason for using $int\_delay(next - get\_time)$ rather than simply $int\_delay(period)$. Proving the invariant confirms that this intent has been realized correctly.

Consider the first statement of the program, including the initialization of the fictitious loop count variable. Using our logic, we add provable assertions before and after:

> $n := 0;$   {Initialize auxiliary counting variable}
> {Real time is assumed equal to $rt_0$ here}
> $next := get\_time;$
> {$next$ in $rt + 0 + [0, t_{max}(get\_time)] + E$ (Section 16.4.2)
> and $RT = rt_0 + T(next := get\_time)$}

From the postcondition, $next = rt_0 + e'_0$, where $e'_0$ in $E'$ ($E' = [0, t_{max}(get\_time)] + E$). Therefore, $next = rt_{start} + n \times period$, where $rt_{start} = rt_0 + e'_0$. Similarly, from $RT = rt_0 + T(next := get\_time)$, we obtain

$$RT = rt_{start} - e'_0 + T(next := get\_time)$$
$$= next - e'_0 + T(next := get\_time) = next + EPS.$$

$EPS$ can be derived from $e'_0$ and $T(next := get\_time)$; a similar derivation is described later in this section. The postcondition of the first statement thus implies that

$$next = rt_{start} + n \times period \text{ and } RT = next + EPS$$

which is our invariant $I$. We have also bounded $rt_{start}$ with respect to $rt_0$.

A bound for $EPS$ is produced by proving the invariant in the loop part of the program, again assuming that $x$ is always appropriately greater than zero (see discussion below). We will use the alternate, but equivalent, notation $rt = next + e, e$ in $EPS$, rather than $RT = next + EPS$, and show that $e$ is canceled each time through the loop, but a one-time residual error is picked up (and canceled the next time through). The minimum and maximum of this residual error (due to statement times and timing errors) and the initial $EPS$ bounds from above are the desired bounds.

**loop**

> {$I$}
> $next := next + period;$   {Call this statement $S1$.}
> {$next = rt_{start} + (n + 1) \times period,$
>     $rt = next - period + s_1 + e,$  $s_1$ in $T(S1)$, $e$ in $EPS$}
> $x := next - get\_time; \{S2\}$
> {$next = rt_{start} + (n + 1) \times period,$  $rt = next - period + s_1 + e + s_2,$

$s_2$ in $T(S2)$,  $x = next - get\_time\}$
$\{x = rt_{start} + (n+1) \times period - (next - period + s_1 + e + e_0'),$
    $e_0'$ in $E' = period - s_1 - e - e_0'\}$
$n := n + 1;$ {Increment auxiliary counting variable.}
$\{x = period - s_1 - e - e_0',\ next = rt_{start} + n \times period,$
    $rt = next - period + s_1 + e + s_2\}$
$int\_delay(x); \{S3\}$
$\{next = rt_{start} + n \times period,\ x = period - s_1 - e - e_0',$
    $rt = next - period + s_1 + e + s_2 + x + e_0 + h,\ \ e_0$ in $E, h$ in $T_{oh}\}$
    {It is assumed that $x \geq \varepsilon$.}
$\{rt = next - period + s_1 + e + s_2 + period - s_1 - e - e_0' + e_0 + h$
    $= next + s_2 - e_0' + e_0 + h\}$
**end loop**  $\{rt = next + s_2 - e_0' + e_0 + h + p, p$ in $T(loop),$
        $next = rt_{start} + n \times period\}$

After $S2$, the details of the assertion for $x$ are derived using primarily the results of the *get_time* analysis in Section 16.4.2. It is assumed that the start event of $S2$ corresponds to the real time $rt$ at the start event of *get_time*, so that the "computer" time returned by *get_time* is equal to $rt + e_0'$. (An alternative realization would result in the addition of another bounded error term.) The rest of the expression is obtained by substituting for $rt$ and $next$. After $S3$, real time is updated using the results of our previous analysis of $int - delay$; substituting for $x$, and assuming that $x \geq \varepsilon$ every time through the loop, we arrive at the assertion just before **end loop**. The final assertion adds in the effects $p$ of transferring back to the beginning of the loop.

Each time through the loop, we have a new error term $del_1 = s_2 - e_0' + e_0 + h + p$. The first time after initialization gives an error $del_0 = -\delta + \gamma$, where $\delta$ in $E'$ and $\gamma$ in $T(next := get\_time)$. For each of these, the expression for real time is of the form:

$$rt = next + a - b$$

where $a$ in $A = [a_1, a_2]$, $b$ in $B = [b_1, b_2]$. With a little analysis, this yields

$$RT = next + EPS$$

with $EPS = [a_1 - b_2, a_2 - b_1]$. ($EPS = A - B$ if we define $A - B = [a_1 - b_2, a_2 - b_1]$.) Two pairs for $EPS$ can be found in this manner:

$$EPS_0 = [eps_{01}, eps_{02}] \qquad \text{(from } del_0)$$

and

$$EPS_1 = [eps_{11}, eps_{12}] \qquad \text{(from } del_1)$$

Our final $EPS$ is then

$$EPS = [min(eps_{01}, eps_{11}), max(eps_{02}, eps_{12})].$$

The analysis does not change substantially if either the execution time of process $P$ or the communication time to $P$ is included. If this time is in $T(S)$, say, then $x$ would receive a value equal to $period - s_1 - e - e'_0 - s, s$ in $T(S)$. Provided that $x \geq \varepsilon$, the invariant would continue to hold. However, if $x < \varepsilon$, the system may not work correctly since the timing errors could then accumulate without bound. This, of course, happens when the overhead and/or $T(S)$ is too large for the period; i.e., whenever $period + \varepsilon < s_1 + \varepsilon + e'_0 + s$, where $e = del_0$ or $e = del_1$.

We have shown how the intent of this common code fragment for controlling a periodic process in real time can be formalized and verified. The example also illustrates the desirability of some machine assistance to keep track of assertions, to verify details (a proof checker), and to compute time bounds.

## 16.5    Synchronization and Communications

The objective is to predict execution times for synchronization and communications software in concurrent systems. Statements and mechanisms that need to be analyzed include semaphores, locks, monitors, events, message passing, input-output, remote procedure call, and rendezvous. Process waiting time, i.e., the interval during which a process is logically blocked, is given explicitly for statements such as the *int_delay* treated in the last section. However, the statements being considered here do not have explicit waiting times, making it more difficult to obtain useful time bounds.

One method is to study the specific context within which one or more of these statements are being used, taking into account the usual overhead times and the details of other processes that interact with the one in question. As an example, consider the following standard producer-consumer system, consisting of two processes that communicate through a bounded buffer and use semaphores for synchronization (e.g., [5]):

producer process:
    **loop**
        $Produce\_Next\_Record;$
        $P(empty); Fill\_Buffer; V(full)$
    **end loop**

consumer process:
    **loop**
        $P(full); Empty\_Buffer; V(empty);$
        $Consume\_Record$
    **end loop**

Initially, the semaphore $empty = n$, the number of buffers, and $full = 0$.

Let us find $T(P(empty)) = [t_{emin}, t_{emax}]$. Assuming that a successful $P$ operation has the pre-determined bounds $T(P_{success}) = [tp_{min}, tp_{max}]$, then $t_{cmin} = tp_{min} \cdot t_{emax}$ is derived by noting that in the worst case, the producer must wait at $P(empty)$ for an entire cycle of the consumer, starting at $Consume\_Record$, before the $V(empty)$ occurs to wake it up. This yields an upper bound $t_{emax}$ equal to the upper bound of the expression:

$$T(P_{fail}) + T(Consume\_Record) + tp_{max} + T(Empty\_Buffer) + T(V\,wakeup)$$

where $T(P_{fail})$ is the predetermined bounds for a $P$ operation that fails (i.e., the time up to the blocking of the process), $tp_{max}$ corresponds to the successful $P(full)$, and $T(V_{wakeup})$ is the time for a $V$ operation that also wakes up a blocked process. A similar analysis can be made for $T(P(full))$. Of course, there are many cases of interest where this approach is not practical.

## 16.5.1    Timeouts

A second method that is guaranteed, in principle, to yield bounds employs timeouts. Associated with each invocation of a synchronization or communication operation is a time, say $t$. If the process is not unblocked by $t$, then a "timeout" occurs, the operation is completed with an appropriate indication, and the process continues. Alternatively, the timeout parameter could be an interval rather than an absolute time. Timeouts are often used as indicators of various kinds of system failures, such as a hardware error, software mistake, or a deadlock. They are also convenient for programming timing constraints, as illustrated below. One commercial example is the VAXElan Toolkit [23], which provides timeouts for waiting on any input-output devices, semaphores, events, or message ports.

Timeouts in operations may be implemented with the same basic clock mechanisms as are used for *int_delay*. That is, a hardware interval timer or absolute timer could be directly employed, or the *get_time* function could be invoked in a busy wait loop. In either case, the implementation details are more complex since the timeout must be coordinated with the primary object or resource that is being requested (message, semaphore, event,...).

**Examples:**

Define a semaphore $P$ operation with timeout as follows:

$P(S, t)$ : Wait until either $S > 0$ or $time = t$, whichever happens first.
If $S > 0$, then $S := S - 1$ and return true.
Otherwise, return false.
{The operation is assumed to be atomic.}

$T(P(S,t))$ must be some function of both the parameter $t$ and the time of the start event for $P(S, t)$ for a particular call of the statement. The lower bound component is almost certainly always $tp_{min}$. (A possible exception is mentioned below.) The upper bound represents the worst-case time when a timeout occurs. Two cases are possible: an "immediate" timeout because $t$ is too small or a later timeout.

In the first case, $t < t_0$ for some computer time $t_0$ that is the *first* one compared against $t$. Execution bounds here are the times for entering $P$, making the tests against $S$ and $t$, and returning. (If the lower bound is smaller than $tp_{min}$, then this also becomes the lower bound for $T(P(S,t))$.)

The failure for the second case occurs at some computer time $ct = rt + \delta, \delta$ in $E$, such that $ct = t + e_1$, where $e_1$ accounts for any missed ticks of $ct$ due to overhead. Therefore, the timeout occurs at real time $ct - \delta = t + e_1 - \delta$. Adding in a term $e_2$ for the time to clean up and return after the timeout, we obtain a final event time $rt_f = t + e_1 - \delta + e_2$. The upper bound is the maximum of $rt_f$ less the time of the start event of $P(S, t)$. The maximum of $rt_f$ is $t + \varepsilon + e_{max}$, where $e_{max}$ is the sum of the maximums of $e_1$ and $e_2$.

One purpose for working out the details in this example is to note that bounds should be derivable for each element in these timing expressions, e.g., $e_1$ or $e_2$.

## 16.5.2   Communications with Timeouts and Time Stamps

Consider a *synchronous* communications mechanism for handling a simple form of events. An event is posted or sent with a send primitive and is obtained or received with a receive operation. Both the sender and receiver are blocked on their respective primitives until either a rendezvous or a timeout occurs. Events are time stamped in the loose sense that the rendezvous time is also returned at the completion of the operations.

The receive function will be used and defined in the following manner:

$$ev := receive(event\_name, t)$$

where *event_name* is an input identifying the type of event, $t$ is an absolute time used as the timeout, and the returned value $ev$ is a pair $ev.name$ and $ev.time$. If a timeout occurs, $ev.name = timeout$ and $ev.time$ is nominally equal to $t$. Otherwise, $ev.name = event\_name$ and $ev.time$ gives the time stamp value, $ts$ say, $ts < t$. $ts$ is some computer time computed sometime between the start and end events of the receive. One could also specify a sender process, a port, or a channel as part of the input of receive, but this is not necessary for our timing analysis purposes. (Aside: In the last section, our definition of $P(S, t)$ permitted a true return, i.e., no timeout, if $time = t$; here, for variety, we assume that $ts < t$ on an event.)

In this section, we will analyze receive and a non-trivial example that uses timeouts and time stamps. The send operation will not be examined or defined in any detail, since we will need it only in a peripheral way.

First consider the no-timeout case for receive, when $ev.time = ts < t$; $ts$ is the rendezvous time obtained by invoking, say, *get_time*, in the receive. The real time corresponding to $ts$ is $ts + \delta$ for some $\delta$ in $E$. Let $T_{roh}$ be the bounds for the software overheads in receive. Then at the end event of $ev := receive(event\_name, t)$, the real time is $rt = ts + \delta + e$, where $e$ in $T_{roh}$.

When the timeout event occurs, computer time $ct \geq t$. Two possibilities arise, similar to those treated in the $P(S, t)$ analysis (Section 16.5.1). If the timeout value $t$ was too small initially, for example, if it was less than computer time at the start event of receive, then the real time at the end event of receive is $rt_{start} + e, e$ in $T_{roh}$, where $rt_{start}$ is the real time at the start event of the receive. The second-case timeout occurs at computer time $ct = t + e_1$, where $e_1$ accounts for any missed ticks of $ct$ due to overhead. Real time at the timeout is therefore $t + e_1 + \delta, \delta$ in $E$.

Finally, real time at the end event of the receive can be expressed as $T + \delta + e, e$ in $T_{roh}$, where we have included $e_1$ in $e$ as well as the other overheads.

The examples to be analyzed are programs to recognize single and double clicks from a button on a mouse input device (e.g., [6]). A user clicks the button by depressing it (D for button *down*) and then letting it go (U for button *up*). If the time between the D and U events is less than some given interval $t_{sc}$, a single-click event is defined. A double-click event is two single clicks separated by an interval less than a given $t_{dc}$; more specifically, $t_{D2} - t_{U1} < t_{dc}$, where $t_{D2}$ is the time of the second click's down event and $t_{U1}$ is the time of the first click's up event. A recognizer for single clicks might be the following program:

```
{Recognize a single click.}
loop
        down := receive(D, inf);  {inf is a very large number.}
        t1 := down.time + tsc;
        up := receive(U, t1);
        if up.name = U then {single click} send(SC)
        else {timeout} receive(U, inf)
end loop
```

Our aim is to show that at the "$send(SC)$," we have $down.name = D, up.name = U$, and $rt_{up} - rt_{down} < tsc + err_1$, where $rt_{up}$ is the real time at the up event, $rt_{down}$ is the real time at the down event, and $err_1$ is some small error term that can be bounded. Similarly, we wish the following assertions to hold at the timeout: $down.name = D, up.name = timeout$, and $rt_{up} - rt_{down} = tsc + err_2$, where $rt_{down}$ is as before, $rt_{up}$ is the real time at the timeout event of $receive(U, t1)$, and $err_2$ is an error term. Note that this formulation also shows the existence of an ambiguous window around $tsc$, where single clicks may be detected or missed depending on the relative values of particular instances of $err_1$ and $err_2$.

Using our timing logic and the results of the analysis of receive, we can annotate the program with provable assertions:

```
loop
        down := receive(D, inf); {S1}
        {down.name = D, rt_down in down.time + E, rt in down.time + E + T_roh}
        t1 := down.time + tsc; {S2}
        {t1 = down.time + tsc, rt_down in down.time + E,
          rt in down.time + E + T_roh + T(S2)}
        up := receive(U, t1); {S3}
        {up.name =
            U ⇒ (rt_up in up.time + E, rt in up.time + E + T_roh, up.time < t1),
            up.name = timeout ⇒ (rt in t1 + E + T_roh or
            (rt in down.time + 2×E + 2×T_roh + T(S2) and
            rt in t2 + E + T_roh, t2 > t1))}
        if up.name = U then send(SC)
        else receive(U, inf)
end loop
```

Since $rt_{down}$ in $down.time + E$ after $S1$, we have $rt_{down} = down.time + \delta_1, \delta_1$ in $E$. Similarly, for the case that $up.name = U$ after $S3$, we have $rt_{up} = up.time + \delta_2, \delta_2$ in $E$. The assertions after $S2$ and $S3$ give

$$down.time = t1 - tsc \text{ and } up.time = t1 - deltat1 \text{ for some } deltat1 > 0.$$

Combining these, we get

$$\begin{aligned} rt_{up} - rt_{down} &= up.time + \delta_2 - down.time - \delta_1 \\ &= tsc - deltat1 + \delta_2 - \delta_1. \end{aligned}$$

Since $\delta_1, \delta_2$ in $E$, the difference can be bounded:

$$rt_{up} - rt_{down} < tsc + err_1, \text{ for } err_1 = 2\varepsilon.$$

When $up.name = timeout$, the situation is slightly more complex because there is the possibility that the interval $tsc$ is smaller than the execution time overhead between the down and up clicks. Provided that $tsc$ is large enough, the first implication on the timeout assertion holds and we also have

$$rt_{up} = t1 + \delta_1 + e, \delta_1 \text{ in } E, \ e \text{ in } T_{roh}.$$

Using the same expressions for $rt_{down}$ and $t1$ as before, we get

$$\begin{aligned} rt_{up} - rt_{down} &= t1 + \delta_1 + e - (t1 - tsc + \delta_2) \\ &= tsc + \delta_1 - \delta_2 + e, \delta_1, \delta_2 \text{ in } E, \ e \text{ in } T_{roh} \\ &= tsc + err_2 \end{aligned}$$

where $err_2$ in $2E + T_{roh}$.

If $tsc$ is too small, the program will always timeout, indicating that the system is not fast enough to recognize a single click. To be safe, $tsc$ should certainly be larger than the maximum of $T(S2) + 2T_{roh} + 2E$.

A recognizer for a double click employs similar ideas:

```
{Recognize a double click.}
down1 := receive(D, inf);
t1 := down1.time + tsc;
loop
        up1 := receive(U, t1);
        if up1.name = U then {first single click}
        begin
                t2 := up1.time + tdc;
                down2 := receive(D, t2);
                if down2.name = D then {Start 2nd single click.}
                begin
                        t1 :— down2.time + tsc;
                        up2 := receive(U, t1);
                        if up2.name = U then {double click} send(DC)
```

$$\textbf{else } up2 := receive(U, inf)$$
$$\textbf{end}$$
$$\textbf{end}$$
$$\textbf{else } up1 := receive(U, inf);$$
$$down1 := receive(D, inf);$$
$$t1 := down1.time + tsc$$
$$\textbf{end loop}$$

The program logic is sufficiently complex to warrant some arguments in favor of correctness. Assuming that computer time and real time are identical and that overhead time is zero, the following assertions hold at the double click send(DC):

$First\_Single\_Click$ :
  $down1.name = D, up1.name = U, up1.time - down1.time < tsc$
$Second\_Single\_Click$ :
  $down2.name = D, up2.name = U, up2.time - down2.time < tsc$ $Double\_Click$ :
  $\{First\_Single\_Click, Second\_Single\_Click, down2.time - up1.time < tdc\}$

Similarly, assertions of correctness can be made and proven at the timeout points and at the single-click event. We can then add in the overhead and timing error terms to obtain the real-time properties, using the same approach as for the single clicker.

# 16.6   Interrupt Handling and Processor Sharing

Our assumption of dedicated processors (Section 16.2.2) applies to some contemporary systems; it can be expected to hold more often for future applications where timing predictability and simplicity are more important than potential cost savings through resource sharing. Still, there are now, and will continue to be, many systems that must deal with processor sharing problems. Typically, a processor may be shared between a user process and a clock process, between a user process and one or more input-output processes, among several user processes, and combinations of these. An operating system is also required in order to regulate the multiplexing among processes. Timer and input-output driver processes are usually driven by or closely connected to hardware interrupts; the code for handling an interrupt often implements the software part of one of these processes. In this section, we show how the timing behavior for *some* of the above sharing can be predicted.

It is worth noting that the techniques for computing $T(S)$ and the timing logic presented in the previous sections can be used without change for those parts of a system that are *not* interruptible, i.e., where interrupts are masked off. Thus, for example, our methods can be employed to analyze the kernel and many higher-level components of an operating system that are global critical sections and uninterruptible. Similarly, our techniques apply to segments of applications processes that are run in a no-interrupt mode because of shared data possibilities or the need for predictable performance.

When interrupts are permitted and both interrupt handling times and frequencies can be bounded, the effects of processor sharing between a user process and one or more interrupt handlers can be included in a timing analysis. The interrupt handler for a clock interrupt, a "tick," might just update a variable representing time; the driver handler for an input-output device might update some state variables, transfer data to or from a buffer, and initiate another operation.

Suppose that an interrupt handler $IH$ can be characterized by the following parameters:

$F = [f_{min}, f_{max}]$ : bounds on the frequency of interrupts (number of times per second)

$T(IH)$ : execution time for the code

The interpretation is that the interval between interrupts is no smaller than $1/f_{max}$ seconds and no longer than $1/f_{min}$ seconds. Let $T(S)$ be the execution time bounds of a statement $S$ running on a dedicated processor and $T'(S)$ be the time bounds for $S$, including processor sharing with the interrupt handler. Then, the upper bound in $T'(S)$ is

$$t'_{max}(S) = t_{max}(S) + t'_{max}S) \times f_{max} \times t_{max}(IH)$$

giving

$$t'_{max}(S) = t_{max}(S)/(1 - f_{max} \times t_{max}(IH)).$$

A similar result is obtained for $t'_{min}(S)$. The proof rule (*) of Section 16.2.4 is changed in a straightforward way to reflect the new execution times:

$$\{P\} < RT_0 := RT; S; RT := RT_0 + T'(S) > \{Q\}.$$

Note that our results for $T'(S)$ should be adjusted upward so that $t'_{max}(S) = t_{max}(S) + k \times t_{max}(IH)$, for some integer $k$, to eliminate "fractional" handling of the last interrupt; a similar downward adjustment should be made for $t'_{min}(S)$. The level of granularity at which these results should be applied depends on $F$; clearly, one wishes to avoid a buildup of rounding-up and rounding-down errors, that would make the final bounds meaningless. Assuming that interrupt handlers are non-interruptible, the effects of more than one handler can also be incorporated using the same ideas.

The interrupt-handling results can also be employed for the analysis of more elaborate instances of processor sharing. One example is the class of slice-based software architectures in common use in hard real-time systems [3]. Processes are broken into non-preemptible units called *slices*; these are scheduled by a cycle executive, driven by a timer, that consults a scheduling table at each clock tick [21]. Each slice can be analyzed for execution times *a priori*, given also some frequency and bounds information on the clock and the input-output interrupt handlers. Slices can be interrupted but not preempted—the slice continues after a handler completes. The cyclic executive itself is a non-preemptible process whose timing behavior can also be obtained. An extreme but practical example of a slice-based system is one where each cycle of a periodic process is non-preemptible and thus constitutes a slice (e.g., [2]).

Timing predictability seems impractical when a process can be preempted at arbitrary points in its code. If processes that are sharing a processor use time-related functions such as *int_delay*, their execution times also appear to be unpredictable in general; for example, if two processes are waiting on an *int_delay* and are "scheduled" to wake up at the same time, then it is not evident how to associate practical time bounds with each process's delay. More study is needed to define particular useful cases that can (or cannot) be analyzed.

## 16.7    Discussion

The methodology for specifying, predicting, and proving assertions about time is new and promising, but still incomplete and untested in practice. The major outstanding issue is whether or not *useful* best- and worst-case execution time bounds can be found for statements in contemporary higher-level languages and their underlying systems.

The obvious next step is to perform some experiments with programs in a suitable implemented language/system. The aim would be to determine whether some combination of measurements and analysis of the language, compiler, run-time system, and target architecture will yield good deterministic bounds and also confirm our definitions of the basic timing elements. In order to compute bounds on structured statements in general and to compute times for statements in particular programs, it would be desirable to build some automatic tools to help in the analysis, for example, tools that are realizations of our algorithms for various statement schemas (e.g., Section 16.3.2). Software for doing interval arithmetic is available (e.g., [16]) and should be a part of these tools.

Structured timing schemas for the components of higher-level languages, such as the schemas proposed in the chapter, correspond well with the philosophy and straightforward code generation of some modern compilers [26]. These seek to improve correctness, understanding, and maintainability by using simple parsing and predictable code generation.

A difficult problem is the determination of tight timing information on instructions and code sequences for contemporary computers; pipelining, caching, and a host of other performance-enhancing features seem to hinder timing predictability. By selecting appropriate granularities for the higher-level language elements, we hope that these and other hardware issues, such as exactly how and where to incorporate worst-case effects of memory and bus contention, can be handled practically. This work may also result in a clearer understanding and definition of those machine architectures and hardware features that permit timing predictability (perhaps in a manner similar to that reported in [27], where some microprocessor architectures are evaluated based on their suitability for compiler code generation).

There is also a need to analyze other types of statements, including standard input-output instructions, other forms of synchronization and communications operations, and guarded commands in conditional and iterative statements. Finding and proving the "right" kinds of assertions has been somewhat difficult; further experiences in reasoning with and about time should simplify this problem. Timing assertions and the associated proofs seem to be relatively simple, leading to optimism about the viability of our approach.

The main results and contributions of this work are the techniques that, in principle, permit the prediction of the timing as well as the logical behavior of programs. We believe that all of the following are novel: the idea and methods for computing time bounds, the ability to deal directly with both real time and computer times, the extension and application of Hoare logic for reasoning about time, and the illustration of specific assertions involving time for common problems.

## Acknowledgments

This chapter is a revised version of [22] and was published in *IEEE Trans. Software Eng.*, vol. 15, pp. 875-889, July 1989. The principal part of the research was accomplished at Laboratoire MASI, University of Paris 6, during the academic year 1986-87. Further work was done during a month's visit in spring 1987 at the Institüt für Informatik, ETH, Zürich, and during summer 1987 at the University of Washington. The research was supported in part by the above institutions, by a Fulbright research grant from the Franco-American Commission, and by the Washington Technology Center. I am grateful to Philippe Chretienne, Serge Fdida, Claude Girault, and John Zahorjan for some helpful discussions. Special thanks go to Kevin Jeffay for a critical and detailed reading of [22]; several of his suggestions have been followed in the revision.

## References

[1] *Military Standard Ada Programming Language*, ANSI/MIL-STD-1815A, U.S. Dept. of Defense, Washington, D.C., Jan. 1983.

[2] L.L. Alger and J.H. Lala, "A real time operating system for a nuclear power plant computer," in *Proc. Real-Time Systems Symp.*, IEEE Computer Society, New York, Dec. 1986, pp. 244-248.

[3] T.P. Baker and G.M. Scallon, "An architecture for real-time software systems," *IEEE Software*, May 1986, pp. 50-58.

[4] G. Berry and L. Cosserat, "The ESTEREL synchronous programming language and its mathematical semantics," in *Lecture Notes in Computer Science 197, Seminar in Concurrency*, S. Brooks, A. Roscoe, and G. Winskel (eds.), Springer-Verlag, New York, 1985, pp. 389-448.

[5] L. Bic and A. Shaw, *The Logical Design of Operating Systems*, 2nd edn., Prentice Hall, Englewood Cliffs, N.J., 1987.

[6] L. Cardelli and R. Pike, "Squeak: a language for communicating with mice," *Proc. SIGGRAPH '85*, ACM SIGGRAPH, vol. 19, no. 3, July 1985, pp. 199-204.

[7] D.R. Cheriton, M.A. Malcolm, L.S. Melen, and G.R. Sager, "Thoth, a portable real-time operating system," *Commun. ACM*, vol. 22, Feb. 1979, pp. 105-114.

[8] R.M. Clapp, L. Duchesneau, R.A. Volz, T.N. Mudge, and T. Schultze, "Toward real-time performance benchmarks for Ada," *Commun. ACM*, vol. 29, Aug. 1986, pp. 760-778.

[9] B. Dasarathy, "Timing constraints of real-time systems: constructs for expressing them, methods for validating them," *IEEE Trans. Software Eng.*, vol. SE-11, Jan. 1985, pp. 80-86.

[10] V.H. Haase, "Real-time-behavior of programs," *IEEE Trans. Software Eng.*, vol. SE-7, Sept. 1981, pp. 454-501.

[11] V.H. Haase, "Modular design of real-time systems," in *System Description Methodologies*, D. Teichroew and G. David (eds.), Elsevier, Amsterdam, 1985, pp. 91-100.

[12] C.A.R. Hoare, "An axiomatic basis for computer programming," *Commun. ACM*, vol. 12, Oct. 1969, pp. 576-580.

[13] F. Jahanian and A.K.-L. Mok, "Safety analysis of timing properties in real-time systems," *IEEE Trans. Software Eng.*, vol. SE-12, Sept. 1986, pp. 890-904.

[14] E. Kligerman and A.D. Stoyenko, "Real-time Euclid: a language for reliable real-time systems," *IEEE Trans. Software Eng.*, vol. SE-12, Sept. 1986, pp. 941-949.

[15] D.E. Knuth, *The Art of Computer Programming*, vol. 1, Fundamental Algorithms, 2nd ed., Addison-Wesley, Reading, Mass., 1973.

[16] U.W. Kulish and W.L. Miranker (eds.), *A New Approach to Scientific Computation*, Academic Press, New York, 1983.

[17] L. Lamport, "Time, clocks, and the ordering of events in a distributed system," *Commun. ACM*, vol. 21, July 1978, pp. 558-565.

[18] A.K.-L. Mok, "Fundamental design problems of distributed systems for the hard real-time environment," Ph.D. Dissertation, M.I.T., May 1983.

[19] R.E. Moore, *Interval Analysis*, Prentice Hall, Englewood Cliffs, N.J., 1966.

[20] A. Pnueli, presentation given at the Real-Time Systems Issues Workshop, Univ. of Texas, Austin, Dec. 1986.

[21] A. Shaw, "Software clocks, concurrent programming, and slice-based scheduling," in *Proc. Real-Time Systems Symp.*, IEEE Computer Society, New York, Dec. 1986, pp. 14-18.

[22] A. Shaw, "Reasoning about time in higher-level language software," Research Report, Laboratoire MASI, University of Paris, Apr. 1984.

[23] *VAXElan Technical Summary*, Digital Equipment Corp., 1983.

[24] R.A. Volz and T.N. Mudge, "Instruction level mechanisms for accurate real-time task scheduling," in *Proc. Real-Time Systems Symp.*, IEEE Computer Society, New York, Dec. 1986, pp. 209-215.

[25] N. Werum and H. Windauer, *Introduction to PEARL*, 2nd ed., Friedr Vieweg & Sohn, Wiesbaden, Germany, 1983.

[26] N. Wirth, "A fast and compact compiler for Modula-2," TR No. 64, Institüt für Informatik, ETH, Zürich, July 1986.

[27] N. Wirth, "Microprocessor architectures: a comparison based on code generation by compiler," *Commun. ACM*, vol. 29, pp. 978–990, Oct. 1986.

# 16.A    Predicting Program Execution Times

## 16.A.1    Introduction

Since the original paper was published, much work has been done by us and others in further developing and testing these and similar ideas. Most of this following research has concentrated on refining and extending the schema approach to predicting execution times and on validity predictions by experiments. This research is summarized for the most part in [11]. Related recent work on execution time prediction include [2–4, 8, 13].

## 16.A.2    Validation Experiments

Several software tools were constructed and a variety of experiments carried out in order to determine the practicality of the idea to use source-program-level schema as the basis for deterministic timing prediction [5–7]. The experiments were done with programs in the C language, using the GNU C compiler running on a Motorola 68010-based SUN2. The tools accept a C program and produce a time bound for the best- and worst-case execution times of the program. Validation is accomplished by comparing predictions with measurements. Hardware interferences such as clock interrupts and dynamic RAM memory refresh are explicitly taken into account.

The first sets of tools and experiments used a static analysis of program paths, as implied by the timing formulas obtained from the source language statement schema. User input in the form of best- and worst-case iteration counts was required for each loop. Two granularities were tried as the basic atomic unit or block for schema decomposition—a small atomic block corresponding to the terminal symbols of the source language (variables, constants, operators, ...) as proposed in our original paper, and a large atomic block corresponding approximately to expressions and control constructs. For the suite of relatively small C programs (the largest was 160 lines of C code) that were analyzed and measured, the results were very good. All timing estimates were "safe," i.e., within their actual best- and worst-case run times, and most bounds were reasonably tight, i.e., close to realizable run times. As expected, better results were obtained with the larger atomic block. When bounds were loose, it was apparent that the cause was the interrelationship among different program parts and within nested loops, which could not be handled by a purely static analysis technique.

A method for specifying dynamic execution paths through a program, but still using the statement schema for prediction, was then developed by Park; this restricted the set of execution paths and eliminated many infeasible paths that had contributed incorrectly to best- and worst-case predictions. Dynamic paths are described in a user language whose underlying basis is an extension of regular expressions, including negation and intersection. The correctness of user specifications can be established by assertional program proving techniques. Software tools were built to test the method with C programs. The approach worked extremely well, producing safe and very tight bounds on all the programs that were tested.

## 16.A.3  Parallel Program Prediction

The timing schema notion was applied to a variety of common parallel program constructs involving fork/joins for spawning and synchronizing the termination of processes; shared variable interactions through critical sections and general semaphores; distributed message passing; and remote procedure calls [10]. Hypothetical implementations were given to demonstrate the potential reasonableness and applicability of the schema. Some initial experiments were made on a shared memory multiprocessor (20-processor Sequent) [1]. The simplest process structures were used, where no process interactions occur except to synchronize the initiation and termination of processes. As above, predictions produced by the schema approach were compared with measured execution times. Predictions were safe and reasonably tight, despite the complexities of the underlying computer system.

## 16.A.4  Conclusion

We have demonstrated that the schema approach works well for relatively small sequential programs. An obvious need is to determine whether the methodology "scales" well to larger software. Much additional work is also required on deterministic timing prediction for parallel systems, and for input-output commands; underlying hardware complexities and variations make the search for generality particularly difficult. We have also applied and extended some of the prediction ideas (not the schema) into the area of executable languages for requirement and design specifications [9, 12].

# References

[1] J. Kim and A. Shaw, "An Experiment on Predicting and Measuring the Deterministic Execution Times of Parallel Programs on a Multiprocessor," Tech. Report #90-09-01, Dept. of Computer Science and Engineering, Univ. of Washington, Sept. 1990.

[2] K. Lin et al., "FLEX: A Language for Real-Time Systems Programming," in *Foundations of Real-Time Computing: Formal Specifications and Methods*, A. van Tilborg and G. Koob (eds.), Kluwer Academic Publishers, Dordrecht, The Netherlands, 1991, pp. 251-290.

[3] A. Mok et al., "Evaluating Tight Execution Time Bounds of Programs by Annotations," *Proc. of the 6th IEEE Workshop on Real-Time Operating Systems and Software*, May 1989, pp. 74-80.

[4] V. Nirkhe and W. Pugh, "A Partial Evaluator for the Maruti Hard Real-Time System," *Proc. of the 12th IEEE Real-Time Systems Symp.*, Dec. 1991, pp. 64-73.

[5] C. Park and A. Shaw, "Experiments with a Program Timing Tool Based on Source-Level Timing Schema," *Proc. of the 11th IEEE Real-Time Systems*

*Symp.*, Dec. 1990, pp. 72-81. (A revised version is also in *IEEE Computer*, vol. 24, no. 5, May 1991, pp. 48-57.)

[6] C. Park, "Predicting Program Execution Times by Analyzing Static and Dynamic Program Paths," Tech. Report #91-12-1, Dept. of Computer Science and Engineering, Univ. of Washington, Dec. 1991. (Also published in *Journal of Real-Time Systems*, 1993.)

[7] C. Park, "Predicting Deterministic Execution Times of Real-Time Programs," Ph.D. Dissertation, Tech. Report #92-08-02, Dept. of Computer Science and Engineering, Univ. of Washington, Aug. 1992.

[8] P. Puschner and Ch. Koza, "Calculating the Maximum Execution Time of Real-Time Programs," *Journal of Real-Time Systems*, vol. 1, no. 2, Sept. 1989, pp. 159-176.

[9] S. Raju and A. Shaw, "A Prototyping Environment for Specifying, Executing, and Checking Real-Time State Machines," Tech. Report #92-10-03, Dept. of Computer Science and Engineering, Univ. of Washington, Oct. 1992. (In publication in *Software-Practice and Experience.*)

[10] A. Shaw, "Deterministic Timing Schema for Parallel Programs," *Proc. of the 5th International Parallel Processing Symp.*, Apr. 1991, pp. 56-63.

[11] A. Shaw, "Towards a Timing Semantics for Programming Languages," *Foundations of Real-Time Computing: Formal Specifications and Methods*, A. van Tilborg and G. Koob (eds.), Kluwer Academic Publishers, 1991, pp. 217-249.

[12] A. Shaw, "Communicating Real-Time State Machines," *IEEE Trans. on Software Engineering*, vol. 18, no. 9, Sept. 1992, pp. 805-816.

[13] A. Stoyenko, "A Real-Time Language with a Schedulability Analyzer," Ph.D. Dissertation, Tech. Report #CSRI-206, Computer Systems Research Institute, Univ. of Toronto, Dec. 1987.

# Part VI

# Fault Tolerance and Architecture

# Part VI

# Fault Tolerance and
Architecture

# Chapter 17

# Action-Level Fault Tolerance

## K. H. (Kane) Kim

Action-level (AL) fault tolerance means to accomplish every critical action (output action of a critical task as specified) successfully in spite of component failures. Therefore, it is aimed for the highest degree of fault tolerance in real-time computer systems. Several basic techniques developed in recent years for realizing action-level fault tolerance in real-time LAN (local area network)-based systems are reviewed in this chapter.

## 17.1   Introduction

Real-time computing is a relatively old branch (at least 35 years old) of computer engineering but has been advancing rather slowly until recently. In the author's opinion the main reason was the small market size for real-time computing. However, in recent years, the researcher population in the field of real-time computing has shown rapid growth for various economic and technological reasons and as a result, the technology started advancing rapidly. Most large-scale real-time computing applications are of safety-critical type and thus require high reliability and fault tolerance properties from the computer systems used.

The most desirable types of fault tolerance techniques for use in real-time computer systems (RTCSs) are those for realizing **action-level (AL) fault tolerance**, which means to accomplish every critical action (output action of a critical task as specified) successfully in spite of component failures. Such techniques are thus aimed for the highest degree of fault tolerance in RTCSs. Several basic techniques developed in recent years for realizing action-level fault tolerance in real-time local area network (LAN)-based systems are reviewed in this chapter.

The chapter starts with the author's personal perspectives of the evolution of the two fields, the RTCS field and the fault-tolerant computer system (FTCS) field, in Section 17.2. Then in Section 17.3, a classification of various fault tolerance properties with respect to their values is discussed. In Section 17.4, two most important cornerstones of the real-time fault-tolerant (FT) distributed computer system (DCS) technology are discussed, and then basic techniques which can be viewed as important representatives of the cornerstone technologies are reviewed. One representative of the first cornerstone technology, the distributed recovery block (DRB) technique for constructing real-time FT processing nodes, is discussed in further detail in Section 17.5. Discussions are focused on the cases of LAN-based DCSs. A representative of the second cornerstone technology, the periodic reception history broadcast (PRHB) scheme for real-time network surveillance and reconfiguration (NSR), is discussed in further detail in Section 17.6. Major remaining research issues are discussed in Section 17.7.

## 17.2  Current States of Real-Time Computing and Fault-Tolerant Computing

### 17.2.1  Real-Time Computer System Technology

A **real-time computer system** (RTCS) is a system which must produce outputs within deadlines in response to stimuli from application environments or spontaneously within specified time intervals. Although the development of computer-based real-time application systems is a profession almost as old as the computer industry is, it is still done by and large in an artistic fashion lacking rigorous engineering disciplines. Most existing large-scale real-time computer systems break down under occasionally occurring peak load conditions. Therefore, design of real-time computer systems is not yet a mature field. There are several major reasons for this relatively slow maturing of the field. To name a few:

(1) Due to the relatively small size of the market that existed for this technology up to the recent past, a major portion of the computer industry has not pursued this technology and instead devoted itself to pursuing the business data processing market.

(2) In computer science and engineering, it has been fashionable to abstract away the timing aspect of computer programs as much as possible. Especially after the emergence of the multiprogramming scheme in the late 1950s through early 1960s, *(execution-)speed-independent analysis of concurrent programs and logical synchronization of asynchronous processes* swept the mainstream computer science field from the late 1960s through the 1980s and they are still the predominant fashions. Time-dependent programs are generally machine-dependent, and without adequate tools which are considered to be very sophisticated by today's standards, such programs cannot easily be ported across different types of machines and across different configurations of the same machine model. Therefore, such programs have been considered to be ugly.

(3) Due to the high cost of computer hardware in the 1960s and 1970s, computer scientists and engineers vigorously sought techniques for optimal utilization of hardware. One feature of many such techniques is that they make the analysis

of the temporal behavior of the computer system a very difficult task. They have thus discouraged computer engineers from dealing with the time domain in an explicit and systematic manner. This has slowed down the development of an effective programming language for real-time programming as well as the development of program analysis and validation tools.

However, dramatic reduction of the hardware cost that occurred in the past two decades made many *hardware utilization optimization techniques* much less significant because a greater portion of the computer system complexity and cost has been shifted from the hardware to the software. In fact, it is now often more cost-effective to design *one-process-per-processor* systems, and such approaches make the temporal behavior analysis easy and encourage high-level optimizations such as those aimed for faster guaranteed response and fault-tolerant high-availability operations.

Therefore, the explicit handling of the timing aspect of real-time programs, including requirement specification, design specification, and validation, has lagged behind in research and development. New ways of looking at the optimal design aspect have not yet been widely accepted in research circles.

## 17.2.2    Fault-Tolerant Computer System Technology

A **fault-tolerant computer system** (FTCS) is a system which can continue to operate reliably by producing acceptable outputs in spite of occasional occurrences of component failures, including those of both hardware and software components.

The main part of the FTCS field started in the late 1960s, although there were a few philosophical or abstract papers published as early as in the early 1950s. Numerous studies done on the techniques for *off-line testing and repair* since the 1950s are not regarded to be in the mainstream part of this field. Research on *coding techniques* for fault tolerance was active in the 1940s through 1970s but has diminished substantially in its fervor since the early 1980s. In the late 1960s and 1970s, most research activities dealt with circuit-level or **register-transfer-level fault tolerance** and in the late 1970s, research issues related to processor-level fault tolerance (i.e., treating a processor as the smallest replaceable unit) started being addressed seriously. In the 1980s, tolerance not only of hardware component failures but also of weaknesses of software components became a subject of serious discussion, and so was born the notion and subfield of **system-level fault tolerance.**

**Hardware fault tolerance** has been maturing rapidly in recent years. Two major reasons are:

(1) The hardware cost has become a relatively insignificant portion of the overall computer system cost, and thus use of hardware redundancy is easily justified in many safety-critical application environments.

(2) Major computer system vendors have succeeded in producing fault-tolerant and yet economic modules of substantial complexity, thereby enabling pro-

duction of "cost-competitive" computer systems with substantial hardware fault tolerance capabilities and opening a market of substantial size.

Therefore, the bigger remaining challenge is in the problem of tolerating design faults, primarily in the software domain. A major class of design faults are the *integration faults*. When a large number of hardware modules are assembled into a distributed computer system (DCS) through both physical interconnection and functional integration by incorporation of system software, the system developer often overlooks the possibilities of the system entering inconsistent states. This is due to the sheer functional complexity of the integrated system. Individual hardware components meet their specifications, but the specifications are often incomplete, if not inaccurate, with respect to their integration with others. Therefore, it is nearly impossible to avoid such integration design faults in developing large-scale DCSs.

One can thus conclude that the **system-level fault tolerance**, which is to tolerate both physical hardware faults and design faults (especially faults in system software effecting functional integration of a large number of hardware modules), is the most challenging area in fault-tolerant computing. Moreover, the challenge becomes greater in the area which is the intersection of the system-level fault tolerance field and the RTCS field. In fact, missing deadlines on the part of a RTCS is quite often as dangerous as producing incorrect values. Therefore, if incorporation of fault tolerance mechanisms increases the chance of a computer system missing deadlines, it would decrease the overall system reliability rather than improving it. In hard real-time computer systems, the boundary between the application software and the system software is often blurred, and thus non-negligible sources of design faults are much greater than in soft real-time computer systems.

## 17.3    Degrees of Fault Tolerance in RTCSs

Fault tolerance is not a property which can be pursued simplistically in an all-or-nothing fashion. In fact, in spite of the old history of fault-tolerant computing, there has been lack of careful distinction between highly desirable types of fault tolerance properties and significantly less valuable fault tolerance properties. The following classification of fault tolerance properties in Table 17.1 is a first step toward closing this gap.

In this classification scheme, five different categories of achievable fault tolerance are recognized. The top category is degree-4 fault tolerance. It is basically **action-level (AL) fault tolerance** in that every *visible action* (i.e., an output action or database update action) or every step of processing a critical input data item takes place successfully in spite of fault occurrences. Therefore, the maximum reliability is assured.

Degree-3 fault tolerance occurs when the recovery from a fault is so slow that there is no choice but to abandon the execution of a visible action which was interrupted due to a fault occurrence. Except for abandoning one or a few interrupted actions due to lack of time remaining in their deadlines after fault containment and restoration of a consistent state, all service functions will be resumed. So,

**Table 17.1  Degree of Fault Tolerance**

| Degree | Assumable Damages | Recovery Capabilities |
|---|---|---|
| < 4 > | No loss of visible actions (i.e., output actions or database update actions) | Action-level fault tolerance (recovery of an interrupted visible action) |
| < 3 > | Loss of one or more visible actions | Slow recovery of a service function (no loss of hardware) |
| < 2 > | Loss of one or more service functions | Partial recovery of hardware (service degradation) |
| < 1 > | Loss of all but a core set of critical service functions | Minimum recovery of core hardware (minimum critical services) |
| < 0 > | Loss of critical service | No fault tolerance |

there is no service degradation after the recovery. Degree-2 fault tolerance results in some service degradation, because in this case, not a full configuration of the hardware needed to sustain the full set of originally designed service functions can be recovered and thus some less critical services are sacrificed. Degree-1 fault tolerance represents the worst case of degree-2 fault tolerance in that it is aimed at sustaining the absolute minimum set of critical service functions with the recovery of a minimum core hardware configuration. If a critical service function cannot be maintained, then there is no longer a fault-tolerant system and one can say that degree-0 fault tolerance or no fault tolerance is facilitated. Of these, degree-4 fault tolerance schemes, i.e., AL fault tolerance schemes, are the most desirable. In fact, fault tolerance of degree 1–3 is less of a challenge now, due to the advances made in the commercial fault-tolerant computer industry during the past decade. On the other hand, only a few basic techniques are available for realizing AL fault tolerance.

# 17.4   Two Cornerstones of FTDCS Technology

A real-time DCS can be viewed as an interconnection of computing stations, where a **computing station** refers to a processing node (hardware and software) dedicated to the execution of one or a few application processes. Two most important cornerstones of the real-time FT DCS technology are:

(1) the set of techniques for constructing "hardened" computing stations which have the capabilities of real-time forward recovery, and

(2) the set of techniques for real-time network surveillance and reconfiguration (NSR), which includes

(2.1)  on-line diagnosis and reconfiguration of both processing nodes and shared communication facilities, and

(2.2)  support for reliable message communication among the computing stations.

Of the two sets of techniques, the most valuable ones are those suitable as basic building blocks of the technology for constructing AL FT systems. Although numerous techniques for construction of FT computing stations and NSR have been developed or have appeared in the literature, those applicable to the construction of AL FT systems are mostly specialized instances, variations, or combinations of the basic techniques reviewed in this section. Not all useful variations or combinations of the basic techniques have been explored, however.

## 17.4.1   Basic Techniques for Construction of Real-Time FT Computing Stations

The techniques can be divided into two groups.

### 17.4.1.1   For Tolerance of Hardware Faults Only

(1) **Voting triple modular redundancy (TMR)** (more generally, voting N-modular redundancy)

The essence of the **triple modular redundancy (TMR)** scheme is to use three copies of a computing component and take a vote with their execution results [3, 31]. When there is discrepancy, the result with a majority vote is used.

(2) **Pair of self-checking processing nodes (PSP) scheme**

The essence of this PSP scheme is to use two copies of a **self-checking computing component** in the form of a **primary-shadow** pair [14, 18] as shown in Figure 17.1.

A computing component is said to be **self-checking** if it possesses the capability of judging the reasonableness of its own computation results. The **internal audit logic** in a processing node, which is responsible for checking the computation results of the node, can be implemented with or without special hardware support. Internal audit hardware mechanisms have been extensively developed [28, 30, 32]. A well-known case of the PSP scheme implemented with a special internal audit hardware mechanism is the **pair of comparing pairs** (PCP) scheme used in the Stratus system [32]. A generic approach to software implementation of the internal audit logic is discussed in Section 17.5.

(3) **Temporary blackout handling**

A system-wide simultaneous disturbance caused by lightning, an unreliable power source, radiation, and so on, is referred to by the generic term **temporary blackout** [15]. In the case of a LAN system, a temporary blackout means a global fault of

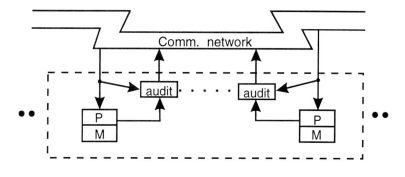

PSP-Structured Computing Station

**Figure 17.1** PSP-Structured Computing Station

the system. This is a unique characteristic since other types of faults usually create some localized damage to distributed computations. Efficiency and timing concerns lead to the selection of a procedure for detecting and recovering from temporary blackouts that is tailored to the detailed application logic. A typical forward recovery procedure involves first restoring critical state variables with the most recently saved values, next reading the current status of the application environment, and finally, establishing the computation to an appropriate state compatible with the current environment.

Therefore, a state saving mechanism is almost indispensable in applications subject to temporary blackouts. Whether AL fault tolerance can be achieved in the presence of temporary blackouts or not depends upon the nature of both temporary blackout events and the application tasks.

### 17.4.1.2    For Tolerance of Both Hardware and Software Faults

The following two basic techniques have been established in this area.

#### (1) Voting N-version scheme

A straight extension of the TMR scheme in the direction toward tolerance of both hardware and software faults results in the **voting N-version** scheme [4, 5]. This scheme uses multiple functionally equivalent versions of each critical software component with the voting approach for fault detection and result selection. Due to the high cost of designing and maintaining multiple versions, the use of three versions is the standard practice in applying the voting N-version scheme. Each version should run on a different node to facilitate hardware fault tolerance. The voting routine must run on all three processing nodes in a cooperative manner.

Moreover, the voting approach requires the design of multiple versions expected to generate *truly identical computation results*, which could be a severe restriction in cases where complexity of a program component is high. A number of experimental studies have been conducted with this scheme [6, 13], but much further research is needed to establish the scheme as a cost-effective technology.

(2) **Distributed recovery block (DRB) scheme**: a generalized active redundancy scheme

The DRB scheme uses the PSP scheme with software-implemented internal audit mechanisms as its core. It also uses the **recovery block** scheme [12, 27] for structuring general forms of software redundancy, including internal audit routines. This scheme is a flexible technique in that

a) a **DRB computing station**, which is a real-time FT computing station consisting of two or more nodes operating as cooperating partners under the DRB scheme, can operate with just two versions of a critical software component and two processing nodes, and

b) the two versions are not required to produce identical results and the second version need not be as sophisticated as the first version.

Several demonstrations of the performance of the scheme in practical application contexts have been conducted [2, 10, 14, 16]. A small company located in Los Angeles (SoHaR, Inc) extended the DRB scheme for use in real-time local area PC networks for nuclear reactor control applications and produced a commercial product prototype [10, 11]. However, further research is needed to establish guidelines for cost-effective design of recovery blocks. The DRB scheme will be discussed in more detail in Section 17.5.

## 17.4.2    Basic Techniques for Real-Time Network Surveillance and Reconfiguration (NSR)

The techniques for real-time NSR aim for minimizing the periods during which faulty components are lurking in DCSs. This means:

(1) to facilitate *fast learning* by each interested fault-free node of the faults or repair completions occurring in other parts of the DCS, which in turn means *diligent network surveillance* performed

(1.1) to detect and locate faulty nodes (crashed nodes and nodes in abnormal states),

(1.2) to detect message loss and ensure reliable message communication, and

(1.3) to recognize newly added or repaired processing nodes; and

(2) to facilitate *fast reconfiguration*, including

(2.1) functional amputation of faulty components, and

(2.2) redistribution of tasks, including assignment of tasks to newly incorporated or repaired nodes.

Basically, the following three types of approaches are conceivable:

(1)  *Centralized* [9, 11, 18],

(2)  *Decentralized* [7, 8, 19, 21], and

(3)  *Hybrid.*

Centralized approaches are simple and have been considered from the beginning days of distributed computing. Yet its integration with the techniques for construction of real-time FT computing stations has not been fully accomplished. In Section 17.5, a case of integrating the DRB scheme with centralized real-time NSR approaches is discussed. Decentralized approaches are much less mature as a technology, although again the basic concept is at least 20 years old. In fact, practical decentralized techniques that have been established so far and possess tightly bounded delay characteristics are scarce. The best examples of practical techniques that can be used in constructing hard real-time FT DCSs seem to be the PRHB (periodic reception history broadcast) technique formulated by Kopetz, Grunsteidl, and Reisinger in [21] and extended in [19] and its variations, such as the TTP scheme [22]. Hybrid approaches can be developed in rigorous forms only after decentralized approaches are well understood.

# 17.5    The DRB Scheme for Real-Time FT Computing Stations

The DRB scheme is one of the most flexible techniques for construction of real-time FT computing stations. The DRB scheme exploits the principle of *parallel replicated execution* to effect AL fault tolerance. Two major parts of the DRB scheme are the PSP scheme and the recovery block scheme.

## 17.5.1    Primary-Shadow PSP Scheme Forming the Core of the DRB Scheme

The DRB scheme uses software-implemented internal audit mechanisms. Such mechanisms are not necessarily substitutes for hardware-implemented internal audit mechanisms, but rather, the former can be supplements to the latter. One of the most versatile and flexible type of internal audit software mechanisms is the **acceptance test**, which is a routine for checking the acceptability of the execution results of a task [12, 27]. Use of this mechanism, possibly in conjunction with some internal audit hardware mechanisms, is the approach adopted in the DRB scheme.

Figure 17.2 illustrates a PSP-structured computing station using the internal audit function implemented in the form of an acceptance test routine. For the sake of simplicity in discussion, Figure 17.2 depicts the special case where the following assumption holds:

(A1)  The arrival rate of data items is such that each time a data item arrives, no other data items are being processed.

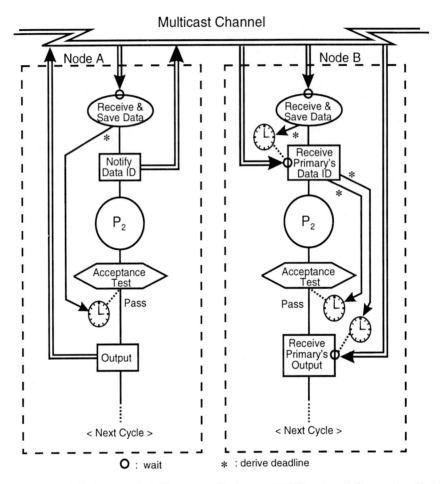

**Figure 17.2** A Fault-Free Task Execution Cycle of a PSP-Structured Computing Station

Node A is the initial *primary* node and node B is the initial *shadow* node within this computing station. Although not shown explicitly in Figure 17.2, each of the partner nodes in a PSP station is assumed to contain its own local database, which keeps persistent information used during more than one task cycle. Although there are many conceivable options in controlling possible times for updating this database, we assume that the database is updated upon sucessful completion of the acceptance test execution, not before the acceptance test time. Both nodes obtain input data from the multicast channel (built on a system-wide multi-access communication network, e.g., [24]). The next step for the primary node A is to inform the shadow node B of the ID of the data item that the former received (or selected in general) for processing in the current task cycle. This step is not essential in this special case subject to (A1). Nodes A and B process their copies of the same data item and perform their self-checking concurrently by using the same acceptance test routine. Since node A passes the test, it delivers the results to both the successor computing station(s) and node B, and then starts the next task cycle. By receiving the output from node A, node B detects the success of node A, and if node B has also succeeded in its acceptance test, it too starts the next task cycle.

Suppose that another PSP station is the successor station. Nodes C and D process the data received from node A and perform their self-checking concurrently, but this time the primary node C fails in passing the acceptance test (or crashes during the processing of the data item), whereas the shadow node D passes. Node D will learn the failure of node C by noticing the absence of output from node C. Node D then becomes a new primary and delivers its task execution results to both its successor computing station(s) and node C. Meanwhile, node C, if alive, attempts to become a new useful shadow node by making a retry of the processing of the saved data item. If node C passes the self-checking test this time, it can then continue as a useful shadow node and proceeds to the next task cycle.

In many applications, assumption (A1) does not hold. It is thus necessary to provide input data queues in each node within a PSP station. Each node may contain multiple input data queues corresponding to multiple data sources. Therefore, it is important for the partner nodes in a PSP station to ensure that they process the same data item in each task execution cycle. This is the main reason why the step of reporting the ID of the selected data item is taken by the primary node in Figure 17.2 .

In addition, in typical DCSs with multicast channels, receiving data and placing them into input data queues within each node are handled by an independent unit (often called a LAN interface processor) operating concurrently with the main processor(s) in the node executing the application task(s). The interaction protocol used by the partner nodes of a PSP station in such DCSs are thus more complicated than those shown in Figure 17.2.

## 17.5.2    The Algorithm Redundancy Component of the DRB Scheme

In order to support handling of not only hardware faults but also software faults, the above primary-shadow PSP scheme can be extended by incorporating the approach of using multiple versions of the application task procedure. Such versions are called **try blocks**. The extended scheme is the **distributed recovery block** (DRB) scheme and it uses the **recovery block** language construct to support the incorporation of try blocks and acceptance tests [12, 27].

The syntax of recovery block is as follows:

*ensure* T *by* $B_1$ *else by* $B_2$ ... *else by* $B_n$ *else error.*

Here, T denotes the **acceptance test**, $B_1$ the **primary try block**, and $B_k$, $2 < k < n$, the **alternate try blocks**. All the try blocks are designed to produce the same or similar computational results. The acceptance test is a logical expression representing the criterion for determining the acceptability of the execution results of the try blocks. A **try** (i.e., execution of a try block) is thus always followed by an acceptance test. If an error is detected during a try (by hardware or operating

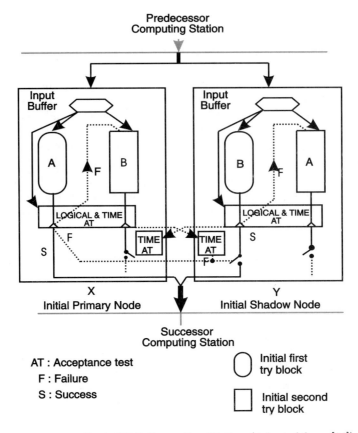

**Figure 17.3** Basic DRB Computing Station (Adapted from [14])

system mechanisms) or as a result of an acceptance test execution, then a rollback-and-retry with another try block follows.

In the DRB scheme, a recovery block is replicated into multiple nodes, forming a **DRB computing station** for parallel redundant processing. In most cases a recovery block containing just two try blocks is designed and then assigned to a pair of nodes as depicted in Figure 17.3. A try not completed within the maximum execution time allowed for each try block due to hardware faults or excessive looping is treated as a failure. Therefore, the acceptance test can be viewed as a combination of both **logic** and **time** acceptance tests.

As shown in Figure 17.3, the roles of the two try blocks are assigned differently in the two nodes. The governing rule is that the primary node tries to execute the primary try block whenever possible, whereas the shadow node tries to execute the alternate try block. Therefore, primary node X uses try block A as the first try block initially, whereas shadow node Y uses try block B as the initial first try block. Until a fault is detected, both nodes receive the same input data, process the data by use of two different try blocks, and check the results by use of the acceptance test concurrently. If the primary node X fails and the two nodes exchange their roles, then the new primary node Y will start executing the primary try block A under the rule mentioned above.

In case the shadow node fails, the primary node is not disturbed. This is based on the principle that the actions of the primary node should not depend on those of the shadow node, so that the execution overhead, which has an adverse impact on the response time of the computer system, may be minimized. Whether the primary node fails or the shadow node fails, the failed node attempts to become an operational shadow node without disturbing the (new) primary node; it attempts to roll back and retry with its second try block to bring its application computation state, including local database, up to date.

## 17.5.3    Recursive Shadowing with $N$ ($> 2$) Try Blocks

In some highly safety-critical applications, the system designer may design more than two try blocks into a recovery block for the sake of increased reliability. Although several approaches to structuring a DRB station equipped with three try blocks are conceivable, one of the most natural approaches is the **recursive shadowing** approach, which is to treat the third node as a shadow node for the team of the first two nodes, as depicted in Figure 17.4 [16, 18].

Node Z in the figure will normally use try block C as its primary try block and deliver its results only when both X and Y fail to produce acceptable results in time. Nodes X and Y behave like a single functional node with respect to interfacing with their shadow node Z. They must share responsibilities for providing their status information to node Z at various points. If node X or Y crashes, then it can be replaced by node Z and thus the computing station can start functioning as an ordinary two-node DRB station. Similarly, crash of node Z will result in the computing station functioning as an ordinary two-node DRB station. If both X and Y fail at their acceptance tests but are alive, then node Z becomes the new primary node and one of the two failed nodes (X and Y) should become the new secondary node (a shadow for node Z) and the other should become the third node (a shadow for the team of Z and the secondary node).

In an $n$-node DRB station, the $n$th node functions as a shadow for the team of the first $n-1$ nodes. A natural consequence of this recursive shadowing organization is the modest increase in the implementation complexity as the number of nodes used in a DRB station increases.

## 17.5.4    Virtual DRB (VDRB) Stations

When the number of nodes in a DCS is less than twice the number of DRB stations to be constructed to support a given real-time application, an option worth exploring is to use the same node pair to form multiple **virtual DRB** (VDRB) stations. Each of the VDRB stations hosted on the same node pair is functionally equivalent to a DRB station when it is in execution using a time slice of the node pair. An interesting requirement imposed on each node pair supporting multiple VDRB stations is that the task schedulers on both partner nodes must schedule the executions of **virtual nodes** (i.e., constituent nodes of VDRB stations) such that

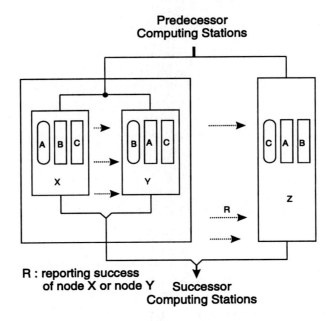

**Figure 17.4** A DRB Station That Uses Three Try Blocks in the Recursive Shadowing Mode (Adapted from [16])

the executions of **partner virtual nodes** (belonging to the same VDRB station) are maximally overlapped in time.

### 17.5.5   Supervisor Station and Worker DRB Computing Stations

In typical LAN-based real-time FT systems using the DRB scheme, there will be several DRB stations among which real-time data flow. These stations are called here **worker DRB stations**. In addition, we may also incorporate a supervisor station which will perform a major part of the real-time NSR [11, 18].

The supervisor station is in general responsible for detection of node crashes, detection of misjudgments by the nodes in DRB stations about the status of their partner nodes (i.e., misjudgments occurring due to communication link faults), supporting reliable message communication among computing stations, and network reconfiguration, including task redistribution. Some of these functions, e.g., detection of node crashes, can be decentralized [21].

## 17.6   The PRHB Scheme for Real-Time NSR

The PRHB scheme is reviewed here because at present the scheme and its variations [8, 19, 21] are the best examples of practical decentralized NSR techniques that possess tightly bounded delay characteristics and thus are suitable as building blocks of AL FT real-time systems.

The PRHB scheme was originally designed for use in TDMA (time-division multiplexed access) bus-based LAN systems [21]. Each node periodically owns the bus, i.e., holds exclusive right for broadcasting through the bus, for a fixed duration called a **bus slot**. The key idea in the PRHB scheme is to have each node listen to the bus all the time and, during its bus slot, broadcast a report on its listening experiences during the most recent TDMA cycle. Each broadcasted report on listening experiences is in the form of a **reception history vector** (RHV) $[v_1, v_2, \ldots, v_n]$, where $n$ denotes the number of bus slots in a TDMA cycle and $v_i$ is 1 if the reporting node heard the most recent broadcast made by the owner node of the $i$ th bus slot and 0, otherwise. The RHV is broadcasted by every active node each time its bus slot arrives, regardless of whether the node has any application message to broadcast. If there is an application message to broadcast, it is combined with the RHV. Each node keeps RHVs received from different nodes in its own data structure called the **reception history matrix** (RHM), and by analyzing this RHM it can discover recent changes in the health status of the constituent nodes of the LAN system quickly and accurately.

An RHM analysis procedure enabling every fault-free node to detect any single fault of either a processor or a link between a processor and the TDMA bus with a minimal delay which is always less than two TDMA cycles was developed in [17]. Here the fault may be of permanent or temporary nature. It may be in a host processor or in a processor-bus link. If a bus slot is 1 ms and there are 16 nodes in the DCS, then two TDMA cycles take 32 ms. Also, once a repaired node is activated, its active status can be recognized by other healthy nodes within two TDMA cycles. In cases where multiple but less than half the nodes in the system experience faults of their processors or processor-bus links, every node can again detect them through analysis of its RHM in time less than two TDMA cycles [19]. In these cases of higher fault rates, recognition of the active status of a repaired node can take up to three TDMA cycles.

Therefore, in the case of a TDMA bus-based LAN system incorporating the PRHB scheme, NSR is very efficient but it is achieved at the cost of the overhead processing power needed for RHM analysis and a small part of the bus bandwidth spent for RHV broadcast. The RHM analysis can be off-loaded to an auxiliary processor. A similar NSR scheme with less communication overhead, called the time-triggered protocol (TTP), was recently formulated by Kopetz in [22]. Further research is needed to find similar efficient NSR schemes that can be implemented on different LAN access schemes, e.g., CSMA with deterministic collision resolution, token ring, and so on.

## 17.7   Major Remaining Issues

**(1) Efficient integration of the schemes for construction of real-time FT computing stations with real-time NSR schemes**

As mentioned in Section 17.4, research in this direction started only in recent years, but research efforts are expected to expand rapidly in the next few years.

## (2) Techniques for hardening groups of computing stations

The basic techniques for structuring real-time FT computing stations discussed in Section 17.4 are designed to prevent errors from crossing computing station boundaries. In some large-scale real-time applications, integration design faults are unavoidable and internal audit mechanisms in computing stations have limited detection coverage. Therefore, the probability of faulty information crossing the computing station boundary cannot be ignored. In such applications, e.g., national defense applications, it may thus be worth employing schemes that make a group of computing stations cooperate in recovery, thereby forming an FT **computing station group**. Such schemes must be considered only as supplements to those techniques discussed in Section 17.4. Some promising schemes [1, 15, 27] have been studied, but their efficient implementation has been insufficiently studied. Also, when a group of real-time computing stations share a persistent database, structuring of *real-time database transactions* is an important issue and much research is needed in this area [29].

## (3) Rigorous validation and evaluation of FT RTCSs

Accurate information on the powers and costs of various fault tolerance schemes is currently lacking. Here **testbed-based evaluation** is most desirable. The availability of low-cost building blocks such as microcomputers and interconnection devices has made the construction of cost-effective DCS testbeds not much more expensive than constructing pure software simulators running on centralized computer systems. Testbeds are capable of representing the operating environment and input scenario more accurately than do software simulators.

An efficient method for validating the schemes aimed at handling design faults is currently lacking. The main difficulty is in the creation of realistic fault conditions.

Modeling and analysis efforts aimed at obtaining more precise understanding of the costs and benefits of the FT distributed computing techniques have started growing in recent years. The most basic issue faced in such scientific pursuit is the selection of a **fault model**, i.e., a characterization of the "non-negligible" patterns of fault occurrences [26].

In a DCS, the modularity is an inherent and valuable characteristic and thus selection of a fault model boils down to characterization of the anomalous symptoms which each replaceable component (typically a processing node or a connection device) may exhibit to the outside. In the literature dealing with the analysis of FT distributed computing algorithms (not in practical design and evaluation of systems), replaceable components have most often been modeled as units of one of the two extreme types. One extreme model which is at the simplest end in the domain of conceivable models is the **fail-silent unit** (FSU) model, which can exhibit only absence of an explicit output upon occurrence of any internal fault [25]. No erroneous values are explicitly sent out from such units. The model which is at the other extreme end in terms of complex faulty output behavior is the **malicious unit** (MaU) model, also called the **Byzantine unit** model [23]. A malicious unit is capable not only of sending out erroneous values but also of sending out sequences of values as if they were carefully manufactured to cause troubles to monitoring and diagnosing units.

Our assessment of the state of the art in this fault modeling area is as follows [20]:

(a) The FSU model is an idealistic component model which should be taken as a 'design goal' for each replaceable component. However, for evaluating many existing DCSs, it is too simplistic a model of components to use, even if absence of software faults can be assured before the modeling step.

(b) The MaU model has been devised to facilitate theoretical investigation of some limits of various FT algorithms. However, for use in practical system design and evaluation, the MaU model (or at least all the versions that have appeared in the literature) appears to have fundamental shortcomings. The main shortcoming is that the probability of malicious behavior occurring in a real system is much smaller than the probability of one of the other assumptions adopted in conjunction with the MaU model being violated. It is an 'unfair' model in that it tends to draw attention to events of negligible occurrence probabilities while taking attention away from events of higher occurrence probabilities.

(c) What is essentially required to advance the state of the art in this important area is a systematic method for laying out possible occurrences of all types of anomalous events in the space of occurrence probabilities and choosing in a fair manner the subset of the possible events to deal with, i.e., choosing events by use of the occurrence probability as the main criterion for selecting or ignoring. Further details are referred to [20].

## (4) Software engineering environment (SEE) for real-time FT DCSs

Effective tools that support systematic design and validation of real-time FT DCSs are lacking. In fact, even the **software engineering environments** (SEEs) for producing non-FT real-time systems have not yet been well established . However, rapid advances appear to be occurring currently in this area. Also, the author believes that powerful graphics tools hold great promise for use in reducing the software engineering problems that are highly troublesome at present in real-time FT computing applications.

# Acknowledgments

The work reported here was supported in part by the US Navy, NSWC Dahlgren Division, under Contract N60921-92-C-0204, in part by the University of California MICRO Program under Grant 93-080, in part by USAF Rome Labs, and in part by a grant from Hitachi Co., Ltd.

# References

[1] Anderson, T., and Knight, J. C., "A Framework for Software Fault Tolerance in Real-Time System," *IEEE Transactions on Software Engineering*, May 1983, pp. 355–364.

[2] Armstrong, L. T., and Lawrence, T. F., "Adaptive Fault Tolerance," *Proc. 1991 NSWC Systems Design Synthesis Technology Workshop*, Silver Spring, MD, Sept. 1991.

[3] Avizienis, A., Gilley, G., Mathur G. C., Rennels F. P., Rohr, J. A., and Rubin, D. K., "The STAR (Self Testing and Repairing) Computer: An Investigation of the Theory and Practice of Fault-Tolerant Computer Design," *IEEE Transactions on Computers*, Vol. C-20, No. 11, Nov. 1971, pp. 1312–1321.

[4] Avizienis, A., "Fault Tolerance and Fault Intolerance: Complementary Approaches to Reliable Computing," *Proc. 1975 Int'l Conf. on Reliable Software*, Los Angeles, Apr. 1975, pp. 458–464.

[5] Avizienis, A, "The N-Version Approach to Fault-Tolerant Software," *IEEE Transactions on Software Engineering*, Vol. SE-11, No. 12, Dec. 1985, pp. 1491–1501.

[6] Avizienis, A., Lyu, M. R., and Schutz, W., "In Search of Effective Diversity: A Six-Language Study of Fault-Tolerant Flight Control Software," *Proc. IEEE Computer Society's FTCS-18*, pp. 15–22.

[7] Cristian, F., "Agreeing on Who Is Present and Who Is Absent in a Synchronous Distributed System," *Proc. IEEE Computer Society's 18th Int'l Symp. on Fault-Tolerant Computing* (FTCS-18), Tokyo, June 1988, pp. 206–211.

[8] Ezhilchelvan, P. D. , and Lemas, R, "A Robust Group Membership Algorithm for Distributed Real-Time Systems," *Proc. IEEE Computer Society's Real-Time Systems Symp.*, Dec. 1990, pp. 173–179.

[9] Garcia-Molina, H., "Elections in a Distributed Computing System," *IEEE Transactions on Computers,* Jan. 1982, pp. 48–59.

[10] Hecht, M., Agron, J., and Hochhauser, S., "A Distributed Fault Tolerant Architecture for Nuclear Reactor Control and Safety Functions," *Proc. IEEE Computer Society's 1989 Real-Time Systems Symp.*, Dec. 1989, pp.214–221.

[11] Hecht, M. et al., "A Distributed Fault Tolerant Architecture for Nuclear Reactor and Other Critical Process Control Applications," *Proc. IEEE Computer Society's 21st Int'l Symp. on Fault-Tolerant Computing*, June 1991, Montreal, pp. 462–469.

[12] Horning, J. J., Lauer, H. C., Melliar-Smith, P. M., and Randell, B., "A Program Structure for Error Detection and Recovery", *Lecture Notes in Computer Science,* Vol. 16, Springer-Verlag, New York, 1974, pp. 171–187.

[13] Kelly, J. P. J., et al., "A Large Scale Second Generation Experiment in Multiversion Software: Description and Early Results," *Proc. FTCS-18*, pp. 9–14.

[14] Kim, K. H., and Welch, H. O., "Distributed Execution of Recovery Blocks: An Approach to Uniform Treatment of Hardware and Software Faults in Real-Time Applications," *IEEE Transactions on Computers*, May 1989, pp. 626–636.

[15] Kim, K. H., "Approaches to System-Level Fault Tolerance in Distributed Real-Time Computer Systems," *Proc. 4th Int'l Conf. on Fault-Tolerant Computing Systems*, Baden-Baden, Germany, Sept. 1989, pp. 268–281 Springer-Verlag, New York, (invited paper).

[16] Kim, K. H. and Min, B. J., "Approaches to Implementation of Multiple DRB Stations in Tightly Coupled Computer Networks and an Experimental Validation," *Proc. IEEE Computer Society's 15th Int'l Computer Software and Applications Conf. (COMPSAC 91)*, Sept. 1991, Tokyo, pp. 550–557.

[17] Kim, K. H., Kopetz, H., Mori, K., Shokri, E. H., and Gruensteidl, G., "An Efficient Decentralized Approach to Processor-Group Membership Maintenance in Real-Time LAN Systems: The PRHB/ED Scheme," *Proc. IEEE Computer Society's 11th Symp. on Reliable Distributed Systems*, Oct. 1992, Houston, TX, pp. 74–83.

[18] Kim, K. H., "Structuring DRB Computing Stations in Highly Decentralized Systems," *Proc. IEEE Computer Society's Int'l Symp. on Autonomous Decentralized Systems*, Mar. 1993, Kawasaki, Japan, pp.305–314.

[19] Kim, K. H. and Shokri, E. H., "Minimal-Delay Decentralized Maintenance of Processor-Group Membership in TDMA-Bus LAN Systems," *Proc. IEEE Computer Society's 13th Int'l Conf. on Distributed Computing Systems*, Pittsburgh, PA, May 1993, pp. 410–419.

[20] Kim, K. H., "Fair Distribution of Concerns in Design and Evaluation of Fault-Tolerant Distributed Computer Systems," *Proc. IEEE Computer Society's Workshop on Future Trends of Distributed Computing Systems*, Lisbon, Sept. 1993, pp. 173–180.

[21] Kopetz, H., Grunsteidl, G., and Reisinger, J., "Fault-Tolerant Membership Service in a Synchronous Distributed Real-Time System," *Proc. IFIP WG 10, 4th Int'l Working Conf. on Dependable Computing for Critical Applications*, Santa Barbara, CA, Aug. 1989, pp. 167–174.

[22] Kopetz, H. and Grunsteidl, G., "TTP-A: Time Triggered Protocol for Fault-Tolerant Real-Time Systems," *Proc. IEEE Computer Society's FTCS-23*, Toulouse, June 1993, pp. 524–533.

[23] Lamport, L., Shostak, R., and Pease, M., "The Byzantine Generals Problem," *ACM Trans. Programming Languages Syst.*," No. 4, Vol. 3, July 1982, pp. 382–401.

[24] Mori, K., "Autonomous Decentralized Systems: Concepts, Data Field Architecture and Future Trends," *Proc. IEEE Computer Society's Int'l Symp. on Autonomous Decentralized Systems,* Mar. 1993, Kawasaki, Japan, pp.28-34.

[25] Powell, D., et al., "The Delta-4 Approach to Dependability in Open Distributed Computing Systems," *Proc. IEEE Computer Society's 18th Int'l. Symp. on Fault-Tolerant Computing,* June 1988, pp. 246–251.

[26] Powell, D., "Failure Mode Assumptions and Assumption Coverage," *Proc. IEEE Computer Society's 22nd Int'l Symp. on Fault Tolerant Computing,* July 1993, pp. 386–395.

[27] Randell, B., "System Structure for Software Fault Tolerance," *IEEE Transactions on Software Engineering,* June 1975, pp. 220– 232.

[28] Siewiorek, D. P., "Fault Tolerance in Commercial Computers," *IEEE Computer,* July 1990, pp. 26–37.

[29] Son, S. H., and Kim, Y. K., "Predictability and Consistency in Real-Time Database Systems," *Proc. InfoScience '93* (Int'l Conf. organized by Korea Information Science Society in commemoration of its 20th anniversary), Seoul, Oct. 22, 1993, pp. 225–232 (Invited paper).

[30] Toy, W. N., "Fault-Tolerant Computing," A Chapter in Advances in Computers, Vol. 26, Academic Press, New York, 1987, pp. 201–279.

[31] Wensley, J. H., "An Operating System for a TMR Fault-Tolerant System," *Digest of Papers FTCS-13, 13th Annual International Symposium on Fault-Tolerant Computing,* Milano, June 1983, pp. 452–455.

[32] Wilson, D., "The STRATUS computer system," Chapter 12 in T. Anderson ed., Resilient Computing Systems, Volume I, John Wiley & Sons Inc., New York, 1985, pp. 45–67.

# Chapter 18

# Run-Time Monitoring of Real-Time Systems

Farnam Jahanian

This chapter presents a framework for formal specification and monitoring of run-time constraints in real-time systems. As embedded real-time systems become more sophisticated, the ability of a system to provide dependable and timely service becomes critical. The unpredictability of the physical environment and the inability to satisfy design assumptions due to the inherent complexity of embedded systems can cause unexpected conditions or violations of system constraints at run time. A monitoring facility can dynamically monitor the system and trigger appropriate action if a constraint is violated. Furthermore, it can be used to test the simulation of an executable specification before the system is operational or even before it is fully implemented.

## 18.1  Introduction

In designing real-time systems, we often make assumptions about the behavior of the system and its environment. These assumptions take many forms, such as upper bounds on interprocess communication delay, deadlines on the execution of tasks, or minimum separations between occurrences of two events. They are often made to deal with the unpredictability of the external environment or to simplify a problem that is otherwise intractable or very hard to solve. Such assumptions may be expressed as part of the formal specification of the system or as scheduling requirements on real-time computations. Despite the contributions of formal verification methods and real-time scheduling results in recent years, the need to perform run-time monitoring of these systems is not diminished, for several reasons: the execution environment of most systems is imperfect and the interaction with the external world introduces additional unpredictability; design assumptions can be violated at run time due to unexpected conditions such as transient overload;

application of formal techniques or scheduling algorithms, in turn, requires assumptions about the underlying system; and it may not be feasible (or impossible) to verify formally some properties at design time, thus further necessitating run time checks.

Run-time monitoring of a system requires the timestamping and recording of relevant event occurrences, analyzing the past history as a computation progresses, and providing feedback to the rest of the system. This chapter presents a general framework for formal specification and monitoring of run-time constraints in real-time systems. The objective is to specify complex system constraints, including timing requirements, and to provide appropriate mechanisms for monitoring these constraints at run time. One can envision a system in which a monitoring subsystem can provide feedback so that the system can adapt to a changing environment or an exception condition. In particular, the information collected by the monitoring facility can be used to detect a violation of system constraints or to manage resources at run time.

The approach presented in this chapter is an event-based model, first presented in [3, 9]. In this model, an application program consists of a set of cooperating tasks, perhaps running on multiple processors. A system computation is viewed as a set of partially ordered *event occurrences*. Informally, events represent state transitions in a system, such as the start or completion of a code segment, a reading of a new sensor value, or an assignment to a variable in the program. The observable events are specified by annotating real-time programs with those events that are to be monitored at run time. The system constraints that must be maintained at run time are expressed as invariant assertions on various events. The invariants are specified using a notation based on real-time logic (RTL) [10]. The system constraints, expressed as RTL-like assertions, are monitored at run time as new event occurrences are generated. A *satisfiability checker*, at the heart of the monitoring subsystem, examines the event occurrences and detects violations of system constraints. In summary, the key components of the framework presented here are:

- an annotation system for specifying observable events in a computation and for expressing system constraints (or assertions) to be monitored,

- a run time system for recording and timestamping relevant events as a computation progresses, and

- a satisfiability checker for detecting violations of system constraints at run time.

This chapter is organized as follows: Section 18.2 introduces an annotation system for labeling observable events that are to be monitored. Section 18.3 discusses synchronous and asynchronous monitoring of real-time systems. It also describes a notation, based on RTL, for specifying complex system constraints as invariant assertions on various events. Section 18.4 considers the problem of detecting violations of timing assertions as event occurrences are recorded. It introduces the conditions under which a timing assertion can be violated. Section 18.5 presents examples of several expressive classes of constraints that require bounded event histories to be maintained for an accurate detection of violations. Section 18.6 discusses operating system support for run-time monitoring. Section 18.7 is the related work, followed by the concluding remarks in Section 18.8.

# 18.2  Program Annotation with Events and Run-Time Assertions

This section addresses the specification of the events and assertions to be monitored. The annotation system presented here is independent of the underlying programming language. In fact, it is intended to provide a formal system that can be superimposed on an existing real-time programming language with the appropriate run-time support.

## 18.2.1  Event Specification

A computation of a real-time system can be viewed as a sequence of event occurrences. Informally, events represent things that happen in a system. An event occurrence defines a point in time in a computation at which a particular instance of an event happens. Thus, timing properties can be expressed as relationships among event occurrences in a computation.

As mentioned earlier, events denote state changes in a system as seen by the monitoring subsystem. Events can be classified into two categories: *task events* and *run-time system events*. Task events denote the state changes of an executing task. Examples of these events include assignment of a value into a variable or receipt of a message. Run-time system events are a set of predefined state changes in the run-time system. Examples of these events include preemption of a task or blocking a task for a resource. Run-time system events are not necessarily visible to an executing task because of the abstract machine that is provided by a programming language implemented on top of a run-time system. Hence, events such as task preemption are independent of the internal state transitions of a task. One can view these events as representing state changes in the run-time system below the application task. In time-critical systems, however, it may be desirable to make certain run-time events visible to the monitoring facility or the tasks themselves. Appropriate operating system support for achieving this will be revisited in a later section. The remainder of this section will focus on the language constructs for specifying task events and the corresponding assertions to be monitored at run time.

The first component of the proposed annotation system allows the specification of the observable events in a real-time system by annotating real-time tasks with those events that are to be monitored at run time.

We distinguish between two classes of observable task events in this model: *label events* and *transition events*. Label events are used to denote the initiation and completion of a sequence of program statements. Intuitively, one can view label

```
...
E1->
S;
<-E2
...
```

**Figure 18.1** Code Fragment with Event Labels

events as denoting the location of the program counter in a task execution. They are defined by inserting labels in appropriate places in the code. The notation in our system for marking programs with label events is illustrated in Figure 18.1, where two event labels are defined, E1 and E2. The right-pointing arrow is a syntactic marker that specifies E1 as the event that denotes the start of statement S. The left-pointing arrow associates event E2 with the end of statement S. Two events may be placed between a pair of statements, one bound to the end of the first statement and the other bound to the beginning of the second. This can be used to make preemption between two consecutive statements observable in an execution.

Transition events denote assignments of values to state variables in a program. A transition event may correspond to reading a new sensor value into a program variable or receiving a message from another task. An assignment to a state variable captures a change in a system state, and it is observable as an event occurrence when monitoring a system. The term *watchable variable* is borrowed from the ORE language [5] to denote those program variables that are to be seen by the monitoring system. Figure 18.2 illustrates our notation for marking programs with transition events. The integer variable a is marked so that each assignment to the variable is recorded as an event occurrence.

Since the state of a program execution can be characterized by the values of its program counter and its state variables, the two types of events in the proposed model, label and transition events, capture the state changes in a computation. System constraints are monitored by examining the observable events at run time.

```
...
event int a;
event int b;
...
a = read_sensor();
```

**Figure 18.2** Code Fragment with Transition Events

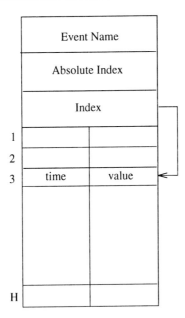

**Figure 18.3**  Event History Data Structure

## 18.2.2    Event Histories

Run-time monitoring of a system requires recording and examining event occurrences as a computation progresses. If it would be sufficient to remember only the last occurrence of each event, then a bound can be imposed a priori on the number of event occurrences that must be kept at any given point in time during a computation. Furthermore, the algorithms for recording and discarding the event occurrences in a system computation would be very simple. However, since examining a property at run time may involve multiple occurrences of the same event, it may be necessary to remember more than one occurrence of an event to detect the violation of a timing property. We use *event histories* to store the times (and values, for transition events) of a bounded number of previous occurrences of each event. As described in the next section, the size of the event history for each event is either specified by the system designer or is determined by examining the assertion to be monitored at run time.

**Manipulating Event Histories.**   Each event history should be viewed as a finite length circular queue of times (and values), with a relative index pointing to the most recent event, as shown in Figure 18.3. An absolute index counts the number of occurrences of the event. The name field identifies each event uniquely in the system of tasks.

Two RTL-like [10] functions for accessing the event histories are provided: the occurrence function @$(e, i)$, which returns the time of the $i$th occurrence of event $e$, and @$val(v, i)$, which returns the value of the $i$th occurrence of the state variable $v$'s transition event. A positive occurrence index is absolute with respect to the beginning of the computation sequence. For example, $@(e, 5)$ refers to the time of the fifth occurrence of event $e$. When the index $i$ is negative, it refers to the $i^{th}$ most recent occurrence of the event in a computation prefix. For example, $@(e, -1)$ denotes the time of the most recent occurrence of $e$. An occurrence index of 0 is undefined. An additional function, $@index(e, i)$, returns the absolute index of an occurrence of event $e$, given an index $i$ relative to the beginning or end of the sequence.

# 18.3   Synchronous and Asynchronous Monitoring

The preceding subsection discussed different classes of events and a notation for specifying events in a program. The programmer should also be provided a notation for specifying complex constraints that are to be monitored at run time. For example, a timing constraint may specify an end-to-end deadline on a set of actions that must be executed upon receiving a new sensor value; or a safety assertion may require that a specific precedence must hold among the actions while the system is in a certain mode. In our model, a system constraint can be viewed as an assertion on the relationship between the occurrences of the observable events. The model distinguishes between two general ways in which event histories can be utilized in specifying and monitoring system constraints: *synchronous* vs. *asynchronous*.

In synchronous monitoring, the programmer can explicitly check for the satisfiability of a constraint at a particular point in the execution of the program and modify the computation accordingly. This is done by directly manipulating the event histories that are shared by the cooperating tasks. Thus, testing and handling of any violation of the constraint is carried out synchronously on the threads of the executing tasks.

Alternatively, in asynchronous monitoring, the constraint is enforced during the entire execution of the program. Thus, testing and handling of exceptions are performed asynchronously. The events generated by the application tasks are sent to the system monitor (a separate task), which is responsible for maintaining the event histories. Whenever an event occurs that may violate the satisfiability of the constraint, the system monitor re-evaluates the expression and invokes the appropriate handler if the constraint is no longer satisfiable. The rationale for asynchronous monitoring is that, for certain assertions, it may be impossible to insert a test at a particular point in the program and synchronously check for its satisfiability.

## 18.3.1   Embedded Constraints

Under the model of embedded constraints, run-time properties are enforced at a particular point in the execution of a program, providing *synchronous* monitoring of constraints. This is done by allowing direct manipulation of the @ functions and occurrence indices through the constructs available in a programming language such as C. As described in [3], an RTL-like notation can be added to a programming language to specify constraints that must be checked synchronously. (Recall that event histories are accessed by two RTL-like functions, *@(e,i)* and *@val(e,i)* .) The primary advantage of this approach is that it permits the programmer to manipulate the @ functions and to access event histories directly, through C constructs. The constraint applies only when it is checked, and at no other time in the execution sequence. For example, suppose that `temp` is a watchable variable denoting the temperature reading from a sensor. Each assignment to `temp` is a new instance of the corresponding event. The code segment in Figure 18.4 specifies an assertion which requires consecutive readings of new temperature values to be within a specific tolerance.

```
temp = read_sensor();
if(@val(temp,-1) - @val(temp,-2) > 200) {
  shutdown_reactor();
}
else {
  raise_rods();
}
```

**Figure 18.4**  An Embedded Constraint

The notation @val(temp,-1) refers to the value of the last temperature reading. Similarly, @val(temp,-2) refers to the second-most-recent reading. The preceding assertion is examined synchronously as each new sensor value is read. It compares the last two temperature readings and invokes *shutdown_reactor* if the specified limit is exceeded.

For embedded constraints, our model consists of a set of application tasks and shared event histories, as shown in Figure 18.5. The model provides for communicating the event occurrences among tasks through the histories. Event occurrences are recorded by tasks in the shared history. The satisfiability of an embedded constraint is tested by retrieving the appropriate values from the history for the corresponding event occurrences. During program execution, application tasks write the event histories by noting event occurrences (both label events and watchable variable assignments), and reading event histories by using the @ and *@val* functions to retrieve the time and value of an event occurrence. @ and *@val* map relative and absolute indices into a location in the event history, and return the requested time or value, or an error, since an expired or non-existent event can be detected easily.

## 18.3.2   Monitored Constraints

A complementary approach to embedded constraints is to make the constraint specification independent of the program. A separate monitoring process runs concurrently with the real-time application tasks and checks the satisfiability of the

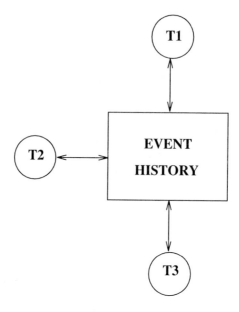

**Figure 18.5** Embedded Model

constraints. Under this model, timing properties may be enforced during the entire execution, providing *asynchronous* monitoring of the constraints. This approach serves two purposes: it separates the timing concerns from the functional specification of the program; and it allows the expression of properties that cannot be checked at a specific point in the execution sequence. An exception that must be raised when a task misses a deadline is an example of a monitored constraint.

The following assertion specifies a deadline constraint which requires every $i$th send message to be acknowledged by a corresponding message within 5 ms:

$$@(send, i) \leq @(ack, i) \ \wedge \ @(ack, i) \leq @(send, i) + 5$$

The constraint is violated if the deadline on the acknowledgment is missed after a message is sent, i.e., the event *ack* is more than 5 ms apart from the corresponding *send* event. One may attempt to enforce the above constraint by inserting the condition to be checked at a specific point in the execution of a task, after an acknowledgment is received, for example. However, there are two potential problems. If the acknowledgment is not received within the required deadline, the violation is not detected until after the acknowledgment. If the acknowledgment is never received, due to a failure, the violation of the property may not be detected at all. Hence, the constraint may be viewed as a property to be enforced when a send occurs, until either an acknowledgment is received, or 5 time units have passed. The latter test can be triggered by a timer interrupt associated with the send event.

For monitored constraints, our model consists of a set of application tasks generating events and a monitoring task. As shown in Figure 18.6, a queue provides interprocess communication between each task and the monitor. Event histories are local to the monitor rather than shared among all tasks. During task execution, as events occur, they are sent to the monitor. The monitor processes each event occurrence and records it in a local repository. The monitor maintains the event histories for the tasks, and arbitrates simultaneous occurrences. Furthermore, as events are recorded, the monitor checks the satisfiability of the corresponding constraint.

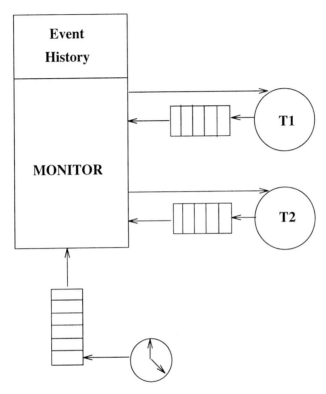

**Figure 18.6**  Monitored Model

# 18.4   Detection of Timing Violations

In this section, we look at the problem of detecting violations of timing assertions at run time. We first discuss the representation of a timing assertion as a directed constraint graph. We then introduce the conditions under which a timing assertion can be violated.

## 18.4.1   Specification of Timing Assertions

In our model, a timing requirement on a system is viewed as an assertion on the events that can occur in the system. We need to provide a notation for specifying complex constraints that are to be monitored at run time. The notation must be expressive enough to capture a variety of complex constraints that may be imposed on a system. As described in an earlier section, we use a notation based on real-time logic (RTL) for specifying timing assertions. We provide two functions for accessing the event histories: the occurrence function $@(e, i)$, which returns the time of the $i$th occurrence of event $e$, and $@val(v, i)$, which returns the value of the $i$th assignment to a variable $v$. A positive occurrence index is absolute with respect to the beginning of the computation sequence. When the index $i$ is negative, it refers to the $i$th most recent occurrence of the event in a computation. A more detailed discussion of the above model can be found in [9]. We present two examples to illustrate how the notation can be used to specify timing assertions.

*Example:* Consider two events $e_1$ and $e_2$ which must always occur in pairs and within 5 time units of each other. The following assertion (or formula) specifies such a constraint. The universal quantifier $\forall$ indicates that the constraint must be satisfied for all corresponding occurrences of $e_1$ and $e_2$.

$$\forall i \quad @(e_1, i) \leq @(e_2, i) + 5 \ \lor \ @(e_2, i) \leq @(e_1, i) + 5 \qquad (18.1)$$

*Example:* The following formula illustrates a deadline constraint which requires every send message to be acknowledged by an acknowledgment message within 5 ms:

$$\forall i \exists j \quad @(send, i) \leq @(ack, j) \ \land \ @(ack, j) \leq @(send, i) + 5. \qquad (18.2)$$

*Example:* The value of the occurrence indices in a timing constraint need not be a variable or a positive integer. It can be relative to the current index in a computation. Consider an event whose successive occurrences must be separated by at least 5 time units. The following RTL formula specifies such a constraint.

$$@(response, -2) \leq @(response, -1) - 5$$

If this constraint is checked whenever a *response* event occurs, then it is equivalent to

$$\forall i > 1 \quad @(response, i - 1) \leq @(response, i) - 5.$$

## 18.4.2   Graph Representation of Timing Constraints

If a timing assertion is in disjunctive normal form as in Formulas (18.1) and (18.2), each conjunct can be represented as a directed, weighted graph, called a *constraint graph*. Each constraint graph represents a conjunction of predicates, and each edge in the graph is a predicate of the form:

$$@(e, i) \leq @(f, j) \pm C$$

such that $i$, $j$ are integer variables/constants and $C$ is an integer constant.

Intuitively, a predicate in a conjunct represents either a delay or a deadline constraint on a pair of events. The vertices of the constraint graph correspond to unique occurrence functions; the weighted edges denote the constraints between event pairs. For example, the following *delay constraint*:

$$@(response, -2) \leq @(response, -1) - 5$$

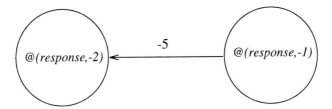

**Figure 18.7**  Delay Constraint

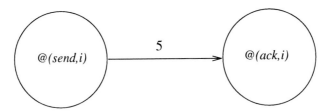

**Figure 18.8**  Deadline Constraint

is represented by an edge with weight -5 as shown in Figure 18.7. A predicate of the form $@(response, 1) \leq C$ where $C$ is an absolute time value is translated to an edge $\mathbf{0} \xrightarrow{C} @(response, 1)$ where $\mathbf{0}$ is a special "zero vertex" designed to take care of constants. Similarly, a predicate of the form $C \leq @(response, 1)$ is represented by an edge $@(response, 1) \xrightarrow{-C} \mathbf{0}$.

As an example of a *deadline constraint*, consider the following assertion:

$$\forall i \;\; @(ack, i) \leq @(send, i) + 5.$$

This constraint specifies that an *ack* event must occur within 5 time units of its corresponding *send* event, and is represented by an edge with positive weight *5* as shown in Figure 18.8.

A *path* between two vertices $u$ and $v$ in the graph is a sequence of edges from $u$ to $v$. The *length* of a path is the sum of the weights of all edges along the path. In the rest of this chapter, without loss of generality, we do not associate any occurrence indices to events. This is possible because a specific constraint graph is instantiated for a set of event occurrence indices before checking for a violation.

### 18.4.3  Implicit Constraints

In addition to the explicit delay or deadline edges in a constraint graph, we can derive certain implicit constraints often as an intermediate deadline or delay. In fact, it is possible that an implicit constraint is violated before an explicit deadline or delay becomes unsatisfiable at run time.

For example, consider the simple constraint graph in Figure 18.9. It consists of two explicit timing constraints: a deadline edge and a delay edge. Events *e1*, *e2*, and *e3* occur on tasks 1, 2, and 3, respectively. There is an explicit deadline from *e1* to *e2*. In addition, since there is a path from *e1* to *e3* of length 6, there is an

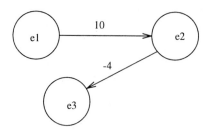

**Figure 18.9** Intermediate Deadline from *e1* to *e3*

implicit, intermediate deadline of 6 from *e1* to *e3*. If the intermediate deadline is not met, then either the explicit deadline or the delay constraint from *e3* to *e2* will eventually be violated. If the violation of the implicit constraint between *e1* to *e3* is detected, the system can be notified before any of the two user-specified constraints are violated. As a result, corrective action can potentially be taken even before the application-level constraint is violated.

### 18.4.4   Checking Constraint Graphs

The constraint graphs must be checked for potential violations at certain discrete points in time. We establish these discrete points of time in this section. When an event occurs that may affect the satisfiability of a timing assertion, a satisfiability checker is invoked to check for violations. The checker instantiates the vertices of the graph from event histories. For example, the vertex *@(response, -1)* will be replaced by the occurrence time of the most recent *response* event. The vertex *@(send,i)* will be replaced by the occurrence time of the current activation of *send* event. Vertices that have been instantiated are merged with the **0** vertex as follows: Every edge with weight $w$ incoming to a vertex, to which a time value $t$ has been assigned, is replaced with an edge with weight *w-t* incident on the **0** vertex. Conversely, every edge with weight $w$ outgoing from a vertex, to which time $t$ has been assigned, is replaced with an edge of weight *w+t* outgoing from the **0** vertex. Vertices that have not yet occurred are not instantiated. Instead, an edge from the uninstantiated vertex to the **0** vertex of weight equal to *-NOW* is added, where *NOW* is the current time. This is an assertion that the event has not happened since system startup. After a constraint graph has been instantiated, it can be checked for violations.

     We state a lemma that establishes the conditions under which a timing assertion (constraint graph) may be violated. The proof of this lemma appears in [12].

**Lemma 18.4.1** *In a constraint graph, the earliest time a constraint can be violated is as follows:*

1. *A delay constraint will be violated if for a path of negative length $-T$ $(T \geq 0)$ from vertex $e_n$ to vertex $\mathbf{0}$, the event corresponding to vertex $e_n$ happens before time $T$.*

2. *A deadline constraint will be violated if the minimum length $T$ ($T \geq 0$) of all shortest paths from vertex* **0** *to all other vertices is to a vertex $e_m$ and the event corresponding to vertex $e_m$ does not happen at or before $T$.*

Lemma 18.4.1 states that delay violations need only be tested whenever an event occurs, and deadline violations need not be tested before some timeout value. Hence, a constraint graph must be checked for violations after the occurrence of any event in the graph. The event occurrence is instantiated in the graph with its occurrence time and the graph is checked for violations. If the graph is not violated, the length of the minimum of the shortest paths from vertex **0** to all uninstantiated vertices is computed. If this length $P$ is not infinity, then a timer that expires at time $P$ is set. The graph is again checked for violations when the timer expires or when an event happens, whichever is earlier.

# 18.5    Bounded Event Histories

As mentioned in Section 18.2.2, detecting a violation of a timing constraint at run time may require examining multiple occurrences of an event that have happened in the past. For example, suppose that a constraint requires a minimum separation of 100 ms between consecutive occurrences of sending a signal, denoted by the event $SEND$:

$$\forall i @(SEND, i) + 100 < @(SEND, i+1).$$

It may be necessary to keep the last two occurrences of the $SEND$ event to detect a violation of the above constraint at run time.

Although one can attempt to keep the entire history for each event, it is impractical (and perhaps impossible) to do so in most nontrivial systems. We observe that there are two distinct ways of establishing a bound on the history of event occurrences. This can be done by calculating the number of distinct occurrences of the same event that must be kept at any point in the execution of a specification, or by determining the length of time that a given event occurrence must be remembered after it happens. For example, consider the property that a system sensor must be sampled at least 10 times during every 500 ms. This minimum sampling rate is expressed by the RTL formula:

$$\forall j @(SAMPLE, j + 10) \geq @(SAMPLE, j) + 500. \tag{18.3}$$

The above timing constraint can be checked for violations if either the last 10 occurrences of event $SAMPLE$ are saved, or each occurrence of the event is kept for at least 500 ms.

The remainder of this section looks at the issue of establishing bounds on event histories by syntactically examining a timing assertion, and it presents a satisfiability checker for a representative class of timing assertions.

## 18.5.1    Classes of Properties with Bounded History

Although a system designer can explicitly specify the maximum length of the history for each event that must preserved at run time, it is often possible to determine a bound by syntactically examining the formula that expresses a timing constraint. The work, reported in [9], describes several powerful classes of properties, expressed in RTL, for which bounds on history of event occurrences can be established. A detailed discussion on each of these classes is beyond the scope of this chapter. However, an informal description of several classes is presented here.

**Constant Occurrence Indices.** This class consists of properties (expressed as RTL-like formulas) that explicitly identify the occurrence index of each event in the formula relative to the first or last occurrence of the event in a computation prefix. In other words, the occurrence indices in this class of properties are integer constants. The RTL formulas in this class allow @ functions of the form:

$$@(e, a) \ or \ @(e, -a)$$

where $e$ is an event and $a$ is a positive integer constant. In particular, recall that when the occurrence index of an @ function is a positive integer constant, the notation $@(e, a)$ refers to the $a$th occurrence of event $e$ from the start of the computation. For example, $@(SIGNAL, 1)$ refers to the time of the first occurrence of event $SIGNAL$. Alternatively, the occurrence index can refer to a particular most recent occurrence of an event. We use the notation $@(e, -a)$ to denote the time of the $a$th most recent occurrence of event $e$ in a computation prefix. For example, $@(SIGNAL, -1)$ is the time of the last occurrence of event $SIGNAL$.

*Example:* Consider a system that executes the action $RESPONSE$ when a $SIGNAL$ event occurs. An exception condition must be raised if another $SIGNAL$ occurs during the execution of a $RESPONSE$ action. The two events $R$ and $R'$ are used to denote the start and stop events corresponding to an execution of the action $RESPONSE$.

$$@(R, -1) \leq @(SIGNAL, -1) \Rightarrow$$

$$@(R, -1) \leq @(R', -1) \ \wedge \ @(R', -1) < @(SIGNAL, -1) \tag{18.4}$$

The above formula specifies that if the last occurrence of action $RESPONSE$ starts before the last occurrence of a $SIGNAL$ event, the action must also complete before that $SIGNAL$ event.

**Unique Occurrence Index Variables.** Another useful class of properties involves formulas that have a unique index variable in all applications of the @ function. Intuitively, the index variable often corresponds to a particular activation of related events. For example, the constraint expressed by Formula (18.1) in an earlier section belongs to this class. The constraint requires that the corresponding instances of the two events $e1$ and $e2$ must occur within 5 time units of each other. The same occurrence index variable is used for $e1$ and $e2$ in Formula (18.1). Similarly, the same index variable $j$ is used for all applications of the @ function in Formula (18.3).

**Exclusion/Inclusion/Overlapping of Intervals.** An event occurrence denotes a point in time. Hence, one can view a pair of distinct event occurrences as a time interval: one denoting the opening of the interval and the other closing of the interval. The assertions in this class specify three types of properties:

- exclusion of two intervals,

- inclusion of an interval within another interval, and

- overlapping of two intervals.

*Definition:* An *endpoint* is defined to be an application of an occurrence function of the form $@(e, i \pm C) + I$ such that $e$ is an event, $i$ is an integer variable, and $C$ and $I$ are non-negative integer constants.

*Definition:* An *interval* consists of two endpoints of the form

$$@(e_1, i \pm C_1) + I_1 \ \wedge \ @(e_2, i \pm C_2) + I_2$$

such that $e_1$ and $e_2$ are events, $i$ is an integer variable, and $C_1$, $C_2$, $I_1$, and $I_2$ are non-negative integers. An *instance* of an interval is an assignment of time values to the endpoints of the interval.

Observe that both endpoints of an interval have the same occurrence index variable. Furthermore, the notions of endpoint and interval are syntactic, which will be used to classify RTL formulas. However, an instance of an interval is a pair of time values which is obtained by observing the appropriate event occurrences in a computation. For instance, $@(P, j)$ and $@(P', j)$ correspond to the opening and closing endpoints of an interval, respectively. The interval defined by the pair of endpoints may define the $j$th execution of a particular action. An instance of the interval is the time values associated with a specific occurrence, e.g., first occurrence of the two events. Similarly, $@(SIGNAL, i) + 100$ and $@(SIGNAL, i + 1)$ are the two endpoints of an interval. They represent the interval between consecutive occurrences of two events.

*Definition:* Suppose that $\rho_1$ and $\rho'_1$ are opening and closing endpoints of *interval*$_1$, and $\rho_2$ and $\rho'_2$ are opening and closing endpoints of *interval*$_2$ such that $i$ and $j$ are the occurrence index variables of *interval*$_1$ and *interval*$_2$, respectively. *Exclusion* of *interval*$_1$ and *interval*$_2$ is expressed by RTL formulas of the form:

$$\forall i \forall j \ \ \rho'_1 < \rho_2 \ \vee \ \rho'_2 < \rho_1$$

$$\exists i \forall j \ \ \rho'_1 < \rho_2 \ \vee \ \rho'_2 < \rho_1.$$

*Inclusion* of *interval*$_2$ within *interval*$_1$ is expressed by RTL formulas of the form:

$$\forall i \exists j \ \ \rho_1 \leq \rho_2 \ \wedge \ \rho'_2 \leq \rho'_1$$

$$\exists i \exists j \ \ \rho_1 \leq \rho_2 \ \wedge \ \rho'_2 \leq \rho'_1.$$

*Overlapping* of *interval*$_2$ with *interval*$_1$ is defined similarly.

*Example:* Mutual exclusion of the execution of two tasks $P$ and $Q$ can be specified by the following assertion:

$$\forall i \exists j \ @(STOP_P, i) < @(START_Q, j) \vee @(STOP_Q, j) < @(START_P, i).$$

The above formula specifies two intervals: one is the interval between the start and completion of task $P$; the other is the interval between the start and completion of task $Q$. Exclusion of the instances of the two intervals denotes that no execution of the two processes overlap.

## 18.5.2   A Satisfiability Checker

The previous section presented several classes of constraints, expressed in RTL-like notation, for which bounded event histories can be established. This section presents a satisfiability checker for one of the classes described earlier. As new event occurrences happen during a computation, a satisfiability checker is invoked at run time to detect timing constraint violations.

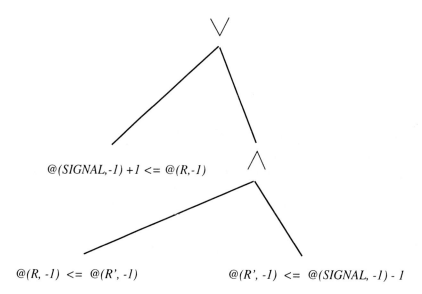

@(SIGNAL,-1) +1 <= @(R,-1)

@(R, -1) <= @(R', -1)

@(R', -1) <= @(SIGNAL, -1) - 1

**Figure 18.10** Parse Tree for Example

Recall the class of timing properties with *constant occurrence indices* presented in Section 18.5.1. The formulas of this class consist of a disjunct of conjuncts of predicates, where each predicate is an inequality of the form $@(e, \pm a) \leq @(f, \pm b) + C$, where $a$ and $b$ are positive integer constants, and $C$ is an integer constant. $C$ corresponds to an offset time value–a delay or deadline. It can be shown that the history length of each event is bounded by the absolute value of the largest negative index associated with the event in all constraints, plus the number of explicitly defined positive indices. To simplify the presentation of a satisfiability checker in this section, it is assumed that constraint formulas are in disjunctive normal form (DNF). This does not limit the expressibility of the language. The disjunctive normal form of the assertion expressed by Formula (18.4) is

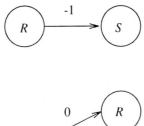

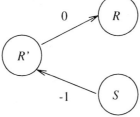

**Figure 18.11**  Uninstantiated Constraint Graph

$$@(SIGNAL, -1) + 1 \leq @(R, -1) \vee$$

$$[@(R, -1) \leq @(R', -1) \; \wedge \; @(R', -1) + 1 \leq @(SIGNAL, -1)]. \qquad (18.5)$$

A formula string is translated by scanner/parser into a parse tree whose leaves are the inequalities, whose root is $\vee$, and whose internal nodes are $\wedge$'s. The parse tree for the assertion above is given in Figure 18.10. Each conjunct subtree can be transformed into an equivalent weighted directed graph, as shown in Figure 18.11.[1] Each unique occurrence function call corresponds to a node on the graph. The predicate $@(SIGNAL, -1) \leq @(R, -1) - 1$ becomes an edge $@(R, -1) \xrightarrow{-1} @(SIGNAL, -1)$. A predicate of the form $@(SIGNAL, 1) \leq C$ where $C$ is an absolute time value is translated to an edge $\mathbf{0} \xrightarrow{C} @(SIGNAL, 1)$ where $\mathbf{0}$ is the special "zero node" designed to take care of constants. Similarly, a predicate of the form $C \leq @(SIGNAL, 1)$ is represented by an edge $@(SIGNAL, 1) \xrightarrow{-C} \mathbf{0}$.

During a system execution, when the satisfiability checker is invoked on a constraint, each conjunct graph is instantiated from the current event histories. *If a negative cycle is found in the instantiated graph, then the conjunct is unsatisfiable.* A shortest-path algorithm can be used to search efficiently for negative cycles in the instantiated graph. A constraint in DNF is violated if all of its graphs are not satisfied for a particular instantiation from the event histories.

Recall that graph instantiation is based on the event histories. Every edge with weight $w$ incoming to a node, to which a time value $t$ has been assigned, is replaced with an edge with weight $w - t$ incident on the "zero node." Conversely, every edge with weight $w$ outgoing from a node, to which a time value $t$ has been assigned, is replaced with an edge with weight $w + t$ outgoing from the "zero node."

---

[1]The letter $S$ is used to denote the event $SIGNAL$ in the remaining figures for this example.

Furthermore, for each node that has no time value associated with it, i.e., the corresponding event has not happened yet, an edge from that node to the "zero node" is added with the weight $-NOW$, where $NOW$ is the current time. This edge denotes that the corresponding event may happen at or after time $NOW$.

Figures 18.12 and 18.13 present an example of an event sequence leading to a constraint violation. Figure 18.12 shows an execution prefix over which we test the constraint formula (18.5) given above. At time 1, Figure 18.13(a), no cycles exist in either graph, so the constraint is satisfiable. At time 2, Figure 18.13(b), a negative cycle is found in the second conjunct. Since the first conjunct has a valid instantiation, the formula remains satisfiable. At time 3, Figure 18.13(c), a $SIGNAL$ event occurs before the end of the $RESPONSE$ action. This violates both conjuncts and causes a negative cycle to appear in both graphs. Observe that since $R'$ has not occurred before time 3, the corresponding node in the graph has no value associated with it. Hence, a dashed edge from the node $R'$ to "node zero" with the value -3 is added during instantiation, as shown in Figure 18.13(c). The constraint remains unsatisfiable at time 4, after the $R'$ event occurs, as shown in Figure 18.13(d).

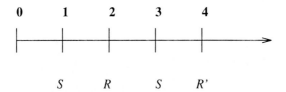

**Figure 18.12**  Execution Prefix

The Floyd-Warshall shortest path algorithm can be used to search for negative cycles on the instantiated graph: if such a cycle is found, the conjunct is unsatisfiable. The complexity of the negative cycle detection algorithm is $O(n^3)$ in the number of nodes in the graph. In many cases, however, it is not necessary to call the algorithm because a one-node negative cycle is detected on the "zero node" during instantiation.

## 18.6   Operating System Support

The issues of operating system support for run-time monitoring is discussed in this section. The discussion is organized around three major issues: (a) the visibility of certain run-time system events, (b) the relationship between the granularity and atomicity of event timestamps, and (c) kernel support for scheduling.

### 18.6.1   Operating System Events

As described in Section 18.2, annotating application tasks with label events and transition events captures the state changes in a computation. However, certain

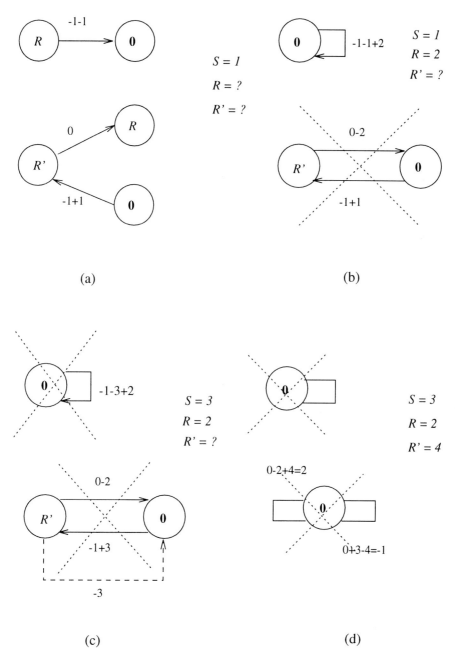

**Figure 18.13**  Instantiated Graph:  (a) Time = 1;   (b) Time = 2;   (c) Time = 3; (d) Time = 4

run-time events, such as task preemption, which are seen by the operating system are independent of the internal state changes in a task execution. In conventional operating systems, most run-time events are hidden from executing programs. In fact, much effort has been devoted to making sure that processes have the illusion of running on a dedicated (abstract) machine. While this is a worthy goal for conventional systems, real-time systems and systems that monitor them have a different set of requirements. These monitoring systems require that certain operating system events be made visible to queries [23]; the ability to determine the timing of certain operations is also necessary.

Events which might be of interest to a monitoring system include: task preemption, task suspension and resumption, task resource changes (i.e., change in number of pages or other resources allocated to a task), certain resource requests, and scheduling events such as task priority changes and frame overrun. Appropriate operating system support must be provided so that these run-time events are recorded and made visible to the monitoring facility and in some cases to the tasks themselves. (An alternative way is to view these events as describing the internal state changes of the operating system. Then the goal is to expose certain operating system events to the run-time monitoring facility.)

The ability to observe operating system events adds substantially to the power of a monitoring system. In particular, if a monitoring system receives notification of these event occurrences for the process being monitored, it may be possible for the monitor to change the behavior of the system by providing feedback to the process being monitored or the resource scheduler. For example, exceeding the maximum computation time estimated for a task can be reported by the monitoring facility. The feedback from the monitoring system to the scheduler can be used to build a robust system that is capable of adapting to the changes in the environment and the system load. For example, some scheduling algorithms can modify process priorities if the failure of a process to meet its deadline is detected [21].

## 18.6.2 Timestamping Events

Monitoring the run-time behavior of a program usually involves examining sequences of timestamped events. This introduces the problem of how and when these timestamps are obtained. Recording event occurrences at run time requires support in the operating system for atomically acquiring a timestamp with an acceptable granularity. In other words, the occurrence of an event and acquiring a timestamp must be seen as an indivisible unit. Otherwise, the comparison between the timestamps of two event occurrences may not be meaningful. This problem is complicated even further in a distributed environment in which events in a real-time system can occur on distinct processors. A comparison between event timestamps is meaningful if the clocks between the processors are synchronized within a known bound when a computation runs in a distributed environment.

A related issue is the granularity of the timestamp for an event occurrence. Suppose that reading the system clock requires 30 $\mu$s (not an unreasonable assumption if a system call is required), then the ordering of events in two processes is indeterminate if the timestamps are closer than 30 $\mu$s from each other. A similar problem arises if the clock being read is updated only infrequently (e.g., updates to the clock might occur at 60 Hz). When events in such a system are timestamped close to each other, the ordering is muddled, and two possible orderings must be considered (assuming no simultaneous occurrences). These problems make it quite desirable to have operating system support for quickly reading a frequently updated accurate clock. For example, certain processors support special hardware clocks that can be accessed by a process without the overhead of a system call. Without these features, analyzing the streams of events is difficult.

## 18.6.3    Support for Scheduling Monitoring Activities

Timing predictability is a fundamental requirement of real-time systems. Therefore, one must quantify the timing intrusiveness of monitoring activities on the behavior of real-time application tasks. One approach is to view monitoring activities as time-constrained tasks and to include them in the scheduling analysis of the system [11]. Scheduling support for run-time monitoring must meet two basic requirements. First, the mechanisms for scheduling the monitoring activities should ideally employ the same scheduling primitives used by the application tasks themselves. Secondly, the monitoring activities must be scheduled such that they do not endanger the deadlines of critical application tasks. If these two requirements can be met, the monitoring activity can be viewed as one or more application tasks scheduled in the system each with its own timing constraints.

For example, if an operating system supports a fixed-priority preemptive scheduler, the rate-monotonic scheduling framework can be used to schedule monitoring activities. The scheduler also needs to avoid unbounded priority inversion when tasks block while accessing event histories. A sporadic server which bounds the amount of time spent on processing monitored constraints is also required. Another key parameter of interest to many scheduling algorithms is the execution time consumed by a task. One way to ensure that decisions made by the scheduler are based upon the actual execution times consumed by a task is to specify the execution time of a task as part of a timing constraint. Eight basic primitives which can support these scheduling abstractions are *Create/Destroy task*, *Get/Set task priority*, *Activate/Suspend task*, and *Get/Set task execution time*.

The granularity of the sporadic server capacity and the time interval for replenishment of the capacity determine the priority at which monitored constraints can be evaluated. Ideally, the monitoring should be performed at the highest priority. Under the rate-monotonic scheduling framework, this implies that the sporadic server should have a shorter period than any of the application tasks. This requires fine timing granularities. At fine granularities, however, the cost of context switching may become large, and kernel support for sporadic servers is desirable. Supporting monitoring activities for real-time systems with predictable timing behavior requires further investigation of the scheduling issues.

# 18.7   Related Work

Despite extensive work on monitoring and debugging facilities for parallel and distributed systems, run-time monitoring of real-time systems has received little attention, with a few exceptions. Special hardware support for collecting run-time data in real-time applications has been considered in a number of recent papers [8, 24]. These approaches introduce specialized co-processors for the collection and analysis of run-time information. The use of special-purpose hardware allows non-intrusive monitoring of a system by recording the run-time information in a large repository, often for post analysis. A related work [7] studies the use of monitoring information to aid in scheduling tasks. The underutilization of a CPU due to the use of scheduling methods based on the worst-case execution times of tasks is addressed by the use of a hardware real-time monitor which measures the task execution times and delays due to resource sharing. The monitored information is fed back to the operating system for achieving an adaptive behavior. A work closer to our approach is a system for collection and analysis of distributed/parallel (real-time) programs [14]. The work is based on an earlier system for exploring the use of an extended E-R model for specification and access to monitoring information at run time [22]. The assumption is that the relational model is an appropriate formalism for structuring the information generated by a distributed system. A real-time monitor developed for the ARTS distributed operating system is presented in [23]. The proposed monitor requires certain support from the kernel, such as notification of the state changes of a process, including waking up, being scheduled. In particular, the ARTS kernel records certain events that are seen by the operating system as the state changes of a process, e.g., waking up, being scheduled. These events are sent periodically by the local host to a remote host for displaying the execution history. The invasiveness of the monitoring facility is included in the schedulability analysis. Monitoring and detecting violations of certain predefined timing constraints have been proposed in real-time languages, such as FLEX [13]. The FLEX language provides the constructs for specifying delay and deadline constraints in a program.

Detecting a violation of a timing assertion in a distributed system is also related to the problem of detecting stable (global) properties of a system. Many snapshot algorithms for establishing a global consistent system state have been proposed in the past (e.g., [2, 15]). A more recent work proposed a method for detecting locally stable properties by constructing sub-states of a system [17]. The goal of the snapshot algorithms is to preserve causality when constructing a global system state. In our case, if a history of event occurrences is maintained, then detecting a violation of a timing assertion can be viewed as detecting a stable property. Of course, a primary motivation for monitoring a real-time system is to detect a violation as early as possible. Recent work on evaluating non-stable global predicates for distributed computations also relate to our work, but to a lesser extent [6, 16]. Reference [16] looks at several techniques for limiting the exponential number of states that must be considered to evaluate a property over computations. Reference [6] considers an alternative approach by restricting the global predicate to one that can be efficiently detected, such as the conjunction and disjunction of local predicates. A well-written chapter on monitoring distributed computations for asynchronous systems appears in [1].

# 18.8    Concluding Remarks

This chapter presented a framework for formal specification and monitoring of run-time constraints in real-time systems. Although the focus has been on run-time monitoring in a multi-tasking shared memory environment, most of the concepts presented are directly applicable to distributed systems. A recent work, reported in [12], discusses the details of extending the approach presented in this chapter to monitoring distributed real-time systems. In particular, it focuses on the problem of detecting violations of timing assertions in an environment in which cooperating real-time tasks run on multiple processors, and timing constraints can be either inter-processor or intra-processor constraints. Since timing constraints may be imposed on events across multiple processors without physical shared memory to store event histories, several additional issues must be addressed. First, it is desirable to detect potential constraint violations at the earliest possible time, because it may allow the system to take corrective action before the violation actually occurs. This is done by deriving and checking intermediate constraints from the user-specified end-to-end constraints. Second, since events happen on different processors and timing constraints can span processors, some form of interprocessor communication is needed to propagate this information. Minimizing the number of extra messages is crucial for reducing overhead. Finally, when an event occurs, there must be a way of recording the occurrence time of the event. The granularity of timestamping determines the minimum observable spacing between two consecutive events on a processor. Timestamping is typically done by reading the clock on the local processor. A distributed system must also deal with the fact that the clocks on different processors are not perfectly synchronized. The processor clocks, however, can be kept synchronized within a known maximum bound on the deviation between them. Clock synchronization allows controlled comparison of timestamps from different clocks. In particular, one must take into consideration the deviation between clocks when evaluating a timing assertion at run time.

The approach to run-time monitoring of real-time systems, presented in this chapter, has been used to check the simulation of an executable specification. References [18, 19] describe the design, implementation, and some experiments with a monitor for a real-time executable specification language called Communicating Real-Time State Machines. The simulation of an executable specification generates a trace of events. The trace can be tested for functional and timing correctness. The advantage of monitoring a simulation is that the specification designer need not manually observe the simulation to find errors. The monitor reports errors as soon as they occur and off-line analysis is not required. Thus the specification can be debugged before moving to design and implementation.

A similar work is under way to use the approach, presented in this chapter, to test specifications of real-time systems described in the Modechart language. One of the features of the Modechart Toolset (MT) is that it can simulate a Modechart specification by generating execution traces [4, 20].[2]  The monitoring approach, presented in this chapter, is being integrated with the Modechart Toolset to test simulation traces and to detect erroneous system behavior.

## Acknowledgments

The author wishes to thank Raj Rajkumar, Sitaram Raju, Sarah Chodrow, and Marc Donner for their contributions to the work that was presented in this chapter. Much of the research was done while the author was at the IBM T.J. Watson Research Center. The author also wishes to thank Ambuj Goyal for his support and technical guidance during that period.

## References

[1]  O. Babaoglu and K. Marzullo. Consistent global states of distributed systems: Fundamental concepts and mechanism. In S. Mullender, editor, *Distributed Systems*, chapter 4, pages 55–96. Addison-Wesley, Reading, Mass., second edition, 1993.

[2]  K.M. Chandy and L. Lamport. Distributed snapshots: determining global states of distributed systems. *ACM Transactions on Computer Systems*, 3(1):63–75, February 1985.

[3]  S. Chodrow, F. Jahanian, and M. Donner. Run–time monitoring of real–time systems. In *Proc. of 12th Real-Time Systems Symposium*, December 1991.

[4]  P. Clements, C. Heitmeyer, B. Labaw, and A. Rose. Mt: A toolset for specifying and analyzing real-time systems. In *Proc. of Real-Time Systems Symposium*, pages 12–22, December 1993.

[5]  M. D. Donner and D. H. Jameson. Language and operating system features for real-time programming. *Computing Systems*, 1(1):33–62, 1988.

[6]  V. Garg and B. Waldecker. Unstable predicate detection in distributed programs. Technical Report TR92-07-82, Dept. of ECE, University of Texas at Austin, 1992.

[7]  D. Haban and K. G. Shin. Application of real–time monitoring for scheduling tasks with random execution times. *IEEE Transactions on Software Engineering*, 16(12):1374–1389, December 1990.

---

[2]MT is a set of tools for the specification, modeling, and analysis of embedded real-time systems using the Modechart language. It has been developed by the researchers at the Naval Research Laboratories in collaboration with the Real-Time Systems Group at the University of Texas.

[8] D. Haban and D. Wybranietz. A hybrid monitor for behavior and performance analysis of distributed systems. *IEEE Transactions on Software Engineering*, 16(2):197–211, February 1990.

[9] F. Jahanian and A. Goyal. A formalism for monitoring real-time constraints at run-time. In *Proc. of Fault-Tolerant Computing Symposium (FTCS-20)*, June 1990.

[10] F. Jahanian and A. K.-L. Mok. Safety analysis of timing properties in real-time systems. *IEEE Transactions on Software Engineering*, 12(9):890–904, 1986.

[11] F. Jahanian and R. Rajkumar. An integrated approach to monitoring and scheduling in real-time systems. In *Proc. of IEEE Workshop on Real-Time Operating Systems and Software*, May 1991.

[12] F. Jahanian, R. Rajkumar, and S. Raju. Run-time monitoring of timing constraints in distributed real-time systems. *Real-Time Systems Journal*, 1994 (also Technical Report, Dept. of EECS, University of Michigan, April 1994).

[13] K.B. Kenny and K.-J Lin. Building flexible real-time systems using the flex language. *IEEE Computer*, 24(5):70–78, May 1991.

[14] C. Kilpatrick, K. Schwan, and D. Ogle. Using languages for capture, analysis and display of performance information for parallel or distributed application. In *International Conference on Computer Language '90*, March 1990.

[15] R. Koo and S. Toueg. Checkpointing and rollback-recovery for distributed systems. *IEEE Transactions on Software Engineering*, pages 23–31, January 1987.

[16] K. Marzullo and G. Neiger. Detection of global state predicates. In *Proceedings of 5th International Workshop on Distributed Algorithms (WDAG-91)*, Delphi, Greece, 1991.

[17] K. Marzullo and L. Sabel. Using consistent subcuts for detecting stable properties. Technical report, Dept. of Computer Science, Cornell University, March 1992.

[18] S.C.V. Raju. *Using Assertions for Validating, Verifying and Monitoring Real-Time Systems*. Ph.D. thesis, University of Washington, 1994.

[19] S.C.V. Raju and A.C. Shaw. A prototyping environment for specifying, executing and checking communicating real-time state machines. *Software: Practice & Experience*, pages 175–195, February 1994.

[20] A. Rose, M. Perez, and P. Clements. Modechart toolset user's guide. Technical Report NRL/MRL/5540-94-7427, Center for Computer High Assurance Systems, Naval Research Lab., Washington, D.C., February 1994.

[21] Wei Kuan Shih, J.W.S Liu, and C.L. Liu. Modified rate monotone algorithm for scheduling periodic jobs with deferred deadlines. Technical Report, Dept. of Computer Science, University of Illinois at Urbana, 1991.

[22] R. Snodgrass. A relational approach to monitoring complex systems. *ACM Transactions on Computer Systems*, 6(2):157–196, May 1988.

[23] H. Tokuda, M. Koreta, and C.W. Mercer. A real-time monitor for a distributed real-time o.s. *ACM SIGPlan Notices*, 24(1):68–77, January 1989.

[24] J. P. Tsai, K.-Y. Fang, and H.-Y. Chen. A noninvasive architecture to monitor real-time distributed systems. *Computer*, 23(3):11–23, March 1990.

# Part VII

# Real-Time Databases

# Chapter **19**

# An Overview of Real-Time Database Systems[1]

# Ben Kao and Hector Garcia-Molina

A real-time database system provides database features such as data independence and concurrency control, while at the same time enforcing real-time constraints that applications may have. In this chapter we give an overview of the problems that arise in designing a real-time database system, and discuss some of the possible solutions. The topics covered include the choice of transaction model, the specification of real-time constraints, processor scheduling, concurrency control, I/O scheduling, and memory management.

## 19.1  Introduction

Traditionally, real-time systems manage their data (e.g., chamber temperature, aircraft locations) in application-dependent structures. As real-time systems evolve, their applications become more complex and require access to more data. It thus becomes necessary to manage the data in a systematic and organized fashion. Database management systems provide tools for such organization, so in recent years there has been interest in "merging" database and real-time technology. The resulting integrated system, which provides database operations with real-time constraints, is generally called a real-time database system (RTDBS) [1].

Like a conventional database system, a RTDBS functions as a repository of data, provides efficient storage, and performs retrieval and manipulation of information. However, as a part of a real-time system, whose "tasks" are associated with time constraints, a RTDBS has the added burden of ensuring some degree of

---

[1]This chapter is based on "An Overview of Real-Time Database Systems," by the same authors that appeared in W. A. Halang and A. D. Stoyenko (Eds.), *Real-Time Computing*, NATO ASI Series F, vol. 127. Berlin, New York: Springer-Verlag, pp. 261–282, 1994.

confidence in meeting the system's timing requirements.

Example applications that handle large amounts of data and have stringent timing requirements include telephone switching (e.g., translating an 800 number into an actual number), radar tracking, and others. Arbitrage trading, for example, involves trading commodities in different markets at different prices. Since price discrepancies are usually short-lived, automated searching and processing of large amounts of trading information are very desirable. In order to capitalize on the opportunities, buy-sell decisions have to be made promptly, often with a time constraint so that the financial overhead in performing the trade actions are well compensated by the benefit resulting from the trade. As another example, a radar surveillance system detects aircraft "images" or "radar signatures." These images are then matched against a database of known images. The result of such a match is used to drive other system actions, for example, in choosing a combat strategy.

Conventional database systems are not adequate for this type of application. They differ from a RTDBS in many aspects. Most important RTDBSs have different performance goals, correctness criteria, and assumptions about the applications. Unlike a conventional database system, whose main objective is to provide fast "average" response time, a RTDBS may be evaluated based on how often transactions miss their deadlines, the average "lateness" or "tardiness" of late transactions, the cost incurred in transactions missing their deadlines, data external consistency (how current the values of data are in reflecting the state of the external world), and data temporal consistency (values of data in the database should be taken from the external world at similar times) [49].

As a real-time system, specifications related to timing constraints are usually supplied by the application designers. For most cases, these timing requirements are expressed as deadlines for transactions. Transactions of this sort, with which explicit time constraints are associated, are termed real-time transactions.

As mentioned above, a RTDBS can be viewed as a value-added database system that supports real-time transactions. A real-time transaction has to be completed by its deadline to be of full benefit to the system. Such guarantees are usually hard to ensure. In case a transaction's deadline is not met, the transaction is called a tardy transaction.

Real-time database systems differ in the way tardy transactions are handled, and this issue is generally referred to as the overload management problem. A tardy transaction may carry positive, zero, or negative residual value to the system. For the positive case, even though the benefit obtained by completing the tardy transaction is usually less than its full-fledged value, the system should still complete it, if possible. The system may, however, choose to lower the transaction's priority so that non-tardy transactions are given preferential treatment, for example, in accessing system resources. When a tardy transaction completely loses its value (zero-residual-value case), it should be dropped to free system resources for the benefit of other transactions. Finally, when a tardy transaction carries negative value, the system may choose to raise the transaction's priority so that it can be completed as soon as possible to diminish the cost incurred due to it tardiness. On the other hand, the system may lower the transaction's priority or even drop it so that other transactions have a better chance of meeting their deadlines. The decision is dependent upon the application semantics. In the extreme case that a system cannot afford having a tardy transaction (e.g., in nuclear power plant control), the system is said to be a hard real-time database system; otherwise, if tardy transactions are tolerated even though they may be undesirable (e.g., arbitrage trading), we say that the system is a soft real-time database system.

It is argued in [50] that with current technology, it is very hard to provide an absolute guarantee on meeting transaction deadlines, and therefore, RTDBSs are mostly limited to soft real-time systems. There are several factors that make it hard for a RTDBS to meet all deadlines. Firstly, the executions of database transactions are usually data and resource dependent. To guarantee satisfaction of transaction deadlines requires enormous excess resources to accommodate the highest system load. Second, full transaction support involves many database protocols which are highly unpredictable in their execution times.[2] Concurrency control protocols, for example, often introduce blocking and restart of transactions over resource contention. Third, disk-based database systems interact heavily with the I/O subsystem. Problems such as disk seek time variation, buffer management, and page faults cause the average-case and worst-case execution times to differ widely. All these add to the unpredictability of transaction execution.

While difficulties for ensuring transactions meet their deadlines certainly exist, since most RTDBSs are used for highly specialized applications, special techniques may be applied to improve the system's real-time behavior. For example, if the database is small enough to fit into main memory, most of the I/O operations can be eliminated. This, in turn, gets rid of the problem of page faults and I/O scheduling. We will discuss main memory database systems later in this chapter.

Also, in some real-time systems, "tasks" or transactions can be preanalyzed. Semantic properties of transactions and data may be known a priori. The knowledge of transaction run-time and resource requirements may lead to more effective scheduling and concurrency control protocols. As an example [37], in a conventional database system the number of constraints is assumed to be large. Checking them individually may be impractical, so instead, serializability is used as the correctness criterion. However, "since real-time systems may have a fixed number of processes and the databases are statically structured, it may be feasible to specify a small set of integrity constraints which are most critical for the system's correctness" [37]. Specialized protocols may then be designed that allow non-serializable but consistent schedules [33].

In the rest of this chapter, we will discuss some problems concerning the design of a RTDBS. We will present some solutions as proposed by the research community. We will also examine the various components of a database system and discuss what features should be added to support real-time transactions.

---

[2]For a brief account of real-time system predictability, see [51].

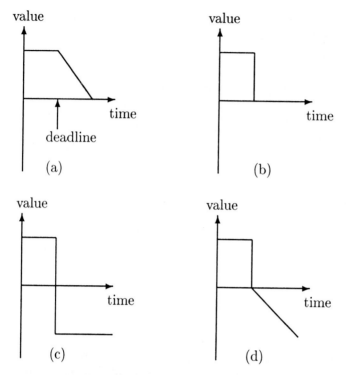

**Figure 19.1** Example Value Functions: Tardy Transaction Has (a) Diminishing Positive Value; (b) Zero Value; (c) Negative Value; (c) Increasingly Negative Value

## 19.2  Transaction Model

In this section, we look at the attributes of real-time transactions and discuss how they affect transaction design. In particular, we will discuss the issue of deadline assignment, and how semantic information can be used to help meet the system's timing constraints.

The following types of information about transactions may be available and may be of use in scheduling and concurrency control:

1. Timing constraints — e.g., deadlines.

2. Criticalness — It measures how critical it is that a transaction meets its deadline. Different transactions may have different criticalness. Note that criticalness is a different concept from deadline. A transaction may have a very tight deadline, but missing it may not cause great harm to the system.

3. Value function — Related to a transaction's criticalness is its value function. A value function of a transaction measures how valuable it is to complete the transaction at some point in time after the transaction arrives. Some typical value functions are shown in Figure 19.1.

4. Resource requirements — This includes the number of I/O operations to be executed, expected CPU usage, etc.

5. Expected execution time. This is usually hard to predict (see Section 19.3).

6. Data requirements — Read sets and write sets of transactions.

7. Periodicity — If a transaction is periodic, what its period is.

8. Time of occurrence of events — At what point in time will a transaction issue a read/write request?

9. Other semantics — Is the transaction read only? Does it conflict with any other transaction? If so, will they ever be executed at the same time? How up-to-date is the data required to be by the transaction?

There are many ways that this information can be used to help the design of real-time transactions. We demonstrate its use by the following examples.

One example concerns database consistency. In a conventional database system, as long as transaction atomicity, consistency, isolation, and durability (the ACID properties) are enforced, transactions can be executed concurrently to increase throughput without jeopardizing correctness. However, insurance of the ACID properties does not come cheap. Special protocols for concurrency control, transaction commitment, and database recovery have to be exercised. Very often, such protocols hamper the system's real-time performance through blocking, transaction abortion, deadlock, and additional I/O due to logging.

Since full transaction support is costly, it has been suggested [50] that real-time data and transactions be categorized into classes depending on their timing, synchronization, consistency, and atomicity properties. Then using the supplied semantic information, devise special minimal transaction supports that are sufficient for the classes.

Another example use of semantic information as suggested in [16] is to analyze transactions and construct contingency plans for each transaction type. Contingency plans are alternate actions that can be invoked whenever the system determines that it cannot complete a task in time. A contingency plan is usually more economical to execute than the original transaction. It provides useful but not optimal results. A related idea on imprecise computations can be found in [14].

Among the attributes of a real-time transaction, deadline is the most important one. This piece of information is used in many aspects of a RTDBS, be it concurrency control, scheduling, or the use of contingency plans and imprecise computations. Usually the deadline of a transaction is specified by the application designers. However, if the transaction model supports nested transactions or subtransactions, there is the question of how time constraints are assigned to individual subtransaction based on the parent transaction's deadline.

To illustrate this problem, let's consider a transaction $T$ with deadline $d$. Further assume that $T$ consists of two subtransactions $T_1$ and $T_2$ to be executed in order. Since $T_2$ is executed last, its deadline should be $d$, the deadline of its parent transaction. But what about $T_1$'s deadline? If we set it to be $d$ minus the expected execution time of $T_2$, $T_2$ is left with no slack[3] and the system runs the risk of missing $T$'s deadline. A probably better but more complicated solution is to assign a tighter deadline to $T_1$. If $T_1$ misses it, its deadline is incremented gradually until it is completed. A problem with this scheme is that transactions with "soft" but tight deadlines (e.g., $T_1$) will interfere with the execution of others that have "harder" deadlines (e.g., $T_2$).

So far we have assumed that real-time constraints are specified on the transactions. Korth, Soparkar, and Silberschatz [32] propose a different model with which deadlines are associated with consistency constraints. In addition to transactions that maintain correct database states, in their model, transactions may be invoked to record the effects of some external event that is generated outside the system (e.g., sensor reading). The ensuing change in the database state may render a consistency constraint invalid (e.g., room temperature $< x°$F), and that constraint may need to be restored within a specific deadline (e.g., the room temperature has to be raised within 30 seconds). Once an inconsistency is detected, a "patch-up" transaction is invoked to attempt to correct the violation. The patch-up transaction, however, may cause other consistency constraints to be violated. This leads to a possible chain of transaction triggering.

In [32], three types of transactions, which have *different atomicity and consistency requirements*, are considered:

1. External-input transactions: These transactions are executed to record relevant events that occur in the external world into the database. They are often simple, write-only transactions with short duration. In order to keep the database externally consistent, external-input transactions should be able to execute promptly without waiting or blocking. They may cause a consistency violation.

2. Internal transactions: These transactions are similar to standard database transactions. They are also invoked to restore consistency of the database. Their execution could be of long duration.

3. External-output transactions: These transactions cause actions to be performed in the external world. Just like the external-input transactions, they are often of short duration.

Their approach to consistency restoration works as follows: First of all, by analyzing the underlying real-time system, a predicate-priority graph (PPG) is constructed. A PPG is a bipartite graph consisting of two kinds of nodes, representing transactions and consistency constraints. An edge emerging from a transaction node, $T_1$, to a constraint node, $C_1$, means that the execution of $T_1$ may cause $C_1$ to be violated. The fanout of a transaction node may be larger than 1, meaning that a transaction can potentially violate several consistency constraints. An edge

---

[3]The slack time of a transaction is the amount of time that the transaction can be delayed in its execution but still be able to meet its deadline. We will have a more precise definition of slack time later in this chapter.

from a constraint node, $C_2$, to a transaction node $T_2$ symbolizes that by executing $T_2$, $C_2$ will be restored. Again, a constraint node may have multiple outgoing links. In that case, *any one* of the transaction nodes that are pointed to by a constraint node is capable of restoring the constraint. A choice is thus possible in selecting a "patch-up" transaction.

Now, when a constraint is violated, a "patch-up" plan is constructed by analyzing the PPG. A "patch-up" plan is represented by an inconsistency-resolution subgraph (IRS) of the PPG, which provides a strategy for resolving any inconsistencies. Intuitively, an IRS gives a partial ordering of transaction execution so that consistency constraints are restored.

Since a constraint violation may be fixed by more than one internal transaction, there may be more than one IRS choice for restoring an inconsistency. Korth's paper suggests several strategies for selecting an IRS. For example, choose an IRS such that:

1. the total execution time of the transactions involved is minimum.

2. the IRS involves the least number of transactions.

3. the IRS violates the least number of consistency constraints.

4. the slack time for restoring consistencies is maximum.

These strategies are engineered toward different system performance metrics. Complexities of problems related to the implementation of these strategies are also studied in [32]. Some of these problems are found to be NP-hard.

# 19.3    Transaction Scheduling

A major part of real-time system research concerns scheduling of jobs (of which transactions are one kind) in a multiprogramming environment. Following Liu and Layland's paper [39], numerous others have been published on the subject. Among these is a series of work done by Lehoczky et al. [34–36]. For a survey on scheduling algorithms in a hard real-time environment, readers are referred to [13].

Much of the work done on real-time job scheduling focuses mainly on CPU scheduling. Transaction scheduling, however, involves not only the CPU. In fact, due to the extensive data processing requirements of a database system, resources such as data, I/O, and memory are also subject to severe competition among concurrently running transactions. Careful scheduling of the use of these resources is very important to the performance of RTDBSs.

In this section, we discuss some general issues of transaction scheduling. Since most of the real-time scheduling protocols revolve around the use of priority, we will discuss how priority is assigned to transactions. We also discuss CPU scheduling and its database-related problems. Algorithms for scheduling other system resources, such as data, I/O, and memory, will be discussed in the following sections on concurrency control, I/O scheduling, and buffer management, respectively.

As a major asset of a computer system, efficient use of CPU cycles is very important. Conventional scheduling algorithms [43], as employed by most of the existing operating systems, aim at balancing the number of CPU-bound and I/O-bound jobs to maximize system utilization and throughput. They are also designed to treat processes fairly; each one gets its fair share of the system resource. Other performance criteria include slow job turnaround time, small waiting time, and fast response time. However elaborated, these algorithms are not adequate for real-time transaction scheduling. This is because in a RTDBS, transactions should be scheduled according to their criticalness and the tightness of their deadlines, even if this means sacrificing fairness and system throughput.

Real-time scheduling algorithms should therefore be based on the "inequalities" of transactions. They should give preferential treatment to transactions which are very critical and with stringent timing constraints. A popular method is to assign a numerical priority to each transaction which reflects its relative urgency. A transaction with higher priority is given an upper hand in gaining access to system resources.

A transaction has many attributes that may affect its priority. Below is a list of those attributes that are most relevant to a RTDBS. The parenthesized variables next to each attribute represent the individual quantitative measure of each concept.

1. Criticalness ($\gamma$) — the more critical a transaction is, the higher is its priority.[4]

2. Deadline ($d$) — the earlier its deadline, the higher is the transaction's priority [22].

3. Amount of unfinished work ($l$) — a transaction with less unfinished work may be given a higher priority than a transaction with large amount of unfinished work. In the extreme case when a transaction has begun its commit phase,[5] its priority could be raised to a higher value. This enables a committing transaction, which requires minimal computation, to finish fast. Resources held by the committing transaction can thus be released sooner to reduce blocking of other transactions [24].

4. Amount of computation already invested ($c$) — a transaction that already has a large amount of computation done may be given a higher priority. Preempting a transaction in a database system requires not only the release of resource but also careful roll-back of the transaction. It is sometime easier and less wasteful of system resources to roll back a transaction that has run for only a short time.

---

[4]Sometimes, the criticalness of a transaction can be expressed as a value function (see Section 19.2). For scheduling algorithms that aim at obtaining high total process value, see [23, 40].

[5]A transaction is in its commit phase after it finishes all the computation. Any data it updates are being written to disk in this phase.

5. Age $(a)$ — a transaction that arrived early should be given a higher priority than those that arrived late. This scheme reduces turnaround time and helps keep data externally consistent.

6. Slackness $(s)$ — slackness measures how long a transaction's execution can be delayed while still making it possible to meet the transaction's deadline. If we denote the arrival time of a transaction by $t_a$, then slackness can be expressed as:

$$s = d - t_a - c - l.$$

The tighter the slackness of a transaction is, the higher should be its priority.

It is generally hard to capture the idea of urgency by only one of the items discussed above. Consequently, it is suggested in [50] that a combination be used to compute a priority value function $(pr())$. In particular, the following formula is suggested as an example:

$$pr(T) = \gamma(w_1 a - w_2 d + w_3 c - w_4 l)$$

where the $w_i's$ are weights reflecting the relative importance of the various factors.

We note that when priority computation is based on the amount of unfinished work and slackness, a good prediction of transaction execution time is needed. We have discussed in Section 19.1 the factors which make a precise prediction hard to achieve. As an attempt, we can generally decompose the execution time $(t_{exec})$ into three components as follows [9]:

$$t_{exec} = t_{fault} + t_{db} + t_{nondb}$$

where $t_{fault}$, $t_{db}$, and $t_{nondb}$[6] denote the times spent in page fault, data-processing operations, and non-data-processing operations, respectively. We look at these terms one by one.

The term $t_{fault}$ represents the amount of time spent in paging data from disk to memory. For periodic transactions, if data prefetching is possible, a memory-resident database can be assumed. This removes any uncertainty on $t_{fault}$ by essentially setting it to zero. Otherwise, $t_{fault}$ includes all the time for I/O operations. Due to the wide gap between memory access time and disk access time, in a disk-based database, the use of a deterministic worst-case bound on $t_{fault}$ is too pessimistic. A probabilistic model on estimating $t_{fault}$ may be more effective in this case. Scheduling algorithms which are based on execution-time prediction, therefore, have to take into account the fact that the estimates are not precise.

The variable $t_{nondb}$ measures the execution time of non-database-related operations while $t_{db}$ measures database-related ones. It is generally harder to estimate $t_{db}$ than $t_{nondb}$ because the amount of data processing usually depends on the state of the database itself. It is suggested that metadata be kept describing the size of each object class [9]. Execution time on data processing is then estimated dynamically with the help of these metadata.

---

[6]This notation is adapted from [9].

Before we end this section, we briefly discuss various scheduler properties and compare their relative merits with respect to RTDBSs. These properties include on-line vs. off-line, conflict avoidance vs. conflict resolution, and preemptive resume schedulings.

Due to the unpredictable job arrival pattern, conventional scheduling algorithms are usually on-line. That is, the order of transaction execution is not pre-computed. However, in RTDBS, if information about the transactions' data access patterns, periodicities, deadlines, and so on, is available, transaction preanalysis should be carried out off-line [9]. Transaction execution order is thus scheduled before transactions arrive. Since off-line schedulers are given more information, and sooner, they are more flexible and usually produce better schedules.

When there are concurrently running tasks in a system, there are potential conflicts on resource access. These resources include data, I/O, memory, and others. When given a job, a conflict-avoidance scheduler detects and resolves conflicts among jobs over resources before the job is released for execution [9]. For conflict avoidance to be applicable, all resource requirements must be known in advance. A conflict-resolving scheduler, on the other hand, handles conflicts when they actually occur. A conflict-resolution protocol, for example, may decide that a resource requester aborts a resource holder if it is determined that the requester has a higher priority over the resource. The penalty of using a run-time conflict resolution strategy is the uncertainty it introduces in transaction execution time [9].

Finally, we note that preemptive resume CPU scheduling may not be suitable for database systems [11]. Under this scheme, a high-priority transaction preempts a low-priority one for CPU. The low-priority transaction is not aborted and does not relinquish any lock held. It simply sleeps and then resumes processing when the high-priority transaction completes. If the low-priority transaction is holding lock on a hot item, a convoy of waiting transactions will be formed, due to the extended period of locking. This convoy, once formed, tends to persist for a long time [8]. The convoy phenomenon causes long waits for locks and should be avoided in a real-time system. A solution based on priority-based round-robin CPU scheduling is suggested in [11], where the length of a CPU slice is determined by the priority of a transaction.

# 19.4   Concurrency Control

Concurrency control refers to the control of interaction among concurrent transactions in such a way that database consistency is not destroyed [31]. Transactions interact with each other mainly through reads and writes of data items. Careful access control on data therefore needs to be exercised. A good deal of work has been done on this subject for conventional databases (see, for example, [42]). The purpose of this section is to discuss the properties of concurrency control protocols that are pertinent to RTDBSs.

Serializability is the most popular correctness criterion in concurrency control. A sequence of database operations is considered serializable if its effect is *equivalent* to a serial transaction schedule. This condition, however, often limits the degree of multiprogramming, and introduces blockings and restarts of transactions.

An argument which supports sacrificing serializability to improve performance in a RTDBS is that data are often short-lived in some real-time applications [47]. The claim is that any inconsistency introduced by concurrent transactions does not spread too much over the database. Since the content of the database does not get corrupted badly, techniques like compensating transactions as discussed in Section 19.2 may be useful.

However, depending on the application semantics, serializability may be a better choice for maintaining database consistency. In this case, the prevalent approaches to concurrency control are lock-based protocols and optimistic concurrency control protocols.

Two-phase locking (2PL) is the most common locking protocol in conventional database systems. With 2PL, a transaction execution consists of two phases. In the first phase, locks are acquired but may not be released. In the second phase, locks are released but new locks may not be acquired. In case a transaction $T_R$ requests a lock that is being held by another transaction, $T_H$, $T_R$ waits.

Conventional locking protocols, like 2PL, are unsatisfactory for RTDBSs. The two main problems encountered are the possibility of priority inversion and deadlock. Let's take a look of the problem of priority inversion first.

Consider the example given above which involves a lock requester $T_R$ and a lock holder $T_H$. If the priority of $T_R$ is higher than the priority of $T_H$, then a high-priority transaction waits for a low-priority one to finish. We call this phenomenon *priority inversion* [2, 4, 27, 45].

Priority inversion is very undesirable in a RTDBS because a high-priority transaction is blocked by a low-priority one. Since the low-priority transaction is discriminated against in its use of system resources, the blocked high-priority transaction is essentially running at an effective priority equal to that of the low-priority transaction. This renders the real-time scheduling algorithms ineffective.

One solution to this problem is to hoist the priority of the lock holder to that of the requester. Referring to our earlier example, $T_H$ will be executed at an elevated priority equal to $pr(T_R)$. This priority lift truly reflects the urgency of completing $T_H$, whose progress means progress of $T_R$. We call this strategy *Wait Promote* [45].

> Wait Promote:
> **IF** $pr(T_R) > pr(T_H)$ **THEN**
>     $T_R$ waits;
>     $T_H$ inherits the priority of $T_R$;
> **ELSE**
>     $T_R$ waits;
> **ENDIF**

We note that the property of priority inheritance, as exhibited by the Wait Promote strategy, should be transitive. It means that if $T_H$ is itself blocked by some other transaction $X$, then we should set $pr(X) = \max \{pr(X), pr(T_R)\}$. Also, if a lock holder is blocking more than one lock requester, the priority of the lock holder should be set to the maximum of the requester's priorities.

The problem with Wait Promote is that we still let a low-priority transaction block a high-priority transaction. If aborting a transaction is not too expensive, we may choose to abort the low-priority lock holder and let the high-priority lock requester proceed. This strategy is called *High Priority* [2].

High Priority:
**IF** $pr(T_R) > pr(T_H)$ **THEN**
    $T_R$ aborts $T_H$;
**ELSE**
    $T_R$ waits;
**ENDIF**

The use of High Priority eliminates the problem of priority inversion. However, a problem arises if the priority function chosen (e.g., least slack) is such that a restarted transaction may have a higher priority than its previous incarnation. In such cases, when the restarted transaction tries to acquire locks, it may abort the transaction that killed it before because the restarted transaction is now running at a higher priority. This leads to the problem of cyclic restart.

To avoid this problem, before a lock requester $T_R$ aborts a lock holder $T_H$, the scheduler should make sure that the next incarnation of $T_H$, $T_H^A$, also has a lower priority than $T_R$. This modified *High Priority* algorithm *without cyclic restart* is shown below [2].

High Priority without Cyclic Restart:
**IF** $pr(T_R) > pr(T_H)$ **AND** $pr(T_R) > pr(T_H^A)$ **THEN**
    $T_R$ aborts $T_H$;
**ELSE**
    $T_R$ waits;
**ENDIF**

The High Priority strategy, although simple, may abort transactions too liberally. This wastes system resource and lower throughput, and should be avoided unless it is necessary. For our example, if it is estimated that the slack time of $T_R$ is longer than the remaining running time of $T_H$, then $T_H$ may be allowed to finish without missing $T_R$'s deadline. In that case, $T_H$ is not aborted to save system resources. This strategy, called *Conditional Restart* [2], is shown below.

Conditional Restart:
$E_H :=$ estimated remaining running time of $T_H$;
$S_R :=$ estimated slack time of $T_R$;
**IF** $pr(T_R) > pr(T_H)$ **AND** $pr(T_R) > pr(T_H^A)$ **THEN**
    **IF** $S_R \geq E_H$ **THEN**
        $T_R$ waits;
        $T_H$ inherits the priority of $T_R$;
    **ELSE**
        aborts $T_H$;
    **ENDIF**
**ELSE**

$T_R$ waits;
**ENDIF**

There are two complications of Conditional Restart. First, if there is a non-trivial probability that the chain of blocked transactions involves more than one transaction, the strategy needs to be modified. For example, if $T_H$ is itself blocked by a transaction $X$, then instead of comparing $E_H$ and $S_R$, we ought to compare the sum of the expected execution times of $H$ and $X$ with $S_R$ instead. Second, estimates of $E_H$ and $S_R$ have to be available.

The above discussion shows that no single strategy excels. The choice is dependent upon the applications, the availability of resource, and the cost of transaction restart.

There are studies on other real-time locking protocols which use delayed transaction commitments to achieve more flexible schedulings, and to produce serialization orders that favor high-priority transactions [6, 38, 48]. In [48], a three-phase real-time locking protocol is proposed. Among its nice properties are strict history [7], high degree of concurrency, and a smaller rate of missed deadlines compared to the basic 2PL-HP protocol. In [6], the problem of blocking and restarts caused by conventional locking protocols, and their adverse effects on a RTDB are discussed. A technique called "ordered sharing" [5] is used to tackle the problem and is shown to be an effective way of ameliorating blockings and restarts, as well as transaction missed deadlines.

As mentioned earlier, the second problem of locking protocols is the possibility of deadlock. Whenever a set of transactions get involved in a circular wait, a deadlock occurs [43]. In such situation, a transaction involved in the deadlock is chosen to be aborted. This victim transaction should be picked such that the largest number of remaining transactions can meet their deadlines. Example strategies for choosing a victim in deadlock resolution include [24]:

1. Abort a transaction that already passed its deadline.

2. Abort a transaction with the longest deadline.

3. Abort a transaction that is least critical.

Finally, empirical studies have shown that when deadlock occurs, it usually involves only two transactions [17]. There are thus not many choices for a victim. Hence, it may not be wise to use a sophisticated but expensive deadlock breaking protocol.

Most commercially available database systems use lock-based concurrency control protocols. Optimistic concurrency control, however, has the advantages of being non-blocking and deadlock free. These properties are very desirable for a real-time system. We devote the rest of this section to a discussion of optimistic concurrency control as applied to RTDBSs [21, 26, 46].

With optimistic concurrency control, the execution of a transaction can generally be divided into three phases: (1) read phase, (2) validation phase, and (3) write phase.

During the read phase, data items are read into memory. Computations based on the values of these data items are performed. New values are computed, but are not written into the database until the write phase. In general, if the concurrency control scheduler has decided that a transaction $T_i$ be serialized before a transaction $T_j$, the following conditions have to be satisfied [26]:

1. R/W rule. Data items to be written by $T_i$ should not have already been read by $T_j$.

2. W/W rule. $T_i$'s writes should not overwrite $T_j$'s writes.

When a transaction finishes its computation, it enters its validation phase in which the R/W and W/W rules are tested. If any one of the rules is violated, conflict resolution, which usually involves aborting one or more transactions, is invoked. One scheme for validating the rules is to check if any one of the following conditions hold:

1. $T_i$ completes its execution before $T_j$ started (no interleaving).

2. The write set of $T_i$ does not intersect with the read set of $T_j$ (thus enforcing the R/W rule), and $T_i$ completes its write phase before $T_j$ starts its validation phase (this enforces the W/W rule).

Readers are referred to [31] for details on this validation scheme.

When validation fails, a conflict resolution scheme is invoked. Several schemes are suggested in [26]. We quote three examples here:

1. Broadcasting Commit. Always let the validating transaction commit and abort all the conflicting transactions. This strategy guarantees that as long as a transaction reaches its validation phase, it will always finish.

2. Abort the validating transaction only if its priority is less than that of all the conflicting transactions.

3. If the priority of the validating transaction is not the highest among the conflicting transactions, wait for the conflicting transactions with higher priority to complete.

Simulation experiments have been carried out in [20] comparing 2PL with High Priority and optimistic concurrency control with Broadcasting Commit. Their results show that under an overload management policy of discarding tardy transaction, optimistic concurrency control can outperform 2PL. An independent study by Huang and Stankovic [26] also compares an optimistic concurrency control algorithm (OCCL_SVW) with 2PL. Their results show that the performance difference between OCCL_SVW and 2PL is sensitive to the amount of data contention, but not to the amount of I/O resource contention. In particular, the optimistic concurrency control protocol performs better than 2PL when data contention is low; otherwise, 2PL has a better performance.

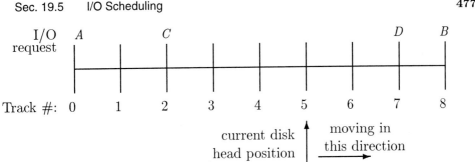

Figure 19.2  Disk Scheduling Example

# 19.5  I/O Scheduling

In a disk-based database system, disk I/O occupies a major portion of transaction execution time. As with CPU scheduling, disk scheduling algorithms that take into account timing constraints can significantly improve the real-time performance [3, 11, 12]. CPU scheduling algorithms, like Earliest Deadline First and Highest Priority First, are attractive candidates but have to be modified before they can be applied to I/O scheduling. The main reason is that disk seek time, which accounts for a very significant fraction of disk access latency, depends on the disk head movement. The order in which I/O requests are serviced, therefore, has an immense impact on the response time and throughput of the I/O subsystem. To illustrate, let's consider the following example, as shown in Figure 19.2.

Suppose that we have four requests $A$, $B$, $C$, and $D$ in the I/O queue with their priorities in the following order:

$$pr(A) > pr(B) > pr(C) > pr(D).$$

The position of the data needed by each request is shown in Figure 19.2. If Highest Priority First (HPF) scheduling is employed, the service order would be:

HPF:      $A$, $B$, $C$, $D$.

We note that in this case, the head sweeps the disk back and forth four times, or 32 tracks. Considering that the requests can be satisfied in only 11-track movement (in the order $D$, $B$, $C$, $A$), apparently HPF is not a very smart way of scheduling the disk head if response time or throughput is a concern.

Algorithms for shortening disk head movement have been devised [52]. The Elevator Algorithm, for example, moves the head from one end of the disk to the other and then back, servicing whatever requests are on its way, and changing direction whenever there are no more requests ahead in its direction. Referring to the example in Figure 19.2, the Elevator Algorithm will produce the following servicing schedule:

Elevator:      $D$, $B$, $C$, $A$

which takes three times less disk head movement than Highest Priority First does.

The problem with the Elevator Algorithm, as applied to real-time systems, is that the priority of requests is not considered. In our example, the highest priority request $A$ is serviced last. There is thus a trade-off between maximizing throughput and meeting system's timing constraints. Methods that combine the properties of HPF and the Elevator Algorithm are very desirable. In what follows, we describe two middle-ground I/O scheduling algorithms: one that puts the Elevator concept on Highest Priority First scheduling, and another which adds the flavor of HPF to the Elevator Algorithm.

When Highest Priority First scheduling is used, the disk head may pass through tracks for which there are other low priority requests. The Elevator principle says "do pick them up because the disk head is already there!" In [3, 4], Abbott presents the FD-SCAN[7] algorithm. Simply stated, FD-SCAN follows HPF in always "targeting" the disk head towards the track with the highest priority request, but also services whatever requests are on its way. Consider the earlier example, the servicing order under FD-SCAN would be:

$$\text{FD-SCAN:} \quad C, \ A, \ D, \ B.$$

We note that in this example, the disk head moves a similar distance as the Elevator Algorithm but the highest priority request $A$ is served sooner.

In Abbott's studies, FD-SCAN is tested against other disk scheduling algorithms including First Come First Served, the Elevator Algorithm, Shortest Seek Time First, and Earliest Deadline First. Simulation results show that FD-SCAN performs best among the algorithms tested in terms of the ability to meet deadlines. This property is most prominent when the load of the I/O subsystem is high. Also, this advantage of FD-SCAN is persistent through a wide range of system parameter settings.

In [11], the problem of long seek time for the Highest Priority First scheduling is addressed. It is argued that the use of fine grain priority gives the HPF scheduler a FCFS-like average seek time (with possibly even worse response time). Their idea (which we will call the Highest Priority Group First (HPGF)) is to blur the boundaries of priority. Disk requests are grouped into a small number of priority levels even though the transactions issuing the I/O requests may have distinct priorities in other parts of the system. Once these groups are formed, the disk is scheduled to service the highest priority group first. In case there is more than one request in the highest priority group, the Elevator Algorithm is used for the intra-group scheduling. Referring to our example, if requests $A$ and $B$ are in a high priority group, and requests $C$ and $D$ are in a low priority group, the service order under HPGF would be:

$$\text{HPGF:} \quad B, \ A, \ C, \ D.$$

We note that in the example, the disk movement is much less than what HPF would require, while the higher-priority requests are served before the lower-priority ones.

---

[7]In [3, 4], deadline is used as a priority measure. FD-SCAN stands for "Feasible Deadline SCAN." Any request whose deadline is determined to be impossible to meet is discarded.

Through a series of experimental studies [11], it is found that HPGF performs better than the Elevator Algorithm in meeting deadlines. This benefit is achieved at a cost of a prolonged *average* response time. However, the study shows that the response-time degradation mainly affects low-priority requests. High-priority requests, on the other hand, experience response times which are very close to what the Elevator Algorithm provides.

# 19.6    Buffer Management and Memory Resident Database

In the last three sections, we have discussed various issues concerning access to CPU, data, and disk I/O in a real-time database system. In this section, we turn our attention to yet another system resource—main memory. We will discuss how memory is managed and how it can be used efficiently to improve the performance of RTDBSs.

This section is divided into two parts. The dividing issue is whether memory space is tight or plentiful. If a real-time system has only a limited amount of memory, *buffer management*, which concerns the allocation of memory space among concurrent transactions, has to be specially designed. The goal here is to ensure that the execution of high-priority transactions is not hindered by the lack of memory. On the other hand, if memory is plentiful, much of the data can reside in main store[8] forming what is called a *memory resident database system* (MRDBS). An MRDBS has many features, such as fast and predictable access time, which make it particularly suitable for real-time applications.

## 19.6.1    Buffer Management

The availability of memory affects transaction response time in two ways. First, before a transaction starts its execution, buffers (memory pages) have to be allocated to the transaction. These buffers are used to store the execution code, copies of files and data paged in from disk, and any temporary objects produced. Depending on the transaction, a certain number of buffers have to be allocated in order to prevent the transaction from *thrashing*.[9] When memory is running low, a transaction may be blocked from execution. The amount of memory available in a system thus limits the number of concurrently executable transactions. Second, some applications, such as image processing, have high demands on memory. Their executions will be significantly slowed down if memory is tight and frequent memory swapping is done.

The job of a buffer manager is to allocate memory buffers to transactions intelligently such that high-priority transactions enjoy shorter response times. A

---

[8]We use the word "store" as a synonym of "memory."

[9]In our context, thrashing refers to the phenomenon in which a transaction spends most of its time swapping data to and from disk [43].

buffer manager is usually specified in terms of its admission policy and buffer replacement policy. We briefly explain each policy in turn below. We will also give examples on how transaction priorities are used to improve the manager's real-time behavior [25].

When a transaction $T$ is issued, the buffer manager will decide whether to admit it for execution. This decision is called the transaction admission policy. We assume that transactions are able to supply the buffer manager with the number of buffers it needs for proper execution. If enough free space is available, transaction $T$ is admitted. Otherwise, $T$ is blocked or else a number of running transactions can be suspended[10] and their buffers reallocated to transaction $T$. For the latter case, the decision of which transactions to suspend can be determined by their priorities. A simple solution would be to suspend transactions with the lowest priorities until either:

1. enough number of buffers have been freed up for $T$ to execute, or

2. there are no more unsuspended transactions with priority less than that of $T$.

In the first case, the freed-up buffers are allocated to $T$ and $T$ is admitted. For the second case, $T$ is blocked due to a lack of memory.

When a transaction references a data item which is not already in memory, a free buffer has to be allocated to page in the data. If no more free buffers are available, some buffer has to be flushed out to disk (if it was dirty) and its content replaced by the needed data. The choice of a buffer for replacement is called the buffer replacement policy.

Traditional replacement policies include Least Recently Used (LRU), Least Frequently Used, and so on [43]. In [11], a new policy, Priority-LRU, is proposed which considers transaction priority as well as buffer recency. This algorithm groups transactions into $m$ priority classes. All buffers which are being used by some transaction in the $i$th class is put into a list $L_i$ and are said to be of priority $i$. The buffer pool is thus organized into $m$ lists: $L_1$, $L_2$, ..., $L_m$ according to buffer priority. The Priority-LRU algorithm can be succinctly described by the following pseudo code:

```
Priority-LRU(W_R):
S := φ;
(* put the least recently used buffer of each list into S *)
FOR i := 1 TO m DO
        x := least recently used buffer in L_i;
        S := S ∪ {x};
END FOR
(* pick the lowest-priority buffer in S that is not one of the W_R
    most recently used buffers *)
WHILE S ≠ φ DO
        x := lowest-priority buffer in S;
```

---

[10]A suspended transaction is swapped out to disk and its execution is halted.

(* test if $x$ has been referenced recently *)
**IF** $x$ is one of the $W_R$ most recently accessed buffers **THEN**
   $S := S - \{x\}$;
**ELSE**
   **RETURN**$(x)$;
**ENDIF**
**END WHILE**
**RETURN**(no suitable page);


The Priority-LRU algorithm takes one parameter, $W_R$, which controls the relative importance of recency and priority. For example, when $W_R$ is set to zero, the least recently used buffer in the lowest-priority group is chosen. A low-priority buffer is always chosen in favor of higher-priority ones. Conversely, if $W_R$ is set high, then low-priority buffers will get a break if they are referenced recently enough.

### 19.6.2   Memory Resident Database System

As discussed in Sections 19.1 and 19.3, one of the major difficulties encountered in designing a RTDBS is the long and often unpredictable disk access delays. As the price of memory continues to drop, one possible remedy is to put data directly into memory, thus eliminating I/O accesses. In this subsection, we give a brief account on memory resident database system design. Interested readers are referred to [10, 18, 19, 47] for further reading.

Compared to disk, main memory access time is much faster (1000 to 10000 times), and is more predictable (no disk seek). These features are very desirable in RTDBSs, and may even be necessary if transactions have extremely tight time constraints.

However, putting all the data in memory is not without its disadvantages. Above all, an MRDBS is more costly than a disk-based system. Even though technology for high-density memory chips is improving and the cost dropping, currently there is still a limit on how much data can be memory resident. For large databases, storing data in main memory has to be done selectively. In a real-time environment, if the transaction data requirement is relatively stable and known, data items that are referenced by high-priority transactions should have preference over low-priority ones in claiming memory residency.

Another problem with main memory is its volatility. Data stored in main memory usually do not survive through a power failure or a CPU failure. An MRDBS, therefore, still requires disks to provide a stable backup storage. Conventional recovery protocols that load the entire database to memory from the disk backup copy and then apply the transaction log to bring the database up-to-date may be too slow for real-time applications. Mechanisms which allow quick restart and the database to function (partially) during recovery have to be employed [28]. For example, in [18], a recovery technique for MRDBS is proposed. Their method assumes that a small part of main memory is made stable by separate battery backup. This stable memory is used to store log records of "pre-committed" transactions. Schemes for check-pointing the database and compressing the transaction log for fast restart are also discussed.

A third MRDBS issue is that their design goals are different from a conventional disk-based system. Data structure and query processing algorithms for traditional database system are optimized to reduce the number of disk accesses and to enhance data clustering [31, 55]. These goals are no longer valid[11] in an MRDBS. When data are memory resident, query optimization and data structure should be designed to minimize CPU processing time and the amount of memory space used. Conventional access methods and database structures have to be revised. A B-tree [15], for example, is found to be less efficient than hashing for MRDBS index search. This is due to the additional space that a B-tree needs to store all the keys and pointers [10]. The sort-merge join algorithm [30], which was designed to reduce the number of disk I/O, is also found to be inferior in performance to the hash-merge algorithm when memory is plentiful [10].

Finally, small data access time also affects the choice of a concurrency control mechanism [47]. Without I/O delay, transaction execution time will be small in an MRDBS. Blocking delays due to data locking will also be reduced. We can thus afford to have a coarser granularity for data lock to reduce memory and processor overhead. Moreover, since memory is an important asset, optimistic concurrency controls that create temporary data objects, and those which store multiple versions of data, may not be attractive in an MRDBS [47].

## 19.7   Conclusions

In this chapter, we have discussed the various issues concerning the design and implementation of real-time databases and transaction processing. We distinguished a RTDBS from a database system and a real-time system by its more demanding goals. We also looked at application semantics and showed how they can be used to improve RTDBSs performance. CPU, data, I/O, and memory scheduling were also discussed. Furthermore, some desirable features of memory resident databases as applied to a real-time environment were also mentioned.

Due to space limitation, some other aspects of RTDBS which deserve special attention are not covered by this chapter (see [44, 53] for additional discussion). These topics include fast and incremental recovery protocols [28], database architectures that support predictable transaction execution, programming languages that provide constructs for timing specifications [54], query processing and optimization techniques that are based on real-time performance goals, scheduling methods that improve data external and temporal consistency [49], and distributed real-time databases [37].

Finally, we note that appropriate deadline assignment to subtransactions is

---

[11]Clustering may still improve data access time in an MRDBS by putting data that are often referenced together in the same "cache line." This increases the cache hit probability. The impact is, however, not as dramatic as data clustering on disk.

very crucial to the success of many real-time database protocols [29, 41]. Relatively little work has been done on this subject. As real-time databases evolve, however, we expect to see more work on this and many other RTDBS problems.

# References

[1] R. Abbott, H. Garcia-Molina: What Is a Real-Time Database System? Abstracts of the Fourth Workshop on Real-Time Operating Systems, IEEE (July 1987), 134–138.

[2] R. Abbott, H. Garcia-Molina: Scheduling Real-Time Transactions: A Performance Evaluation. Proceedings of the 14th VLDB Conference (Aug. 1988), 1–12.

[3] R. Abbott, H. Garcia-Molina: Scheduling I/O Requests with Deadlines: A Performance Evaluation. IEEE Real-Time System Symposium (Dec. 1990), 113–124.

[4] R. Abbott: Scheduling Real-Time Transactions: A Performance Evaluation. Ph.D. Dissertation, Princeton University (1991).

[5] D. Agrawal, A. El Abbadi, A. E. Lang: Performance Characteristics of Protocols with Ordered Shared Locks. Proceedings of the 18th IEEE International Conference on Data Engineering (1991).

[6] D. Agrawal, A. El Abbadi, R. Jeffers: Using Delayed Commitment in Locking Protocols for Real-Time Databases. Proceedings of the ACM SIGMOD International Conference on Management of Data (1992), 104–113.

[7] P. A. Bernstein, V. Hadzilacos, N. Goodman: Concurrency Control and Recovery in Database Systems Addison-Wesley, Reading, Mass. (1987).

[8] M. Blasgen, J. Gray, M. Mitoma, T. Price: The Convoy Phenomenon. Operating Systems Review (1979), Vol. 13, number 2, 20–25.

[9] A. P. Buchmann, D. R. McCarthy, M. Hsu, U. Dayal: Time-Critical Database Scheduling: A Framework for Integrating Real-Time Scheduling and Concurrency Control. IEEE, New York (1989)

[10] M. J. Carey, T. J. Lehman: Query Processing in Main Memory Database Management Systems. Proceedings of ACM SIGMOD (1986), 239–250.

[11] M. J. Carey, R. Jauhari, M. Livny: Priority in DBMS Resource Scheduling. Proceedings of the 15th VLDB Conference (1989), 397–410.

[12] S. Chen, J. A. Stankovic, J. F. Kurose, D. Towsley: Performance Evaluation of Two New Disk Scheduling Algorithms for Real-Time Systems. Real-Time Systems Journal (1991), Vol. 3, number 3, 307–336.

[13] S. C. Cheng, J. A. Stankovic, K. Ramamritham: Scheduling Algorithms for Hard Real-Time Systems — A Brief Survey. Hard Real-Time Systems, IEEE (1988), 150–173.

[14] J. Chung, J. Liu, W. Shih: Fast Algorithms for Scheduling Imprecise Computations. IEEE Real-Time System Symposium (Dec. 1989), 12–19.

[15] D. Comer: The Ubiquitous B-Tree. ACM Computing Surveys (June 1979), Vol. 11, number 2.

[16] U. Dayal et al.: The HiPAC Project: Combining Active Databases and Timing Constraints. SIGMOD Record (March 1988), Vol. 17, number 1, 51–70.

[17] C. Devor, C. R. Carlson: Structural Locking Mechanisms and Their Effect on Database Management System Performance. Information Systems (1982), Vol. 7, number 4, 345–358.

[18] D. Dewitt, R. Katz, F. Olken, L. Shapiro, M. Stonebraker, D. Wood: Implementation Techniques for Main Memory Database Systems. Proceedings of ACM SIGMOD (1984), 1–8.

[19] H. Garcia-Molina, K. Salem: System M: A Transaction Processing Testbed for Memory Resident Data. IEEE Transactions on Knowledge and Data Engineering (Mar. 1990), Vol. 2, number 1 161–172.

[20] J. Haritsa, M. Carey, M. Livny: On Being Optimistic about Real-Time Constraints. Proceedings of the 9th ACM symposium on Principles of Database Systems (April 1990).

[21] J. Haritsa, M. Carey, M. Livny: Dynamic Real-Time Optimistic Concurrency Control. IEEE Real-Time Systems Symposium (Dec. 1990), 94–103.

[22] J. R. Haritsa, M. Livny, M. J. Carey: Earliest Deadline Scheduling for Real-Time Database Systems. IEEE Real-Time System Symposium. (1991), 232–242,

[23] J. R. Haritsa, M. J. Carey, M. Livny: Value-Based Scheduling in Real-Time Database Systems. VLDB Journal (Apr. 1993), Vol. 2, number 2, 117–152.

[24] J. Huang, J. Stankovic, D. Towsley, K. Ramamritham: Real-Time Transaction Processing: Design, Implementation and Performance Evaluation. University of Massachusetts COINS TR 90-43, (May 1990).

[25] J. Huang, J. Stankovic: Buffer Management in Real-Time Databases. University of Massachusetts COINS TR 90-65, (July 1990).

[26] J. Huang, J. A. Stankovic: Experimental Evaluation of Real-Time Concurrency Control Schemes. Proceedings of the 17th VLDB Conference (Sept. 1991), 35–46.

[27] J. Huang, J. Stankovic: On Using Priority Inheritance in Real-Time Databases. IEEE Real-Time Systems Symposium (Dec. 1991), 210–221.

[28] B. Iyer, P. Yu, Y. Lee: Analysis of Recovery Protocols in Distributed On-line Transaction Processing Systems. IEEE Real-Time Systems Symposium (Dec 1986), 226–233.

[29] B. Kao, H. Garcia-Molina: Deadline Assignment in a Distributed Real-Time System. Proceedings of the 13th International Conference on Distributed Computing Systems (1993), 428–437.

[30] D. Knuth: The Art of Computer Programming: Sorting and Searching. Addison-Wesley, Reading, Mass. (1973).

[31] H. F. Korth, A. Silberschatz: Database System Concepts. McGraw Hill, New York (1986).

[32] H. F. Korth, N. Soparkar, A. Silberschatz: Triggered Real-Time Databases with Consistency Constraints. Proceedings of the 16th VLDB Conference (1990), 71–82.

[33] T.-W. Kuo, A. K. Mok: Application Semantics and Concurrency Control of Real-Time Data-Intensive Applications. IEEE Real-Time System Symposium (1992), 35–45.

[34] J. P. Lehoczky, L. Sha, R. Rajkumar: Solutions for Some Practical Problems in Prioritized Preemptive Scheduling. Proceedings of IEEE Real-Time Systems Symposium (1986), 181–189.

[35] J. P. Lehoczky, L. Sha, J. K. Strosnider: Enhanced Aperiodic Responsiveness in Hard-Real-Time Environment. Proceedings of IEEE Real-Time Systems Symposium (1987), 261–270.

[36] J. P. Lehoczky, L. Sha, B. Sprunt: Aperiodic Task Scheduling for Hard-real-time Systems. Journal of Real-Time-Systems (1989), 27–60.

[37] K. Lin, M. Lin: Enhancing Availability in Distributed Real-Time Databases. ACM SIGMOD Record (Mar. 1988), 34–43.

[38] Y. Lin, S. H. Son: Concurrency Control in Real-Time Databases by Dynamic Adjustment of Serialization Order. IEEE Real-Time System Symposium (1990), 104–112.

[39] C. L. Liu, J. W. Layland: Scheduling Algorithms for Multiprogramming in a Hard Real-Time Environment. Journal of the ACM (1973), Vol. 20, number 1, 46–61.

[40] E. D. Jensen, C. D. Locke, H. Tokuda: A Time-Driven Scheduling Model for Real-Time Operating Systems. IEEE Real-Time System Symposium (1985), 112–122.

[41] H. Pang, M. Livny, M. J. Carey: Transaction Scheduling in Multiclass Real-Time Database Systems. IEEE Real-Time System Symposium (1992), 23–34.

[42] C. H. Papdimitriou: The Theory of Database Concurrency Control. Computer Science Press, New York (1986).

[43] J. L. Peterson, A. Silberschatz: Operating System Concepts. Addison-Wesley, Reading, Mass., (1985).

[44] K. Ramamritham: Real-Time Databases. Distributed and Parallel Databases Journal (Apr. 1993), Vol 1, number 2, 199–226.

[45] L. Sha, R. Rajkumar, J. P. Lehoczky: Priority Inheritance Protocols: An Approach to Real-Time Synchronization. IEEE Transaction on Computers (1990), Vol. 39, number 9, 1175–1185,

[46] L. Sha R. Rajkumar, J.P. Lehoczky: Concurrency Control for Distributed Real-Time Databases. ACM SIGMOD Record (Mar. 1988), 82–98.

[47] M. Singhal: Issues and Approaches to Design of Real-Time Database Systems. ACM SIGMOD Record (Mar. 1988), 19–33.

[48] S. H. Son, S. Park, Y. Lin: An Integrated Real-Time Locking Protocol. Proceedings of the 18th IEEE International Conference on Data Engineering (1992), 527–534.

[49] X. Song, J. Liu: How Well Can Data Temporal Consistency Be Maintained? Proceedings of IEEE Symposium on computer-Aided Control System Design (Mar. 1992).

[50] J. Stankovic W. Zhao: On Real-time Transactions. ACM SIGMOD Record (Mar. 1988), Vol. 17, 4–18.

[51] J. A. Stankovic, K. Ramamritham: What Is Predictability for Real-Time Systems? Editorial, Real-Time Systems Journal (Nov. 1990), Volume 2, number 4, 247–254.

[52] T. J. Teorey, T. B. Pinkerton: A Comparative Analysis of Disk Scheduling Policies. Communications of the ACM (Mar. 1972), Vol. 15, number 3, 177–184.

[53] Özgür Ulusoy: Current Research on Real-Time Databases. SIGMOD Record (Dec. 1992), Vol. 21, number 4, 16–21.

[54] P. van der Stok: The Feasibility of a Relational Database Programming Language in Process Control. IEEE Real-Time Systems Symposium (Dec. 1984), 105–113.

[55] G. Wiederhold: Database Design. McGraw-Hill, New York (1983).

# Chapter 20

# Real-Time Databases: Issues and Applications

Bhaskar Purimetla, Rajendran M. Sivasankaran, Krithi Ramamritham, and John A. Stankovic

Data in real-time databases has to be logically and temporally consistent. The latter arises from the need to preserve the temporal validity of data items that reflect the state of the environment that is being controlled by the system. Some of the timing constraints on the transactions that process real-time data come from this need. These constraints, in turn, necessitate time-cognizant transaction processing so that transactions can be processed to meet their deadlines. This chapter explores the issues in real-time database systems and studies two real-time database applications: Cooperative distributed navigation systems and network services database systems. The purpose of the chapter is to discuss the general characteristics of data and transactions in real-time database systems and further explore them in the context of these two applications. Cooperative distributed navigation systems appear in several complex applications, such as road following and robot navigation. Network services databases provide support for the services in an intelligent network (IN). These services include dialed number services (800 service), personal mobility service, virtual business group service, and televoting.

## 20.1 Introduction

Many real-world applications involve time-constrained access to data as well as access to data that has temporal validity. For example, consider autonomous navigation systems, telephone switching systems, network management, program stock trading, managing automated factories, and command and control systems. More specifically, consider the following activities within these applications: obstacle detection and avoidance, looking up the "800 directory," radar tracking and recognition of objects, and determining the appropriate response, as well as the automatic tracking and directing of objects on a factory floor. All of these involve gathering data from the environment, processing of gathered information in the context of information acquired in the past, and providing *timely* response. Another aspect of these examples is that they involve processing both temporal data, which loses its validity after a certain interval, as well as archival data.

Our goal in this chapter is to delve into the details of two such applications that can benefit from RTDB technology, point out the special characteristics, in particular the temporal consistency requirements, of data in these applications, and show how these lead to the imposition of time constraints on transaction execution.

This chapter is divided into three parts. The first part, corresponding to Section 20.2, introduces real-time database systems. Section 20.2.1 discusses the characteristics of *data* in real-time database systems, while Section 20.2.2 presents the characteristics of *transactions* in real-time database systems. Many of these characteristics are typical of active databases. Hence, Section 20.3 is devoted to an examination of the relationship between active databases and real-time databases to point out the additional features we need in active databases in order to make them suitable for use in a real-time database context.

The second part of the chapter, contained in Sections 20.4 and 20.5, discusses the two real-time database applications in detail, especially their data and transaction characteristics.

The third part of the chapter, contained in Section 20.6, presents some research issues in real-time databases.

Section 20.7 summarizes the chapter.

## 20.2   Real-Time Databases

In this section, we examine those characteristics of databases and real-time systems that are relevant to real-time database systems. We also point out the advantages of using databases to deal with data in real-time systems.

*Traditional databases*, hereafter referred to simply as databases, deal with persistent data. Transactions access this data while maintaining its consistency. Serializability is the usual correctness criterion associated with transactions. The goal of transaction and query processing approaches adopted in databases is to achieve a good throughput or response time.

In contrast, *real-time systems*, for the most part, deal with temporal data, i.e., data that becomes outdated after a certain time. Due to the temporal nature of the data and the response-time requirements imposed by the environment, tasks in real-time systems possess time constraints, e.g., periods or deadlines. The resulting important difference is that the goal of real-time systems is to meet the time constraints of the activities.

One of the key points to remember here is that real time does not just imply fast. Also, real-time does not imply timing constraints that are in *nano*seconds or *micro*seconds. For our purposes, real time implies the need to handle *explicit* time constraints in a predictable fashion, that is, to use time-cognizant protocols to deal with deadlines or periodicity constraints associated with activities.

Databases are useful in real-time applications because they combine several features that facilitate (1) the description of data, (2) the maintenance of correctness and integrity of the data, (3) efficient access to the data, and (4) the correct executions of query and transaction executions in spite of concurrency and failures. Specifically,

- database schemas help avoid redundancy of data and its description,

- data management support, such as indexing, assists in efficient access to the data, and

- transaction support, where transactions have ACID (atomicity, consistency, isolation, and durability) properties, ensures correctness of concurrent transaction executions and ensure data integrity maintenance even in the presence of failures.

However, support for real-time database systems must take into account the following. First, not all data in a real-time database are permanent; some are temporal. Second, *temporally correct* serializable schedules are a subset of the serializable schedules. Third, since timeliness is sometimes more important than correctness, in some situations, precision can be traded for timeliness. Similarly, atomicity may be relaxed. For instance, this happens with *monotonic* queries and transactions, which are the counterparts of monotonic tasks [12] in real-time systems. Furthermore, many of the extensions to serializability that have been proposed in databases are also applicable to real-time databases (see [15] for a review of these proposals). Some of these assume that isolation of transactions may not always be needed.

In spite of these differences, given the many advantages of database technology, it will be beneficial if we can make use of them for managing data found in real-time systems. In a similar vein, the advances made in real-time systems to process activities in time could be exploited to deal with time-constrained transactions in real-time database systems.

As illustrated by the examples discussed in this chapter, many real-time applications function in environments that are inherently distributed. Furthermore, many real-time systems employ parallel processing elements for enhanced performance. Hence, parallel and distributed architectures are ubiquitous in real-time applications, and hence real-time database systems must be able to function in the context of such architectures.

## 20.2.1   Characteristics of Data in Real-Time Database Systems

A real-time system consists of a a *controlling system* and a *controlled system*. The controlled system can be viewed as the *environment* with which the computer and its software interacts.

The controlling system interacts with its environment based on the data available from various sensors, e.g., distance and speed sensors. It is imperative that the state of the environment, as perceived by the controlling system, be consistent with the actual state of the environment to a high degree of accuracy. Otherwise, the effects of the controlling systems' activities may be disastrous. Hence, timely monitoring of the environment as well as timely processing of the sensed information is necessary. In many cases the sensed data is processed to derive new data. For example, the distance and speed information pertaining to a vehicle may be used to derive the pressure to be applied on the brakes for stopping safely before an obstacle. This derivation typically would depend on past trends and so some of the needed information may have to be fetched from archival storage (a temporal database [19]). Based on the derived data, where the derivation may involve multiple steps, actuator commands are set. In general, the history of the environment and the interactions with it are also logged in archival storage.

In addition to the timing constraints that arise from the need to continuously track the environment, timing correctness requirements in a real–time (database) system also arise because of the need to make data available to the controlling system for its decision-making activities. For example, if the computer controlling a vehicle does not command it to stop or turn on time, the vehicle might collide with another object on the path. Needless to say, such a mishap can result in a major catastrophe.

The need to maintain consistency between the actual state of the environment and the state as reflected by the contents of the database leads to the notion of temporal consistency. Temporal consistency has two components [2, 20]:

- *Absolute consistency*—between the state of the environment and its reflection in the database.

  As mentioned earlier, this arises from the need to keep the controlling system's view of the state of the environment consistent with the actual state of the environment.

- *Relative consistency*—among the data used to derive other data.

  This arises from the need to produce the sources of derived data close to each other.

Let us define these terms formally. Let us denote a data item in the real-time database by

$$d : (value, avi, timestamp)$$

where $d_{value}$ denotes the current state of $d$, and $d_{timestamp}$ denotes the time when the observation relating to $d$ was made. $d_{avi}$ denotes $d$'s *absolute validity interval*, i.e., the length of the time interval following $d_{timestamp}$ during which $d$ is considered to have absolute validity.

A set of data items used to derive a new data item form a *relative consistency set* $R$. Each such set $R$ is associated with a *relative validity interval* denoted by $R_{rvi}$.

Assume that $d \in R$. $d$ has a correct state iff

1. $d_{value}$ is logically consistent—satisfies all integrity constraints.

2. $d$ is temporally consistent:

- Absolute consistency:
  $(current\_time - d_{timestamp}) \leq d_{avi}$.

- Relative consistency:
  $\forall d' \in R, \mid d_{timestamp} - d'_{timestamp} \mid \leq R_{rvi}$.

Consider the following example: Suppose that $temperature_{avi} = 5$, $pressure_{avi} = 10$, $R = \{temperature, pressure\}$, and $R_{rvi} = 2$. If $current\_time = 100$, then (a) $temperature = (347, 5, 95)$ and $pressure = (50, 10, 97)$ are temporally consistent, but (b) $temperature = (347, 5, 95)$ and $pressure = (50, 10, 92)$ are not. In (b), even though the absolute consistency requirements are met, $R$'s relative consistency is violated.

Whereas a given $avi$ can be realized by sampling and updating the database with the corresponding real-world parameter often enough, realizing an $rvi$ may not be that straightforward. This is because achieving a given $rvi$ implies that the data items that belong to a relative consistency set have to be observed at times close to each other. Details can be found in [14].

To satisfy *logical consistency* we can use standard concurrency control techniques such as two-phase locking [3] and to satisfy *temporal consistency* requirements we need to use *time-cognizant* transaction processing—by tailoring the traditional concurrency control and transaction management techniques to deal explicitly with time.

## 20.2.2 Characteristics of Transactions in Real-Time Database Systems

In this section, transactions are characterized along three dimensions: the manner in which data is used by transactions, the nature of time constraints, and the significance of executing a transaction by its deadline, or more precisely, the consequence of missing specified time constraints. Subsequently, we show how the temporal consistency requirements of the data can lead to some of the time constraints for the transactions.

Real-time database systems employ all three types of transactions discussed in the database literature. For instance,

- *Write-only transactions* obtain the state of the environment and write into the database.

- *Update transactions* derive new data and store it in the database.

- *Read-only transactions* read data from the database and transmit that data or derived actions based on that data to actuators.

The above classification can be used to tailor the appropriate concurrency control schemes.

Some transaction-time constraints come from temporal consistency requirements and some arise from requirements imposed on system reaction time. The former typically take the form of periodicity requirements: For example,

> *Every 10 seconds*: Sample wind velocity.
> *Every 20 seconds*: Update robot position.

It should be noted that the periodicity requirements can be derived from the *avi* of the data.

System reaction requirements typically take the form of deadline constraints imposed on aperiodic transactions: For example,

> If *temperature* > 1000
> > *within 10 seconds* add coolant to reactor.

In this case, the system's action in response to the high temperature must be completed by 10 seconds.

Transactions can also be distinguished based on the effect of missing a transaction's deadline. In this chapter, we use the terms *hard*, *soft*, and *firm* to categorize the transactions. This categorization tells us the *value* imparted to the system when a transaction meets its deadline. In systems which use priority-driven scheduling algorithms, value and deadline are used to derive the priority. Whereas arbitrary types of value functions can be associated with transactions [8], the following simple functions occur more often:

- *Hard* deadline transactions are those which may result in a catastrophe if the deadline is missed. One can say that a large negative *value* is imparted to the system if a hard deadline is missed. These are typically safety-critical activities, such as those that respond to life or environment-threatening emergency situations.

- *Soft* deadline transactions have some value even after their deadlines. Typically, the value drops to zero at a certain point past the deadline.

- *Firm* deadline transactions impart no value to the system once their deadlines expire; i.e., the value drops to zero at the deadline [6].

For example, if components of a transaction are assigned deadlines derived from the deadline of the original transaction, then even if a component misses its deadline, the overall transaction might still be able to make its deadline. Hence, these deadlines are soft. Another example is that of a transaction that is attempting to recognize a moving object. It must complete acquiring the necessary information before the object disappears from its view and hence has a firm deadline.

The processing of real-time transactions must take their different characteristics into account. Since meeting time constraints is the goal, it is important to understand how transactions obtain their time constraints. Since handling *avis* is quite involved [14], in the rest of this section, we discuss how absolute validity requirements on the data induce periodicity requirements.

Suppose that the *avi* of *temperature* is 10, i.e., the *temperature* must be no more than 10 seconds old. Consider one of the many possible semantics of transactions with period $P$: One instance of the transaction must execute every period; as long as the start time and completion time lie within a period, the execution is considered to be correct with respect to the periodicity semantics. Suppose that a simple transaction takes at most $e$ units of time to complete ($0 \leq e \leq P$). Thus, if an instance starts at time $t$ and ends at $(t + e)$ and the next instance starts at $(t + 2 * P - e)$ and ends at $(t + 2 * P)$, then we have two instances, which are separated by $(2 * P)$ units of time in the worst case. This, for example, will be the case if the rate monotonic static priority approach, extended to deal with resources [17], is used to schedule periodic transactions executing on a main memory database. Thus, it follows from the above periodicity semantics that to maintain the *avi* of *temperature*, the period of the transaction that reads the *temperature* must be no more than half the *avi*, that is, 5.

Many concurrency control protocols have been developed to process transactions with time constraints. The reader is referred to [1, 6, 7, 11, 17, 20] for more details.

## 20.3    Relationship to Active Databases

Many of the characteristics of data and transactions discussed in the last two sections may remind a reader of active databases. This section is devoted to a discussion of the specific distinctions between active databases and real-time databases.

The basic building block in active databases is the *Event-Condition-Action* (ECA) paradigm, which has the following semantics:

> ON *event*
>    IF *condition*
>       DO *action*.

Upon the occurrence of the specified *event*, if the *condition* holds, then the specified *action* can be taken. This construct provides a good mechanism by which integrity constraints can be maintained among related or overlapping data or by which views can be constructed [5]. The *event* can be arbitrary, including external events (as in the case of real-time events generated by the environment), timer events, or transaction-related events (such as the begin, commit, or abort of transactions). The *condition* can correspond to conditions on the state of the data or the environment. The *action* is said to be *triggered* [4, 10] and it can be an arbitrary transaction or set of transactions.

Given this, it is not difficult to see that active databases provide a good model for the *arrival* (i.e., triggering) of periodic/aperiodic activities based on events and conditions which is so typical of real-time systems. Even though the above construct implies that an active database can be made to react to timeouts, time constraints are not *explicitly* considered in the above construct nor by the underlying transaction processing mechanism.

However, as we have discussed before, the primary goal of real-time database systems is to *complete* the transactions on time. One can thus state the main deficiency in active databases in relation to what is required for them to deal with time constraints on the completion of transactions: time constraints must be *actively* taken into consideration.

Consider a system that controls the landing of an aircraft. Ideally, we would like to ensure that once the decision is made to prepare for landing, necessary steps, such as lowering the wheels, decelerating, and reducing altitude, are completed within a given duration, say 10 seconds. Here the steps may depend on the landing path, the constraints specific to the airport, and the type of aircraft, and hence may involve access to a database containing the relevant information. In those situations where the necessary steps have not been completed in time, we would like to abort the landing within a given deadline, say within 5 seconds; the abort must be *completed* within the deadline, presumably because that is the "cushion" available to the system to take alternative actions. This requirement can be expressed as follows:

ON (*10 seconds after* "initiating landing preparations")
        IF (steps not completed)
                DO (*within 5 seconds* "Abort landing").

In summary, while active databases possess the necessary features to deal with many aspects of real-time database systems, the crucial missing ingredient is the active pursuit of the timely processing of actions. As our two examples discussed in the following sections illustrate, real-world database applications possess both active and timeliness characteristics and hence it is important to deal with active real-time databases.

## 20.4   Cooperative Distributed Navigation Systems

Cooperative navigation systems usually consist of multiple semi-autonomous sensor-based agents, which are coordinated by a high-level controller to cooperatively and distributedly achieve a particular goal. The agents sense the environment (e.g., by capturing images through a camera) and relay the data back to the high-level controller if necessary. Each of the agents has an onboard front-end system which filters data before sending it to the high-level controller. Also a limited amount of control knowledge is incorporated in the front-end system in order to perform some reflexive actions, i.e., actions which immediately react to sensed values without involving the high-level computational model and the database. The front-ends may prefetch maps of their current position from the controller. Each of the agents perform some local matching in parallel to verify their position and pose (angle of placement). The high-level controller handles events which the front-end cannot handle with its limited capabilities and preserves them correctly in stable storage for future perusal. The events of different agents can be handled in parallel by the controller. The high-level controller also acts as a coordinator of the multiple agents. The high-level controller may be a real-time active database (RTADB), with control knowledge incorporated into it. The high-level controller also maintains a map database and associated data, such as the positional information of the agents, the pathplans of the various agents, destination information, archival data

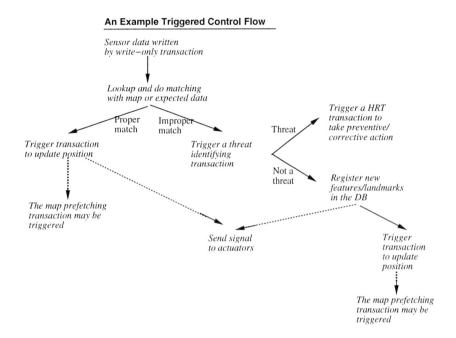

*Lookup and do matching
with map or expected data*

**Figure 20.1**  An Example Triggered Control Flow

for future processing, various index structures which support efficient access, and so on. The control knowledge consists of the various actions that need to be taken upon the occurrence of some pre-specified events.

## 20.4.1   Application Characteristics

In this section we discuss the high-level details of the navigation application. Then we discuss the data and transaction characteristics present in the application. We also discuss how the transactions derive their deadlines and also how the ECA paradigm of active databases helps in encoding the control knowledge in the system.

We now discuss the common case control loop of the navigation application and the triggered flow of transactions which might occur if we implement it using the ECA paradigm of active databases. The flow diagram is shown in Figure 20.1. An instance of the loop is initiated when the sensors write the image data into the system. This usually occurs at the front-ends and can be implemented with periodic write-only transactions. Once the image data is available, it is processed and compared with the expected scene constructed using the map data and considering the present position and direction. This matching can also be done at the front-end system. If the matching is successful, then there is no need for the agent to contact the high-level controller. The position is updated and, if necessary, new map data is prefetched from the high-level controller. The transaction control flow can be coded using the ECA rules.

If the front-end system does not detect a successful match, then the data can be relayed to the high-level controller for more sophisticated analysis. The controller can do the matching of the images from different agents at the same time in parallel. Here the data is analyzed to identify any new landmarks or features or any perceivable threats/obstacles. The controller then relays the appropriate commands back to the agent. A landmark or feature is any environmental feature of sufficient distinction to allow robust recognition from a large range of viewpoints. The set of possible threats/obstacles an agent can come across in the environment can be stored in the database.

Similarly, the map data is annotated with the set of landmarks/features known to be present in the scene. If present, the threats/obstacles trigger a hard real-time (HRT) transaction which sends appropriate corrective/preventive commands to the actuators. The deadline of the transaction depends upon the position, velocity, and direction of movement of the agent and the type of the threat.

For example, a car coming in the opposite direction on the same lane demands a tighter deadline than a stationary vehicle in the path, since the relative velocity is larger in the first case, and the value of the velocity itself affects the choice of transaction deadlines. The entire control loop has timing constraints which depend on the position, direction, and velocity of motion of the agent. Also the operator can query and intervene in the proceedings by issuing queries/commands to the high level controller. This is needed for emergency situations and manual overruling by an operator. Once a threat is identified, the mode change can be done to execute in a crisis mode if the threat demands this. If there are multiple threats, then either they are processed in order of value or an action to counter all of them is taken. If there is no threat, then any new permanent landmarks/features are consistently entered into the database using update transactions. These are necessary for future use as well as to aid cooperation among the agents. In the case of multiple threats/landmarks there may be a requirement to identify as many of them as possible in a short time. In this case there is no need to identify all of the threats/landmarks before proceeding further. But the time available for doing the job may be constrained by the present velocity of the vehicle and other physical parameters. This leads to firm real-time transactions. It may be useful to borrow ideas from the theory of imprecise computation [18] if a threat cannot be completely identified. The system can roughly identify the characteristics of the threat and assume a worst-case threat possibility. An incomplete result may be useful here.

In addition, there will be *time-triggered* as well as *periodic* actions, which can also be conveniently specified using the ECA model. For example, periodically, the system verifies whether proper progress is being made toward a goal, and if not, a new plan can be calculated and activated. Similarly, if we detect a moving object for the first time while it is a safe distance away, we can keep track of its movements relative to the agent until it materializes as a threat or it exits the sensor range. This can be done by triggering a periodic transaction as soon as we recognize a potential threat which is quite far away. Archival data may be very useful here to monitor the situation progressively. The characteristics of a moving threat, including its velocity, can be determined from the previous snapshots along with their temporal relationship. The high-level controller may need to maintain such archival data. Another example is the periodic reception of information about the status of a traffic accident. The system analyzes it periodically and may do alternative planning depending upon the extrapolated trend.

## 20.4.2    Data Characteristics

The navigation application has data of different characteristics with varying consistency criteria, recovery criteria, access patterns, and durability needs. Here we will discuss the different data present in the application and their various characteristics.

As has been mentioned earlier the data in a real-time database not only has to be consistent but also be temporally correct, since the contents of the database have to reflect the current status of the outside world. The input to the system consists of sensor data obtained from cameras and other sensors. This data has absolute temporal consistency requirements as they have to reflect the real world closely. In addition, absolute validity intervals may vary depending upon the speed of the agent as well as the mode it is in. A crisis mode may demand a smaller validity interval, as we need to sample the world faster. Similarly, when the agents are traveling at a high speed, there will be tighter absolute consistency requirements. If absolute consistency is not satisfied and the mode is normal, then extrapolation of archival data can be used to maintain consistency. The concept of invoking contingency transactions for compensation has applicability here [9]. If two or more sensors from one or more agents are used to track a common target, then relative consistency among the data from these sensors needs to be maintained in order to make correct decisions. Again, the relative consistency requirements may vary depending upon the mode of the system. As to the conventional consistency requirements, the sensor data is written by only one transaction type and no concurrency control is needed. Also, sensor data is strictly temporal in nature and may not require conventional recovery. If a transaction which updates this data is aborted then instead of doing a conventional rollback, the data can be declared invalid since the data will be updated during the next sampling period. This simplifies the recovery protocols.

The control loop attempts to identify the changes in the observed scene from the expected scene on a best-effort basis. The system tries to identify as many of the threats/landmarks as possible before the deadline. This data is derived from the sensor data. The absolute validity intervals may also have to be derived from the sensor data it uses. Also, multiple firm real-time transactions may be used to compare and analyze different sections of the image. The different landmarks/threats may be identified by different transactions. This leads to relative consistency requirements on the data, that all these transactions finish within a certain interval. Since there is only one transaction which updates this data, there is no need for any concurrency control. The system archives the threats/landmarks identified in the present scene for future perusal. This data may need the property of permanence.

The map data and the data of possible threats do not have any temporal consistency requirements. They require the conventional consistency criteria, as both reads and writes are possible by multiple transaction types. Recovery is required to maintain the durability of the data. Also, this data is the target of interactive queries and off-line updates.

The path plans of various agents also do not have any temporal consistency requirements. Since they can be updated by both the operator and the system, they require the conventional consistency to be maintained. Conventional recovery may be needed to ensure atomicity and durability.

The output data of the system consists of the actuator commands for steering and stopping the agents. They have absolute consistency requirements since the data has to be updated once every command interval. The requirements may vary according to the speed of the agent as well as the mode of the system. The same recovery criteria applicable to the sensor data are valid here too.

### 20.4.3   Transaction Characteristics

A wide variety of transactions occur in this application.

Transactions updating sensor data are periodic hard real-time transactions with their periods and deadlines dependent on the absolute consistency requirements of the sensor data. They are write-only transactions with known data requirements. They don't face any data contention.

Similarly, the image-matching transactions and position update transactions are aperiodic hard real-time transactions. They do not encounter any data contention, as their data requirements are fixed and only they update the data. These transactions are triggered by the completion of the sensor update transactions. In essence, they are triggered once every period of sensor value update transactions.

The threat or landmark identification transactions are aperiodic transactions which are triggered only when a successful match does not occur. These are firm real-time transactions which are capable of giving incomplete results which can be used to construct a worst-case scenario. If there are multiple threats, then a subset of them can be identified and returned by the deadline. The measure of success is the percentage of landmarks in the scene that are identified by the deadline. Deadlines depend on the type of the threat and the speed of the agents. Since the type of threat is unknown, assuming the worst, a very high value is associated with such transactions. They do not have any data contention, as they are append-only transactions.

Threat-handling transactions are hard real-time transactions whose deadlines vary according to the type of threat and speed of the agent. They have to be completed by the deadline in order to avoid a catastrophe. For example, if the agent is moving at 55 mph and a 0.5 $g$ deceleration is possible, then it takes 22.5 m to come to a stop. The deadline must depend upon the distance between the threat and the agent, and whether the threat is static or moving.

The map data prefetching transactions are aperiodic firm real-time transactions with deadlines based on the speed of the vehicle. The frequency of invocation depends on the speed as well as the terrain type. If we are moving on a road full of curves, then we may need to prefetch more often than when traveling on a straight section of highway. They are read-only transactions.

The actuator update transactions are periodic with period and deadlines derived from the absolute consistency requirements of the output data. If the actuator commands have to be sent every 10 sec, then the period will be appropriately defined. Since they are just update transactions and do not share data, there will be no data contention. These transactions, depending upon the result of the matching cycle and the map data, give the appropriate commands for moving the agent forward.

Apart from these there are operator interactive transactions such as for overruling plans and updating, which are aperiodic. The overruling transaction will be run at highest value for responsiveness and safety reasons. These face some potential data contention and can be handled by a simple concurrency control mechanism.

In summary, a cooperative distributed navigation system is a challenging application for real-time databases. It has a rich variety of data and transaction types. The various concepts developed as part of real-time database research have applicability in this application. The main goal of a real-time database system would be to provide integrated support for all these different data and transaction types and exploit their semantics to meet the performance goals of such systems.

## 20.5    Network Services Database

The telecommunication industry plans to provide numerous services like the 800 number service and personal mobility service. They require a robust, evolvable intelligent network (IN) architecture to serve as the backbone of such services. The features for IN that they desire are a service-independent architecture, flexible distribution of service logic[1] and service supporting functions, user-friendly and flexible service creation functions, open architecture with a set of standard interfaces, compatibility with existing networks, self-awareness, and self-adapting and self-provisioning capabilities [21, 22].

### 20.5.1    Characteristics of the 800 Service—A Typical IN Service

Current implementation of the 800 number service network consists of five major components, as shown in Figure 20.2. They are Service Switching Points (SSPs), Signal Transfer Points (STPs), Service Control Points (SCPs), the Signal Engineering and Administration System (SEAS), and the Service Management System (SMS) [16]. The SSPs are simple electronic switches and the STPs are highly reliable packet switches. The SCPs are on-line, fault-tolerant, real-time databases containing 800 records. They handle inquiries from a SSP and return data to the SSP for call processing. Supporting the STP in a geographic area is the SEAS, which the STP uses to route queries to the appropriate SCP. SEAS also collects traffic data from STP that is used for network management and engineering. The last architectural component is the SMS, an interactive operations support system

---

[1]Code to process the service.

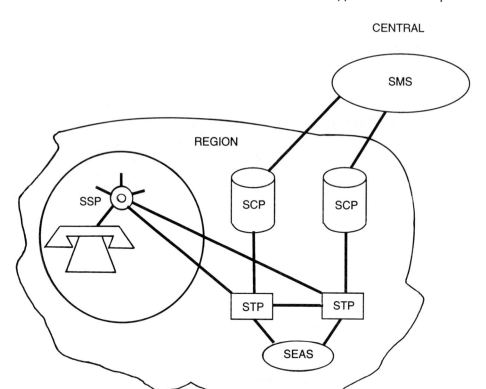

**Figure 20.2** 800 Service Network

that is used to maintain the network services customer records. The underlying network connecting these systems is the Common Channeling System (CCS) network, which uses the Signaling System #7 (SS7) protocol. When an 800 number is dialed, the call is routed to a SSP. The switch launches a query via the CCS network, which routes it to the SCP. The query contains both the 800 number and the originating station number. The SCP acts as the database that provides the answer for the query.

In the future, service processing in the IN is expected to be more complicated and demanding than the 800 number call processing. When a request for service is sensed at a call processing node,[2] depending on the request, the node could process the request locally, or transfer it to another node, or get the service processing logic from an appropriate node. Once a node starts to process a service it may have to read/write data from/to appropriate databases or transfer processing to

---

[2]In the 800 service network, a call is first processed at Service Switching Points (SSP) which are electronic switches that contain the service logic required to send queries to the centralized database. We will use the term *node* to indicate any entity on the service network that is involved in call processing.

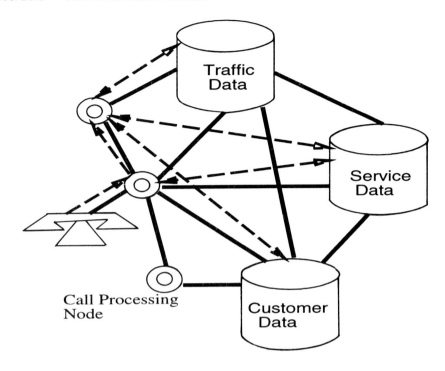

**Figure 20.3** Intelligent Network

another node to complete the service. After the completion of service the account information is updated. We need a flexible distribution of service processing logic, service related data, and accounts data. The network must be self-adapting and fault-tolerant.

So, whenever a node queries a database, or transfers processing or routes a query, it will have to look at the network request (or query) traffic[3] and configuration so that it can query the database that will take the least time to respond, or transfer processing or route the query to the node that will take the least time to respond. It should be noted that the traffic and configuration data could reside in a database from where the nodes could obtain them. Figure 20.3 shows the different databases present in the intelligent network.

## 20.5.2   Data Characteristics

The different data entities that are in the IN are service logic, customer service records, account records, operations support data, and network traffic management (NTM) data. All these data are distributed and subject to concurrent accesses. Data such as the service logic is mostly read-only and is subject to infrequent

---

[3]When we mention traffic and routing we do not mean the network-layer-level packet traffic and routing, but the service-level query traffic and routing.

updates. There is read/write data like the customer record base and account information base. The most dynamic of all this data is the NTM data, which provides the ability for real-time monitoring of the network, contributing to the self-adapting and fault-tolerant requirements.

NTM data has to be *temporally consistent*; i.e., there is a need to maintain consistency between the actual state of the network and the NTM data. The notions of *absolute consistency* and *relative consistency* are applicable to NTM data. The sampled data of the real world (NTM data) should not lag behind the actual data of the real world (network traffic) by more than a specified time. This specified time is the *absolute validity interval (avi)*. The NTM data used to derive other data should not differ from each other by more than the *relative validity interval (rvi)*.

The dynamic data that is used for real-time monitoring is temporal. Failure of a transaction that updates such data may not require conventional rollback and recovery protocols because the next transaction that updates this data will restore it to a consistent value. The best way to recover is to trigger a transaction to sense the value again in such a way that the logical and temporal consistency of the data item are not violated.

Non-dynamic data such as the service logic, customer records, and accounts information do not have temporal consistency requirements. It is possible in the case of account information to relax the isolation[4] property of the accessing transactions, for instance, using epsilon serializability[5] to give approximate account information.

## 20.5.3   Transaction Characteristics

This application includes all of the transaction types discussed in Section 20.3 except for hard real-time transactions.

Examples of periodic transactions include those responsible for obtaining the traffic data, and those responsible for generating bills. Let us briefly look at the transaction that obtains the NTM data for real-time surveillance. The *avi*s of the NTM data require these transactions to be executed with a period that will maintain the temporal consistency. These transactions have soft deadlines, because failure to meet the deadline is not catastrophic and obtaining the traffic data after expiration of deadline might be useful for later routing of requests. There are other transactions, such as the monthly billing and accounting, that are periodic and have soft deadlines.

The transactions that are executed to process a service call are aperiodic in nature. All the transactions that are part of this larger call processing transaction are aperiodic. The call processing transactions have firm deadlines because they impart no value to the system once their deadlines expire. The transaction that

---

[4]Isolation of the atomicity, consistency, isolation and durability (ACID) properties of transactions.

[5]Epsilon serializability [13] is a weaker form of the consistency criterion that allows transactions to view inconsistent data in a controlled way, thus providing more concurrency.

queries the database about the loads which is a subtransaction of a call processing transaction is monotonic in nature. It is advantageous to know the load characteristics of as many nodes as possible for optimal routing of requests. The quality of the response increases with the length of the transaction completed. In such transactions we can relax the atomicity property. Partial completion of such transactions is not totally undesirable. The transactions that are part of a call processing transaction have soft deadlines. It might still be possible to complete a call after missing a deadline of one of the many queries processed as part of the call. It does not make sense to give up and respond with a failure message to a caller just because a query to obtain the service logic is delayed. There are other aperiodic transactions, such as the ones executed to process a call for information on accounts. As mentioned earlier, in these transactions it is possible to relax the isolation property if the customers are satisfied with approximate information. Even in transactions that query the traffic data (part of call processing) approximate information might be sufficient, thus permitting the relaxation of their isolation property.

There are different kinds of transactions with varying access patterns (read-only, read-write, and write-only). The transaction that reads the network configuration for efficient routing of service query is a read-only transaction. Report-generating transactions are read-only. The transaction that does accounting is an example of a read-write transaction.

It should be noted that the application is conducive to use of the Event-Condition-Action (ECA) paradigm from active databases [4]. We can set triggers to update routing data when the traffic load reaches a minimum or a maximum value. A service request may be forwarded to different nodes depending on the time of the day. The physical address of the node to which a request is forwarded will change depending on the time of the day. We can set triggers to update the address translation database when the time of the day is a certain value. We can trigger transactions to do the billing when certain events occur. For instance, we can trigger transactions at the end of the month to calculate the monthly bill.

In summary, Network Services Databases is a soft/firm real-time system that contains rich data and transaction semantics which can be exploited to design better protocols for concurrency control, recovery, and scheduling. It has data with varying consistency criteria, recovery criteria, access patterns, and durability needs. This can potentially lead to development of various relaxed consistency and correctness criteria with different degrees of relaxation that will improve the performance of such systems.

## 20.6    Research Issues

In this section we outline some open research issues in the area of real-time active databases.

Numerous interesting questions arise when we try to assign deadlines and priorities to actions triggered by a transaction. For instance, in the IN application when the traffic reaches a particular level we can trigger actions to update the routing table. The problem of assigning value and deadline to this transaction is nontrivial. The assignment strategy will have a significant impact on the performance of the system as the triggered actions will contend with ongoing transactions for both data and CPU and I/O resources. An action can be a subtransaction or an independent transaction depending on the type of coupling mode chosen [4]. Hence, we may have to consider the coupling mode in the assignment of priorities and deadlines of the actions. Moreover, rules can have deadlines specified for their actions when a constraint has to be restored within a certain time from the point where the constraint has been violated. This explicit deadline specified for the action has to be considered in the assignment.

The actions triggered by a transaction make its execution time unpredictable if immediate or deferred coupling modes are used. It may be possible to preanalyze a transaction to determine the potential rules it can trigger and if it can finish before the deadline, and if it can, assign an appropriate value so that it can finish by its deadline. Under normal circumstances, i.e., when the transaction does not trigger any rules, the transaction may finish before its deadline with a low value. But due to increased execution time (because of rule triggering) it may be unable to finish before the deadline with a lower value. We can design a transaction model where potential rules that are triggered can be specified. This information can be used to assign a transaction a higher value than usual so that it can meet its deadline.

Recovery is a complex, unexplored issue in the context of real-time databases and has great impact on the predictability of the system. For instance, in the undo/redo recovery model, undoing the effects of a transaction consumes resources that can interfere with ongoing transactions. Hence RTDB recovery must consider resource availability to determine the most opportune time to do recovery. Moreover, we can exploit data characteristics to simplify recovery and minimize overheads. Given an application, we might be able to classify its data depending on their recovery and their permanence properties and develop appropriate recovery protocols. For instance in the IN, data for real-time monitoring need not be permanent. An aborted transaction that updates this data can recover just by updating the value again. If a transaction that is updating the routing table fails and the updating is monotonic (i.e., accuracy of data increases with the fraction of update done), then we may not need undo the effects, but just use the data and let the next updating transaction update it to the correct value or run a compensating transaction that reconciles the values later when there is less load on the system (opportune moment).

There are various other research issues that have to be looked at, such as trading off quality of response for timeliness. We can compromise on the completeness of transactions, accuracy of results, consistency of the data, and currency of the data to gain timeliness. Another issue of interest is the performance of time-cognizant CPU scheduling and CC protocols in a distributed setting. Most of the studies until now have been done in single-site systems.

Many real-time database transactions use past trends in the environment to determine their output. For instance, in network management, one examines past behavior of the controlled system to determine subsequent responses from the controlling system. Temporal databases provide the necessary facilities to maintain this historical information. They also have the notion of validity, which has its counterpart in real-time databases, in the form of temporal consistency. What temporal databases do not have is an active means to maintain validity with respect to the current time, but real-time databases make this their primary concern. So temporal databases and real-time databases complement each other in their capabilities, and a lot is to be gained by considering the two in conjunction [23].

## 20.7   Conclusions

In this chapter, we presented the characteristics of data and transactions in real-time database systems and discussed the differences between real-time database systems and traditional databases. Many of the differences arise because temporal consistency requirements are imposed on the data in addition to the usual integrity constraints. Maintaining temporal consistency imposes time constraints on the database transactions. In addition, the reaction requirements demanded by the environment also give rise to time constraints. The performance of real-time database systems is measured by how well the time constraints associated with transactions are met. The system must meet all hard deadlines and minimize the number of transactions whose soft deadlines are missed. This is a crucial difference from traditional databases and necessitates *time-cognizant* transaction processing and resource management.

Distributed cooperative navigation and network services databases are rich and challenging applications for real-time active databases. The first one has many hard real-time constraints, whereas the latter is primarily a soft real-time system. They contain rich data and transaction semantics which can be exploited to design better protocols for concurrency control, CPU scheduling, and recovery. Different data have different recovery, consistency, and permanence characteristics, which aids in the design of tailored protocols for the data. There are many interesting issues which have to be considered. Given the complexity of transactions, how does one preanalyze the rule set to guarantee predictable response times? If the system's integrity constraints are implemented using triggers, then how does one assign deadlines to the transactions? Does the restoration of consistency, which takes several transactions, as a whole have a deadline, or does each individual transaction have a deadline? Many similar questions arise whose answers may require the preanalysis of rule sets. In conclusion we can say that real-time active database systems simplify the design and maintenance of such distributed applications which need access to large amounts of data and also desire data consistency. But, as of now, few studies have addressed the problem of making the active databases actively consider time constraints in their design and implementation.

## Acknowledgments

This work was supported in part by NSF under Grants IRI-9114197 and IRI-9208920.

# References

[1] R. Abbott and H. Garcia-Molina. "Scheduling I/O Requests with Deadlines: A Performance Evaluation". *Proceedings of the Real-Time Systems Symposium*, Dec. 1990.

[2] N. Audsley, A. Burns, M. Richardson, and A. Wellings. "A Database Model for Hard Real-Time Systems." *Technical Report*, Real-Time Systems Group, Univ. of York, U.K., July 1991.

[3] P. A. Bernstein, V. Hadzilacos, and N. Goodman. *Concurrency Control and Recovery in Database Systems.* Addison-Wesley, Reading, MA, 1987.

[4] U. Dayal et al. "The HiPAC Project: Combining Active Databases and Timing Constraints." *SIGMOD Record*, 17 (1), March 1988, 51-70.

[5] K. R. Dittrich and U. Dayal. "Active Database Systems (Tutorial Notes)". *The Seventeenth International Conference on Very Large Databases*, September 1991.

[6] J. R. Haritsa, M. J. Carey and M. Livny. "Dynamic Real-Time Optimistic Concurrency Control." *Proceedings of the Real-Time Systems Symposium*, December 1990.

[7] J. Huang, J.A. Stankovic, K. Ramamritham, D. Towsley, and B. Purimetla. "Priority Inheritance in Soft Real-Time Databases". *Real-Time Systems Journal*, 4(3), September 1992.

[8] E. D. Jensen, C. D. Locke, and H. Tokuda. "A Time-Driven Scheduling Model for Real-Time Operating Systems." *Proceedings of 1985 IEEE Real-Time Systems Symposium*, pp. 112-122.

[9] H. F. Korth, E. Levy, and A. Silberschatz. "Compensating Transactions: A New Recovery Paradigm." *Proceedings of the Sixteenth International Conference on Very Large Databases*, pp. 95–106, Brisbane, Australia, August 1990.

[10] H. F. Korth, Soparkar, and A. Silberschatz. "Triggered Real-Time Databases with Consistency Constraints." *Proceedings of the Conference on Very Large Data Bases*, 1990.

[11] Y. Lin and S. H. Son. "Concurrency Control in Real-Time Databases by Dynamic Adjustment of Serialization Order." *Proceedings of the Real-Time Systems Symposium*, December 1990.

[12] J. Liu, K. Lin, W. Shih, A. Yu, J. Chung, and W. Zhao. "Algorithms for Scheduling Imprecise Computation." *IEEE Computer*, 24(5), May 1991.

[13] K. Ramamritham and C. Pu. "A Formal Characterization of Epsilon Serializability." To appear in *IEEE Transactions on Knowledge and Data Engineering*.

[14] K. Ramamritham. "Real-Time Databases." *International Journal of Distributed and Parallel Databases*, 1(2), 1993.

[15] K. Ramamritham and P. Chrysanthis. "In Search of Acceptability Criteria: Database Consistency Requirements and Transaction Correctness Properties". *Distributed Object Management*, Ozsu, Dayal, and Valduriez Ed., Morgan Kaufmann Publishers, San Mateo, CA, 1993.

[16] N. Redding. "Network Services Databases." *Globecom '86*, 1986.

[17] L. Sha, R. Rajkumar, and J. P. Lehoczky. "Concurrency Control for Distributed Real-Time Databases." *ACM SIGMOD Record*, March 1988.

[18] K. P. Smith and J. W. S. Liu. "Monotonically Improving Approximate Answers to Relational Algebra Queries." *Proceedings of Compsac*, September 1989.

[19] R. Snodgrass and I. Ahn. "Temporal Databases." *IEEE Computer*, 19 (9), September 1986, 35-42.

[20] X. Song and J. W. S. Liu. "How Well Can Data Temporal Consistency Be Maintained?" To appear in *Proceedings of the IEEE Symposium on Computer-Aided Control Systems Design*, 1992.

[21] AT&T Technical Journal. "Intelligent Networking: Network Systems." 70, Summer 1991.

[22] IEEE Computer. "Special Issue on Telecommunications." August 1993.

[23] K. Ramamritham. "Time for Real-Time Temporal Databases?" *International Workshop on an Infrastructure for Temporal Databases*, June 1993.

# Chapter 21

# Predictability and Consistency in Real-Time Database Systems

## Young-Kuk Kim and Sang H. Son

Real-time database systems (RTDBS) have transactions with explicit timing constraints, such as ready time, deadlines, and temporal constraints. Conventional database systems lack features for supporting these real-time transactions. Meeting the requirements of RTDBS requires a balanced and coordinated effort between concurrency control and transaction scheduling. Current research efforts in RTDBS have been focused on scheduling transactions with soft or firm deadlines with serializability as the sole correctness criterion. In this chapter, we focus on predictability and consistency of RTDBS. We first discuss characteristics and requirements of RTDBS. Then we present a framework to support predictability for real-time transactions and address consistency issues to explore non-serializable semantics of real-time applications.

## 21.1 Introduction

As our society becomes more integrated with computer technology, information processing for human activities necessitates computing that responds to requests in *real-time* rather than just with *best-effort*. Many computer systems are now used to monitor and control physical devices and large complex systems which must have predictable and timely behaviors. We call such systems *real-time systems*. Some real-time systems must maintain and manipulate data shared by many tasks; thus they need to have databases which can provide the services needed by real-time computations.

Real-time database systems (RTDBS) have (at least some) transactions with explicit timing constraints, such as deadlines and temporal distances. RTDBS are becoming increasingly important in a wide range of applications, such as aerospace and weapon systems, computer-integrated manufacturing, robotics, nuclear power plants, network management, and traffic control systems. Unfortunately, conventional database systems are not adequate for time-critical applications since they lack features required to support real-time transactions. They are designed to provide good average performance, while possibly yielding unacceptable worst-case response times. In addition, since the real world is constantly evolving, it is very important for real-time databases always to keep up with the real world. Although much work has been done on the topics of real-time transaction processing, it is generally agreed that there is a lack of fundamental theory for real-time database systems [1, 22, 24].

Most real-time database operations are characterized by (1) their time constrained access to data, and (2) access to data that has temporal validity. These operations involve gathering data from the environment, processing the gathered information in the context of information acquired in the past, and providing timely responses. The operations also involve processing not only archival data but also temporal data which loses its validity after a certain time duration. Both the temporal nature of the data and the response-time requirements imposed by the environment define the transaction timing constraints and may be expressed as either the periods or the deadlines. Therefore, the correctness of real-time database operations depends not only on the logical computations carried out but also on the time at which the transaction results are delivered. The goal of RTDBS is to meet the timing constraints of transactions.

The design and implementation of RTDBS introduces many unique and interesting problems. For example, what is an appropriate model for real-time transactions and data? What language constructs can be used to specify real-time constraints? What is the best concurrency control scheme that handles real-time constraints and importance of transactions? Is serializability a useful correctness criterion for RTDBS? In this chapter, we focus on two issues, *predictability* and *consistency*, which are fundamental to real-time transaction processing, but sometimes demand for conflicting actions. To ensure consistency, we may have to block certain transactions. However, blocking these transactions may cause unpredictable transaction execution and may lead to violation of timing constraints.

The remainder of this chapter is organized as follows. In Section 21.2, we describe some of the characteristics and requirements of RTDBS, especially focusing on predictability and consistency issues. In Section 21.3, we introduce a real-time database model. Section 21.4 presents a predictable transaction processing scheme under the proposed model, which can maintain temporal consistency of real-time data objects as well as real-time transactions' response-time requirements. Finally, concluding remarks are given in Section 21.5.

## 21.2   Characteristics and Requirements

Real-time systems in general try to meet the timing constraints of individual *tasks*, but may ignore data consistency problems. Task in real-time systems and transaction in RTDBS are similar abstractions in the sense that both are units of work as well as units of scheduling. However, tasks and transactions are different computational concepts, and their differences affect how they are controlled. In real-time task scheduling, it is usually assumed that all tasks are preemptable. Preemption of a transaction that uses a file resource in an exclusive mode of writing, however, may result in subsequent transactions reading inconsistent information. In addition, while the run-time behavior of a task is statistically predictable, the behavior of a transaction is dynamic, making it difficult to predict its execution time with accuracy.

The reasons why conventional database systems are not used in real-time applications include their poor performance and their lack of predictability. In conventional database systems, transaction response time is often affected by disk access delays, which are slow and unpredictable. Since real-time systems are often used in safety-critical applications, an unpredictable system can do more harm than good under abnormal conditions. There are other reasons why traditional database systems may have unpredictable performance. For example, to ensure the data consistency, traditional database systems often block certain transactions from reading or updating data if these data are locked by other transactions. It is difficult for a transaction to predict how long the delay will be since there may be cascaded blockings when the blocking transactions themselves are blocked by other transactions. Consequently, the response time for a transaction in conventional database systems is often unpredictable.

In the following, we further investigate the characteristics of real-time data and transactions, and discuss the requirements of RTDBS.

## 21.2.1   Real-Time Data

Since real-time systems are used to monitor and to control physical devices, they need to store a large amount of information about their environments. Such information includes input data from devices as well as system and machine states. In addition, many embedded systems must also store the system execution history for maintenance or error recovery purposes. Some systems may also keep track of system statistics like average system load or average device temperature. Depending on the applications, real-time systems may have to handle multi-media information like audio (for sonar devices), graphics (for radar devices), and images (for robots). Since systems are constantly recording information, data must have their temporal attributes recorded. Also, some input devices may be subject to noise degradation and need to record the quality of the attributes along with the data.

Often a significant portion of a real-time database is highly perishable in the sense that it may contribute to a mission only if used in time. In addition to deadlines, therefore, other kinds of timing constraints could be associated with data in RTDBS. For example, each sensor input could be indexed by the time at which it was taken. Once entered into the database, data may become out-of-date if it is not updated within a certain period of time. To quantify this notion of "age," data may be associated with a *valid lifespan*. Data outside its valid lifespan does not represent the current state. What occurs when a transaction attempts to access data outside its valid lifespan depends on the semantics of data and the particular system requirements.

## 21.2.2   Real-Time Transactions

Real-time applications can be grouped into three categories: *hard deadline*, *firm deadline*, and *soft deadline*. The classification is based on how the application is affected by the violation of timing constraints. For a hard deadline application, missing a deadline is equivalent to a catastrophe. In general, a large negative value is imparted to the system if a hard deadline is missed. For firm or soft deadline applications, however, missing deadlines leads to a performance penalty but does not entail catastrophic results.

We believe that this conventional categorization of real-time applications is not enough for real-time database applications and also some of the terms used in conventional real-time systems should be redefined or clarified in the context of RTDBS, since the latter have quite different characteristics from the former. First of all, the term "hard" should have different semantics from the conventional real-time systems, since RTDBS must maintain not only transactions' timing constraints but also real-time data consistency constraints. What if a real-time transaction meets its hard deadline but losing the validity of the data (i.e., the result of the transaction does not meet the given real-time data consistency constraints)?

In this chapter, we define a *hard real-time transaction* as a transaction that has hard response-time requirement and temporal data consistency constraints. The RTDBS must guarantee that both timing and consistency requirements will always be met before it starts, since a failure to meet those hard timing requirements will lead to a system failure.

To our knowledge, no dynamic method can achieve both requirements at the same time. One approach to this problem is to associate temporal data consistency constraints with timing constraints. That is, one can determine a deadline of a real-time transaction so that once the deadline is met, the temporal data consistency is maintained. Note that in most research work on real-time transaction processing, deadlines are usually determined by considering only execution-time estimates.

A *soft/firm real-time transaction* is defined as a transaction which does not have critical timing constraints but has less or no value if it does not meet those constraints. But it must still maintain data consistency constraints.

Furthermore, there may be some real-time database applications which cannot be classified into either category. Consider a transaction that has a critical response-time requirement but cannot be guaranteed to meet the deadline due to its indeterministic data access behavior or unknown data requirement. This kind of transaction can be regarded as neither hard nor soft. To include such transactions, we introduce the concept of *guarantee level* of real-time transactions. The guarantee level of a real-time transaction is determined by the degree of criticality of its constraints and has a value between 0 and 1. If the guarantee level of a transaction is $x$, the system should meet its constraints at least $10 * x$ out of 10 instances (or with $100 * x$ % probability). For example, the guarantee level of a hard and soft real-time transaction should be 1 and 0, respectively.

### 21.2.3    Predictability

Real-time computing is not equivalent to *fast* computing [29]. Rather than being fast, more important properties of RTDBS should be *timeliness*, i.e., the ability to produce expected results early or at the right time, and *predictability*, i.e., the ability to function as deterministically as necessary to satisfy system specifications, including timing constraints. Fast computing which is busy doing the wrong activity at the wrong time is not helpful for real-time computing. Fast is helpful in meeting stringent timing constraints, but fast alone does not guarantee timeliness and predictability.

Since the performance requirements may be different for each class of real-time applications, the term *predictability* should be interpreted in a specific context. A hard real-time system must be predictable in the sense that we should be able to know beforehand whether its tasks will complete before their deadlines. This prediction will be possible only if we know the worst-case execution time of a task and the data and resource needs of the task. However, in real-time database applications, it is not always possible to get this information in advance, since, unlike the conventional real-time applications, there are more factors which contribute to the unpredictability of transaction execution in database systems, such as interactions with indeterministic subsystems, data dependence of transaction execution, data and resource conflicts among transactions, and conventional recovery mechanisms.

Thus, we cannot give this kind of guarantee to all real-time transactions. Instead, we should provide a different level of guarantee to each class of real-time transactions. For example, for a group of real-time transactions, we should be able to *predict* at least what percentage of the transactions will meet the deadlines.

Predictability is also important for soft real-time transactions, albeit to a lesser degree. For instance, using some scheduling policies designed for on-line scheduling, a system may provide an earlier feedback on whether a transaction can be completed before its deadline. This allows the system to discard *infeasible* transactions (i.e., transactions which may not complete before its deadline) even before they begin execution so that wasted computations, aborts, and restarts can be avoided [1, 17].

### 21.2.4    Operating System and Architectural Support

Most research efforts on real-time database systems have concentrated on developing and evaluating real-time transaction scheduling algorithms, including priority assignment, disk I/O scheduling, concurrency control, and conflict resolution schemes, all of which performance goals are to minimize the deadline miss ratio of transactions [1, 4, 9–13, 17, 20]. However, less attention has been paid to architectural and operating system aspects of the system, supporting the predictable behavior of a real-time transaction. We believe that without adequate support in the underlying subsystems, none of the scheduling algorithms can guarantee predictable system performance. The major difficulty is the lack of a reasonable paradigm for cooperation between real-time operating systems and real-time database management systems. The result is a duplication of some common services, not only leading to a degradation in system performance, but also making the system even more unpredictable. Clearly, this is intolerable for real-time applications. Real-time database building blocks must be integrated with the real-time operating system kernel and other run-time environment building blocks in order to avoid wasteful duplication and provide predictable services.

## 21.2.5   Correctness Criteria of Real-Time Transactions

Another limitation of current real-time transaction scheduling algorithms is that most of them rely on serializability to preserve the logical consistency of the database, but they fail to address how to maintain temporal consistency of real-time data.

To facilitate more timely executions of transactions to meet their deadlines, we may extend the definition of correctness in database systems. Since real-time systems are used to respond to external stimuli (e.g., in combat systems) or to control physical devices (e.g., in auto-pilot systems), a timely and useful result is much more desirable than a serializable but out-of-date response. As long as the result of a transaction is consistent with the situations of the real world, whether or not the database is internally consistent may not be important to the application. Depending on the semantics and requirements of data and transactions, a RTDBS may use different correctness criteria under different situations.

## 21.2.6   Real-Time Database Applications

A *real-time database system* is often defined as a database system where transactions are associated with real-time constraints, typically in the form of deadlines. However, with this definition, it is not clear what its applications wiil be.

Unlike conventional general-purpose computing systems, it is extremely difficult, if possible, to develop general-purpose real-time computing systems that can be used for all kinds of time-critical applications, since each real-time application has different characteristics and performance requirements. Thus, a real-time system is often designed and configured for a specific type of application to achieve the desired performance. Or, a system must be adaptable, providing a variety of options to process different kinds of applications.

We consider that a real-time database system can be used in two different types of applications: first, real-time process control systems which manage large amounts of real-time data, and second, information management systems in which at least some transactions have deadlines. Each type of application has totally different characteristics from the other. For example, a real-time transaction in a process control system often has hard timing constraints, accesses highly perishable and predefined set of data objects, requires only simple database functions, and arrives with a fixed period, while a real-time transaction in an information management system usually has a soft deadline, may request highly complex queries, and arrives aperiodically.

Even though there has been a considerable amount of research work done in the real-time database area so far, no research work deals with both types of applications. Some of them assume process control systems having highly perishable data and hard deadline transactions as their target applications. The others consider full-fledged information management systems supporting only soft or firm deadline transactions.

The real-time database system model proposed in the following section supports all possible real-time transactions, including both hard and soft real-time transactions.

### 21.2.7   Our Approach

Our research is motivated by the limitations of current real-time database systems research as described above and thus will address some of the important issues in a real-time database system's development which have not been investigated thoroughly in the current research. The goal is to provide a framework to realize a predictable real-time transaction processing system which also maintains consistency of real-time data objects.

Our approach to achieving this goal is as follows: We identify the sources of unpredictability in a database system and try to eliminate or avoid them by providing deterministic subsystems and a proper RTDBS model.

First, we analyze the characteristics of data and transactions in typical real-time database applications, and categorize them into several classes, giving different assumptions and requirements to each class. Second, we provide an adequate architectural and operating system support for the proposed real-time database and transaction model, which guarantees a deterministic behavior of the subsystems. Our intention is to make a transaction's execution time (pure computation and data access time) deterministic by minimizing the variance between the worst-case and average-case execution time of a transaction or by removing the sources of the variance. We observe that hard real-time database systems become feasible only when the worst-case execution times of hard real-time transactions are available. If the desired level of predictability can be achieved, the performance of soft or firm real-time transactions can also be significantly improved. Finally, based on the above framework, we develop an integrated real-time transaction management scheme which can guarantee the given performance requirements of real-time applications and maintain consistency requirements of a real-time database.

## 21.3   The Real-Time Database Model

Most real-time database scheduling algorithms have been developed and evaluated under almost the same workload and operating environment model used in conventional database systems [1, 10, 12, 25]. That is, transactions are assumed to arrive in a Poisson stream at a specified mean rate. Each transaction consists of a random sequence of pages to be read, a subset of which are also updated. In addition, a conventional disk-based database environment is assumed. The general approach is to utilize existing concurrency control protocols, especially two-phase locking, and to apply time-critical transaction scheduling methods that favor more urgent transactions [23]. While this model is suited to some real-time database applications with soft or firm deadlines (e.g., airline reservation system, telephone directory service system, etc.), typical hard real-time database applications do not fit into this model, since they require predictability and semantically consistent data which may not satisfy serializability.

## 21.3.1   Characterization of Real-Time Data Objects

In our model, a real-time database consists of a set of data objects representing the state of an external world controlled by a real-time system. There are two types of data objects in a RTDBS: *continuous* and *discrete*.

Continuous data objects are related to external objects continuously changing in time. The value of a continuous data object can be obtained directly from a sensor (*image object*) or computed from the values of a set of image data objects (*derived object*) with a regular period. Discrete data objects are static in the sense that their values do not become obsolete as time passes, but they are valid until update transactions change the values.

Different from non-real-time data objects found in traditional databases, continuous data objects are related with the following additional attributes:

- A *timestamp* tells when the current value of the data object was obtained.

- An *absolute validity duration* is the length of time during which the current value of the data object is considered to be valid. The value of a continuous data object $x$ achieves *absolute temporal consistency* (or *external consistency*) only when $t_{now} - t_x \leq avd_x$, where $t_{now}$ is the current time, $t_x$ is the timestamp of $x$, and $avd_x$ is the absolute validity duration of $x$.

- A *relative validity duration* is associated with a set of data objects $\Sigma_y$ used to derive a new data object $y$. Such a set $\Sigma_y$ has a *relative temporal consistency* when the timestamp difference (or *temporal distance*) between the data object $y$ and any data object in the set is not greater than the relative validity duration $rvd_y$. The value of a derived object $y$ has *temporal consistency* only when all the values of data objects in $\Sigma_y$ are externally consistent and $\Sigma_y$ satisfies relative temporal consistency.

A continuous data object is in a *correct state* if and only if the value of the object satisfies both absolute and relative temporal consistency, while a discrete data object is in a correct state as long as the value of the object is logically consistent (i.e., satisfies all integrity constraints).

Observe that there is only one writer for each continuous data object and that its value can be used as long as it maintains temporal consistency. Thus, serializability and recoverability of transactions, on which most conventional databases depend to maintain their correctness, may not be necessary for these kinds of data objects.

For later use, suppose that a real-time database $\mathcal{R}$ consists of the following data objects:

1. A set of image objects $X = \{x_1, x_2, \ldots, x_n\}$,

2. A set of derived objects $Y = \{y_1, y_2, \ldots, y_m\}$, and

3. A set of discrete data objects $Z = \{z_1, z_2, \ldots, z_l\}$.

A set of data objects which is used to compute the value of a derived object $y$ is denoted as $\Sigma_y = \{\sigma_1, \sigma_2, \ldots, \sigma_k\}$, $\sigma_i \in X \cup Y \cup Z$, $1 \le i \le k$.

## 21.3.2    Characterization of Real-Time Transactions

Generally, a real-time transaction $\tau$ can have the following attributes:

1. Arrival time $(a_\tau)$

2. Periodicity: a period $(P_\tau)$ if periodic, or a minimum inter-arrival time $(M_\tau)$ if sporadic

3. Timing constraints: Deadline $(D_\tau)$

4. Priority $(p_\tau)$

5. Execution time requirement $(C_\tau)$

6. Data requirement: Read set $(RS_\tau)$ and Write set $(WS_\tau)$

7. Criticalness $(w_\tau)$

8. Value function $(v_\tau(t))$

Based on the values of the above attributes, the availability of the information, and other semantics of the transactions, a real-time transaction $\tau$ can be characterized as follows:

1. Implication of missing deadline $D_\tau$: *hard*, *critical*, or *soft* (*firm*) real-time

2. Arrival pattern: *periodic*, *sporadic*, or *aperiodic*

3. Data access pattern: predefined (*write-only*, *read-only*, or *update*) or *random*

4. Data requirement: *known* or *unknown*

5. Runtime requirement (pure processor and data access time):
   *known* or *unknown*

6. Accessed data type: *continuous*, *discrete*, or *both*

We believe that if a RTDBS utilizes the unique characteristics of real-time data and transactions, it can make more efficient decisions in processing transactions and thus improve overall system performance. Considering the above characterization of real-time data and transactions, there are hundreds of possible transaction classes. However, some of them are infeasible (e.g., a hard real-time transaction with random arrival pattern, random data access set, and unknown execution time), and others can be grouped together to be processed differently. In our model, a typical real-time database application consists of the following classes of transactions:

**Class I Transactions.**   This class includes all the *hard* real-time *periodic* transactions. Since all the data and run-time requirements are supposed to be available for Class I transactions in advance and they write only continuous data objects which require only temporal consistency, it is feasible to guarantee their hard timing constraints under an appropriate scheduling algorithm.

This class can be further divided into three subclasses according to the transaction's semantic information:

*Class IA Transactions.* A transaction of this class maintains the *absolute temporal consistency* of the database by writing a sampled value of an external object to the corresponding image object with a regular interval ($WS_\tau \subset X$). It is a *write-only* ($RS_\tau = \emptyset$) transaction. We assume that the transaction is the only writer to the corresponding image object (*single-writer* property). Thus, there is no *ww*-conflict with other transactions.

*Class IB Transactions.* Transactions of this class read some data objects (mainly, continuous data objects), compute new values of derived objects, and write them to the database ($RS_\tau \subset X \cup Y \cup Z$, $WS_\tau \subset Y$). They do not conflict with other Class I transactions, since there can be only one writer for a derived object. Note that in order to strictly maintain the correctness of the derived objects written by a Class IB transaction, the values of data objects read by the transaction must be in a correct state until the completion of the next instance of the transaction. However, we may be able to relax this condition to be less conservative, depending on the semantics of a specific application.

*Class IC Transactions.* Class IC transactions periodically retrieve the values of data objects ($RS_\tau \subset X \cup Y \cup Z$) and send either some control decisions to actuators or the retrieved data to display monitors. They are *read-only* transactions ($WS_\tau = \emptyset$) with hard deadlines. They have different validity requirements from Class IB transactions: the values of data objects read by a Class IC transaction must be in a correct state until the transaction is completed.

**Class II Transactions.**   Transactions of this class are *read-only* transactions with some critical timing constraints. Their timing constraints come from response-time requirements of the transactions, not from the attributes of data. Different from the Class IC transactions, they are not *periodic*, and their run-time estimates and read sets are not always available in advance. Also, they may access some discrete data objects which require serializable accesses. Thus, we cannot always guarantee a Class II transaction to meet its deadline. This is the transaction class in which each transaction can have different *guarantee level* as its performance requirement.

The main idea to achieve the specified guarantee level of a Class II transaction is to reduce the sources of unpredictability down to one dimension, making the transaction execution time a function of only one variable (i.e., an indeterministic transaction attribute such as data requirement). We assume that each transaction of this class has a specified minimum inter-arrival time $M_\tau$ (i.e., *sporadic*) and a known *selectivity distribution* $S_\tau$. An appropriate run-time estimate for a Class II transaction can be determined, and using a scheduling scheme proposed in the next section, the specified guarantee level can be achieved.

Note that a Class II transaction can be made to either a hard or a soft real-time transaction depending on its required guarantee level (i.e., a hard real-time if the guarantee level is 1, and soft real-time if it is 0). Determining the guarantee level of a Class II transaction is application-dependent.

**Class III Transactions.**    All real-time transactions not belonging to any of the above classes can be categorized in this group. They have either soft (Class IIIA) or firm (Class IIIB) deadlines, their data and run-time requirements are not always known, and they can access both continuous and discrete data objects. Since data conflicts between Class III and Class II transactions can occur, an appropriate resolution scheme is required.

In fact, Class III transactions can be further divided into several classes and processed differently. For example, a priori knowledge of a transaction's attributes is sometimes available for some soft real-time transactions and should be utilized to improve the system performance. However, we decide not to further categorize soft real-time transactions but to concentrate on Class I and II transactions. Much work has been already done for this class of transactions [1, 10, 12, 25]. Moreover, all Class III transactions are supposed to have the same level of importance (non-critical) and not to require an individual performance guarantee.

Non-real-time conventional transactions which do not have any timing constraints and access only discrete data objects also can be included in this class as if they have *infinite* deadlines.

This classification is summarized in Table 21.1. There may be some exceptions in this classification: for example, aperiodic update transactions with hard deadlines and unknown data and run-time requirements. However, we exclude these cases from our consideration because it is not feasible to guarantee their timing constraints, and thus they should not be hard real-time transactions.

Most real-time database research uses the models which include only a subset of the above classes (e.g., {Class I} [3, 22, 26] or {Class III} [1, 10, 12, 25]), and never discriminate among transactions in the system. However, in practice, all kinds of transactions can coexist in one system.

Consider a medical information system as an example: Class IA transactions are transactions which update the dynamic physical status of a critical patient from the sensor devices, such as blood pressure, heart rate, and body temperature. Transactions that write derived information from the raw data about the patient's physical status are Class IB transactions. Class IC transactions may include the transactions monitoring the physical status of the patient to provide information to life support devices. A decision-making transaction during a critical operation on a patient can be regarded as a Class II transaction. It may access not only the patient's current physical status but also his or her medical history. Conventional record-keeping transactions on patient data, such as retrieving their weight or height, can be classified as Class III transactions.

Table 21.1  Classification of Real-Time Transactions

| Property | Class I | | | Class II | Class III |
|---|---|---|---|---|---|
| | A | B | C | | |
| Timing constraints | Hard | | | Critical | Soft or firm |
| Arrival pattern | Periodic | | | Sporadic | Aperiodic |
| Data access pattern | Write-only | Update | Read-only | Read-only | No restriction |
| Data requirement | Known | | | Unknown | Unknown |
| Runtime requirement | Known | | | Unknown | Unknown |
| Updated data type | Image | Derived | N/A | N/A | Discrete |
| Correctness criteria | Temporal consistency | | | Both | Logical consistency |
| Transaction schedule | Non-serializable | | | Both | Serializable |
| Performance goal | 100% guarantee | | | Statistical guarantee | No guarantee, but best-effort |

## 21.4   Predictable Transaction Processing Scheme

Our model for a RTDBS supports all of the above classes of transactions. The performance goal of such a RTDBS is first to guarantee all the hard timing constraints of Class I transactions, to achieve the specified guarantee levels of Class II transactions, and finally, to minimize the deadline miss ratio of Class III transactions (or maximize the total values of the completed transactions if value functions can be defined for each transaction).

To achieve this performance goal, it is necessary to apply different transaction scheduling and concurrency control algorithms for each class of transactions. In this section, we present our approach to determining a transaction's attributes (period and priority) and to process each class of transaction differently for maintaining database consistency (logical or temporal) as well as satisfying the given timing constraints.

## 21.4.1   Maintaining Temporal Consistency

There are two possible approaches to maintaining temporal consistency of real-time data objects: one is a *static* approach which carefully assigns the periods of Class I transactions in order to automatically maintain temporal consistency of the continuous data objects accessed by the transactions as long as they meet the deadlines [15, 19, 21], and the other is a *dynamic* approach which either uses multiple versions of data objects [26] or delays some transactions so that all the active transactions can meet the temporal consistency requirements [16].

In this section, we present a static approach under the proposed real-time transaction classification framework.

**Class IA Transactions.**   A Class IA transaction $\tau_x$ is responsible for maintaining the absolute temporal consistency of an image object $x$. To do this, its period must satisfy the following condition:

$$avd_x \geq P_x + D_x, \qquad (21.1)$$

where $avd_x$ is the absolute validity duration of $x$, $P_x$ is the period of $\tau_x$, and $D_x$ is the deadline of $\tau_x$. This is because the worst-case update time for an image object at the beginning of a certain period is the deadline of the next period. If the deadline equals the period, a transaction's period must be less than or equal to the half of the absolute validity duration of the related image object to maintain its absolute temporal consistency.

**Class IB Transactions.**   The value of a derived object $y$ is correct only while the value of each data object $\sigma_i$ in $\Sigma_y$ is correct (i.e., temporally consistent) and $y$ maintains its correctness until the next instance of the transaction updates the value. Unfortunately, it is extremely difficult, if possible, to ensure this dynamically. However, we approach this problem by giving some restrictions on a transaction's attributes and applying a fixed-priority scheduling algorithm.

Assuming that the first periods of all transactions begin at the same time (*in phase*), we find a sufficient condition for this purpose. A derived object $y$ always has a correct value if each transaction $\tau_{\sigma_i}$ which writes a data object in $\Sigma_y$, always meets the deadlines and satisfies the following condition:

$$P_y = P_{\sigma_i} = D_{\sigma_i} \leq \min\{rvd_y, 0.5*\min_j(avd_{\sigma_j})\} \text{ for all } \sigma_i \in \Sigma_y \cap (X \cup Y), \quad (21.2)$$

where $rvd_y$ is the relative validity duration of $\Sigma_y$, and $\tau_{\sigma_i}$ must have a higher priority than $\tau_y$. In this way, $\Sigma_y$ maintains its relative temporal consistency and each $\sigma_i$ read by $\tau_y$ will be valid until the next update of $y$.

However, since this condition is too restrictive, we investigate how to relax this condition, considering the semantics of a specific application. Suppose the given application allows the following temporal consistency criteria of derived objects:

1. The values of $\sigma_i$ in $\Sigma_y$ have only to be valid until the completion of $\tau_y$.

2. The derived object $y$ has its own absolute validity duration $avd_y$.

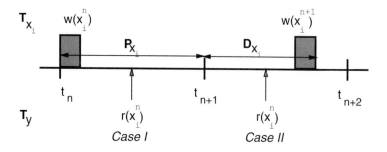

**Figure 21.1**

3. $\Sigma_y$ must satisfy the relative temporal consistency requirement (i.e., temporal distance $d(y, x_i) \leq rvd_y$ for any $x_i \in \Sigma_y \cap (X \cup Y)$).

Then, we can derive the following conditions for a Class IB transaction's period in order to maintain temporal consistency of derived objects, assuming that transactions are scheduled and guaranteed to meet the deadlines based on the *deadline-monotonic* scheduling algorithm [2] and if $D_{x_i} = D_y$, then the priority of $\tau_y$ must be higher than that of $\tau_{x_i}$:

$$P_{x_i} + D_{x_i} \leq avd_{x_i}, \tag{21.3}$$

$$P_y + D_y \leq avd_y, \tag{21.4}$$

$$D_y \leq D_{x_i}, \text{ and} \tag{21.5}$$

$$P_{x_i} + D_{x_i} \leq rvd_y \text{ for all } x_i \in \Sigma_y \cap (X \cup Y). \tag{21.6}$$

That is, unlike Equation (21.2), all $P_{x_i}$, $D_{x_i}$, $P_y$, and $D_y$ do not have to be the same as long as $D_y$ is less than or equal to the smallest $D_{x_i}$. Considering the cases in Figure 21.1, we can justify the above conditions as follows:

**Case I:** $\tau_y$ reads $x_i$ *after* the current instance of $\tau_{x_i}$ updates $x_i$ (i.e., writes $x_i^n$).

In this case, the value $x_i^n$ will be valid at least until the time $t_{n+1} + D_{x_i}$ from Equation (21.3) and the completion of $\tau_y$ comes before that time since $D_y \leq D_{x_i}$ from Equation (21.5). Thus, $x_i^n$, the value read by $\tau_y$, will be valid until $\tau_y$ completes.

**Case II:** $\tau_y$ reads $x_i$ *before* the current instance of $\tau_{x_i}$ updates $x_i$ (i.e., writes $x_i^{n+1}$).

In this case, the value $x_i^n$ read by $\tau_y$ will be valid at least until the time $t_{n+1} + D_{x_i}$ from Equation (21.3). Furthermore, $\tau_y$ should complete before that time (i.e., the deadline of $\tau_{x_i}$), since the priority of $\tau_y$ is higher than the priority of $\tau_{x_i}$ from Equation (21.5) and the deadline-monotonic scheduling. Thus, $x_i^n$, the value read by $\tau_y$ will be valid until the completion of $\tau_y$.

Also, since the maximum temporal distance between the data object $y$ and any data object in $\Sigma_y \cap (X \cup Y)$ is

$$\max_{\forall x_i \in \Sigma_y \cap (X \cup Y)} (P_{x_i} + D_{x_i}),$$

$\Sigma_y$ satisfies its relative temporal consistency requirement, as long as $P_{x_i} + D_{x_i} \leq rvd_y$ for all $i$ in $\Sigma_y \cap (X \cup Y)$ (i.e., if Equation (21.6) holds).

**Class IC Transactions.**  Since a Class IC transaction is read-only, the values of data objects read by the transaction have only to be in a correct state until the transaction finishes.

Suppose $O_\tau = \{o_i\}$ is a set of data objects that are read by a Class IC transaction $\tau$, $rvd_\tau$ is a relative validity duration of the set, and $\tau_{o_i}$ is responsible for updating the data object $o_i$. The set $O_\tau$ must satisfy its relative temporal consistency requirement (i.e., temporal distance between any two data objects in $O_\tau$ must be less than or equal to $rvd_\tau$) as well as the absolute temporal consistency of each data object in the set. The following conditions are sufficient to maintain the above temporal consistency requirements by a Class IC transaction, assuming that the first periods of all transactions begin at the same time (*in phase*):

$$P_{o_i} = D_{o_i} \leq \min\{rvd_\tau, 0.5 * \min_j(avd_{o_j})\}, \tag{21.7}$$

$$P_\tau = n * P_{o_i}, \quad n = 1, 2, 3, \ldots, \text{ and} \tag{21.8}$$

$$D_\tau \leq 2 * P_{o_i} \text{ for all } o_i \in O_\tau \cap (X \cup Y), \tag{21.9}$$

where $rvd_\tau$ is the relative validity duration of $O_\tau$ and $\tau$ has a lower priority than any $\tau_{o_i}$. With these conditions, $O_\tau$ satisfies its relative temporal consistency, and each $o_i$ read by $\tau$ will be valid at least until $\tau$ finishes (in the worst-case, the deadline of $\tau$).

Again, however, these conditions may be too restrictive for some applications. Alternative conditions for Class IC similar to those of Class IB can be given as follows, assuming that transactions are scheduled and guaranteed to meet the deadlines based on the *deadline-monotonic* scheduling, and if $D_{o_i} = D_y$, then the priority of $\tau$ must be higher than that of $\tau_{o_i}$:

$$P_{o_i} + D_{o_i} \leq avd_{o_i}, \tag{21.10}$$

$$D_\tau \leq D_{o_i}, \text{ and} \tag{21.11}$$

$$P_{o_i} + D_{o_i} - R_\tau \leq rvd_\tau \text{ for all } o_i \in O_\tau \cap (X \cup Y), \tag{21.12}$$

where $R_\tau$ is the worst-case response time of $\tau$. The justification for the equations (21.10) and (21.11) can be given similar to that of Class IB. Note that since a Class IC transaction writes no data object, there is no restriction on its period.

Equation (21.12) can be justified as follows: if the arrival time of $\tau$ is $a_\tau$, the oldest possible timestamp of $o_i$ read by $\tau$ is $a_\tau + R_\tau - \max_{\forall o_i \in O_\tau \cap (X \cup Y)}(P_{o_i} + D_{o_i})$ since $o_i$ must be valid until the completion of $\tau$, and the latest possible timestamp of $o_i$ read by $\tau$ is less than $a_\tau$ since $\tau$ has higher priority than any $\tau_{o_i}$. Thus, the maximum temporal distance between any two data objects in $O_\tau \cap (X \cup Y)$ is

$$\max_{\forall o_i \in O_\tau \cap (X \cup Y)} (P_{o_i} + D_{o_i}) \; - \; R_\tau,$$

and if it is less than or equal to $rvd_\tau$ (i.e., if Equation (21.12) holds), $O_\tau$ satisfies its relative temporal consistency requirement.

## 21.4.2    Integrated Transaction Scheduling

Suppose that a real-time application consists of a set of transactions

$$\mathcal{T} = \{T_I, T_{II}, T_{III}\},$$

where $T_X$ is a set of Class $X$ transactions ($X \in \{I, II, III\}$). Each class of transactions in $\mathcal{T}$ can be scheduled by the following integrated transaction scheduling algorithm.

**Class I Transactions.**   For all transactions of Class I, the computation and data requirements are known in advance. Also, there is no blocking due to data conflicts with other transactions (i.e., these transactions access only a fixed set of continuous data objects, and any values of the data objects can be used as long as they maintain temporal consistency). Thus, no concurrency control is required and the *deadline-monotonic* scheduling algorithm can be applied for this group of transactions. Schedulability tests for deadline-monotonic scheduling theory have been developed in [2].

**Class II Transactions.**   With deterministic subsystem support, we can bound the time to fetch one instance of the data objects accessed by a Class II transaction $\tau$ ($t_{fetch}$). Then, the pure execution time of $\tau$ (denoted as $C_\tau$) can be written as

$$C_\tau = t_{init} + (t_{fetch} + t_{comp}) * N * S_\tau + t_{close},$$

where $N$ is the size of the database, $S_\tau$ is a random variable of the selectivity distribution of $\tau$, and $t_{init}$, $t_{comp}$, and $t_{close}$ are the transaction initialization time, the pure computation time of $\tau$ per data object, and the transaction closing time, respectively.

We can compute the probability that the worst-case execution time of $\tau$, $C_\tau$, is $t_s$:

$$Prob\,[C_\tau \leq t_s] \; = \; Prob\,[S_\tau \leq s] \; = \; p_s,$$

where $t_s = t_{init} + (t_{fetch} + t_{comp}) * N * s + t_{close}$.

A method for guaranteeing deadlines of sporadic processes with correct runtime estimates within deadline-monotonic scheduling framework is shown in [2]. By using this method, it can guarantee that if the value $t_s$ is used as the transaction's run-time estimate, the transaction will meet its deadline with the probability no less than $p_s$ (i.e., it will achieve the given guarantee level $p_s$).

However, in order to get more precise performance characteristics for this class of transactions, we need to study the effect of underestimating the worst-case execution time of a transaction on the system performance (e.g., deadline miss ratio) under the given transaction scheduling algorithm.

The transaction processing protocol for Class II transactions can be summarized as follows:

1. Derive the selectivity $s$ of a transaction $\tau$ from the given performance requirement (the *guarantee level*, $p_s$) and the selectivity distribution ($S_\tau$), and calculate the run-time estimate $t_s$ using $s$.

2. Regard $\tau$ as a periodic transaction with the period $M_\tau$ (the minimum inter-arrival time of $\tau$), the run time $t_s$, and the given deadline $D_\tau$. Then, schedule $\tau$ under the deadline-monotonic policy.

3. Keep track of the consumed run time by $\tau$. If $\tau$ has spent the estimated run time $t_s$ but is not completed yet, it must be treated as a Class III transaction with the highest priority until its deadline. In this way, overrunning Class II transactions never affect the other hard real-time transactions in $T_I \cup T_{II}$.

Even though a basic schedulability analysis for the deadline-monotonic scheduling algorithm has been presented in [2], a more realistic off-line schedulability analysis must be performed on transactions in $T_I \cup T_{II}$, which includes all the possible system overheads occurred in the underlying scheduling mechanism [5, 6]. Assume that the transactions in $T_I \cup T_{II} (= \{\tau_1, \tau_2, \ldots, \tau_n\})$ are ordered according to priority with $\tau_1$ having the highest priority and $\tau_n$ having the lowest and they are scheduled by a *timer-driven* scheduler [14] (i.e., the scheduler is invoked by a regular timing interrupt with a period denoted by $P_{clk}$).

For each $\tau_i$, the following relationship holds:

$$R_i = C_i + B_i + I_i + IS_i + IH_i, \tag{21.13}$$

where $R_i$ is the worst-case response time of $\tau_i$, $C_i$ is the worst-case execution time of $\tau_i$, $B_i$ is the worst-case blocking time of $\tau_i$, $I_i$ is the interference that $\tau_i$ experiences from higher-priority transactions in $T_I \cup T_{II}$, $IS_i$ is the computational overheads due to the scheduler, and $IH_i$ is the sporadic interrupt handler overheads.

Each term in Equation (21.13) can be determined as follows:

$$I_i = \sum_{\forall j \in hpp(i)} \left\lceil \frac{R_i}{P_j} \right\rceil C_j + \sum_{\forall s \in hps(i)} \left\lceil \frac{R_i}{M_s} \right\rceil C_s,$$

$$IS_i = K * C_{clk} + \min(K, V) * C_{QL} + \max(V - K, 0) * C_{QS}, \text{ and}$$

$$IH_i = \sum_{\forall h \in sih} \left\{ C_{IH} + \left\lceil \frac{R_i}{M_h} \right\rceil C_{IH} \right\},$$

where $K$ is the maximum number of times the scheduler is invoked in a given interval $(0, R_i]$ and $V$ is the maximum number of transactions moved from the

**Table 21.2   Parameters and Notations**

| Notation | Description |
| --- | --- |
| $P_j$ | Period of $\tau_j$ in $T_I$ |
| $C_j$ | Worst-case computation time of $\tau_j$ in $T_I$ |
| $D_i$ | Deadline of $\tau_i$ in $T_I \cup T_{II}$ |
| $M_s$ | Minimum inter-arrival time of $\tau_s$ in $hps(i)$ |
| $C_s$ | Worst-case computation time of $\tau_s$ in $hps(i)$ |
| $P_{clk}$ | Clock interrupt handler period |
| $C_{clk}$ | Fixed overhead associated with a clock interrupt |
| $C_{QL}$ | Cost of moving one process between queues |
| $C_{QS}$ | Additional cost (per transaction) of moving more than one transaction at a time |
| $hpp(i)$ | The set of higher-priority transactions than $\tau_i$ in $T_I$ |
| $hps(i)$ | The set of higher-priority transactions than $\tau_i$ in $T_{II}$ |
| $sih$ | Set of all sporadic interrupt handlers |
| $M_h$ | Period of a sporadic interrupt handler in $sih$ associated with a transaction $\tau_s$ in $hps(i)$ |
| $C_{IH}$ | Computing cost of a sporadic interrupt handler |

delay queue to the run queue in the interval, which can be bounded by:

$$K = \left\lceil \frac{R_i}{P_{clk}} \right\rceil \quad \text{and} \quad V = \sum_{\forall j \in T_I \cup T_{II}} \left\lceil \frac{R_i}{P_j} \right\rceil.$$

Then, the schedulability of a transaction $\tau_i$ can be assessed by comparing the worst-case response time $R_i$ with the deadline:

$$R_i \leq D_i.$$

Note that transactions in $T_I \cup T_{II}$ will not be blocked due to data contention with other transactions, but we may need $B_i$'s to account for the blockings caused by unavoidable critical sections in the kernel and the servers.

The parameters and notations used in the above equations are summarized in Table 21.2.

**Class III Transactions.**   Within the fixed-priority preemptive scheduling framework, a number of approaches have been developed for scheduling soft real-time tasks along with the guaranteed hard real-time tasks [8, 18, 27, 28]. Our scheduling algorithm for Class III transactions is based on a *dynamic slack stealing* algorithm presented in [7, 8], since it is based on the deadline-monotonic analysis and is claimed to show better flexibility and performance than any other approaches.

The transaction processing protocol for Class III can be described as follows:

1. Find the maximum amount of slack time, $S_i^{max}(t)$ during $[t, t + D_i(t))$.

2. Class III transaction processing is permissible only at priority level $k$, while there is slack present at priority level $k$ and all lower levels:

$$\min_{\forall j \in lp(\tau)} S_j^{max}(t) > 0.$$

3. Whenever slack time is available, the highest-priority runnable Class III transaction is scheduled.

If we assume that all Class III transactions have the same values when they complete, the obvious goal of the scheduler is to meet as many of the deadlines as possible. In this case, we can assign priorities to Class III transactions using one of the following methods: Earliest Deadline First (EDF) or Least Slack First (LSF). Otherwise, we need to define a *priority value function* for each transaction:

$$p_\tau(t) = f(v_\tau(t), t - a_\tau, D_\tau, c_\tau, C_\tau - c_\tau),$$

where $c_\tau$ is the consumed execution time budget for the current invocation of transaction $\tau$.

### 21.4.3  Semantic-Based Concurrency Control and Conflict Resolution Scheme

As presented in Section 21.3, the real-time database model does not always require *serializable schedules* for transactions to maintain consistency of the database. Utilizing the inherent semantic information about transactions in specific classes, the real-time transaction scheduler can make different control decisions for different classes of transactions, in order to meet both timing and consistency constraints of the system.

In this section, we present a semantic-based concurrency control and conflict resolution scheme under our real-time database model. The scheme is based on the optimistic real-time concurrency control (OPT-CC) framework [10, 17], since it can be easily integrated with non-serializable transaction scheduling.

**Class I Transactions.**  Since Class I transactions write only continuous data objects which do not require serializable accesses as long as they are temporally consistent, there is no data conflict among them. Thus, it is never necessary to block or abort transactions in this category, due to data contention.

Especially, no concurrency control (CC) is required for a Class IA transaction, since it is a *write-only* transaction on some image objects and it is the one and only writer to the objects.

However, Class IB and IC transactions may experience *read-write* conflict with Class III transactions, since they are allowed to read discrete data objects. Even in this case, the Class I transactions can continue without blocking, while the conflicting Class III transactions must wait until the conflicting Class I transactions commit. Note that the Class III transactions do not have to be aborted or restarted as long as they can feasibly meet the deadlines, since the Class I transactions are not going to write discrete data objects.

In conclusion, Class I transactions bypass the validation phase of OPT-CC and always commit without blocking.

**Class II Transactions.**   We can also claim that Class II transactions do not experience any blocking due to data contention, since:

- They never conflict with Class I transactions, since serializable access is not necessary for continuous data objects which can be shared by both classes of transactions. Class IB, IC, and II transactions may share some discrete data objects, but they do not conflict with each other, since the accesses are read-only.

- There is no conflict among Class II transactions, since they are *read-only* transactions.

- Even though a conflict occurs with a Class III transaction, the Class II transaction keeps going. The conflicting Class III transaction must wait until the Class II transaction commits.

Thus, no priority ceiling protocol (PCP)-based synchronization scheme [21] is necessary to solve priority inversion problem due to shared data objects. Class II transactions can also bypass the validation phase of OPT-CC and always commit.

**Class III Transactions.**   As described above, if a Class III transaction conflicts with a Class I or II transaction, it just waits until the conflicting Class I or II transaction commits as long as it is still feasible. However, if a conflict occurs with other Class III transactions, it should be resolved based on their priorities (e.g., *WAIT-50* [10] and *OCC-TI* [17]).

# 21.5   Conclusions

Transactions with soft or firm deadlines can be processed successfully by using *time-cognizant* transaction scheduling algorithms without making any special assumptions as to data and transaction semantics. This is because the performance goal of the scheduler is not to guarantee timing constraints of individual transactions, but rather to make a best effort to minimize the deadline miss ratio of transactions (or to maximize the total value of finished transactions when transactions have different values).

However, if there exist some hard deadline transactions in a real-time database application, the scheduling algorithm must guarantee that all the hard deadline transactions will complete by their deadlines and then try the best with the remaining soft or firm deadline transactions. This goal cannot be achieved without the support of a deterministic subsystem and *a priori* analysis of its data and transactions.

We observe that no transaction scheduling algorithms proposed so far address this problem completely even though several papers in the real-time database field have pointed it out. In this chapter, we have examined some of the characteristics and requirements of RTDBS, introduced a real-time database model which classifies real-time data and transactions considering their attributes and the application semantics and requirements, and provided a framework to realize predictable real-time transaction processing under the assumption of a deterministic subsystem support.

Future work includes implementing a deterministic real-time database server, developing a real-time transaction workload generator based on the proposed transaction model, and evaluating the performance of our transaction processing scheme. Currently, we have a real-time database server supporting only firm real-time transactions, running on Real-Time Mach 3.0 [30]. We will extend the current system to have a deterministic software structure as proposed in [15] and support the real-time database and transaction model presented in this chapter.

# Acknowledgments

This work was supported in part by ONR, by IBM, and by CIT.

# References

[1] R. Abbott and H. Garcia-Molina. Scheduling Real-Time Transactions: A Performance Evaluation. *ACM Transactions on Database Systems*, 17(3):513–560, September 1992.

[2] N. C. Audsley, A. Burns, M. F. Richardson, and A. J. Wellings. Hard Real-Time Scheduling: The Deadline Monotonic Approach. In *Proceedings of the 8th IEEE Workshop on Real-Time Operating Systems and Software*, Atlanta, GA, May 1991.

[3] N. C. Audsley, A. Burns, M. F. Richardson, and A. J. Wellings. Absolute and Relative Temporal Constraints in Hard Real-Time Databases. In *Proceedings of the 1992 IEEE EuroMicro Workshop on Real Time Systems*, February 1992.

[4] A. Buchmann et al. Time-Critical Database Scheduling: A Framework for Integrating Real-Time Scheduling and Concurrency Control. In *Proceedings of the 5th International Conference on Data Engineering*. IEEE, New York, February 1989.

[5] A. Burns and A. J. Wellings. Implementing Analysable Hard Real-Time Sporadic Tasks in Ada 9X. Technical Report YCS209, Department of Computer Science, University of York, September 1993.

[6] A. Burns, A. J. Wellings, and A. D. Hutcheon. The Impact of an Ada Runtime System's Performance Characteristics on Scheduling Models. In *Proceedings of the 12th Ada Europe Conference, LNCS 688*, pages 240–248. Springer-Verlag, New York, 1993.

[7] R. I. Davis. Approximate Slack Stealing Algorithms for Fixed Priority Pre-emptive Systems. Technical Report YCS217, Department of Computer Science, University of York, November 1993.

[8] R. I. Davis, K. W. Tindell, and A. Burns. Scheduling Slack Time in Fixed Priority Pre-emptive Systems. In *Proceedings of the 14th Real-Time Systems Symposium*, pages 222–231, Raleigh-Durham, NC, December 1993.

[9] J. Haritsa, M. Carey, and M. Livny. Dynamic Real-Time Optimistic Concurrency Control. In *Proceedings of the 11th Real-Time Systems Symposium*, pages 94–103, Orlando, FL, December 1990.

[10] J. R. Haritsa. *Transaction Scheduling in Firm Real-Time Database Systems*. Ph.D. thesis, University of Wisconsin–Madison, August 1991.

[11] J. R. Haritsa, M. Livny, and M. J. Carey. Earliest Deadline Scheduling for Real-Time Database Systems. In *Proceedings of the 12th Real-Time Systems Symposium*, pages 232–242, December 1991.

[12] J. Huang. *Real-Time Transaction Processing: Design, Implementation, and Performance Evaluation*. Ph.D. thesis, University of Massachusetts at Amherst, May 1991.

[13] J. Huang, J. A. Stankovic, et al. Experimental Evaluation of Real-Time Transaction Processing. In *Proceedings of the 10th Real-Time Systems Symposium*, Santa Monica, CA, December 1989.

[14] D. I. Katcher, H. Arakawa, and J. K. Strosnider. Engineering and Analysis of Fixed Priority Schedulers. *IEEE Transactions on Software Engineering*, 19(9), September 1993.

[15] Young-Kuk Kim and Sang H. Son. An Approach towards Predictable Real-Time Transaction Processing. In *Proceedings of the 5th Euromicro Workshop on Real-Time Systems*, pages 70–75, Oulu, Finland, June 1993.

[16] Tei-Wei Kuo and Aloysius K. Mok. SSP: A Semantics-Based Protocol for Real-Time Data Access. In *Proceedings of the 14th Real-Time Systems Symposium*, pages 76–86, Raleigh-Durham, NC, December 1993.

[17] Juhnyoung Lee and Sang H. Son. Using Dynamic Adjustment of Serialization Order for Real-Time Database Systems. In *Proceedings of the 14th Real-Time Systems Symposium*, pages 66–75, Raleigh-Durham, NC, December 1993.

[18] J. P. Lehoczky and S. Ramos-Thuel. An Optimal Algorithm for Scheduling Soft-Aperiodic Tasks in Fixed-Priority Preemptive Systems. In *Proceedings of the 13th Real-Time Systems Symposium*, pages 110–123, Phoenix, AZ, December 1992.

[19] K.-J. Lin, F. Jahanian, A. Jhingran, and C. D. Locke. A Model of Hard Real-Time Transaction Systems. Technical Report RC 17515, IBM T.J. Watson Research Center, January 1992.

[20] Y. Lin and S. H. Son. Concurrency Control in Real-Time Databases by Dynamic Adjustment of Serialization Order. In *Proceedings of the 11th Real-Time Systems Symposium*, pages 94–103, Orlando, FL, December 1990.

[21] H. Nakazato. *Issues on Synchronization and Scheduling Tasks in Real-Time Database Systems*. Ph.D. thesis, University of Illinois at Urbana-Champaign, January 1993. Also available as UIUCDCS-R-93-1786.

[22] L. Sha, R. Rajkumar, S. H. Son, and C. Chang. A Real-Time Locking Protocol. *IEEE Transactions on Computers*, 40(7), July 1991.

[23] S. H. Son. Real-Time Database Systems: A New Challenge. *IEEE Data Engineering*, 13(4):39–43, December 1990.

[24] S. H. Son, J. Lee, and Y. Lin. Hybrid Protocols Using Dynamic Adjustment of Serialization Order for Real-Time Concurrency Control. *Journal of Real-Time Systems*, 4(3):269–276, September 1992.

[25] S. H. Son, S. Park, and Y. Lin. An Integrated Real-Time Locking Protocol. In *Proceedings of the 8th IEEE International Conference on Data Engineering*, pages 527–534, Phoenix, AZ, February 1992.

[26] X. Song and J. Liu. Performance of Multiversion Concurrency Control Algorithms in Maintaining Temporal Consistency. In *Proceedings of the IEEE 14th Annual International Computer Software and Applications Conference (COMPSAC)*, October 1990.

[27] B. Sprunt. *Aperiodic Task Scheduling for Real-Time Systems*. Ph.D. thesis, Department of Computer Science, Carnegie-Mellon University, August 1990.

[28] B. Sprunt, J. Lehoczky, and L. Sha. Exploiting Unused Periodic Time for Aperiodic Service Using the Extended Priority Exchange Algorithm. In *Proceedings of the 9th Real-Time Systems Symposium*, pages 251–258, December 1988.

[29] J. Stankovic. Real-Time Computing Systems: The Next Generation. Technical Report TR-88-06, University of Massachusetts, Amherst, January 1988. Also available as Misconceptioins about Real-Time Computing, *IEEE Computer*, October 1988.

[30] H. Tokuda, T. Nakajima, and P. Rao. Real-Time Mach: Towards Predictable Real-Time Systems. In *Proceedings of the USENIX 1990 Mach Workshop*, October 1990.

# Index

absolute validity duration, 516
active databases, 493
active real-time databases, 493
actual schedule, 205
admissible, 302, 303
admissible timed trace, 302
admission control, 105
admission test, 111
arbitrary deadlines, 233, 235
assertional techniques, 299
asynchronous communication, 82
asynchronous monitoring, 440
atomic computations, 40, 63
atomic invocations, 43, 45
atomicity, 57
ATP execution delay operator, 305
attributes, 50
augmented timed automaton, 327
autonomous navigation, 488
average breakdown utilization, 119

backward recovery, 42, 49, 50
backward simulation, 306
best-effort scheduling, 226, 243
blocking, 251
bounded clock system, 303
bounded delay, 423, 429
buffer management, 479

calendar, 97
channel establishment, 108
Chaos, 348
clock synchronization algorithm, 308
code scheduling, 362
compilation, 77, 87
compiler, 336, 345

completion time, 200, 202
completion time test, 164
complex objects, 62
computational model, 240
computing stations, 419
concurrency control, 41, 50, 65, 472, 491
    optimistic, 527
    semantic-based, 527
configurability, 40
conflict resolution
    semantic-based, 527
constraint graph, 444, 446
continuous data objects, 516
cooperative scheduling, 230
counting automaton, 321
counting process, 321
critical instant analysis, 365
critical section, 251
CSP interrupt operator, 305

database systems, 464
deadline, 309, 464, 512
    firm, 512, 519
    hard, 512
    soft, 512, 519
deadline-monotonic, 522
    schedulability analysis, 524, 525
    sporadic processes, 524
deferred preemption, 230, 231
delay bound, 107, 109, 110
delay jitter bound, 107
derived object, 516
detection, 421, 428
deterministic delay bound, 110
Dicon, 340
discrete data objects, 516